Communication and Society
Editor: Jeremy Tunstall

The manufacture of news
Social problems, deviance and the mass media

In the same series

Journalists at work
Jeremy Tunstall

The making of a TV series
Philip Elliott

The political impact of mass media
Colin Seymour-Ure

The manufacture of news (rev edn)
Stanley Cohen, Jock Young (editors)

Children in front of the small screen
Grant Noble

The Fleet Street disaster
Graham Cleverley

The silent watchdog
David Murphy

The media are American
Jeremy Tunstall
(published by Columbia University Press USA)

Putting reality together
Philip Schlesinger

The sociology of rock
Simon Frith
(published by Pantheon Books USA)

Newspaper history
George Boyce, James Curran, Pauline Wingate (editors)

The international news agencies
Oliver Boyd-Barrett

Deciding what's news
Herbert Gans
(published by Pantheon Books USA)

The bounds of freedom
Brian Lapping (editor)
(Not for sale USA)

---

*This book is a revised edition of the fourth volume in a series
edited by Jeremy Tunstall and devoted to
explorations of the interrelationships between
society and all forms of communication media.*

STANLEY COHEN AND JOCK YOUNG
(editors)

The manufacture of news

Social problems, deviance and the mass media

REVISED EDITION

CONSTABLE
London

SAGE Publications
Beverly Hills, California

Books by the same authors:

by Stanley Cohen
Images of deviance (Editor)
Folk devils and moral panics
Psychological survival: The experience of
long-term imprisonment
(with Laurie Taylor)
Escape attempts
(with Laurie Taylor)
Prison secrets
(with Laurie Taylor)

by Jock Young
The drugtakers
The new criminology
(with I. Taylor and P. Walton)
Critical criminology (Co-editor)
Abortion in demand
(with V. Greenwood)
Know your own society
(with M. Fitzgerald and K. Margolis)

First published in Great Britain 1973
by Constable and Co Ltd
10 Orange Street, London WC2H 7EG
hardback ISBN 0 09 463780 6
paperback ISBN 0 09 463790 3

Published in the United States of America 1973
by Sage Publications Inc
275 South Beverly Drive
Beverly Hills California 90212
hardback ISBN 0-8039-1636-1
paperback ISBN 0-8039-1637-X
Library of Congress Catalog Card No. 81-50585

Reprinted 1974
Reprinted 1976 (twice)
Reprinted 1978
Completely revised 1981

Printed in the United States of America

'Up till now it has been thought that the growth of the Christian myths during the Roman Empire was possible only because printing was not yet invented. Precisely the contrary. The daily press and the telegraph, which in a moment spread inventions over the whole earth, fabricate more myths . . . in one day than could have formerly been done in a century.'

KARL MARX
(writing on atrocity stories in the British
press during the Paris commune—
in a letter to Kugelmann, 27 July 1871)

Acknowledgements

The editors would like to thank the following for their kind permission to reproduce from material mentioned below: Tavistock Publications Ltd for Leslie Wilkins' *Social deviance, social policy, action and research;* Bob Roshier for 'The selection of crime news by the press'; The International Institute for Peace and Conflict Research for Johan Galtung's and Mari Ruge's 'Structuring and selecting news'; Paul Rock for 'News as eternal recurrence'; Collins and Viking Press for Michael Frayn's *The tin men;* The British Sociological Association for Steve Chibnall's 'The production of knowledge by crime reporters'; *Social Problems* for Mark Fishman's 'Crime waves as ideology'; *The Insurgent Sociologist* for Harvey Molotch's and Marilyn Lester's 'News as purposive behaviour'; *Industrial Relations Journal* for Paul Edwards' 'The awful truth about strife in our factories'; Stuart Hall and *New Society* for 'A world at one with itself'; Gaye Tuchman and Oxford University Press, New York for 'The symbolic annihilation of women by the mass media'; A. S. Linksy and *Public Opinion Quarterly* for 'Theories of behaviour and the image of the alcoholic in popular magazines'; Holt, Rinehart & Winston Inc. for Jum C. Nunnally's *Popular conceptions of mental health;* Graham Murdock for 'Political "deviance": press presentation of a militant mass demonstration'; Stuart Hall for 'The determinations of news photographs'; E. P. Thompson and *New Society* for 'Sir, Writing by candlelight . . .'; The Institute of Race Relations for Paul Hartmann's and Charles Husband's 'The mass media and racial conflict' which first appeared in *Race;* Frank Pearce for 'The British press and the "placing" of male homosexuality'; The Centre for Contemporary Cultural Studies, University of Birmingham, for Helen Butcher's 'Images of women in the media'; Macmillan for Stuart Hall's 'The social production of news'; *Sociological Review* for David Morley's 'Industrial conflict and the mass media'; Allen Lane, the Penguin Press and Beacon Press Inc. for extracts from Philip Slater's *The pursuit of loneliness;* also the editors of the *Daily Mail* and *The Guardian* for articles on Sir John Waldron's annual report of 1972.

The editors would also like to acknowledge help received from Juliet Ash, Dave Chaney, Arlene Chung, Glynis Cousin, Stuart Hall, Paul Hartmann, Sonny Mehta, Graham Murdock and Jeremy Tunstall.

Contents

8

Preface to Second Edition

When we first started to assemble this book in 1972, the notion of connecting mass media studies on the one hand, with the sociology of deviance and social problems on the other, was somewhat novel. This is no longer the case and the guiding connecting principle we used—a search for the overall models of society implied in the media's selection and presentation of stories about crime, deviance and social problems—has now become well established in research and theory.

Consequently our remarks in the original edition about the size, weakness and idiosyncracy of the pool of material we could draw upon now apply with less force, and a second edition is needed to represent at least some of this recent material. We have included twelve completely new items; rewritten our linking sections and Part Four (on "Do-it-yourself media sociology"); and updated the references and suggestions for further reading. Where possible, we have chosen to give particular emphasis to two notable developments in the last few years: the theoretical work associated with the Centre for Contemporary Cultural Studies at the University of Birmingham and empirical work in two areas underrepresented in the original edition: industrial conflict and women's studies.

Purely for reasons of space, this has unfortunately meant dropping seven of the papers in the first edition[1]: two standard but dated American articles, one on the representation of ethnic minorities in magazine fiction, the other on crime reporting; Eamonn McCann's polemical analysis of British press reporting on Northern Ireland (a topic on which unfortunately and surprisingly there is very little current research available)[2]; Jerry Palmer's reading of Mickey Spillane's thrillers—now expanded into a book[3]; Phillips' paper on the media reporting of pop festivals; extracts from Cirino's book on bias in the American press and Knopf's article on media myths about sniping.

A feature of much recent work on the media is an interest in the active social processes by which news is selected and created—rather than just analysing the content of what is finally presented. This interest is reflected in many of our new papers (Fishman, Chibnall, Edwards, Molotch and Lester, Hall, Tuchman) particularly those included in the enlarged Part One (on *Selection*). Both at this level and in Part Two (which covers *Models of presentation*), there are still some notable gaps in the literature: on race, poverty, white collar crime and mental illness, for example, there are still many empirical questions to be answered. More notably, though, it is the question of *Effects* which remains unresolved: how media images actually enter into social consciousness. More research along the lines of Hartmann's (reprinted in Part Three) is needed to deal with this problem.

A major objective of the First Edition was to indicate directions for further work. This Revised Edition retains the same objective.

S. C.

J. Y.

January 1980

1. B. Berelson and P. J. Salter, 'Majority and minority Americans: an analysis of magazine fiction', *Public Opinion Quarterly*, Vol 10, (1946) pp. 169–190; F. J. Davis, 'Crime news in Colorado newspapers', *American Journal of Sociology* LVII (June, 1952), pp.325–330; E. McCann, *The British press and Northern Ireland* (Pluto Press, 1971); J. Palmer, 'Mickey Spillane: a reading' and D. Phillips, 'The press and pop festivals: stereotypes of youthful leisure'.
2. See, though, P. Elliott, 'Reporting Northern Ireland' in *Ethnicity and the media* (Paris, Unesco, 1977).
3. Jerry Palmer, *Thrillers: Genesis and structure of a popular genre* (London, Edward Arnold, 1978).

Introduction

UNDER THE PAVING STONES THE BEACH	ANGRY BRIGADE: SEX ORGIES AT THE COTTAGE OF BLOOD
CONSUME MORE? THEN YOU LIVE LESS	A DREAM CAR FOR YOU!
THERE'S NOTHING THEY WON'T DO TO RAISE THE STANDARD OF BOREDOM	HAPPINESS IS fi SHAPED
PLAY WITHOUT RESTRAINTS AND LIVE WITHOUT DEAD TIME	NEW 'GET TOUGH' MEASURES ON DRUG PROBLEM
ALL POWER TO THE IMAGINATION	WHO ARE BRITAIN'S SMUT PEDLARS?
BE REALISTIC, DEMAND THE IMPOSSIBLE	'MILITANT TEACHERS INFILTRATING SCHOOLS' CLAIMS HEADMASTER

Two sets of slogans: one found on the walls of Paris in May 1968, the other in the headlines and advertisements carried in our national newspapers every day. They represent not just degrees of bias from a taken-for-granted social reality but—in their very words and syntax—radically alternative and oppositional realities. One conjures up a world that might be and deplores the façade of what is, the other accepts the present façade and its monolithic certainty and caricatures all deviations from it.

Just as the slogans on the Paris walls represent a created image of society, so the mass media are in the business of manufacturing and reproducing images. They provide the guiding myths which shape our conception of the world and serve as important instruments of social control. These processes are, of course, extremely complex: the media neither simply supply information and entertainment nor do they mechanically implant attitudes into the heads of their recipients. Just what effects the mass media do have on attitudes, values and behaviour, has been the subject of much popular and scientific debate and this book is not meant to provide a comprehensive or representative selection of such

12

arguments. Even to draw only on sociological work would have meant lumping together an eclectic sample of the vast literature.

Rather, by concentrating on how the media treat certain forms of deviance and social problems, we have chosen to emphasize a particular theoretical perspective. We have deliberately biased the book away from some of the standard questions on the subject, particularly those concerned with the supposed direct effects on behaviour of media exposure: for example, does the viewing of TV violence lead to increased aggressiveness? Instead we have concentrated on a somewhat neglected aspect, but one which we believe to have much greater sociological potential and practical importance, namely: the conceptions of deviance and social problems revealed in the mass media and the implicit view of society behind such conceptions.

The writings on this aspect of the media debate are informed by a number of different theories and rely on different methods of investigation. For our purposes, two polarized traditions are important to distinguish: the Mass Manipulative model and the Market or Commercial model. In the Manipulative model, the public is seen as an atomized mass, passive receptacles of messages originating from a monolithic and powerful source. In the left-wing political version of this model, the source is controlled by and represents the interests of the ruling class. Those in power use the media to mystify and manipulate the public. In some right-wing versions, the media are also seen as powerful, but their influence is in the direction of lowering cultural standards and propagating values of permissiveness. Each of these versions carries its logical implications for how the media *select* and *present* information and for what *effects* this might have on the public.

The Commercial or Market model emerged largely as a critique of the manipulative picture: it is mostly adhered to by journalists themselves and it tends to be more optimistic. It argues that there is variety and diversity in information and opinions presented in the mass media and that such variation minimizes the chances of manipulation. Principles such as 'give the public what it wants' (and their commercial implications) rather than some manipulative conspiracy, are what determine how the media select and present information. Indeed the public themselves, as consumers, can actively select or selectively perceive those media (or parts of the media) which already fit existing positions and preconceptions. The effects of the media then are seen as less awesome than in the Manipulative model: people's opinions might be reinforced, but rarely changed in an opposite direction and moreover the primal source of attitude formation and change is personal experience and face-to-face contact.

Our own position is one that will emerge as we compare how these models 'work' in the three areas of social problem imagery the book covers: *selection, presentation* and *effects*. In the case of selection—Part One of the book—we concern ourselves with the problem of how and why certain events are selected as news in the first place. The second Part is the longest and consists of separate case studies—using diverse sources and methods—on the modes of presentation and underlying models of deviance and social problems employed in the media. Most of the articles or extracts refer to Britain or America and most are contemporary or as near to comtemporary as we could find.

Part Three is concerned with the likely effects of the mass media both on people's conceptions of social problems and on the groups themselves designated as deviant or socially problematic. It draws, amongst other sources, upon some of our own work in this area and attempts to pull together some of the arguments advanced in the first two parts of the book.

It would have made our task as editors much easier if we had confronted a field where most of the important areas had been explored and analyzed. But this is not the case—the very fact that we draw so much on our own research in limited areas makes the volume atypical—and our major aim is to point to the areas of media research which have been ignored, despite a proliferation of research institutes, commissions and grants. We hope to interest enough people to fill these gaps and get involved themselves in what is a very open research field. Consequently, the last Part of this book consists of suggestions for do-it-yourself research which can be carried out with very few resources. We believe that much mainstream media research is on the wrong lines; a major objective in putting this volume together is to suggest some new ones.

PART ONE

The process of selection

There are two questions which confront us when we deal with the problem of how news is selected from the multitude of events which occur in the world. The first is: what is selected? What are the *criteria* of newsworthiness? Why are certain events headlined and others omitted altogether? The second is that of objectivity: namely, how *accurately* does such a selection reflect the real world?

In terms of the Market model of the media, the answers to such questions are seen to be obvious. News is a natural category of event which must—in good professional journalism—be reported as objectively as possible. The journalist, therefore, goes out in the objective world of events to pursue news which she/he captures in his or her notebook or newsreel and takes back triumphantly to his or her editor. To be sure, there are bad journalists—but then, so are there inadequate doctors or lawyers. This does not call into question the timeless role of the competent professional journalist: to reproduce, as faithfully as possible, those parts of reality which are news.

The criterion for selecting these nuggets of news out of the dross of everyday events is public interest. This means both what interests the public and what is in the public's interest. To give the public what it wants demands a sense of what it is that *naturally* grabs people's attention: this 'news sense' is a capacity which the capable journalist builds up over his or her career. Now the Market model is only too ready to admit that these two sorts of public interest need not necessarily coincide: what the public wants may not be totally in its best interest. Indeed the major debate *within* Market theories of the media is between on one hand a social responsibility school of thought which sees the roles of the professional journalist and the 'quality' media as public educators and, on the other, the 'libertarians' who would give the public what it is supposed to want.[1] What both sides of this internecine debate agree on, however, is that, in the last analysis, it is market forces which will guarantee a media free to present that vital democratic commodity, news, to the public at large. The Market model then maintains that the responsible journalist selects those events which are in the public interest to know and then objectively portrays reality within the format and genre of the particular media concerned.

The Manipulative model has an almost opposite understanding of the process of selection. Here the media and journalists are seen as acting directly in the interest of the owners, whose interests in turn are quite opposed to the public at large and to any true presentation of events in the world. The journalists are ideological hacks who select news according to the criterion of whether it serves the interests of their paymaster, omitting all else. They distort reality in order to fit the propagandistic needs of their employers. They purvey a tissue of lies directed at misleading the masses as to their true interests. If the apex of Market journalism is the exposé, that in the Manipulative model is the cover-up. News is the patina which obfuscates reality.

Now despite these contrasts it is important to stress what both Market and Manipulative models have in common. Both have an unproblematic conception of what is news (in the Market model it is what is revealed, in Manipulation it is what is concealed) and of the objective reality which should be reported (in the Market model reality is reflected whilst in Manipulation it is distorted). It is against such uncontentious notions of selectivity—as applied to criteria for newsworthiness or standards of objectivity—that the articles in this section have been collected.

It might help at this stage for us to express diagramatically the problem of selection. We are interested here in the relationship between events (reality) and news, thus:

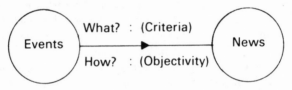

We introduce this section with Leslie Wilkins' classic article on information about deviance. If we ignore the author's rather mechanistic application of cybernetic theory to human behaviour, two interesting observations can be gleaned regarding the selection of news. First, Wilkins suggests that the criterion of selection is the unusualness of an event but that unusualness is a function of the information stock that the members of an audience have from direct experience about a particular class of events. That is, it is not unusualness in some *natural, objective* sense but the unexpected in terms of what is thought of as usual. Secondly, Wilkins notes that the information relayed by the mass media is one-dimensional compared to the multi-dimensional knowledge derived from direct experience. The stereotype carried of deviants by the media is a way of simplifying reality. This is neither a calculated distortion of the real world nor an accurate reflection of real events but rather a *translation* of reality into stereotypes.

Bob Roshier makes a detailed examination of what types of crime become news. He finds four factors of importance: seriousness; ironic and unusual circumstances; dramatic events and high status of the actors involved. This corroborates Wilkins' notion of unusualness being judged against a standard or stereotype of usualness. His finding that there is a consistent tendency to over report high status offenders is of particular interest (and old offenders compared to young) because it is the opposite of what a Manipulative model would suggest and is in clear violation of the accuracy claimed by the Market model. What seems to be happening is a selection of the unusual or *anomalous* against the background of the 'usual' criminal—the low status and the youthful.

But clearly not everything which is anomalous or stereotypically unusual is reported. For instance Robert Cirino presents a quite different position.[2] His case is that the American news media use bias, distortion and censorship to manipulate public opinion and he notes that the journalist does not merely make an inspired guess about the potential interest of an item. Powerful commercial and political interests direct his or her attention to particular issues while shutting out awareness of others. The massive deaths from lung cancer caused by cigarette smoking, widespread poverty, environmental pollution and the inadequate safety precautions in cars which result in unnecessarily severe road accidents were four of the many areas cited by Cirino as being (presumably) of acute public concern, but which had been systematically ignored by the American mass media. To take an example of a different order from Britain: for some two years before the story became big news in the conventional media, most working journalists knew (and the satirical magazine *Private Eye* had already published) the information about the then Home Secretary Mr Maudling's suspicious financial involvements which was to lead to his resignation in 1972. The same applied to the Jeremy Thorpe story in 1978. Many unusual and startling events are concealed for long periods of time—and by no means just because of libel laws—before other events force some discussion of them, while many 'events' such as comments of politicians, amazing only in their lack of surprise and interest, are reported in great detail. Or to take as a further example the news reporting of the British Royal Family: as any avid reader of the foreign press will know, the Royal 'good news' stories which are obligatory in the British Press stand in stark contrast to the news angle in continental papers. Nor are all of these stories speculative: witness the manner in which the breakup of Princess Margaret and Lord Snowdon's marriage was widely discussed in continental papers months ahead of their British counterparts.

Now such an argument is on the face of it, in line with Manipulation theory and a serious objection to any Market model. This is, moreover, reinforced when one details the extreme degree of oligopilisation of the mass media in all advanced capitalist societies. For example Murdoch and Golding[3] in 1973 produced the following table summarising the concentration of ownership in selected mass media sectors in Britain:

PROPORTION OF THE TOTAL MARKET ACCOUNTED FOR BY THE
FIVE LEADING COMPANIES IN SELECTED MASS MEDIA SECTORS

(Percentages are rounded off to the nearest whole number)

	percent
National morning newspapers: % of circulation	86
National Sunday newspapers: % of circulation	88
Network television: % of television homes served	73
Paperbacks: % of domestic production (1971)	86
Mid-price long-playing records:* % of market	69†
Cinema exhibition: % of admissions:**	78

†denotes estimate   *Mid-price = 99p to £1.98   **Top four companies

Thus the two arguments hang together: certain news is excluded where it is dangerous to the *status quo* and then there is a high ownership of the media by precisely such interests. This is an important connection, but to point solely to the concentration of ownership of the mass media and its overlap with wider industrial and commercial interests is far from being a cast-iron critique of the Market model. The model depends, it is true, on the notion of a free market for news: namely, that the mass media are merely in the business of supplying the demand for news, and that wherever a particular desire for certain information grows to a size that is commercially feasible, a section of the media will develop in order to cater for it. And such a competition between news sources is unlikely to occur in a situation where ownership is in a few hands. But—the defenders of the commercial position will retort—the simple fact of a limited number of news outlets does not imply that the various magazines, newspapers and broadcasting stations will not compete with each other in order to increase their respective audiences. The owners are only interested in maximising specific audiences—and thus advertising revenue—and they maintain a commercial laissez-faire rather than a dictatorial relationship to their editors. Ownership of the means of transmitting news does not imply control of the criteria of the selection of news. This is true, Manipulation theorists may in turn reply, but the evidence is that the criteria for selecting news show little regard for the public interest: important news is manifestly disregarded and, furthermore, there is little variation in the news that is proffered.

The problem though with such a Manipulative position is that it is true only up to a point. The exclusion of news by political, legal and social pressures obviously is a form of direct manipulation. But this does not rule out the possibility that the news that actually does get through this web of censorship is a fairly accurate depiction of the world. Nor is it admissible to criticize market theory by simply pointing to the lack of variation in the news reporting of significant items, and thus the impossibility of the audience shopping around in a market place of different opinions. An advocate of the commercial model need merely argue that this is because the existing monolithic portrayal is *correct*. There is a true reality without variation and the media show it thus.

The more compelling evidence against Market theories derives from systematic comparisons between the assessment of reality by outside informed opinion and that which occurs within the mass media. Numerous comparative studies indicate that such a lack of correspondence is commonplace—that the media consistently get things wrong. We will return to this discussion later, but let us note here a few examples from the area of crime. The media's portrayals here are very often mythological—depicting worlds with well-structured delinquent gangs, an all-embracing Mafia, crazed dope fiends, drug pushers who corrupt their innocent victims, women who deliberately invite rapists, muggers who hold law-abiding communities in terror, police who spend most of their time on the streets investigating crime. . . . These are all characterizations which criminological research has consistently contradicted. Even on the question of basic statistical information (as Roshier notes) there is little relationship between the relative frequency by which crime is reported in the press and the actual statistics, and there is an exaggerated impression about the amount of crime cleared up.

Now this is not merely a question of the journalists deliberately getting and giving the wrong end of the stick. Indictment of the market model it may be but this does not drive us into the ranks of crude manipulative theory. For if the news items on crime were mere lies there would be—if we are to exclude the paranoid assumption that all the media are directed from one source—less consistency in their presentation and more obvious propaganda value in their content. But instead of this we have repeated patterns of presentation and recognizable models of interpretation which often do not have an obvious manipulative point—and indeed are often quite radical and subversive in their own way. How then are we to explain these patterned stereotypes which mediate in the selection process between the world of events and the eventual news that confronts us in the media? We might illustrate the question this way:

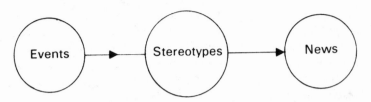

This is the sort of question to which Johan Galtung and Mari Ruge address themselves. They first list, somewhat eclectically, a series of factors found to be criteria of newsworthiness in the selection of foreign news. Two groups of factors are most relevant to our discussion: *bureaucratic* and *cultural*.

In terms of bureaucratic criteria, Galtung and Ruge state that an item of news is more likely to be reported if its frequency is similar to that of the media. That is, a daily newspaper will prefer to describe stories that occur within a period of a day—or if a news item takes longer to develop, it will only report the climaxes. This criterion may be termed *periodicity*. Similarly, definite proportions of a newspaper will be allocated to carrying types of news (e.g. crime, foreign, sport): the threshold for incorporating into the paper a particular type of news will depend on the relative scarcity of this sort of news at that time. All in all, the standard *composition* or balance between different types of news will be maintained— despite the variation of occurrences in the real world.

Among the cultural factors of significance are *consonance* and *expectedness*. An item will be more readily assimilated if it is consonant with the mental set or image of the newsman. As a corollary to this, new events without immediate precedent may be assimilated into the frame of reference of earlier accepted images. For example, Galtung notes how the Norwegian Broadcasting Company interpreted the Russian invasion of Czechoslovakia in terms of the previous invasion of Hungary.[4] Similarly, Graham Murdock (in his paper in Part Two of this book), notes how the 27th October 1968 Vietnam demonstration in London was cast in the scenario of the May events in Paris or the demonstrations surrounding the Chicago Convention, both occurring earlier that year. Within the factor of consonance, however, it is the *unexpected* that will be preferentially selected. That is (in line with Wilkins' suggestions): an unusual event in terms of the media's definition of usualness will find itself in the news.

It is not difficult to apply these bureaucratic and cultural factors to the selection of deviance and social problem news—say about crime, suicide, drug-taking, political corruption, pornography or pollution. What Galtung and Ruge importantly suggest is that the organizational set-up for gathering news and the cultural set by which journalists view the world have profound effects in determining the acceptability of incoming information. In other words, that bureaucratic and cultural exigencies mediate between events and the news. Periodicity and consonance are the two filters which determine the criteria of selection and, thereby, the mode in which news is 'objectively' reported. Thus:

This formulation, however over-mechanistic one might find it, recognizes that journalists are not merely tools in the invisible hand of the newsmarket—as the extreme commercial model would have it—but play a much more active, selective role. Moreover—to invoke the cultural dimension—they are creatively selecting and interpreting events to fit their preconceived models of the social universe. In a real sense, the court correspondent going through the daily list, the crime reporter phoning up the police desk, the London editor of the TV news deciding whether to run an item on a Birmingham bank robber, the editor selecting a news story on abortion statistics as suitable for an editorial: all are involved in *making* news.

This view of the media as active agents and not passive recipients or gatherers obviously goes against the commercial model. But equally, it raises problems for the Manipulative model which presents an over-simplified view of the domination of owners and controllers over creators. It, too, ignores the organizational and cultural mediations. Moreover, bias—which no doubt does exist, as our readings in Part Two demonstrate—may not necessarily be impelled by a conscious machiavellianism. Along with the more blatant censorship by others—which operates very much in such areas as violence and sex—goes the more important 'self-censorship' of the journalist as he or she systematically attempts to fit events into a particular world view whose basic premises are seen as embodying a faithful portrayal of society. So 'objectivity' becomes a matter of interpreting and analysing the event dispassionately in the light of the accepted paradigm of 'how things happen' and 'what the social universe looks like'. Now there is nothing wrong with this *per se*. It is impossible to approach reality with an open or empty mind; preconceptions are always there and indeed necessary, in order to make sense of what is going on around us. However, whereas some paradigm is always necessary, the question of whether the paradigm prevalent in the media may be *false* is one which occurs only on very rare occasions.

Paul Rock in his paper in this section, explores the nature of news as an organized response to routine bureaucratic problems. He expands on the criteria such as those used by Galtung and Ruge, noting how the demand for a regular news intake of a consistent and reliable nature leads to the mass media feeding off each other. Their shared product becomes reified as possessing an especially 'objective' quality but this is within the series of close relationships between official news generating agencies. Rock illustrates with great clarity how news consists of the unusual event occurring within the rubric of the 'usual' characterizations of journalists and press officers. The paradigm of the usual 'taken for granted' world view of the journalist becomes stylized into a number of almost reflexive clichés evoked effortlessly in the face of the deluge of events which face him in his work. In his fine satirical novel set in some futuristic Research Institute, Michael Frayn simply carries this notion to its logical conclusion by conjuring up the idea of a digital computer which could effortlessly produce entertaining news without any contact with 'the raw, messy offendable real world' at all.

The final articles in this section challenge the simple flow model of selection that we have developed so far. The assumption has been as Steve Chibnall nicely puts it, that the reporter 'goes out gathering news, picking up stories, as if they were fallen apples'. But only very rarely does he or she directly perceive events in this way: accounts are selected from the selective accounts of others and then they, in turn, are selected and transferred by the subeditors—the gatekeepers of the news. Specifically, Chibnall shows us how the link between crime reporters and the police almost completely structures this pre-conceptualisation of news: for events have *already* been turned into news accounts when the crime reporter receives them.

Now this process has two sides to it: on one level it serves the interests of those attempting to influence public opinion about themselves (in this case the police), on the other, it provides a steady flow of 'reliable' information to the news-hungry media. Gaye Tuchman in a series of influential articles and in her recent book *Making news*[5] has highlighted this central contradiction in the manufacture of news, namely that newswork involves the 'routinization of the unexpected'. That is, like any bureaucracy, the mass news media must routinely process information—

they must be capable of planning *ahead* so as not to be at the mercy of unexpected events. This, despite the fact that the media's very currency is the unusual and the unexpected. She indicates how this problem is resolved through various bureaucratic mechanisms and extends such concepts as 'periodicity' by situating them more clearly in the business of making news. In so doing, Tuchman goes beyond the Galtung-Ruge and Rock analyses by looking for the ways the established order legitimates itself through this work process. She tries, in other words, to weld together the two variables hitherto separated: 'power in the outside world' and 'power within the newsroom' by discussing the practical problems of manufacturing news:

> . . .news both draws upon and reproduces institutional structures. Through its arrangement of time and space as intertwined social phenomena, the news organization disperses a news net. By identifying centralized sources of information as legitimated social institutions, news organisations and newsworkers wed themselves to specific beats and bureaus. Those sites are then objectified as the appropriate sites at which information should be gathered. Additionally, those sites of news gathering are objectified as the legitimated and legitimating sources of both information and governance. Through naive empiricism, that information is tranformed into objective facts—facts as a normal, natural, taken-for-granted description and constitution of a state of affairs. And through the sources identified with facts, newsworkers create and control controversy; they contain dissent.

The dispersion of reporters to glean facts generates its own organisational structure replete with assigned responsibilities and priorities. These are the territorial, institutional, and topical chains of command. Distinctions between and among these three spheres, which necessarily overlap one another, require ongoing negotiations of responsibility and newsworthiness. At least in part, newsworthiness is a product of these negotiations intended to sort out strips of everyday occurrences as news. These negotiations also legitimate the status quo. Each day the editors reproduce their living compromise—the hierarchy among the editors. They also re-establish the supremacy of the territorial chain of command, which incorporates political beats and bureaus but excludes topical specialities such as women's news and sports. These sorts of news are thus rendered institutionally uninteresting. In contrast, the topics of the territorial chain of command—stories about legitimated institutions—receive attention and so substantiate the power of those institutions.

Social actors also produce the rhythm of daily life, which they base in societal institutions. In newswork that rhythm is embedded in the intersection of news organizations and legitimated institutions. Faced with a glut of information by the dispersion of the news net, newsworkers and news organizations battle to impose a uniform rhythm of processing upon occurrences. They impose deadlines on defined states of processing, and so objectify a news rhythm. They draw on the way occurrences are thought to happen, in order to reproduce a state of affairs conducive to news processing. Using past experiences as guides for the present, they typify occurrences as news events.[6]

How does Tuchman's conception of the 'news net' contribute to our discussion of the problem of selection? Note, first, that the net is aimed only at certain pools of events; secondly, that the mesh is geared to pick up only certain topics; thirdly, that the net is connected to the institutional structures of the powerful, and finally that the events themselves are precast by such institutional sources.

To change metaphor: the one-directional inductive flow from events to news (criticized by Chibnall) is replaced by a notion of a conductor from events to news. And the conductor is bent by the pressure of institutional power and practical concerns, carrying messages already preshaped by the powerful. Our diagram changes once more:

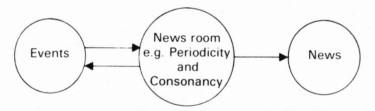

Two articles in this section, that of Fishman and Molotch and Lester reflect this type of 'radical phenomenological' theory in some recent American media analysis.[7]

Mark Fishman commences his article by pointing, like Roshier, to the disparity between police statistics and crime news but he extends this to examine how and why news organizations construct crime waves. How are a series of individual crimes constructed into crime waves and how does this relate to the process of news gathering and interpretation? He argues that news workers cope with the glut of crime news coming in at them, by grouping them into themes: for example, a crime wave of mugging, or of vandalism, or of Mafia violence. They 'routinize the unexpected' by clustering the disparate items into themes—rejecting those that do not fit as being of little interest. That is, they are dealing with their problems of periodicity (what can be coped with: *bureaucratically*) by utilizing a notion of consonance (what is expected: *conceptually*). Thus news is selected which fits these themes (the problem of criteria: *what* is selected?) and is shaped in order to fit these thematic categories (the problem of objectivity: *how* it is selected?). Furthermore, the result is not so much the statistically unusual—the atypical as judged against stereotypes of the typical—but that which is judged as initially atypical and *then* characterized stereotypically. It is the *typical atypical* event.

Fishman then explores the source of the journalist's knowledge of crime events and, like Chibnall, points to the major source as being the information relayed to them by the police (a subordinate source being news refracted from other news organisations). Thus it is street crime, for example, rather than white collar crime that is deemed news by the police, for that is what the police focus their manpower on. Furthermore, even within this restricted focus, crimes selected out are those which the police think are of interest to journalists and the public. Thus domestic violence and 'common' crimes against women are omitted.

Once such 'crime waves' become launched, politicians and police then proceed to use their news-making powers (given their strategic placement at centres of information) to augment or to attempt to halt the sequence. It is this creation and channelling of news which is the focus of the article by Molotch and Lester reproduced here. News is constructed reality, it does not simply exist 'out there', ('the objectivity assumption') but is a product which is pre-constituted by the powerful. But the possibility is there that through accident or scandal, the real nature of events can be modified by the population and forced on the newsmakers.

There is a danger inherent in some ethnomethodologically influenced research that reality itself can come to be viewed as infinitely interpretable.[8] Thus although Molotch and Lester in actuality construct their argument by contrasting the world of real events (e.g. the Santa Barbara Oil spill and the interlocking of Federal and Corporate bureaucracies) with the world of managed news, they commence with an attack on the objectivity assumption, namely the notion that: 'there is a world out there to be objective about'. Similarly, both Gaye Tuchman in *Making news* and Mark Fishman in the article in this volume, cite approvingly the Glasgow Media Group's commentary on the following quote:

'The week had its share of unrest. Trouble in Glasgow with striking dustmen and ambulance controllers, short time in the car industry, no *Sunday Mirror* or *Sunday People* today and a fair amount of general trouble in Fleet Street and a continuing rumbling over the matter of two builders' pickets jailed for conspiracy. (BBC, 18.55, 19 January 1975).'

In this piece of news talk the category 'unrest' is used simultaneously to gloss such diverse phenomena as different strikes, short-time working, and a conspiracy case. The preferred hearing is clearly that we see (since we are talking of television) all of these as merely cases of 'unrest'.[9]

Now the problem here is that such a position comes near to suggesting that any such categorization—or grouping together of events—is *necessarily* arbitrary, subjective or the product of mere folk or value judgement. The implication, in other words, of such relativistic theories is that there are no such things (can never be such things?) as crime waves or that manifestations of industrial unrest do not (and can never have?) any common links. Our position is at variance with this extreme relativism: we argue that objectivity in this context is quite possible and that conceptual categories (such as 'unrest') may be quite appropriate.

To point correctly to events in the world being social constructions does not imply: (a) that they are not real in their consequences (although people create social reality this reality comes to dominate them) nor (b) that this reality dominates them in the way that an illusion dominates a dreamer; (homicide rates do involve people actually being killed, strikes do involve the withdrawal of labour, theft rates do involve the violation of real property relations etc). As Norman Geras remarks about the arch-subjectivists, Berger and Pullberg:

> in an article on the sociology of knowledge, they formulate the following stupefying definition: '. . alienation is the process by which man forgets that the world he lives in has been produced by himself'. What they themselves 'forget' is that, if forgetfulness were all that was involved, a reminder should be sufficient to deal with the constituent problem of alienation.[10]

Let us return now to our twin problems of selection criteria (what?) and objectivity (how?). To point to the pre-processed nature of news-events and the ultimate meshing of power in the world and in the newsroom should not lead to a relativism which denies us the platform to argue that there are more and less appropriate criteria of newsworthiness in terms of the public interest nor that objective reality is a mere folk artifact. On the contrary, our task is to analyse the means by which the social constructions of the powerful distort news criteria and undermine objectivity.

This being said, the sort of media analysis which points to the social construction of news during and prior to the news gathering process obviously represents a considerable breakthrough. The concept of the natural event which is naturally newsworthy becomes less and less viable. Indeed a group working at the Centre for Contemporary Cultural Studies push this position even further in discussing definitions of crime:[11]

What in fact we are dealing with is the relation between three different *definitions* of crime: the *official*, the *media* and the *public* definitions of crime. Each of these definitions is socially constructed—a social event not a fact in Nature; each is produced by a distinctive social and institutional process. The *official* definition of crime is constructed by those agencies responsible for crime control—the police, the courts, the statisticians, the Home Office. This definition is the result of the rate of reported crime, the clear-up rate, the focused and organised police response to certain crimes, the way the patterns and rates of crime are interpreted by judges and official spokesmen in the crime control institutions and so on. The *media* definition of crime is constructed by the media, and reflects the selective attention of news men and news media to crime, the shaping power of 'news values', the routines and practices of news gathering and presentation. The *public* definition of crime is constructed by the lay public with little or no direct experience or 'expert' knowledge of crime. It is massively dependent on the other two definitions—the official and the media definitions. The selective portrayal of crime in the mass media plays an important part in shaping public definitions of the 'crime problem', and hence also (through further feed-back) in its 'official' definition. So we must replace the simple equation, crime = apprehension = news about crime with a more complex model, which takes full account of the shaping power of the intervening institutions. Thus:

crime ▸	'crime' ▸	news values ▸	'crime-as- ▸	public definition
(volume &	(product	(the selec-	news'	of crime
incidence	of insti-	tive insti-	(the se-	(the consequence
unknown)	tutional	tutional	lective	of information
	definition	practices of	portrayal	provided by
	by crime	'news	of crime	official and
	control	making')	in the	media sources)
	agencies		media)	

So a series of social constructions occur, each compounding typification upon typification. Indeed, the above illustration even underestimates
this process given that the major source of crime known to the police is, in
fact, public reporting—itself a function of the definitions of crime held
by different 'publics'.

There is nothing at all idiosyncratic about the complex twists which
such a model reveals—indeed it is the folklore image about the nature of
both investigative journalism and investigative police work which happens so rarely. Most other forms of news are also the products of public
initiation—whether from an individual member of the public (rare) or
calculated press releases from institutions and organizations. Indeed a
peculiar characteristic of modern news is that it is frequently a doubly
manufactured commodity. It is a characterization of an event packaged so
as to be 'sold' to the media and it is such a characterization repackaged so
as to be 'sold' to an audience. Thus:

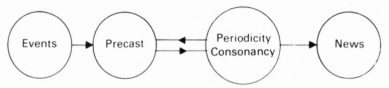

Critical research calls for some counterposing of objective reality
against such news commodities. Of interest, here, because it analyses
how a piece of social science research is reported by the media, is the
article by Paul Edwards on the way in which a study of industrial relations
in Britain was refurbished in the press. Edwards notes, in particular, how
the 'awful truth' that strike statistics do not contain every industrial disturbance was picked upon as evidence that the statistics concealed the true
extent of 'strife in our factories' and how a correlation between the rate of
strikes and the level of shop steward organisation came to be interpreted as the causal sequence: agitators lead to strikes. 'To any serious
student of the "strike problem" '—Edwards notes—'the finding that official figures do not record every strike is notable solely for its obviousness'. That is, strike rates like crime rates are social constructs, they are
not natural objects as the media would have us believe. In order to make
objective comparisons, it is necessary to employ social constructs involving agreed definitions and cut off points whilst allowing for variation in
reporting and interpretation of such indices. And just like news organizations, the periodicity (bureaucratic problems) and consonance (social
constructs) of such statistic-collecting agencies shape their eventual
product.

Both the notion of a national strike figure which is high and alarming and the causal sequence (militants cause strikes) fit the preconceptions of the media on industrial relations. Important to note is that here is an example of contradiction between news source and the news gatherers. This is close to what Molotch and Lester call an 'accident'. What Edwards is tracing here is the fashion in which the conceptually unexpected is transformed into a message consonant with the ideological structures of the media.[12] Normally, this doesn't have to be done; in a journalist's words about police information: 'generally what we write is parallel and complementary to what the police are saying; but this is not a deliberate policy—it just happens that so often the interests of the press, the police and the public are complementary.'[13] But in the instances of 'accidents' or in the work of critical researchers or organizations, a recasting of the message is more likely to occur. This can be seen, for example, in the case of some recent War correspondents—who will build into their reports an account of the difference between the army press release and the 'news' as they see it from other sources.

Let us return finally to the problems of periodicity and consonance and the relationship between these principles of news gathering. As Tuchman stresses, the conduits of information are, of course, laid primarily to those established news sources which provide the expected interpretation of events—and in this sense alone consonance has a determinate influence over the periodicity. Furthermore, in their attempt to 'sell' their own particular interpretation of the news to the news gatherers, large institutions with public relations departments will—whether they be industrial corporations, trade unions, the police or the army—attempt to pre-package a commodity which argues their particular case in terms consonant with the discourse or terms of debate used by the media. It is only the minority event (the accident, the critical research report etc.) which sounds a discordant note and these, as we have seen, tend to have their messages and implications recast. Such messages, with their lack of periodicity and consonance with the media, must pass a greater threshold before they will be selected as news items.

It is obviously not enough to see consonance (or the 'themes' which Fishman discusses) as arising purely from the problems of information glut and periodicity. Granted that the bureaucratic and cultural structure of the media demands a well-timed, correctly phrased product, where does the *content* of the stereotypes used in this selection and packaging of events come from? Stuart Hall confronts this problem of the implicit and unstated rules of journalism, by examining one of its products, the daily radio news, in the light of its ideological significance. He argues that its

basic model of society is that of a democratic consensus where a considerable measure of agreement occurs over the legitimate nature of the existing political and economic arrangements. This paradigm might in fact
'work' for many events but the problems and contradictions arise when
the media are asked to explain those groups and phenomena which
explicitly deny the consensual world view, for example, Black Power,
the New Left, the Woman's Movement, unofficial strikes, the Gay Liberation and the formation of prisoners' unions. That is just as periodicity
demands the routinization of the unexpected so does consonance. To face
this challenge, the media adopt an analysis—and hence, implicitly, a
mode of selection—which defuses the reality of alternative conceptions
of social order. It does not allow such phenomena an integrity of their
own, but instead characterizes them as 'meaningless', 'immature' or
'senseless', as involving a *misunderstanding* of reality rather than an
alternative interpretation of its nature. Thus Hall finds in the structures
used to select and analyse events in the mass media important ideological
significance for the maintenance of the *status quo* of power and interest.

The conceptualisation used by the mass media is thus causally linked to
the power structure of the outside world. In the next section we will
examine the nature of such explanatory models and critically discuss the
limits of this sort of analysis of the cultural structures used to manufacture
news.

REFERENCES

1. See F. S. Siebert, T. Peterson and W. Schramm, *Four theories of the press,*
   (University of Illinois Press, 1963) for a discussion of libertarian and social
   responsibility theories.
2. See R. Cirino, *Don't blame the people* (Los Angeles: Diversity Press, 1971)
   extracts from which we reprinted in the first edition.
3. G. Murdock and P. Golding, 'For a political economy of mass communication' in *Socialist Register 1973* (eds.) R. Milliband and J. Saville (London,
   Merlin Press, 1974) and 'The structure, ownership and control of the press
   1914–1976' in G. Boyce *et al.* (eds.), *Newspaper History* (London, Constable, 1978).
4. Cited in J. Halloran, P. Elliott and G. Murdock, *Demonstrations and communications* (Harmondsworth, Penguin Books, 1970), p. 26.
5. 'Objectivity as strategic ritual', *American Journal of Sociology,* 77 (1972) pp
   660–79; 'Making news by doing work', *American Journal of Sociology,* 79
   (1973) pp 110–31; 'Introduction' to *The TV establishment* ed. G. Tuchman
   (New Jersey, Prentice-Hall, 1974) and *Making news* (New York, The Free
   Press, 1978).
6. Ibid. pp. 210–11.

7. Besides these and Tuchman's work, see E. Epstein, *News from nowhere* (New York, Random House, 1973). H. Molotch and M. Lester, 'Accidental news', *American Journal of Sociology* 81 (September 1975) pp. 235–260. Note also the discussion in Philip Elliott, 'Media organizations and occupations' in *Mass communication and society,* ed. J. Curran, M. Gurevitch and J. Woollacott (London, Arnold, 1977).

8. For a crude example of such a position see D. Anderson and W. Sharrock, 'Biasing the news', *Sociology* 13 (September 1979, pp. 367–385). For them, there can never be objectivity or bias.

9. Glasgow Media Group, *Bad news* (London, Routledge & Kegan Paul, 1976), p. 23.

10. N. Geras, 'Marx and the critique of political economy', in *Ideology in social science* ed. R. Blackburn (London, Fontana, 1972), p. 292. The article they refer to is P. Berger and S. Pullberg, 'Reification and the sociological critique of consciousness', *New Left Review*, No. 35 (Jan. –Feb. 1966) p. 61.

11. S. Hall, J. Clarke, C. Critcher, T. Jefferson and B. Roberts, 'Newsmaking and crime' CCCS pamphlet No. 37. This pamphlet was part of the collective work which led up to the book *Policing the crisis,* S. Hall *et al.* (London, Macmillan, 1978) (see the selection from this volume in Section 2).

12. Young gives an additional example of this in Section 2 when he deals with the press reception to the Wootton Report on Cannabis.

13. Cited in S. Harris, 'Are the police a special case?' MA thesis, Middlesex Polytechnic, March 1978.

Information and the definition of deviance*

LESLIE WILKINS

The experience which forms the basis for classification of usual and unusual events is obtained in different ways and its content will differ. Experience is coded and stored as information, this the mind retrieves from the store as and when required. In the retrieval process the information may become distorted owing to its interaction with other information stored at earlier periods. Some discussion of the ways in which information influences classifications of deviance is necessary in presenting the general theory.

It would appear that information may be classified for the current purpose according to three types of consideration:

(a) content
(b) amount
(c) channel

By 'channel' is meant the different means of receiving information, particularly the difference between directly and indirectly received information. Some information may be regarded as trivial because of its content, or it may have no impact because the amount was small or the channel through which the information was received regarded as unreliable. What is regarded as trivial will relate to the perception of the culture in which the observer lives as much as to the degree of unusualness.

As an example of the trivial, but perhaps also unusual, the following might suffice. If I am unaccustomed to eating without wearing a jacket, I will perceive a person so eating as acting 'abnormally'. According to my interpretation of the action in relation to the culture and my status within the culture I may take a different seat at the restaurant, go to a different restaurant, or demand that the person be arrested! In general the dimen-

*Extract from Leslie T. Wilkins, *Social deviance: social policy, action and research* (London, Tavistock, 1964), pp. 59–65.

sion of 'unusualness' and the dimension of triviality will be negatively correlated. It is difficult to think of something that would be defined by every person as a trivial deviation from normality but that, at the same time, is an extremely rarely observed deviation. If an event or an act committed by any person is *sufficiently* rare, the rare nature of the event would normally be taken to imply lack of triviality. If I have never seen a thing in my life before, and it is very different from anything else I have ever seen, I am not likely to regard the matter as trivial unless I have other information to confirm the triviality.

A shopkeeper who notes that 2 per cent of his annual turnover seems to disappear in unaccountable ways may perceive this as normal, although he may know that it is due to shoplifting and staff pilfering. Depending upon his experience of variation about the 2 per cent, he may define 3 per cent loss as abnormal and take action which could result in an increase in the number of reported crimes, and perhaps also of arrested criminals.

It will be obvious that the hypothetical shopkeeper would adjust his behaviour and his definitions if he had further information regarding his expected losses. If, for example, he knew that the majority of stores in his particular chain experienced, say, only 1 per cent unaccountable loss, he would begin to consider ways and means of reducing his losses (2 per cent) to around the average or adjusted perception of 'normal' figures for his company. If he had other information enabling him to point to other 'abnormalities' in his district or type of trade, it might be possible that the two abnormalities would be perceived to cancel out to a total situation representing 'normality'.

As another example of the influence of information on the perception of normality, consider the following experience of the author. Rather late one Saturday evening he was returning to his home from central London. He joined a bus queue, which seemed to him to consist of some six or seven tough and probably delinquent gang members. He inferred this from the way they stood, and particularly from the manner of their dress. They had not spoken. His knowledge of the delinquent sub-culture did not relieve him of certain feelings of anxiety, or at least of a defensive attitude towards the members of the group. However, immediately they spoke he was able completely to modify his perception of 'abnormality' or deviance of the group—they spoke in French. From his knowledge of the habitual dress of French youth on holiday in England, he was able to fit this apparently 'deviant' behaviour and dress symbolism into a 'normal' or expected context. It would seem, therefore, that we may claim that what is defined as deviant is determined by our subjective experience of 'non-deviant' or 'normal', but that our experience and the resulting classifications can be changed by certain types of information. It would appear that information acts upon our expectations through our storage system and modifies the classifications which provide the basis for our prediction of behaviour.

The amount of information may influence the base against which events are considered with regard to their unusualness. The more odd experiences I may have, the less odd they will seem to be. The quantity of information available to an individual may increase his tolerance because it may increase the range of his experience of all forms of behaviour, or it may decrease his tolerance because his experience has been limited to more of the same kinds of observation. The shopkeeper may, for example, be tolerant of a loss of 2 per cent if he has information that only two or three other stores in his chain have a lower rate, but he may be less tolerant if he has information only from those with the lower rates; in the latter case his information is not only less but also biased. Increase in tolerance of events which would otherwise be defined as deviant is not a direct function of increased knowledge.

In recent years technological advance has mainly resulted in speedier communications between places in different parts of the world; highways, railways, and air travel have increased the range of communications both between nationalities and cultures and between different subcultures within the same nation. The shopkeeper of the 2 per cent loss store can no longer be unaware of the loss rate of other stores. The behaviour of people living in groups in what were once far-away mountains is now observable by tourists, administrators, and social agencies. In times gone by, deviant groups were able to establish their own cultures with reference only to their own sets of norms. Except for the intrusion of an occasional itinerant anthropologist they were left without contact with the norms of other societies. There have been numerous cultures where the total definitions of normality were out of accord with existing Western values. It was not until the increase in transport and the increased speed of movement brought these communities into contact with other communities having different concepts of normality that their deviance was defined. The definition of 'deviance' was, of course, provided by the more powerful forces.

Types of Information

Let us refer to the analogy of bridges. In total, the experience of bridges possessed by the population in 1600 would be much smaller than the experience of bridges possessed by the population today. The base of experience to which any new bridge could be referred for comparison by persons living in 1600 would be a sample of a much smaller *(n)* than would be the case now. The increase in speed of transport has increased the sample of bridges available to the population. The individual who travels widely will personally travel over and *directly* experience a large number of bridges in addition to those he may read about in the press. But the increase in travel may not be expected to increase his direct experience of crime. This is an example of a general point. The experience people have of *things* has tended to increase rapidly—things have to be extremely unusual to occasion surprise today. But the base of experience of *people* available by which we may be able to assess *people* may have diminished. In the village community were included all kinds of people, but the modern housing development tends to be limited in both class structure and age. There are communities where hardly an elderly person can be seen on the streets, and there are zones where children do not play in the public places. In the small local communities the farmer and the labourer and even the slave in feudal times were in direct contact with each other. Today more selective living is possible. The middle and upper classes do not necessarily *have* to know how the working classes live. There is no need even to give them their orders directly. Intermediary communications systems have been established so that the direct contact which was essential in earlier times is not now required.

The telephone makes it possible to talk to people without personally seeing them; the fact that even the lowest social classes can now be expected to read means that they may be sent letters and forms to complete. The administration may ask them whether they have a bathroom or not without seeing (and smelling) for itself. The insane, the criminal, and the deviant can now be isolated from society so that the normal members of the culture do not gain any experience of the non-normal. The unpleasant smell of the bathroomless homes contaminates a different sector of the town from that where the authorities concerned are likely to live. Even a world authority in criminology may not necessarily ever meet a criminal in order to become informed or to keep up to date.

In earlier times the young and the old were continuously in touch with each other; youth was aware of the problems of age, and age was aware of the problems of youth. The village was aware of the problems of mental deficiency—each village had its village idiot who was part of the total culture. Everybody knew 'Jack' who stood at the corner of the cross-roads and drooled. The newcomer to the village might feel threatened by Jack's behaviour, but immediately he spoke with a member of the village culture he would be assured, 'Oh! Jack's all right, he's just a little weak in the head—he was dropped on it when a baby.' Thus, apart from indirect experience derived from newspapers and other mass media, our modern culture has led to the isolation (and alienation) of deviant groups. The nature of the information obtained from direct experience and that obtained from mass media differs in both quality and type. The sample of experience obtained in the village contains different information, covers a wider range, and is of a different order from information indirectly obtained in the urban environment.

In urban societies the isolation of deviants has become institutionalized. Even the direct experience of one social class by visits for 'charitable purposes' has been reduced so that the paid social worker, quietly and decently, away from the normal citizen, is charged with the pacification of Jack, and the society has lost its direct information about and feeling for the problems of mental deficiency. The wealthy have moved from the downtown areas and have lost their direct experience of the problems of the idle youth, and so on. This is not merely a replacement of face-to-face communication and the information derived from such situations by other means, but a quantitative and qualitative change in the nature of the information. Clues may be picked up in face-to-face communication covering many dimensions and the information related to the situations which occur in a wide variety of ways. In a real sense members of the urban culture have suffered a *loss of information,* even though Jack may now be better cared for than previously. If it were possible for the urban culture to receive the *same type and quantity* of information regarding deviants as is obtained in the village, it might be possible for the urban cultures to accept a greater range of deviance. But, as will be noted later, the difference between rural and urban communication systems (face-to-face as compared with mass media and the like) necessarily involves also a difference in the type and the quantity of information received.

No value judgements are made here: we merely wish to bring out the point that information is a factor to be considered in explanations of definitions of deviance, and of societies' reactions to it. Value systems come into this discussion when we consider the mechanisms which people have constructed to insulate themselves from information—the ways in which societies' defects and shortcomings may be hidden because the deviants can be isolated and information regarding them rejected and distorted.

If the information individuals within a social system receive about the workings and expectations of the system is biased, they will be robbed of reinforcement of their definitions of normality. The effect of propaganda has been well documented in this regard. The individual's store of information, which serves as the reference for individual definitions of normal and abnormal behaviour, is today easily derived from the mass media. The larger units of society do not provide a set of information sufficiently varied for the individual to rely upon his own direct experience except within some limited range of activities. The average middle-class citizen living in the urban environment may be supposed to have information from his own experience, plus the information he derives from newspapers that is defined by their editors as 'newsworthy' . . . . The model used to describe deviant behaviour may perhaps be used to describe the differences between the nature of 'news' and the nature of information derived directly by experience, as shown in *Figure 1*. The region of overlap, where the individual has both direct experience of events and the experience of reading the news presentation of the same event, provides a check on the validity of the press comment and a base-line for the integration of the two types of information into a coherent 'experience' information set against which further events may be matched. Where there is no common ground between the two types of information intake, there may be a tendency to sum them simply together, ignoring the difference.

The selection of
crime news by the press*

BOB ROSHIER

There are two processes at work in the selection of crime news by the press: first, there is the extent to which crime news is actually selected for publication in competition with other categories of news; secondly, there is the way in which particular types of crimes (and criminals) are selected for publication out of the total pool of potentially reportable crime (i.e. officially recorded crime). This study is concerned with both processes. An additional underlying concern is with the impact of this double process of selection on the recipients of crime news, in particular its effect, if any, on public perceptions of crime and criminals.

The reason for these concerns is that they are tied up with the general process whereby the 'official' picture of crime is itself constructed. For the nature of this crime picture is shaped by the decisions of the public to report potential criminal events to the police, and these decisions are obviously influenced by public definitions of the nature and extent of crime. In turn, these definitions are likely to be influenced by the type of information fed back to the public through the mass media (since most people very rarely actually experience crime except in this secondhand way). In other words, it is at least plausible that the selective portrayal of crime in the mass media plays an important part in shaping public definitions of the 'crime problem' and hence also its 'official' definition. This can be explored by comparing the relationship between the three different definitions of the nature of crime and criminals: that shared by the public, that portrayed in the official statistics and that portrayed in the mass media. This study attempts to do this, in a limited way, with reference to press portrayals of crime and criminals.

The first process of selection (of crime news in preference to other types of news) is examined through quantitative measures of the amount of news space devoted to crime. In addition, these measures have been repeated for different time periods when the crime rates were different

*Paper prepared especially for this volume.

and moving in opposite directions, in order to see whether these variations were reflected in the levels of crime news coverage. This was done in order to check one possible manifestation of media influences on public and official definitions suggested by Leslie Wilkins' concept of *deviance amplification*.[1] One aspect of this process is that during periods of rising crime rates, feedback of information about this rise increases public sensitivity to crime which is reflected in increased reporting, hence amplifying the initial increase. Since the media are the main source of this information feedback, the theory suggests that rising crime rates should be accompanied by increased media concern and coverage, and vice-versa.

The second process of crime news selection is the way in which particular types of crimes, criminals and circumstances are selected for reporting. Where possible, the 'facts' portrayed in this way have been compared with the 'facts' as they appear in the criminal statistics to see whether there are any consistent variations. In addition, an attempt is made, through a qualitative analysis, to assess the common underlying factors which appear to account for the way in which news items are selected.

The study is based on a content analysis of crime news in the press (still the most detailed purveyor of crime news) and concentrates on three national dailies—the *Daily Mirror,* the *Daily Express* and the *Daily Telegraph* together with the *Newcastle Journal* (an important local daily newspaper in the area where this study was carried out). Some further information was collected from the Sundays, in particular the *News of the World*. The period covered was September 1967 (September to November for the Sundays). The same information was also collected for the national dailies (and some for the *News of the World*) for September 1955 and September 1938. These two years were chosen to see what quantitative and qualitative changes in press coverage had taken place since the present post-war 'crime wave' really got under way, and to test the 'amplification' hypothesis. 1955 was chosen since it was the last year of a five-year period during which the crime rate had been declining. Hence this would give useful comparative information as to how press coverage was influenced by a downward trend in crime rates. The information collected was: percentage of news space (i.e., total space minus advertisements) devoted to crime news, types of crime reported, stage at which items were reported (pre- or post-arrest), sentences given and information on offenders (age, sex and social class). In addition, information was collected on qualitative aspects of crime reporting. An attempt was made to classify the factors associated with the newsworthiness of crimes, and to assess how factually or otherwise crime news items were dealt with.

To supplement the content analysis data, a postal questionnaire was sent to a random sample of the adult population of Newcastle upon Tyne. This was used to assess public perceptions of crime and criminals using as far as possible the same variables as were measured in the content analysis. Also, the respondents were asked directly about their perceptions of crime reporting in the newspapers they read.

Finally, the official *Criminal Statistics* for each of the years were used for comparative purposes in relation to both the content analysis data and the survey data.

In the first section of the questionnaire respondents were asked various questions about the crime news in the newspapers they read. They were asked whether they thought their newspapers

(i) contained too much/too little/about right amount of crime news?
(ii) made crime appear attractive and profitable?
(iii) were too sympathetic/too hard/neither/on criminals?
(iv) made heroes out of criminals?
(v) put ideas into people's heads about how to commit crimes?
(vi) increase/decrease/have no effect/on people's tendencies to commit crime?

On all these questions the majority of each readership group (with the exception of *News of the World* readers) took the favourable view of their newspapers. A majority of *News of the World* readers thought that their newspapers contained too much crime and gave people ideas about how to commit crime. On the other variables the majority took the favourable view. These generally favourable findings are in marked contrast to the findings of a recent National Opinion Poll survey which showed, for example, that 70 per cent of respondents thought press coverage of crime increased criminal tendencies.[2] However, there is an important difference: in the National Opinion Poll study respondents were critical of 'the press' in general while in this study they were replying in relation to the newspapers they themselves read (there was evidence in the questionnaires that they differentiated the two). Thus, although people view the press in general unfavourably, they view their own newspapers favourably. Paradoxically, this seems to apply whichever newspapers they read (including the *News of the World* for most of the variables).

The respondents were also asked what crimes they thought their newspapers concentrated on and this was checked against what they actually concentrated on. In most cases there was very little relationship between the two. The exception, once again, were *News of the World* readers who were remarkably accurate (and not just because they got sex crimes right). I will return to this point later.

Finally, the respondents were asked to estimate what percentage of the total news space in their newspapers was devoted to crime news. Interestingly, in all cases the estimates were wildly high. For all readership groups the mean estimate was at least four times the actual figure (this was despite the fact that the legal definition of crime used in this study meant that the newspaper figures were, if anything, an over-estimate since they included a substantial proportion of minor offences which might well have been viewed as 'crime' by the readers). There is one obvious explanation for this: people perceive more crime in their newspapers than there actually is because they are more likely to read it. In fact, there is some evidence to support this view. In the various 'reading and noting' studies that have been carried out crime items were among those which obtained high 'thorough readership' scores. As James Curran[3] has pointed out, there is a marked discrepancy between what people actually read in their newspapers (human interest items with entertainment value) and what they say, in interviews, they think their newspapers ought to contain (serious social and political news items). This points to an interesting dilemma for the press which is rather well illustrated by the case of *News of the World* readers in this study. The *News of the World* contained the highest proportion of crime news. Its readers were exceptionally accurate in assessing the types of crimes it reported, suggesting that it caters particularly well for their tastes and hence is read less selectively. This all adds up to a clear impression of a newspaper that knows what its readers want and is giving it to them (as indeed its circulation figures suggest). Yet alone among the newspapers considered, it had a clear majority of its readers who thought it had too much crime news in it. In addition, its readers were noticeably more censorious of the way it reported crime compared with the other newspapers. It seems unlikely that the *News of the World* has recruited among its readers a majority of moral crusaders dedicated to its reform. A more likely conclusion is that there is a discrepancy between what *News of the World* readers say they want of their newspaper with what they actually read in it. Further, it suggests that people feel guilty about what they read in their newspapers and that one of the categories they read and feel guilty about is crime. If this is true it has rather ominous implications for newspaper producers: if they concentrate on what people actually read and hence presumably want to buy, they are likely simultaneously to incur the maximum public disapproval.

These findings have an important implication for the main concerns of this study. That is, whatever the quantity of crime news contained in the newspapers, it is more significant in terms of readership than the simple quantitative measure suggests. In fact, as can be seen from the table, the actual percentages are very small for all the newspapers for all three periods. The exception, once again, is the *News of the World*, especially in the earlier periods. One criticism of this type of data is that simple quantitative measures such as these ignore the prominence that may be given to the items (such as large headlines and position on front page). Consequently, an 'attention score' (devised by R. Budd)[4] was calculated for each crime news item. The overall findings were that, on average, crime news items were not especially prominently displayed in any of the newspapers.

From the point of view of quantitative coverage the figures give little support to the amplification hypothesis suggested earlier. The figures for the dailies seem to have remained surprisingly stable, while for the *News of the World* there has been a marked decline, particularly since 1955. Thus the post-war 'crime wave' does not seem to have been accompanied by an increase in press coverage, nor was the decline in the official rate between 1950 and 1955 accompanied by a decrease. This, of course, does not deny the amplification hypothesis. However, it does suggest that it is not simply a matter of feedback of increasing amounts of information in the form of crime news items.

It has been suggested to me that the small amount of crime in the national press reflects the fact that it is the local press that is the main purveyor of crime news. This certainly did not appear to be the case in this study for the *Newcastle Journal* whose pattern of crime coverage was very similar to the national press (despite reporting predominantly crime in the north east). However, the *Journal* is an unusual local newspaper in that it is a daily with a large circulation over a relatively wide area. In these respects it is closer to a national newspaper than a local. It may well be that the more directly local press does play this role.

For all the newspapers for all three periods, the relative frequency with which different types of crime were reported bore no relationship to their relative frequency in the *Criminal Statistics*. This applied even when motoring offences (which account for two thirds of official crime) were excluded from both sets of figures. On these data, an interesting finding was that the types of crime over-reported remained constant for all newspapers for all three periods. These were: all crimes against the person, robbery, fraud, blackmail and drugs (1967 only). However, the only crime very markedly over-reported was murder (including manslaughter). An important point is that in all the newspapers a substantial proportion of the total (up to one third) consisted of a wide variety of trivial offences. The only very significant variation between newspapers was the very high proportion of sex crimes in the *News of the World,* although even this was only really marked in 1967 when it accounted for one third of the total (as against less than 5 per cent for all the other newspapers). The general conclusion, however, was that the newspapers do give a distorted impression of the relative frequency of different types of crime and this distortion is in the direction of over-representation of more serious offences (or offences of serious topical concern in the case of drugs). If this seems a rather obvious finding, it is worth pointing out that this was not found to be the case in a study of Oslo newspapers by Ragnar Hauge.[5]

TABLE 1

PERCENTAGE OF TOTAL NEWS SPACE (MINUS ADVERTISEMENTS) DEVOTED TO CRIME NEWS, FEATURES AND ARTICLES

Newspaper	Sept. 1938	Sept. 1955	Sept. 1967
Daily Mirror	5·6	7·0	5·6
Daily Express	4·4	5·6	4·4
Daily Telegraph	3·5	3·4	2·4
Newcastle Journal	—	—	2·0
News of the World	17·8	29·1	11·0*

*Sept.-Nov.

A unanimous tendency for all the newspapers was to concentrate on solved crimes. In all three periods all the newspapers included far more reports at the post-arrest stage than was warranted from the actual 'clear-up' rate. In addition, where sentences were reported, there was a very marked tendency, again in all cases, to over-report the more serious punishments, particularly imprisonment. In other words, all the newspapers gave an exaggerated impression of the chances of getting caught and, when caught, of getting a serious punishment. This is obviously relevant to the often-voiced view that the press glorifies crime or makes it appear attractive and profitable. From these data the opposite seems to be the case.

Very little information was usually given about offenders. The only information that could be at all consistently collected was sex, age and social class and in the last case this was only possible for the minority of offenders whose occupations were given. However, on these characteristics it was obviously possible for the newspapers to give a false impression of offenders. In fact, once again there was considerable consistency both between newspapers and over the three periods. The sex ratio of reported offenders was very close to the official picture. The age structure, on the other hand, over-represented older, adult offenders. Finally, there was a consistent tendency to over-report higher social class offenders. The last two findings are of particular interest since they are perhaps the opposite of what might be expected from a more jaundiced view of newspapers (although they do fit in with the findings of Ragnar Hauge's study of Oslo newspapers). It seems, then, that the press does not exaggerate the extent of youthful crime, nor does it purvey a lower-class stereotype of offenders as has sometimes been suggested (at least, not in simple quantitative terms).

In general, then, two main conclusions emerge: first, that newspapers do give a distorted impression of crime and criminals through their process of selection (although not always in the way that might be expected): secondly, that these distortions show remarkable consistency both over time and between newspapers.

An attempt was also made to assess some of the qualitative aspects of crime reporting. First, why are some crimes selected in preference to others? What are the factors associated with newsworthiness?

From those aspects which were 'played up' in the reports, it was possible to discern four sets of factors:

(1) The seriousness of the offence. Sometimes this, on its own, would account for the newsworthiness (although usually only in the case of murders or large-scale robberies).

(2) 'Whimsical' circumstances, i.e. humorous, ironic, unusual. Examples are items headed:

'Flower people take blooms in raid on cemetery.'

'Jail man's first job—in a bank!'

'Thief pinches detective car.'

'Bank was tricked by boy of ten.'

This category, perhaps surprisingly, seemed to be probably the most important in relation to crime reporting in general.

(3) Sentimental or dramatic circumstances. These could be associated with either the victim or the offender, arousing feelings of either sympathy or outrage:

'Boys take Arthur's budgies. 25 years' work ruined.'

'Mother lied to protect daughter.'

'Man pleads in vain for woman who cheated him.'

(4) The involvement of a famous or high status person in any capacity (although particularly as offender or victim).

It is impossible to quantify these categories separately, since they were usually involved in varying mixtures in particular reports. They seem to account for nearly all the reports in the *Daily Mirror* and the *News of the World*, the vast majority in the *Daily Express* and a large proportion in the *Daily Telegraph*. The last mentioned, however, did have a substantial proportion of reports which did not seem to be accounted for by any of these factors or, indeed, by any factors which differentiated them from a multitude of similar offences which were not reported. Interestingly, the categories seemed to apply even more comprehensively in the earlier periods, particularly 1938. The earlier periods were also characterized by a greater concentration on drama and sentiment. This was generally the case, but an interesting example was the very much greater emphasis on suicide reports, with extracts from suicide notes (rarely reported in 1967). Reports with headlines such as: 'I prayed while he attacked me, sobs girl in court' which are difficult, although not impossible, to come by today, were quite commonplace in 1938 (with the exception of the *Daily Telegraph,* although even this newspaper was noticeably different in 1938).

'Sensationalism' in its usual sense of a contrived appeal to the 'baser' human emotions emerges from this as only one aspect of newsworthiness. Trivial, light entertainment is equally if not more important. In fact, anything which has entertainment value and contains human interest in the widest sense (appealing to the nobler as well as the baser human emotions) makes crime newsworthy. Indeed, if the evidence mentioned earlier is correct, this is what people want to read in their newspapers generally.

As this suggests, it is difficult to accuse any of the newspapers of taking a consistent line on crime reporting. There were, however, two notable exceptions: the reporting of drug offences and football hooliganism in all the newspapers in 1967. In these two categories there was a noticeable tendency to dramatize the seriousness and extensiveness of these problems and to publicize 'get tough' statements. In the case of football hooliganism this was achieved through various techniques such as grouping together a large number of separate (often trivial) offences in a wide variety of places into one report with a joint heading, '40 arrested in football riots', and also by publicizing statements from magistrates and football managers saying how serious the problem was and how something needed doing about it. This is not suggesting that there would be no football hooliganism problem without the press. It is suggesting, however, that the press does use the considerable power at its disposal to keep alive, direct and to some extent exaggerate the problem as it is purveyed to the public. Similarly, the approach to drug offences was universally condemnatory using everything from ridicule to spurious 'facts' and unsubstantiated opinions. The idea, again often voiced, that the press aggravates the drug problem by making drug use attractive or exciting did not gain support from a single item in this study. The important point about both these cases is that they suggest that there is a significant distinction between the way the press handles day-to-day, run-of-the-mill crime reporting (which usually includes most crime) and the way it handles areas of particular topical concern (the concern itself being, at least in part, a product of the press).

Another exception to the general points made so far was the *News of the World*. Although in all three periods the *News of the World* contained more sex crimes than the other newspapers, this was by far the most marked in 1967 (although in that year the total amount of crime news was much the lowest). But most interesting was the trend, over the three periods, towards a particularly characteristic style of reporting these crimes which makes it distinctive from all the other newspapers. 'Titillating' is perhaps the term which most people would use to describe this approach and, in fact, this is the term that most readily springs to mind from this study. It is achieved by the use of relatively long reports with a literary style that often carefully unfolds the plot like a novelette, with headlines which are suggestive without giving much away. A few examples from this period are:

LOVE IN THE SAND DUNES

DEEP IN THE SHADOWS SOMETHING STIRRED

THE PLOTTERS IN THE HOUSE OF SIN

THE STRIPPER, A P.C. AND A POWDER PUFF

A note was made of crime news items (and features) which expressed an opinion about the causes of or cures for crime in all the newspapers. The findings were very much in keeping with those of an earlier study by Peter Scott:[6] there is a great variety of often contradictory views expressed within any of the newspapers studied. This is not to deny an overall bias towards punitiveness or otherwise which may characterize particular newspapers. But there is a large amount of evidence today to suggest that people use the mass media selectively in such a way as to reinforce existing attitudes that they hold. The data here suggest that there is sufficient variety of implicit or explicit views in any of the newspapers to reinforce practically any viewpoint (although not always about particular offences, as the earlier data on drugs and football hooliganism suggested). This point is supported later by the lack of relationship between the overall bias of the newspapers studied and the views of their readers.

The final section of this study deals with public perceptions of crime and criminals and how these relate to newspaper presentations on the one hand and the official picture in the *Criminal Statistics* on the other. The overall finding is that public perceptions do not seem to be influenced by the biases in their newspapers but, in fact, are surprisingly close to the official picture.

First, however, respondents were asked what crimes they thought were the most serious. Most of the crimes selected were also those that were over-reported in the newspapers. The exceptions were robbery and fraud which were not rated as particularly serious. In general, though, there was some evidence that the newspapers concentrated on the crimes which their readers view as particularly serious.

Respondents were then asked to rate the relative frequency with which different types of offence occurred. These were then compared with the relative frequencies in the newspapers they read and in the *Criminal Statistics*. In all cases the estimates were very much closer to the official picture (they were surprisingly accurate in this respect). The accuracy was positively related to the socio-economic status of the respondents, but all groups correlated strongly with the official picture. Also, insofar as the different readership groups did differ from the *Criminal Statistics* they were not in the direction that would be expected from their newspapers' deviations.

One area where respondents were closer to their newspapers was in their estimates of the percentage of crimes cleared up. All groups over-estimated the clear-up rate. This is in keeping with the fact that all the newspapers over-represented solved crimes.

On the characteristics of offenders there was again very little relationship between readers' views and their newspapers' presentations. All groups tended to slightly over-estimate the relative frequency of female crime compared with the official picture, while their newspapers did not. Their estimates of the relative propensity of the different age groups to commit crime was close to the official picture, while their newspapers over-represented older offenders. On the social class of offenders, there was some evidence that respondents did over-estimate the extent of crime among the higher status groups (compared with the official picture, although in this case the official picture is not itself very clear). This was in line with their newspaper portrayals, but the tendency was not very marked.

In general, then, on these characteristics public perceptions of crime and criminals appeared to be very more much influenced by the official picture than by their newspapers. This is more or less encouraging depending on how sceptically one view the meaningfulness of the official picture. However, there certainly seems to be very little evidence of any direct influence by the newspapers on their readers' views.

News of the World readers, however, presented an interesting case. They rated sexual crimes as being particularly serious and particularly frequent (there was in fact a general tendency to rate sexual crimes very high on these dimensions, but *News of the World* readers were the most marked). Thus, in one respect they did appear to share their newspaper's relative preoccupation with sex (although, as we saw earlier, they disapproved of this). Whether this reflects an influence by the *News of the World* on its readers, or whether it simply means that the *News of the World* caters particularly well for those who share an extreme form of a general preoccupation is impossible to say. However, in view of other findings, the latter probably seems more likely.

Respondents were also asked what they thought was necessary to reduce the crime rate. Their answers were rated as 'predominantly punitive', 'predominantly reformative' or 'neutral'. In line with the National Opinion Poll findings the respondents were generally predominantly punitive. This, however, was strongly related to socio-economic status, the lower groups being markedly more punitive. Interestingly, it did not relate directly to the newspapers they read. Thus, for example, *Daily Mirror* readers far more frequently mentioned the need for the return of capital punishment than did *Daily Telegraph* readers despite the opposite policies of the two newspapers on this issue. The difference was entirely accounted for by the different socio-economic status of the readership groups. Once again, then, it appears that newspaper presentations have not been very influential on their readers' views.

Well over 90 per cent of respondents agreed that the crime rate had been rising in recent years and a generally high level of concern about 'the crime problem' was reflected in the answers to the previously mentioned question. This has obvious implications for the 'amplification' question. Although the rising crime rate had not been reflected in increased crime reporting it was clear that the increase had been more than adequately conveyed to the public. This was presumably through the communication of crime trends in the official *Criminal Statistics* (hence the general accuracy of public perceptions). It is still possible, then, that feedback of official information may play a significant amplifying function.

In conclusion, the findings in this study suggest that although the press does present a consistently biased impression of crime and criminals through its process of selection, there is little evidence to suggest that this is very influential on public perceptions of, and opinions about, these phenomena. In general the findings support the view that the simple deterministic conception of the effects of the mass media whether on attitudes, knowledge or behaviour grossly underestimates the abilities of the recipients to differentiate and interpret the information they receive. Not only do they not confuse media fiction with reality but nor, it seems from this study, do they take media presentations of real events to be necessarily representative of reality.

REFERENCES

1. L. T. Wilkins, *Social deviance* (London, Tavistock, 1964).
2. *National Opinion Poll, Attitudes toward crime, violence and permissiveness in society* (1971).
3. J. Curran, 'The impact of television on the audience for national newspapers 1945–68', in J. Tunstall (ed.), *Media sociology* (London, Constable, 1970).
4. R. W. Budd, 'Attention score: a device for measuring news "play"', *Journalism Quarterly* Vol. 41, No. 2 (Iowa, 1964).
5. R. Hauge, 'Crime and the press', in N. Christie (ed.), *Scandinavian studies in criminology* Vol. 1 (London, Tavistock, 1965).
6. P. D. Scott, 'Public opinion and juvenile delinquency', *British Journal of Delinquency* (July 1950).

Structuring and selecting news*

JOHAN GALTUNG AND MARI RUGE

Imagine that the world can be likened to an enormous set of broadcasting stations, each one emitting its signal or its programme at its proper wavelength. (Another metaphor might be of a set of atoms of different kinds emitting waves corresponding to their condition.) The emission is continuous, corresponding to the truism that something is always happening to any person in the world. Even if he sleeps quietly, sleep is 'happening'[1]—what we choose to consider an 'event' is culturally determined. The set of world events, then, is like the cacophony of sound one gets by scanning the dial of one's radio receiver, and particularly confusing if this is done quickly on the medium-wave or short-wave dials. Obviously this cacophony does not make sense, it may become meaningful only if one station is tuned in and listened to for some time before one switches on to the next one.

Since we cannot register everything, we have to select, and the question is what will strike our attention. This is a problem in the psychology of perception and the following is a short list of some obvious implications of this metaphor:

(F_1) If the frequency of the signal is outside the dial it will not be recorded.

(F_2) The stronger the signal, the greater the amplitude, the more probable that it will be recorded as worth listening to.

(F_3) The more clear and unambiguous the signal (the less noise there is), the more probable that it will be recorded as worth listening to.

(F_4) The more meaningful the signal, the more probable that it will be recorded as worth listening to.

(F_5) The more consonant the signal is with the mental image of what one expects to find, the more probable that it will be recorded as worth listening to.

*Extract from 'The structure of foreign news: The presentation of the Congo, Cuba and Cyprus crises in four foreign newspapers', *Journal of International Peace Research*, 1 (1965), pp. 64–90.

(F_6) The more unexpected the signal, the more probable that it will be recorded as worth listening to.

(F_7) If one signal has been tuned in to, the more likely it will continue to be tuned in to as worth listening to.

(F_8) The more a signal has been tuned in to, the more probable that a very different kind of signal will be recorded as worth listening to next time.

Some comments on these factors are in order. They are nothing but common-sense perception psychology translated into radio-scanning and event-scanning activities. The proper thing to do in order to test their validity would be to observe journalists at work or radio listeners operating with the dial—and we have no such data. For want of this the factors should be anchored in general reasoning and social science findings.

The first factor is trivial when applied to radio sets, less so when applied to events in general. Since this is a metaphor and not a model we shall be liberal in our interpretation of frequency and proceed as follows. By the 'frequency' of an event we refer to the time-span needed for the event to unfold itself and acquire meaning. For a soldier to die during a battle this time-span is very short; for a development process in a country to take place the time-span may be very long. Just as the radio dial has its limitation with regard to electro-magnetic waves, so will the newspaper have its limitations, and the thesis is that *the more similar the frequency of the event is to the frequency of the news medium, the more probable that it will be recorded as news by that news medium*. A murder takes little time and the event takes place between the publication of two successive issues of a daily, which means that a meaningful story can be told from one day to the next. But to single out one murder during a battle where there is one person killed every minute would make little sense— one will typically only record the battle as such (if newspapers were published every minute the perspective could possibly be changed to the individual soldier). Correspondingly, the event that takes place over a longer time-span will go unrecorded unless it reaches some kind of dramatic climax (the building of a dam goes unnoticed but not its inauguration). Needless to say, this under-reporting of trends is to some extent corrected by publications with a lower frequency. A newspaper may have a habit of producing weekly 'reviews', there are weeklies and monthlies and quarterlies and yearbooks—and there are *ad hoc* publications. If we concentrate on dailies, however, the thesis is probably valid and probably of some heuristic value when other aspects of news communication are to be unravelled.

The second thesis is simply that there is something corresponding to the idea of 'amplitude' for radio waves. What this says is only that the bigger the dam, the more will its inauguration be reported *ceteris paribus;* the more violent the murder the bigger the headlines it will make. It says nothing about what has greater amplitude, the dam or the murder. It can also be put in a more dichotomous form: there is a threshold the event will have to pass before it will be recorded at all.[2] This is a truism, but an important one.

The third hypothesis is also trivial at the radio level but not at the news level. What is 'signal' and what is 'noise' is not inherent; it is a question of convention,[3] as seen clearly when two radio stations are sending on the same frequency. Clarity in this connection must refer to some kind of one-dimensionality, that there is only one or a limited number of meanings in what is received. Thus interpreted the hypothesis says simply the following: the less ambiguity the more the event will be noticed. This is not quite the same as preferring the simple to the complex, but one precization of it; rather an event with a clear interpretation, free from ambiguities in its meaning, is preferred to the highly ambiguous event from which many and inconsistent implications can and will be made.[4]

The fourth hypothesis also deals with meaning but not with its ambiguity. 'Meaningful' has some major interpretations. One of them is 'interpretable within the cultural framework of the listener or reader' and all the thesis says is that actually some measure of *ethnocentrism* will be operative: there has to be *cultural proximity*. That is, the event-scanner will pay particular attention to the familiar, to the culturally similar, and the culturally distant will be passed by more easily and not be noticed. It is somewhat like the North European radio listener in say, Morocco: he will probably pass by the Arab music and speech he can get on his dial as quaint and meaningless and find relief in European music and French talk.

The other dimension of 'meaningful' is in terms of *relevance*: an event may happen in a culturally distant place but still be loaded with meaning in terms of what it may imply for the reader or listener. Thus the culturally remote country may be brought in via a pattern of conflict with one's own group.[5]

The fifth hypothesis links what is selected to the mental pre-image, where the word 'expects' can and should be given both its cognitive interpretation as 'predicts' and its normative interpretation as 'wants'. A person *predicts* that something will happen and this creates a mental matrix for easy reception and registration of the event if it does finally take place. Or he *wants* it to happen and the matrix is even more prepared, so much so that he may distort perceptions he receives and provide himself with images consonant with what he has wanted. In the sense mentioned here 'news' are actually 'olds', because they correspond to what one expects to happen—and if they are too far away from the expectation they will not be registered, according to this hypothesis of consonance.[6]

The sixth hypothesis brings in a corrective to the fourth and fifth. The idea is simply that it is not enough for an event to be culturally meaningful and consonant with what is expected—this defines only a vast set of possible news candidates. Within this set, according to the hypothesis, the more unexpected have the highest chances of being included as news. It is the unexpected *within the meaningful and the consonant* that is brought to one's attention, and by 'unexpected' we simply mean essentially two things: *unexpected* or *rare*. Thus, what is regular and institutionalized, continuing and repetitive at regular and short intervals, does not attract nearly so much attention, *ceteris paribus,* as the unexpected and *ad hoc*—a circumstance that is probably well known to the planners of summit meetings.[7] Events have to be unexpected or rare, or preferably both, to become good news.

The seventh hypothesis is the idea that once something has hit the headlines and been defined as 'news', then it will *continue* to be defined as news for some time even if the amplitude is drastically reduced.[8] The channel has been opened and stays partly open to justify its being opened in the first place, partly because of inertia in the system and partly because what was unexpected has now also become familiar. Thus F_7 is, in a sense, deducible from F_3 and F_6.

The eighth and final hypothesis refers to the *composition* of such units as evening entertainment for the family around the radio set, the front page of a newspaper, the newscast on radio, the newsreel on TV or in the cinema, and so on. The idea is this: imagine the news editor of a broadcasting station has received only news from abroad and only of a certain type. Some minutes before he is on the air he gets some insignificant domestic news and some foreign news of a different kind. The hypothesis is that the threshold value for these news items will be much lower than would otherwise have been the case, because of a desire to present a 'balanced' whole. Correspondingly, if there are already many foreign news items the threshold value for a new item will be increased.

As mentioned, these eight factors are based on fairly simple reasoning about what facilitates and what impedes perception. They are held to be culture-free in the sense that we do not expect them to vary significantly with variations in human culture—they should not depend much on cultural parameters. More particularly, we would not expect them to vary much along the east-west, north-south or centre-periphery axes which we often make use of to structure the world. In particular, these factors should be relatively independent of some other major determinants of the press. A newspaper may vary in the degree to which it caters to mass circulation and a free market economy. If it wants a mass circulation, all steps in the news chain will probably anticipate the reaction of the next step in the chain and accentuate the selection and distortion effects in order to make the material more compatible with their image of what the readers want. Moreover, a newspaper may vary in the degree to which it tries to present many aspects of the situation, or, rather, like the partners in a court case, try to present only the material that is easily compatible with its own political point of view. In the latter case selection and distortion will probably be accentuated and certainly not decrease.

But there is little doubt that there are also culture-bound factors influencing the transition from events to news, and we shall mention four such factors that we deem to be important at least in the north-western corner of the world. They are:

(F_9)The more the event concerns élite nations, the more probable that it will become a news item.

(F_{10})The more the event concerns élite people, the more probable that it will become a news item.

(F_{11}) The more the event can be seen in personal terms, as due to the action of specific individuals, the more probable that it will become a news item.

(F_{12}) The more negative the event in its consequences, the more probable that it will become a news item.

Again, some comments are in order.

That news is *élite-centred,* in terms of nations or in terms of people, is hardly strange. The actions of the élite are, at least usually and in short-term perspective, more consequential than the activities of others: this applies to élite nations as well as to élite people. Moreover, as amply demonstrated by the popular magazines found in most countries, the élite can be used in a sense to tell about everybody. A story about how the king celebrates his birthday will contain many elements that could just as well have been told about anybody, but who in particular among ordinary men and women should be picked for the telling of the story? Élite people are available to serve as objects of general identification, not only because of their intrinsic importance. Thus in an élite-centred news communication system ordinary people are not even given the chance of representing themselves. *Mutatis mutandis,* the same should apply to nations.

More problematic is the idea of *personification.* The thesis is that news has a tendency to present events as sentences where there is a subject, a named person or collectivity consisting of a few persons, and the event is then seen as a consequence of the actions of this person or these persons. The alternative would be to present events as the outcome of 'social forces', as structural more than idiosyncratic outcomes of the society which produced them. In a structural presentation the names of the actors would disappear much as they do in sociological analysis and for much the same reason—the thesis is that the presentation actually found is more similar to what one finds in traditional personified historical analysis. To the extent that this is the case the problem is *why,* and we have five different explanations to offer:

(1) Personification is an outcome of *cultural idealism* according to which man is the master of his own destiny and events can be seen as the outcome of an act of free will. In a culture with a more materialistic outlook this should not be the case. Structural factors should be emphasized, there will be more events happening to people or with people as instruments than events caused by people.

(2) Personification is a consequence of the need for meaning and consequently for *identification:* persons can serve more easily as objects of positive and negative identification through a combination of projection and empathy.

(3) Personification is an outcome of the *frequency-factor:* persons can act during a time-span that fits the frequency of the news media, 'structures' are more difficult to pin down in time and space.

(4) Personification can be seen as a direct consequence of the *élite-concentration* but as distinct from it.

(5) Personification is more in agreement with modern techniques of news gathering and news presentations. Thus, it is easier to take a photo of a person than of a 'structure' (the latter is better for movies—perhaps), and whereas one interview yields a necessary and sufficient basis for one person-centred news story, a structure-centred news

story will require many interviews, observation techniques, data gathering, etc. Obviously, there is an egg-chicken argument implied here since it may also be argued that personification came first and that techniques, the whole structure of news communications, were developed accordingly.

We only offer those explanations without choosing between them; first of all because there is no reason to choose as long as they do not contradict each other, and secondly because we have neither data nor theory that can provide us with a rational basis for a choice. It is our hunch that future research will emphasize that these factors reinforce each other in producing personification.

When we claim that *negative* news will be preferred to positive news we are saying nothing more sophisticated than what most people seem to refer to when they say that 'there is so little to be happy about in the news', etc. But we can offer a number of reasons why this state of affairs appears likely, just as we did for the factor of personification. We shall do so using the other factors relatively systematically:

(1) Negative news enters the news channel more easily because it satisfies the *frequency* criterion better. There is a *basic asymmetry* in life between the positive, which is difficult and takes time, and the negative, which is much easier and takes less time—compare the amount of time needed to bring up and socialize an adult person and the amount of time needed to kill him in an accident: the amount of time needed to build a house and to destroy it in a fire, to make an aeroplane and to crash it, and so on. The positive cannot be too easy, for then it would have low scarcity value. Thus, a negative event can more easily unfold itself completely between two issues of a newspaper and two newscast transmissions—for a positive event this is more difficult and specific. Inaugurating or culminating events are needed. A PR-minded operator will, of course, see to that—but he is not always present.

(2) Negative news will more easily be *consensual and unambiguous* in the sense that there will be agreement about the interpretation of the event as negative. A 'positive' event may be positive to some people and not to others and hence not satisfy the criterion of unambiguity. Its meaning will be blurred by other overtones and undertones.

(3) Negative news is said to be more consonant with at least some dominant pre-images of our time. The idea must be that negative news fulfils some latent or manifest needs and that many people have such

needs. Of the many theories in this field we prefer the cognitive dissonance version because it is falsifiable. The theory, however, presupposes a relatively high level of general anxiety to provide a sufficient matrix in which negative news can be embedded with much consonance. This should be the case during crises,[9] so a test of this theory would be that during crises news that is not related to the crises tends to be more negative and not more positive (as a theory of compensation rather than of dissonance/reduction would predict).

(4) Negative news is more *unexpected* than positive news, both in the sense that the events referred to are more rare, and in the sense that they are less predictable. This presupposes a culture where changes to the positive, in other words 'progress', are somehow regarded as the normal and trivial thing that can pass under-reported because it represents nothing new. The negative curls and eddies rather than the steady positive flow will be reported. The test of this theory would be a culture with *regress* as the normal, and in that case one would predict over-reporting of positive news. This is exemplified by news about the illness of an important person: the slightest improvement is over-reported relative to a steady decline.

Again we do not have sufficient theory to make a choice between these possible explanations—nor do we have to do so since they do not exclude each other.

As to these last four factors it was mentioned that they seem to be of particular importance in the northwestern corner of the world. This does not mean that they are not operating in other areas, but one could also imagine other patterns of relationship between the set of events and the set of news. Table 1 shows some examples:

TABLE 1

SOME PATTERNS OF NEWS STRUCTURE

Pattern	F_9 nation	F_{10} people	F_{11} personification	F_{12} negativization
I	élite centred	élite centred	person centred	negative centred
II	élite centred	élite centred	structure centred	positive centred
III	élite centred	élite centred	both	negative centred
IV	non-élite centred	élite centred	person centred	positive centred

Pattern I is the pattern we have described above. Pattern II would, where the last two aspects are concerned, be more in agreement with socialist thinking, and where the first two are concerned, with big-power thinking. It might fit the news structure of the Soviet Union, but with the important proviso that one would probably use Pattern III to describe Western powers. Similarly, a newly independent developing nation might use Pattern IV for itself, but also receive Pattern III for former colonial powers. But all this is very speculative.[10]

Let us then list systematically the twelve factors we have concentrated on in this analysis; with subfactors:

Events become news to the extent that they satisfy the conditions of

(F_1)　frequency
(F_2)　threshold
$(F_{2.1})$　absolute intensity
$(F_{2.2})$　intensity increase
(F_3)　unambiguity
(F_4)　meaningfulness
$(F_{4.1})$　cultural proximity
$(F_{4.2})$　relevance
(F_5)　consonance
$(F_{5.1})$　predictability
$(F_{5.2})$　demand
(F_6)　unexpectedness
$(F_{6.1})$　unpredictability
$(F_{6.2})$　scarcity
(F_7)　continuity
(F_8)　composition
(F_9)　reference to élite nations
(F_{10})　reference to élite people
(F_{11})　reference to persons
(F_{12})　reference to something negative

As mentioned, these twelve factors are not independent of each other: there are interesting inter-relations between them. However, we shall not attempt to 'axiomatize' on this meagre basis.

Let us now imagine that all these factors are operating. This means, we hypothesize, three things:

(1) The more events satisfy the criteria mentioned, the more likely that they will be registered as news *(selection)*.

(2) Once a news item has been selected what makes it newsworthy according to the factors will be accentuated *(distortion)*.

(3) Both the process of selection and the process of distortion will take place at all steps in the chain from event to reader *(replication)*.

Thus the longer the chain, the more selection and distortion will take place according to this—but the more material will there also be to select from and to distort if one thinks of the press agencies relative to special correspondents. In other words, we hypothesize that every link in the chain reacts to what it receives fairly much according to the same principles. The journalist scans the phenomena (in practice to a large extent by scanning other newspapers) and selects and distorts, and so does the reader when he gets the finished product, the news pages, and so do all the middle-men. And so do, we assume, people in general when they report something, and, for instance, diplomats when they gather material for a dispatch to their ministry—partly because they are conditioned by their psychology and their culture partly because this is reinforced by the newspapers.

In general this means that the cumulative effects of the factors should be considerable and produce an image of the world different from 'what really happened'—for instance in the ways indicated by Östgaard.[11] However, since we have no base-line in direct reports on 'what really happened' on which this can be tested we shall proceed in a different direction. Our problem is how the factors relate to each other in producing a final outcome.

NOTES AND REFERENCES

1. For an impression of what sociologists can get out of the condition of sleeping see Vilhelm Aubert and Harrison White, 'Sleep: a sociological interpretation', *Acta Sociologica*, Vol. 4, No. 2, pp. 46–54 and Vol. 4, No. 3, pp. 1–16.

2. This, of course, is a fundamental idea in the psychology of perception. Actually there are two separate ideas inherent here: the notion of an absolute level that must not be too low, and the notion of the increase needed to be noticed—the 'just noticeable differences' (jnd's). The jnd increases with increasing absolute level; the stronger the amplitude, the more the difference is needed to be noticed (whether this is according to Weber's principle or not). This principle probably applies very explicitly to news communication: the more dramatic the news, the more is needed to add to the drama. This may lead to important distortions. The more drama there already is, the more will the news media have to exaggerate to capture new interest, which leads to the hypothesis that there is more exaggeration the more dramatic the event—i.e., the less necessary one might feel it is to exaggerate.

3. N. R. Ashby in *An introduction to cybernetics* (New York, Wiley, 1957) defines noise simply as distortion that may create differences in interpretation at the sender and receiver ends of a communication channel. But one may just as well say that the signal distorts the noise as vice versa.

4. B. Berelson and G. A. Steiner in their *Human behavior: an inventory of scientific findings* (New York, Harcourt, Brace & World, 1963) mention a number of principles under 'Perceiving', and two of them are (p. 112 and p. 100):

> B7:   The greater the ambiguity of the stimulus, the more room and need for interpretation.
>
> B3.3a: There may also be decreased awareness of stimuli if it is important *not* to see (perceptual defence).

What we have been doing is to combine these theorems (but not deductively) into the idea of defence against ambiguity. There are several reasons for this. Modern newspapers are mass media of communication, at least most of them, and publishers may feel (justifiably or not) that increase in ambiguity may decrease the sales. Moreover, to the extent that news shall serve as a basis for action orientation ambiguity will increase rather than reduce the uncertainty and provide a poorer basis for action.

5. The common factor behind both dimensions of what we have called 'meaningfulness' is probably 'identification'.

6. Again, some findings from Berelson and Steiner are useful (op. cit., p. 101 and p. 529):

> B3.2: With regard to expectations, other things equal, people are more likely to attend to aspects of the environment they anticipate than to those they do not, and they are more likely to anticipate things they are familiar with.
>
> B3.3: With regard to motives, not only do people look for things they need or want; but the stronger the need, the greater the tendency to ignore irrelevant elements.
>
> A1:   People tend to see and hear communications that are favourable to their predispositions; they are more likely to see and hear congenial communications than neutral or hostile ones. And the more interested they are in the subject, the more likely is such selective attention.

7. For a discussion of this see Johan Galtung, 'Summit meetings and international relations', *Journal of Peace Research* (1964), pp. 36–54.

8. For a discussion of this factor see E. Ostgaard, *Nyhetsvandering* (Stockholm: Wahston and Widstrand, 1968), p. 151.

9. Festinger has a very interesting account of how Indians selected rumours following an earthquake, and consistent with the fear provoked by the earthquake: 'Let us speculate about the content of the cognition of these persons. When the earthquake was over they had this strong, persistent fear reaction but they could see nothing different around them, no destruction, no further threatening things. In short, a situation had been produced where dissonance existed between cognition corresponding to the fear they felt and the knowledge of what they saw around them which, one might say, amounted to the cognition that there was nothing to be afraid of. The vast majority of the

rumours which were widely circulated were rumours which, if believed, provided cognition consonant with being afraid. One might even call them "fear-provoking" rumours, although, if our interpretation is correct, they would more properly be called "fear-justifying" rumours.' Leon Festinger, 'The motivating effect of cognitive dissonance,' in Gardner Lindzey (Ed.), *Assessment of human motives* (New York, Grove Press, 1958), p. 72.

10. As an example some impressions can be given from three months' systematic reading of the Moroccan newspaper *Le Petit Marocain*. In very summarized form: the first page contained news about progress in Morocco, the second about decadence, murder, rape and violence in France—so that anybody could draw his conclusion. Of course, such things will depend rather heavily on the value-systems of the editorial staff—but we nevertheless postulate the existence of general patterns. Ola Mårtensson, in a mimeographed report (in Swedish) of a content analysis of three major papers in the USSR, indicates both personification and élite concentration. Ola Mårtensson, *Pravda, Izvestija och Krasanaja Zvezda under våren hösten 1964* (Lund, Institute for Political Science, Lund University, Sweden, 1965), 26 pp. mimeo.

11. Östgaard, op. cit., pp. 52 ff.

News as eternal recurrence*

PAUL ROCK

News is a peculiar form of knowledge: its character derives very much from the sources and contexts of its production. With few exceptions, those sources and contexts are bureaucratic, and news is the result of an organized response to routine bureaucratic problems. So obvious is this interpretation that it has informed numerous treatments of news. Those treatments have, however, been dominated by one particular perspective on organized communication. The newspaper office has been portrayed as a network of communication channels, and news itself has been explained by concepts which revolve loosely around the cybernetic properties of such channels.[1] This mode of analysis neglects what is distinctive about news as *bureaucratic* knowledge; it fails to recognize that the communications of a newspaper office constitute a special system. In this paper, I shall examine one consequence of knowledge being transformed into a work material that can be practically managed by a complex organization.

The business of any bureaucracy is the routine production of sequences of activity that are anticipated and guided by formal rules. Those rules can never be exhaustive. They explicitly and implicitly define the limits of variation in the material that can be processed by the bureaucracy. When an organization does not exercise total control over that material, there is always the possibility that it will fall outside the defined limits of variation. In such a case, the formal rules are rendered inappropriate. The roles that were established to superintend normal work will lose their usefulness. The understandings that informed activity become irrelevant or misleading. An organization can respond by attempting to force the obdurate materials into a workable form; it may modify some of its practices; it may destroy the materials; or it may simply refuse to handle them. Yet it is apparent that anomalous or ambiguous cases can be disruptive and that some bureaucratic effort must be directed at their control.

*Paper prepared especially for this book.

The basic product of a newspaper office is knowledge about particular events in the world. Those events must have some extraordinary quality that makes them worthy of being reported to a large audience. They may be extraordinary and repetitive like dealings on the stock exchange, or extraordinary and uncommon like a disaster at sea. In either case, their reporting signifies that they have been identified as an important departure from the familiar and the everyday.

It would seem, however, that the identification process is not simple. Journalists and sociologists alike maintain that the world does not appear to reporters as a clearly structured entity.[2] A few of its happenings have become remarkable by convention. Aircraft crashes and elections are routinely reported.[3] Other happenings are so engineered that they become eminently reportable.[4] The rest is ambiguous and perplexing. It is not laid out before the reporter as a landscape composed of transparently ordinary and extraordinary occurrences.

This experience of confusion is compounded by the largely solipsistic nature of the identification process. News is held to be distinguished by its objective facticity. It is a social fact that is not open to much negotiation or manipulation. The readership of a newspaper is taken to be capable of recognizing and demanding accounts of such social facts. Its interest grows and wanes in response to changes in the natural world of social events. The reporter's own perspective on those events acknowledges both their facticity and their lack of immediate significance. However, it cannot rely on the public's interpretative procedures for clarification because they tend to be inaccessible to the reporter.[5] In the absence of such directives, the staff of a newspaper office are thrown back on themselves. They become a surrogate for the unreachable public.[6] Thus, while much news becomes what the office has itself decided to treat as news, 'newsworthiness' is still regarded as an independent quality of autonomous events.

The world does not seem to be arranged for reporting purposes, and the strategies which would make it describable reflect its confusion. They are not amenable to reflective analysis by those who use them. Journalists seem unable to explain how they impose order on flux. In consequence, the procedures which are employed to identify and record news are not regulated by formal rules.[7] They are, instead, governed by an interpretative faculty called 'news sense' which cannot be communicated or taught.[8] A newspaper office, then, is regarded by its members as a bureaucracy which cannot generate formal rules for all its important areas of activity. Such a lack of structure creates a great potential for anarchy.

The critical task of capturing news is entrusted to an indescribable skill whose workings are uncertain.

The world reported as news is ambiguous and elusive. Unless it can be translated into a succession of coherent events, the entire reporting exercise would fail. The process of translation must, moreover, be mechanical enough to ensure that a constant volume of news is produced at regular and frequent intervals. The organization of newspaper work cannot rely on a random search for news. It cannot permit lengthy explorations which might be fruitless. Certainty must be built into reporting processes.

The apparent formlessness of much journalism is lent a shape by its organizational setting. The explicit rules which fail to emerge in the quest for news are remedied by institutional imperatives that emanate from the more manageable areas of the industry. What seems unregulated is, in fact, controlled. These imperatives relate chiefly to issues of the mapping out and timetabling of newspapers. They give structure to the schemes which journalists use to confront an ambiguous world. They provide the categories that underlie 'news sense'. If journalists themselves are unable to articulate those categories, it is perhaps because they do not fully understand the larger contours of the context in which they work.

Space

Policies affecting the layout of a newspaper predetermine what can be reported about the world. They map out the rough system of priorities which will be allocated to the description of unrealized events; decide the proportions that those reports will occupy in the total presentation; and limit the entire volume of events which can evoke a journalistic reaction.[9] Newspapers do not vary substantially in size from day to day; neither do they vary in their composition. The inclusion of photographs, advertising and standardized matter such as cartoons and stock-exchange reports further defines what is recordable. Although policies differ between newspaper organizations, each one imposes a firm grid on the distribution of events that will be recognized. Such a grid enhances the probability that consistent amounts of crime, sport, foreign conflict and so on will journalistically occur. If the anticipated amount does not obviously manifest itself, the definition of what might properly be reported becomes negotiable.[10] The conception of what is newsworthy will grow elastic enough to encompass relatively nebulous or insignificant events. After all, it is this layout policy which supports the journalistic division of labour. Crime reporters, sports commentators and foreign correspondents are occupationally committed to producing a relatively constant output of knowledge about their particular worlds.

Of course, the overall spacing scheme is not immutable. The changing expertise of a newspaper's staff, novel events which seem to be unambiguously important, or perceived changes in a public's demands can all bring about shifts in the scheme. These shifts are, however, likely to be calculated and orderly. Once a newspaper has acquired a new focus, it will tend to retain it for some while. The movement from focus to focus will not minutely reflect the fluid character of the world that is under observation.[11]

Although the scheme organizes journalistic responses, it is evident that the way in which a newspaper allots space is itself based on some initial definition of the absolute and relative importance of different areas. In part, that definition may be explained by convention: newspapers record crime and sport because other newspapers record crime and sport.[12] Indeed, it may be regarded as the essence of a newspaper that it covers such phenomena. Other features of the scheme may be attributed to journalistic understandings of popular morality and culture. For instance, crime news has traditionally been defined as attractive to readers.[13] Yet, in the absence of effective feedback from a readership, the solipsistic element of selection remains and, once formulated, the scheme tends to serve as its own authority. What has been news in the past is likely to be news again.[14]

Time

Not only are events seen to occur in relatively stable proportions, they are also expected to occur in definite sequences. Newspapers are published in editions which succeed one another in time. Each edition must convey a coherent and persuasive portrait of the world; each must be significantly differentiated from its predecessors and successors; and each one must have some thematic continuity with other editions. The timetable of newspaper production imposes itself upon what can be recorded.

Developments which unfold very gradually tend to be unreportable by the daily press unless some distinctive stage is reached.[15] Phenomena which do not change appreciably have a lesser chance of being recorded unless they were expected to develop.[16] There is thus a constant strain within the reporting enterprise to adapt the world of events to the timetable of the newspaper. Such an adaptation may be achieved by a deliberate scheduling of newsworthy occurrences,[17] by delays in reporting, or by negotiation with those who are responsible for initiating action.[18] Newspapers must demonstrate that significant change has occurred during the time interval that elapsed between editions. This requirement may lead to nothing more than a special selection of what is newsworthy, but it may lead to the imposition of development upon recalcitrant phenomena. Western newspapers are unable to contend with slow-moving historical cycles; they are far better equipped to accommodate rapid, expected change.[19] They are, moreover, generally incapable of reporting what seems to be an indeterminate or fluid situation. Process may be forced on occurrences whose direction is indecisive.[20]

Thus, in the place of random search, newsgathering takes routine forms. Those forms can be continually maintained only if they are supported by a set of operating assumptions about the world and about the newspaper's place in that world. The assumptions transform a possible anarchy into a more or less stable universe of events in which there is some predictability and rationality. The events are linked together in a discernible manner, and their emergent properties observe an established time-scale. These assumptions maintain and are maintained by a corresponding allocation of resources. In the main, journalists position themselves so that they have access to institutions which generate a useful volume of reportable activity at useful intervals. Some of these institutions do, of course, make themselves visible by means of dramatization, or through press releases and press agents.[21] Others are known regularly to produce consequential events. The courts, sports grounds and parliament mechanically manufacture news which is effortlessly assimilated by the press.[22]

When these assumptions are applied, news can acquire a cyclical quality. If resort is made to developments which are institutionalized, predicted, short-lived and in continual production, news will itself become a series of cycles. The content may change, but the forms will be enduring.[23] Much news is, in fact, ritual. It conveys an impression of endlessly repeated drama whose themes are familiar and well understood.[24]

The ambiguity of events is thus considerably dispelled by trapping the activities of reliable and permanent organizations. News is less likely to be made by ephemeral groups of people, by ill-structured groups or by groups whose behaviour does not appear on a suitable schedule.

An interesting consequence of the search for an objectified and sure world of news is that the solipsism of the newspaper office may feed upon itself and transform newspapers into authoritative sources themselves. Once some newspaper ratifies an event as news, others may accept that ratification and treat the event as independently newsworthy. Journalists religiously read their own and others' newspapers;[25] they consult one another;[26] and look for continuities in the emerging world which their reporting has constructed. In this process, a generally consistent interpretation is maintained and built up. It possesses an independent and impersonal quality which makes it seem compelling.

These self-generated paradigms may, in time, become virtually autonomous. They may become progressively detached from their base and then unfold in accord with an internal logic of their own. In this fashion, the press can create 'pseudo-disasters'[27] which may have no discernible relation with events as they are known by outsiders. Pseudo-disasters, crime waves[28] and panics create a reality which is organized by the structure of the newspaper office alone. Most probably, these autonomous news cycles are more conveniently constructed than any other to meet the space and timetabling demands of a newspaper organization. They are likely to be discrete, brief, well structured, and pregnant with intelligible, consistent development.

I have done no more than impose a slightly different construction on themes which are familiar in the writings on newspapers and news. Yet the ritualized and cyclical nature of much reporting is a critical feature of the way in which the world is made known. It conveys an impression of eternal recurrence, of society as a social order which is made up of movement but no innovation. Change occurs in a series of small occurrences of small duration. There is no grand design.

REFERENCES

1. The prototype for such work was D. White, 'The "gatekeeper": a case study in the selection of news', *Journalism Quarterly* (Fall 1950), Vol. 27, No. 4.
2. Cf. J. Carey, 'The communications revolution and the professional communicator', in P. Halmos (ed.), *The sociology of mass-media communicators, Sociological Review Monograph*, No. 13, University of Keele (1969), esp. p. 33; J. Tunstall, *Journalists at work* (London, Constable, 1971), esp. p. 6.
3. Cf. B. Cohen, *The press and foreign policy* (New Jersey, Princeton University Press, 1963), esp. p. 55.
4. Cf. D. Boorstin, *The image* (London, Weidenfeld & Nicolson, 1961), esp. pp. 9–11.
5. Cf. W. Gieber, 'News is what newspapermen make it', in L. Dexter and D. White (eds.), *People, society, and mass communications* (New York, Free Press, 1964), p. 176; J. Tunstall, *The Westminster Lobby correspondents* (London, Routledge & Kegan Paul, 1970), p. 67; W. Gieber, 'Two communicators of the news', *Social Forces* (October 1960), Vol. 39, No. 1, p. 80; C. Lindstrom, 'Sensationalism in the news', *Journalism Quarterly* (Winter 1956), Vol. 33, p. 9; W. Gieber, 'Across the desk', *Journalism Quarterly* (Fall 1956), Vol. 33, p. 431.

6. Cf. G. Gerbner, 'Institutional pressures upon mass communicators', in P. Halmos (ed.), op. cit., p. 242; W. Gieber, 'Two communicators of the news', op. cit., p. 80; T. Burns, 'Public service and private world', in P. Halmos (ed.), op. cit., p. 65.

7. Cf. W. Breed, 'Newspaper opinion leaders and processes of standardization', *Journalism Quarterly* (Summer 1955), Vol. 32 p. 282; M. Warner, 'Decision-making in network television news', in J. Tunstall (ed.), *Media sociology* (London, Consable, 1970), p. 63.

8. Cf. B. Cohen, op. cit., p. 54.

9. Cf. R. Casey and T. Copeland, 'Current "news hole" policies of daily newspapers: a survey', *Journalism Quarterly* (Spring 1957), Vol. 34, pp. 175–6; W. Gieber, 'Across the desk', op. cit., pp. 429–30.

10. Cf. W. Breed, 'Social control in the newsroom', *Social forces* (May 1955), Vol. 33, No. 4, p. 331.

11. Cf.B. Cohen, op. cit., p. 99.

12. Cf.W. Breed, 'Newspaper opinion leaders', op. cit., p. 278.

13. Cf. J. Frank, *The beginnings of the English newspaper: 1620–1660*, (Massachusetts, Harvard University Press, 1961), pp. 202, 212, 237.

14. Cf. B. Cohen, op. cit., p. 59.

15. Cf. H. Hughes, *News and the human interest story* (Chicago, University of Chicago Press, 1940), p. 80.

16. Cf.J. Galtung and M. Ruge, 'The structure of foreign news: The presentation of the Congo, Cuba and Cyprus crises in four foreign newspapers', *Journal of International Peace Research*, 1 (1965), pp. 64–90. Extract reprinted in this Reader.

17. Cf. D. Boorstin, op. cit., pp. 9–11.

18. Cf. P. Murphy, 'Police-press relations', in A. Brandstatter and L. Radelet, *Police and community relations* (California, Glencoe Press, 1968).

19. Cf. H.Hughes, op. cit., pp. 55–6; W. Gieber, 'How the "gatekeepers" view local civil liberties news', *Journalism Quarterly* (Spring 1960), pp. 199–205.

20. Cf. S. Cohen, 'Hooligans, vandals and the community' (Unpublished Ph.D. dissertation, University of London, 1969).

21. Cf. W. Lippmann, *Public opinion* (New York, Free Press, 1949).

22. Ibid.

23. Cf. H. Hughes, op. cit., p. 210.

24. Cf. H. Duncan, *Communication and social order* (New York, Bedminster Press, 1962), p. 305.

25. Cf. W. Breed, 'Newspaper opinion leaders', op. cit., p. 278.

26. Cf. D. Grey, 'Decision-making by a reporter under deadline pressure', *Journalism Quarterly* (Autumn 1966), Vol. 43, p. 427.

27. Cf. N. Medalia and O. Larsen, 'Diffusion and belief in a collective delusion: The Seattle windshield pitting epidemic', *American Sociological Review*, Vol. 23, No. 2; D. Johnson, 'The phantom anesthetist of Matoon', *Journal of Abnormal and Social Psychology* (April 1945), Vol. 40; N. Jacobs, 'The phantom slasher of Taipei', *Social Problems* (Winter 1965), Vol. 12, No. 5.

28. Cf. M. Wiseheart, 'Newspapers and criminal justice', in R. Pound and F. Frankfurter (eds.), *Criminal justice in Cleveland* (Cleveland, Cleveland Foundation, 1922); F. Davis, 'Crime news in Colorado newspapers', *American Journal of Sociology* (January 1952), Vol. 57, No. 4.

The complete stylization of news*

MICHAEL FRAYN

The soporific quiet which filled Goldwasser's laboratory in the Newspaper Department was disturbed only by the soft rustle of tired newsprint. Assistants bent over the component parts of the Department's united experiment, the demonstration that in theory a digital computer could be programmed to produce a perfectly satisfactory daily newspaper with all the variety and news sense of the old hand-made article. With silent, infinite tedium, they worked their way through stacks of newspaper cuttings, identifying the pattern of stories, and analysing the stories into standard variables and invariables. At other benches other assistants copied the variables and invariables down on to cards, and sorted the cards into filing cabinets, coded so that in theory a computer could pick its way from card to card in logical order and assemble a news item from them. Once Goldwasser and his colleagues had proved the theory, commercial interests would no doubt swiftly put it into practice. The stylization of the modern newspaper would be complete. Its last residual connection with the raw, messy, offendable real world would have been broken.

Goldwasser picked up a completed file waiting for his attention. It was labelled 'Paralysed Girl Determined to Dance Again'. Inside it were forty-seven newspaper cuttings about paralysed girls who were determined to dance again. He put it to one side. He had picked it up, looked at the heading, and put it to one side every day for a week, waiting for a day when he felt strong.

He picked up the next file instead, labelled 'Child Told Dress Unsuitable by Teacher'. Inside there were ninety-five cuttings about children who had been told their dress was unsuitable by their teacher, an analysis of the cuttings into their elements, and a report from the researcher who had prepared the file. The report read:

'V. Satis. Basic plot entirely invariable. Variables confined to three. (1) Clothing objected to (high heels/petticoat/frilly knickers). (2)

*From Michael Frayn, *The tin men* (London, Collins, 1965), Chapter 7.

Whether child also smokes and/or uses lipstick. (3) Whether child alleged by parents to be humiliated by having offending clothing inspected before whole school.

'Frequency of publication: once every nine days.'

Nobbs, Goldwasser's Principal Research Assistant, shambled over and threw some more files on to Goldwasser's desk. He wore a beard, to identify himself with the intelligentsia, affected a stooped, lounging gait to establish parity of esteem with the aristocracy, and called everyone except the Director and Deputy-Director 'mate', to demonstrate solidarity with the proletariat. He had a powerful effect on Goldwasser, causing a helpless panic to seize him.

'Here you are, mate,' said Nobbs, ramming the word 'mate' into Goldwasser like a jack-knife. 'I'm just doing the "They Think Britain is Wonderful" file now. Seems all right. Variables are mainly who's doing the thinking—American tourists, Danish *au pair* girls, etc.'

'Are you going to cross-index it with "British Girls Are Best, Say Foreign Boys"?' said Goldwasser, 'I mean, to avoid using them both on the same day?'

'It wouldn't matter, would it, mate?' said Nobbs. 'We're trying for an upbeat tone overall, aren't we?'

'I suppose so,' muttered Goldwasser, unable to bring himself to argue with anyone as horrible as Nobbs. 'But cross-index it with "Boomerang, Bustling Britain", then. We can't have them *all* in on the same day.'

'Your word is law, O master,' said Nobbs. 'Mate.'

O God, prayed Goldwasser humanely, let Nobbs be painlessly destroyed.

'Have you checked "Paralysed Girl Determined to Dance Again" yet?' asked Nobbs.

'Not yet,' said Goldwasser.

'Well, don't blame me when we're a week behind schedule at the end of the month,' said Nobbs. 'That's all I ask, mate. And what about "I Plan to Give Away My Baby, Says Mother-to-be"? We can't do anything more on that until we've got a policy decision from you.'

'I'll look at that now,' said Goldwasser. Nobbs slouched away. Goldwasser lifted his eyes from the pencil jar, where they had taken refuge from the sight of Nobbs, and watched Nobbs shamble back to his office, knocking over chairs and sweeping files off the corners of desks as he went. He turned to the 'I Plan to Give Away My Baby, Says Mother-to-be' file.

'Difficulty here,' said the researcher's report. 'Frequency of once a month, but in fifty-three cuttings examined there are no variables at all.

Even name of mother-to-be the same. May possibly involve fifty-three different foetuses, but no way of telling from cuttings. Can we use story with no variables?'

Goldwasser put it to one side. One had to wait for decisions as big as that to ambush one unexpectedly. He looked at his watch. He had the impression that he had been working continuously for an exceedingly long time. Perhaps he had earned a break; perhaps he could slip across to play with the loyal leader cards for five minutes.

Goldwasser sometimes took himself out of himself by pretending to be a computer, and going through one of the completed sets of cards observing the same logical rules and making the same random choices that a computer would to compose a story from them. The by-election set and weather story set soon palled. So did 'I Test New Car' and 'Red Devils Fly In to Trouble Spot'. But the set for composing a loyal leader on a royal occasion seemed to Goldwasser to have something of that teasing perfection which draws one back again and again to certain pictures.

He opened the filing cabinet and picked out the first card in the set. *Traditionally,* it read. Now there was a random choice between cards reading *coronations, engagements, funerals, weddings, coming of age, births, deaths,* or *the churching of women.* The day before he had picked *funerals,* and been directed on to a card reading with simple perfection *are occasions for mourning.* Today he closed his eyes, drew *weddings,* and was signposted on to *are occasions for rejoicing.*

The wedding of X and Y followed in logical sequence, and brought him a choice between *is no exception* and *is a case in point.* Either way there followed *indeed.* Indeed, whichever occasion one had started off with, whether coronations, deaths, or birth, Goldwasser saw with intense mathematical pleasure, one now reached this same elegant bottleneck. He paused on *indeed,* then drew in quick succession *it is a particularly happy occasion, rarely,* and *can there have been a more popular young couple.*

From the next selection Goldwasser drew *X has won himself/herself a special place in the nation's affections,* which forced him to go on to *and the British people have clearly taken Y to their hearts already.*

Goldwasser was surprised, and a little disturbed, to realize that the word 'fitting' had still not come up. But he drew it with the next card—*it is especially fitting that.*

This gave him *the bride/bridegroom should be,* and an open choice between *of such a noble and illustrious line, a commoner in these democratic times, from a nation with which this country has long enjoyed a particularly close and cordial relationship*, and *from a nation with which this country's relations have not in the past been always happy.*

Feeling that he had done particularly well with 'fitting' last time, Goldwasser now deliberately selected it again. *It is also fitting that*, read the card, to be quickly followed by *we should remember*, and *X and Y are not merely symbols—they are a lively young man and a very lovely young woman.*

Goldwasser shut his eyes to draw the next card. It turned out to read *in these days when.* He pondered whether to select *it is fashionable to scoff at the traditional morality of marriage and family life* or *it is no longer fashionable to scoff at the traditional morality of marriage and family life.* The latter had more of the form's authentic baroque splendour, he decided. He drew another *it is fitting that*, but thinking three times round was once too many for anything, even for a superb and beautiful word like 'fitting', he cheated and changed it for *it is meet that*, after which *we wish them well* followed as the night the day, and the entertainment was over.

What a piece of work had the school of Goldwasser wrought here! What a toccata and fugue! How remote it was from the harsh cares of life!

Goldwasser started all over again with the churching of women. He had got as far as choice between *it is good to see the old traditions being kept up* and *it is good to see old usages brought more into line with our modern way of thinking,* when Nobbs came shambling out of his room, the word 'mate' written all over his face.

'Now look here, mate,' started Nobbs, 'this Paralysed Girl Determined to Dance Again . . .'

But at this point, as it said on one of the cards in the 'They Are Calling It the Street of Shame' story cabinet, *our investigator made an excuse and left.*

The production of knowledge by crime reporters*

STEVE CHIBNALL

Commercial knowledge and communications research[1]

In a highly differentiated society we look to the mass media to provide us with information about those areas of social life of which we have little direct experience. The media are our central repositories of knowledge, but that knowledge is of a particularly problematic kind. It is commercial knowlege, a saleable product designed to meet the perceived requirements of its consumers. In the case of the press, it is knowledge cast in the form of news, and as such it reflects the routine practices, assumptions and conventional wisdoms of its producers—the professional communicators. We cannot hope to understand the process of mass communication without examining the role of these professional communicators; but while media sociologists have accepted, in principle, the necessity of studying the world of the communicator, in practice they have concentrated their attention on the social effects of his products. Media content has been accepted as an independent variable with only cursory attempts to understand the processes which shape its production. Moreover, those studies which have looked at the production of news (the particular form of commercial knowledge with which this paper will be concerned) have operated with a central concept which is dangerously simplistic—the 'gatekeeper' concept.[2] Its deficiencies stem from its foundation in a model of news production which is apparently unable to cope with the creative aspects of communicative work. That model is essentially mechanistic in its conception of the process of news production as a system of cybernetic filters reducing the flow of information reaching the audience. Professional communicators are dichotomized into 'newsgatherers' and 'newsprocessors' whose activities relate to the two stages of production. In the first stage reporters collect the news stories and pass them on to the

*This paper was originally published in *Sociology*, vol. 9, no. 1, 1975, under the title 'The crime reporter: a study in the production of commercial knowledge'.

gatekeepers in their news bureaucracies. Here, in stage two, the stories undergo a process of selection, abbreviation and organization and those lucky enough to survive in some form emerge at the end of the news funnel and are received by the audience.

While superficially attractive, this model is misleading and can blind us to vitally important elements and processes of news manufacture. The reporter does not go out gathering news, picking up stories as if they were fallen apples, he *creates* news stories by selecting fragments of information from the mass of raw data he receives and organizing them in a conventional journalistic form. As Curtis MacDougall has correctly pointed out: 'The news is the account of the event, not something intrinsic in the event itself.'[3]

But in the process of news construction the reporter will only rarely utilize his own direct perception of an event. More usually, his raw materials will be the selected and selective accounts of others—his sources. In most reporting situations, the reality of events must be processed by others before the reporter can render his own account. It is within this context of reporter/source interaction, a context largely taken-for-granted by the conventional news flow model,[4] that the significant 'gatekeeping' takes place. If we wish to understand the selection and construction of news stories, we must examine the procedures which journalists adopt to identify potential stories and select appropriate sources, as well as the ideologies and stocks of knowledge which inform those decisions. We must scrutinize the process of exchange which takes place between the journalist and his source, the bonds which bind the one to the other, and the interests and predispositions of each. This is not to ignore the role of sub-editors and news room executives, for their importance lies in the occupational socialization of the reporter rather than in the selection of his copy.[5] By the time that copy reaches the sub-editor the most significant decisions have been made—events have occurred, they have been experienced, accounts of experiences have been constructed for particular audiences, accounts of those accounts have been fashioned, and these have either been stored away or transformed into fully-fledged news stories. At every stage selection and processing has taken place.

This paper presents a case study in these processes, outlining the procedures and relationships through which one group of specialist correspondents comes to produce public accounts. Although many of their procedures and experiences will be common to other journalists, no claims are made for the general representativeness of crime reporters. Crime reporting is the most deeply-entrenched and conservative bastion of traditional Fleet Street reporting.[6] Its specialists represent the old guard of hard-bitten, self-educated and politically-conservative newspapermen who are increasingly experiencing the arrival of a 'new breed' of university-educated journalists whose political beliefs and approach to news are significantly more radical.[7] Their impact on crime reporting has not been direct, as they have not been recruited into the field (new recruits are generally well-established and experienced journalists), but they are having an indirect liberalizing effect through their influence on the general ethos of the profession, encouraging a more sceptical and critical approach to news:

> Journalists over the last few years have become far more political animals. Before they only wanted stories, something to fill their paper, keep them in work. They are now questioning editorial policies much more. They are more critical of the police. (Journalist).

Crime reporters as specialist correspondents[8]

Crime reporters are an elite corps of professional communicators occupying a strategically-important position in the process of news creation and dissemination. There are, perhaps, 60 or 70 journalists who regularly report on crime and the police for Fleet Street papers, but only one-third of these are full-time crime reporters. These specialists form an exclusive inner circle, and the control they exert over our knowledge of the worlds of criminal and policeman is extensive. The portrait of reality they provide may be fragmentary and superficial but for most of us it is the most complete and detailed available. Because his knowledge is relatively exclusive the crime reporter's public accounts are *powerful* accounts, alternative sources are few. The power and exclusivity of the accounts make the processes, relationships and ideologies which shape their construction doubly significant to the media sociologist.

If we are to successfully understand the way in which the crime reporter selects and manipulates materials in his account construction we must first pay some attention to the developments within his specialization. The history of crime reporting is characterized by:

(i) An increasing reliance on one major institutional source—the Police.
(ii) A long-standing tradition of source suspicion and secrecy.
(iii) The increasing autonomy and complexity of the crime reporter's role.

The term 'crime reporters' is really a misnomer. They are essentially *police* reporters. They rely on the police rather than criminals for the vast majority of their information, and their frame of reference extends beyond crime to police politics, pay, conditions and public relations. The roots of their specialization lie not so much in court reporting[9] (although many crime reporters gained experience of this in their provincial days) as in what one of my informants described as 'foot-slogging'. The forerunner of the modern crime reporter was a 'leg man' who used to wander round London police stations in search of scraps of information for the use of more senior colleagues. His responsibilities were limited, but his increasing contact with the police and the relationships he began to form on his beat steadily contributed to the security of his role and the extension of his autonomy. The use of the police as a news source poses acute problems for the pressman. It is an essentially cautious and secretive organization whose members generally regard journalists with a deep-seated suspicion, but it also controls a great deal of potentially newsworthy information and, therefore, cannot be ignored. Fleet Street's solution to this problem was to employ specialists to work with the police on a regular basis in the hope that the barriers of suspicion and hostility could be broken down by frequent interaction with individual journalists who could prove themselves trustworthy and sympathetic. Thus the primary task of the crime reporter was the winning of trust and respect from sources who were generally not predisposed to accept him. If he failed in this task his professional existence was in jeopardy. As we shall see, this obligation to cultivate and protect his relationships with his sources still imposes a powerful constraint on his public accounts. But to understand why source relationships are so salient to the crime reporter we must examine the police's institutional arrangements for the release of information.

The inadequacy of official sources and the need for personal contacts

The police made their first half-hearted attempt to institutionalize dealings with the press in the 1920s when the Scotland Yard Press Bureau was founded—as a response partly to the growth of crime as a field of specialist reporting and partly to parliamentary compliants about the existing system of informal information dissemination (consisting typically of policemen selling information to reporters in pubs). The new arrangements consisted of just one civil servant issuing twice-daily bulletins. Since the war, successive attempts to improve press relations have resulted in greatly-improved Bureau facilities, but it is still regarded by crime reporters as grossly inadequate for their purposes.

Firstly, the Bureau still lacks the full co-operation of senior CID officers who control the information journalists seek. Many are content to sit back and wait to be asked for information and often regard such requests as an annoying hindrance to their investigations. The Bureau's civilian staff lack the authority to demand the release of information, and must be careful not to offend senior officers.

Secondly, despite the fact that some of the press officers have had experience in journalism, some crime reporters still doubt their ability to identify news:

> Some of these chaps can tell a good story and some of them just can't. It's a thing you learn and they've not really got much chance to learn it down there if they've never been out on the street working. (Crime reporter).

Thirdly, when information is released it may come too late to be of use to the crime reporter—either because his publication deadline has passed or because the police investigation to which it refers has passed the point where legal constraints on newspaper reports become operative:

> A lot of stuff we could use comes out too late. The important thing for us is to get the job in the situation where we can write most about it, and that is when it's just happened, no one is caught, or if anyone is caught, no one is charged. You are then free to write screeds about it. (Crime reporter).

Fourthly, the values of universalism which the Bureau has institution-alized mitigate against the interests of crime reporters who are seeking information which is relatively exclusive. And, although the familar and trusted crime reporter usually benefits from what little discretion the press officer is able to exercise, the extra tit-bits of information he does get from that source are insufficient to prevent him seeking alternative sources who can provide more detailed and exclusive accounts.[10] He uses the Bureau mainly as a source of *routine* information and, more frequently, as a means of checking information acquired elsewhere. As one press officer put it:

> Typically we are confirming information put to us rather than us initiating information. Competition being what it is, the press learn

information before we do . . . the crime reporters all tend to discount this place and use it only as an occasional source of reference.

In Fleet Street circles the Bureau retains a reputation for censorship—it is jokingly referred to as the SUppress Bureau and its mobile representatives—Divisional Liaison Officers—are sometimes known as the Don't Let Ons. I was told of one DLO at the scene of the Shepherds Bush police killing in 1966 who, when questioned by crime reporters about the murders, refused to say anything except 'Foul play cannot be ruled out'.

Thus, more often than not, the crime reporter is obliged to go directly to the men who control the information he requires, and comes to rely on the cultivation of close personal contacts, generally with CID officers. To quote the reporters themselves:

> The Press Bureau is all right for piddling little things, and it's useful for checking information, but when it comes to big stories you need help and guidance and this is where the Press Bureau falls down . . . . As a privileged crime man I can by-pass the Press Bureau more or less whenever I like . . . . Personal contacts are vital.

> The information you get with police contacts is so much more important and interesting and penetrating.

The cultivation of informal personal contacts is vital to the professional survival of the crime correspondent and the number and quality of these relationships are criteria for the allocation of status within the field. But the necessity of their cultivation also protects the territory of the crime specialist from attack by non-specialists. Thus, there may be a vested interest in the inadequacy of official sources:

> The traditional crime reporter welcomes police secrecy because it gives him a special position in the news organization, because it gives him a chance to get information which other reporters cannot get hold of, information which is not available any other way. (Crime reporter).

Before examining source relationships in more detail we should pause to note four points of general significance which have emerged thus far:

(i) *Sources* are the primary gatekeepers of information.
(ii) The selection of appropriate sources is a central concern of the journalist and is based on the quality of the accounts they can offer.

(iii) The quality of source accounts is assessed according to a number of implicit criteria. These include:
   (a) Relevancy—The degree to which the accounts conform to current rules about what is news. These rules of relevancy will be discussed later.
   (b) Depth—Does the account contain sufficient detail to construct a rich story?
   (c) Exclusivity—How many journalists have access to the account?
   (d) Timing—Is the account acquired at an appropriate time with regard to legal and bureaucratic constraints?
(iv) Access to high quality information depends on the reporter's ability to cultivate relationships with strategically well-placed sources.

Source relationships

Clearly is it impossible to untangle the instrumental and affective bonds which bind together the crime reporter and his police informants. The pursuit of information promotes a growth of friendship which is reinforced by a reciprocation of help and co-operation. Over drinks or a meal, usually at a pub or restaurant but often in one another's homes, the crime reporter and the detective will exchange information, comment and advice. But they do not always 'talk shop' and inevitably often develop an intimate knowledge of each other's family life. As one crime reporter put it:

> Over the years you get to know a copper . . . . They're not just business contacts, they're friends—you meet them socially, you go out to dinner, you meet them for a drink, not to discuss business but just to meet them like you meet your pals.[11]

They usually get to know each other through working on the same cases. Sometimes the original contact will be by telephone but the detective may want to meet the crime reporter privately to discuss a particularly delicate piece of information. There is also a system of sponsorship by which senior specialists introduce contacts to new recruits in the field, but this is not as significant as we might expect because most journalists establish a number of basic contacts as general reporters and apply for specialization on the basis of their connections. The crime reporter usually invests a considerable amount of time in the cultivation of contacts (although perhaps not quite so much now as in the past) with the expectation of long-term rather than short-term gain. As one of my informants commented:

> I'm having lunch with a contact today. I'm not expecting any information, but we'll have lunch and a chat and at the end of that I shall know him a bit better and he will be more likely to tell me things in the future. The time will have been well spent.

Before being accepted by a policeman the crime reporter must usually undergo a lengthy period of probation:

> In the old days, a policeman would try you out over a period— sometimes it might be a couple of years—he'd feed you stories to see how you wrote them up, to see if you could be trusted. They tried you out for a long time before they trusted you and that's still true today, really. (Crime reporter).

As he steadily builds up relationships with individual policemen the crime reporter acquires a more generalized reputation for dependability among policemen which helps him to obtain information from unfamiliar sources. When he becomes a full-time specialist he is entitled to join the highly-exclusive Crime Reporters Association. Membership provides him with a metaphorical badge of trustworthiness which can be especially useful in overcoming the suspicion of sources in provincial forces, but the trust and co-operation won by CRA membership numbers does not really compare with that won by years of patient source cultivation. It would be a mistake, however, to regard the relationship between the powerful senior detective and the crime specialist as one of patronage. They normally interact on a basis of equality and recognize mutual obligations. The crime reporter has much to offer the detective and can be a useful professional asset. To quote a former Metropolitan Police Commander:

> Often the man from the Yard can stand in real need of a crime reporter's help and good will. Sometimes the crime reporter, because of his greater freedom to question people, can actually help to uncover evidence which would be difficult for a policeman to obtain.[12]

The experienced crime correspondent is usually highly respected in police circles and retiring detectives may seek his assistance when they write their memoirs. One detective had this to say of a crime reporter whose help and friendship he had found valuable:

Throughout my years of police service I have on many occasions had good reason to be grateful for help I have received from senior news-papermen during my investigations. One journalist, Norman Lucas, Chief crime reporter of the *Sunday Mirror,* was at my side during almost all the investigations I led. In the 24 years he has been a Fleet Street crime reporter and author he has deservedly gained the respect of all ranks of the police forces throughout Britain.[13]

Thus, to a large extent, the relationship between detective and crime reporter is characterized by exchange. But this exchange is rarely formal or overt. Reciprocal obligations are implicit in the relationship, it is taken for granted that favours will be returned and friends will be helped:

> We don't expect them to tell us anything, there's no reason why they should, but under the 'Old Pals Act' which works in other businesses as well as ours you do expect a little bit. It's not a question of buying drinks to curry favour, it's a question of having drinks with them to be sociable. (Crime reporter).

> I would urge my editor not to publish a story if I knew that if it were published a criminal would get away or it would cause three or four weeks extra police work. But, in return, I'd hope that the policeman would make sure I had the tip-off about the arrest when it happened. I think this is *quid pro quo,* we can help each other. Similarly, I would hope that if you have knowledge of a crime you can favour a police contact. (Crime reporter).

Clearly, then, the quantity and the quality of informal source accounts is influenced to some degree by what the reporter can offer in exchange.

The most obvious exchange resource the journalist has at his disposal is money. But, although direct payment of certain types of sources is recognized as legitimate, it is generally considered an inappropriate (although not unknown) method of obtaining information from the police. It is far too crass and unsubtle and defines the reporter/source relationship as one of business rather than friendship. The offer of food and drink, on the other hand, carries connotations of sociability rather than commerce or corruption:

> I never give them money. I'll take them out for a meal, something like that. That's legitimate entertaining. Mind you, taking a couple of coppers usually costs as much as bunging them twenty quid. Still, the paper pays the expenses of course.(Crime reporter).

The purchase of food and drink is used merely as a means of lubricating social interaction, but the crime reporter controls other, more powerful, exchange resources. These derive from his position within an organization offering the possibility of instant communication with the public. For the police, such communication makes the task of crime prevention and investigation considerably easier than it would otherwise be. Moreover, mass communication creates the opportunity for members of an organization to promote their interests and disseminate their ideas on a large scale. The crime reporter is able to act as intermediary between the press and the police, offering the police both informational and promotional assistance.

Informational aid

Informational aid is of two broad types—solicited and unsolicited. Solicited aid usually takes the form of direct appeals to the public to supply the police with intelligence about specific crimes. These appeals have become a taken-for-granted part of criminal investigation; but the public is generally less aware of the extent to which the police also use the press to communicate with specific individuals or minority groups. In these cases the aim is usually to supply rather than receive intelligence. 'Appeals' directed at the criminal underworld, for instance, usually take the form of threats—that the homes of known criminals will be raided until someone informs on a wanted man. The strategic 'leaking' of information is a method employed by a wide variety of organizations which are engaged in some form of external conflict. The police are no exception. Crime reporters are usually willing accomplices to the type of deception that involves, say, the police declaring that bank raiders have stolen a million rather than half a million pounds, in the hope of causing the thieves to fall out:

> The police can use us with our knowledge. They can say, 'Look, can you jolly this one along, stir things up a bit, get a bit of agitation going', and we can write along those lines without saying that the coppers said it. You'd be surprised as well the number of times it stirs up the old hornets' nest. . . . It's good fun—it's fun for us and it also does the job for the police.

Occasionally ethical scruples will restrain the crime reporter from publishing information he knows to be untrue, but conflict with professional ethics can usually be avoided by the ready acceptance of the veracity of police statements and the assertion of news values.[14]

Often the police will issue information which makes a good story and say, 'Well, if you print this it may help us catch this guy.' Say if he's hiding and the police don't know where he is they may say, 'If you print this he may start running.' Usually it's a case of leaking information that the police are getting closer and that, say, an arrest is expected in the next 36 hours. Well, when he hears this the guy gets jumpy. (Crime reporter).

Unsolicited informational aid is most often a result of crime reporters' relationships with underworld contacts who are more likely to give information to a journalist than to a policeman. Here again, the crime reporter fulfils an important intermediary function, facilitating 'the anonymous tip-off':

Joe Smith might know a lot of details about a certain robbery and, for whatever reasons, he wants to tell . . . He won't go to a policeman and tell him direct, but he'll tell me in the full knowledge that I would tell whoever is investigating the job. But he wouldn't want to be revealed as the man giving the information. (Crime reporter).

Promotional aid

Police are coming increasingly to believe in the power of the mass media over public opinion and are, hence, increasingly concerned with the image of the force in the media and the promotion of its interests through the media. Such concerns lie at the root of the Metropolitan Police's new 'open' press relations policy.[15] The role of the crime reporter in promotional activities is partly as intermediary and facilitator, interviewing policemen and liaising between newspaper and Scotland Yard; but also as copy writer—he makes public police activities, and he can portray those activities favourably or unfavourably. Thus, an important exchange resource for the crime reporter are his accounts themselves. Although explicit bargains are rarely negotiated he can still exchange favourable comments for source co-operation by means of tacit mutual understandings.[16] Having briefly examined the bargaining power of the crime reporter[17] we are now ready to return to the problem of public account production.

Account construction

Earlier, it was suggested that journalists do not gather news; they construct second order accounts of reality from materials provided by sources (first order accounts). If we wish to understand this process we must examine not only journalism's conventional wisdoms and stocks of knowledge but also the journalist's relationships with his sources. This section of the paper examines the selection and interpretation of materials in terms of the constraints which occupational ideology and source relationships impose on those procedures.

1. Occupational ideology

(A) Selection—Researchers have often noted that all journalists learn to identify newsworthy material according to implicit rules of relevancy (generally termed 'news values') which they find difficult to explicate.[18] They learn these rules through a process of informal socialization—reading newspapers, talking to more experienced colleagues, and observing the selection procedures of sub-editors.

> There is this intangible thing called a news story—I don't know how your recognize it, it's experience, I suppose. It's an odd quality. You can put six reporters in a court and they can sit through six hours of court verbiage and they'll all come out with the same story. (Crime reporter).

The rules remain essentially taken-for-granted and lie behind the more conscious typifications of news stories with which reporters also operate *(e.g.* the typification 'Man Bites Dog' is derived from a number of rules concerning the relevancy of the unusual, the unexpected, the dramatic, etc.) For one crime reporter, news stories were really 'simple clichés set to music—you select the right cliché and write it up to suit the particular circumstances. Something like "tug-of-love" identifies a particular type of story and its theme.'[19] There is no space here to examine these rules and typifications in any detail, but one or two observations are possible:

(i) There are generalized rules common to most news organizations, and there are also particular rules which are fashioned to fit the requirements of individual news organizations. The latter are a guide to the organization's implicit policy which may well lack more formal institutionalization.[20] As one crime reporter put it:

You write on the basis of what your paper's interests are and we are expected to know those interests.

(ii) Rules of relevancy and news typifications are believed to be little understood by sources:

Policemen don't know a story when they see one. You can go for a beer with a policeman and talk for an hour and have an interesting chat but get nothing. And then, in the last two minutes, he will say something which would obviously make a good story but he just didn't realize its potential. (Crime reporter).

(iii) The rules of relevancy become associated with audience expectations and are legitimated in terms of audience desires. For the journalist who sees himself as a representative of his audience observance of the rules thus becomes mandatory.[21]

(iv) The operation of the rules and news typifications ensures that large segments of the social world are systematically excluded from representation and discussion in the media, and thus public knowledge of those segments is effectively impoverished. For example, there appear to be rules stressing the relevancy of: The Present, The Unusual, The Dramatic, Simplicity, Actions, Personalities and Results; this means that The Past, The Normal, The Mundane, Complexity, Ideas, Structures, Cultures and Processes are all neglected in the news media. Our knowledge of certain types of crime also suffers:

Company fraud is a difficult thing to write about, you can't work the clichés into it, there's no violence, no drama. Crime has to have colour about it, something to make people react. (Crime reporter).

(B) Interpretation—It might appear misleading to separate selection and interpretation because (a) the materials from which selections are made are already, themselves, interpretations and (b) the implicit rules and assumptions which constrain selection also constrain interpretation, such that certain selections invite 'obvious' interpretations (*e.g.* the journalist selects accounts suitable for dramatic interpretation). But the distinction is useful because it enables us to focus on specific structures of meaning which recur in journalistic accounts. These recurrent interpretations take the form of conventional explanations, legitimations and evaluations of social phenomena which have been incorporated into journalism's stocks of knowledge.[22] As such, they constitute both a source on which the journalist may draw in arriving at understandings of phenomena, and a conservative constraint on the construction of accounts in that they provide 'ready-made' interpretations of new phenomena. As conventional wisdoms, there are two ways in which they can 'work' for the journalist. Firstly, they can enhance his personal understanding of social phenomena, enable him to make sense of the world. Or, secondly, knowledge of conventional interpretations can enable the journalist to produce *public* accounts acceptable to his various audiences (editors, readers, sources) while allowing him to employ alternative interpretations in his *private* construction of reality. Crime reporters are much more likely to employ conventional interpretations in their private as well as their public constructions of reality. The discontinuity of private thoughts and public words is characteristic of the generalist rather than the specialist—the strong element of natural selection in specialist recruitment sees to this.[23] As one crime reporter put it: 'It's horses for courses and any good executive will realize this.' Crime reporters are generally ideally suited to their own particular course, and generally exhibit a strong normative commitment to their work, but there still remains an element of ambivalence, deriving from their own realization that news is essentially commercial knowledge:

> I regard news as a commodity—it's there to buy, it's there to report, it's there to be processed, and packaged and sold. That's to say, I'm in much the same position as the man who goes to work at Ford's—I do my work, how it's sold by the company is someone else's responsibility.

> A paper is an economic concern, it's got to pay, it's got to be successful. Any journalist who says his only job is serving the public interest is not telling the truth.[24]

2. Source relationships

(A) Selection—It has already been suggested that crime reporters control valuable exchange resources in their relationships with sources. They do help the police more than is often realized, but, in the final analysis, the policeman is in a superior negotiating position because the reporter who cannot get information is out of a job, whereas the policeman who retains it is not. Therefore, it is usually the crime reporter who initiates interaction and actively cultivates the relationship. Thus, as the relationship develops, it is the reporter's world which is drawn towards that of the policeman rather than vice versa. Gieber and Johnson in their study of reporter and source roles call this process 'assimilation'. It is, in fact, a complex process of socialization by which the journalist's frame of reference, methods of working and personal system of perceptions and understandings are brought into line with the expectations of his sources. The importance of mutual trust, confidence and understanding is emphasized and the journalist is encouraged to conform to his source's model of the 'good reporter'—he exercises and values 'responsibility', he does not pester for information at inconvenient times, he sympathizes with his source's problems, he identifies with his source's interests, he accepts what he is told and reports it faithfully. As one crime reporter said of his police contacts: 'You get to know them. You understand how they think, how they are likely to act. You talk the same language.' By fulfilling his sources' expectations, the reporter not only receives good copy, he also earns the respect of his sources. He becomes a confidant and drinking companion. Obviously the degree of assimilation varies, but no crime reporter remains entirely unaffected by his relationships with police informants.[25]

When it comes to the selection of materials for accounts, source relationships introduce a variety of complications. Firstly, there is the obligation not to damage ongoing police inquiries which ensures the introduction of secondary selection procedures and reinforces the need for information storage:

> It's a continual tussle if you're a crime reporter and getting information in a backdoor way not to harm an inquiry by printing information that's given to you . . . You've got to be careful of coppers shooting their mouths off and getting you into trouble. But we go into it with our eyes open. We've got a sort of built-in computer which tells us what we can and can't use. It's an automatic reaction. We make mistakes, of course, but usually the computer gets it right . . . . You can't always print what coppers tell you, but it's a case of storing things away for future reference. (Crime reporter).[26]

Secondly, there are the complexities introduced by source attempts to insert information into the reporter's final account which would normally be rejected according to the rules of relevancy:

> I'm not bothered about upsetting people, but you have to be a bit careful about upsetting coppers because they're my bread and butter. Officially they can't influence me at all, but in practice I try very hard to play it their way, providing there is a story in it. But what is a news point is often not what they want me to include. But, having got a news point and a basic story, I'll co-operate as much as I can in putting over what they want. (Crime reporter).

Thirdly, there are the complications that arise from a direct conflict between source interests and journalistic obligations.[27] The clearest example, here, is that of police deviance. Exposés of police deviancy are a severe embarrassment to crime reporters. Police sensitivity to criticism is such that the reporter who allows himself to be directly associated with this kind of story is likely to lose potentially valuable sources. Three options are usually open to a crime reporter who has information about police deviancy and who wishes to avoid a 'freeze out':

   (i) He can write the story up anonymously.
  (ii) He can pass the information to a colleague who is able to write the story because he does not rely on the police for information.
 (iii) He can suppress the information.

One reporter on a Sunday paper with a reputation for running exposés of police deviancy favoured the second option:

> I, probably more than anybody else on this paper, have quite a number of police contacts and it would completely destroy my role to have my by-line on a story knocking the police . . . If such a story does come my way I hand it over to my colleagues to handle, I wash my hands of it . . . . Quite frankly, I think it's hypocritical, but I've got to live a long time in Fleet Street doing this kind of work. What alternative is there for me?

A little later in the interview I asked if crime reporters on other papers ever offered him stories they were unable to handle:

> It does happen in other fields . . . but I can never remember a crime reporter offering me a story and I don't think that any crime reporter would do this. You see, if it's a good story about the police they'd have it in their papers, if it's a bad story they'd tend to forget it.

Ostracism is a powerful sanction and suppression is usually the safest course. But the crime reporter does not necessarily see the non-publication of this type of information as suppression. Often the process of assimilation means that definitions of situations and codes of conduct derived from sources replace those of journalism. The informal ethics of police work dominate the formal ethics of journalism. The process may result in police deviancy being seen by the crime reporter as an essentially private affair, unsuitable for public scrutiny. But this does not mean that the reporter takes no action when cases of police deviancy come to his notice. It means that he allows his response to be governed by the expectations and codes of his unofficial sources—he sorts out the situation:

I've had two or three cases . . . where the guy (an informant) has ended up saying, 'Look, I've arranged to meet this copper at such and such a pub tomorrow and I'm going to get him to accept this bribe'. And, in that case, I've got straight on to a pal in that particular division to say to him, 'Look, one of your chums has got a meet tomorrow at 6:30—no need for me to tell you who or where it is, you find out who it is and perhaps you'd make other arrangements for him. In other words, make sure he doesn't keep the meet. And, in this way, the guy who is *allegedly* going to accept a bribe will not keep the meet. His boss has got no proof of what he has done before and the guy who was allegedly going to take the bribe has got the wind put up him because he knows that somebody else knows about it. So everything's hunky dory in the end, or at least I like to think it is.
(Probe) You wouldn't go to A10?[28]
What me? No, not at all—that's grassing going to A10. I haven't been a good boy all my life, I'm sure you haven't.

(B) Interpretation—The same source constraints which operate on the selection of materials also operate on the organization and transformation of those materials into public accounts. It is, of course, difficult for crime reporters to admit that their accounts are constrained in this way, given their professional ethic of integrity and detachment which continues to exert a powerful influence over their public statements and private perceptions. When asked if they feel that their close association with police informants could perhaps impair their ability to criticize the police, they usually evoke the rhetoric of this same professional ethic:

> I am a reporter, not a policeman, nor a civil servant, nor a copper's nark . . . . After 20 years of dealing with this subject you should have enough experience to know when to criticize.

> If it came to the crunch, I would rather ditch a contact than suppress information it would be in the public interest to know.

However, some crime specialists are prepared to admit that the reporter's critical faculty can be undermined:

> There are some crime reporters of the old school . . . who have been in the game so long that they have completely sold out to the police.

> I wouldn't get myself involved in commenting on jobs that involved people I know—I don't particularly want to stick my bloody neck out, I'd lose all the friends I've ever made.

But it is not usually a case of inability to criticize when the occasion demands it, it is rather a general reluctance to criticize, a desire not to offend those whose help and friendship one values, the ready acceptance of the police version of the story, the undermining of the *will* to criticize. All this is a consequence of long association and common experience, shared perspectives, values and interests:

> Certainly I'm on the side of the police. I don't go around looking for trouble in the police force. I'm not looking for that kind of bother, but if I find it I'll report it. Fortunately, it doesn't happen very often. We do not make it our business to criticize the police—there are plenty of other people in Fleet Street who do that sort of thing. (Crime reporter).

It is not that crime reporters actively promote the interests of the police to the detriment of others, or that they deliberately ignore conflicts in their role; it is rather that they often simply do not perceive these conflicts. As one informant put it, the crime reporter may sometimes be 'the guy in the middle', but 'usually everybody is marching in the same direction' and consequently 'there aren't generally many crises of loyalty'. Other comments emphasized the same point:

> Generally, what we write is parallel with and complementary to what the police are saying; but this is not a deliberate policy, it just happens that so often the interests of the press, the police and the public are complementary.

The interests of the police are identified with those of the public and the role of the responsible journalist is seen as the promotion of those interests:

> It's important to support the police and make sure that public confidence in the force is not damaged . . . They must have public support or they can't do their job properly.

> I feel a responsibility to help the police in their job. I don't want to put crime into people's minds. I won't encourage crime . . . naturally I'm against it and feel it's wrong, just like anybody else.

> Crime is anti-society, anti-social, and newspapers can't possibly line themselves up with something like that . . . . Everybody is anti-crime, except criminals.

Most crime reporters see their professional responsibilities towards the public as entailing the support of the police in their battle against crime. This means they are obliged to defend and promote the interests of the police unless they can be clearly shown to be in conflict with the interests of the public. The demonstration of conflict will obviously depend upon the assumptions made about the nature of the public's interests. Certainly, crime reporters believe that an open exposure of 'the facts' is not always in the public interest, and one thing that is in its long-term interest is the maintenance of its faith and confidence in the police force. Such beliefs reinforce already existent pre-dispositions to construct public accounts which are generally favourable to agencies of social control and highly unfavourable to the deviant and those who represent a threat to the established order.

Summary

This paper, then, has focused on the construction of public accounts by professional communicators. In particular, it has emphasized the importance of occupational ideology and source relationships in shaping this construction and has attempted to highlight the deficiencies of the 'gatekeeper' tradition of media research which, on the whole, has failed to appreciate the way in which news is *created*.

There has, unfortunately, been insufficient space to explore other important influences on journalistic account construction such as legal restrictions and deadline pressures, or the wider socio-economic contexts within which knowledge production occurs; but it is recognized that a consideration of these constraints would be an essential part of a more comprehensive discussion of the problem.

NOTES AND REFERENCES

1. I am indebted to Professor Stanley Cohen (University of Essex) for his help and guidance during the formative stages of this paper.
2. The origin of the concept lies in Kurt Lewin's studies of food marketing ('Forces behind food habits', *Bulletin of the National Research Council*, 1943), but was first introduced into media sociology by D. M. White in a seminal paper in *Journalism Quarterly* ('The gate keeper: a case study in the selection of news', 27, 1950, pp. 383–90). The concept has since undergone numerous refinements, (cf. W. Gieber, 'Across the desk: a study of 16 Telegraph editors', *Journalism Quarterly*, 33, 1956, pp. 425–32; R. E. Carter, 'Gatekeepers and news sources', *Public Opinion Quarterly*, 22, 1958,

pp. 133–44; L. Donahew, 'Newspaper gatekeepers and forces in the news channel', *Public Opinion Quarterly*, 31, 1967, pp. 61–8; Z. A. Bass, 'Refining the gatekeeper concept', *Journalism Quarterly*, 46, 1969, pp. 69–72), but it remains a major constraint on a fully-developed sociology of journalism.

3. C. MacDougall, 'Interpretative reporting' (New York, Macmillan, 1968), p. 12.

4. There are, of course, exceptions. Cf. W. Gieber, 'Two communicators of the news: a study of the roles of sources and reporters', *Social Forces*, 39, 1960, pp. 76–83; W. Gieber and W. Johnson, 'The City Hall beat: a study of reporter and source roles', *Journalism Quarterly*, 38, 1961, pp. 289–97; R. P. Judd, 'The newspaper reporter in a suburban city', *Journalism Quarterly*, 38, 1961, pp. 35–42, B. C. Cohen, 'The press and foreign policy', Princeton University Press, 1963; J. Tunstall, 'The Westminster Lobby correspondents' (London, Routledge & Kegan Paul, 1971); L. V. Sigal, 'Reporters and officials' (Lexington, D. C. Heath & Co.), 1973.

5. In Jeremy Tunstall's study, *Journalists at work* (London, Constable, 1971), p. 130, 71% of the specialist correspondents surveyed claimed that over 80% of their copy appeared in the paper. This included 13 of the 14 crime reporters consulted. Non-specialists and inexperienced reporters are perhaps less likely to get their copy past the sub-editors unchanged, especially on mass-circulation papers.

6. Tunstall's study also suggested that crime reporters were older, more politically conservative, and had left school earlier, than any other specialist group.

7. In recent years, Fleet Street's lines of specialization have become somewhat blurred. There are a number of reasons for this; one is an increasing financial instability which will not allow editors the luxury of a specialist for every story, and another is the influx of radical journalists who wish to retain broad and flexible frames of reference. This is particularly noticeable on a paper like *The Guardian* which has no specialist crime correspondent.

8. The materials which form the basis of the remainder of this paper are drawn from a series of 31 interviews with journalists on Fleet Street newspapers. These included 13 with crime correspondents. The interviews were part of a wider research project on crime and police news; cf. S. J. Chibnall, 'Law-and-Order News'.

9. Fleet Street papers either employ specialist reporters to cover trials or, more usually, rely on general reporters and agency copy. In the case of a major trial, the crime reporter will not generally sit through the entire proceedings but may arrive in time for the verdicts, having already prepared a background piece, anticipating the outcome ('It's no good going too early because you get fogged by a mass of irrelevant information.') Court reporting as a specialization has been declining over the last decade and many of its leading practitioners have now retired—Charles Doherty, Arnold Latcham, etc. The Association of Central Criminal Court Journalists is an enclave of conservatism whose members are prepared to resist challenges to their shared values, perceptions and understandings. Something of the character of the organization can be gleaned from its reaction to the *Evening Standard*'s decision to ask underground journalist, Richard Neville, to cover the case of

Regina vs. Prescott and Purdie in 1971. Part of its letter of protest to the *Evening Standard*'s Editor reads:

Our members are reporters of long experience in Fleet Street and elsewhere, who are justly proud of their reputation of providing responsible day-to-day coverage of trials at a place that the Lord Chancellor described last month as ' . . . par excellence, the premier criminal court in the Commonwealth, and perhaps the world.' We object, therefore, to being identified . . . with a person who has a conviction for sending an obscene article, *viz. Oz*, No. 28, Schoolkids issue, through the post . . . . Our members feel that in these days of declining standards, our voice must be raised in the hope that eventually, with others, it will be heard.

Compared with crime reporting, court reporting is highly structured, offering the journalist less scope for innovation, autonomy, source selection and exclusivity. This means that, while conflicts of interest are by no means absent, source relationships and the negotiation of accounts are less significant.

10. The idea that reporters thrive on 'scoops' is a truism. Exclusive material creates problems of validation and involves the journalist in risk-taking behaviour. A major channel for testing both the veracity and relevancy of information—the opinions of other journalists—is effectively closed. Cf. W. Breed, 'Newspaper opinion leaders and processes of standardization', *Journalism Quarterly*, 32, pp. 277–84; Cohen, *op. cit.*, pp. 81–2; Sigal, *op. cit.*, pp. 71–2.

11. Police biographies and autobiographies occasionally reveal something of the quality of these relationships. The biographer of Deputy Commander Reginald Spooner of Scotland Yard produces this anecdote:

Tom Tullett, crime reporter of the *Daily Mirror*, but once a CID officer himself, recalls that one evening he was having a drink with Spooner in a public house near Scotland Yard when Spooner suddenly said, 'Here, what are you doing here drinking with me tonight? It's your wedding anniversary.' 'It was too', says Tullett. (I. Adamson, *The Great Detective* (London, Muller, 1966), p. 46).

12. E. Millen, 'Specialist in crime' (London, Harrap, 1972), p. 221. For a graphic account of the way in which a crime reporter can participate in a police investigation cf. N. Lucas, *The child killers* (London, A. Barker, 1979), Chapter 6.

13. I. Forbes, *Squad man* (London, W. H. Allen, 1973), p. 1.

14. For their practical purposes, journalists are not so much interested in discovering the reality of events as in the acquisition of source accounts and theories. Cf. J. Halloran *et al., Demonstrations and communication: a case study* (London, Penguin, 1970), pp. 137–8; G. Murdock in this Reader.

15. The new policy was set out in an internal Scotland Yard memo from Commissioner Robert Mark in Spring 1973. One passage reads:

It is my firm belief that the Metropolitan Police have a great deal more to be proud of than the public know and that a little more openness with the news media, heightening trust, confidence and co-operation, is all that is required to correct that ignorance. In particular, there is convincing evidence that, given the opportunity to do so, the press . . . . will give a great deal of support to the Force.

16. The crime reporter may be able to promote the interests of individual officers, but my informants were generally uncertain of the influence of their reports on the career prospects of policemen. Most felt that senior officers at the Yard are suspicious of publicity seekers, but some were prepared to entertain the possibility that press reports might influence the decision to promote an officer.

17. For other discussions of exchange between journalists and sources, cf. Tunstall, *Journalists at work, op. cit.*, pp. 198–200; Sigal, *op. cit.*, Chapters 3, 6 and 7. Peter Blau's work, of course, remains the dominant body of theory in the area of social exchange ('Exchange and Power in Social Life', Wiley, 1964).

18. Cf. Breed, Cohen, *op. cit.*, pp. 54–8; J. Galtung and M. Ruge, 'The structure of foreign news', *Journal of International Peace Research*, 1, 1965, pp. 64–90; Halloran, *op. cit.*, Chapter 1; Tunstall, *Journalists at work, op. cit.*, pp. 261–5.

19. Cf. G. Tuchman, 'Making News by Doing Work: Routinizing the Unexpected', *A.J.S.*, 79, 1973, pp. 110–31.

20. For more extensive discussions of policy constraints and the socialization of the reporter see: W. Breed, 'Social control in the news room', *Social Forces*, 33, 1955, pp. 326–35; R. W. Stark, 'Policy and the pros: an organizational analysis of a metropolitan newspaper', *Berkley Journal of Sociology*, 17, 1962, pp. 11–31; A. Matejko, 'Newspaper staff as a social system', *Polish Sociological Bulletin*, 1967, pp. 58–68; M. Warner, 'Organizational context and control of policy in a television newsroom', *B.J.S.*, 12, 1971, pp. 283–94; L. Sigelman, 'Reporting the news: an organizational analysis', *A.J.S.*, 79, 1973, pp. 132–51; Sigal, *op. cit.*

21. Journalists receive relatively little feedback from their general audiences, compared with that received from colleagues and sources. (Cf. Gieber and Johnson, *op. cit.*; Cohen, *op. cit.*, p. 111; Tunstall, *The Westminster Lobby correspondents, op. cit.*, p. 67; R. C. Flegel and S. H. Chaffee, 'Influences of editors, readers and personal opinions on reporters', *Journalism Quarterly*, 48, 1971, pp. 645–51). In my experience, journalists on 'popular' papers generally see their readers as essentially conservative beings, living snugly within the illusion that all is well with the world as long as they are protected from 'the wreckers in their midst':

The average reader likes to feel he's safe in his bed at night and this gentleman in size 13 boots pounding up and down the street is the only line of protection he has against the ravaging hordes of vicious thugs, drug pushers and negroes who want to rape his 16-year-old daughter (who's had it so many times she's forgotten anyway). Therefore, they don't like their peace disturbed and they tend to react to stories against the police.

22. Cf. S. Hall, 'Deviance, politics and the media', in P. Rock and M. McIntosh (eds.), *Deviance and social control* (London, Tavistock, 1974), pp. 261–306, for a similar conceptualization.
23. Sigelman, *op. cit.*, contains a more extensive discussion of natural selection in journalism.
24. The exploration of the way in which economic changes, interests and considerations are reflected in media content has recently been promoted by a perceptive article by Graham Murdock and Peter Golding, 'For a political economy of mass communications', in R. Miliband and J. Saville, eds., *Socialist Register* (London, Merlin Press, 1973).
25. For other discussions of assimilation in this context, cf. Gieber and Johnson, *op. cit.*; Judd, *op. cit.*; Cohen, *op. cit.*, pp. 144–53; Turnstall, *Journalists at work, op. cit.*, pp. 173–201; Sigal, *op. cit.*, Chapter 3.
26. One crime reporter told me of a major story he had known about for three or four weeks before writing up:

    I agreed on a code with this bloke who would phone me. I was in the city somewhere, and my wife phoned and said, 'I've just had this strange phone call. He wouldn't give his name, he just said, The Dog is barking.' 'Course, I was able to write up the story and it was all over the front page within a couple of hours.

27. Cf. Tunstall, *Journalists at work, op. cit.*, pp. 200–1, for another discussion of the management of 'news dilemmas'.
28. A10 is the department at Scotland Yard which investigates complaints against police officers.

Crime waves as ideology*

MARK FISHMAN

When we speak of a crime wave, we are talking about a kind of social awareness of crime, crime brought to public consciousness. It is something to be remarked upon at the corner grocery store, complained about in a community meeting, and denounced at the mayor's press conference. One cannot be mugged by a crime wave, but one can be scared. And one can put more police on the streets and enact new laws on the basis of fear. Crime waves may be 'things of the mind', but they have real consequences.

Crime waves are prime candidates for ideology. This study analyzes a specific crime wave that occurred in New York City in late 1976. This case both illustrates and informs my analysis that the crime waves which periodically appear in the press are constructs of the mass media and contribute to an ideological conception of crime in America.[1]

My use of the term ideology follows Dorothy Smith.[2] All knowledge is knowledge from some point of view, resulting from the use of procedures for knowing a part of the world. Ideological accounts arise from 'procedures which people use as a means *not to know*'[3] (emphasis mine). Routine news gathering and editing involve 'procedures not to know'. The business of news is embedded in a configuration of institutions. These include a community of news organizations from which journalists derive a sense of 'what's news now', and governmental agencies upon which journalists depend for their raw materials. Through their interactions and reliance on official sources, news organizations both invoke and reproduce prevailing conceptions of 'serious crime'.

Crimes against the elderly

In late 1976, New York City experienced a major crime wave. The city's three daily newspapers and five local television stations reported a surge of violence against elderly people. The crime wave lasted approximately

*This paper originally appeared in a slightly different version in *Social Problems*, vol. 25, no. 4., 5 June 1978.

seven weeks, eventually receiving national television and newspaper coverage.

One consequence of this was the public definition of a new type of crime.[4] 'Crimes against the elderly' became a typical crime with typical victims, offenders, and circumstances. Reported muggers, murderers, and rapists of the elderly were usually black or Hispanic youths with long juvenile records. They came from ghetto neighbourhoods near enclaves of elderly whites who, for various reasons (usually poverty), had not fled the inner city. Using this scenario, journalists reported incident after brutal incident throughout November and December 1976.

The outcry against these crimes was immediate. The Mayor of New York City, who was preparing to run for re-election, criticized the juvenile justice system and the criminal courts. The New York City Police Department gave its Senior Citizens Robbery Unit (SCRU) manpower to extend plain-clothes operations. Camera crews from local news stations filmed SCRU officers dressed as old people and arresting muggers. Local police precincts held community meetings to advise the elderly how to protect themselves. New York State legislators introduced bills to make juvenile records available to a judge at the time of sentencing, to deny sixteen to nineteen-year-olds juvenile status if they victimized an old person, and to mandate prison sentences for crimes of violence against the aged. These proposals were passed in both the State Senate and Assembly, but were eventually vetoed by the Governor on 19 August 1977—nine months after the crime wave had ended.

A May 1977 Harris poll suggested the crime wave also had a nationwide effect on people's fear of crime. Moreover, it had an effect on the crime categories which the Harris organization used in its surveys; this poll included a new type of crime, crimes against the elderly, not previously present in Harris polls. Harris found that 60% of his respondents felt that assaults against elderly people in their home areas had been going up, and that 50% of those aged fifty or older said they were more uneasy on the streets than they had been one year ago.[5]

It is doubtful that, in fact, there was any unusual surge of violence against the elderly at the end of 1976. No one really knows, least of all the journalists who reported the crime wave. For those types of crime most publicized (homicides, robberies, and purse snatchings), statistics from the NYPD actually show *decreasing* rates of victimization of the elderly relative to victimization of the general population. In the second half of 1976, when the wave of publicity occurred, reported robberies were down .2% from the previous six months; purse snatchings were down 1.5%; and homicides were down 1.9%.[6]

This paper, however, is not a study in the disparity between police statistics and crime news. Prior studies of crime news and crime waves[7], as well as anecdotal reports,[8] have shown the irony of crime waves: although the public is alarmed and politicians respond to media reports of a dramatic increase in crime, such 'waves' have no basis in police statistics. This study goes beyond sociological irony to examine *how and why news organizations construct crime waves.* Crime waves are taken to be waves of coverage of some topic in crime. Crime waves as *media waves* may or may not be related to something happening 'on the streets' or in the police crime rates. Studying crime waves means studying processes in the mass media.

Method

I collected two kinds of data. First, two student researchers and I conducted participant observation from November 1976 to April 1977 on a New York City local television station, WAVE (a pseudonym). One student was a full-time WAVE journalist who worked as a news writer, programme producer, and assignment editor. We focused on how the assignment editor assembled the daily news programme by deciding what major stories would be covered for the day and assigning reporters and camera crews to these stories. In addition, we conducted interviews with journalists from WAVE and the New York *Daily News.*

Secondly, we kept a record of all news relating to crimes against the elderly reported from September 1976 to February 1977 in two newspapers, the New York *Daily News* and the *New York Post,* and on WAVE, which aired a one-hour newscast in the evening. This enabled us to 'locate' the New York crime wave, to determine when it began and ended, and to determine the kind of coverage crimes against the elderly received before, during, and after the crime wave period.

The crime wave: a view from the outside

Over the six-month period of observation the *News,* the *Post,* and WAVE presented eighty-nine stories of crimes against the elderly. Fifty-six stories or 63% occurred during the crime wave period. The weekly frequencies of news stories from all three media are shown in the appendix. This graph clearly indicates a wave of media reporting that began in the last week of October and trailed off by the second week of December. It shows a sharp, swift rise in coverage for the first two weeks, then a slow, uneven decline for the remaining five weeks.

Examining the individual patterns of coverage for each news organization reveals that prior to the crime wave each organization was reporting approximately one story of crime against the elderly every other week. After the wave, coverage in all three media was sporadic, but heavier than coverage during the pre-wave period, indicating that the media appear to have been sensitized to the topic.

The three patterns of reporting in the *News*, the *Post*, and WAVE show that the marked increase in coverage did not coincide in all three media. The *News* had a sudden increase in the third week of October; WAVE and the *Post* did not increase their coverage until the fourth week of October. Further, in this fourth week the two 'latecomers' began their increase *simultaneously*. Prior to their increased coverage, the *Post* and WAVE did not parallel each other. It was only after the *News* began reporting a wave that the others developed a synchronous pattern. This trend suggests that the other media simultaneously responded to the *Daily News'* portrayal of a wave of violence against the elderly.

All three media show different crime wave profiles. WAVE steeply increased coverage to a single peak, then had an equally steep decline (seventeen days rising and sixteen days falling). In contrast, the *Daily News* and the *Post* show bimodal curves. In the *News* there was a swift initial rise (ten days), from which coverage subsided slowly, then it turned upward to a second peak (lower than the first), and finally declined.

The unevenness of the *Daily News's* wave was echoed in the *Post*. The *Post* participated less actively in the crime wave than did the *News* or WAVE. We might even say that the *Post* did not show a crime wave, except that the period of its heaviest coverage coincided with the crime wave period in the other media. Moreover, the *Post's* pre- and post-wave patterns were similar to the other media, and during the crime wave it showed a bimodal wave which paralleled that of the *Daily News*. Thus, the *Post's* wave seems to have been a weak reflection of the *Daily News's* curve.

How can we explain these bimodal patterns? The likely reason why the *News* and *Post* reduced their coverage after the first peaks involves a major news event coinciding with this drop: the 1976 Presidential Election of 2 November. The elections seem to have crowded out crimes against the elderly from the newspapers, but not from local TV news, since stations like WAVE were not trying to compete with network coverage of the Presidential race. Thus, during the slow news period after the elections, the *News* and *Post* seemed to have 'rediscovered' the crime wave, which was still present in local TV news.

In other words, it seems the *News'* and the *Post's* second peak was a response to the continuing crime wave in the television media (assuming other TV stations behaved like WAVE). Just as the initial appearance of the crime wave in the *Daily News* seems to have spurred increased coverage by the *Post* and WAVE, so the continuing coverage of the crime wave on television seems to have 're-awakened' interest in the topic by the *Daily News* and the *Post.* Thus, *the behaviour of each news organization during the crime wave seems to have been in response to the other media.*

Seeing themes in crime: a view from the inside

How do individual crimes come to be seen as a crime wave? The answer is found in the methods by which news is organized. News workers make crime waves by seeing 'themes' in the news. Crime waves are little more than the continued and heavy coverage of numerous occurrences which journalists report as a single topic (for example, 'crimes against the elderly').

News themes are various: 'everything Jimmy Carter did today,' 'the taxi cab strike,' 'Vietnam,' 'the disintegrating American family,' or 'labour disputes'. A news theme is a unifying concept. It presents a specific news event, or a number of such events in terms of some broader concept. For example, the mugging of an eighty-two-year-old Bronx woman can be reported as 'the latest instance of the continuing trend in crimes against the elderly'. A news theme allows journalists to cast an incident as an *instance* of something.

The Glasgow Media Group[9] provides an interesting example of thematized news events from one British television newscast:

> The week had its share of unrest. Trouble in Glasgow with striking dustmen and ambulance controllers, short time in the car industry, no *Sunday Mirror* or *Sunday People* today and a fair amount of general trouble in Fleet Street and a continuing rumble over the matter of two builders' pickets jailed for conspiracy.

As the authors point out, disparate incidents are reported together under the single theme of 'unrest'. Calling these things 'unrest' imposes order on the events reported. Audience members are meant to see the events as unified, as instances of a single theme.

Themes give news shows and newspapers a presentational order. Items are presented in groups organized around a theme. Some themes are related to others, making it possible for groups of news stories to be placed near each other. For instance, during the crime wave against the elderly, the first ten minutes of a sixty-minute news programme at WAVE was organized around interrelated themes:

1. Police apprehend three youngsters who allegedly mugged an elderly Queens couple.
2. Police and senior citizens meet at a Queens precinct to discuss fighting crimes against the elderly.
3. A feature report on the Senior Citizens Robbery Unit.
4. Police seize guns and drugs intended for warring gangs in the Bronx.
5. Two members of a youth gang are arrested for robbing someone at knifepoint.
6. ROTC cadet charged in the stabbing death of another cadet.
7. New York State audit finds the city police have been mishandling $9.1 million of federal funds.
8. New York City and the police union are still working on a new contract, at the same time that some laid-off firemen and subway cops will be rehired.

First, there are small groups of stories, each containing a theme that the stories in the group share in common (the first three stories are about 'crimes against the elderly' and the next three about 'youth crime'). Second, groups of stories are placed next to other groups, since the different themes of each group share common features (the group of crimes against the elderly and the group of youth crimes both can be seen to be about youthful perpetrators and police responses to them).

Journalists do not create themes merely to show an audience the appearance of order. News themes are very useful in newswork itself. In particular, editors selecting and organizing the day's stories need themes.[10] Every day, news editors face a glut of 'raw materials' (wire service reports, press releases, police crime dispatches) out of which they must fashion relatively few news stories. This task involves a selection process which operates somewhat differently in television and newspaper newsrooms. The essentials of the process are the same: individual news items are identified and sorted according to possible themes.

The chances that any event or incident will be reported increase once it has been associated with a current theme in the news. Crime incidents are rarely reported unless news workers see them related to a past or emerging trend in criminality or law enforcement. A brief description of how the assignment editor at WAVE developed the first segment of the news show just cited illustrates this point. The assignment editor determined the top stories for the day when he noticed that several previously unrelated stories were all part of the same current newsworthy theme: crimes against the elderly. And the discovery of this theme was no coincidence: that day's programme was in the midst of the crime wave period.

The assignment editor did not begin his day knowing that crime news, and, in particular, that crimes against the elderly, would receive top billing in the evening's news show. When he started work at 8:45 a.m. he already knew of two stories that he would most likely cover:[11] One was a feature report on the Senior Citizens Robbery Unit fighting crimes against the elderly. This feature, which eventually ran as the third story in the evening newscast, had been taped days before; it was part of a continuing series on SCRU the station had been airing for the past few weeks. The second story was a feature report on a 'food fair' that afternoon in Manhattan. The editor planned to send a reporter and camera crew to cover it, but also wanted to line up, as he put it, 'some better stories' for the day.

Ten minutes after he arrived in the newsroom the assignment editor began scanning his news sources for lead stories. He sifted through reams of wire service news that had collected overnight under the wire machines; he scanned the police dispatches of the previous night's and that morning's crime incidents (about ten or twelve) received through a teletype called 'the police wire'. He also looked to other news media for story ideas: he read the *Daily News* and *New York Times* and he listened to an all-news radio station.

In the *Daily News* he found a small story about rehiring firemen and Transit Authority police who had been laid off. He thought this would be a good story because 'this indicates things may be turning around in the city'. This incident became newsworthy when the assignment editor could see it as part of a current newsworthy theme (New York's fiscal crisis).

Still, the assignment editor despaired that he had 'no real news', that this was 'a slow news day'. However, around 10 a.m. two things happened. First, when scanning the police crime dispatches, the assignment editor found that in the 113th precinct in Queens an elderly couple had been mugged, and that one perpetrator was wounded by police. As he was clipping this dispatch, he heard over the all-news radio that the 112th precinct in Queens, very close to where the mugging occurred, was holding a crime prevention meeting with senior citizens. He now knew what his lead stories for the day would be, and he knew what he had to do to line them up:

1. He would send a reporter out to the 113th precinct to find, and get on film, whatever he could about the mugging (interviews with police, perhaps with some witnesses or with the victims themselves; and, if he was lucky, film of any suspects that were apprehended).

2. Then the reporter could go over to the nearby 112th precinct to film the police meeting with senior citizens.

3. These two reports would be followed by the pre-taped feature on SCRU.

4. The story on rehiring firemen and Transit police, as well as a few other brief wire service reports relevant to crime which might come in during the rest of the day, would all follow the above three lead stories in some as yet undetermined order. The story on the 'food fair' would be placed further back in the show.

Each story, seen independently, might not have merited attention. But seen together, all of them were made newsworthy by the perception of a common theme. The editor's 'discovery' of the theme of crime against the elderly made the day's news come together. He knew how to assign a schedule to his reporter and camera crew; and he knew pretty much what the day's news was going to be.

The selection of news on the basis of themes is one component in the ideological production of crime news. It constitutes a 'procedure not to know'. This procedure requires that an incident be stripped of the actual context of its occurrence so that it may be relocated in a new, symbolic context: the news theme. Because newsworthiness is based on themes, the attention devoted to an event may exceed its importance, relevance, or timeliness were these qualities determined with reference to some theory of society. In place of any such theoretical understanding of the phenomena they report, newsworkers make incidents meaningful only as *instances of themes*—themes which are generated within the news production process. Thus, something becomes a 'serious type of crime' on the basis of what is going on inside newsrooms, not outside them.

From crime themes to crime waves

Crime themes are potential crime waves. A news organization cannot make a crime wave without the collaboration of other media reporting the same crime theme. Crime waves emerge out of an interaction among news organizations.

The indefinite overlapping character of news judgments.

All newsworkers depend on other media organizations for their sense of 'what's news today'. For example, the WAVE assignment editor began his day by reading the morning papers, the *Daily News* and *The New York Times,* and by listening to an all news radio station. He later read the *New York Post* and watched when other TV stations aired their news. This editor told me that he did not mind using 'anything, any source of news. I'm not proud. I'll steal any source of news.'

In reality, stories were not stolen wholesale; rather, the other news media provided an important pool of ideas for story assignments. The noon and evening TV news shows rarely were used for this purpose because, by the time these shows were aired, most of the editor's news was set. The news on other stations mainly confirmed the assignment editor's news judgments, since his planned 10 p.m. news was, with few exceptions, identical to what his competitors were broadcasting. It seems his competitors were doing just what he was doing: reading the *Times* and the *News,* listening to the all-news radio, and taking stories from the same news sources (wire services, police news dispatches, and press releases).[12]

News judgments continuously overlap in space and time. Editors of afternoon and evening media look for, and are oriented by, the news in the morning media. Editors of the morning media derive their sense of news from afternoon and evening media. Since these media may be in different regions and different cities, news judgments spread throughout an indefinite expanse of territory. The wire services and a few nationally-read newspapers, *The New York Times* and *Washington Post,* increase the diffusion of news judgments throughout the USA.

Moreover, this overlap provides a continuity of news judgments. A specific incident or theme presented in the morning will be covered in the evening, perhaps with fresh incidents, more details, a new development or a 'local angle' on the story. The process may repeat itself the next day, reproducing the theme of the previous evening.

The crime wave dynamic.

When journalists notice each other reporting the same crime theme, it becomes entrenched in a community of media organizations. Reporters and editors will know that 'this kind of crime is news'. To use Sacks' term[13], journalists have established a 'consistency rule': *every crime incident that can be seen as an instance of the theme, will be seen and reported as such.* The rule is used to identify the newsworthiness of certain crimes. Reporters and editors will know, for example, that a certain incident is 'another one of those crimes against the elderly' and not just an incident that can be categorized in a variety of ways.

Each use of the consistency rule reestablishes the rule. Any use of the principle invites readers or viewers of the news, including other journalists, to use the same principle. In order to recognize a crime incident as an instance of a theme, readers or viewers must use the same consistency rule which was used to produce that news.

Journalists who have not yet seen a particular crime theme learn to see it simply by watching their competition. They are able, using the consistency rule, to report the same crime theme their competition taught them to see. At this point, when a crime theme is beginning to spread through more and more media organizations, the 'reality' of the theme is confirmed for the media organizations who first reported it. They now see others using the theme. Moreover, as the theme persists, news organizations already using the theme will not hesitate to report new instances, because they confirm a past news judgment that 'this thing really is a type of crime happening now'. Thus, each use of the theme confirms and justifies its prior uses.

If it continues long enough, the process constitutes a crime wave dynamic. All crime waves begin as simple themes but by means of this dynamic can swell into waves. Crime themes constantly appear in the media and few reach the proportions of full-scale crime waves. After all, it only takes one editor with a little imagination to introduce a new theme into the news. Why is it that few crime themes go beyond a few days of coverage by one or two news organizations?

Clearly, something more than the crime wave dynamic is necessary for a theme to grow into a wave: *There must be a continuous supply of crime incidents that can be seen as instances of a theme*. Journalists may be primed to report a wave of crime incidents, but they also must know of enough incidents to report the wave. (During the period of my research, New York City journalists had been frustrated in reporting an expected 'mafia war'. This theme never persisted long for lack of enough incidents. Thus, 'mafia war' was a hungry crime theme, starved of enough incidents to make it the crime wave it could have become.) The supply of incidents is crucial in determining the growth of crime waves. What are journalists' sources of crime news?

Perpetrators of crime could be a source, but news workers rarely learn of crimes directly from offenders. The primary source is law enforcement agencies.[14] In the newsroom of WAVE, journalists first learned of crime incidents through three sources:[15] the 'police wire', the police radio, and other news organizations (wire service reports, the all-news radio station, and the *Daily News*). The first two of these were direct links to the city police. Crime news is really police news. Thus, *the media's supply of crime incidents is a function of the crime reporting practices of law enforcement agencies*. This reliance on law enforcement agencies constitutes another component of the ideological production of crime news. News workers will not know what the police do not routinely detect or transmit to them. What journalists do know of crime is formulated for them by law enforcement agencies.

The pool of potential crime waves

The police supply news organizations with an assortment of crime incidents every day. For media organizations in towns and small cities this assortment often consists of *all* crimes known to the police in a 24-hour period. But in large urban areas there are far too many crimes known to the police for any reporter to know them all. Therefore, urban journalists depend on the police to provide a 'summary' of these incidents.

In New York City, the daily summary is known as the 'police wire'. All the city's major media have a teletype that receives crime dispatches from the NYPD's Office of Public Information. In one day, this police wire types out anywhere from 12 to 25 messages. The crime items appearing over the police wire constitute a 'crime wave pool': a collection of crime incidents known to the media and having the potential of being seen as certain crime themes. Crime themes steadily supplied with instances over the police wire can become crime waves.

While journalists may invent crime themes (I suspect the police suggest and encourage many of them), a crime wave needs enough incidents on the police wire to support it. The police have power both to veto and promote the media's construction of crime waves. The collection of crime incidents the police provide to news organizations may systematically preclude certain themes from becoming waves (the veto power). Moreover, the same collection of incidents may contain enough crime items of a certain type to allow only a restricted class of crime themes to become crime waves (the enabling power).

For three 10-day periods from mid-February to the end of March 1977, a copy of all crime dispatches of the police wire was kept. Over this 30-day period, 468 individual dispatches (averaging 15.6 per day) were received. Of these, I ignored 97 (21%) which the police and journalists did not consider crime items. (They were mostly traffic advisories and non-suspicious fires.)

The remaining 371 crime dispatches reveal that the police wire provides journalists with a heavy and steady diet of 'street crimes'. 246 items or 66.3% of the crime items consisted of: (a) robberies and burglaries (85 items or 23% of all crime items), (b) unspecified shootings and stabbings (156 items or 42%) and (c) a sprinkling of other assaults (5 items or 1%—mostly rapes).

The remaining 33% of the police wire consisted of a variety of incidents: 13 bombings; 9 police suspended or arrested; 6 demonstrations requiring police action; 5 hostage situations; 4 raids for gambling, pornography, and drugs; 3 people run over by subway trains; 1 arson; and 1 hit-and-run. In addition, this third contained incidents which, I assume, the police considered 'strange' and consequently of interest to the media (for example, a bus stolen, the theft of a large amount of poisons, a man threatening to set himself on fire, a person crushed by an elevator, and the discovery of a disembodied head.)

This first thing worth noting about the police wire is what it does *not* contain: incidents of price-fixing, consumer fraud, sub-standard housing, unhealthy food, environmental pollution, political bribery and corruption, and the like. None appear in this pool of crime incidents from which crime waves arise, yet all of these may occur enough to constitute a crime wave if the media were to have routine access to knowledge of their occurrence.

One reason why these do not appear over the police wire is that agencies other than the city police enforce the laws governing these kinds of crime. Because police manpower is devoted to street crimes, it is street crime reports that the police wire carries. If journalists are to report other kinds of crime, they must draw on other sources (usually the wire services and other media organizations) which provide instances of such crime only sporadically.

Moreover, in the police wire one is unable to find a number of very common crimes which local police *do* know about, but consider 'uninteresting' and, thus, not worth transmitting to the media.[16] These included what journalists told me were 'too common' to be news: everything from bicycle theft, liquor store stick-ups and rapes, to wife beating, child molesting and other 'family matters' not resulting in homicide or hospitalization.

It is likely that a large number of the street crimes reported over the police wire were, in fact, family disputes, crimes against women, and racial conflict. But it was difficult to tell this from the information in the crime dispatches. This is particularly true of the large number of shootings and stabbings, which reporters tended to ignore.

Any descriptive features in a crime dispatch provide important clues to newsworkers looking for themes in crime. From reading the police wire, I was struck by the lack of detail. Victims, if they were identified at all, and if they were persons not businesses, were identified by sex and age. When more was told, they were described as: (1) 'elderly' (for homicides and robberies), (2) policemen (for any assaults), or (3) banks (for robberies). Perpetrators (and in the police wire these were always persons, not businesses) were usually identified by sex and a specific age. When more was said, it was almost always in connection with a 'youth gang' or the offender's youth. Victim-offender relationships were rarely mentioned. It was quite difficult to identify cases where the victim and offender knew each other. Thus the police wire gives one the impression most crimes occur between strangers. Finally, the location of a crime was usually provided in terms of a specific address or intersection. But a *type* of location was mentioned only when it could be said the incident occurred in a public or semi-public place, for example, a street, a subway, a schoolyard, or an apartment hallway.

Thus, the kinds of crime items and the descriptions of them in the police wire support only special sorts of crime themes that journalists may report. Crime in public places, crimes between strangers, and crime specific to age are themes that the police wire can and does provide numerous instances of. 'Crimes against the elderly' is one theme that has already blossomed into a crime wave with the help of the police wire. But other themes such as 'youth gang crime', 'subway crime', and 'school yard crime', have an excellent chance of becoming new crime waves.[17]

Apparently, the police who transmit crime dispatches to the media select incidents that they think will interest journalists.[18] This criterion of selectivity has two consequences, both keeping the present image of 'serious crime' from changing in the news. First, when the police perceive that the media are interested in a certain type of crime (for example, crimes against the elderly), they include instances of it in the police wire whenever they can. Thus, the police bolster emerging crime waves as long as those waves pertain to crimes the police routinely detect (that is, street crime). Second, the police decide what the media are interested in on the basis of what the media have reported before.

The police-supplied incidents that make up the media's crime wave pool all support prevailing notions of 'serious crime'. The crime wave pool leads the media to reproduce a common image that 'real crime' is crime on the streets, crime occurring between strangers, crime which brutalizes the weak and defenceless, and crime perpetrated by vicious youths. Such crimes exist, but this imagery becomes *the only reality of crime* which people will take seriously because it is the only reality impressed upon them in the media. And it is the only reality newsworkers are able to report continuously as themes in crime, and, periodically, as full-scale crime waves.

The role of authorities

I have described the crime wave pool as if it were only composed of crime incidents. This description is only partially true. During the initial phase of crime waves, media organizations mostly report crime incidents as instances of their theme-becoming-a-wave. But as soon as a crime theme looks like it is catching on and becoming a wave, journalists have another kind of news to report: the responses of politicians, police, and other officials.

The first signs of New York's crime wave against the elderly appeared in the last week of October 1976, when the city's media began reporting incidents of crime against old people. There was widespread coverage of three incidents: the murder of two aged sisters in their Bronx apartment, the rape-murder of an 85-year-old Manhattan woman, and the release on 50 dollars bail of a youth who beat an elderly person. After this third incident, the first official response appeared: Mayor Beame called a news conference and, with the Police Commissioner at his side, he vowed to make the city safe for old people by beefing up the police's Senior Citizens Robbery Unit and by working for reforms in the criminal justice system. From this point on, 'crimes against the elderly' became a favourite topic for political rhetoric and proposed reforms.

Starting from the very first week of the crime wave, the media could report both crimes against the elderly *and* stories of what the authorities were saying and doing about it. The entire wave was bolstered throughout its seven-week course by coverage of official statements, possible reforms of the criminal justice system, legislative debate and action, the formation of new police programmes, and community conferences on the problem. These kinds of stories made up 35% of the crime-wave-related news published during the period.

Officials and authorities were willing to assume from the outset that the crime wave represented something real or, at least, they were unwilling to express any doubts in public. Thus, by making public statements and taking official action on the basis of this assumption, authorities made the wave look even more real. And they guaranteed that the wave would go on for some time. As official responses to 'the problem' trailed off in mid-December, so did the number of crime incidents known to the media from the police wire and other police sources. The wave finally died.

It is clear that officials with a stake in 'doing something' about crime, have power over crime waves. Whether or not they inspire crime waves, they can attempt to redirect the focus of coverage of a crime wave already being reported. Nowhere is this clearer than in the first four weeks of *Daily News* coverage of the wave of crimes against the elderly. *News* headlines during the first week emphasized 'the problem', citing instance after instance. But in the next three weeks the stories (starting with the Mayor's first press conference) shifted focus to 'what is being done about the problem'.

Politicians and police use their news-making power to channel the coverage of social problems into a definite direction[19]: news of the problem becomes news of how the system is working to remedy the situation. Authorities may also use their newsmaking powers to stop certain crime themes from becoming crime waves. There is tentative data indicating that another crime theme, 'crimes on the subways', was stopped from becoming a full-scale crime wave by the New York City Transit Authority.

In the third week of February 1977, the *Daily News,* the *New York Post,* and WAVE all suddenly increased their coverage of murders and muggings in subways. In the middle of that week the Police Chief of the Transit Authority told a *Daily News* reporter there was no crime wave and, soon thereafter, three senior Transit officials called a news conference to assert that the subways were safer than the city streets. From that point on, coverage of subway crime steadily decreased to its pre-wave level.

If an unwanted crime wave should arise, officials can use their newsmaking powers to deny the wave's existence or to redirect crime coverage into a 'safe' direction. There is some evidence, however, that crimes against the elderly were not an 'unwanted crime wave'—at least for some officials in the New York City Police Department.

The *Daily News* reporter who wrote the feature articles which turned out to be the beginning of the crime wave, told me that he received 'considerable help' from the Senior Citizens Robbery Unit, whose job it was to catch muggers and murderers of the elderly (and the same unit that the Mayor expanded early in the crime wave). On 7 October, the reporter first wrote a story on two crimes with elderly victims that appeared over the police wire on the same day. This story was published 8 October, two weeks before the wave. At that time, a *Daily News* editor thought it would be a good idea for the reporter to do a series of feature stories on 'this kind of crime'. (Such features had shown up periodically in other media organizations before.)

While he was first researching these feature stories, the reporter was in frequent contact with SCRU. This police unit let him know they felt beleaguered, under-staffed, and that they were fighting a battle that deserved more attention. (According to the reporter, 'They proselytized a lot.') After he had written his feature stories, police from SCRU began calling him whenever they knew of a mugging or murder of an elderly person. This enabled the reporter to follow up his series with reports of specific crime incidents. Finally, it was SCRU which first told the reporter about the youth who was let out on 50 dollars bail after beating an elderly person. All major media in New York quickly picked up this story after the *News* reported it. At that point, the crime wave had begun.

I do not want to assert from this brief history of one crime wave that all waves are inspired by the police or politicians. It is not that simple. The crime wave against the elderly in New York seems to have resulted from a mixture of happenstance and police assistance. The history of this crime wave, however, does show that officials can and do use their positions to nurture fledgling crime themes first identified by journalists. Equally, they may use their position to deny the reality of crime waves.

Summary and conclusions

Crime waves begin as crime themes that journalists perceive in the process of organizing and selecting news to be presented to a public. Because journalists depend on one another for their sense of 'what's news', a crime theme can spread throughout a community of news organizations. As each news organization sees the theme presented by other organizations, they learn to use the theme and present it in their news.

But for this crime wave dynamic to occur, journalists must be able to associate a crime theme with a continuous supply of incidents that can be seen as instances of the theme. Media organizations know of crime almost exclusively through law enforcement agencies. The media's major source of supply for crime incidents in New York City is the NYPD's police wire. Crime dispatches over this wire are largely reports of street crimes: robberies, burglaries, shootings, stabbings, and other assaults. These constitute a pool of potential crime waves, excluding the possibility of certain themes. Non-street crime themes, if they were to receive massive

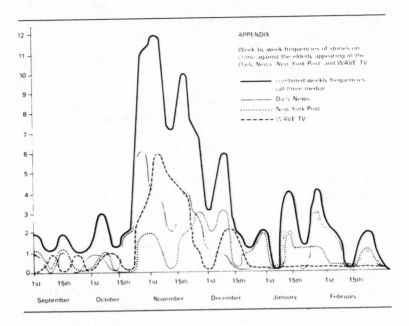

publicity as crime waves, might challenge prevailing notions of 'serious crime' in this society.

Moreover, once crime themes receive heavy coverage in the media, authorities can use their power to make news in an attempt to augment, modify, or deny a burgeoning crime wave. Thus, official sources not only control the supply of raw materials upon which crime news is based, but also the growth of crime waves.

While this study has dealt with the generation of crime waves, the news-making processes it reveals have broad implications. News plays a crucial role in formulating public issues and events, and in directing their subsequent course. Just as the interplay between local politics and local media organizations brought about New York City's crime wave, so the interplay between national elites and national media organizations may well have given rise to a number of social issues now widely accepted as fixtures in the recent American political scene.

Consider Watergate. As a few investigative reporters persisted in digging up news about the illegal activities of the Nixon administration, national elites competed among one another to halt, support, or redefine the growing Watergate news theme. Eventually, special prosecutors and Congressional committees were formed; that is, a bureaucratic apparatus was set up which began to feed the media with fresh instances of the Watergate theme. Once Nixon was deposed, this apparatus was dismantled, and so was the Watergate 'news wave'.

Watergate, the Bert Lance affair, the 'death' of political activism of the 1960s, and many other accepted political 'realities' may have been produced by the same ideological machinery that underlies crime waves.

NOTES AND REFERENCES

1. This paper focuses on the generation of crime waves, not their effects. Thus, I infer that media crime waves contribute to existing images and fears of crime in society. To substantiate this inference would require a study of crime wave effects with a different method from that used here. There is, however, research indicating that people's fears and images of crime derive, in large part, from the news media. See, for example: Albert Biderman, Louise Johnson, Jennie McIntyre and Adrianne Weir, 'Report on a pilot study in the District of Columbia on victimization and attitudes toward law enforcement' (Washington, DC, US Government Printing Office, 1967) and F. James Davis, 'Crime news in Colorado newspapers; (1952) *American Journal of Sociology* 57: 325–30.
2. Dorothy Smith, 'The ideological practice of sociology.' (Unpublished paper, 1972, Department of Sociology, University of British Columbia.)
3. Ibid.
4. While the New York City crime wave represents the first widely publicized formulation of 'crimes against the elderly,' the issue was not first defined by the New York media. Fredric DuBow (personal communication) has pointed out that the law enforcement establishment had formulated crimes against the elderly as a new type of crime at least two years prior to the crime wave: since 1974 it was an important funding theme of LEAA; in 1975 it was the subject of a major conference; and in February 1976 *Police Chief* devoted a special issue to it.

    These earlier law enforcement formulations probably led to the creation of the New York Police Department's Senior Citizens Robbery Unit (SCRU) well before the city's crime wave. As we shall see, SCRU played a crucial role in directing media attention to crimes against the elderly in the first stages of the crime wave. Thus, it seems that early 'professional formulations' led to the establishment of a specialized agency which, in turn, enabled the media publicly to formulate a category for crimes against the elderly.

5. Reported in the *New York Post*, 9th May 1977.
6. These figures are based on measuring the rate of crimes against the elderly as a proportion of crimes against the total population. If, however, one measures the rate in terms of the number of elderly victimizations per 1,000 senior citizens in New York, then the statistical picture is less clear. Murder and purse-snatching still declined (down 21% and 11%, respectively), but robbery increased (up to 3.4%).
7. See Davis (1952) and Bob Roshier, 'The selection of crime news in the press' (1973) and reprinted on p. 40.
8. Lincoln Steffens, *The Autobiography of Lincoln Steffens* (New York, Harcourt Brace, 1931).
9. Glasgow Media Group, 'Bad news' (1976) *Theory and Society* 3: 339–63.
10. The editor's use of news themes is part of the more general tendency of newsworkers to code and categorize news events in order to 'routinize their unexpectedness'. See Gaye Tuchman, 'Making news by doing work: routinizing the unexpected' (1973) *American Journal of Sociology* 79: 110–31.
11. The assignment editor started with these two stories because his superior in the newsroom had suggested that they be covered.
12. While my example of overlapping news judgments is drawn from a local television station, the same phenomenon occurs both on newspapers—see Bernard Cohen, *The press and foreign policy* (Princeton University Press, 1963), pp.54–65, and Leon V. Sigal, *Reporters and officials* (Lexington, Mass., D.C. Heath, 1973), p.103—and national network news—Edward Jay Epstein, *News from nowhere* (New York, Random House, 1973), p.150.
13. Harvey Sacks, 'On the analyzability of stories by children,' in J. Gumperz and D. Hymes (eds), *Directions in sociolinguistics* (New York, Holt, Rinehart & Winston, 1972), pp.325–45.
14. The only exception that comes to mind is the coverage of mafia news by specialized reporters on large New York publications: *The New York Times*, the New York *Daily News*, the *New York Post*, the *Wall Street Journal*, and *Newsday*.
15. There was an occasional fourth source: phone calls from the police.
16. There were some exceptions. A handful of common crimes did appear over the police wire (e.g. 4 rapes in a 30-day observation period). The journalists I observed could not explain why these were there, and they ignored them.
17. In fact, one year after I wrote this, New York City experienced a major 'wave' of crime in its subways.
18. For a more detailed discussion of how the police select incidents for inclusion in the police wire, see Mark Fishman, *Manufacturing the news* (Austin, University of Texas Press, 1980); 'Police news: constructing an image of crime.' (Paper presented at the Annual Meeting of the Society for the Study of Social Problems, Boston, August 1979.)

19. Harvey Molotch and Marilyn Lester, 'News as purposive behavior: the strategic use of routine events, accidents, and scandals.' (1974) *American Sociological Review* 39: 101–12, and reprinted here on p. 118.

News as purposive behaviour; on the strategic use of routine events, accidents, and scandals*

HARVEY MOLOTCH AND MARILYN LESTER

Everyone needs news. In everyday life, news tells us what we do not experience directly and thus renders otherwise remote happenings observable and meaningful. Conversely, we fill each other with news. Although those who make their living at newswork (reporters, copy editors, publishers, typesetters, etc.) have additional needs for news, all individuals, by virtue of the ways they attend to and give accounts of what they believe to be a pregiven world, are daily newsmakers.

News is thus the result of this invariant need for accounts of the unobserved, this capacity for filling-in others, and the production work of those in the media. This paper seeks to understand the relationships between different kinds of news needs and how it is that news needs of people differently situated vis à vis the organization of news work produce the social and political 'knowledge' of publics.[2]

Theoretical groundings

Humans schedule and plan.[3] We learn from the experience of a sociologist-patient in a tuberculosis sanitorium[4] that whether, from the standpoint of the outside observer, anything is 'really happening' and whether there is any 'real reason' to create calendars, reckon time, or scheme a future, people nonetheless provide accounts of activities which make those activities observable as real and patterned happenings. In a manner analogous to the creation of a meaningful spatial world, those happenings are used as temporal points of reference for ordering a past and future.

Pasts and futures are constructed and reconstructed, as a continuous process of daily routines. In such constructions an infinite number of

* This paper was originally published in the *American Sociological Review*, vol. 39, February 1974.

available activities are not attended to, and a certain few become created observables. These few become resources—available as practically needed—to break up, demarcate, and fashion lifetime, history, and a future.

Our conception is not of a finite set of things that 'really happened out there' from which selection is made; our idea is not analogous to selective perception of the physical world. We propose (following Garfinkel[5] and others) that what is 'really happening' is identical with what people attend to. Our conception thus follows Zimmerman and Pollner's description of the work of 'assembling the occasioned corpus':

> By the use of the term occasioned corpus, we wish to emphasize that the features of socially organized activities are particular, contingent accomplishments of the production and recognition work of parties to the activity . . . The occasioned corpus is a corpus with no regular elements, that is, it does not consist of a stable collection of elements. The work of assembling an occasioned corpus consists in the ongoing 'corpusing and decorpusing' of elements rather than the situated retrieval or removal of a subset of elements from a larger set transcending any particular setting in which that work is done.[6]

Thus pasts and futures are not accomplished once and for all, with new 'additions' embellishing an established 'whole'. A new happening reinforms what every previous happening was; in turn each happening gets its sense from the context in which it is placed.

An *occurrence* is any cognized happening; it can be infinitely divided and elaborated into additional happenings and occurrences. 'Important' occurrences are those which are especially useful in demarcating time. In their individual lives, Americans conspicuously use such rites of passage as birthdays, anniversaries, employments, promotions, geographical moves, and deaths for this end. Depending upon the context, other occurrences may serve the same function (e.g. the date the house was painted, the time one's son was arrested, the year the crop failed). We will use the term 'events' to refer to occurrences which are creatively used for such purposes. Once such use occurs, an occurrence becomes, to a degree, reified as an object in the social world[7] and thus available as a resource for constructing events in the future.

Doing events

The everyday activities of constituting events are guided by one's purposes-at-hand. A much oversimplified analogy to fact-making about the

physical world may be helpful here. Individuals 'see' chairs when they
enter a room because of the recurrent need to sit. Sociologists sometimes
'see' religion as an explanatory variable in their data because it sometimes
'works'. The analogous process in creating temporal points of reference
means that occurrences *become events* according to their usefulness to an
individual who is attempting on a particular occasion to order her or his
experience.[8] But the creation of temporal points of reference varies over
time. Each time there is a need to carve up reality temporally, the reason
for doing so constrains what kind of carving will be done. Events may
thus, to a degree, persist, but they are not intrinsically durable. Any
occurrence is a potential resource for constructing an event, and the event
so constructed is continuously dependent on purposes-at-hand for its
durability.

Collectivities of people—communities, klans, societies, civiliza-
tions—similarly appear to create (or have created for them) temporal
demarcations which are assumed to be shared in common among those
who are deemed and deem themselves to be competent individuals in the
collectivity.[9] *Public Time* is the term which we will take to stand for that
dimension of collective life through which human communities come to
have what is assumed to be a patterned and perceptually shared past,
present and future. Just as the rudiments of an individual lifetime consist
of private events, so public time is analogously constituted through public events. Thus the content of an individual's conceptions of the history
and the future of his or her collectivity comes to depend on the processes
by which public events get constructed as resources for discourse in
public matters. The work of historians, journalists, sociologists and political scientists helps to accomplish this task for various publics by
making available to citizens a range of occurrences from which to construct a sense of public time.

To the degree to which individuals or collectivities have differing
purposes, rooted in diverse biographies, statuses, cultures, class origins,
and specific situations, they will have differing and sometimes competing uses for occurrences. An *issue* arises when there are at least two such
competing uses, involving at least two parties having access to event-
creating mechanisms. For public issues, these mechanisms are the mass
media.

Conflicting purposes-at-hand lead to competing accounts of what happened or, what is a variant of the same question, to dispute over whether
anything significant happened at all. Under these circumstances an *issue*
takes form. The thirtieth birthday, or the thirteenth birthday, or meno-

pause, or the signing of a lease, will become an issue if there are competing interpretations of what really happened. That is, a struggle takes place
over the nature of the occurrence, and embedded in that struggle are
differing interests in an outcome. It is currently being disputed, for example, whether menopause is a 'real' event. Women's liberationists assert
that although it is in fact an occurrence, that is, it 'simply' happens, it is
not an event. It should not serve as a time-marking feature of the environment *through which certain consequences* (e.g. no woman should hold
important responsibility) *should follow*. Others (usually men) assert the
contrary; and in these differing accounts of the meaning of the occurrence
(i.e. whether it is or is not an event) an issue resides.

In all public issues, analogous processes are at work. We debate, for
example, whether the 'My Lai massacre' 'really' happened or whether it
was 'only' a routine search and destroy mission. That choice between
accounts determines the nature of the occurrence, and at the same time,
the degree to which it was special enough to be used to reorder past
occurrences and events, change priorities, and make decisions. Any
public issue involves a similar struggle over an occurrence and similar
interests in the outcome: Did the ITT lobbyist send that memo as specified? Is the crime rate so high that now 'you-can't-walk-the-streets'? The
existence of an issue demonstrates that competing *event needs* exist with
respect to a given occurrence. Sometimes, in fact, the issue itself can
become an issue. For example, a politician might charge that his opponents have deliberately 'cooked up' a 'phony issue' to deflect voter attention from the 'real issue'. In such instances, the issue of the issue becomes
an event.

The work of promoting occurrences to the status of public event
springs from the event needs of those doing the promoting. Unlike the
case of private events, it involves making experience for great numbers of
people. This potential public impact means that the social multiplier
effect of the work of those who do news for publics is much greater than
the effect of people who do news for themselves and their face-to-face
associates. Although analogous processes and distinctions exist for private and public events, this greater impact of the latter leads us to focus
our discussion on public events.

Career lines of public events

In the career pattern of a public event, an occurrence passes through a set
of agencies (individuals or groups), each of which helps construct,

through a distinctive set of organizational routines, what the event *will have turned out to be* using as resources the work of agencies who came before and anticipating what successive agencies 'might make out of it'.[10]

For simplicity, we view events as being constituted by three major agencies.[11] First, there are the *news promoters*—those individuals and their associates (e.g. Nixon, Nixon's secretary; Kuntsler, Kuntsler's spokesman; a-man-who-saw-a-flying-saucer) who identify (and thus render observable) an occurrence as special, on some ground, for some reason, for others. Secondly, there are the *news assemblers* (newsmen, editors, and rewritemen) who, working from the materials provided by the promoters, transform a perceived finite set of promoted occurrences into public events through publication or broadcast. Finally, there are the *news consumers* (e.g., readers) who analogously attend to certain occurrences made available as resources by the media and thereby create in their own minds a sense of public time. Each successive agency engages in essentially the same kind of constructing work, based on purposes-at-hand which determine given event needs. But the work accomplished at each point closes off or inhibits a great number of event-creating possibilities. In this closing off of possibilities lies the power of newswork and of all accounting activity. We now turn to a detailed examination of the newswork done by each agency in the newsmaking process and the power implications of that work.

1. Promoting

There are interests in promoting certain occurrences for public use, as well as interests in preventing certain occurrences from becoming public events. By 'promoting' we merely mean that an actor, in attending to an occurrence, helps to make that occurrence available to still others. In some instances, the promoting may be direct, crass, and obvious—as in public relations work[12] or transparently political activity (e.g., a candidate's press conference). In others, promotion work is less crassly self-serving as when a citizen tries to publicize a health danger. Commonly, promotion work revolves around one's own activity which like all social activity is accomplished with its prospective and retrospective potential uses in mind. Thus, the press conference is held for the benefits which its public impact are assumed to provide; a protest demonstration is, in the same way, geared for its selection as an event[13]. Similarly, a decision to bomb North Vietnam is conducted with what-will-be-made-of-it and what-it-really-was-all-along (e.g. its deniability) as two of its constituent features. In our language, then, doing and promoting are part of the same process; indeed, the career of the occurrence will, in the end, constitute what was 'done'. That is, if the bombing is not widely reported or is reported as 'bombing selected military targets', the nature of the act itself, from the perspective of the agent (Nixon), will radically differ from the result of prominent and widespread coverage which stipulates 'indiscriminate massive bombing'. Thinking through these possible coverages is part of the work of a newsmaker and is essential to competent event creation.[14]

Although promoters often promote occurrences for which they themselves are responsible, they also have access (within limits) to promote the activities of others—including individuals whose purposes are opposed to their own. Thus, a political candidate can 'expose' the corrupt occurrence work of a political rival or take credit for its beneficent consequences. Similarly, Richard Nixon could promote letters from P.O.W. mothers which were written as private communications and perhaps not envisioned by their authors as public events. The richness and irony of political life is made up of a free-wheeling, skilled competition among people having access to the media, trying to mobilize occurrences as resources for their experience-building work.

2. Assembling

Media personnel form a second agency in the generation of public events. From their perspective, a finite number of things 'really happen', of which the most special, interesting or important are to be selected. Their task involves 'checking a story out' for worthiness, a job which may involve months of research or a fleeting introspection or consultation with a colleague. The typical conception of the media's role, then, at least in western, formally uncensored societies, is that the media stand as reporter-reflector-indicators of an objective reality 'out there', consisting of knowably 'important' events of the world. Armed with time and money, an expert with a 'nose for news' will be led to occurrences which do, indeed, index that reality. Any departure from this ideal tends to be treated as 'bias' or some other pathological circumstance.

To suggest the view that assemblers' own event needs help to constitute public events, is also to imply the importance of the organizational activities through which news is generated. The nature of the media as formal organization, as routines for getting work done in newsrooms, as career mobility patterns for a group of professionals, as profit-making institutions, all become inextricably and reflexively tied to the content of published news.[15] The extent to which news organizations generate event

needs among news assemblers that vary from those of occurrence promoters is the extent to which the media have an institutionally patterned
independent role in newsmaking. How then does the construction work
of the media coincide or conflict with the construction work of promoters? Assemblers' purposes-at-hand, as they contrast or coincide with
the purposes-at-hand of different types of promoters, will determine the
answers to such a question.

Powerful promoters may attempt to increase the correspondence between their event needs and those of assemblers by pressuring media into
altering their work routines. The sanctions which the powerful exercise to
control media routines may be direct and crude (e.g. threatening
speeches, advertising boycotts, anti-trust suits against broadcasters) or
subtle (e.g. journalism awards, and the encouragement, through regular-
ized interviews, leaks and press conferences of newsroom patterns which
inhibit follow-up, experimentation and deviation). Thus, for example, all
television networks have abandoned their habit of 'instant analysis' of
presidential speeches, as a response, we assume, to White House pressure. What may eventually evolve as a journalistic 'professional canon'
will have been historically grounded in an attempt by the institutionally
powerful to sustain ideological hegemony. In this instance, the event
needs of assemblers come to closely resemble those of promoters who
affect journalistic work routines.

In societies having a formally-controlled press, the substantive relationship between news promoters and assemblers is less obscured. In
such societies, media are organized to serve a larger purpose (e.g. creating socialist man or maintaining a given regime). Validity thus tends to be
equated with utility. Presumably, career advancement and survival depend on one's ability to mesh her or his 'nose for news' with the bosses'
conceptions of the general social purpose and thus of the utility of a given
occurrence.

Because Western conceptions of news rely on the assumption that there
is a reality out-there-to-be-described, the product of any system which
denies this premise is termed 'propaganda'. Thus, in the Western mind,
the distinction between news and propaganda lies in the premise seen to
be embedded in the assemblers' work: those with purposes produce propaganda; those whose only purpose is to reflect reality produce news.

As Tuchman[16] has argued, the assumption of an objective reality allows Western newsmakers at all levels to have an ever available account
of their activities—i.e. they report (or at least try their best to report)
what is there. But this kind of self-definition by practitioners should not
be allowed to obscure the purposiveness of media work. In fact, that self-

definition as an account is itself part of the very organizational activities through which newswork gets done. By choosing to suspend belief in an ability to index 'what really happened'[17] we make manifest the basic similarities between newsmaking in any social or political context.

In the West as in the East, parallels exist between the event needs of assemblers and promoters. These parallels do not necessarily result from plots, conspiracies, 'selling out' or even ideological communalities.[18] While not ignoring these, we are intrigued by the possibility of news generated through the parallel needs of promoters and assemblers which arise for different reasons. Though perhaps unaware of the implications of one another's work, they somehow manage to produce a product which favours the event needs of certain social groups and disfavours those of others.

3. Consuming

Members of publics, glutted with the published and broadcast work of the media, engage in the same sort of constituting activity as news assemblers. A residue of biography, previous materials made available by media, and present context, all shape the consumer's work of constructing events. Their newswork is procedurally identical with that of promoters and assemblers, but with two important differences: the stock of occurrences available as resources has been radically truncated through the newswork of other agencies; and, unlike assemblers, they ordinarily have no institutional base from which to broadcast their newswork.

A typology of public events

Despite the overarching similarity of individuals' and organizations' methods of newsmaking, we find it useful to describe certain substantive differences in the ways in which occurrences are promoted to the status of public event.[19]

In using this typology, we are imposing ideal types on data. Consistent with that fact, any event which we may pull from a newspaper's front page for illustrative purposes may be seen to contain some features of each event type. Similarly, the category which any kind of event 'fits' may similarly shift with changing features or schemes of interpretation, which may lead to a revision of what 'really happened'.

We distinguish between events by the circumstances of the promotion work which makes them available to publics. The answers to two questions which can be asked of any event provide the basis for our typology.

First: Did the underlying happening come into being through intentional or unintentional human activity? And second: Does the party promoting the occurrence into an event appear to be the same as the party who initially accomplished the happening upon which the event is based? The relevance of these questions will become clearer as each event type is described.

Routine events

Routine events are distinguishable by the fact that the underlying happenings on which they are presumably based are purposive accomplishments and by the fact that the people who undertake the happening (whom we call 'effectors') are identical with those who promote them into events. The prototypical routine event is the press conference statement, but the great majority of stories appearing in the daily press fall in this category; hence, on grounds of frequency, we term them 'routine'.[20]

Whether or not a given promoter is the 'same' as the effector can be difficult to determine in some instances. It is clear, for example, that if Richard Nixon's Press Secretary promotes the President's trip to China or Russia, the effector (Nixon) and the promoter (Press Secretary) can be taken as identical for all intents and purposes. If, however, Nixon reads a letter on TV written to him by a P.O.W.'s wife, the degree of identity between Nixon, the promoter, and P.O.W. wife, as effector, is less clear. To the extent to which it can be assumed that both party's purposes are identical—e.g. to bring public attention to P.O.W.s and/or to mobilize support for the war—the promoter and agent can be deemed identical and the written letter as a public event can be classified as routine. Of course, it may be that Nixon wants to bring attention to the P.O.W.s for other long-range ('ulterior') purposes not shared by the P.O.W. wife. In such a case, Nixon is not merely using his position to advance the effector's public event needs, but is fostering a new occurrence of his own and promoting it as a public event. After noting that kind of constructing work, the 'new' occurrence is analytically the same as any other.

While all routine events share certain features, elucidating those features does not tell us what makes for a successful routine event. Each day a multitude of activities is done with a view to creating routine events. But those intentions must complement the work done by news assemblers if a public event is to result. The success of a potential routine event is thus contingent on the assembler's definition of an occurrence as a 'story'. Put another way, those who seek to create public events by promoting their activities (occurrences) must have access to that second stage of event-creation. With respect to this accessibility, various subtypes of routine events can be discussed;

(a) those where the event promoters have *habitual access* to news assemblers;
(b) those where the event-promoters are seeking to *disrupt* the routine access of others to assemblers in order to make events of their own; and
(c) those where the access is afforded by the fact that the promoters and news assemblers are *identical*.

(a) *Habitual access*. As the term implies, habitual access exists when an individual or group is so situated that their own event needs routinely coincide with the newsmaking activities of media personnel. Thus, for example, the President of the United States is always assumed to say 'important' things. This 'importance' is taken for granted, and a Washington reporter who acts on the opposite assumption will probably lose his job. Habitual access is likely limited in this country to high government officials, major corporate figures, and, to a lesser extent, certain glamour personalities.[21] Such people, especially those in political life, must be concerned with keeping their podia alive and organizing the news so that their goals do not suffer in the continuing competition to create publics. That competition may involve occasional struggles with other powerful figures, or, on the other hand, with insurgent groups seeking to provide a different set of public experiences. Intra- or inter-group competitions notwithstanding, habitual access is generally found among those with extreme wealth or other institutionally-based sources of power. Indeed, this power is both a result of the habitual access and a continuing cause of such access. Routine access is one of the important sources and sustainers of existing power relationships.

The function of habitual access is illustrated by a routine event such as Richard Nixon's 'inspection' of a Santa Barbara beach after the calamitous 1969 oil spill.[22] Nixon was depicted leaving his helicopter on a section of the sand, 'inspecting' the beach beneath his feet. Needless to say, Nixon's talented assistants could have done the inspection for him; furthermore, Nixon is scientifically incompetent to 'inspect' beaches. The activity was an attempt to generate an event so as to inform the American public that Richard Nixon was personally concerned about oil on beaches. His efforts and inspection were meant to instruct the public that the beaches were in fact clean. When Fidel Castro visits a hospital or Mao checks up on a generator, a similar dynamic is at work. When this type of occurrence becomes a successful public event, the results are seen as close to those first envisioned by the effector/promoter.

Although news assemblers commonly act upon the assumption that those with official authority are the most newsworthy[23], other individuals and groups are occasionally in the position to generate events. Yet, whereas the U.S. President's access to the media continues across time and issue, the access of other groups—e.g. spokespeople for women's rights, civil rights, and youth—will ebb and flow over time and place.[24] For this reason, the ideal-typical routine event is taken to be the generating of a public experience by those in positions to have continual access to asserting the importance and factual status of 'their' occurrences.

(b) *Disruptive access.* Those lacking habitual access to event-making who wish to contribute to the public experience, often come to rely on disruption.[25] They must 'make news', by somehow crashing through the ongoing arrangements of newsmaking, generating surprise, shock, or some more violent form of 'trouble'. Thus, the relatively powerless disrupt the social world to disrupt the habitual forms of event-making. In extreme cases, multitudes are assembled in an inappropriate place to intervene in the daily schedule of occurrence and events. Such activities constitute, in a sense, 'anti-routine' events. This 'obvious' disruption of normal functioning and its challenge to the received social world prompts the coverage of the mass media.

The disruptive occurrence becomes an event because it is a problem for the relatively powerful. We would argue that a protest event—e.g. a student sit-in or a Jerry Rubin remark—receives media play precisely because it is thought to be an occurrence which 'serious people' need to understand. What does a sit-in mean? Have students gone berserk? Will secretaries be raped? Is order in jeopardy? People interested in maintaining the ongoing process need to answer these questions before developing strategy and plans for restoration of order. The coverage which results typically speaks to these implications—not to the issues which raised the protest in the first place. Thus, to the extent that student protest activity continues as an issue, it does so because important parties disagree about what the protest means and how it should best be handled. Important liberals think it means that certain institutions need to be reformed (e.g. a particular war ended, stepped-up counselling in the Dean's office, improved student-faculty ratios); important conservatives think it means that students are bums and should be coddled less. Issues exist through this disagreement on meaning-methods among parties with access. The focus is typically on how to handle dissidents, and not on the points raised by the dissidents. That is why the leaders of campus revolts almost never find themselves quoted *substantively* in the press.[26]

We would argue that coverage of student protest fades as the event needs of one or the other important party decline. The mystery of the student protest declines as the scenario becomes increasingly typified through repetition: buildings are taken—speeches made—administrations respond—cops are called—heads are cracked—ringleaders arrested—trials proceed. No rapes, little destruction, token reform (maybe). People can go back to their everyday activities; the strategic need to know is satisfied.

There is a second reason this type of routine event declines in usefulness to important people. The very reporting on the occurrence may come to be seen as precipitating the creation of more such occurrences. Thus, an interest develops in eliminating such events from the news—either by taking actions to prevent them (e.g. softening resistance to student demands) or by agreeing not to report them. Police, for example, may bar reporters from the sites of ghetto riots, and be supported in doing so by politicians, civic leaders, and publishers as well. Certain canons of the 'responsibility of the press' are readily available to editors who choose to bypass anti-routine events. The purposiveness underlying all routine events can be selectively perceived at appropriate moments to justify cancelling a story because it is viewed as promoted precisely for its media effects.[27] When important people see a potential event as too costly, given their purposes-at-hand, there are various resources for eliminating it.

(c) *Direct access.* Some news stories are generated by assemblers who go out and 'dig up' the news. Feature stories are often of this sort but many 'straight news' articles can be of the same type. For example, assemblers in scrutinizing the police blotter may detect that 'crime is rising' or may interview or poll a population for attitude shifts. This newswork is routine in that creating the occurrence (e.g. record checking, attitude polling) is a purposive activity promoted as a public event by the effector. It is distinctive, however, in that the promoter and the assembler are identical. When this identity is sufficiently transparent, the media involved may be castigated for lacking 'objectivity' or for engaging in 'muckraking' or 'yellow journalism'. A tenet of the 'new journalism' is that such newsmaking is indeed appropriate. This controversy is, in our terms, a conflict over whether or not media personnel can legitimately engage in transparent news promotion, or whether they must continue to appear to be passively reporting that which objectively happens.[28]

Accidents

An accident differs from a routine event in two respects: (1) the underlying happening is not intentional, and (2) those who promote it as a public event are different from those whose activity brought the happening about. In the case of accidents people engage in purposive activity which leads to unenvisioned happenings which are promoted by others into events. Accidents thus rest upon miscalculations which lead to a breakdown in the customary order.

Events such as the Santa Barbara oil spill, the Watergate arrests, the release of nerve gas at Dugway Proving Ground, and the inadvertent U.S. loss of hydrogen bombs over Spain all involve 'foul ups' in which the strategic purpose of a given activity (e.g. oil production, political espionage, gas research, national defence) becomes unhinged from its consequences.

The accident tends to have results which are the opposite of routine events. Instead of being a deliberately planned contribution to a purposely developed social structure (or in the language of the literature, 'decisional outcome'), it fosters revelations which are otherwise deliberately obfuscated by those with the resources to create routine events.

For people in everyday life, the accident is an important resource for learning about the routines of those who ordinarily possess the psychic and physical resources to shield their private lives from public view. The Ted Kennedy car accident gave the public access to that individual's private activities and dispositions. As argued elsewhere[29] an accident like the Santa Barbara oil spill provided the local public analogous insights into the everyday functioning of American political and economic institutions.

When accidents surface as public events, they do so in 'error'; we can expect that, unless the needs of powerful people differ, routine event-making procedures subsequently and increasingly come into play to define the accident out of public politics. But the suddenness of the accident and its unanticipated nature mean that event makers are initially not ready and thus the powerful could give uncoordinated, mutually contradictory accounts. This process of accidental disruption, followed by attempts to restore traditional meanings can, we have found, be observed empirically; and thus, *we take accidents to constitute a crucial resource for the empirical study of event-structuring processes.*[30]

In their realization as events, accidents are far less contingent than are routine events on the event needs of the powerful. Given the inherent drama, sensation, and atypicality of accidents, it is difficult to deny their existence; and typically nonimportant groups can more easily hold sway in the temporal demarcation process. Thus, the outflow of a small sea of oil on the beaches of California is for 'anybody' a remarkable occurrence; and a reporter or newspaper which ignored it would, owing to the physical evidence widely available to direct experience, be obviously 'managing the news'. That is, if newsmaking results in published accounts considered by a multitude to differ from 'what happened' as determined by their own event needs, the legitimacy of newsmaking as an objective enterprise is undermined. Of course, not all accidents become public events. Oil spills off the Gulf of Mexico, almost as large as the Santa Barbara spill, received far less coverage; similarly, the massive escape of nerve gas at Dugway Proving Ground[31] could easily be conceived as far more disastrous to the natural environment and to human life than any oil spill; yet again, relatively little coverage occurred.[32] All this attests to the fact that all events are socially constructed and their 'newsworthiness' is not contained in their objective features.

Scandals

Scandals share features of both accidents and routine events but differ from both as well. A scandal involves an occurrence which becomes an event through the intentional activity of individuals (we call them 'informers') who for one reason or another do not share the event-making strategies of the occurrence effectors. Like a routine event, the precipitating happening is intended and the event is promoted; but unlike a routine event, the promoting is not done by those who originally brought about the happening. In fact, the event's realization typically comes as a surprise to the original actors. Thus, Ronald Reagan deliberately paid no state income tax 1970–71, but did not expect, in so doing, to read about it in newspapers. Dita Beard did, we assume, write the notorious 'ITT Memo', but again, did not envision it as a public event. (The ITT *issue* derives from an attempt by ITT to destroy the scandal by denying the precipitating occurrence.) A scandal requires the willing cooperation of at least one party having power and legitimacy which derive either from first-hand experience (the eye-witness) or position in the social structure (e.g. a 'leaker' of memos or Pentagon papers). The more both circumstances are fulfilled, the greater the capacity to generate a scandal. Again, this capacity is disproportionately in the hands of élites, but their trusted hirelings are also strategically well situated. Like the accident, the scandal reveals normally hidden features of individual lives or institutional processes.

The My Lai massacre is one of the more dramatic examples of scandal. It is not a routine event in that those originally involved in making it happen—whether defined as the troops in the field or the President and Generals—did not intend that the mass murder become a recorded phenomenon. The tortuous route the occurrence followed (it was twenty months becoming a public event) has been elucidated in some detail.[33] My Lai was originally reported as a successful, routine offensive against Viet Cong soldiers; only later was it transformed into a 'massacre'. In other scandals, high status people 'fink' on each other—as, for example, when political reformers expose 'the machine', or when political leaders wage internecine war to eliminate opponents (e.g. the Fortas, Dodd, Goldfine scandals). Of course, scandals can also occur when statuses are more asymmetrical; it may have been a clerk who exposed Reagan; it was an Army corporal who exposed My Lai. Also, when the informer is of relatively low status and unsupported by a group with power, the scandal-making business can be quite arduous (e.g. My Lai) and often a complete failure. Frequently, an accident can stimulate a series of scandals, as in the instance of the Santa Barbara oil spill, and in the McCord and Dean testimony in the aftermath of the Watergate arrests.

Serendipity

A fourth type of event, the serendipity event, shares features of both the accident and the routine. The serendipity event has an underlying happening which is unplanned (as with accidents) but is promoted by the effector himself (as with routine events). Examples of the serendipitous event are hard to come by precisely because one of its features is that the effector/promoter disguises it to make it appear routine. Self-proclaimed heroes are perhaps a variant of those who effect serendipitous events: one inadvertently performs a given act which results in the accomplishment of some courageous and socially-desired task. Thus, through self-promotion (or at least tacit approval), one converts an accident into a deliberate act.

Unlike the accident, the underlying happening in the serendipity event remains unobserved and perhaps unobservable for members of publics. Because the agent can transform the unintended happening into a routine event through his promotion activities, people are not given the kinds of information which accidents and scandals afford. Because serendipity events are difficult to differentiate from routine events, they are as irretrievable for sociological investigation as accidents are retrievable. They are the least sociologically useful of any event type.

TABLE 1

EVENT CLASSIFICATORY SCHEME

	Happening accomplished intentionally	Happening accomplished not intentionally
Promoted by Effector	Routine	Serendipity
Promoted by Informer	Scandal	Accident

By way of summary, Table 1 displays the four event types, distinguished by the degree to which their underlying happening is accomplished intentionally and by whether the occurrence effector or an informer does the promotion work.

Summary Discussion

Consistent with Gans'[34] urgings, we attempt a new departure for the study of news. We see media as reflecting not a world out there, but the practices of those having the power to determine the experience of others. Harold Garfinkel made a similar point about clinical records he investigated; rather than viewing an institution's records as standing ideally for something which happened, one can instead see in those records the organizational practices of people who make records routinely. Garfinkel concludes that there are 'good organizational reasons for bad clinical records. Following Garfinkel, our interest in their 'badness' does not rest in spell out the clinic's social organization.

We think that mass media should similarly be viewed as bad clinical records. Following Garfinkel, our interest in its 'badness' does not rest in an opportunity for criticism and depiction of irony, but rather in the possibility of understanding how the product comes to look like it does, i.e., what the 'good reasons' are. We advocate examining media for the event needs and the methods through which those with access come to determine the experience of publics. We can look for the methods through which ideological hegemony is accomplished by examining the records which are produced.

Seen in this way, one approach to mass media is to look not for reality, but for purposes which underlie the strategies of creating one reality instead of another. For the citizen to read the newspaper as a catalogue of the important happenings of the day, or for the social scientist to use the newspaper for uncritically selecting topics of study, is to accept as reality the political work by which events are constituted by those who happen to currently hold power. Only in the accident, and, secondarily, in the scandal, is that routine political work transcended to some significant degree, thereby allowing access to information which is directly hostile to those groups who typically manage public event making. Future research on media and on the dynamics of power would be strengthened by taking this 'second face of power'[35] into consideration. More profoundly, sociologists who habitually take their research topics and conceptual constructs as they are made available through mass media and similar sources may wish to extricate their consciousnesses from the purposive activities of parties whose interests and event needs may differ from their own.

NOTES AND REFERENCES

1. We would like to thank Aaron Cicourel, Mark Fishman, Lloyd Fitts, Richard Flacks, Eliot Friedson, Richard Kinane, Milton Mankoff, Hugh Mehan, Linda Molotch, Milton Olin, Charles Perrow, Michael Schwartz, David Street, Gaye Tuchman, John Weiler, Eugene Weinstein and Don Zimmerman. Financial support was provided through a faculty senate grant, University of California, Santa Barbara.

2. The term 'public' throughout this essay is used in the sense John Dewey used it: a political grouping of individuals brought into being as a social unit through mutual recognition of common problems for which common solutions should be sought. Information thus does not merely *go to* publics, it *creates* them. See John Dewey, *The public and its problems* (New York, Holt, Rinehart, 1927).

3. George Miller, Eugene Galanter and Karl Pribram, *Plans and the structure of behavior* (New York, Holt, Rinehart & Winston, 1960).

4. Julius Roth, *Timetables: structuring the passage of time in hospital treatment and other careers* (New York, Bobbs-Merrill, 1963).

5. Harold Garfinkel, *Studies in ethnomethodology* (Englewood Cliffs, Prentice Hall, 1967).

6. Don Zimmerman and Melvin Pollner, 'The everyday world as phenomenon,' in Jack Douglas (ed.), *Understanding everyday life* (Chicago, Aldine, 1970), pp. 94–97.

7. Cf. Richard Appelbaum, 'Social mobility: a study in the reification of sociological concepts,' (1973) Department of Sociology, University of California, Santa Barbara (mimeographed).

8. Schutz draws a similar parallel between the world of space and the world of time constituting the natural attitude of everyday life. Cf. Alfred Schutz, *Collected papers*, Vol. I, Pt III (The Hague, Martinus Nijhoff, 1966).

9. As we imply above, while members assume that meanings are shared, we view that sharedness as yet another accomplished feature of the process of creating events.

10. Aaron Cicourel makes an analogous argument with respect to the creation of a juvenile delinquent. A delinquent is constituted by a set of accounts produced by a series of law enforcement agencies motivated by the need to appear rational to others in the processing system. Any youth's activities will be made (through a course of accounting work) to tally with or violate some law. Thus a delinquent is an accomplishment of a chain of processing agencies who need to do a 'competent job for all practical purposes'. That is, what the act, the person, (or event) 'really is', is as it is attended to through members' practical work. See his book, *The social organization of juvenile justice* (New York, Wiley, 1968). This view departs fundamentally from the gate keeping theory of newswork, which sees the selfsame happening as acted upon by a series of newsworkers (cf. Tamotsu Shibutani, *Improvised news,* New York, Bobbs-Merrill, 1966). For a discussion of gate keeping, see D. M. White, 'The gatekeeper: a case study in the selection of news,' and Walter Gieber, 'News is what newspapermen make it,' in L. A. Dexter and D. M. White, *People, society and mass communication* (New York, Free Press, 1964).

11. These agencies, as here presented, are generally consistent with Holsti's six 'basic elements': source, encoding process, message, channel of transmission, recipient, decoding process. See Ole R. Holsti, *Content analysis for the social sciences and humanities* (Reading, Mass., Addison-Wesley, 1969), p. 24.

12. Cf. Daniel Boorstin, *The Image: a guide to pseudo events in America* (New York, Harper & Row, 1961).

13. Cf. Barbara Myerhoff, 'The revolution as a trip: symbol and paradox,' in Philip G. Altbach and Robert S. Laufer (eds), *The new pilgrims: youth protest in transition* (New York, David McKay, 1972).

14. Our mention of policy statements by public figures raised the question of *lies* for readers of earlier drafts of this paper. Based on the principle that event creation universally stems from contextually constrained purposes, our schema does not make an objective distinction between telling a truth and telling a falsehood. For us, a lie is a meaning accomplished for purposes at hand, including those involved in having to deal with others. A lie to us is distinguishable by the fact that another party (observer) sees it as a deliberate move to effect a purpose done without respect for the conditions of an assumed, objective reality. This assumed lack of correspondence to reality is typically invoked when the second party has purposes contrary to the liar's. Lies, like any meanings, are thus created because they are 'looked for' by the second party. When a liar is 'caught'—that is, when he cannot persuade others that his promoted account corresponds to an objective reality—he attempts to handle the situation by: (a) demonstrating that the second party was, in fact, looking for the lie, being 'picky', or making a mountain out of a molehill; or (b) minimizing the effect of the objectivity assumption by selectively claiming inherent ambiguity in the present case, as expressed in the claims, 'it all depends on how you look at it,' or 'if you knew what I knew at the time, you would see it as indeed corresponding to what is, to all intents and purposes, the truly relevant reality.' A selective assertion of a subjective world thus becomes a resource like any other.

15. Breed, Gieber and Tuchman have provided important insights into the assembling process. See: Warren Breed, 'Social control in the newsroom,' *Social Forces* 33 (May 1955): 326–35; Gieber (1964) and 'Across the desk: a study of 16 telegraph editors,' *Journalism Quarterly* 43 (Fall 1956): 423–32; and Gaye Tuchman, 'Objectivity as strategic ritual,' *American Journal of Sociology* 77 (January 1972): 660–79, 'News as controlled conflict and controversy,' New York, Department of Sociology, Queens College (mimeographed) (1972), and 'Making news by doing work: routinizing the unexpected,' *American Journal of Sociology* 79 (July 1973): 110–31.
16. Gaye Tuchman (1972) *op. cit.*
17. Cf. Thomas Wilson, 'Conceptions of interaction and forms of sociological explanation,' *American Sociological Review* 35 (August 1970): 697–710.
18. A. J. Liebling in *Mink and red herring: the wayward pressman's casebook* (Garden City, Doubleday, 1949), provides anecdotal illustrations of the occurrence of such plots and related chicanery. See also almost any issue of *Chicago Journalism Review* or *(More): A Journalism Review*, or Robert Cirino, *Don't blame the people: how the news media use bias, distortion and censorship to manipulate public opinion* (Los Angeles, Diversity Press, 1970).
19. That is, following the ethnomethodological instruction, we have heretofore attempted to suspend our belief in a normative order. However, to extend our analysis to a common-sensically useful approach to news, and to provide tools of concise description for mundane, practical work, we enter the 'attitude of everyday life' in this section of the essay.
20. Roger Manela in 'The classification of events in formal organizations' (Ann Arbor: Institute of Labor and Industrial Relations, mimeographed, 1971), in an analogous typology of events, treats events as objective phenomena which are categorized in terms of how well they fit ongoing formal organization rules and routines.
21. Cf. Gaye Tuchman (1972) *op. cit.*
22. Cf. Harvey L. Molotch, 'Oil in Santa Barbara and power in America,' *Sociological Inquiry* 40 (Winter 1970): 131–44.
23. Gaye Tuchman (1972) *op. cit.*
24. Cf. Harvey Molotch and Marilyn Lester, 'Accidents, scandals and routines' (1972, presented at the American Sociological Association meetings, New Orleans).
25. Cf. Barbara Myerhoff (1972) *op. cit.*
26. Cf. Kirkpatrick Sale, 'Myths as eternal truths,' *(More): A Journalism Review 3* (June 1973): 3–5. This situation eventually changed in reference to anti-war activity, because the position and event needs of the American press and a substantial portion of the élite became sympathetic with the movement. Thus, the event needs of a segment of the élite came to correspond to those of the protesters; accordingly, the war became the issue, not the protest itself.
27. In response to a complaint that his newspaper was holding back an important story, a reporter for the *Los Angeles Times* wrote Molotch the following defence: 'We have not run an extensive story on _____ because of the judgment of my editors that because the _____ case has not become an issue of major proportions enveloping the campus community, we might be accused of creating an issue if we give it full-blown treatment at

this point in time. It is not a case of holding back information, but the concern that my editors have for trying to avoid the situation where something becomes a major issue *because* a large daily newspaper has written about it at length'. (Personal communication to the author, 8th January 1971.)

28. What is or is not a transparently non-objective technique changes historically. Fishman (in Forthcoming, *News of the world: what happened and why*, unpublished doctoral dissertation, Department of Sociology, University of California, Santa Barbara) details how the use of interview in straight news came as a radical departure from objective news coverage. The technique was introduced as part of the yellow journalism movement and was denounced by the more traditional papers.

29. Harvey L. Molotch (1970) *op. cit.*

30. It is precisely these forms of events which tend to be excluded in community power research using the decisional technique (cf. Edward Banfield, *Political influence*, New York, Free Press, 1962). By uncritically accepting those stories which appear in newspapers over an extensive time period as corresponding to the basic local political conflicts, use of the decisional technique guarantees that only those matters on which the élites do internally disagree will emerge as study topics. Thus, pluralistic findings are guaranteed through the mode of case selection.

31. Seymour Hirsch, 'On uncovering the great nerve gas cover-up,' *Ramparts* 3 (July 1969): 12–18.

32. Marilyn Lester, 'Toward a sociology of public events' (1971, unpublished master's paper, University of California, Santa Barbara).

33. See *New York Times*, 20th November 1969; *The Times* (London), 20th November 1969.

34. Herbert Gans, 'The famine in American mass communications research: comments on Hirsch, Tuchman and Gecas,' *American Journal of Sociology* 77 (January 1972): 697–705.

35. Cf. Peter Bachrach and Morton Baratz, 'The two faces of power,' *American Political Science Review* 56 (Dec. 1962): 947–52; and Murray Edelman, *The symbolic uses of politics* (Urbana, University of Illinois Press, 1964).

'The awful truth about strikes in our factories': a case study in the production of news*

PAUL EDWARDS

There is a growing literature on the ways in which the mass media select and interpret particular aspects of the world for presentation as 'news', for example, Cohen and Young[1]; Glasgow University Media Group[2]; Beharell and Philo[3]. This paper examines the production of one significant story, as a further contribution to this literature. But it departs in two main respects from the usual type of sociological account. Firstly, it concentrates on the social processes whereby the story came to be written, to reveal in some detail *how* a given piece of news was produced. Secondly, it asks whether it is possible to solve the conflict between journalists' accounts of industrial relations and an account which would emerge from a fuller and more disinterested examination of the issues involved.

The newspaper story which is discussed here appeared on 12 November 1978 on the front page of the *Sunday Times*, under the headline which has been borrowed for the title of the present paper. As will be seen below, the story was subsequently taken up by other papers. The following three sections examine the background of the *Sunday Times* article, the appearance of the article itself, and the development of the story by other papers.

Background

A fortnight before the appearance of the report in question, *The Sunday Times* had carried a full-page article on industrial conflict. This had suggested that official Department of Employment statistics underestimate the number of strikes in Britain, and went on to discover as many strikes as possible during one week in September 1978. To any serious student of the 'strike problem', the finding that official figures do not

*This paper was first published in *Industrial Relations Journal*, vol. 10, Spring 1979.

record every strike is notable solely for its obviousness. It is consistent with many previous studies—for example, Turner *et al*[4], and Daniel[5]— and is almost wholly unsurprising. The authors of the article, however, were surprised by it and used it to suggest that the Department of Employment plays down Britain's strike problem. Moreover, they said that the Department 'deliberately' ignores some strikes. (Incidentally, they got this slightly wrong, since they said that strikes lasting less than a day or involving fewer than ten workers are omitted from the official figures, forgetting that such strikes would be counted if they involved the 'loss' of 100 working days.)

The implication is that Britain is somehow worse than other countries and that there is a deliberate cover-up of the strike figures. However, if other countries are affected by short stoppages to the same degree as Britain, Britain's *relative* position in the 'international league table' of strikes would be unaltered. There is some evidence to support this possibility (see Herding[6]). Moreover, the exclusion of small strikes is done largely for statistical reasons: to obtain a series of observations which is *reliable* in that the same sorts of strikes are recorded from one year to the next. Similar devices are used in most countries which produce strike statistics.

These points could be taken further, but are mentioned simply to show that *The Sunday Times* had developed a 'view' on strikes and that in its original article it sought to stress a particular aspect of the official reporting of strikes. That aspect was the limited validity of the figures, a point which is familiar to students in the area but which was employed as if it were a surprising and sensational piece of news.

The 'awful truth'

In the course of writing their original article, *The Sunday Times* team discovered that a survey of industrial relations had recently been carried out by IFF Research Limited and the Industrial Relations Research Unit, and obtained a copy of a report entitled 'Workplace industrial relations in manufacturing industry, 1978: key results'. This report is a brief (13 pages) summary of the findings of a large-scale survey, and covered several areas of industrial relations such as employers' organisations, disputes procedures and manpower planning.

In its piece on the 'awful truth', however, *The Sunday Times* concentrated on the evidence on strikes and industrial action. This can be explained by the paper's existing view on strikes. (The article explicitly notes that the 'Key Results' 'bear out in general' the findings of the paper's earlier article.) Without this interest in strikes by *The Sunday Times,* it is doubtful whether the 'Key Results' would ever have been defined as newsworthy.

On the whole, the summary was quoted accurately, although there was a misconception about industrial action other than strikes: *The Sunday Times* said that the use of such action has become more prevalent, whereas the 'Key Results' stated that "there is no marked trend . . . in the popularity of strikes as against other forms of action". The problem is that the summary was no more than that, with the result that it gives rather bald statements of findings. Thus, a direct association between the level of shop steward organisation and the frequency of industrial action was noted, and repeated in *The Sunday Times.* The summary did, however, contain a guarded sentence saying that causal links between these two things cannot be established on the basis of survey evidence. *The Sunday Times* interpreted this statement as meaning that it was impossible to say 'whether a lot of strikes occur in a plant because there are full-time shop stewards, or whether there are full-time shop stewards because the plant has a lot of strikes'.

The paper was clearly trying to render the term 'causal links' into language which is readily understood. However, several points must be made about this gloss. Firstly, *The Sunday Times* team contacted the people at IFF and the IRRU who were concerned with the evidence of strikes, and had to be persuaded to include any reservation about causal links. Secondly, any reading of the 'Key Results' would indicate that the problem of causal links was not posed in terms of whether a lot of shop stewards cause a lot of strikes or *vice versa:* the sentence interpreted in this light by *The Sunday Times* referred to the "links between the role of stewards and the amount and type of industrial action" and not to the number of stewards. In other words, the original reservation was about the whole role of shop stewards in industrial conflict, and not just about the correlation between numbers of stewards and numbers of strikes.

Moreover, an attempt was made to persuade *The Sunday Times* team that the findings of the 'Key Results' must be seen in context. Thus, it was pointed out that fieldwork in progress suggests that many strikes occur over small issues, are often over within an hour or two, and do not lead to the loss of *any* production. For example, a stoppage may be called over working conditions to indicate to management that the workers are concerned about an issue and think that it is time for something to be done about it. Indeed, local management may well agree a stoppage is the only way to put pressure on other parts of management to resolve the problem.

Such disputes do not reveal any 'awful truth' about industrial conflict, but are part of the mundane reality of day-to-day negotiation at shopfloor level.

Similarly, in relation to the earlier interest of *The Sunday Times* in strike statistics, it was pointed out that it is neither new nor surprising for the spread of industrial action, as recorded by workplace surveys, to be wider than official statistics might suggest. Problems of improving the coverage of official figures without endangering the reliability of the record were also mentioned.

These points were, however, largely ignored. As will be apparent from the studies cited at the start of this paper, the mass media have an image of the 'problem of strikes' which is constantly being projected. The two *Sunday Times* articles were more serious than many reports in this area, and the original piece involved some thorough research into the nature of strikes during the selected week in September 1978. But the underlying image still broke through: there was little in the 'Key Results' as a whole to suggest any 'awful truth', and the points made verbally to *The Sunday Times* team stressed above all that great caution is needed regarding the significance which is attached to findings about the prevalence of industrial action. But these points, and the status of the 'Key Results' as a brief summary of results (which will be analysed at length in a book due to be produced by the IRRU in 1979), were ignored. The implications of this will be considered when the development of the story by other papers has been considered.

The story is taken up by other papers

On 13 November 1978 *The Daily Telegraph* published a piece entitled 'Plants with shop stewards "have more disputes"'. This was based on the 'Key Results' summary, which was attributed to the 'Industrial Research Unit' of the SSRC. *The Sunday Times* mentioned several findings of the summary, including those relating to the closed shop and the growth in the number of shop stewards; but, for the *Telegraph,* the sole point of interest was the correlation between the presence of full-time shop stewards and the frequency of industrial action. The *caveat* about imputing causality was simply ignored. *The Daily Telegraph* also reported that 'small businesses have been almost as badly affected as notorious trouble spots like the car industry'. This confused the effects of plant size (on which the summary reported that small *establishments* (not businesses) were *less* likely than large ones to experience industrial action) and of technology. On the latter, the summary reported that mass production industries were not particularly strike prone, a finding which *The Daily Telegraph* would have been wiser using to argue that the 'notorious' reputation of the car industry is somewhat unjustified.

The interpretation placed on the 'Key Results' by the *Telegraph* was thus technically inaccurate as well as highly selective. Even the limited caution displayed by *The Sunday Times* was lost. Instead of noting problems of interpretation itself, the *Telegraph* approached David Basnett, of the General and Municipal Workers Union, for his comments. He said that "the appearance of a simplistic analysis does not help" and that shop stewards are concerned to promote good industrial relations. These points are quite justified, but they must be seen as criticisms of the *Telegraph's* use of the 'Key Results' and not of the results themselves. The analysis was certainly limited, but this was explicitly stated; it was the use of the figures by the *Telegraph* which was simplistic.

One further illustration of the *Telegraph's* approach is the paper's reference to data on the reporting of strikes to the Department of Employment. It attributes evidence on this matter to the 'Key Results', whereas that summary said nothing on the subject. The *Telegraph's* source of information was *The Sunday Times* article, which reported results which were not even available when the 'Key Results' summary was written.

A second example of the distortions which can occur as a story is developed by the press is a piece in the new *Daily Star,* also for 13 November 1978. This attributes the study to the SSRC, with no mention of IFF or the IRRU, and again concentrates on the link between shop stewards and strikes. Peter Grimsditch, the writer of the story, feels that the finding was "a load of pompous piffle" because, in factories without stewards, there is no one to organise "industrial aggro": conditions may be no better in such plants than in those where there are shop stewards. There can be no quarrel with the substance of this, and Mr. Grimsditch's view of industrial relations is clearly far more sophisticated than that of *The Daily Telegraph*. But there are two problems. Firstly, Mr. Grimsditch notes the rise in the number of shop stewards reported by the 'Key Results' and says that the summary has "the good grace to add that it cannot show whether more shop stewards have produced more strikes or whether more strikes have produced more shop stewards". This is a confusion, however, since the growth in the number of shop stewards has occurred *over time,* whereas the correlation between the presence of full-time shop stewards (and not the number of stewards and the presence of stewards as Mr. Grimsditch says) and frequency of industrial action was noted in a *cross-sectional* analysis. Secondly, and more importantly, the 'experts' whom Mr. Grimsditch chastises are naturally aware of points such as the one he mentions. Had he read the 'Key Results' with more care or checked on it with the authors, he would have found that no one was suggesting that plants without shop stewards were utopias simply because they had few strikes.

A final example of the process of distortion is an article by Alfred Sherman in *The Daily Telegraph* for 22 November 1978 entitled "When it is time to restore the balance of bargaining". This attributes the 'Key Results' to the Department of Employment and claims that it shows a "marked correlation between numbers of full-time shop stewards and industrial conflict" (which presumably means a marked *positive* correlation). This displays the same confusion between number of stewards and the presence of stewards which was made by Mr. Grimsditch; and, although used to support a different argument, follows the same procedure of ignoring all the caveats of the 'Key Results', and even the more limited caution displayed by *The Sunday Times*.

Discussion

This detailed analysis of the 'awful truth' story is consistent with other studies of the coverage of industrial news by the media. A simple image of strife-torn factories, with shop stewards as the agents of disruption, is frequently presented. The 'awful truth' story provided one new angle on this long-running saga, with the benefit, from the viewpoint of the press, of being attributable to official or quasi-official sources; this enabled the 'Key Results' findings to be presented as authoritative confirmation of the standard media line on the subject.

The present analysis goes further than this, however. It shows how the 'awful truth' story came to be defined as news in the first place. A key element in this process was the original interest of *The Sunday Times* in official statistics on strikes. This interest led to the discovery of the 'Key Results'. But even then this summary as a whole could not be seen as newsworthy: certain items in it were abstracted because they appeared to fit into an existing interpretive scheme. In this process, the status of the 'Key Results' as a brief summary of very complex findings became somewhat obscured; the finding that some form of industrial action in the previous two years was reported in 46 percent of the plants was treated as a novel and shocking fact; and the caveat about imputing causal links was distorted.

In the normal way, the production of a document such as the 'Key Results' would be unlikely to create even a mild ripple of interest in Fleet Street. It was only because certain features of the document came to the attention of a group of journalists in a particular context that it was granted the status of being newsworthy. Once one paper had performed the gatekeeper function of admitting it to the charmed circle, other papers followed the lead. As the previous discussion has shown, several confusions and distortions were introduced. These became so great (e.g. the *Telegraph's* statement that the summary contained evidence on the reporting of strikes to the Department of Employment and Mr. Sherman's ignorance as to the authorship) that doubts are raised about the sources of the stories in the *Telegraph* and *Daily Star*. If their authors had read the 'Key Results', there is certainly no evidence of this.

The story in *The Sunday Times*, while stressing the 'awful' side of the picture, did at least attempt a balanced account. This is not so of the other papers, which developed that story for their own purposes, and in the process introduced the simple errors of fact which were noted in the previous section.

Matters of interpretation are more difficult to assess, since the reader of a set of findings is free to place whatever construction on them which he sees fit. However, the reader of the press reports of the 'Key Results', as distinct from the document itself, was clearly being given a powerful message about 'strife in our factories' which he would find hard to disentangle from the facts on which the reports were based. This is a familiar aspect of 'news', which need not be laboured further. But the present case also shows how attempts to place the 'Key Results' in context were ignored or distorted. Thus the points made to *The Sunday Times* about the nature of many strikes and their lack of 'shock value' were ignored. The paper said that "one factory in five (the figure should be one in six— P. K. E.) had 'lightning strikes' of less than a day". In using the term 'lightning strikes' in quotation marks, the paper implied that this phrase was used in the 'Key Results' (which it was not) and that such strikes had a particular significance: the term 'lightning' implies that they were sudden and disruptive. Thus, even the phraseology of the press report conveyed a particular message; a message, moreover, which the authors of the 'Key Results' had attempted to play down in favour of a more reasonable interpretation.

Similarly, the correlation between the presence of full-time shop stewards and industrial action was stressed, and the caveat that this says *nothing* about the role of stewards in industrial action distorted. Thus, even a careful and reasonably full press report carried a message which was at variance with the total message which was *received* by *The Sunday Times*. In terms of communication theory, a signal can be transmitted and then relayed, in the course of which parts of it may be lost, distorted, or drowned by interference. In the present case, the total set of signals sent to *The Sunday Times* were subject to a much more important process: systematic selection of various parts of their signal, and their re-coding into a new and different message. As this message was passed on through the other papers, the process continued until even the message produced by *The Sunday Times* was virtually unrecognisable.

Conclusions

Journalists face a conflict between producing 'news' and stories which give a reasonable account of a particular phenomenon. The dilemma is illustrated by a telephone conversation between the writer and a reporter for a provincial daily paper, who had been given the *Daily Telegraph* story and asked to follow it up at local level. The reporter was clearly aware of the limitations of the simple correlation between shop stewards and strikes, and was receptive to the idea that industrial disputes are often part of day-to-day negotiations and that they do not necessarily reflect the breakdown of order on the shop floor. However, the problem was to take account of these points and yet produce a piece which would find a ready response among the paper's readers.

There is no easy solution to this problem, although *The Sunday Times* itself provides an interesting illustration of a possible way out. On the same page as the 'awful truth' article, the paper took up a comment by Prince Charles that papers should report the good news as well as the bad. It produced a column of interesting tit-bits, but concluded "Sorry about the bad news that has crept into other parts of this page, notably the story about strikes, but that's life, that's news". In other words, the paper accepted the naive distinction between good and bad news, and put its report on strikes firmly in the latter category. If the good and the bad were less sharply distinguished, journalists' problems in this area might at least be eased.

But they are not simply problems for journalists. Researchers cannot happily shrug their shoulders and say 'of course, as soon as the press get hold of anything, it's always distorted'. It is true that journalists work to take up a news angle and that, as previous comments have shown, they tend to ignore the careful qualifications and reservations which are the academic's stock-in-trade. But there are many who, like the provincial paper's reporter, want an account which can bring over the complexities of an issue in everyday language. The present case may serve as an object-lesson to academics as well as journalists. In retrospect, the present writer, in speaking to *The Sunday Times*, did not make enough of the points of qualification and interpretation which have been mentioned above. In other words, a signal was transmitted, and should have been picked up by *The Sunday Times*. But a signal which was coded in a different way would have had a greater chance of being received and, more importantly, retransmitted.

There are limitations to this, however. There is no guarantee that any given message will be relayed. As has been seen, it took some persuasion to have *any* note of caution about imputing causality introduced into *The Sunday Times* report, let alone a lengthy statement of interpretation. And, as noted in the previous section, images of industrial relations are well-established in the media. It may be possible to improve matters on the margins, but journalists' perceptions of what is newsworthy (and their perceptions of what their readers will want to see) will not be easily changed.

Although there is no easy way out of this problem, it is a matter which needs to be faced. But a lengthy discussion would go beyond the bounds of the present paper. This has sought to contribute to an understanding of how news is produced by examining the processes whereby one topic became defined as newsworthy, and the process which then selected certain aspects of the topic for presentation as the final story. The 'awful truth' came not from the original sources of the story, but from the interpretation placed on parts of those sources by the press itself.

NOTES AND REFERENCES

1. Stanley Cohen and Jock Young (eds), *The manufacture of news. Deviance, social problems and the mass media* (London, Constable, first edn, 1973).
2. Glasgow University Media Group, *Bad news* (London, Routledge and Kegan Paul, 1976).
3. Peter Beharell and Greg Philo (eds), *Trade unions and the media* (London, Macmillan, 1977).
4. H. A. Turner, Garfield Clack and Geoffrey Roberts, *Labour relations in the motor industry* (London, Allen & Unwin, 1967).
5. W. W. Daniel, *Wage determination in industry,* PEP Report, Vol. XLII, No. 563 (London, PEP, 1976).
6. R. Herding, *Job control and union structure* (Rotterdam University Press, 1972).

A world at one with itself*

STUART HALL

The issue of violence in the mass media has been posed in the familiar terms of the fantasy or fictional portrayal of violence there. But if the media are playing a role in the alleged escalation of social violence, it is almost certainly not *Z Cars, The Virginian, Callan* or *Codename* which are 'responsible'. What is at issue is not the fantasy role of fictional violence, but the alleged real effects of real violence. The area of broadcasting in question is that traditionally defined as 'news/current affairs/features/documentaries'. It is, for example, the only too real bodies of only too real Vietnamese, floating down an all too real Cambodian river, which some as yet unstated informal theory of cause and effect links in the minds of television's critics with questions of 'law and order'. Thus it is to the question of *news* that we must turn.

As it happens, news has just undergone an enormous expansion in the new radio schedules. In the philosophy of streamed radio which underpins the BBC's *Broadcasting in the Seventies,* news got a privileged place. Under the new dispensation, the avid listener is never more than half an hour away from the next news bulletin. But the really striking development is the growth of the news-magazine styles of programme, on the *World At One* model.

What constitutes the definition of news currently employed on radio programmes of this new type? I put the point in this way, and not in the more familiar terms of 'coverage' or 'bias/objectivity', because this constitutes the heart of the matter. Journalists throughout the media are notoriously slippery and defensive when thus confronted. 'The news', they assume, is clearly what it is: newsworthy people and events, happening 'out there' in the real world, at home and abroad.

The relevant questions are always technical ones: 'How adequately can we cover these events?', 'Is the coverage biased or objective?' This view is legitimated by a body of journalistic folklore, with its ritual references to copy, deadlines and news angles. These sanction professional practice and keep non-professional busybodies at bay.

*From *New Society* (18 June 1970), pp. 1056–8.

Of course, newsmen agree, the news can be either 'hard' or 'soft', graphically or neutrally presented (sensationalism/objectivity), a report from the front or a background analysis (actuality/depth). But these are matters of treatment—of form and 'flavour'—not of content or substance. It is worth observing that all these routine ways of setting up the problem are drawn from the press, reflecting both the common background of media newsmen in Fleet Street, and, more important, the powerful hold of models borrowed for radio or television from the press.

The notion that the news somehow discovers itself may be of service to the harassed newsgatherers and editors. Such professional 'common-sense constructs', such *ad hoc* routines, are employed in most large-scale organizations. They enable hard-pressed professionals to execute their tasks with the minimum of stress and role-conflict.

These idiomatic shorthands give the professional a map of the social system, just as the categories of classification in mental hospitals (Erving Goffman), the clinical records of hospitals (H. Garfinkel) and the note-books and case records of police and probation officers (Aaron Cicourel) witness to the moral order and the system of meanings which other professionals use to give sense to their tasks.

But against this defensive strategy, it needs to be asserted that the news is a *product,* a human construction: a staple of that system of 'cultural production' (to use Theodor Adorno's phrase) we call the mass media. Journalists and editors select, from the mass of potential news items, the events which constitute 'news' for any day. In part, this is done by implicit reference to some unstated and unstatable criteria of *the significant.* News selection thus rests on inferred knowledge about the audience, inferred assumptions about society, and a professional code or ideology. The news is not a set of unrelated items: news stories are coded and classified, referred to their relevant contexts, assigned to different (and differently graded) spaces in the media, and ranked in terms of presentation, status and meaning.

The process of news production has its own structure. News items which infringe social norms, break the pattern of expectations and contrast with our sense of the everyday, or are dramatic, or have 'numerous and intimate contacts with the life of the recipients', have greater news salience for journalists than others. As a highly reputable reporter observed to an irate group of student militants, who were questioning her as to why her paper reported every vote cast during the period of a university occupation, but nothing of the weekend teach-in: 'Votes represent decisions: decisions are news: discussion is not.'

The role of the news journalist is to mediate—or act as the 'gate-keeper'—between different publics, between institutions and the individual, between the spheres of the public and the private, between the new and the old. News production is often a self-fulfilling activity. Categories of news, consistently produced over time, create public spaces in the media which have to be filled. The presence of the media at the birth of new events can affect their course and outcome. The news is not only a cultural product: it is the product of a set of institutional definitions and meanings, which, in the professional shorthand, is commonly referred to as *news values*.

Statistics of crime represent not only the real movement of the crime rate, but the changing definition of what constitutes crime, how it is recognized, labelled and dealt with. To label as 'violent' every incident from skinhead attacks on Pakistanis, to Ulster, to protests against the South African tour, is to establish a certain way of seeing and understanding a complex set of public events.

Once the category of 'law and order' has come into existence as a legitimate news category, whole different orders of meaning and association can be made to cluster together. Terms of understanding—such as the criminal categories reserved for acts of collective social delinquency ('hooligans', say, or 'layabouts')—become transferred to new events like the clashes between citizens and the army in Ulster. It may be that there has been some objective increase in real-world violence; but the effect on news values is *even greater* than that would justify.

This shift is difficult to pinpoint in the brief radio or television news bulletin, though if we take a long enough stretch of time, we can observe changes both in the profile and in the style of news reports. But in the format of the radio news magazine, which approximates more closely to the profile and treatment of a daily newspaper, the amplifying and interpretative function of the media comes into its own.

News magazines include studio interviews, reports from correspondents, replies to attacks, features and 'human interest' stories. This is where background classifying and interpretative schemes register most forcefully. In terms of direct bias, there seems less cause for concern. Within its limits, radio shows little direct evidence of intentional bias. It treats the spokesmen of the two major political parties with scrupulous fairness—more, in fact, than they deserve. But the troublesome question is the matter of unwitting bias: the institutional slanting, built-in not by the devious inclination of editors to the political right or left, but by the steady and unexamined play of attitudes which, via the mediating structure of professionally defined news values, inclines all the media towards the *status quo*.

The operation of unwitting bias is difficult either to locate or prove. Its manifestations are always indirect. It comes through in terms of who is or who is not accorded the status of an accredited witness: in tones of voice: in the set-up of studio confrontations: in the assumptions which underlie the questions asked or not asked: in terms of the analytical concepts which serve informally to link events to causes: in what passes for explanation.

Its incidence can be mapped by plotting the areas of *consensus* (where there is a mutual agreement about the terms in which a topic is to be treated), the areas of *toleration* (where the overlap is less great, and the terms have to be negotiated as between competing definitions) and the areas of *dis-sensus* or *conflict* (where competing definitions are in play).

Unwitting bias has nothing directly to do with the style of 'tough' interviewing, since, even in the areas of consensus issues, the professional ethic sanctions a quite aggressive, probing style (Hardcastle with Heath, Robin Day with Wilson), though the probe does not penetrate to underlying assumptions.

Areas of *consensus* cover the central issues of politics and power, the fundamental sanctions of society and the sacred British values. To this area belong the accredited witnesses—politicians of both parties, local councillors, experts, institutional spokesmen.

Areas of *toleration* cover what might be called 'Home Office issues'— social questions, prisoners who can't get employment after discharge, little men or women against the bureaucrats, unmarried mothers, and so on. The more maverick witnesses who turn up in this group get, on the whole, an off-beat but sympathetic 'human interest'—even at times a crusading—kind of treatment. Guidelines in this sector are less clear-cut. When such topics edge over into the 'permissive' category, they can arouse strong sectional disapproval. But here even the scrupulously objective news editor can presume (again, a matter of negotiation and judgment, not of objective fact) on a greater background of public sympathy, more room for manoeuvre.

Areas of *conflict* have their un-accredited cast of witnesses too: protesters of all varieties; shop stewards, especially if militant, more especially if on unofficial strike; squatters; civil rights activists; hippies; students; hijackers; Stop the Seventy Tour-ers; and so on. In dealing with these issues and actors, interviewers are noticeably sharper, touchier, defending their flanks against any predisposition to softness.

One could plot the hidden constraints of this informal ideology in the media simply by noting the characteristic arguments advanced against each of these groups. Unofficial strikers are always confronted with 'the national interest', squatters with 'the rights of private property', civil rights militants in Ulster with the need for Protestant and Catholic to 'work together', Stop the Seventy Tour-ers with the way their minority actions 'limit the right of the majority to enjoy themselves as they wish'.

I am not arguing here that these arguments should not be accorded some weight. I am remarking how, in the handling of certain issues, the assumptions which shape an interview item are coincident with official ideologies of the *status quo*. I recall numerous instances when Ulster civil rights militants were confronted with the consequences of violence. But I cannot recall a single instance when an Ulster Moderate or politician was confronted with the equally tenable view, succinctly expressed by Conor Cruise O'Brien, that since Ulster society has for long been based on the dominance of a minority over a majority, no fundamental change in that structure can be expected without its accompanying release of the 'frozen violence' inherent in the situation.

I know that Ulster is a particularly sensitive matter, that the BBC's impartiality came under direct fire during the events of September 1969, and that in this period a close executive watch was maintained over the news output. But then, my criticism is not of the wilful, intentional bias of editors and newscasters, but of the institutionalized ethos of the news media as a whole. The influence exerted by this ethos over actual broadcast programmes is precisely to be found on those occasions when men of quite varying temperaments and political views are systematically constrained in a certain direction.

I recall William Hardcastle's phrase, when reporting the American Anti-Vietnam demonstrations last year: 'the so-called Vietnam Moratorium Committee'. William Hardcastle's objectivity is not in question. But I await, without much confidence, the day when *The World At One* will refer to 'the so-called Confederation of British Industries' or the 'so-called Trades Union Congress' or even the 'so-called Central Intelligence Agency'.

The sources for this hidden consensus must be located outside the broadcasting media proper, at the heart of the political culture itself. It is a view of politics based on the relative absence of violence in British political life, the relative degree of integration between the powerful corporate interest groups within the state. This negotiated consensus is both a historical fact and a source of ideological comfort. The sociologist,

Paul Hirst, in a recent paper, 'Some problems of explaining student militancy', gave a succinct sketch of this political style:

> What is the nature of this consensus? It is that parliamentary democracy is founded upon legitimate procedures of political action, and that primary among these procedures is that parliament is the mode of pursuit and accommodating interests within the society. It provides legitimate means for the pursuance of interests without resort to open conflict . . . British democracy raises the means of political action to the level of ends: the primary values of British political culture are specified by a body of existing institutions. These institutions and their maintenance have become the primary political goals.

We can only understand the limits and constraints within which 'objectivity' functions in the media when we have grasped the true sources of legitimation in the political culture itself.

We are now at the crunch. For the groups and events upon which, increasingly, the media are required to comment and report, are the groups in conflict with this consensual style of politics. *But* these are precisely the forms of political and civil action which the media, by virtue of their submission to the consensus, are consistently unable to deal with, comprehend or interpret. The nervousness one has observed in the treatment of these issues reflects the basic contradiction between the manifestations which the media are called on to explain and interpret, and the conceptual/evaluative/interpretative framework which they have available to them.

Whereas the core value of the political consensus is the adherence to 'legitimate means for the pursuance of interests without resort to open conflict', the highly heterogeneous groups I have mentioned are characterized either by political militancy, leading through extra-parliamentary politics to the varying types of 'confrontation', or by social disaffiliation, leading through collective and expressive acts of rebellion to the various types of civil disturbance. Civil righters, students, Black Power militants, political hijackers and kidnappers, shop stewards fall into the political militancy category. Skinheads, hippies, squatters, soccer hooligans, psychedelic freak-outs fall into the social disaffiliation category.

The collective label of 'violence'—and its twin metaphor, 'law and order'—is, at one and the same time, both a staggering confusion of new and old meanings and a penetrating insight. As symbolic categories they only make sense when the issues they refer to are shifted from the explanatory context of media to the content of *politics*.

The effective question about the role of the media, then, is not Callaghan's—'Do the media *cause* violence?'—nor Wedgwood Benn's—'Is politics too important to be left to the broadcasters?' (with its obvious retort); but rather, 'Do/can the media help us to understand these significant real events in the real world?' 'Do the media clarify them or mystify us about them?'

Actuality versus depth is not a simple technical choice. The distinction is already built into the structure of the national press. In the arena of news and foreign affairs, popular journalism does not permit systematic exploration in depth. In the 'quality' press, some measure of background interpretation and analysis is more regularly provided. Both these things are legitimated by the professional folk-wisdom. Thus, for the populars: 'The Great British Public is not interested in foreign news'—though how the regular reader of the *Mirror,* the *Express* or the *News of the World,* our circulation front-runners, could develop an intelligent interest in foreign affairs is a matter for speculation. And for the quality press there is 'the rigid separation of "hard" news from comment'.

Distinctions of format and depth of treatment flow, via the grooves of class and education, into the papers we get, and they are hardened and institutionalized in the social structure of the national press. But the relevance of this fragmented universe of press communication for a medium like radio at this time is highly questionable. The audience for news through the day is far less stratified by class and education than the readership of newspapers. Radio must operate as if its potential audience is *the whole nation*.

It follows that radio must find ways of making *both* the foreground event *and* the background context core aspects of its working definition of the news. Otherwise, the radio audience, whatever its range of interests, will be consigned effectively to getting a perpetual foreground.

This becomes a critical issue when the coverage is of groups and events which consistently challenge the built-in definitions and values enshrined in the political culture of broadcasters and audiences alike. This position redefines the concept of 'public service', in relation to radio, in a way which runs diametrically counter to the philosophy of rationalization which infected *Broadcasting in the Seventies*. The press has little to contribute to the development of appropriate models.

Judged in these terms, the manifest tendencies in radio are not encouraging. A heady, breathless immediacy now infects all of the news-magazine programmes. In terms of their profile of items, these programmes progressively affiliate to the model of the daily newspaper. As events like political confrontation and civil disturbance escalate, so the coverage is doubled, quadrupled. As coverage expands, so we become even more alive to the actual 'violent' events and overwhelmed by the vivid sound and image. But as this coverage takes the characteristic form of *actuality without context,* it directly feeds our general sense of a meaningless explosion of meaningless and violent acts — 'out there' somewhere, in an unintelligible world where 'no legitimate means' have been devised 'for the pursuance of interests without resort to open conflict'.

'Out there', let us note, is a rapidly expanding area, covering most of the rest of the globe—Indo-China, Latin America, the Middle East, Africa, the Caribbean, Berkeley, Chicago, Tokyo—as well as some growing enclaves closer home. Events of this order play straight into an *ideological gap* in the media — and in public consciousness. That gap is not filled by the media — or, rather, it is now being filled in a systematically distorted way.

Let me conclude with two examples. Take the spate of kidnappings of foreign diplomats in Latin America. These events were endlessly covered on radio and television, usually by reporters on the spot. There was some studio discussion; but the thrust was consistently towards actuality coverage: has he been shot? will the government pay the ransom? will West Germany break off diplomatic relations? The model? Essentially: the front page of the *Daily Express.* What this coverage lacked was some framework which would make this bizarre series of events meaningful or intelligible.

I have been told that this kind of 'background piece' would be provided by the longer reports at the weekend by BBC foreign correspondents. But this is like telling a man whose regular and only newspaper is the *Mirror,* 'If you want to understand the politics of Guatemala, read the *Sunday Times*'. The example is not fortuitous. For during the kidnappings the *Sunday Times* did print a fairly full background article on Guatemala — and a hair-raising, all too intelligible, story it turned out to be.

An even better example, and one where the press performed as badly as radio and television (with the exception of *24 Hours*) was the recent Black Power rioting in Trinidad. The most generally agreed judgment among intelligent West Indians about Trinidad and Jamaica is that the political situation there is highly explosive. Indeed, the real question is why either society has not, before now, gone down in a wave of riots by underprivileged blacks against the privileged coloured middle class. The answer is not unconnected with the presence of both Cuba and of the American fleet within easy striking distance of Kingston and Port of Spain.

The background to the foreground-problem of riots in Trinidad is the persistent grinding poverty of the mass of the people, intensified by basic conflicts of interest between the coloured middle class inheritors of the 'end of colonial rule' (one of the most conspicuous-consumption classes anywhere in the Third World) and the mass of peasants, workers and urban unemployed, who also happen to be black. Without this knowledge, the large-scale migration from the Caribbean to Britain, which has occupied so much 'foreground' space in recent months is, literally, unintelligible. It is another of those meaningless events, leading to the expected confrontations, and ultimately to 'violence'.

This gap between the urban and rural masses and a native bourgeoisie, grown flush in the hectic, post-colonial years of neo-imperialism, is *the* political fact about vast tracts of the Caribbean and Latin America. Yet radio discussions in studio uniformity expressed puzzlement at how Black Power could become an organizing slogan in a country where the government is 'black'. The fact which needs clarification, of course, is that in the West Indies (unlike the United States, where the permanent presence of a white power structure creates solidarity between all 'black brothers'), the emergent lines of social conflict are laid down precisely by the overdetermined coalescence of class, power and gradations of colour.

Unfortunately, neither of the two accredited witnesses—Sir Learie Constantine, who regarded the riots as inexplicable, and Alva Clark, who regarded them as 'a tragedy'—contributed to this process of conceptual clarification. When faced with this sudden eruption of yet another incidence of political violence, the explanatory concepts of 'neo-colonialism' and 'native bourgeoisie' were not available—nor anything else which could do duty for them—in the world of radio. Instead, the ingredients of the consensual view were quickly wheeled into place: 'The Prime Minister' . . . 'resignations from the government' . . . 'state of emergency' . . . 'small groups of vandals roaming the streets' . . . 'disaffection in the army' . . . 'detachment of marines from nearby Puerto Rico' . . . violence/law and order.

In one event after another, now, the same informal theories—supported by the same ideological commitments, and functioning as an 'objective' set of technical-professional routines—produce the same mysterious product with systematic regularity.

REFERENCES

1. A. Cicourel, *The social organisation of juvenile justice* (New York, John Wiley & Sons, 1968).

2. H. Garfinkel, *Ethnomethodology* (New Jersey, Prentice Hall, 1967).
3. P. Berger and T. Luckmann, *The social construction of reality* (New York, Doubleday Anchor, 1967).
4. R. Clausse, *Les nouvelles* (Brussels, Centre National d'Etude des Techniques de Diffusion Collective, 1963).
5. U. Saxer, 'News and publicity' in *Diogenes*, No. 68 (1969).
6. W. Breed, 'Social control in the newsroom', *Social Forces*, vol. 33 (1955).
7. D. White, ' "The gatekeeper": a case in study the selection of news' in Dexter and White (ed.), *People, society and mass communications* (Glencoe, The Free Press, 1964).
8. K. and G. Lang, 'The inferential structure of political communications' *Public Opinion Quarterly*, vol. 19 (1965).
9. P. Hirst, 'Some problems of explaining student militancy' (paper delivered to the BSA Conference (Durham, 1970) unpublished).
10. W. Breed, 'Analysing news: some questions for research', *Journalism Quarterly*, vol. 33 (1956).
11. H. Hughes, 'The social interpretation of news', *Annals*, vol. 219 (1942).

PART TWO

Models of presentation

In Part One we raised some problems about how events are selected by the journalist. We criticized the Commercial or Market model of this process for suggesting that news was 'discovered' and that the institutions dealing with the news merely supplied existing public demand. News, rather, is manufactured by journalists through interpreting and selecting events to fit pre-existing categories, themselves a product of the bureaucratic exigencies of news organizations and the particular concentration of media control and ownership. To stress this creative nature of journalism is not to imply a Mass Manipulative model: distortion is not limited to the heavy hand of direct censorship but is a less obvious process—often unconscious and unstated—of interpreting the event in terms of a conventionally acceptable world view.

In Part Two, we discuss various ways of analyzing and explaining such world views. What models of society—and specifically, of deviance and social problems—are implicit in the news or stories produced for the media? Our readings fall into three groups: those which limit themselves to a description of the content of media items; those which relate the various items to a coherent image seen as a function of the problems of the journalist as a member of a corporate bureaucracy, and finally those which explain the images in terms of the relationship between ideology and reality.

The quantity and quality of deviance and social problems

The first set of readings describes the content of the images presented to the public by the mass media, contrasting this, where possible, with evidence from alternative sources. Thus Gaye Tuchman surveys research on the presentation of women in the mass media and concludes that women are 'symbolically annihilated'. Quantitatively, men have dominated the television screen whilst qualitatively women have been portrayed as incompetent or inferior to males. In magazine stories they are portrayed as dependent and ineffectual; they are disproportionately over-presented as housewives and under-represented as workers. This sort of analysis parallels the work of Berelson and Salter who in an article written 30 years ago compared the portrayal of minority and majority Americans in magazine fiction.[1] They noted how heroes or heroines were almost exclusively of 'pure' American or Anglo-Saxon/Nordic stock and that minority group members played wicked or servile roles. They traced the stereotypical depiction of minority groups and noted how their numbers were consistently under-represented. For example, 9.8 per cent of the American population were black yet only 1.9 per cent found roles in these stories. Such fiction portrays a world where good motives, success and decency are the monopoly of American White who exists in a world where most lower status minority members are servile to or subversive of his interests.

Such research is complementary to the work of F. James Davis who, in a classic article on the crime news coverage in Colorado newspapers, showed that the quantity of crime news in the newspapers was unrelated to that reflected in the criminal statistics.[2] Similar conclusions were reached by Bob Roshier and Mark Fishman (Part One) who show in addition that the relative proportions assigned to various types of crimes were considerably unbalanced. The total impression from such studies is of a series of distortions about the quantity and quality of crime and the type of person likely to be criminal.

Two further articles examine other social problem areas, namely mental illness and alcoholism. Nunnally contrasts the stereotype of the mentally ill person as presented in the mass media (using fictional and nonfictional material) to that of public and expert opinion. The mass media are found to distort causes, symptoms, methods of treatment prognoses and social effects of mental illness. The mentally ill person is cast in a stereotype different from that held both by public and expert opinion (although we do not agree with Nunnally's implication that the experts must be 'right'). Linsky makes his comparisons within the media over time, comparing the changes in the explanations of alcoholism between 1900 and 1966. He finds a radical shift from a free will notion of human nature to an extreme determinist conception of the aetiology of social problems. Linsky suggests that the mass media not only provide a system for categorizing the quality and quantity of deviance, they also contain implicit explanatory models of how such deviance came about.

Such elementary content analyses of the mass media, illuminating although they may be, suffer from two major shortcomings. First, they fail to separate out the *total* messages which the media carry. That is they discuss the stereotype of the particular group in isolation, they do not discuss its relationship to others within the particular universe being considered. This has been a failure of much sociological analysis of the media. For it is only by delineating the whole underlying structure of the media's message that we can understand the world view that is being diffused. This relates to the second criticism, namely, that it is necessary to relate this message to the actual business of production occurring within the media organization.

Periodicity and consonancy

The second group of readings in Part Two attempt to separate out the underlying structures implicit in news item and relate them to the organizational and ideological problems of the media. Students of mass communication have only begun to do the sort of research necessary to illuminate just what organizational and professional mediations are involved in presenting certain images to the audience.[3]

We have shown in Part One how one of the central concerns of the journalist is to handle the mass of events which confront him or her. One way of doing this is actively to phase events to fit the bureaucratic schedules of the news organization *(periodicity)*; another is to draw on existing analytical models to interpret the events *(consonancy)*. The daily periodicity of a newspaper will result in what Graham Murdock calls an event-orientation: information which can be gathered, processed and dramatized within a 24-hour cycle stands a better chance of being incorporated than news which is gradual and undramatic. Murdock's example is the coup or assassination attempt compared to the drawn out guerrilla war. But even if the phenomenon does not 'naturally' present itself in a series of dramatic events, the mass media may well create such events. Even if *nothing happens,* what Daniel Boorstin calls 'our extravagant expectations' about the amount of novelty in the world, will ensure that something is turned into news.[4] One technique of presenting such 'pseudo events' is to run a story which has died or even a non-story by extracting the maximum drama through the technique of 'Unit Headline Language' invented by Michael Frayn's computer expert, Goldwasser.

The 'event orientation' of the media closely relates to another tendency, that of personalizing the news. This, as Galtung and Ruge (Part One) indicate, is not an absolute characteristic of all mass media but a function in part of cultural idealism of the Western media. That is, events are seen to occur because of the intervention of important figures while collective action and wider social determinants are ignored. This is in stark contrast to the Soviet media where historical process is emphasized and event orientation is so insignificant that a large proportion of newspapers such as *Pravda* is written weeks ahead of a particular issue.[5] Even within the Western media these events and personality orientations vary widely, showing again that they are not just inevitable bureaucratic tendencies. Thus many papers or feature programmes make worthy attempts to 'fill in' the background for the reader or viewer. A brief comparison between the contrasting styles of popular and quality newspapers would make this clear.

All in all, then, the argument that the images presented in the mass media are a function of technical/ bureaucratic problems *in the abstract* ignores the fashion in which particular analytical models (in the examples we have cited: culturally idealist, event-oriented and personalized) transfigure this process. This concurs with our argument in Part I, pointing to the importance of consonancy over periodicity. But to merely stop at a description of the content of the structures that lie behind consonancy is insufficient. There are indeed weighty forces which impose upon the journalist the need to make snappy last minute analyses of events and all this will create a tendency to utilize unreflectingly a preconceived stereotype. This does not explain though (just as the notion of periodicity fails to do) the nature of that stereotype, its ideological significance, nor the pressures against the journalist changing the model he or she uses. To take an example: when marijuana use was first reported in the British newspapers (in the Fifties) it was categorized in terms of the 'dope fiend', a stereotype based on opiate addicts. Because of this, certain items of information were more readily assimilated and accredited as truthful (e.g. craving, eventual death from use), while others were more readily ignored (e.g. aesthetic pleasure, harmlessness). A new 'social problem' was squeezed, pummelled and distorted into the already grotesque and inaccurate category of 'dope fiend'. No sooner was the word 'drug' mentioned than the well-trained journalist proceeded to search for the exploitative pusher (the corrupter) in order to complete the *Gestalt*—the total world view—that his story demanded.

William Braden, a reporter for the *Chicago Sun-Times,* presents us with an illuminating illustration of this process. LSD was first categorized in the early 'Sixties as a 'miracle drug' used in the treatment of alcoholism, drug addiction and mental illness, and only later as a 'killer drug' similar to other illicit psychotropic substances. Braden notes how the transition between these two stereotypes corresponded to the increasing advocacy of LSD as a 'consciousness expander'. The ineffable mystical feeling claimed to be experienced by LSD users could not be easily categorized as a product of a therapeutic 'miracle drug' or as being within the realm of 'normal' religious experience. For a while, the drug's qualities did not fit existing media categories and caused a degree of unease. The arrival at last of 'proof' that it was dangerous in terms of chromosome damage and its suicidogenic qualities came as a relief to the journalists who could now easily place it within the 'killer drug' category.

Such examples illustrate the fashion in which consonancy operates and underlies media stories. But they stop short of explaining why particular paradigms are utilized and what is the motivation behind the journalist's reluctance to change directions and reconceptualize the phenomenon that he faces. Graham Murdock's paper starts to do this. By showing how underlying structural and ideological factors shape the journalist's definition of the situation when faced with political deviance and mass demonstrations, his argument links our earlier group of papers (which are descriptive or leave explanations at the bureaucratic level) and our later group which moves to the ideological level. A similar link is provided by Stuart Hall's account of the determination of news photos. He discusses both the operational practices which allow editors, working over a set of prints, to select, rank, classify and elaborate the photo in terms of his 'stock of knowledge' as to what constitutes 'news' *and* the further determinants which exist at an ideological level.

The Consensual Paradigm

We wish to argue that the phenomenon of consonancy is best viewed as an explanatory paradigm. That is, it is not that events are wilfully distorted as the Manipulative model would suggest nor that they are a more or less accurate reflection of reality as the Market model would maintain but they are a *translation* of reality into a paradigm or world view. This contains, a preconceived notion of social order (a consensus), a concept of 'normal' human nature (free and voluntaristic) and a conception of deviance (it is either a determined sickness or an act of corruption). It is not that the facts are either distorted or reflected, it is that they are given a frame of reference within this consensual paradigm. For example, Crutchley and Young in their study of the 1973 strike in Britain against the Industrial Relations Act[6] found that it was not that the number of demonstrators was inaccurately reported nor that the details of the strike were ignored; rather it was that the contextualization of the event was radically altered. Thus instead of being portrayed as an event in the (subsequently successful) struggle to overthrow the Conservative government, this massive political strike was presented as an ahistorical irrelevancy, a piece of madness in the consensus of modern industrial relations.

Kurt and Gladys Lang refer to such a consensual paradigm as an inferential structure.[7] This is the key concept used by Halloran, Elliott and Murdock in their study of the television coverage of 27th October 1968 demonstration against the war in Vietnam. Thus they write:

> . . . events will be selected for news reporting in terms of their fit or consonance with pre-existing images—the news of the event will confirm earlier ideas. The more unclear the news item and the more

uncertain or doubtful the newsman is in how to report it, the more likely it is to be reported in a general framework that has already been established.[8]

And again:

Once selected a framework will structure the subsequent coverage. That is, events which are consonant with the basic image are likely to be given prominence whereas contradictory developments will be played down or excluded altogether.[9]

The consensual paradigm, then, is a lens through which reality is seen: it focuses on certain events, it obscures or obfuscates others, it leads to certain questions being asked and others being ignored. This is not, of course, to imply that the images thus engendered are wholly fictitious: Mods and Rockers, Teddy Boys, Skinheads, violent criminals, hippies, drug addicts are after all not just inkblots on to which fantasies are projected. Thus as Terry Ann Knopf in an article[10] on distortions in press reports of racial violence in America (in the direction of grossly exaggerating supposedly 'new' elements of planning, organization, sniping and leadership) concludes:

Unwittingly or not, the press has been constructing a scenario on armed uprisings. The story line of this scenario is not totally removed from reality. There *have* been a few shoot-outs with the police, and a handful may have been planned. But no wave of uprisings and no set pattern of murderous conflict have developed—at least not yet.

Using the notion of a 'constructed scenario' Cohen compares what happened at the initial Mods and Rockers events with their fantasy portrayal in the mass media. He suggests that much of the inventory of qualities ascribed to these actors was putative. However, none of these readings—and this is particularly clear in Murdock's and Hall's articles—argues that there is nothing 'out there', that the journalist sits in his or her office wilfully and maliciously inventing stories. What is being scrutinized is the process of construction which transforms what happens 'out there' into news. The wider societal reasons for such constructions bring us to our next group of readings.

In discussing the relationship between the internal dynamics of the news organization and the events which it confronts, we argued that an explanatory point outside the bureaucracy was necessary for an adequate explanation of the particular images and the selection procedures used.

Neither periodicity nor consonance are sufficient to explain the *content* of the consensual paradigm or inferential structures. The way the media make sense of things, must be related to wider ideological maps of meaning.

Thus Graham Murdock's paper presents an explicit theory about the media's role in managing political conflict and dissent. Similarly, E. P. Thompson, in his analysis of the letters chosen by the press to depict public attitudes to the 1970 power workers' strike, develops the same theme. He detects a scenario created by the media which caricatures the strikers as irrational and ignorant and the effect of their strike as being directed against the *whole* of the nation and causing casualties among the *weak*. Class conflict becomes recast into the conservative imagery of a small group of men trampling on the poor and damaging the national interest. The vast majority of men are seen to agree with the economic system as it stands, disturbances are due to the machiavellianism of a few. Real conflict of interests *is* possible in this model but it tends to be reserved for those cases where the 'real' indigenous population is portrayed as being threatened by the 'alien' members in their midst. Thus Hartmann and Husband note the constant depiction of race relations in terms of this supposed conflict. The media's handling of the 'invasion' by the Ugandan Asians in 1972 reflects a similar image.

An even more explicit attempt to relate media models to broader societal conflict is made in Frank Pearce's analysis of the media's characterization of homosexuality. Only the 'normal' categories of sexuality relating to male and female are allowed. Homosexuality is a deviant form which violates the male/female bifurcation and is grouped as an aberration, as an almost non or semi-human activity. Pearce thus attempts to explore the total *structure* of sexual categorization utilized rather than merely depict the appearance of each category. A related—and even more transparent—area for examining the media's refraction of wider ideological structures is the way women are portrayed. As the extract from Butcher *et al.* suggests (see also the references cited in Part Four) a sexist projection of women serves to maintain their subordinate position in society.

All these paradigms and models, though, have to do some work to make themselves work: however much the media would like the world to be simple, they cannot help but register all sorts of complexities, paradoxes and contradictions. The model might break down if too many of these were left unresolved. Thus Young sees that certain contradictions are being actively worked out in the media's depiction of drug taking. The media must solve the problem of advocating a consensus model, yet explain the prevalence of widespread deviation, for example, drug use, strikes, student militancy. The solution is to suggest that deviancy is never freely chosen. It is either the result of sickness, or if it is widespread, a function of the corruption of the ignorant or innocent by a wicked minority. The typical citizen is thus represented as freely choosing normality—and the deviant as ineluctably impelled by forces beyond his or her knowledge or control into transgression. A morality play unfolds where the normal is seen to prosper and the abnormal inevitably to suffer pain and hardship.

Such studies of the mass media move from a mere description of the dramatis personae involved in what is categorized as a social problem, to a study of the play itself, examining its implicit structures and tracing the fashion in which it justifies the world 'as it is'. The suggestion here, then, is that news is not merely a series of lies fabricated in order to protect ruling class interests but that it is a subtle and deceptive mythology attractive to the audience.

Problems with the consensual paradigm

The last selection of readings in this section point to problems with the 'consensual paradigm' approach to the media. We commence with a piece taken from *Policing the Crisis*[11]—a study of the media reporting of mugging and the law and order debate in the 1970s. Hall *et al.* note the *relative autonomy* of the mass media from the powerful despite the fact that very often it is not the media who are the *primary definers* of events. That is—in line with our conclusion in Part One—inferential structures about particular events are often created by the powerful prior to the media using them in the manufacture of news. The media, however, manage a relative autonomy in two ways: first, in terms of the media culture with its notions of balance, lack of bias, propriety, the proper range of coverage, etc. and secondly, in terms of the news being a commodity sold to an audience. For example, Hall *et al.* point to how newspapers address their audience in a *public idiom*, that is in their perception of the language of their audience. With this in mind even the powerful—the primary definers of reality—must phrase their interventions and pronouncements in a fashion which takes account of the relative autonomy of the media. They must 'sell' their news commodities to the media just as the media must 'sell' to their audience. Now such a position begins to undermine a widespread assumption within the consensual paradigm approach: that there is a one-to-one functional relationship between the contents of the mass media and the interests of the powerful. Young, in the final article in this section, castigates this assumption as 'left functionalism' and points to its theoretical, methodological and political drawbacks. Indeed the Middlesex Mass Media Group in a recent analysis of the 'Winter of discontent'—the industrial disputes in Britain in the winter of 1978–1979—point to a degree of variation within the media quite inconsistent with the monolithic unanimity that functionalism would suggest. Furthermore, they argue, the mode of reporting the effects of the road haulage strike by exaggerating the impact could have precipitated a more decisive and speedy victory for the drivers. In this instance, then, reporting may have been decidedly dysfunctional to ruling class interests.[12]

Such an argument for the relative autonomy of the media places them in a linked but separate relationship to both the powerful and to the audience. David Morley, in an illuminating piece on industrial relations in the media, stresses this autonomy and points to what he sees as the most important link between the message carried by the mass media and the audience. Namely, that the message is persuasive because it makes cognitive sense to the audience. This is not manipulation nor a simple reflection of reality but a one-sided accentuation of a social reality which is itself contradictory. It is neither lie nor reflection but a message ultimately grounded in the world of appearances.

On all these scores consensual paradigm theory, with its notion of a message which is illusory, uncontradictory, functional and a direct expression of ruling class interests, can be faulted. But its central insight remains a powerful one: the way the mass media provide a frame of reference, an inferential structure for understanding the world. This insight can best be understood by decoding what the media actually say— and leave out—about deviance and social problems. All the diverse readings that follow, variously address themselves to this point.

REFERENCES

1. B. Berelson and P. Salter,'Majority and minority Americans. An analysis of magazine fiction', *Public Opinion Quarterly*, Vol. 10 (1946) pp 169–90. For an elaboration of Tuchman's position see G. Tuchman, 'Women's depiction by the mass media' *Signs* 4 (1979) No 3 pp 528–542
2. F. James Davis, 'Crime news in Colorado newspapers', *American Journal of Sociology*, LVII (June 1952) pp. 325–30

3. For an excellent case study of how a television documentary—in this case, on the nature of prejudice—was made, from the emergence of the idea to its ultimate realization in the studio, see Philip Elliott, *The making of a television series: a case study in the sociology of culture* (London, Constable, 1972).

4. Daniel J. Boorstin, *The image* (Harmondsworth, Penguin, 1963). For numerous examples, see particularly Chapter I entitled 'From news gathering to news making: a flood of pseudo events'.

5. See F. S. Siebert, T. Peterson and W. Schramm, *Four theories of the press* (University of Illinois Press, 1963).

6. J. Crutchley and J. Young, 'May Day madness' in *Trade unions and the media* (eds) P. Beharrell and G. Philo (London, Macmillan, 1977).

7. K. Lang and G. E. Lang, 'The unique perspective of television and its effect: a pilot study', *American Sociological Review*, Vol.18 (1953), pp. 3–12.

8. James D. Halloran, Philip Elliott and Graham Murdock, *Demonstrations and communications* (Harmondsworth, Penguin, 1970) p.26.

9. G. Murdock, 'Mass communication and the construction of meaning', in *Reconstructing Social Psychology* (ed.) N. Armistead (Harmondsworth, Penguin, 1974) pp.208–9.

10. See Terry Ann Knopf, 'Sniping—A new pattern of violence'.

11. S. Hall *et al.*, *Policing the crisis* (London, Macmillan, 1978).

12. An initial report on this research is at present in preparation, 'The Winter of Discontent', S. Harris, T. Jones and J. Young, Middlesex Mass Media Group, Middlesex Polytechnic.

The symbolic annihilation of women by the mass media*

GAYE TUCHMAN

Two related ideas are central to our discussion. These are *the reflection hypothesis* and *symbolic annihilation*. According to the reflection hypothesis, the mass media reflect dominant societal values. In the case of television[1], the corporate character of the commercial variety causes programme planners and station managers to design programmes for appeal to the largest audiences. To attract these audiences (whose time and attention are sold to commercial sponsors), the television industry offers programmes consonant with American values. The pursuit of this aim is solidified by the fact that so many members of the television industry take those very values for granted: dominant American ideas and ideals serve as resources for programme development, even when the planners are unaware of them, much as we all take for granted the air we breathe. These ideas and ideals are incorporated as *symbolic representations of American society, not as literal portrayals*. Take the typical television family of the 1950s: mother, father, and two children living in an upper middle-class, single-residence suburban home. Such families and homes were not the most commonly found units in the 1950s, but they were the American ideal. Following George Gerbner[2], we may say that 'representation in the fictional world', such as the 1950s ideal family, symbolizes or 'signifies social existence'; that is, representation in the mass media announces to audience members that this kind of family (or social characteristic) is valued and approved.

Conversely, we may say that either condemnation, trivialization, or 'absence means symbolic annihilation'[3]. Consider the symbolic representation of women in the mass media. Relatively few women are portrayed there, although women are 51 per cent of the population and are well over 40 per cent of the labour force. Those working women who are portrayed

*Extracts from Gaye Tuchman, 'Introduction: The symbolic annihilation of women by the mass media' in Gaye Tuchman, Arlene Daniels and James Benet (eds.), *Hearth and home: Images of women in the mass media* (New York, Oxford University Press, 1978), pp. 3–38.

are condemned. Others are trivialized: they are symbolized as child-like adornments who need to be protected or they are dismissed to the protective confines of the home. In sum, they are subject to *symbolic annihilation*.

Television: symbolic annihilation of women

To say television is the dominant medium in American life is a vast understatement. In the average American household, television sets are turned on more than six hours each winter day. More American homes have television sets than have private bathrooms, according to the 1970 census. Ninety-six per cent of all American homes are equipped with television, and most have more than one set. By the time an American child is fifteen years old, she has watched more hours of television than she has spent in the classroom. And since she continues watching as she grows older, the amount of time spent in school can never hope to equal the time invested viewing television.

The use of television by children is encouraged because of parental use. The average adult spends five hours a day with the mass media, almost as much time as she or he spends at work. Of these five hours, four are occupied by the electronic media (radio and television). The other hour is taken up with reading newspapers, magazines, and books. Television consumes 40 per cent of the leisure time of adult Americans.

What are the portrayals of women to which Americans are exposed during these long hours? What can the pre-school girl and the school-girl learn about being and becoming a woman?

From children's shows to commercials to prime-time adventures and situation comedies, television proclaims that women don't count for much. They are under-represented in television's fictional life—they are 'symbolically annihilated'. From 1954, the date of the earliest systematic analysis of television's content, through 1975, researchers have found that males dominated the television screen. With the exception of soap operas where men make up a 'mere majority' of the fictional population, television has shown and continues to show two men for every woman. Figure 1 indicates that proportion has been relatively constant. The little variation that exists occurs between types of programmes. In 1952 68 per cent of the characters in prime-time drama were male. In 1973, 74 per cent of those characters were male. Women were concentrated in comedies where men make up 'only' 60 per cent of the fictional world. Children's cartoons include even fewer women or female characters (such

as anthropomorphized foxes or pussycats) than adult's prime-time programmes do. The paucity of women on American television tells viewers
that women don't matter much in American society.

The symbolic annihilation of women by the mass media

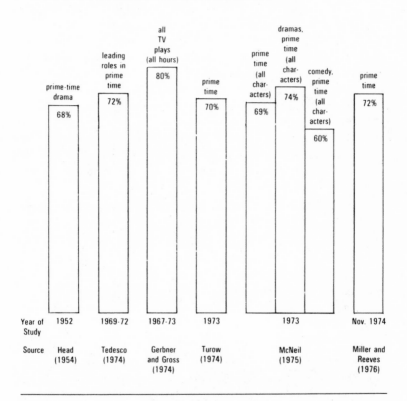

	prime-time drama	leading roles in prime time	all TV plays (all hours)	prime time	prime time (all characters)	dramas, prime time (all characters)	comedy, prime time (all characters)	prime time
	68%	72%	80%	70%	69%	74%	60%	72%
Year of Study	1952	1969-72	1967-73	1973	1973			Nov. 1974
Source	Head (1954)	Tedesco (1974)	Gerbner and Gross (1974)	Turow (1974)	McNeil (1975)			Miller and Reeves (1976)

FIGURE 1   Percentage of males in TV programmes, 1952–1974.

That message is reinforced by the treatment of those women who do
appear on the television screen. As seen in Figure 2, when television
shows reveal someone's occupation, the worker is most likely to be male.
Someone might object that the pattern is inevitable, because men constitute a larger share of the pool of people who can be professionals. But that
objection is invalidated by the evidence presented by soap operas, where
women are more numerous. But the invariant pattern holds there too,
despite the fact that men have been found to be only about 50 per cent of
the characters on the 'soaps'.[4]

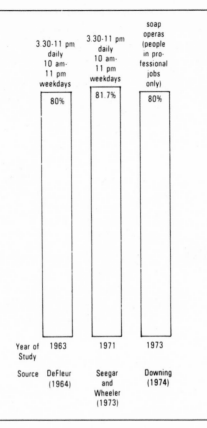

FIGURE 2   Percentage of males among those portrayed as employed on TV, 1963–1973.

Additionally, those few working women included in television plots are symbolically denigrated by being portrayed as incompetent or as inferior to male workers. Pepper, the 'Policewoman' on the show of the same name (Angie Dickinson) is continually rescued from dire and deadly situations by her male colleagues. Soap operas provide even more powerful evidence for the portrayal of women as incompetents and inferiors. Although Turow[5] finds that soap operas present the most favourable image of female workers, there too they are subservient to competent men. On 'The Doctors', surgical procedures are performed by male physicians, and although the female M. D.'s are said to be competent at their work, they are primarily shown pulling case histories from file cabinets or filling out forms. On other soap operas, male lawyers try cases and female lawyers research briefs for them. More generally, women do not appear in the same professions as men: men are doctors, women, nurses; men are lawyers, women, secretaries; men work in corporations, women tend boutiques.

The portrayal of incompetence extends from denigration through victimization and trivialization. When television women are involved in violence, unlike males, they are more likely to be victims than aggressors[6]. Equally important, the pattern of women's involvement with television violence reveals approval of married women and condemnation of single and working women. As Gerbner[7] demonstrates, single women are more likely to be victims of violence than married women, and working women are more likely to be villains than housewives. Conversely, married women who do not work for money outside the home are most likely to escape television's mayhem and to be treated sympathetically. More generally, television most approves those women who are presented in a sexual context or within a romantic or family role[8]. Two out of three television-women are married, were married, or are engaged to be married. By way of contrast, most television men are single and have always been single. Also, men are seen outside the home and women within it, but even here, one finds trivialization of women's role within the home.

According to sociological analyses of traditional sex roles[9], men are 'instrumental' leaders, active workers and decision-makers outside the home; women are 'affective' or emotional leaders in solving personal problems within the home. But television trivializes women in their traditional role by assigning this task to men too. The nation's soap operas deal with the personal and emotional, yet Turow[10] finds that on the soap operas, the male sex is so dominant that men also lead the way to the solution of emotional problems. In sum, following the reasoning of the reflection hypothesis, we may tentatively conclude that for commercial reasons (building audiences to sell to advertisers) network television engages in the symbolic annihilation of women.

Two additional tests of this tentative conclusion are possible. One examines non-commercial American television; the other analyses the portrayal of women in television commercials. If the commercial structure of television is mainly responsible for the symbolic annihilation of women, one would expect to find more women on public than on commercial television. Conversely if the structure of corporate commercial television is mainly responsible for the image of women that is telecast, one would expect to find even more male domination on commercial ads.

To an even greater extent than is true of programmes, advertising seeks to tap existing values in order to move people to buy a product.

Unfortunately, few systematic studies of public broadcasting are available. The best of these is Caroline Isber and Muriel Cantor's work[11], funded by the Corporation for Public Broadcasting, the source of core programming in the Public Broadcasting System. Cantor asks, 'Where are the women in public television?' Her answer, based on a content analysis of programming is 'in front of the television set'. Although a higher proportion of adult women appear on children's programming in public television than is true of commercial television, Cantor finds 'both commercial and public television disseminate the same message about women, although the two types of television differ in their structure and purpose'. Her conclusion indicates that commercialism is not solely responsible for television's symbolic annihilation of women and its portrayal of stereotyped sex roles.

Male domination has not been measured as directly for television commercials, the other kind of televised image that may be used to test the reflection hypothesis. Since so many of the advertised products are directed toward women, one could not expect to find women neglected by commercials. Given the sex roles commercials play upon, it would be bad business to show two women discussing the relative merits of power lawn mowers or two men chatting about waxy buildup on a kitchen floor. However, two indirect measures of male dominance are possible: (1) the number of commercials in which only men or only women appear; and (2) the use of males and females in voice-overs. (A 'voice-over' is an unseen person speaking about a product while an image is shown on the television screen; an unseen person proclaims 'two out of three doctors recommend' or 'on sale now at your local. . . .')

On the first indirect measure, all-male or all-female commercials, the findings are unanimous. Schuetz and Sprafkin[12], Silverstein and Silverstein[13], and Bardwick and Schumann[14] find a ratio of almost three all-male ads to each all-female ad. The second indirect measure, the use of voice-overs in commercials, presents more compelling evidence for the acceptance of the reflection hypothesis. Echoing the findings of others, Dominick and Rauch[15] report that of 946 ads with voice-overs, 'only 6 per cent used a female voice; a male voice was heard on 87 per cent.' The remainder use one male and one female voice.

The commercials themselves strongly encourage sex-role stereotypes. Although research findings are not strictly comparable to those on television programmes because of the dissimilar 'plots', the portrayals of women are even more limited than those presented on television dramas and comedies. Linda Busby[16] summarized the findings of four major studies of television ads. In one study,

—37.5% of the ads showed women as men's domestic adjuncts
—33.9% showed women as dependent on men
—24.3% showed women as submissive
—16.7% showed women as sex objects
—17.1% showed women as unintelligent
—42.6% showed women as household functionaries.

Busby's summary of Dominick and Rauch's work reveals a similar concentration of women as homemakers rather than as active members of the labour force:

—Women were seven times more likely to appear in ads for personal hygiene products than not to appear [in those ads]
—75% of all ads using females were for products found in the kitchen or in the bathroom
—38% of all females in the television ads were shown inside the home, compared to 14% of the males
—Men were significantly more likely to be shown outdoors or in business settings than were women
—Twice as many women were shown with children [than] were men
—56% of the women in the ads were judged to be [only] housewives
—43% different occupations were coded for men, 18 for women.

As Busby notes, reviews of the major studies of ads[17] emphasize their strong 'face validity' (the result of real patterns rather than any bias produced by researchers' methods), although the studies use different coding categories and some of the researchers were avowed feminist activists.

In sum, then, analyses of television commercials support the reflection hypothesis. In voice-overs and one-sex (all male or all female) ads, commercials neglect or rigidly stereotype women. In their portrayal of women, the ads banish females to the role of housewife, mother, homemaker, and sex object, limiting the roles women may play in society.

What can the pre-school girl, the school-girl, the adolescent female and the woman learn about a woman's role by watching television? The answer is simple. Women are not important in American society, except *perhaps* within the home. And even within the home, men know best, as the dominance of male advice on soap operas and the use of male voice-

overs for female products, suggests. To be a woman is to have a limited
life divorced from the economic productivity of the labour force.

Women's magazines: marry, don't work

As the American girl grows to womanhood, she, like her counterpart
elsewhere in industrialized nations, has magazines available designed
especially for her use. Some, like *Seventeen,* whose readers tend to be
young adolescents, instruct on contemporary fashions and dating styles.
Others, like *Cosmopolitan* and *Redbook,* teach about survival as a young
woman—whether as a single woman hunting a mate in the city or a young
married coping with hearth and home.

This section reviews portrayals of sex roles in women's magazines,
seeking to learn how often they too promulgate stereotypes about the role
their female readers may take—how much they too engage in the symbolic annihilation of women by limiting and trivializing them. Unfortunately, our analyses of images of women in magazines cannot be as
extensive as our discussion of television. Because of researchers' past
neglect of women's issues and problems, few published materials are
available for review.

Like the television programmes just discussed, from the earliest content analyses of magazine fiction[18] to analyses of magazine fiction
published in the early 1970s, researchers have found an emphasis on
hearth and home and a denigration of the working woman. The ideal
woman, according to these magazines, is passive and dependent. Her fate
and her happiness rest with a man, not with participation in the labour
force. There are two exceptions to this generalization: (1) The female
characters in magazines aimed at working-class women are a bit more
spirited than their middle-class sisters. (2) In the mid-1970s, middle-
class magazines seemed less hostile toward working women. Using the
reflection hypothesis, particularly its emphasis upon attracting readers to
sell advertisements, we will seek to explain the general rule and these
interesting exceptions to it.

Like other media, women's magazines are interested in building their
audience or readership. For a magazine, attracting more readers is *indirectly* profitable. Each additional reader does not increase the
magazine's profit margin by buying a copy or taking out a subscription,
because the cost of publication and distribution per copy far exceeds the
price of the individual copy—whether it is purchased on the newsstand,
in a supermarket, or through subscription. Instead a magazine realizes its
profit by selling advertisements and charging its advertisers a rate ad-

justed to its known circulation. Appealing to advertisers, the magazine specifies known demographic characteristics of its readership. For instance, a magazine may inform the manufacturer of a product intended for housewives that a vast proportion of its readership are homemakers, while another magazine may appeal to the producer of merchandise for young working women by lauding its readership as members of that target group. Women's magazines differentiate themselves from one another by specifying their intended readers, as well as the size of their mass circulation. Additionally, they all compete with other media to draw advertisers. (For example, *Life* and *Look* folded because their advertisers could reach a larger group of potential buyers at a lower price per person through television commercials.) Both daytime television and women's magazines present potential advertisers with particularly appealing audiences, because women are the primary purchasers of goods intended for the home.

Historically, middle-class women have been less likely to be members of the labour force than lower-class women. At the turn of the century, those married women who worked were invariably from working-class families that required an additional income to assure adequate food, clothing, and shelter[19]. The importance of this economic impetus for working is indicated by the general adherence of working-class families to more traditional definitions of male and female sex roles[20]. Although middle-class families subscribe to a more flexible ideology of sex roles than working-class families, both groups of women tend to insist that the man should be the breadwinner. The fiction in women's magazines reflects this ideology.

Particularly in middle-class magazines, fiction depicts women 'as creatures . . . defined by the men in their lives'[21]. Studying a random sample of issues of *Ladies' Home Journal, McCall's,* and *Good Housekeeping* between the years 1940 and 1970, Helen Franzwa found four roles for women: 'single and looking for a husband, housewife-mother, spinster, and widowed or divorced—soon to remarry'. All the women were defined by the men in their lives, or by their absence. Flora[22] confirms this finding in her study of middle-class (*Redbook* and *Cosmopolitan*) and working-class (*True Story* and *Modern Romances*) fiction. Female dependence and passivity are lauded; on the rare occasions that male dependence is portrayed, it is seen as undesirable.

As might be expected of characterizations that define women in terms of men, American magazine fiction denigrates the working woman. Franzwa says that work is shown to play 'a distinctly secondary part in women's lives. When work is portrayed as important to them, there is a concomitant disintegration of their lives'[23]. Of the 155 major female characters depicted in Franzwa's sample of magazine stories, only 65 or 41 per cent were employed outside the home. Seven of the 65 held high-status positions. Of these seven, only two were married. Three others were 'spinsters' whose 'failure to marry was of far greater importance to the story-line than their apparent success in their careers'[24]. One single woman with a high status career was lauded: She gave up her career to marry.

From 1940 through 1950, Franzwa found, working mothers and working wives were condemned. Instead, the magazines emphasized that husbands should support their spouses. One story summary symbolizes the magazines' viewpoint: 'In a 1940 story, a young couple realized that they couldn't live on his salary. She offered to work; he replied, "I don't think that's so good. I know some fellows whose wives work and they might just as well not be married" '[25]. Magazines after 1950 are even less positive about work. In 1955, 1960, 1965, and 1970 not one married woman who worked appeared in the stories Franzwa sampled. (Franzwa selected stories from magazines using five-year intervals to enhance the possibility of finding changes.)

Since middle-class American wives are less likely to be employed than their working-class counterparts, this finding makes sociological sense. Editors and writers may believe that readers of middle-class magazines, who are less likely to be employed, are also more likely to buy magazines approving this life-style. More likely to work and to be in families either economically insecure or facing downward mobility, working-class women might be expected to applaud effective women. For them, female dependence might be an undesirable trait. Their magazines could be expected to cater to such preferences, especially since those preferences flow from the readers' life situations. Such, indeed, are Flora's findings, presented in Table 1.

TABLE 1

FEMALE DEPENDENCE AND INEFFECTUALITY BY CLASS,
BY PERCENTAGE OF STORIES*

	FEMALE DEPENDENCE			FEMALE INEFFECTUALITY		
	Undesir-able	Desir-able	Neu-tral	Undesir-able	Desir-able	Neu-tral
Working Class	22	30	48	38	4	58
Middle Class	18	51	31	18	33	49
Total	20	41	40	28	19	53

*Adapted from Flora (1971).

However, this pattern does not mean that the literature for the working-class woman avoids defining women in terms of men. All the women in middle-class magazines dropped from the labour force when they had a man present; only 6 per cent of the women in the working-class fiction continued to work when they had a man and children. And Flora explained that for both groups 'The plot of the majority of stories centered upon the female achieving the proper dependent status, either by marrying or manipulating existing dependency relationships to reaffirm the heroine's subordinate position. The male support—monetary, social, and psychological—which the heroine gains was generally seen as well worth any independence or selfhood given up in the process'[26].

Such differences as do exist between working-class and middle-class magazines remain interesting, though. For they indicate how much more the women's magazines may be responsive to their audience than television can be. Because it is the dominant mass medium, television is designed to appeal to hundreds of millions of people. In 1970, the circulation of *True Story* was 'only' 5,347,000, and of *Redbook*, a 'mere' 8,173,000. Drawing a smaller audience and, by definition, one more specialized, the women's magazines can be more responsive to changes in the position of women in American society. If a magazine believes its audience is changing, it may alter the content to maintain its readership. The contradictions inherent in being women's magazines may free them to respond to change.

A woman's magazine is sex-typed in a way that is not true of men's magazines[27]. *Esquire* and *Playboy* are for men, but the content of these magazines is, broadly speaking, American culture. Both men's magazines feature stories by major American writers, directed toward all sophisticated Americans, not merely to men. Both feature articles on the state of male culture as American culture or of male politics as American politics. Women's magazines are designed in opposition to these 'male magazines'. For instance, 'sports' are women's sports or news of women breaking into 'men's sports'. A clear distinction is drawn between what is 'male' and what is 'female'.

Paradoxically, though, this very limitation can be turned to an advantage. Addressing women, women's magazines may suppose that some in their audience are concerned about changes in the status of women and the greater participation of women in the labour force. As early as 1966, before the growth of the modern women's movement, women who were graduated from high school or college assumed they would work until the birth of their first child. Clarke and Esposito[28] found that magazines published in the 1950s and addressed to these women *(Glamour, Made-*

moiselle, and *Cosmopolitan)* stressed the joys of achievement and power when describing working roles for women and identifying desirable jobs. Magazines addressed to working women were optimistic about these women's ability to combine work and home, a message that women who felt that they should or must work would be receptive to. Indeed, in 1958 Marya and David Hatch criticized *Mademoiselle, Glamour* and *Charm* as 'unduly optimistic' in their 'evaluation of physical and emotional strains upon working women'. Combining work and family responsibilities may be very difficult, particularly in working-class homes, since working-class husbands refuse to help with housework[29]. But even working-class women prefer work outside the home to housework[30] since it broadens their horizons. Wanting to please and to attract a special audience of working women, magazine editors and writers may be freed to be somewhat responsive to new conditions, even as these same writers and editors feature stereotyped sex roles in other sections of their magazines.

Additional evidence of the albeit limited responsiveness of women's magazines to the changing status of women in the labour force is provided by their treatment of sex-role stereotypes since the advent of the women's movement. The modern women's movement is usually said to begin in the mid-1960s with the founding of the National Organization for Women. The date is of consequence for the study of sex roles in women's magazines because of Betty Friedan's involvement in the National Organization for Women. Her book, *The feminine mystique,* published in 1963, provided much of the ideology for the young movement. And, its analysis of sexism ('the problem with no name') was based in part on an analysis of the portrayal of sex roles in women's magazines. In an undated manuscript cited in Busby[31], Stolz and her colleagues compared the image of women in magazines before and after the advent of the women's movement. Like others, they found no changes between 1940 and 1972. However, a time-lag ('culture lag') is probably operating, since non-material conditions (ideas and attitudes) change more slowly than do material conditions (such as participation in the labour force).

Several very recent studies affirm that women's magazines may be introducing new conceptions of women's sex roles that are more conducive to supporting the increased participation of women in the labour force. Butler and Paisley[32] note that at the instigation of an editor of *Redbook,* 28 women's magazines published articles on the arguments for and against the Equal Rights Amendment, a constitutional change prompted by the women's movement and the increased participation of

women in the labour force. Franzwa's impression of the women's magazines she had analyzed earlier is that they revealed more sympathy with
working women in 1975[33]. Sheila Silver[34] indicates that a 'gentle support'
for the aims of the women's movement and a 'quiet concern' for working
women may now be found in *McCall's*. By the terms 'gentle support' and
'quiet concern', she means to indicate that the magazine approves of equal
pay for equal work and other movement aims, although it does not
approve of the women's movement itself. That magazine and others, such
as the *Ladies' Home Journal,* continue to concentrate upon helping
women as housewives: they still provide advice on hearth and home. The
women's magazines continue to assume that every woman will marry,
bear children and 'make a home'. They do not assume that every woman
will work some time in her life.

In sum, the image of women in the women's magazines is more responsive to change than is television's symbolic annihilation and rigid type-
casting of women. The sex roles presented are less stereotyped, but a
woman's role is still limited. A female child is always an eventual mother,
not a future productive participant in the labour force.

Newspapers and women: food, fashion, and society

Unlike the women's magazines, newspapers seek to appeal to an entire
family. Historically, they have sought to attract female readers by treating
them as a specialized audience, given attention in a segregated women's
page, an autonomous or semi-autonomous department whose mandate
precludes coverage of the 'hard news' of the day. Although women's
magazines have been published in the United States since the early nineteenth century, it took the newspaper circulation wars of the 1880s to
produce the notion of 'women's news'. At that time, it appeared that every
man who would buy a newspaper was already doing so. To build circulation by robbing each other of readers and attracting new readers, newspapers hired female reporters to write about society and fashion, as well as
to expand 'news' to include sports and comic strips. Items of potential
interest to women were placed near advertisements of goods that women
might purchase for their families. The origin of women's news reveals
how long newspapers have traditionally defined women's interests as
different from men's and how items of concern to women have become
non-news, almost oddities. That view continues today. The budget for
women's pages rarely provides for updating those pages from edition to
edition, as is done for the general news, sports, and financial pages,
sections held to be of interest to men. Finally, as is true of other depart-

ments as well, women's page budgets are sufficiently restricted to force that department's dependence upon the wire services.

For now, a characterization of women's pages provided by Lindsay Van Gelder[35] seems apt. She speculates thus: suppose a Martian came to earth and sought to learn about American culture by reading the women's pages. Bombarded by pictures of wedding dresses, the Martian might suppose that American women marry at least once a week. After all, a Martian might reason that newspapers and their women's pages reflect daily life. That view, we might add, would seem justified by the women's pages' intense involvement with the social life of the upper class, because upper-class power is a daily aspect of American life. Women's pages feed upon the parties, marriages, engagements and clothing and food preferences of the wealthy and the celebrated. In this, like newspapers in general[36], the women's pages encourage all citizens to emulate the upper class and to chase after positions of high status and institutionalized importance.

Newspapers' very emphasis upon established institutions and those with institutionalized power may account in part for their denigration of women and the women's movement[37]. Most information in the general sections of newspapers concerns people in power, and newspapers justify this emphasis by stressing that such people work in or head societal institutions that regulate social intercourse. But communications researchers view the matter somewhat differently. They argue that newspapers exercise social control: by telling stories about such people, newspapers lend status to approved institutions and chastise lawbreakers. Historically, those few women mentioned in the general news pages belonged to the powerful groups in society. Gladys Engel Lang[38] suggests 'the most admired woman' list probably reflects the publicity given to specific women. They are mainly wives of the powerful, celebrities and stars, and the few women who are heads of state. But women are mainly seen as the consorts of famous men, not as subjects of political and social concern in their own right.

This situation appears to be changing. Once ignored or ridiculed[39], the women's movement has received increasing coverage as it has passed through the stages characteristic of any social movement. As the women's movement became sufficiently routinized to open offices with normal business hours, some newspapers established a 'women's movement beat' that required a reporter to provide at least periodic coverage of new developments[40]. When increased legitimation brought more volunteers and more funds to wage successful law suits against major corporations and to lobby for the introduction of new laws, newspapers concerned with major institutions were forced to cover those topics[41]. In turn, these successes increased the movement's legitimation. Legitimation also brought support of sympathizers within other organizations who were not movement members[42]. Reporters having those other organizations as their beats are being forced to write about the ideas of the women's movement and women's changing status. For instance, the position of women and minorities in the labour force is becoming a required topic for labour reporters and those who write about changing personnel in the corporate world.

On the whole, though, despite coverage of women forcibly induced by the legitimation of the women's movement, newspapers continue to view women in the news as occasional oddities that must be tolerated. Attention to women is segregated and found on the women's page. As a recent survey of women's pages demonstrates[43], most women's pages continue to cater to a traditional view of women's interests. They emphasize home and family, only occasionally introducing items about women at work. And those items are more likely to concern methods of coping with home and office tasks than they are with highlighting problems of sex discrimination and what the modern women's movement has done in combating it. Like the television industry, appealing to a common denominator encourages newspapers to engage in the symbolic annihilation of women by ignoring women at work and trivializing women through banishment to hearth and home.

NOTES AND REFERENCES

1. Gaye Tuchman, *The TV establishment: programming for power and profit* (Englewood Cliffs, NJ, Prentice-Hall, 1974); 'Media values', *Society* (1976, November/December), pp. 51–4.
2. George Gerbner, 'Violence in television drama: trends and symbolic functions' in G. A. Comstock and E. A. Rubinstein (eds), *Media content and control*, Television and social behavior, Vol. 1 (Washington, DC, US Government Printing Office, 1972), p. 44.
3. Ibid., p. 44.
4. Mildred Downing, 'Heroine of the daytime serial', *Journal of communication* (1974, Vol. 24, No. 2, pp. 130–7); N. Katzmann, 'Television soap operas: what's been going on anyway?', *Public opinion quarterly* (1972, Vol. 35, pp. 200–12)
5. Joseph Turow, 'Advising and ordering: daytime, prime time', *Journal of communication* (1974, Vol. 24, No. 2, pp. 138–41):
6. Gerbner, ibid.
7. Ibid.

8. Ibid., and cf. R. M. Liebert, J. M. Neale and E. S. Davidson, *The early window: effects of television on children and youth* (Oxford and New York, Pergamon, 1973).

9. Talcott Parsons, 'Age and sex in the social structure of the United States', *Essays in sociological theory* (New York, The Free Press, 1949).

10. Turow, ibid.

11. Caroline Isber and Muriel Cantor, *Report of the task force on women in public broadcasting* (Washington, Corporation for Public Broadcasting, 1975).

12. Schuetz and Sprafkin, in G. Tuchman, A. Daniels and J. Benét (eds), *Hearth and home: images of women in the mass media* (New York, Oxford University Press, 1978).

13. Arthur Jay Silverstein and Rebecca Silverstein, 'The portrayal of women in television advertising', *FCC Bar Journal* (1974, No. 1, pp. 71–98).

14. Judith Bardwick and Suzanne Schumann, 'Portrait of American men and women in TV commercials', *Psychology* (1967, Vol. 4, No. 4, pp. 18–23).

15. Joseph Dominick and Gail Rauch, 'The image of women in network TV commercials', *Journal of broadcasting* (1972, Vol. 16, No. 3, pp. 259–65).

16. Linda J. Busby, 'Sex-role research on the mass media', *Journal of communication* (1975, Vol. 25, No. 4, pp. 107–31).

17. Such as A. E. Courtney and T. W. Whipple, 'Women in TV commercials', *Journal of communication* (1974, Vol. 24, No. 2, pp. 110–18).

18. P. Johns-Heine and H. Gerth, 'Values in mass periodical fiction, 1921–1940', *Public opinion quarterly* (1949, Vol. 13, Spring, pp. 105–13).

19. Valerie Kincaid Oppenheimer, *The female labor force in the United States: demographic and economic factors governing its growth and changing composition*, Population Monograph, Series No. 5 (Berkeley, University of California, Institute of International Studies, 1970).

20. Lillian Rubin, *Worlds of pain. Life in the working-class family* (New York, Basic Books, 1976).

21. Helen Franzwa, 'Working women in fact and fiction', *Journal of communication* (1974(a), Vol. 24, No. 2, p. 106); see also *idem*, 'Pronatalism in women's magazine fiction' in Ellen Peale and Judith Senderowitz (eds), *Pronatalism: the myth of motherhood and apple pie* (New York, T. Y. Crowell, 1974(b), pp. 68–77); and *idem*, 'Female roles in women's magazine fiction, 1940–1970' in R. K. Unger and F. L. Denmark (eds), *Woman: dependent or independent variable* (New York, Psychological Dimensions, 1975, pp. 42–53).

22. Cornelia Flora, 'The passive female: her comparative image by class and culture in women's magazine fiction', *Journal of marriage and the family* (1971, Vol. 33, August, pp. 435–44).

23. Franzwa, 1974(a), p. 106.

24. Ibid., pp. 106–7.

25. Ibid., p. 108.

26. Flora, p. 441.

27. Margaret Davis, *'The Ladies' Home Journal* and *Esquire:* a comparison' (unpublished manuscript, Stanford University, Dept. of Sociology, 1976).

28. P. Clarke and V. Esposito, 'A study of occupational advice for women in magazines', *Journalism quarterly* (1966, Vol. 43, pp. 477–85).
29. Rubin.
30. Ibid., and Joann Vanek, *Married women and the work day: time trends* (Baltimore, Maryland, Johns Hopkins Univ. Press, forthcoming), ch. 4.
31. Busby.
32. Matilda Butler and William Paisley (personal communication, Autumn 1976).
33. Personal communication 1976.
34. Sheila Silver, 'Then and now—content analysis of *McCall's* magazine' (paper presented at the annual meeting of Association for Education in Journalism, College Park, Maryland, August 1976).
35. Lindsay Van Gelder, 'Women's pages: you can't make news out of a silk purse' (*Ms*, 1974, November, pp. 112–16).
36. Paul F. Lazarsfeld and Robert K. Merton, 'Mass communication, popular taste and organized social action' in L. Bryson (ed.), *The communication of ideas* (New York, Harper Brothers, 1948, pp. 95–118).
37. Monica B. Morris, 'The public definition of a social movement: women's liberation', *Sociology and social research* (1974, Vol. 57, pp. 526–43).
38. See ch. 8 of *Hearth and home: images of women in the mass media*.
39. Morris.
40. See ch. 11 of *Hearth and home: images of women in the mass media*.
41. Ibid, ch. 12.
42. Maren Lockwood Carden, *The new feminist movement* (New York, Russel Sage, 1973).
43. Zena B. Guenin, 'Women's pages in contemporary newspapers: missing out on contemporary content', *Journalism quarterly* (1975, Vol. 52, Spring, pp. 66–69, 75).

Mental illness:
what the media present*

JUM C. NUNNALY

The media of mass communication are commonly thought to exert a powerful influence on what the general public feels and believes. Consequently, we studied presentations dealing with mental-health phenomena in the mass media and the impact of the media on public opinion. This chapter will describe a content analysis of the mass media.

Content-analysis procedure

Our content analysis counted the number of times that particular points of view about mental health were portrayed in samples of mass media presentations.

Coding categories

In a content analysis, the people who do the counting are referred to as *coders* and the things that they count are referred to as *coding categories*. Usually coding categories are determined *a priori,* or 'rationally', rather than deduced from empirical observations. Our content analysis departed from the customary dependence on 'rational' categories. One of the principles which guided our study of information held by our three sources (the public, the experts, and the media) was that comparable measures should be used for all three. Consequently, the ten information factors that were used to study the public and the experts were also used to study the content of the media.

How the information factors were used to analyse the content of media presentations can be illustrated with one of the television programmes 'caught' in our sample. The programme was a 15-minute crime drama. As the scene opens, a thief is sneaking through a clock shop. The shop is filled with ticking clocks and swinging pendulums. The thief enters a

---

*Extracted from Jum C. Nunnally, *Popular conceptions of mental health* (New York, Holt, Rinehart & Winston, 1961).

barred enclave in the room where the safe is placed. The barred door accidentally closes and locks, and the unfortunate thief must spend the night looking at and listening to a room full of clocks. When the proprietors arrive in the morning, the thief is staring glassy-eyed and mumbling incoherently. In the final scene he is carted away to a mental hospital.

How the content of this television presentation was analysed will illustrate our general procedures. It was first necessary to decide whether any relevant material occurred. (How relevance was determined will be discussed later.) Relevant material was then coded on the ten information factors. A judgment was made as to whether the material affirmed each factor, repudiated each factor, or portrayed a neutral viewpoint (a neutral presentation either said or portrayed nothing relating to the ten factors or was a balance of pro and con). Scores of plus, minus, and zero were given for the results.

The television drama described above is relevant to our problem because the thief was referred to several times as being 'out of his mind' and because he was placed in a mental hospital. The presentation was particularly relevant to two of our factors, 'look and act different' (Factor I) and 'immediate external environment versus personality dynamics' (Factor VII). The thief assumed a very bizarre appearance, which, if characteristic of the mentally ill at all, would be found only in the most severely ill. Consequently, the programme was scored plus on Factor I. In the drama, the thief was 'driven mad' by the ticking clocks. He entered the shop an apparently normal person (except for an unfortunate occupation) and left with a severe mental illness. Consequently, the programme was scored 'plus' on Factor VII. The details of the programme supplied information enough to score some of the other information factors as either plus or minus, and zeros were given to the remaining information factors because no related ideas were presented.

In addition to the ten factors, five supplementary content categories were employed. Counts were made of the number of portrayals of *supernatural* causes and cures associated with mental-health problems. Although supernatural explanations were generally rejected by the public, it was thought that some of the media presentations might deal with evil omens, visions, magic spells, and the like. The second supplementary category concerned the *approval of mental-health professions and facilities*. A plus was recorded if the portrayal suggested, for example, that psychiatrists usually do an effective job. An example of a minus situation is one in which the psychiatrist was in league with crooks and used his position to confine hapless victims in a mental hospital. Similarly, codings were made of portrayals relating to psychotherapy, mental hospitals, and specific forms of treatment. The third supplementary category concerned the *incidence* of mental-health problems: whether or not the presentation suggested that mental-health problems occur frequently in our society. For the fourth supplementary category, *methods of prevention and treatment,* coders simply listed all the suggested methods encountered in the media presentations. For the fifth supplementary category, *whom to approach for help* when mental problems occur, coders listed the kinds of persons suggested in the media presentations, such as ministers, psychiatrists, and lawyers.

In addition to the content categories, coders applied a number of space and time categories. For the printed media, the coders determined the amount of space taken up by each relevant message. For radio and television, coders noted the amount of time consumed by each relevant presentation—an hour, a half-hour, or only five minutes. The space and time categories were broken down in terms of the places in which relevant material appeared. For example, in the analysis of newspapers, each relevant item was classified into one of the following 'location' categories: (1) news stories, features, and pictures, (2) paid advertising, (3) entertainment such as fiction, comics, and puzzles, (4) personal-advice columns on health and psychology and for the 'lovelorn', (5) editorials, including political cartoons and 'letters to the editor', and (6) all factual 'how to' items, such as recipes, financial guides, and home-repair columns.

The ten factors and the supplementary categories were intended to measure the information stated and implied by mass media presentations. In addition to these information-type measures, part of the content analysis was concerned with the attitudes suggested by the media presentations. For this, coders were asked to make judgments about the portrayals of the mentally ill and the persons who treated the mentally ill. Each character appearing in the media was rated on a series of seven-step attitude scales. The scales were bounded by polar adjectives such as safe-dangerous, strong-weak, and valuable-worthless. . . . The coders were not asked to rate their personal reactions to the characters portrayed but to try to make impartial judgments about the nature of the portrayals themselves.

Coder selection and training
The main job of the coders was to analyse media content on the basis of the ten information factors. Consequently, the coders had to be familiar

with psychological concepts. . . . The meanings of the information factors were explained in detail. One form of practice was to make a 'blind' sorting of the 180 information items (the ones used in the original factor analysis) into their proper factors. Thus, given a statement like 'The eyes of the insane are glassy', the coders had to guess the corresponding factor (in this case the correct answer was Factor I, 'look and act different'). On the average the coders assigned 75 per cent of the items correctly, giving us some confidence in their understanding and use of the factors. As another form of practice, the coders made content analyses of excerpts from newspaper articles and of contrived written messages. The results were compared with the codings made by psychologists on the research staff, which resulted in more exact specification of the procedures of analysis and continued training for coders.

Media samples
A truly representative sampling of the content of the mass media would be an enormous research undertaking. Not only are there numerous arms of the media (films, books, newspapers, radio, television, and others), but there are numerous classifications of each. Even a representative sample of one arm alone, such as magazines, would require a diverse and extensive collection. In comparison with a truly representative sampling of media content, our sample was relatively weak.

Television. Television coverage was the most restricted of our media samples, because of the difficulties and expenses of content-analysing television programmes as compared with newspapers, magazines, and other media. The television sample was restricted to the total output— about 111 hours of transmission time—of a single VHF station, WCIA in Champaign, Illinois, for one full week, 31 January to 6 February 1955. In addition to local productions, this station offered more than 100 CBS, nearly 20 NBC, and several DuMont programmes.

As was true in all of the content analyses, every minute of the telecasting was considered for material relevant to mental health. Thus our coders watched such apparently unrelated presentations as basketball games, stock-market quotations, and commercials, but we did not want to judge in advance where relevant presentations would be found.

Coders worked in shifts to analyse television programmes, with one shift of three coders watching at all times. A room equipped with clocks, two television sets (in case one fell into disrepair), and partitions separating the coders from one another was specially prepared for the analysis. Supervisors were available to distribute and collect coding sheets and to answer coders' questions about technical procedures.

Radio. The radio sample consisted of one week's total broadcasting by four stations, affiliated with four different networks, in four widely separated geographic areas of the United States. The broadcasts had been recorded in November and December 1953 for another project. It proved much less tedious to analyse the radio recordings than it was to analyse 'live' television. The coders were also able to play back portions of the programme recordings to help them form judgments about the content categories.

Magazines. In this sample were 91 different magazines, one issue of each, which were displayed on news-stands at about the same time in March 1955. These included comic books, news, pictorial, digest, 'quality', health, women's, men's, teenage, sports, farm, romance and confession, detective, film, and other magazines. We tried to gather as diverse a collection as possible, excluding only such highly specialized magazines as photography and 'how to' publications. About 351,000 column inches of space were included.

Newspapers. Our newspaper sample was both the most extensive and the most representative for the country as a whole. The sample consisted of one week's home editions of 49 daily newspapers. The newspapers were proportionately representative of the geographic regions in the United States and proportionately representative of circulation size. The issues were spread over the month of October 1954. Involved were 317 separate issues with a total of 12,419 pages, containing approximately 2,086,423 inches—and every inch was searched for material relating to mental health.

Confession magazines. In gathering the magazine sample discussed above, we found that 'confession' magazines are saturated with material relating to mental illness, neurosis, and emotional disturbance. Consequently, a separate study was made of the mental-health content of confession magazines. Different methods of content analysis were used on the confession magazines and the results were not combined directly with those from our four other media samples. . . .

Content-analysis results

How seriously can the results of the content analysis be taken? We have pointed out some of the frailties of the procedures that were used. Much of the data is judgmental and is no better or no worse than the subjective processes of the coders. Also, the content samples were, at best, only moderately representative of the media as a whole. In spite of the limitations of the content analysis and the modest proportions of our media samples, however, the results are so lopsided that we can reach some strong conclusions about the mental-health content of the mass media.

Time and space

Seeking material directly related to mental-health problems (as we defined them) in the mass media is like looking for a needle in a haystack. If you search every inch of space in three different daily newspapers, the odds are that you will find only one item which is relevant. To find one relevant item it would be necessary to read, on the average, the entire content of two magazines. If you listened to one entire day of broadcasting of a radio station, you would, on the average, find about 2·3 programmes with information or portrayals relevant to mental-health problems. An almost identical number of relevant programmes would be expected in the entire daily telecasting of one station—2·4 programmes which in some way relate to mental-health problems. Thus we can conclude that: *Information concerning mental illness appears relatively infrequently in mass media presentations.*

The findings here contradict our original estimates of the prevalence of mental-health presentations in the mass media. We had guessed that relevant material was presented more frequently than it is. Before doing the study we tried to recall the number of presentations relating to mental-health issues that we had seen recently in newspapers, television, and the other media, but in so doing we did not fully consider the many programmes that were irrelevant. Consequently, we overestimated, percentagewise, the occurrence of related material.

In all of the media samples combined, we found a total of 202 relevant items (items being defined as separate whole programmes in radio and television and as columns, stories, and features in the printed media). Of the total, we found 120 items in newspapers, 49 in magazines, 16 in radio, and 17 in television. There were not enough items for us to compare their content similarities and differences or to demonstrate differences among subclassifications of the media. For example, it would have been interesting to determine whether the mental-health content of newspapers is generally different from that of television programmes or whether the mental health content of television news programmes is different from that of evening drama programmes. Because there were not enough relevant items to analyse separately, all of the relevant material was lumped together, providing an average profile of the information presented in the mass media.

Although we did not study the issue directly, it seemed to us that information relating to 'physical' disorders—cancer, heart trouble, physical injury, and so forth—appeared more frequently than information relating to mental health. Perhaps the apparent relative scarcity of information relevant to mental-health problems is related to the findings that public information is unstructured and uncrystallized. Problems of mental health may not be discussed sufficiently in the media, in schools, and in private conversation to permit the individual to develop a firm system of beliefs. More research is needed, however, to determine the amount of mental-health information in the media and, if, as our data indicate, such information is relatively scarce, to test the effect of this scarcity on public beliefs.

The information factors

To review: Two out of three coders had to be in agreement before material was classed as relevant and before content was coded on the information factors. Although basing the analysis on majority decisions reduced the total amount of data, it probably produced a more valid set of results.

While the data on the information held by the public and the experts was in seven-step-scale form and could be compared directly, the data from this content analysis had to be converted to the seven-step scale for comparison purposes. The data consisted of ratings by coders of the number of times that one pole of a factor was portrayed as compared with the other pole. For example, 80 instances were found in which the 'immediate external environment' (Factor VII) was portrayed as being at the root of particular mental disorders. The opposite pole of the factor, 'personality dynamics', was portrayed only 29 times. Thus Factor VII was attributed to be the cause in 73 per cent of the classified presentations. Percentages of this kind were then converted to a seven-point scale (see Nunnally, 1957, for a description of the scaling procedure used). From these converted results we were able to compare the results from the mass media with the opinions held by the public and the experts (see Figure 1).

The scaled factor scores for the media, represented by circles, are shown in Figure 1. Three factors (will power, sex distinction, and age function) occurred less than ten times in the media presentations and consequently offered insufficient grounds for making comparisons. The factor scores for the media are compared with the average responses given by experts and by members of the general public. The results are quite clear. Not only are the views that the media present generally incorrect according to expert opinion but they are also far less accurate than the beliefs of the average man. *The media of mass communication generally present a distorted picture of mental-health problems.*

Although some mass media presentations, especially those specifically designed to convey information about mental health, provide a valid picture of mental illness, the number of such programmes is very small in comparison with those which incidentally portray mental illness in a misleading light. An individual is more likely to see some aspect of neurotic behaviour portrayed on television in an evening drama programme than in a public-information programme.

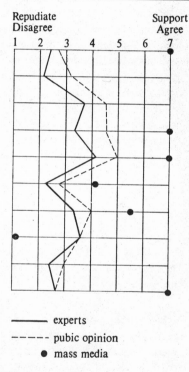

1 Look and act different

2 Will power

3 Sex distinction

4 Avoidance of morbid thoughts

5 Guidance and support

6 Hopelessness

7 External causes vs. personality

8 Non-seriousness

9 Age function

10 Organic causes

——— experts

– – – – pubic opinion

● mass media

FIGURE 1
Comparisons of experts, the public, and the mass media
on the ten information factors

In general, the causes, symptoms, methods of treatment, prognoses, and social effects of mental illness portrayed by the media are far removed from what the experts advocate. . . . In particular, media presentations emphasize the bizarre symptoms of the mentally ill. For example, information relating to Factor I was recorded 89 times. Of these, 88 affirmed the factor, that is, indicated or suggested that people with mental-health problems 'look and act different'; only one item denied Factor I. In television dramas, for example, the afflicted person often enters the scene staring glassy-eyed, with his mouth widely agape, mumbling incoherent phrases or laughing uncontrollably. Even in what would be considered the milder disorders, neurotic phobias and obsessions, the afflicted person is presented as having bizarre facial expressions and actions.

The occurrence of mental disorder is explained in the media most often by pressures in the immediate external environment (Factor VII). The soap-opera heroine develops a neurosis because her husband dies in a plane crash, her little daughter is afflicted with an incurable disease, and all the family savings are lost in a fire. The 'neurosis' goes away with a brighter turn of events. If the pressures of the immediate external environment are not brought in as causal explanations, organic factors are cited. A magazine fiction story might explain neurotic or psychotic behaviour in terms of an old battlefield injury, a head wound in childhood, physical privation such as thirst or hunger.

In the media, the person with a mental disorder most often receives help from some strong person in the environment who lends guidance and support. The strong individual may be a person who is professionally trained—a psychiatrist, 'doctor', or nurse; equally often the guiding hand is that of a homespun philosopher who manages to say the right thing at the right time. Such cogencies as 'The world is what you make of it' and 'The past cannot hurt you' are portrayed as profoundly influencing the course of a disorder.

Supplementary categories
Because only a few examples of the items in the media contained material which was related to the supplementary categories, there is little to report. For example, in the category 'whom to seek for advice', we found that only eight psychiatrists, two 'doctors', one psychologist, and one nurse were mentioned. These categories did provide one interesting bit of negative evidence: although we had thought that the media might portray religion as being related to mental-health issues, it was seldom mentioned as an important variable. The same results held in a separate study of confession magazines. In this case, the media are in line with public

opinion: our studies show that very few people associate mental-health phenomena with religion.

Attitude ratings

The media samples portrayed 41 persons who could be classified as mentally ill. Of these, 21 displayed typical neurotic symptoms and 20 displayed typical psychotic symptoms. Three coders made attitude ratings of the 41 portrayals, and the median rating of the three coders on each Semantic Differential scale was used in the analysis. The resulting profile of the mentally ill in the mass media closely resembles the public's attitudes toward the mentally ill. Both psychotics and neurotics are portrayed as relatively ignorant, dangerous, dirty, unkind, and unpredictable. Neurotics are pictured as less dangerous, dirty, and unkind than psychotics, the latter being pictured as stronger and more active.

For what they are worth, the coders also made attitude ratings of the portrayals of the 12 'therapists' mentioned above. The resulting average profile is much the same as the attitude profile of the general public toward psychologists and psychiatrists. The media portrayals depict the therapist as being intelligent, kind, and valuable.

Summary

Our results point to a seeming paradox: the ideas about mental health portrayed in the mass media are less 'correct' compared with expert opinion than are the beliefs of the public at large. Where then did the public get its present body of information? Certainly not from an uncritical acceptance of media presentations. Perhaps, as has been suggested, the public is able to discriminate between 'valid' information and unrealistic portrayals. If this is so, then the public probably does learn something from the 'better' media presentations, although the number of such programmes is relatively small.

The media are, of course, commercial ventures whose policies and presentations are determined in part by their internal needs. Presentations related to mental health are shaped by numerous hands—writers, editors, directors, media executives, commercial sponsors, and others. Perhaps it is necessary to emphasize bizarre symptoms in order to make the presentations more exciting and to enlarge their audience appeal. Perhaps the relatively restricted time period or space available is responsible for much of the oversimplified treatment of mental disorders. If the media took the time to illustrate the complexities of the learning processes that experts deem to be the important components in personality disorders, they might produce some very dull programmes.

The communications media have adopted a stylized picture of mental-health problems which distorts reality, but is a useful device in drama, comedy, and other programmes for the public. It would be a great waste, however, if the communications media did not eventually help to promote a healthy set of public attitudes and improve public understanding of mental-health phenomena. It is also to be hoped that more accurate information can be incorporated into effective forms of entertainment. Our content analysis was performed in 1954 and 1955. Presentations in the mass media may have begun to incorporate more adequate viewpoints about mental health since then.

Theories of behaviour and the image of the alcoholic in popular magazines 1900–1966*

ARNOLD S. LINSKY

In his satirical novel *Erewhon*, Samuel Butler describes a mythical society in which criminals are sympathetically treated in hospitals at the public expense while diseased persons are sent to prisons and punished according to the seriousness of their illness.[1] Butler's satire illustrates the tenuous linkage which may exist between the form of deviance and public definitions and response to that deviance.

The changes in public views of alcoholism during the twentieth century provide a graphic illustration of how a form of deviance may be rapidly redefined. This shift of 'moral passage' does not make alcoholism unique among forms of deviance, but in this case the shift has begun so recently and advanced so rapidly the possibility exists for objectively charting its course.[2] These changes are believed to reflect both the specific moral history of alcohol problems as well as basic cultural changes in popular conceptions of man's nature and his social relationships which go far beyond the problems of alcohol and which affect views of both normal and abnormal behaviour.

The current study investigates changes in public views on alcoholism during the last seven decades through content analysis of popularly oriented magazine articles dealing with alcohol problems. Popular magazines have long exhorted and advised the public on a variety of social problems, including alcoholism. It is assumed that positions expressed in these magazines are broadly consistent with or at most slightly in advance of beliefs held by their readership, in keeping with the need of such magazines for wide reader acceptance.

The study examines first changes in the methods of treatment advocated and in the aetiological theories of alcoholism presented. Secondly, the

*From Arnold S. Linsky, 'Theories of behaviour and the image of the alcoholic in popular magazines 1900–1966', *Public Opinion Quarterly* 34 (Winter 1970–1), pp. 573–81.

study attempts to bring some empirical data to bear on Charles Y. Glock's thesis that a quiet revolution has been occurring with respect to man's view of human nature.[3] Glock posits a shift away from a moralistic and 'free will' conception of human nature which has traditionally informed American public opinion toward a more deterministic and naturalistic view.

The universe for the present study consists of articles on the subject of alcoholism and alcohol problems listed in *Reader's guide to periodic literature* from 1900 to 1966. Random samples of thirty articles were drawn from each of the six decades from 1900 through 1959, and 60 articles were drawn for the seven-year period 1960–1966. Each article was rated independently on several dimensions by at least two judges.

Causal theories of alcoholism

Causal theories presented in articles are classified according to two central dimensions: (1) a *locational* dimension, i.e. whether the causal agent is seen as inside the alcoholic or located in his environment; (2) and a *moral* dimension, i.e. whether the causal agent is evaluated moralistically in the article or interpreted naturalistically, i.e. in scientific terms.[4]

Each article was rated independently on both locational and moral dimensions from (1) to (5). On the locational dimension a rating of (1) indicates that the cause is viewed as exclusively within the individual, while a (5) indicates that the cause is completely external. On the moral dimension (1) represents a highly moralistic evaluation of the causal agent while (5) represents an entirely naturalistic orientation.[5]

Locational dimension

Table 1 indicates important shifts in the perceived locational origins of alcoholism. For the first three decades of the twentieth century the causal agent was seen as clearly outside of the alcoholic, resting in environmental forces. A decisive change occurred by the 1940s when the focus shifted to factors inside the alcoholic, principally psychological. Since the 1940s there appears to be a moderate trend away from strictly internal explanation, with articles often citing both internal and external factors.

The types of external causes cited in the 1950s and 1960s, however, differed from types cited earlier in this century. Current articles citing external causes focus on diffuse cultural and social patterns such as cocktail parties, tensions of fast-paced living, and breakdown of social controls, as opposed to the liquor traffic, the tavern, the poverty of the working class focused on by earlier articles.

Moral dimension

Attribution of moral blame to the agent causing alcoholism has declined steadily over the last seven decades. The most decisive decline occurred between the decades of 1930–1939 and 1940–1949. It is evident from Table 1 that this period also witnessed the major changes on the locational dimension. Later articles for the most part either denied the relationship of alcoholism to moral weakness or ignored the question of the moral responsibility of the causal agent.

TABLE 1

EXPLANATIONS OF ALCOHOL PROBLEMS IN POPULAR
MAGAZINES: LOCATION AND MORAL DIMENSION BY
DECADE (MEDIAN RATINGS)

Decade	Number of articles	Location score* (internal-external)	Moral score† (Moralistic-naturalistic)
1960–66	30	2·77	4·44
1950–59	30	2·50	3·50
1940–49	30	2·17	3·50
1930–39	30	3·76	2·50
1920–29	30	4·20	2·14
1910–19	30	3·83	2·13
1900–09	30	4·20	2·04

*Ratings may range from (1) 'inside the alcoholic' to (5) 'outside the alcoholic'.
†Ratings may range from (1) 'moralistic' to (5) 'naturalistic'.

Complete causal theories

Most articles on alcoholism include both a stand on the location of the causal agent and a moral evaluation of that agent. The foregoing analysis has focused on the trend for the locational and moral dimensions separately. The distribution of articles on both dimensions jointly is considered in this section. These two dimensions dichotomously treated result in four possible combinations. Each combination, represented by a cell in Figure 1, contains a logically distinct aetiological theory of alcoholism.

Cell (a) represents the traditional free-will theory which holds that the cause of alcoholism is internal to the alcoholic and that he is morally at fault for his condition. Cell (b) represents the social criticism approach which views morally corrupt individuals, groups, and institutions in the external social environment of the alcoholic as the cause of alcoholism. In cell (c) psychological and biological theories are represented, which explain alcoholism on the basis of internal but naturalistic factors, such as emotional, genetic, or physiochemical agents, without blaming the alcoholic. Finally, cell (d) represents sociological explanation, which, like cell (b). explains alcohol problems as originating in the social environment of the alcoholic, but unlike (b) views these environmental factors within a morally neutral, naturalistic framework.

FIGURE 1
THEORIES OF THE AETIOLOGY OF ALCOHOLISM BY
MORAL AND LOCATIONAL DIMENSIONS

Moral dimension	Locational dimension	
	Within the alcoholic	External to alcoholic
Moralistic	(a) Traditional free will position	(b) Social criticism
Non-moralistic (or naturalistic)	(c) Psychological and biological explanation	(d) Sociological explanation

Table 2 presents the distribution of these four aetiological positions for four consecutive time periods. The social criticism approach dominated the explanation of alcoholism during the first twenty years of the century. The cause of alcoholism was placed clearly in the alcoholic's environment, and these environmental agents were unequivocally condemned. Explanations emphasizing the free will of the alcoholic were second in importance, but ran far behind the social criticism approach.

By 1940 a significant shift had occurred toward naturalistic internal explanations of alcoholism. Almost 72 per cent of articles written during this period fell within cell (c), psychological-biological explanation. This continued to be the dominant category of explanation during the 1960s.

There is some evidence that a further shift toward sociological explanation has been occurring since the 1940s but psychological explanations still predominate. Naturalistic explanations, cells (b) and (d) together, account for 81·3 per cent of the articles written between 1940 and 1959, and 86·4 per cent written between 1960 and 1966.

TABLE 2

AETIOLOGICAL THEORIES OF ALCOHOLISM AND ALCOHOL
PROBLEMS PRESENTED IN POPULAR MAGAZINE ARTICLES
BY PER CENT OF TOTAL ARTICLES* IN FOUR PERIODS†

Theoretical position‡	Period			
	1900–1919	1920–1939	1940–1959	1960–1966
	%	%	%	%
'Free will'	11·1	5·6	6·2	8·1
Social criticism	75·0	58·3	12·5	5·4
Psychological and biological explanation	5·6	16·7	71·9	54·0
Sociological explanation	8·3	19·4	9·4	32·4
Number of articles	36	36	32	37

* The number of articles is less than the 60 original articles for each period since articles which received a rating of 3 on either the locational or the moral dimension could not be sorted into the dichotomized table and were excluded from this analysis.
† Decades are consolidated into 20-year periods because of small frequencies in some cells.
‡ See Figure 1 for the derivation of these positions.

Recommendations for dealing with alcohol problems

Treatment recommendations changed markedly during the period covered. Table 3 contains a detailed analysis of these changes. A sharp increase in advocacy of rehabilitation-reform measures is evident for the period of study. Rehabilitation-reform refers to attempts to control the alcohol problem by bringing about changes within the alcoholic himself. Within this major category, therapeutic measures have shown the most dramatic increase. For the most recent decade Alcoholics Anonymous was the most frequently endorsed method of treatment, followed by psychiatric care, medical care, and clinical-institutional care. Neither the traditional measures, such as will power and religious conversion, nor punitive measures have ever assumed major importance in popular articles of this century.

Suggestions oriented toward preventing alcoholism, such as education, social change, and control of the availability of alcohol, have declined, especially since 1939. In the prevention group, only education on alcoholism has gained increased endorsement during the twentieth century. Advocacy of prevention by control of alcohol itself, through moderation, abstinence, and Prohibition, has declined markedly from 50 per cent for the period 1900–1919 to 6 per cent for 1960–1966.[6]

TABLE 3

METHODS ADVOCATED FOR DEALING WITH ALCOHOLISM
AND ALCOHOL PROBLEMS DURING FOUR PERIODS,
BY PER CENT*

Method	1900–1919	1920–1939	1940–1959	1960–1966
	%	%	%	%
REHABILITATION-REFORM	11·2	19·4	62·9	62·0
Therapeutic	5·6	8·8	52·8	53·0
Alcoholics Anonymous	—	—	14·6	20·0
Medical	2·8	3·5	12·4	11·0
Psychiatric	—	1·8	19·1	15·0
Clinical-institutional	2·8	3·5	6·7	7·0
Traditional (will power, moral change, religious)	5·6	5·3	9·0	6·0
Punitive (jails, fines, social pressure)	—	5·3	1·1	3·0
PREVENTION	81·9	73·6	32·5	31·0
Social and cultural change	23·6	17·5	10·1	9·0
Educational	8·3	14·0	11·2	16·0
Control of alcohol	50·0	42·1	11·2	6·0
Moderation	8·3	15·8	1·1	2·0
Abstinence	11·1	1·8	9·0	3·0
Prohibition	30·6	24·6	1·1	1·0
OTHER	6·9	7·0	4·5	7·0
Total per cent	100·0	100·0	100·0	100·0
Number of treatments suggested	72	57	89	100

*Some articles suggest no treatments, others may suggest more than one. Percentages are based on total number of methods suggested. Chi-square equals 107·05 with 15 degrees of freedom, $p < \cdot 001$ (based on four categories: rehabilitation-reform, social and cultural change, education, and control of alcohol).

Interpretation

Mass media have undoubtedly played a part in changing public opinion on alcoholism. A community survey by the author found evidence that exposure to mass media was directly related to 'enlightened' attitudes on alcoholism among the public.[7] Any changes that occur in the mass media, however, should be considered instrumental rather than basic causes of change in public attitudes, since both the reasons for changes in content and the reasons for public receptivity remain unexplained.

Despite the rapid growth of scientific research on alcoholism during the last three decades, neither the aetiology of alcoholism nor the efficacy of modern therapeutic treatment has been established. Current views of alcoholism would seem to derive more from broad social and philosophical considerations than from scientific evidence.

Earlier in this paper it was suggested that changes in public attitudes on alcoholism might be related to a changing view of human nature. According to Glock, the basic factor governing the images of man that have prevailed historically is how much free will man is believed to have.[8] He maintains that the traditional image of man, a view grounded in the history of Western theological thought, sees him as possessing almost unlimited free will and thereby in no sense '. . . a victim of his environment'.

Glock sees a decline in this view beginning in the nineteenth century and accelerating in the last three or four decades. Under the influence of the behavioural sciences this traditional view has, according to Glock, been modified to the view that man cannot entirely escape the influence of his inherited attributes and his social environment. Among the consequences of this shift in the image of man Glock includes the changes in attitudes toward Negroes, and toward such deviants as the delinquent, the poverty stricken, the mentally ill, and the criminal.

Our data have some bearing on Glock's thesis. A somewhat restricted view of Glock's free-will orientation would equate it with cell (a) in our Figure 1. We reserved this cell for inside-moralistic explanations, where the cause is seen as within the alcoholic himself, and he is held morally responsible for his condition. According to Glock's thesis we would expect the free-will position to be relatively important for the early period surveyed, but declining in importance in more recent years. The findings in Table 2 indicate that this interpretation was employed more frequently in the period 1900–1919 than in subsequent periods, but there is no consistent trend over the four periods covered in Table 2. Even during the period 1900–1919 only 11.1 per cent of the articles represented the free-will view, compared with 75 per cent which took the social criticism approach. Our findings do not exclude the possibility that the free-will orientation was dominant at some point prior to the beginning of the twentieth century.

A somewhat broader interpretation of Glock's free will versus determinism dimension would equate it with the moralistic-naturalistic dimension of this study. Explanations of behaviour are considered naturalistic in our study if they employ a natural science frame of reference, i.e. alcoholism is viewed as the consequence of preceding events and conditions such as the genetic, biochemical, and psychological make-up of the individual and his social and cultural environment.

Under this broader definition our findings support Glock's thesis. The evaluation of drinking problems was highly moralistic in the first decade of the study but became progressively more naturalistic with each succeeding decade. For the latest period, the years 1960–1966, the average ratings for the 60 articles surveyed approached the naturalistic end of the continuum.

The timing of the change also supports Glock's contention that this change accelerated approximately 35 to 40 years ago. The dramatic shift that occurred during the period roughly between the 1930s and 1940s is evident in Table 1.

In summary, this study has traced broad changes in public views of alcoholism, alcohol problems, and treatment as presented in popular magazines during the twentieth century. The pattern of changes found is interpreted as reflecting in part cultural changes in popular conceptions of man's nature and social relationships which go far beyond the problems of alcohol, and which affect views of both normal and abnormal behaviour.

NOTES AND REFERENCES

1. Samuel Butler, *Erewhon* (London, Cape, 1922). (First published 1872.)
2. The term 'moral passage' refers to a transition of a behaviour from one moral status to another. Gusfield argues in a recent essay that drinking has undergone two such passages since the early nineteenth century: first from the 'repentant drinker' to the 'enemy drinker' and from the 'enemy drinker' to the 'sick drinker'. Joseph R. Gusfield, 'Moral passage: The symbolic process in public designations of deviance', *Social Problems*, Vol. 15 (1967), pp. 175–88. See also Harold Pfautz, 'The image of alcohol in popular fiction: 1900–1904 and 1946–1950', *Quarterly Journal for Studies on Alcoholism*, Vol. 23, (1962), pp. 131–46.
3. Glock, 'Images of man and public opinion', *Public Opinion Quarterly*, Vol. 28 (1964), pp. 539–46.
4. The following quotes illustrate 'internal' explanations. At this point only the location dimension is considered; the moral dimension is temporarily ignored:

    (1) '. . . drinking is only a symptom of a deeper-seated malady, the source of which is a maladjustment in the drinker's personality, that is in the full circle of his physical, mental, emotional make-up.'

    (2) 'Long days of soul searching followed his recognition that the causes of his excessive drinking were wrong moral values and character defects.'

    Following are examples of the 'external' orientation:

    (3) 'According to one pub manager, the British working man used to drink to forget his hardships. Today the labourer boasts a much better standard of living.'

(4) 'Two great factors contribute toward alcoholism, says Dr Block. One is the necessity for drinking, almost an obligation on the part of a person to drink in our culture. . . . The second factor seems to stem from the extreme toleration on the part of the general American public for drunken behavior.'

It should be remembered that articles are judged independently on both moral and locational dimensions. Some examples of the moral orientation include:

(5) '. . . but drunkenness being an insanity deliberately induced carries a moral stigma'.

(6) 'The booze traffic has been driven underground. It is surreptitious, predatory, evil. The potency of its evil, the weight of the menace it exerts, cannot be determined definitely. . . . The illnesses due to illicit liquor are not made public.'

Two examples of statements reflecting morally neutral or naturalistic explanations follow:

(7) 'Alcoholism is not a vice but a disease. The alcoholic is not a moral weakling. He is tragically ill with a mental malady.'

(8) 'Causes may come under such headings as psychological, medical, economic, and sociological.'

5. Reliability of ratings between the two principal judges on locational dimensions was tested in two pretests of 30 articles each. Gamma between judges for the two samples was $\cdot$73 and $\cdot$70. In the first sample 40$\cdot$0 per cent of the items were identically rated by both judges while a total of 93$\cdot$3 per cent were rated within one point of each other. On the second sample 51$\cdot$7 per cent of the ratings were identical, while a total of 89$\cdot$7 per cent fell within one rating of each other.

Reliability on the moral dimension for the two pretest samples is indicated by a gamma of $\cdot$74 and $\cdot$75. In the first sample 53$\cdot$3 per cent of ratings were identical by both judges while a total of 86$\cdot$6 per cent of the ratings were within one point of each other. In the second sample 69$\cdot$0 per cent of ratings were identical by both while 89$\cdot$7 per cent of ratings were within one point.

Inter-judge reliability, although reasonable, was undoubtedly reduced by the method of assigning a single rating to an entire article, rather than rating sentences. Many articles were internally inconsistent in the explanations which they used. In a few cases a causal sequence was not directly articulated, but implied.

6. This decline corresponds with Joseph Gusfield's report of the collapse of broad-based middle-class support for the Prohibition movement after repeal of the 18th Amendment in 1933. See his *Symbolic crusade: Status politics and the American temperance movement* (Urbana, The University of Illinois Press, 1963).

7. Arnold S. Linsky, 'Changing public views on alcoholism', *Quarterly Journal of Studies on Alcoholism,* in press.

8. Glock, op. cit., pp. 540–1.

Political deviance: the press presentation of a militant mass demonstration*

GRAHAM MURDOCK

Consensus, Conflict and Coincidence

For much of the post-war period, British political life was underpinned by the proposition that fundamental conflicts of interest arising out of historically structured inequalities in the distribution of wealth and power were a thing of the past. It was supposed that full employment and rising real wages had brought about a coincidence of interests between workers and owners, rulers and ruled, in which both parties had an equal stake in increasing the 'rate of economic growth' and raising the general level of 'affluence'. Once this basic framework of agreement on ends had been assumed, it followed that the only legitimate area for dissent was on the question of means. Consequently, 'politics' was identified with the procedures of parliamentary debate and trade union negotiation through which elected representatives debated the 'issues' and arrived at 'businesslike' compromises. Together, these notions served to define the period as one of 'consensus politics'.

Increasingly, during the last five or six years, however, various groups have rejected some or all of the basic notions of 'consensus politics'. Instead they have begun to define their situation in terms of fundamental conflicts of interest which cannot be satisfactorily articulated or resolved through the existing machinery of political and industrial representation. Increasingly, therefore, these groups have turned to direct forms of political action. Examples include: the urban guerilla insurgency and bombing of Ulster; the occupation of work places; student sit-ins; squatting and rent strikes; together with militant industrial strikes and mass demonstrations. In varying degrees, each of these actions presents a radical challenge to both procedures and underlying assumptions of 'consensus politics', a challenge which those in power must actively contest and

*Paper prepared especially for this volume.

overcome, and labelling these actions as illegitimate and 'deviant' is a necessary part of this process. Labelling serves a dual function; first, it reasserts the existence of a basic set of shared assumptions and interests, and secondly, it clarifies the nature of 'consensus' by pointing to concrete examples of what it is not. Both these elements, the celebration of consensus and the denigration of dissent, are indispensable to the process through which power is legitimated in corporate capitalist states. Edward Heath's prime ministerial broadcast following the settlement of the miners' strike in February 1972 provides a good example.

In the kind of country we live in there cannot be any 'we' or 'they'. There is only 'us'; all of us. If the Government is 'defeated', then the country is defeated, because the Government is just a group of people elected to do what the majority of 'us' want to see done. That is what our way of life is all about.

It really does not matter whether it is a picket line, a demonstration or the House of Commons. We are all used to peaceful argument. But when violence or the threat of violence is used, it challenges what most of us consider to be the right way of doing things. I do not believe you elect any government to allow that to happen and I can promise you that it will not be tolerated wherever it occurs.[1]

Once a definition of the situation in terms of the absence of basic structural conflicts and the presence of a common community of interests is accepted, the specific elements involved in the labelling of radical direct action fall into place. Given a basic agreement on ends and on the framework within which means should be debated, any redefinition of either or both must inevitably appear as an essentially transitory 'deviation' by a minority. Secondly, if there are no structured inequalities in the distribution of wealth and power, there can be no fundamental reason for radical action. Consequently, attention is directed away from the underlying issues and the definitions of the situation proposed by radical groups, and fixes instead on the forms which this action takes. The 'issue' therefore becomes one of forms rather than causes. Again, given that the process of 'peaceful argument' within the electoral/representative system is sufficient to resolve the disagreements which might arise, any basic challenge to this system necessarily appears as potentially 'violent'. Despite this concentration on form, the problem of explaining causes still remains. The solution, however, is simple. If radical activity is not generated by contradictions within the system, it must originate outside. In his speech, Mr Heath talked of an 'invisible danger' which is 'undermining our way of life'. Other politicians have been more specific and have located the genesis of radical action either among groups from outside (e.g., foreign infiltrators) or among groups who identify themselves with non-British 'ways of doing things' (e.g., Communist subversives). Together these elements form a coherent definition of the situation which serves to label radical activities as an essentially transitory deviation by a small minority of outsiders. Further, by segregating and ostracizing these groups and defining them as a threat, the act of labelling prepares the way for controlling action.

The definitions provided by the legitimated holders of power appear in the national press in three forms. First, the political speeches are themselves widely reported; secondly, many of the basic themes are reiterated in editorials, and, thirdly, the underlying definition of the situation permeates the texture of news reporting. This paper is concerned with the mechanisms involved in this last process.

It is all too easy to look for a conspiracy. Certainly, newspapers are enmeshed in the present economic and political system both directly through interlocking directorships and reciprocal shareholdings, and indirectly through their dependence upon advertising. They therefore have a vested interest in the stability and continuing existence of the present system. However, the links between this general framework and the day-to-day business of gathering and processing news material are oblique rather than direct. Journalists, in fact, explicitly define themselves in terms of their autonomy and independence of vested political and economic interests, and stress the role of the press as the tribune of the people. Neither is this argument entirely without foundation. Newspapers frequently do expose corruption, graft and miscalculation among the powerful and rich. Nevertheless, despite this element of autonomy, the basic definition of the situation which underpins the news reporting of political events, very largely *coincides* with the definition provided by the legitimated power holders. In order to explain how this coincidence comes about it is necessary to examine the process through which events come to be selected for presentation as 'news' and the assumptions on which this process rests.

This paper approaches this general problem through an analysis of the way in which one particular incidence of radical political activity—the mass demonstration against the Vietnam War in London on 27 October 1968—was presented in the national press.[2] As with all case studies, this research can be accused of picking on an atypical incident to illustrate a general case and it is always possible to find other cases which don't seem to fit. One commentator, for example, has contended that the Demonstration study over-emphasized the 'sensational' elements in the reporting, and that by contrast the coverage of the Aberfan disaster was characterized by 'restraint'.[3] This is to miss the basic point that the Demonstration was an explicitly political event whereas Aberfan was not. A senior *Guardian* reporter recognized this when he remarked that the two biggest news stories he could remember in recent times were the Demonstration and the General Election. This is not accidental, for both stories are fundamentally related to the definition of consensus in a period of increasing conflict. The Election coverage celebrated participation, acceptance and the management of disagreement, while the Demonstration story served to define and explain the dynamics of militant refusal.

The events of 27 October
The main demonstration on 27 October was organized by a committee representing a coalition of various student, trade union, religious, peace and anti-war groups. The publicity and manifestos issuing from the militant core of this organizing committee clearly challenged the basic assumptions of consensus politics. First, they asserted that there were fundamental conflicts of interest arising out of economic exploitation and the inequalities in the distribution of power and argued that these constituted the true locus of 'violence' in the system. Secondly, they maintained that the 'failure' of the Labour government had demonstrated the impossibility of initiating structural change through the parliamentary system and proposed that left-wing groups should unite to form an extra-parliamentary opposition. The 'militant' solidarity of the demonstration was seen as a first step in this long-term strategy. In terms of the immediate tactics of the situation, however, the organizers explicitly rejected a policy of direct confrontation with the police. Consequently, on the day, the demonstration followed the pattern established by the Campaign for Nuclear Disarmament and an estimated 70,000 people marched peacefully along the agreed route through central London to a rally in Hyde Park.

The organizers of the breakaway march to Grosvenor Square also rejected the tactics of confrontation but announced their intention of registering their protest by their physical presence outside the American Embassy, and by the burning of an American flag. This they did. Of the estimated 3000 people who went to Grosvenor Square, approximately

50, supported by a further 200 pushing from behind, attempted to break through the police cordon around the Embassy.

The events of 27 October were situated at a point of transition for the British Left. Following the disillusionment with the 1966 Labour government, young radicals were increasingly moving away from the 'reformism' of the Labour Left and of the Peace Movement, and moving towards the more radical perspectives developed by the international student and anti-war movements. This process was by no means complete by 27 October, however, and consequently, both the consciousness of the participants and the form of events were characterized by an uneasy and essentially ambivalent amalgam of reformist, radical and revolutionary elements. However, it is exactly this ambivalence which makes the Demonstration story a particularly interesting case study. For as Stuart Hall has pointed out, the role of the media in the labelling process is at its maximum in situations which are unfamiliar or ambiguous.[4]

The development of the demonstration story

On 5 September, over one and a half months before the event, *The Times* carried a front-page story headed, MILITANT PLOT FEARED IN LONDON, describing how detectives had discovered that 'militant extremists' planned to use the main march as a cover for attacks on police and public buildings. The plotters were identified as anarchists and American students and the expected level of violence was explicitly compared to the situation in Paris in May. Several elements in this initial story are worth noting. First, the peaceful nature of the main march is contrasted with the expected violent behaviour of 'militant extremists'. This definition of the situation served to concentrate attention on the form of actions to the neglect of underlying causes. More particularly, the implicit equation of militancy with violence bypassed the counter-definitions of these terms offered by the participants. In this way the march was emptied of its radical political content and the way was left open for its appropriation into the consensus on the grounds of its peaceful form. This same exclusive attention to form also characterized the choice of the May *événements* as a context within which to situate the events of 27 October. At the level of form both situations are linked by the image of street fighting between police and student demonstrators, but at the level of underlying causes then are crucial differences. The immediate point is that the fighting in Paris originated in a 'police riot' in which police attacked a peaceful student demonstration with tear gas and baton charges, whereas in London the demonstrators were expected to initiate the confrontation.

More fundamentally, however, the Paris street fighting was only one manifestation of a widely based opposition to De Gaulle's government which culminated in a general strike. In *The Times* story, however, this crucial context was cut away, leaving only the image of street fighting. This same basic image was further reinforced and amplified by the reference to American students studying in Britain. This simultaneously served to evoke the police-demonstrators confrontations at the Democratic Party Convention in Chicago which had occurred a few weeks before in August, and to attribute the violence expected in London to the intervention of outsiders. These elements were reiterated and confirmed when *The Guardian* published essentially the same story on 11 October. From this point on, the press coverage was devoted to extending and amplifying these basic themes.

The main preoccupations of the press coverage in the two weeks preceding 27 October were summed up in the heading of a *Guardian* feature, THE WHO AND THE HOW OF PROTEST. What was missing was any consideration or analysis of the historical context or of the political perspective offered by the organizers. Instead, attention concentrated on the likely form of events, on how much violence could be expected, and on the identity of the organizers. It was made clear that the 'militants' came from 'outside' Britain and therefore outside the consensus. A great deal was made of the fact that French students were expected to participate in the Demonstration, and it was repeatedly pointed out that the leading organizers of both the main and breakaway marchers, Tariq Ali and Abhimanya Manchanda, were not English. The Demonstration was also firmly linked to the Student Movement through the attention given to the planned occupation of the London School of Economics. This stress on students to the neglect of other groups involved served to define the event as essentially part of a passing fashion, rather than as arising out of permanently structured conflicts of interest. The *Daily Express* extended this theme with a story headed, MISS TIMPSON: DEB DEMONSTRATOR, about a débutante who saw the main march as a new and fashionable addition to the 'season'. She was not against the Vietnam War, she told reporters, only against the Wealth Tax. This idea that participants were essentially play-acting and had no consistent political perspective was reinforced by the frequent use of imagery from the cinema and theatre, viz.: ' . . . the Leading Performers', 'supporting cast' *(Daily Express)* 'a Hollywood mock-up' *(The Guardian)*.

The image of the event presented by the national press on 26 October was essentially that set out in the original *Times* story. The 'newsworthiness' of the event was identified with the expectation that 'militant students' led by 'foreign agitators' would use the cover of the main march to engage in extensive street fighting with the police and to attack public buildings. The main march itself was emptied of its radical political content and defined as a performance—bizarre, but essentially within the framework of consensus politics.

On the day there were relatively few incidents of confrontation between police and demonstrators but having committed themselves to a news image based on this expectation, the newspapers proceeded as though the event had been characterized by street fighting. Of the six national dailies studied in detail, *The Times, Daily Express, Sun* and *Daily Sketch* devoted over 60 per cent of their coverage to the events in Grosvenor Square, the *Daily Mirror* 55 per cent and *The Guardian* 41 per cent. Further, events were described in terms of how the police, representing 'us', the consensus, faced and overcame the violent challenge of militant outsiders.

Headlines included:

POLICE WIN BATTLE OF GROSVENOR SQUARE AS 6,000 ARE REPELLED
(The Times)

FRINGE FANATICS FOILED AT BIG DEMONSTRATION—WHAT THE BOBBIES FACED *(Daily Express)*

THE DAY THE POLICE WERE WONDERFUL *(Daily Mirror)*

This definition of the situation was underlined by a news photograph of a policeman apparently being held by one demonstrator and kicked in the face by another. All the papers except *The Times* featured this picture on the front page. Despite this concentration on confrontation, the newspapers recognized that there was a considerable gap between the prediction and the actuality. As the *Daily Mirror* caption to the 'kick' picture put it:

the boot goes in on a policeman already bent almost double as he grappled with a demonstrator. Provocative incidents like this . . . were not commonplace.

Two explanations were provided for the relative infrequency of confrontation. It was argued that the police had been both more efficient and more restrained than those in Paris or Chicago, and secondly it was suggested that the majority of demonstrators had rejected the violent tactics advocated by the 'militants' and foreign elements and had accepted the 'British way of doing things' through peaceful protest.

Summing up we may say that the image and explanation of the event presented by the news coverage coincided and served to reinforce the more general definition of the overall political situation elaborated by parliamentary politicians and other legitimated holders of political power. Further, it is important to recognize that, despite difference of emphasis and presentation, the same basic news image of the event was shared by all the Fleet Street dailies. It cut right across the conventional, 'quality/popular', 'Right/Left' distinctions. It was also shared by both television networks.

The organization of the news process: Sources of coincidence

Journalists generally resist any suggestion that there is an underlying pattern to news production. As one reporter commented on the Demonstration study:

> Our product is put together by large and shifting groups of people, often in a hurry, out of an assemblage of circumstances that is never the same twice. Newspapers and news programmes could almost be called random reactions to random events. Again and again, the main reason why they turn out as they do is accident—accident of a kind which recurs so haphazardly as to defeat statistical examination.[5]

The results of the Demonstration study, however, clearly contradict this viewpoint. From observation of the cumulative process of selection and interpretation which precedes the final news presentation, it is clear that far from being 'random reactions to random events', the selections made are the logical outcome of particular ways of working and of a shared set of criteria of what makes material newsworthy. These routines and assumptions are common to all newsmen and combine to produce both the basic uniformity of news output and the coincidence between the news image of political events and the more general definition of the situation as one of consensus. This section is therefore devoted to examining these routines and criteria of news value.

The first determinant of the news process is the fundamental fact that newspapers operate on a 24-hour cycle. This means that situations about which information can be gathered and processed during this time space, stand a much better chance of being selected for presentation as news than situations which take longer to unfold. This 'event orientation' of news has several important consequences. First, it means that certain aspects of a situation pass the news threshold while others remain more or less permanently below it. A coup or an assassination attempt in a developing country, for example, is far likelier to be reported than a continuing guerrilla war. Similarly, the 27 October Demonstration passed the news threshold whereas the gradual development of disillusionment with the parliamentary process among an increasing number of radicals did not. Secondly, by focusing attention on the immediate form of contemporary events, on what happened and who was involved, news ignores the underlying content of the situation. The coverage of the Demonstration, for example, focused almost entirely on incidents of violence and on the personalities involved, and bypassed completely any consideration of the demonstrators' political perspective. Thirdly, the 'event orientation' of news means that the situations portrayed inevitably appear to be short-lived and transitory. Lastly, in the absence of any analysis of the underlying structural preconditions, events are presented as being 'caused' either by the intervention of natural forces (e.g., floods, earthquakes) or by the immediately preceding actions of particular individuals or groups. As a consequence of the 'event orientation' therefore, the definitions and explanations of situations offered by news presentation coincide with those provided by the political élite. Thus, radical political activity appears as essentially ephemeral, and confined to a small group of outsiders, rather than as the product of historically structured and continuing inequalities in the distribution of wealth and power.

Because it offers no analysis of the relationship between particular events and underlying structural processes, news is fundamentally ahistorical. However, this does not mean that news contains no view of the relationship between events occurring at different times. On the contrary it presents a very specific version of these links. In order to explain this news version of history, however, it is necessary to turn to the other major factor governing the news process—the newspapers' need to attract readers.

In order to remain commercially viable in an increasingly competitive situation it is not enough for a newspaper to reproduce itself once a day, it must also offer a product which is attractive to sufficient readers to maintain sales and advertising revenue. This need to produce something which is both intelligible and interesting to readers, therefore, becomes the main criterion governing the selection and presentation of material.

The need to render information intelligible to the reader means that despite their fundamentally ahistorical nature news stories cannot be presented in a complete vacuum. The journalist must therefore situate the event within a framework which is already familiar to the reader. This is especially necessary if the situation is new or ambiguous as was the case with the Demonstration. As Galtung put it, all 'news' is to some extent 'olds'.[6] Thus, the Dominican crisis of 1965 was approached from within the image of Cuba; Prague in 1968 was translated into Hungary in 1956,[7] and the Attica prison shootings were seen as another 'Riot in Cell Block 11'. In each case, both the structural preconditions of the situation and the political perspectives of the participants were cut away leaving only the immediate image. In the case of Attica for example, the news coverage bypassed the fact that the situation was part of the long-term politicization of American prisons and that the demands of the Attica inmates were explicitly radical (e.g., free passage to a non-Imperialist country), and concentrated instead on the familiar scenario of guards, shotguns and rioting prisoners.[8]

The choice of the May events in Paris, and later the Chicago riots, as a context for the Demonstration story, had several obvious advantages in news terms. First, their comparative recency guaranteed that they were still both familiar and salient to readers. Secondly, they encapsulated all the essential themes of the Demonstration story—street fighting, students and foreign militants—in a single dramatic image which made immediate sense of an ambiguous situation. The news process therefore establishes its own links between situations, links not at the level of underlying structures and processes but at the level of immediate forms and images. Situations are identified as the same if they look the same. In this way news rewrites history for immediate popular consumption.

Having selected a basic framework within which to interpret an event, the next problem is to capture the readers' interest. The solution is to present the material as a dramatic performance in which the action is unfolded through the actions and speech of certain central characters and the conflicts between them. Readers are therefore placed in the role of spectators, encouraged to participate vicariously in the performance through projecting themselves into the situation and/or identifying with the central characters. In many ways therefore newspapers are part of the entertainment business. Certainly, there is a constant and unending search for the offbeat, the bizarre, the 'new', the spectacular, but like the pornography trade, the number of basic situations and plots offered by news presentations is strictly limited.

The presentation of events in terms of the theatrical and spectacular follows logically from journalists' conceptions of what attracts their readers, but it nevertheless has important consequences. As noted above, by presenting the Demonstration participants as performers within a spectacle, the press coverage emptied their actions of their radical political content. For once the Demonstration was conceived as play-acting and therefore both transitory and 'not for real', it became simultaneously both entertaining and capable of being contained and assimilated. To some extent the problem is implicit in the form of mass demonstrations. As John Berger has pointed out, militant mass demonstrations are intended as dramatic 'rehearsals of revolutionary awareness', expressions of 'political ambitions before the political means necessary to realize them have been created'.[9] This was certainly the case with the 27 October Demonstration. However, by choosing to work through the medium of public spectacle, demonstrations invariably open themselves to the possibility that they will be appropriated as entertainment.

The conception of news as dramatic entertainment working through the presentation of personalized conflict is certainly not novel, but it has recently been considerably reinforced by changes in the general economic situation of the national daily press.

The mid-1950s saw the simultaneous ending of wartime restrictions on newsprint and the introduction of commercial television as an alternative news medium and advertising outlet. As a result newspapers, especially the 'populars', found themselves involved in an increasingly stringent competition for a declining number of readers against a background of steadily rising costs. In order to survive, therefore, newspapers had to broaden their readership base. This had a number of consequences.

In order to attract readers with a wide range of political views, papers could not afford to be too obviously partisan. This meant that newspapers like the *Daily Mirror* and *Daily Herald* which had hitherto supported the Labour Party, the trade unions and the Co-operative Movement ceased to ventriloquize these sections of working-class interest, and sought instead to attract new consumer groups.[10] This competition for the 'middle ground' readership had several consequences for the content and presentation of material. In the first place emphasis shifted away from the public sphere of production to the private sphere of consumption and leisure. There were fewer political stories and more human interest items and more attention was given to areas such as fashion, holidays and entertainment.[11] Thus, newspapers became more and more a part of the entertainment business, part of the society of the spectacle. This shift coincided with the general ideological proposition that in an era of full employment and increasing leisure, the primary focus of social life and interests was no longer the work place but the privatized family.

In addition to this shift in emphasis, the search for new readership also reinforced the notion of news as the 'objective' reporting of a pre-existing and definable social reality. This notion had long been a component of the journalistic ethos but was greatly strengthened by the fact that when television news was introduced both channels were placed under a statutory obligation to be impartial. Increasingly, therefore, newspapers were obliged to work within this definition of news. Inevitably 'objectivity' in newspaper terms boiled down to an increased concentration on events as this avoided the partisanship implicit in the consideration of underlying issues. Thus, the presentation of stories in terms of 'Us' (the workers and people) versus 'Them' (the bosses and politicians) was replaced by a definition in terms of 'The National Interest'. Only the *Morning Star* retained its political affiliations and with them the rhetoric of conflict. The difference is evident from the following two extracts from editorials on the clash between the Government and railwaymen over the use of the Industrial Relations Act during the rail go-slow in April 1972:

> The Tories have decided on a showdown with the Unions to try to safeguard and increase the profits of Big Business. This is what lies behind all their talk of 'the public interest'. *(Morning Star)*.

> We are not confronted with a case of the Government versus the Unions but of the People versus the People—confrontation in which all will equally suffer. *(Daily Mirror)*.

The *Morning Star* was the only national daily to reject the prevailing news image of the Demonstration and to give extended coverage to both the underlying causes of the situation and to the political perspective of the participants. As we have seen the other papers avoided any discussion of these aspects and concentrated instead on the form of events and the issue of violence. This stress follows logically from the notion of 'objectivity' and the perceived need to avoid partisanship, but it nevertheless coincides with the fundamental proposition of consensus politics—that there are no longer any fundamental conflicts of interest.

Finally, the fact that newspapers are increasingly in competition for an overlapping audience tends to increase the similarities in their reporting. The development of the Demonstration story, for example, shows a clear pattern in which one paper followed another by carrying the latter's story either in its own late editions or on the following day. There is an almost obsessive concern with being scooped. The printing of the original *Times* story, for example, was stimulated by the fact that the London *Evening News* had carried a similar story the previous evening. As the *Evening News* does not have a complete national circulation this did not constitute a full scoop and consequently *The Times* gave essentially the same story a front-page splash the following day. This element of competition means that newspapers, especially those with a small reporting staff relative to the space that has to be filled, will print a story while it is still 'soft', i.e., still at the stage of rumour and probability rather than 'hard fact'. During the development of the Demonstration story, for example, *The Guardian* consistently picked up stories a day or so before the other papers. Having once appeared in print however, both the basic themes of the story and the context within which it is interpreted become 'set' and subsequent coverage is obliged to work within this framework. This was clearly the case with the Demonstration story. Only those elements that fitted the image presented in the original *Times* story were selected for printing. In this process newspapers become locked in a cycle of self-infatuation which takes them further and further from the underlying reality of the situation.

Important as reader interest is, however, as Jeremy Tunstall has pointed out, it is not the only criterion governing news selection, for some areas of news bear little or no direct relationship to revenue.[12] Foreign correspondents, for example, are expensive to maintain and the stories which they provide have only limited appeal to the general reader. Yet, in May 1971, of the two leading popular dailies, the *Daily Express* had twenty foreign correspondents (the same number as *The Times*) and the *Daily Mirror* had thirteen.[13] Similarly, compared with sports and crime news, parliamentary stories are known to have low reader appeal. Yet, within the newspapers themselves, foreign and Lobby correspondents have the highest status and are disproportionately represented among editors.[14] Thus a hierarchy of newsworthiness is established in which the actions of members of the legitimated political élites have the highest rank. There are a number of obvious advantages in a newspaper concentrating on the actions and speeches of politicians. Firstly, they conserve the organization's resources and they can be comfortably handled within the daily cycle of news production. In fact most politicians actively attempt to gear their actions and speeches to newsroom deadlines. Secondly, they can be defined as events and presented in terms of personalized conflicts within and between the two major parties epitomized in the gladiatorial combat between the two leaders: HEATH SLAMS WILSON, WILSON ACCUSES HEATH. Thirdly, the structure of parliamentary politics, of dissent and debate within and between the parties, fits perfectly into the structure of news, of drama and conflict within a familiar framework, of 'news' within 'olds'. In fact the one is an analogue of the other. Fourthly, reporting political speeches, shifts the responsibility for the accuracy of the substantive content away from the newspaper and on to the source. On Wednesday 16 October, for example, *The Guardian* carried a report that Mr Arthur Carr (prospective Conservative candidate for East Ham South) claimed to have information from 'impeccable sources' that students on three educational flights from Britain to Cuba were in fact going 'to learn the techniques of insurrection and sabotage'. Thus, the fact that a political figure with high credibility had made this accusation, enabled the paper to print a highly newsworthy story without having to take the responsibility for its substantive accuracy. Lastly, the feeling of 'being where the action is' reinforces newspapers' image of themselves as being both an indispensable and influential channel of political communication and a necessary watchdog on the abuses of power. These factors therefore combine to make parliamentary events and diplomatic exchanges prominent categories of news. However, simply by defining parliament as the focus of power and political action and by identifying parliamentary debate as the most appropriate and efficient way of resolving issues and managing dissent, news coverage reinforces the essential definitions of consensus politics. Of course the press is not an entirely passive channel for parliamentary opinion. Its persona as the Fourth Estate stimulates a continual search for corruption and miscalculation. However, exposés are as event- and personality-oriented as any other sort of news story. Consequently, corruption is presented as the result of the personal failings or machinations of particular individuals or groups, and the solution offered is to replace the bad apples with good ones. In this way the consensus is presented as self-regulating, as much able to identify and deal with threats from within as challenges from outside. The labelling process is essentially the same in both cases and the end result is to leave the basic framework of assumption undisturbed.

The various criteria and assumptions underlying the definition of news are not generally made explicit within the news organization, but remain as the implicit basis of daily decision making. Hence they are absorbed gradually and more or less unconsciously through the process of building successful careers as a journalist. A reporter must constantly 'second guess' what the editor wants, and each time he sees his copy being accepted, modified or 'spiked' he learns a little more about what it means to be a reporter. More specifically, he learns what it means to work for a particular paper with a particular image of itself. An interesting example of inadequate 'second guessing' occurred during the actual Demonstration.

The *Daily Mirror* had drafted in a *Sunday Mirror* reporter to do a background 'colour' story on the rally in Hyde Park. Unfortunately, his ideas of what was worth selecting and presenting did not coincide with those of the *Mirror* news desk. Because there is always far more copy than space to print it, reporters are expected to provide basic information which the sub-editor can then re-arrange or re-write as a coherent story. The house reporting style therefore tends toward the deadpan, and questions of style and presentation are considered a matter for the 'subs'. Unfortunately, the *Sunday Mirror* reporter was not aware of this basic but unwritten rule, and turned in a piece full of 'purple patches' viz:

> Here and there boys and girls began to neck on the littered bruised grass and lips that had shortly before spat out the four letter words now pressed against other lips in the dark.

This piece was politely but firmly rejected. At a paper like *The Guardian* with more news space to fill and a much smaller staff, reporters are required to present completed stories and consequently they are expected to pay more attention to style. Despite these differences of emphasis, however, the basic assumptions which guide the selection and presentation of material are shared by both types of paper. Even before he gets to Fleet Street, a young reporter on a local paper is likely to absorb a number of crucial tenets. The stress on competency with shorthand, for example, implies not only an attachment to formal accuracy but also to the notions of 'objectivity' and personalization.[15] More importantly, the self-image of local papers as representing the interests of the local community implies an acceptance of the central notion of consensus.[16] On graduating to Fleet Street the young reporter finds himself in increasingly stringent competition for a declining number of prestigious jobs as specialist correspondents or editors. Promotion therefore involves the internalization of the norms of these élite news groups, and as we have suggested, these tend to coincide with those of the political élite.

This socialization process is not entirely automatic, however, for a number of reporters are aware of the dynamics involved and in varying degrees resist the role they are expected to play. This may lead to a prolonged guerrilla war between reporters and editors. During the Demonstration for example, a senior *Daily Mirror* reporter sent to cover Grosvenor Square refused to phone any copy to the news desk. This he argued demonstrated his independence of the editorial staff and their essential dependence on him. However, as a reporter's career prospects depend largely on his ability to get the story before, or at least at the same time as, his rivals, the tactic of withholding information is of limited applicability. Another possible tactic is for a reporter to get his own view of the situation across by 'playing the system'. Gaye Tuckman relates how by manipulating the criteria of objectivity and putting quotation marks around terms such as 'New Left', a radical young American reporter managed to persuade the conservative news editor to print an account of a draft resistance demonstration.[17] This tactic is ultimately self-defeating however, for the quotation marks still serve to cast doubt on the legitimacy and status of the radical groups involved, and the event-orientation still excludes consideration of the underlying issues and causes. The possibilities of 'playing the system' are limited, however, and, ultimately, a reporter who remains in Fleet Street is likely to resolve the contradictions between his professional role and his personal convictions through resort to self-censorship. As one reporter explained to Eamonn McCann:

> No journalist I have met writes what he knows will be cut. What would be the point? If he has a story which he knows will cause controversy back at the news desk he will water it down to make it acceptable.[18]

Some of this self-censored material finds its way into publications like *Private Eye* or *Open Secret,* but more often than not it is forgotten. He may not like this situation but if he is to be successful as a journalist working for a capitalistically based national daily, he must eventually accept it. As Marx complained to Engels, about the *New York Tribune,* 'It is really loathsome to have to think oneself lucky that a filthy rag like that takes one on . . . ' but 'For all the talk about independence one is tied to the newspaper and its public, especially if one gets paid cash as I do.'[19]

Towards the audience

I have argued that various general factors within the process of news production served to bring about a coincidence between the news image of the 27 October Demonstration and the more general definition of the political situation evolved by the political élite, with the consequence that the two became mutually reinforcing. It now remains to see how far this definition of the situation was accepted first by the participants (the police and the demonstrators) and secondly by the general public.

Certainly on 27 October both the police and the demonstrators expected violence, and these expectations found their concrete expression in the very extensive police preparations and in the establishment of a medical centre at the London School of Economics, then occupied by the demonstrators. However, although there was a general acceptance of the likely form of events there were diametrically opposed views of the likely causes. Thus, the police prepared on the assumption that the demonstrators would initiate violence, while the marchers assumed that the violence was likely to come from the police, as it had in Paris and Chicago. At a more general level, however, evidence suggests that a sizeable proportion of the marchers rejected the overall definition of the situation provided by the news media and the political élite and accepted instead the radical political perspectives of the organizers. The question remains, however, as to how long radical groups can continue to act both within and against the spectacle without internalizing and acting out their ascribed role as 'deviants' and outsiders and hence reinforcing the very processes they are seeking to challenge. In order to answer this question we need to study the development of radical groups over time in order to see how far they take the news presentation of themselves and their motivations into account when formulating their strategy.

As part of the Demonstration study, a small survey was undertaken to see how a sample of non-participants received the story. Despite the many limitations of the resulting information, there were clear indications that these members of the audience, at least, defined and interpreted the event from within the framework provided by the news coverage. Recent studies of white adolescents' definitions of race relations in Britain, and of adults' images of crime and criminals, have produced similar findings.[20] Again these results are indicative rather than conclusive, but the evidence now beginning to accumulate strongly suggests that the news media do provide many people with the framework of definitions and explanations with which they approach situations. Further, this process is self-perpetuating. Thus, the fact that particular images and definitions are known to have wide popular currency makes them more likely to be selected by news organizations as a framework within which to present novel or ambiguous situations. This in turn serves to amplify these images and to keep them circulating as part of the common pool of available stereotypes. On 7 February 1972 for example, over three and a half years after the Demonstration, the *Sun* ran a feature on police heroism in the face of criminal violence. This feature was headed by the 'kick' picture from Grosvenor Square, thus both evoking and further reinforcing the original news image of the event as a confrontation between police and violent extremists. It also served to underline the identification of 'militant' political action with both violence and criminality.

Conclusion

In this paper I have argued that the image of the 27 October Demonstration coincided with, and reinforced, the more general definition of the political situation evolved by the political élite and that in this way the press played an indispensable role in the process of managing conflict and dissent, and legitimating the present distribution of power and wealth within British capitalism.

However, I have also suggested that this coincidence is best explained as the result not of any direct collusion or conspiracy between the press and the politicians, but as the logical outcome of the present organization of news gathering and processing and the assumptions upon which it rests. This is not to say that legitimated power holders do not exercise any direct control over the news process: they do. In the first place, legal restrictions such as the Official Secrets Act, 'D' notices and *sub judice* rulings impose considerable limitations on what newspapers can print and when. In addition there are undoubtedly occasions when politicians bring various forms of moral suasion to bear on newspapermen. These occasions are relatively rare, however, and in most cases are strongly resisted. Certainly they are neither sufficiently frequent nor sufficiently widespread to account for the consistency of newspaper coverage. Rather, the resort to direct intervention may be seen as indicative of a breakdown in the 'normal' working relationship between journalists and politicians through which information and 'stories' are exchanged for coverage and publicity. This day-to-day reciprocity is maintained because it is functional for both parties, newspapers need information and politicians need publicity, but it nevertheless serves to sustain and reinforce the coincidence between the definitions of the situation given by the legitimated politicians and those presented in the national press.

This paper has dealt exclusively with newspapers, but the Demonstration study clearly showed that television news tends to work within the same basic framework of routines and assumptions. This is scarcely surprising since most television newsmen have worked on newspapers. However, the fact that television is first and foremost a visual medium means that television news output is primarily determined by the availability of film footage and that the commentary is written around the screen images. Consequently, television news coverage tends to be even more 'event-oriented' than the corresponding press coverage. Interestingly enough, this limitation is often elevated to a virtue by stressing the immediacy of television coverage as against the *déjà vu* of newspaper reporting. Any discussion of television news would be incomplete without an analysis of the unique position of the BBC and more particularly of the nature of the 'special relationship' between the corporation and the government of the day. Such an analysis is however beyond the scope of the present paper.

I have attempted to illustrate some general points with examples drawn from one particular case study and it may well be that this case was to some extent atypical. However, recent studies of newspaper and television news output on race relations, industrial strikes, student sit-ins and drug taking[21] suggest that many of the forms of presentation discussed in this paper are common to a whole range of news stories and may be a feature of 'news' *per se*. Whether or not this is the case is a question which deserves urgent study.

REFERENCES

1. Quoted in *The Times*, Monday, 28 February 1972, p. 2.
2. The research reported here is part of a larger study which is fully reported in *Demonstrations and communication: A case study* (Harmondsworth, Penguin Books, 1970). This study was the result of a collaborative effort by members of the Centre for Mass Communication Research at Leicester University. I am particularly indebted to my co-authors, Professor James D. Halloran and Philip Elliott, for their comments on the press study. I am also indebted to Peter Golding, Stan Cohen and Jock Young for their comments on previous drafts of this present paper.
3. Jeremy Tunstall, *Journalists at work* (London, Constable, 1971), pp. 264–5.
4. See: Stuart Hall 'Watching the box', *New society,* No. 411, 3 August 1970, pp. 295–6. Also Stuart Hall, 'Deviancy, politics and the media', in *Deviance and social control,* M. McIntosh and P. Rock (eds.) (London, Tavistock Publications, 1973).
5. John Whale, 'News', *The Listener,* 15 October 1970, Volume 84, No. 2168, p. 510.
6. Johan Galtung and Mari Ruge (1955) 'The structure of foreign news', *Journal of International Peace Research,* No. 1, 1965, pp. 64–90. Extract reprinted in this Reader.
7. Theodore Draper, 'The Dominican Crisis', *Commentary,* December 1965, J. Galtung (1968) *The role of television in the time of international crisis,* Paper given at September 1968 seminar on Television as a Political Power Factor, at Hanko.
8. The example of the Attica shootings was suggested by Stan Cohen.
9. John Berger, 'The nature of mass demonstrations', in *Selected articles and essays: The look of things* (Harmondsworth, Penguin Books, 1972), pp. 246–8.
10. See for example, Mark Abrams, *The newspaper reading public of tomorrow* (London, Odhams Press Ltd., 1964).
11. This shift was pointed out by Mr James Curran of the Open University during a discussion of his recent research on the British press since 1945.
12. Jeremy Tunstall (1971), op. cit., p. 7.
13. Philip Elliott and Peter Golding, *The news media and foreign affairs* (University of Leicester, Centre for Mass Communication Research, mimeo, 1971), p. 15.

14. Jeremy Tunstall (1971), op. cit., p. 47 and Table 3:13, p. 110.
15. Oliver Boyd-Barrett, 'Journalism recruitment and training: problems in professionalization', in Jeremy Tunstall (ed.) *Media sociology* (London, Constable, 1970), pp. 181–201.
16. Ian Jackson, *The provincial press and the community* (Manchester University Press, 1971), pp. 40, 87.
17. Gaye Tuckman, *Objectivity as strategic ritual: An examination of newspapermen's notions of objectivity.* (Paper presented to the 66th Annual Meeting of the American Sociological Association, 1971).
18. Quoted in Eamonn McCann, *The British press in Northern Ireland* (Northern Ireland Socialist Research Centre, 1971), p. 26.
19. Quoted in Werner Blumberg, *Karl Marx* (London, New Left Books, 1972), p. 127.
20. Paul Hartmann and Charles Husband, 'The mass media and racial conflict', *Race,* XII (January 1971), pp. 267–82. Reprinted in this Reader. The findings on images of crime result from the as yet unpublished research of Mr Paul Croll of the Leicester Centre.
21. See Stuart Hall (1973) op. cit., Jock Young, 'Mass media drugs and deviancy', in McIntosh and Rock, *Deviance and social control;* John Downing, *'Class' and 'Race' in the British news media* (unpublished mimeo communication, 1971).

The determinations of news photographs*

STUART HALL

I. The level of signification in photographs

In the modern newspaper, the text is still an essential element, the photograph an optional one. Yet photographs, when they appear, add new dimensions of meaning to a text. As Roland Barthes has observed, 'pictures. . . . are more imperative than writing, they impose meaning at one stroke, without analysing or diluting it'.[1]

II. The codes of connotation

First, we must turn to the *codes* which make signification possible. It is principally codes of connotation which concern us here. Connotative codes are the configurations of meaning which permit a sign to signify, in addition to its denotative reference, *other, additional implied meanings*. These configurations of meaning are forms of social knowledge, derived from the social practices, the knowledge of institutions, the beliefs and the legitimations which exist in a diffused form within a society, and which order that society's apprehension of the world in terms of dominant meaning-patterns. Codes of denotation are precise, literal, unambiguous: the photo-image of a sweater *is* (denotes) an object to be worn, recognizable as a sweater and not as a coat, a hat or a walking stick. Codes of connotation are more open-ended. In the connnotative domain of everyday speech *sweater* may also connote 'keeping warm', a 'warm garment'—and thus by further elaboration 'the coming of winter', a 'cold day', and so on. But in the domain of the specialized discourse (sub-code) of fashion, *sweater* may connote 'a fashionable style of *haute couture'*, a certain 'informal style' of dress, and so on. Set against the right background, and positioned in the domain of romantic discourse, *sweater* may connote 'long autumn walk in the woods'.[2]

---

*Extracts from 'The determinations of news photographs' by Stuart Hall which appeared in *Cultural Studies,* no. 3 (Centre for Cultural Studies, University of Birmingham).

At the expressive level, the photo signifies within the lexicon of expressive features distributed throughout the culture of which the reader is a member. This lexicon is not restricted to photography, or indeed to the domain of visual representation. The same 'cues' which allow us to decode the expressive features of the photographed subject are also employed by almost everyone when they 'read' everyday subjects and occasions in an expressive way. Expressive codes depend on our competence to resolve a set of gestural, non-linguistic features (signifiers) into a specific expressive configuration (signified)—an accomplishment which is cultural, not technical. It is part of the 'social stock of knowledge at hand' in any culture that a set of bodily or physical features serves as indices of recognizable expressions. Members of a culture are competent to use this 'knowledge' whether face-to-face with the living subject or a visual transcription of it. The main difference is that in social situations we have available to us a richer set of signifying cues from which to distinguish an expressive pattern: in addition to body position, facial expression, gesture, we have movement, situation, interaction and speech. The photograph therefore represents a *truncated version* of this cultural code.

The front-page photos of Mr Maudling on the day of his resignation over the Poulson affair provide us with a good example of this. The *Daily Mail*, for example, interpreted Mr Maudling as 'angry': MAUDLING—THE ANGRY MAN. The photo—head on hands only—certainly supports this reading, though other descriptions are equally plausible: 'thoughtful', for example, or 'listening patiently'. The interpretation is therefore strengthened by a caption—*Mr Reginald Maudling—angry, disgusted, strongly resentful*. Here the caption selects and prefers one of the possible readings, then amplifies it. The *Sun*, however, interprets Mr Maudling's resignation as 'tragedy': THE TRAGEDY OF MR MAUDLING. It is almost the same photo as the *Mail's*—certainly the same occasion (a Tory Party Conference?). But a tilt in the angle, a shift of the position of the head, above all, a lowering of the eyes and a slight suggesting of 'misting over', tilts the reading from 'anger' to 'tragedy'. The *Express* story has overtones of tragedy too—*Reginald Maudling sacrificed his political career yesterday. . .* —but its headline and sub-head is more non-committal: I'LL QUIT—MY WAY. *Exit—Alone in a Car*. The photo—of Maudling 'exiting alone in a car'—reads less tragically than the *Sun* photo—tense, abstracted, looking 'to one side', preoccupied by inner turmoil. But the 'tragic' face on the *Express* front page is not Maudling's but Heath's! *Mr Heath After His Commons Announcement*

DAILY MAIL

Photo: Associated Newspapers

SUN

Photo: United Press International

DAILY EXPRESS

Photo: London Express

DAILY MIRROR

DAILY TELEGRAPH

Photo: United Press International

(caption, below an extremely solemn Heath photo—this time it is the Prime Minister's eyes which tend to 'mist over with emotion'). The *Mirror* and the *Telegraph* use the same photo: the *Telegraph* denotatively, the *Mirror* to support a 'reading'. But since this photo is generalized enough to be linked with a vast range of expressions, it requires, in the *Mirror,* an extra linguistic anchor, which the caption supplies: *A look of resignation. . . from Maudling.* It is a very common practice for the captions to news photographs to tell us, in words, exactly how the subject's expression *ought to be read*.

In all five instances, the type of exposition is 'head-and-shoulders-only', enlarged. Both the composition—excluding other inessential details of body and setting—and the enlargement—which highlights the face and eyes, the most expressive parts of the body—enhance the power of the expressive dimension. This has an ideological significance, since its function is to exploit the expressive code in such a way as to inflect or displace the story, away from its political point, towards some aspect of Maudling, *the man*. The exposition seems to pose an implicit question—'what do we most want to know about the Maudling affair at this moment?'—and answers it implicitly: 'how does *he* feel?', 'how is *he* taking it?' The exception to this treatment is *The Times,* which produces a version of the now-classic photo of 'public figure relaxing at home after momentous decision'. Mr Maudling, himself, gave the lead to this angle, with his reference, in his resignation letter, to 'the glare of publicity which. . . engulfs the private life even of [my] family'. *The Times,* then, picks up this interpretation, and elaborates it. Its photo—of *Mr Maudling, who resigned yesterday as Home Secretary, photographed last year with his wife in their home at Essendon, Hertfordshire*—shows him in short-sleeved check shirt, standing with his wife, who is holding the cat, in their breakfast room before a table laden with fruit, peppers etc. This photo, rich enough in connoted social detail, also makes an ideological point: it produces the classic counterposition—public figure/private man—which is such a central myth in our learned wisdom about men weighed-down-by/freed-from the cares and burdens of high office. It generates what we might call the *sentimental effect,* one of the most compelling ties which bind the governed to the governors.

In each case, then, the newspaper has slightly inflected the story towards a different 'news-angle' by exploiting the expressive code. But each is an inflection on a single, common theme: the displacement or mystification of the political event 'through the category of the subject'. This is the essence of the ideology of personalization. Expressive codes

THE TIMES
Photo: The Times

are one of the most powerful vehicles in the rhetoric of the news-photo for the production of *personalizing transformations*.

III. The signification of news

It is necessary to distinguish *two aspects* to the signification of news. The first is the *news value* of the photographic sign. The second is the *ideological level* of the photographic sign. 'News value' consists of the elaboration of the story (photo + text) in terms of the professional ideology of news—the common-sense understandings as to what constitutes the news in the newspaper discourse. The ideological level consists of the elaboration of the story in terms of its connoted themes and interpretations. *Formal* news values belong to the world and discourse of the newspaper, to newsmen as a professional group, to the institutional apparatuses of news-making. *Ideological* news values belong to the realm of moral-political discourse in the society as such. Ideological themes will be inflected in different ways according to the particular construction which each newspaper selects. This *inflection* will, in turn, be governed by the newspaper's policy, political orientation, its presentational values, its tradition and self-image. But behind the particular inflections of a particular news 'angle' lie, not only the 'formal' values as to 'what passes as news in our society', but the ideological themes of the society itself. Thus the death of the Duke of Windsor meets the requirement of 'formal news values' because it is unexpected, dramatic, a recent event, concerning a person of high status. But, at the ideological level, this event connotes a powerful, resonant 'set' of themes: 'Prince Charming', the 'King with the people at heart', the monarch who 'gave up the throne for the woman I love', the celebrity life of the Windsors in retirement, the late reconciliation with the Queen, the death and national burial—'the King who came Home'.

Different newspapers will inflect the news-story differently, by picking up one or more of these ideological themes. Nevertheless, in general, *any* of these particular 'news angles' intersects directly with the great ideological theme: *the Monarchy itself*. This is a point which that great chronicler of the British ideology, Bagehot, would have relished:

> The best reason why Monarchy is a strong government is that it is an intelligible government. The mass of mankind understand it, and they hardly in the world understand any other. It is often said that men are ruled by their imaginations; but it would be truer to say they are governed by the weakness of their imaginations. . . . We have no

slaves to keep down by special terrors and independent legislation. But we have whole classes unable to comprehend the idea of a constitution—unable to feel the least attachment to impersonal laws. . . . A republic has only difficult ideas in government; a Constitutional Monarchy has an easy idea too; it has a comprehensible element for the vacant many, as well as complex laws and notions for the inquiring few.[3]

The structure of 'news values' appears as a neutral, operational level in news production. It 'naturally' connects stories and events with persons: it attaches qualities, status, positions in the social world to anonymous events: it searches out the 'drama', the 'human interest', behind impersonal historical forces. Yet, these operational values are not, in the end, neutral values. As Althusser has argued, it is precisely by operating with 'the category of the *subject*', and by producing in the reader 'familiar recognitions', that a discourse becomes ideological.[4]

It appears, then, that the news-photo must lend itself to exploitation at the level of what we have called 'formal news values' first, before— secondly—it can signify an ideological theme. Thus the photo of a demonstrator kicking a policeman has news value because it witnesses to a recent event, which is dramatic, unusual, controversial. It is then possible, by linking this so-to-speak 'completed message' with an interpretation, to produce 'second-order meanings' with powerful ideological content: thus AND THEY TALK ABOUT PROVOCATION! *(The Sketch)*, WHAT THE BOBBIES FACED *(Express)*, VICTORY FOR POLICE *(Telegraph)*, THE DAY THE POLICE WERE WONDERFUL *(Mirror)*. Halloran, Elliot and Murdock[5] note how this 'kick-photo' (taken by a free-lance photographer for Keystone Agency) selectively reinforced both a previous interpretation—that the demonstration against the Vietnam War would be a 'violent' one—and a specific 'news angle'—'the editorial decision to make the police the centre of the story'.[5] In news-value terms, the police are signified as the 'centre' for the story—that is its *formal* news exploitation, grounded by the 'Kick-Photo'. In ideological terms, the police are signified as the *heroes* of the story—an interpretation connotatively amplified by the photo.

In practice, there is probably little or no distinction between these two aspects of news production. The editor not only looks at and selects the photo in terms of impact, dramatic meaning, unusualness, controversy, the resonance of the event signified, etc. (formal news values): he considers at the same time how these values will be treated or 'angled'—that is, interpretatively coded.

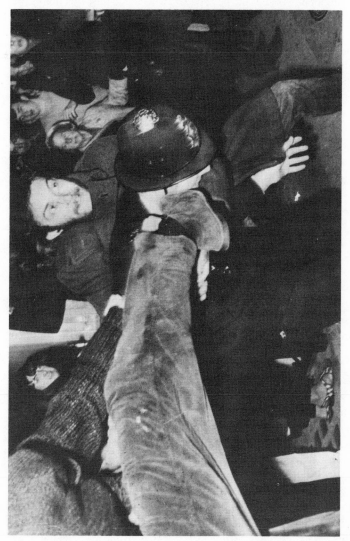

THE KICK-PHOTO

Photo: Keystone Agency

It is this double articulation—formal news values/ideological treatment—which binds the inner discourse of the newspaper to the ideological universe of the society. It is via this double articulation that the institutional world of the newspaper, whose manifest function is the profitable exchange of news values, is harnessed to the latent function of reproducing 'in dominance' the major ideological themes of society. The formal requirements of 'the news' thus appear as 'the operator' for the reproduction of ideology in the newspaper. Via 'news angles', the newspaper articulates the core themes of bourgeois society in terms of *intelligible representations*. It *translates* the legitimations of the social order into faces, expressions, subjects, settings and legends. As Bagehot observed, 'A royal family sweetens politics by the seasonable addition of nice and pretty events. It introduces irrelevant facts into the business of government, but they are facts which speak to "men's bosoms" and employ their thoughts.'

Newspapers trade in news stories. But though the need to harness a multitude of different stories and images to the profitable exchange of news values is 'determining in the last instance', this economic motive never appears on its own. The ideological function of the photographic sign is always hidden within its exchange value. The news/ideological meaning is the *form* in which these sign-vehicles are exchanged. Though the economic dialectic, here as elsewhere, determines the production and appropriation of 'symbolic' values, it is 'never active in its pure state'. The exchange value of the photographic sign is, necessarily, over-determined.

News values

By news values we mean the operational practices which allow editors, working over a set of prints, to select, rank, classify and elaborate the photo in terms of his 'stock of knowledge' as to what constitutes 'news'. 'News values' are one of the most opaque structures of meaning in modern society. All 'true journalists' are supposed to possess it: few can or are willing to identify and define it. Journalists speak of 'the news' as if events select themselves. Further, they speak as if which is the 'most significant' news story, and which 'news angles' are most salient are divinely inspired. Yet of the millions of events which occur every day in the world, only a tiny proportion ever become visible as 'potential news stories': and of this proportion, only a small fraction are actually produced as the day's news in the news media. We appear to be dealing, then, with a 'deep structure' whose function as a selective device is untransparent even to those who professionally most know how to operate it.

A story, report or photo which has the potential of being used to signify the news, seems, in the world of the daily newspaper, to have to meet at least *three* basic criteria. The story must be linked or linkable with an event, a happening, an occurrence: the event must have happened recently, if possible yesterday, preferably today, a few hours ago: the event or person 'in the news' must rank as 'newsworthy'. That is to say, news stories are concerned with *action,* with *'temporal recency'* and *'newsworthiness'.*

These three basic rules of *news visibility* organize the routines of news gathering and selection. They serve as a filter between the newspaper and its subordinate structures—special correspondents, agencies, 'stringers' in far-away places. Once these ground-rules have been satisfied, a more complex set of parameters come into play. These govern the elaboration of a story in terms of *formal news values.* Formal news values have been widely discussed in recent years, but almost always in terms of a simple list of common attributes. Thus Ostgaard[6] suggests that the most newsworthy events are unusual, unexpected events with a problematic or unknown outcome. Galtung and Ruge's[7] list is longer. It includes recency, intensity, rarity, unpredictability, clarity, ethnocentricity: also more presentational features, such as continuity, consonance, 'élite' persons and 'élite' nations, personalization, and so on. These lists help us to identify the formal elements in news making, but they do not suggest what these 'rules' index or represent. News values appear as a set of neutral, routine practices: but we need, also, to see formal news values as an ideological structure—to examine these rules as the formalization and operationalization of *an ideology of news.*

News values *do* have something to do with 'what is not (yet) widely known': with the scarce, rare, unpredictable event. In French the news— *les nouvelles*—means literally 'the new things'. This suggests that news values operate against the structured ignorance of the audience. They take for granted the restricted access of people to power, and mediate this scarcity. News stories often pivot around the unexpected, the problematic. But an event is only unexpected because it 'breaches our expectations about the world'. In fact, most news stories report minor, unexpected developments in the expected continuity of social life and of institutions. They *add to* what we already know or could predict about the world. But, whether the news dramatizes what we really do not know, or merely adds an unexpected twist to what is already known, the central fact is that news values operate as a foreground structure with a hidden 'deep structure'. News values continually play against the set of on-going beliefs and constructions about the world which most of its readers share. That is, news values require *consensus knowledge* about the world. The preoccupation with change/continuity in the news can function at either a serious or a trivial level: the breaking of the truce by the IRA or the latest model on the bonnet of the latest model at the Motor Show. Either the wholly a-typical (the IRA) or the over-typical (the Motor Show) constitute 'news' because, at the level of 'deep structure' it is the precariousness or the stability of the social order which most systematically produces visible news stories.[8]

Without this background consensus knowledge—our 'routine knowledge of social structures'—neither newsmen nor readers could recognize or understand the foreground of news stories. Newspapers are full of the actions, situations and attributes of 'élite persons'. The prestigious are part of the necessary spectacle of news production—they people and stabilize its environment. But the very notion of 'élite persons' has the 'routine knowledge of social structures' inscribed within it. Prime Ministers are 'elite persons' because of the political and institutional power which they wield. Television personalities are 'newsworthy' because celebrities serve as role-models and trend-setters for society as a whole. 'Elite persons' make the news because power, status and celebrity are monopolies in the institutional life of our society. In C. Wright Mills' phrase, 'élite persons' have colonized 'the means of history making' in our society.[9] It is this distribution of status, power and prestige throughout the institutional life of class societies which makes the remarks, attributes, actions and possessions of 'élite persons'—their very being-as-they-are—naturally newsworthy. The same could be said of 'élite nations'. If we knew nothing about Britain's historical connections throughout the world, or the preferred map of power relations, it would be difficult to account for the highly skewed structure to the profile of foreign news in British newspapers. In setting out, each day, to signify the world in terms of its most problematic events, then, newspapers must always *infer what is already known,* as a present or absent structure. 'What is already known' is not a set of neutral facts. It is a set of commonsense constructions and ideological interpretations *about* the world, which holds the society together at the level of everyday beliefs.

Regularly, newspapers make news values salient by *personifying* events. Of course people are interesting, can be vividly and concretely depicted in images, they possess qualities and so on. Personalization, however, is something else: it is the isolation of the person from his relevant social and institutional context, or the constitution of a personal subject as exclusively the motor force of history, which is under consideration here. Photos play a crucial role in this form of personification, for people—human subjects—are *par excellence* the content of news and feature photographs. 'There is no ideology except for the concrete subjects, and the destination for ideology is only made possible by the subject: meaning, *by the category of the subject* and its functioning.'[10] A newspaper can account for an event, or deepen its account, by attaching an individual to it, or by bringing personal attributes, isolated from their social context, to bear on their account as an explanation. Individuals provide a universal 'grammar of motives' in this respect—a grammar which has as its suppressed subject the universal qualities of 'human nature', and which manipulates subjects in terms of their 'possessive individualism'.[11]

The most salient, operational 'news value' in the domain of political news is certainly that of *violence*. Events not intrinsically violent can be augmented in value by the attribution of violence to them. Most news editors would give preference to a photo signifying violence in a political context. They would defend their choice on the grounds that violence represents conflict, grips the reader's interest, is packed with action, serious in its consequences. These are formal news values. But at the level of 'deep structure', political violence is 'unusual'—though it regularly happens—because it signifies the world of politics *as it ought not to be*. It shows conflict in the system at its most extreme point. And this 'breaches expectations' precisely because in our society conflict is supposed to be regulated, and politics is exactly 'the continuation of social conflict without resort to violence': a society, that is, where the legitimacy of the social order rests on the absolute inviolability of 'the rule of law'.

Formal news criteria, though operated by professionals as a set of 'rules of thumb', are no less rooted in the ideological sphere because these transactions take place out of awareness. Events enter the domain of ideology as soon as they become visible to the news-making process. Unless we clarify what it is members of a society 'normally and naturally' take as predictable and 'right' about their society, we cannot know why the semantization of the 'unpredictable' in terms of violence, etc., can, in and of itself, serve as a criterion of 'the news'.

The ideological level
This brings us directly to the second aspect of news construction—the elaboration of a news photo or story in terms of an interpretation. Here,

the photo, which already meets and has been exposed within the formal criteria of news, is linked with an interpretation which exploits its connotative value. We suggest that, rhetorically, the ideological amplication of a news photo functions in the same manner as Barthes has given to the exposition of 'modern myths'.[12] By ideological elaboration we mean the insertion of the photo into a set of thematic interpretations which permits the sign (photo), via its connoted meanings, to serve as the index of an ideological theme. Ideological news values provide a second level of signification of a ideological type to an image which already (at the denotative level) signifies. By linking the completed sign with a set of themes or concepts, the photo becomes an ideological sign. Barthes' example is of a Negro soldier in a French uniform, saluting, his eye fixed on the tricolour. This sign already conveys a meaning: 'a black soldier is giving the French salute'. But when this complete sign is linked with ideological themes—Frenchness, militariness—it becomes the first element in a second signifying chain, the message of which is that France is a great Empire, that all her sons, without colour discrimination, faithfully serve under her flag, and that there is no better answer to the detractors of an alleged colonialism than the zeal shown by this Negro in serving his so-called 'oppressors'. The photographic sign serves, then, both as the final term of the visual/denotative chain, and as the first term in the mythical/ideological chain. On this model, all news photos use the signifiers of the photographic code to produce a sign which is the denotative equivalent of its subject. But for this sign to become a news commodity, it must be linked with a concept or theme, and thus take on an interpretative or ideological dimension.

We may take two examples here. (i) The photo of the Nixons, arm in arm, walking in the White House garden. The President is smiling, giving an 'it's O.K.', 'spot on' gesture. Here the ideological message requires little or no further elaboration. The President's in a happy mood: a figure of world prominence relaxes just like other men: Nixon's on top of the world. There is no accompanying text, only a caption: and the caption, apart from identifying the actors and occasion (their daughter Tricia's wedding), redundantly mirrors the ideological theme: 'Everything in the garden's lovely'. This is very different from (ii) the 'kick-photo', where the denoted message—'a man in a crowded scene is kicking a policeman'—is ideologically 'read'—'extremists threaten law-and-order by violent acts', or 'anti-war demonstrators are violent people who threaten the state and assault policemen unfairly'. This second-order message is fully amplified in the captions and headlines.

But note also that it is slightly inflected to suit the position, presentational tradition, history and self-image of each individual newspaper. It is the linking of the photo with the themes of *violence, extremists and law-and-order, confrontation* which produces the ideological message. But this takes somewhat different forms in each paper: *The Times* inflects it *formally*—POLICE WIN BATTLE OF GROSVENOR SQUARE: the *Express* inflects it *sensationally,* accenting the 'marginal' character of the demonstrators—FRINGE FANATICS FOILED AT BIG DEMONSTRATION; the *Mirror* inflects it *deferentially*—THE DAY THE POLICE WERE WONDERFUL. Here the text is crucial in 'closing' the ideological theme and message.

It is difficult to pin down precisely how and where the themes which convert a photo into an ideological sign arise. Barthes argues that 'The concept is a constituting element of myth: if I want to decipher myths, I must somehow be able to name concepts.' But he acknowledged that 'there is no fixity in mythical concepts: they can come into being, alter, disintegrate, disappear completely'. This is because the dominant ideology, of which these themes or concepts are fragments, is an extremely plastic, diffuse and apparently a historical structure. Ideology, as Gramsci argued, seems to consist of a set of 'residues' or preconstituted elements, which can be arranged and rearranged, *bricoleur*-fashion, in a thousand different variations.[13] The dominant ideology of a society thus frequently appears redundant: we know it already, we have seen it before, a thousand different signs and messages seem to signify the same ideological meaning. It is the very mental environment in which we live and experience the world—the 'necessarily imaginary distortion' through which we continually represent to ourselves 'the [imaginary] relationship of individuals to the relations of production and the relations that derive from them'.[14] The ideological concepts embodied in photos and texts in a newspaper, then, do not produce new knowledge about the world. They produce *recognitions* of the world as we have already learned to appropriate it: 'dreary trivialities or a ritual, a functionless creed'.

Barthes suggests[15] that we can only begin to grasp these ideological concepts reflexively, by the use of ugly neologisms: e.g. 'French-ness', 'Italian-ness'. Or by the naming of very general essences: e.g. militarism, violence, 'the rule of law', the-state-of-being-on-top-of-the-world. Such concepts appear to be 'clearly organized in associative fields'. Thus 'Italian-ness' belongs to a certain axis of nationalities beside 'French-ness', 'German-ness' or 'Spanish-ness'. In any particular instance, then, the item—photo or text—perfectly indexes the thematic of the ideology it elaborates. But its general sphere of reference remains diffuse. It is there and yet it is not there. It appears, indeed, as if the general structure of a dominant ideology is almost impossible to grasp, reflexively and analytically, *as a whole*. The dominant ideology always appears, precisely, diffused in and through the particular. Ideology is therefore both the specific interpretation which any photo or text *specifies,* and the general ambience within which ideological discourse itself is carried on. It is this quality which led Althusser to argue that, while ideologies have histories, ideology as such has none.

Ideological themes exhibit another quality which makes them difficult to isolate. They appear in their forms to link or join *two* quite different levels. On the one hand they classify out the world in terms of immediate political and moral values: they give events a specific ideological reference in the here-and-now. Thus they ground the theme *in* an event: they lend it faces, names, actions, attributes, qualities. They provide ideological themes with actors and settings—they operate above all in the realm of the *subject*. The photo of the demonstrators and the policeman is thus *grounded* by its particularity, by its relation to a specific event, by its temporal relevance and immediacy to a particular historical conjuncture. In that photo the general background ideological value of the 'rule of law', the generalized ethos of attitudes against 'conflict by violent means' were *cashed* at a moment in the political history of this society when the 'politics of the street' was at its highest point, and where the whole force of public discourse and disapproval was mobilized against the rising tide of extra-parliamentary opposition movements. Yet, in that very moment, the ideological theme is distanced and universalized: it becomes *mythic*. Behind or within the concrete particularity of the event or subject we seem to glimpse the fleeting forms of a more archetypal, even archaeological-historical, knowledge which universalizes its forms. The mythic form seems, so to speak, to hover within the more immediate political message. The smiling face of Nixon is of that very time and moment—an American President at a particular moment of his political career, riding the storms of controversy and opposition of a particular historical moment with confidence. But, behind this, is the universal face of the home-spun family man of all times, arm in arm with his lady-wife, taking a turn in the garden at his daughter's wedding. In the handling of the 'kick-photo', *The Times* picks out and specifies the immediate political ideological theme—POLICE WIN BATTLE OF GROSVENOR SQUARE. But, within that message, the *Mirror* glimpses, and elaborates, a more mythic, universal theme—one which may underpin a hundred different photographs: the myth of 'our wonderful British police'.

We seem here to be dealing with a double movement within ideological discourse: the movement towards propaganda, and the movement towards myth. On the one hand, ideological discourse shifts the event towards the domain of a preferred political/moral explanation. It gives an event an 'ideological reading' or interpretation. Barthes puts this point by saying that the ideological sign connects a mythical schema to history, seeing how it corresponds to the interests of a definite society. At this level, the rhetoric of connotation saturates the world of events with ideological meanings. At the same time, it disguises or *displaces* this connection. It asks us to imagine that the particular inflection which has been imposed on history *has always been there:* is its universal, 'natural' meaning. Myths, Barthes argues, dehistoricize the world so as to disguise the motivated nature of the ideological sign. They do not 'unveil historical realities': they inflect history, 'transforming it into nature'. At the ideological level, news photos are continually passing themselves off as something different. They interpret historical events ideologically. But in the very act of grounding themselves in fact, in history, they become 'universal' signs, part of the great storehouse of archetypal messages, nature not history, myth not 'reality'. It is this conjuncture of the immediate, the political, the historical and the mythic which lends an extraordinary complexity to the deciphering of the visual sign.

News photos have a specific way of passing themselves off as aspects of 'nature'. They repress their ideological dimensions by offering themselves as literal visual-transcriptions of the 'real world'. News photos witness to the *actuality* of the event they represent. Photos of an event carry within them a meta-message: 'this event really happened and this photo is the proof of it'. Photos of people—even the 'passport' type and size—also support this function of *grounding and witnessing:* 'this is the man we are talking about, he really exists'. Photos, then, appear, as records, in a literal sense, of 'the facts' and speak for themselves. This is what Barthes calls[16] the 'having-been-there' of all photographs. News photos operate under a hidden sign marked, 'this really happened, see for yourself'. Of course, the choice of *this* moment of an event as against that, of *this* person rather than that, of *this* angle rather than any other, indeed, the selection of this photographed incident to represent a whole complex chain of events and meaning, is a highly ideological procedure. But, by appearing literally to reproduce the event as it *really* happened, news photos suppress their selective/interpretive/ideological function. They seek a warrant in that ever pre-given, neutral structure, which is beyond question, beyond interpretation: the 'real world'. At this level, news photos not only support the credibility of the newspaper as an accurate medium. They also guarantee and underwrite its *objectivity* (that is, they neutralize its ideological function). This 'ideology of objectivity' itself derives from one of the most profound myths in the liberal ideology: the absolute distinction between fact and value, the distinction which appears as a common-sense 'rule' in newspaper practice as 'the distinction between facts and interpretation': the empiricist illusion, the utopia of naturalism.

The ideological message of the news photo is thus frequently displaced by being *actualized*. At first this seems paradoxical. Everything tends to locate the photo in historical time. But historical time, which takes account of development, of structures, interests and antagonisms, is a different modality from 'actuality time', which, in the newspaper discourse, is foreshortened time. The characteristic *tense* of the news photo is the *historic instantaneous*. All history is converted into 'today', cashable and explicable in terms of the immediate. In the same moment, all history is mythified—it undergoes an instantaneous mythification. The image loses its motivation. It appears, 'naturally', to have selected itself.

But few news photos are quite so unmotivated. The story of the Provisional IRA leader, Dutch Doherty, under the headline ULSTER WANTS DOHERTY EXTRADITED, speculates within the story-text on moves against IRA men in the Republic, pressures on the Lynch Government not to shelter wanted men, and so on: but it carries only a small, head-and-shoulders 'passport-photo' of the man in question, with the simple caption *Anthony 'Dutch' Doherty*. Yet the 'passport photo', with its connotation of 'wanted men', prisoners and the hunted, is not without ideological significance. This photo may not be able, on its own, to produce an ideological theme. But it can *enhance, locate* or *specify* the ideological theme, once it has been produced, by a sort of reciprocal *mirror-effect*. Once we know who the story is about, how he figures in the news—once, that is, the text has added the themes to the image—the photo comes into its own again, refracting the ideological theme at another level. Now we can 'read' the meaning of its closely-cropped, densely compacted composition: the surly, saturnine face: the hard line of the mouth, eyes, dark beard: the tilted angle so that the figure appears hunched, purposefully bent: the black suit: the bitter expression. These formal, compositional and expressive meanings reinforce and amplify the ideological message. The ambiguities of the photo are here not resolved by a caption. But once the ideological theme has been signalled, the photo takes on a signifying power of its own—it adds or situates the ideological theme, and grounds it at another level. This, it says, is the face of one of the 'bombers and gunmen': this is what today's headline, of another 'senseless' explosion in downtown Belfast, is all about. This its subject, its author. It is *also* a universal mythic sign—the face of all the 'hard men' in history, the portrait of Everyman as a 'dangerous wanted criminal'.

REFERENCES

1. Roland Barthes, 'Myth today', *Mythologies* (London, Cape, 1972).
2. The example is from Barthes, *Elements of semiology* (London, Cape, 1967).
3. Walter Bagehot, 'The English constitution'. *Walter Bagehot,* ed. N. St John Stevas (London, Eyre & Spottiswoode, 1959).
4. L. Althusser, 'Ideology and the State', *Lenin and philosophy and other essays* (London, New Left Books, 1971).
5. J. Halloran, P. Elliott & G. Murdock, *Demonstrations and communication* (Harmondsworth, Penguin, 1970). See also G. Murdock's paper in this Reader.
6. E. Ostgaard, *Nyhetsvandering* (Stockholm, Wahlston & Widstrand, 1968).
7. J. Galtung & M. Ruge, 'The structure of foreign news'. *Journal of International Peace Research,* no. 1, 1965. Extract reprinted in this Reader.
8. Cf. Jock Young, 'Mass media, drugs & deviancy', in McIntosh and Rock, op. cit.
9. C. Wright Mills, *The power elite* (Oxford, Univ. Press, 1956).
10. L. Althusser, 'Ideology and the State', op. cit.
11. Cf. J. O'Neil, *Sociology as a skin trade* (London, Heinemann, 1972). The phrase is from C.B. MacPherson, *The political theory of possessive individualism* (OUP, 1962).
12. R. Bathes, 'Myth today'. *Mythologies,* op. cit.
13. Gramsci, *Selections from the Prison Notebooks.* Ed. G. Nowell-Smith (London, Lawrence & Wishart, 1971). Cf. also *Beliefs in society,* Nigel Harris (London, Watts, 1968).
14. L. Althusser, op. cit.
15. R. Barthes, 'Rhetoric of the image', *Working papers in Cultural Studies* no. 1 (Birmingham, Centre for Cultural Studies).
16. R. Barthes, ibid.

Unit headline language*

MICHAEL FRAYN

If Goldwasser was remembered for nothing else, Macintosh once told Rowe, he would be remembered for his invention of UHL.

UHL was Unit Headline Language, and it consisted of a comprehensive lexicon of all the multi-purpose monosyllables used by headline-writers. Goldwasser's insight had been to see that if the grammar of 'ban', 'dash', 'fear', and the rest was ambiguous they could be used in almost any order to make a sentence, and that if they could be used in almost any order to make a sentence they could be easily randomized. Here then was one easy way in which a computer could find material for an automated newspaper—put together a headline in basic UHL first and then fit the story to it.

UHL, Goldwasser quickly realized, was an ideal answer to the problem of making a story run from day to day in an automated paper. Say, for example, that the randomizer turned up:

STRIKE THREAT

By adding one unit at random to the formula each day the story could go:

STRIKE THREAT BID

STRIKE THREAT PROBE

STRIKE THREAT PLEA

And so on. Or the units could be added cumulatively:

STRIKE THREAT PLEA

STRIKE THREAT PLEA PROBE

STRIKE THREAT PLEA PROBE MOVE

STRIKE THREAT PLEA PROBE MOVE SHOCK

STRIKE THREAT PLEA PROBE MOVE SHOCK HOPE

*Chapter 13 of Michael Frayn, *The tin men* (London, Collins, 1965).

STRIKE THREAT PLEA PROBE MOVE SHOCK HOPE STORM

Or the units could be used entirely at random:

LEAK ROW LOOMS

TEST ROW LEAK

LEAK HOPE DASH BID

TEST DEAL RACE

HATE PLEA MOVE

RACE HATE PLEA MOVE DEAL

Such headlines, moreover, gave a newspaper a valuable air of dealing with serious news, and helped to dilute its obsession with the frilly-knickeredness of the world, without alarming or upsetting the customers. Goldwasser had had a survey conducted, in fact, in which 457 people were shown the headlines:

ROW HOPE MOVE FLOP

LEAK DASH SHOCK

HATE BAN BID PROBE

Asked if they thought they understood the headlines, 86·4 per cent said yes, but of these 97·3 per cent were unable to offer any explanation of what it was they had understood. With UHL, in other words, a computer could turn out a paper whose language was both soothingly familiar and yet calmingly incomprehensible.

Goldwasser sometimes looked back to the time when he had invented UHL as a lost golden age. That was before Nobbs had risen to the heights of Principal Research Assistant, and with it his beardedness and his belief in the universal matehood of man. In those days Goldwasser was newly appointed Head of his department. He had hurried eagerly to work each day in whatever clothes first came to hand in his haste. He had thought nothing of founding a new inter-language before lunch, arguing with Macintosh through the midday break, devising four news categories in the afternoon, then taking Macintosh and his new wife out to dinner, going on to a film, and finishing up playing chess with Macintosh into the small hours. In those days he had been fairly confident that he was cleverer than Macintosh. He had even been fairly confident that Macintosh had thought he was cleverer than Macintosh. In those days Macintosh had been his Principal Research Assistant.

It was difficult not to believe the world was deteriorating when one considered the replacement of Macintosh by Nobbs. Goldwasser sometimes made a great effort to see the world remaining—as he believed it did—much as it always was, and to see Nobbs as a potential Macintosh to a potential incoming Goldwasser. It was not easy. Now that Macintosh had gone on to become Head of the Ethics Department, Goldwasser no longer invented his way through a world of clear, cerebral TEST PLEA DASH SHOCK absolutes. Now his work seemed ever more full of things like the crash survey.

The crash survey showed that people were not interested in reading about road crashes unless there were at least ten dead. A road crash with ten dead, the majority felt, was slightly less interesting than a rail crash with one dead, unless it had piquant details—the ten dead turning out to be five still virginal honeymoon couples, for example, or pedestrians mown down by the local J.P. on his way home from a hunt ball. A rail crash was always entertaining, with or without children's toys still lying pathetically among the wreckage. Even a rail crash on the Continent made the grade provided there were at least five dead. If it was in the United States the minimum number of dead rose to twenty; in South America 100; in Africa 200; in China 500.

But people really preferred an air crash. Here, curiously enough, people showed much less racial discrimination. If the crash was outside Britain, 50 dead Pakistanis or 50 dead Filipinos were as entertaining as 50 dead Americans. What people enjoyed most was about 70 dead, with some 20 survivors including children rescued after at least one night in open boats. They liked to be backed up with a story about a middle-aged housewife who had been booked to fly aboard the plane but who had changed her mind at the last moment.

Goldwasser was depressed for a month over the crash survey. But he could not see any way of producing a satisfactory automated newspaper without finding these things out. Now he was depressed all over again as he formulated the questions to be asked in the murder survey.

His draft ran:

1. Do you prefer to read about a murder in which the victim is *(a)* a small girl *(b)* an old lady *(c)* an illegitimately pregnant young woman *(d)* a prostitute *(e)* a Sunday school teacher?

2. Do you prefer the alleged murderer to be *(a)* a Teddy boy *(b)* a respectable middle-aged man *(c)* an obvious psychopath *(d)* the victim's spouse or lover *(e)* a mental defective?

3. Do you prefer a female corpse to be naked, or to be clad in underclothes?

4. Do you prefer any sexual assault involved to have taken place before or after death?

5. Do you prefer the victim to have been *(a)* shot *(b)* strangled *(c)* stabbed *(d)* beaten to death *(e)* kicked to death *(f)* left to die of exposure?

6. Do you prefer the murder to have taken place in a milieu which seems *(a)* exotic *(b)* sordid *(c)* much like your own and the people next door's?

7. If *(c)* do you prefer the case to reveal that beneath the surface life was *(a)* as apparently respectable as on the surface *(b)* a hidden cesspit of vice and degradation?

Nobbs enjoyed the survey. '"Do you prefer a female corpse to be naked, or to be clad in underclothes?"' he repeated to Goldwasser. 'That's what I call a good question, mate. That's what I call a good question.'

LSD and the press*

WILLIAM BRADEN

There is a legend, hallowed in journalism, about a newspaper photographer who was assigned to cover an anniversary of the first sustained nuclear reaction at the University of Chicago. Arriving on campus, the photographer addressed himself to the assembled scientists, including Vannevar Bush, Enrico Fermi, Arthur H. Compton, and Harold C. Urey. 'Now, fellows,' he said, 'I got three pictures in mind. First, you guys putting the atom in the machine. Then splitting the atom. And finally all of you grouped around looking at the pieces.'

I had always supposed the story was apocryphal—until just the other day, when I was approached by an excited photographer who works for the same Chicago newspaper I do. 'I've got a terrific idea,' he said. 'You take me out some night to one of those LSD parties. I'll set up my camera and take pictures of the whole thing. All this weird stuff that happens. Who knows? We might come back with a picture of God.'

I like to think he was putting me on. Taken together, however, the two anecdotes provide a reasonably accurate idea of the befuddled manner in which the press has often groped to understand anything radically new and complex—including nuclear energy, space flight, and now psychedelic drugs.

We are able now to cover the atom and space beats with a high degree of competence and sophistication, due in large part to the development of specialist reporters. At my own newspaper, for example, we do not have simply a science writer: we have one reporter who is assigned exclusively to the physical sciences and a second reporter assigned to the biological sciences. A third reporter is a nationally respected authority on evolution and DNA.

It seems fair to say, however, that the nation's newspapers as a whole are still befuddled about LSD. And there are several reasons for this state of affairs.

Extracted from William Braden, 'LSD and the press' in B. Aaronson and H. Osmond (eds.) *Psychedelics* (New York, Doubleday, 1970).

Consider first the plight of a typical city editor. Assuming he wants to provide responsible coverage of LSD phenomena, who might he assign to the job?

The medical writer? Perhaps. But that would certainly limit the scope of the investigation, and the writer would probably tend to reflect the attitudes and concerns of the medical establishment.

The religion editor? Well, he or she is pretty busy as it is putting together the Saturday church page and trying to deal with the day-to-day hard news generated by the ecumenical movement and squabbles over birth control and priestly celibacy. The overworked religion editor seldom has the time, space, or inclination to dabble in metaphysics.

The police reporter at detective headquarters? Unfortunately, he is often enough the final choice. But obviously not a very good one.

What about that new cub reporter with the degree in sociology? He could explore the subject from the standpoint of its social impact and social origins. Not a bad idea maybe. But again, too limited.

The travel editor? He's never taken that kind of trip.

The difficulty with the psychedelics, of course, is that they cut across so many areas—law and psychology, physiology and philosophy, Eastern and Western religions. As a result, the city editor may decide to fall back on the talents of that jack-of-all-knowledge, the general-assignment reporter.

In the old days, any reporter worth his pay cheque was supposed to be capable of handling any story on any subject. The theory was that he would ask himself the same questions that the uninformed layman would ask, and that he would supply the answers in terms that could be understood by a Kansas City milkman or a little old lady in Dubuque. For years, reporters all over America were writing stories with these two mythological readers in mind. And the theory in fact was not such a bad one, until we got quite deep into the twentieth century. I still remember, however, the night the first Sputnik flashed across our innocent Western skies. There was turmoil in the city room as the general-assignment reporters placed frantic telephone calls to sleepy astronomers and physicists. We didn't even know what questions to ask. After only a few days of struggling with apogees and perigees, it became all too evident that we needed our own rocket expert, and in time a top investigative reporter was groomed to take over the field. I don't know if the little old lady in Dubuque can understand every word he writes, but she can rest assured at least that her information is accurate.

The late Professor Jacob Scher used to tell his journalism students: 'Do all you can to simplify. But keep in mind there are some things that are just damned hard to understand. They're difficult. And if you simplify beyond a certain point, you won't be telling the truth about them.' Obviously the issues raised by the psychedelics are incredibly complex and damned hard to understand. A general-assignment Da Vinci would have trouble enough explaining all of them, if he understood them himself, and here again it is clear that complexity demands at least a degree of specialization and a fundamental background in a number of areas.

Newspapers in recent years have produced their experts on outer space, as well as education, labour, politics, urban planning, and human relations, to the point where major city rooms have come to resemble mini-universities. As yet, however, they have not developed any comparable authorities on inner space, if such a thing is possible, and it must be admitted in consequence that newspapers in general have done a bum job in telling the many-faceted story of LSD.

Some patterns are revealed by a visit to a newspaper morgue, where the files contain hundreds of clippings about LSD. The clippings were scissored from newspapers across the country, and there are very few of them that date prior to 1963. The few early ones are optimistic, and they tend to treat LSD as a possible new wonder drug:

DRUG HELPS MENTALLY ILL RECALL PAST (1960)

HOW 'NIGHTMARE' DRUG AIDS ADDICTION FIGHT (1961)

As early as 1951, readers of the Chicago *Daily News* were informed that a psychiatrist had told 'how a white powder given in so tiny an amount it could not be seen by the naked eye transformed normal people into strange, psychotic-like individuals in thirty minutes [and] hinted at the exciting possibility that mental illness could be caused by a toxic substance produced in the bodies of people who have broken down under stress'. A NEW SHOCK DRUG UNLOCKS TROUBLED MINDS, readers of the *This Week* newspaper supplement were told in 1959. 'It has rescued many drug addicts, alcoholics, and neurotics from their private hells—and holds promise for curing tomorrow's mental ills.' It has 'excited psychiatric workers all over the world'.

By 1963, however, the pattern had shifted, and the volume of stories since then has appeared to multiply almost in geometric progression. It is not a coincidence, moreover, that 1963 was the year Dr Timothy Leary took his departure from Harvard University. That was the year the press really discovered LSD, having first discovered Dr Leary, and until recently there has been little success in divorcing the one subject from the other. As far as the drug is concerned, the change in emphasis can be detected from a sampling of 1963 headlines:

A WARNING ON LSD: IT CARRIES WILD KICK

DRUG BRINGS HALLUCINATIONS; USE IS GETTING OUT OF HAND

MEDICS WARN THRILL DRUG CAN WARP MINDS AND KILL

Of psychedelic drugs in general, readers of the *Washington Post* learned in 1963: 'They have been blamed for at least one suicide, and for causing a respectable married secretary to appear nude in public.' Since that year, newspaper readers on the whole have learned very little else of consequence about the drugs; the coverage by and large has been of the cops-and-robbers variety, concentrating on police raids, drug-control bills, suicides, and fatal plunges.

As indicated, this sort of treatment can be attributed in part to a lack of reportorial expertise. Before taking a closer look at newspaper handling of the subject, however, another important factor should be pointed out.

It might be argued that the current emphasis on the negative aspects of LSD is at least partially inherent in the very nature of that curious stuff we call 'news'.

There is a common complaint that every newspaperman must have heard at least a thousand times in his lifetime. It goes something like this: 'Why do you always print bad news? Why is the front page always full of war and crime, murders and disasters? Why don't you print some of the *nice* things that happen? Why don't you write stories about all the good people who lead decent lives?'

'Because you wouldn't buy our paper any more' is an obvious and an honest answer. 'You'd run right out and buy some other paper.' And why? Because a newspaper is supposed to print the news, and news is based on conflict. Dog bites man: that's news. More to the point, news deals with *exceptions*. Its stock in trade is the exceptional event that runs counter to ordinary experience, and that is why man bites dog is *really* news. In the same sense, war, crime, and disasters are all exceptions to the normal rule, and therefore they are news. If a man rises in the morning and does not murder his wife, that is not news. If people live in harmony and do good works, that also is not news. I believe a satirist once wrote a Walter Lord type of book titled *The Day Nothing Happened,* offering an hour-by-hour chronicle of events in some hypothetical American city. One by one, with murderous suspense, these ordinary events built up to a shattering climax in which the sun went down and everybody went peacefully to bed. I can't imagine the book sold very well, but there is probably a lesson in it for those people who complain about news content.

Many complain that the 'good teenager' has had a bad press, that his image has been ruined by a few bad teenagers. The fact is that the good teenager is not news, because he is not exceptional. By the same coin, a good trip on LSD is not news either. But a bad trip: that's news. And a bad trip that ends in suicide or a psychotic break: that's really news.

Newspapers since World War II have been giving more and more space to interpretation of news events—to what is known in the business as 'think pieces'. But their primary function, as it has always been, is still to tell the news—to record the daily glut of occurrences; and since news by definition is almost certain to be bad, it is perhaps unfair to fault the newspapers too much for doing what they are supposed to do.

Having said this, however, I must add that the run-of-mill coverage of LSD has more often than not been superficial at best and violently distorted at worst. Since 1963, the newspapers had had almost nothing to say about the potential benefits of psychedelics in psychotherapy and related fields, including the treatment of alcoholism. As evidence of the breakdown in communications, reflecting also the breakdown in legitimate research in this country, witness this pathetic little column-closer, which was filed in 1967 by an Associated Press reporter in Germany:

> HAMBURG (AP)—The hallucinatory drug LSD is being used by Czech authorities as a possible cure for alcoholism, according to Radio Free Europe monitors.

End of story, in the paper where I read it. Americans can no doubt be thankful at least that they still have Radio Free Europe to keep them posted.

Two news stories in particular were probably of major importance in turning the tide of public opinion decisively against LSD. They broke within a week of each other, in April of 1966. One involved a five-year-old Brooklyn girl who suffered convulsions after swallowing an LSD sugar cube that had been left in a refrigerator by her uncle. The other concerned a former medical-school student, Stephen H. Kessler, who was charged with the stabbing to death of his mother-in-law, also in Brooklyn. 'Man,' he told police, 'I've been flying for three days on LSD. Did I rape somebody? Did I kill my wife?' (It was at this point that Sandoz Pharmaceuticals withdrew its new-drug application, citing unfavourable publicity, and thus cut off most legitimate LSD research in this country.)

Kessler vanished into Bellevue Hospital for mental tests, and that was the last news I have seen about him. But the case since then has been cited repeatedly in newspaper columns to support the assertion that LSD 'can lead to murder'. *Post hoc, ergo propter hoc*, of course. If indeed it was a case of *post hoc*.

Later in the year, in a story on the League for Spiritual Discovery, writer Thomas Buckley noted rather wistfully in the *New York Times,* ' . . . the increasing use of LSD poses social, medical, and religious questions that do not seem to be receiving the attention they deserve'. Soon after that, however, the drug was to receive considerable attention in the very influential pages of the *Times:*

LSD SPREAD IN U.S. ALARMS DOCTORS AND POLICE

AUTHORITIES SEE EDUCATION AS KEY HOPE IN
CURBING PERIL OF THE HALLUCINATORY DRUG

Under the three-column headline, in a lengthy story that attracted widespread attention, Gladwin Hill wrote on 23 February 1967, that LSD had become 'the nation's newest scourge'. Setting out to prove it, he reported some horrifying examples—including the case of a teenage driver whose car had crashed into a house and killed a child; in a trance-like state, trying to climb the walls of his cell, the youth shouted: 'I'm a graham cracker. Oops, my arm just crumbled off.' There was no refer-ence to any possible beneficial uses of LSD. As for the drug's supposed consciousness-expanding qualities, the article quoted an expert on the subject, California's Attorney General Thomas Lynch, who said that LSD represents 'a flight from reality'. Lynch did not say what reality is; but then Hill apparently neglected to ask him.

Reporters who wonder if LSD has any mystical or insight-producing properties can always find out by asking a cop, a doctor, or a legislator. Illinois State Senator Robert Cherry, for example, has been quoted as stating, 'This drug puts these people in the world of nothing'. Dr J. Thomas Ungerleider has said flatly, 'There is no basis in fact for their claims'. John Merlo, an Illinois state representative, has observed that the mystical claims for LSD are 'pure bunk', which he may have picked up from Commissioner James L. Goddard of the Food and Drug Administra-tion, who told a House Government Operations subcommittee in Wash-ington that mind-stretching claims for LSD are 'pure bunk'. (Presumably it takes a subcommittee to study a subculture.)

If there are no experts available, the reporter can always decide for himself. Thus, one reporter gave the subject a fair shake recently. He watched an LSD party and even went so far as to listen to a Jefferson Airplane record, all of which led him to conclude concerning 'the mys-tique' of LSD, 'Tomorrow will come, and that other world—the straight world, the world of reality—will take over.' Or as another reporter saw it, the hippies take LSD 'to elude a world they don't like, and to create an artificial one in which they feel more comfortable'. Nobody has yet suggested that hippies may take LSD to elude reporters.

The newspapers indeed are full of news about psychedelics:

MYSTERY OF NUDE COED'S FATAL PLUNGE

NAKED IN A ROSE BUSH

HER SON'S TRAGIC TRIP

STRIP-TEASING HIPPIE GOES WILD IN LAKESPUR ON LSD

'NIGHTMARE' DRUG PERIL GROWS

HOME DRUG LAB RAIDED IN BRONX

BOBBY BAKER KIN IN TREE NUDE

BANANA SMOKING UNDER U.S. STUDY

Some terrible things are reported. A team of investigators in California, for example, came across a former disc jockey who said he had lost his job after taking LSD, and what's more, he didn't care. A medical man found: ' . . .LSD users are suddenly overcome with religion.' As far back as 1960, *This Week* had recovered from its original optimism, and Dr Franz E. Winkler was warning readers of the supplement that he had detected certain 'ominous symptoms' in some LSD users. 'LSD', the doctor noted,

breaks the fetters of our disenchanted existence and releases the mind to a flight into a fairyland sparkling with colours and sounds and sensations of unearthly beauty. Under its influence, all confinements and separations fade, and the world becomes a place in which individuals need no longer be lonely but become members of an all-encompassing whole. Under such influences, people receive creative inspirations, become inclined to accept the reality of a spiritual world, and at times, even sense the existence of a supreme being.

And this is all wrong and immoral, of course. Because it's too easy. In fact, it's a sin.

Parents, do you know the danger signs? You do if you read a 1967 syndicated series by Ann Honig, which ran among other places in *Chicago's American:*

Parents who suspect their offspring are turned on via LSD should be suspicious if the youngsters suddenly espouse a oneness with God and the universe, if they are suddenly superknowledgeable about life and love, if they hear and see things no one else does, if their pupils are dilated.

Of course there are real LSD tragedies, and nobody should minimize them. Certainly the press cannot be accused of minimizing them.

BAD LSD TRIPS INCREASE, the headline over an Associated Press story reported in May of 1967. And so they probably had. But this raises an interesting possibility I remember discussing one time with Jean Houston, and I believe we agreed that the press might be partly responsible for creating a sort of self-fulfilling prophecy. One dimly recalls a halcyon time, in the beginning, when nobody spoke much about bad trips, and the psychedelic experience was almost always very nice and rewarding. Perhaps that was never the case, or it could be that fewer bad trips in the past were merely a result of a smaller drug population and/or far less publicity. But the other possibility remains.

Just suppose. Here all of a sudden is this Greek chorus of doctors and psychiatrists warning young people to avoid LSD: it might drive them crazy. And the warnings are dutifully passed on by the press. This doesn't stop the young people from taking LSD, of course; but it could possibly create a subliminal anxiety that results in either a bad trip or in a panic reaction at some later date. Since LSD subjects are so highly suggestible, as well known, it could be that they oblige the doctors and the press by doing exactly what they were told they would do. They flip out.

In my own case, I was having dinner one night with a bearded psychiatrist of formidable appearance. This was some months after I had participated in a legal psychedelic experiment at a psychiatric hospital, for a newspaper story, and while the trip had not been a pleasant one, I had not given it any thought for some time, and I had not been worried about it in any way. Between courses, the psychiatrist declared: 'The real tragedy of LSD has only now come to light. People think they might have a bad trip for a few hours, and that's all they have to worry about. But we now know the frightening truth that *nobody comes back unharmed*. In *every* case there is some degree of brain damage.' Oh? And where had the good doctor heard that? Well, he said, he had heard it just the other day at a medical-school symposium. And whom had he heard it from? He had heard it from this doctor sitting right next to him at the symposium, he forgot his name. And where had *he* heard it? He had heard it on a recent visit to the West Coast, where the research had been done. Where on the West Coast? My dinner companion didn't know. Who had done the research, and how was it done? He didn't know that either. He called for the dessert menu.

Driving home, like the man in the joke, I kept telling myself: 'Now is not the time to panic. Now is not the time to panic.' And then, finally: 'Now. *Now* is the time to panic!' Without dwelling on the details, I will say only that I spent a very bad week, and I can certainly understand now those stories about rational Westerners who mentally disintegrate under the suggestive curse of an African witch doctor. In my own mind at least, the experience lends credence to the hypothesis that the press and the medical profession between them may have contributed to a similar situation by continually emphasizing the dangers and negative aspects of the psychedelic experience.

One might ask why the press has been so willing to go along with the doctors in this connection, to the point of distorting the overall truth about LSD. There is in fact a fundamental dilemma involved here, and it is one that editors run into rather frequently. In short, should a newspaper tell the truth, or whole truth, when the public safety might be better served by silence or half-truths?

An obvious example is the development of a riot situation in a community. Should the local newspapers call attention to the situation and thereby possibly aggravate it by directing other malcontents to the scene? In most cases, newspapers withhold such stories during the early stages of mob action, and especially so if the disorder is still on a relatively small scale.

It would be hard to argue with that decision. But I recall a less-obvious version of the same basic problem. A rare solar eclipse was soon to occur, and our newspaper was flooded with urgent messages from individuals and organizations dedicated to the prevention of blindness. We were urged to tell our readers there was no safe way to look directly at the eclipse. It so happens that a safe eclipse viewer can be made with exposed photographic negatives, but the anti-blindness lobby said the procedure was too complicated, and many people undoubtedly would botch the job. Well, what should we do? Should we, in effect, fib and play it safe? Those who wanted us to do so were interested only in preventing blindness—not an unworthy motive, certainly—but the eclipse, on the other hand, was a phenomenon of considerable interest. Did we have the right to deny people the experience of seeing it and studying it? In the end, we decided to tell the truth. We published carefully worded instructions telling how to construct a safe viewer. (To my knowledge, nobody went blind.)

The parallel to psychedelic drugs is obvious. Medical men quite properly are interested in the prevention of suicide and psychosis, and there are strong pressures on a newspaper editor to conform. Besides, there is no foolproof method to guarantee a safe view of the psychedelic world, and editors, in addition, are often cowed by the medical profession. If a doctor says LSD is a deadly peril, how is an editor to argue with him? The result sometimes is a certain timidity on the part of the press in any situation involving a medical judgment. It is understandable, then, if many editors decide to play it safe and treat LSD simply as something that flew out of Pandora's box.

Still, there is no obligation to overdo it.

There was widespread rejoicing when the first study was published in 1967 indicating that use of LSD might result in abnormal chromosome breakage. That would certainly solve the problem very neatly, obviating the necessity to deal with all those sticky questions the psychedelics had raised, and the press in some cases did its best to improve upon the findings. The syndicated series by Ann Honig began with the observation, 'LSD may cause cancer in drug users—and deformity and death in their children.' But the series itself was relatively restrained in comparison with the headlines and advertising that accompanied it in *Chicago's American*. There was an interesting escalation from story to headline to promotional copy. For example the headline:

LSD: FOR THE KICK THAT CAN KILL

Then the printed advertising blurbs:

LSD: THE 'FLY NOW, DIE LATER' DRUG

Although many acid-users have committed suicide or murder while high on LSD, an even grimmer indictment has been placed against it. A well-known genetics expert has found that 'harmless' LSD damages human chromosomes . . . and eventually causes cancer! Find out the frightening facts. Read 'LSD: The Tragic Fad' starting Sunday in *Chicago's American*.

Why does a young person suddenly want to jump out of a window? Or shoot a number of people? Or eat the bark from a tree? Learn what the use of the drug LSD can do to a person . . . .

And finally the spot radio announcements, prefaced with the remark that acid-heads think LSD is harmless:

'Well, they're wrong—*dead wrong*. People who take LSD eventually get cancer.'

In the series, writer Honig sought to analyse why so many young people turn to LSD. The conclusion: 'LSD offers a new mystique, a new entrée to the in-group, a new rebellion against their elders, a new thrill. Also it's cheap, easy to make.' And so much for that. The writer went on to comment upon the experience of a San Mateo high school superintendent who raised $21,000 to finance an 'anti-LSD film' and then asked the students 'whom they would trust as the narrator'. He was 'shocked' by their answer.

'Nobody', said the students.

Small wonder, one might add.

This isn't to say that all newspapers in all cases have taken a limited and wholly negative view of psychedelics. There have been thoughtful pieces, here and there, now and then. My own newspaper, for example, devoted a four-page section to the religious implications of LSD experience, and it also offered vigorous editorial opposition to proposed legislation making LSD possession a crime in Illinois. Occasionally one comes across an isolated headline:

LSD CHEERS UP DYING PATIENT,
DOCTOR FINDS DRUG BRINGS A NEW ZEST FOR LIFE

There has, however, been very little of substance printed. Seldom is any attempt made to explain the nature of the LSD experience, except in terms of the acting-out behavior it sometimes produces. Even in the *New York Times,* one may be told simply that LSD ' . . . produces hallucinations or alters thought processes in various ways'. At best, a reader may find that the experience enhances sensory perception—pretty colours are seen—and sometimes he is told that the experience breaks down the ego and produces a 'mystical' state of mind. But what constitutes a mystical state of mind is left to the imagination. Now and then a perceptive reporter notices that LSD cultists talk a lot about Hinduism and Buddhism. They are interested in something called Zen, and they like to read *The Tibetan Book of the Dead.* But the implications of all this are not pursued; no effort is made to explore or explain the Eastern ideas that hold such fascination for the drug takers. The newspapers report that young drug users are in revolt; they do not say precisely what values are challenged by that revolt, and they do not say what alternatives exactly are offered by the drug movement. This is partly the fault of the cultists themselves— 'mumblers about Reality', a *Life* reporter called them—and it is also due in part to the ineffable character of the psychedelic experience. But it is the fault, too, of the press. It is easy to see why the attractions of LSD seem so inexplicable to those puzzled adults who get all their information from the newspapers. There is one LSD question that is rarely asked in the press, and when it is asked it isn't answered in any depth. In the case of psychedelics, many reporters seem to remember only Who? What? Where? and When? They forget the most important question of all, which is Why?

One split-off of this has been the emergence of the underground press to represent the non-straight viewpoint—the San Francisco *Oracle,* the Berkeley *Barb,* the *Seed* in Chicago, and the *East Village Other* in New York, to name but a few. These improbable newspapers even have their own Underground Press Syndicate (UPS) to service them with news and features. Colourful sheets, sometimes highly original in their content and design, they are of course just as much out of balance on the one side as the regular press is on the other. But if nothing else, they indicate that newspaper readers abhor a vacuum just as much as nature does, and reporters who are still concerned about the fifth W might find a few clues in the pages of the underground journals. (I did like the classified ad I saw in one of them: 'You're welcome, St Jude.')

Recently, a modification in press attitudes seems to have occurred, with the development of a distinct drug subculture focused in such areas as San Francisco's Haight-Ashbury, New York's Greenwich Village, and Chicago's Old Town. The newspapers in these cities have been fascinated by the psychedelic hippies, and at times the fascination has verged on obsession. In New York, the *Times* has devoted many columns of newsprint to their doings, and in San Francisco, the *Chronicle* sent a bearded reporter out to spend a month prowling the acid dens. (You guessed it: 'I Was a Hippie.') Even the 78-year-old historian Arnold Toynbee showed up mingling with the flower children of Haight-Ashbury, where he wrote a series of dispatches for the London *Observer.*

In general, the tone of most stories has been sympathetic. United Press International produced a long feature that compared the hippies favourably with their beatnik predecessors, and a similar piece by the Associated Press seemed to agree with the assessment of a San Francisco florist it quoted: 'These kids are good kids. They don't steal and they don't fight. But they should wash their feet more often.'

Toynbee thought the hippies were just splendid, seeing in them certain similarities to St Francis. I think seriously that the flowers had a lot to do with taming the savage press—it's hard to badmouth a little girl who hands you a posy—but even more important perhaps is the fact that the concentration of amiable hippies has taken the publicity spotlight off Dr

Leary, on whom it had been shining almost exclusively. He's a very nice fellow. But no single individual can dominate a situation without rubbing many people the wrong way, and he is perhaps a trifle old for his role. The kids as a whole come off better.

In any case, the press at times has seemed on the verge of suggesting that the hippies might just possibly have something to say. They have nudged at least a few observers to inquire into their motivations—'Why do they act like that?'—and the newspapers have actually reported a few efforts to answer that question. Toynbee said that the hippies are rebelling against American conformism, which he blamed partly on the Puritans and partly on Henry Ford (a nation of car drivers has become habituated to regimentation by traffic cops, who tell them where and how they may drive). One columnist concluded that hippies ' . . . suffer from something the more fashionable sociologists call "anomie" '. And of course somebody, in this case a psychiatrist, had to drag Marshall McLuhan out of the wings: 'We must understand that we are dealing with the first generation raised on TV, and everything is instant. It is a generation that expects instant gratification.'

Not very good, so far. But better than nothing.

So much for the newspapers. Summing up, we have suggested that the essentially negative attitude toward LSD in this area may be attributed to three primary factors: (1) no experts, (2) the nature of news, (3) eclipse syndrome. And we have proposed that newspapers may be partly responsible for the bad trips and panic behaviour they fill their pages with.

Turning briefly to radio and television, there is little to say, since these media have virtually ignored the drug movement. The one important exception has been the 'talk shows', both on radio and television. Some of the talk programmes run up to three hours or longer, often with audience participation by telephone, and they have produced many excellent debates and discussions by experts representing every conceivable point of view on psychedelics. In other areas of programming, however, one would never guess that such a thing as LSD existed. I have never seen or heard any reference to it in a dramatic presentation, and that is understandable perhaps when you consider the fire television comes under when it shows a young person smoking even a Lucky Strike. In fact, the only substantial network show I recall on LSD was the CBS documentary, narrated by Charles Kuralt, on the psychotherapeutic sessions at the Spring Grove (Maryland) State Hospital. That was very good. But, also, that was in May of 1966. And, to my knowledge, there has been nothing since.

It is painful to admit that the major magazines have probably done a better job than newspapers in reporting on LSD, and that *Time* and *Life* between them have possibly done the best job of all. Between 1963 and 1967, *Life* carried at least ten pieces on LSD, including an important cover story on 25 March 1966. (Another cover story, on psychedelic art, appeared on 9 September 1966.) *Time* discovered LSD in 1954 and has since published at least eighteen pieces on the drug. Other major stories have appeared in such magazines as *Newsweek, Look, Playboy, Reader's Digest, The Saturday Evening Post, The Nation, New Republic, The Atlantic,* and *Harper's.* In fact I recall the first time I learned about LSD—in a 1963 article by Noah Gordon in *The Reporter* magazine.

With some exceptions, the magazines have plumbed the subject to a far greater depth than most newspapers have. They, too, have given heavy play to the dangers involved—as the *Reader's Digest* saw it, 'LSD will remain about as safe and useful as a do-it-yourself brain surgery kit for amateurs'—but they also have been willing to examine psychedelics from other viewpoints, and in general they have treated the drugs with a balanced perspective. To my knowledge, incidentally, *Look* senior editor Jack Shepherd did the one thing journalistic reporters on LSD almost never do: he took the drug himself (and had a detestable trip).

A curious and significant by-product of the fuss over LSD came in 1967 in the form of a widespread effort, especially in the magazines, to give a better image to marijuana, the psychedelic near beer. The proliferation of articles provoked a suspicious complaint from a hippie friend of mine who prefers his fruit forbidden: 'Man, are you aware there's a *conspiracy* in the magazines to make pot legal?' And indeed I could appreciate his growing paranoia on the subject; in July alone, *Life, Newsweek,* and *Look* carried stories sharply questioning the wisdom of marijuana penalties, and *Newsweek* devoted a cover story to the issue.

Life has described marijuana as 'a mild euphoric drug', adding: 'Pot is not physically addicting, nor need it lead to crime, immorality, or stronger drugs.'

Newsweek: 'Indeed, the prohibitive laws against marijuana in America today, like those against alcohol in the 1920s, have not significantly diminished its use and, in fact, may have increased it.'

Look: 'The severity of the Federal marijuana law far exceeds the danger of the drug. The law needs an overhaul, with smoking marijuana reduced from a felony to a misdemeanour, as with LSD.'

The Nation: 'It is difficult to fashion a serious case against smoking marijuana, except that a user will find himself in serious trouble with the police.'

New Republic: 'The worst thing about marijuana is the laws against it, which should be repealed.'

While the magazines outshine the newspapers in reporting on LSD, their coverage is good only by comparison, and nobody could truly grasp all the varied implications of the psychedelics just by flipping through the slicks. In the last analysis, however, anybody in America today who is really interested in the subject can learn what is accurately known about it, which isn't much, by reading both the magazines and the newspapers (underground and above), by listening to the radio and television discussions, by dipping into the large number of books such as this one. And that, perhaps, is all one can ask. As for those who are not really interested, they will resist the best efforts of the media to inform them. As somebody has said, you can't reason people out of an opinion they did not arrive at by reason to begin with.

Mods and Rockers:
the inventory as manufactured news*

STANLEY COHEN

The scene for the first Mods and Rockers 'event', the one that was to set the pattern for all the others and give the phenomenon its distinctive shape was Clacton, a small holiday resort on the East Coast. This was the traditional gathering place over Bank Holiday weekends for kids from the East End and the North East suburbs of London.

Its range of facilities and amusements for young people is strictly limited and Easter 1964 was worse than usual.

It was cold and wet, and in fact Easter Sunday was the coldest for 80 years. The shopkeepers and stall owners were irritated by the lack of business and the young people had their own boredom and irritation fanned by rumours of café owners and barmen refusing to serve some of them. A few groups started scuffling on the pavements and throwing stones at each other. The Mods and Rockers factions—a division initially based on clothing and life styles, later rigidified, but at that time only vaguely in the air—started separating out. Those on bikes and scooters roared up and down, windows were broken, some beach huts were wrecked and one boy fired a starting pistol in the air. The vast number of people crowding into the streets, the noise, everyone's general irritation and the actions of an unprepared and undermanned police force had the effect of making the two days unpleasant, oppressive and sometimes frightening.

Immediately after a physical disaster there is a period of relatively unorganized response. This is followed by what disaster researchers call 'the inventory phase' during which those exposed to the disaster take stock of what has happened and of their own condition. In this period, rumours and ambiguous perceptions become the basis for interpreting the situation. Immediately after the Aberfan coal tip disaster, for example, there were rumours about the tip having been seen moving the night

*This is an abbreviated form of material that appears in Chapter 2 of *Folk devils and moral panics: The creation of the Mods and Rockers* (London, MacGibbon & Kee, 1972).

263

before and previous warnings having been ignored. These reports were to form the basis of later accusations of negligence against the National Coal Board, and the negligence theme then became assimilated into more deep-rooted attitudes, for example, about indifference by the central government to Welsh interests.

I am concerned here with the way in which the situation was initially interpreted and presented by the mass media, because it is in this form that most people receive their pictures of both deviance and disasters. Reactions take place on the basis of these processed or coded images: people become indignant or angry, formulate theories and plans, make speeches, write letters to the newspapers. The media presentation or inventory of the Mods and Rockers events is crucial in determining the later stages of the reaction.

On the Monday morning following the initial incidents at Clacton, every national newspaper, with the exception of *The Times* (fifth lead on main news page) carried a leading report on the subject. The headlines are self-descriptive: DAY OF TERROR BY SCOOTER GROUPS *(Daily Telegraph)*, YOUNGSTERS BEAT UP TOWN—97 LEATHER JACKET ARRESTS *(Daily Express)*, WILD ONES INVADE SEASIDE—97 ARRESTS *(Daily Mirror)*. The next lot of incidents received similar coverage on the Tuesday and editorials began to appear, together with reports that the Home Secretary was 'being urged' (it was not usually specified exactly by *whom*) to hold an enquiry or to take firm action. Feature articles then appeared highlighting interviews with Mods or Rockers. Straight reporting gave way to theories especially about motivation: the mob was described as 'exhilarated', 'drunk with notoriety', 'hell-bent for destruction', etc. Reports of the incidents themselves were followed by accounts of police and court activity and local reaction. The press coverage of each series of incidents showed a similar sequence.

Overseas coverage was extensive throughout; particularly in America, Canada, Australia, South Africa and the Continent. The *New York Times* and *New York Herald Tribune* carried large photos, after Whitsun, of two girls fighting. Belgian papers captioned their photos, 'West Side Story on English Coast'.

It is difficult to assess conclusively the accuracy of these early reports. Even if each incident could have been observed, a physical impossibility, one could never check the veracity of, say, an interview. In many cases, one 'knows' that the interview must be, partly at least, journalistic fabrication because it is too stereotypical to be true, but this is far from objective proof. Nevertheless, on the basis of those incidents that were observed, interviews with people who were present at others (local reporters, photographers, deck-chair attendants, etc.) and a careful check on internal consistency, some estimate of the main distortions can be made. Checks with the local press are particularly revealing. Not only are the reports more detailed and specific, but they avoid statements like 'all the dance halls near the seafront were smashed' when every local resident knows that there is only one dance hall near the front.

The media inventory of each initial incident will be analysed under three headings: (i) Exaggeration and distortion, (ii) Prediction, and (iii) Symbolization.

Exaggeration and distortion

Writing when the Mods and Rockers phenomenon was passing its peak, a journalist recalls that a few days after the initial event at Clacton, the Assistant Editor of the *Daily Mirror* admitted in conversation that the affair had been 'a little over-reported'.[1] It is this 'over-reporting' that I am interested in here.

The major type of distortion in the inventory lay in exaggerating grossly the seriousness of the events, in terms of criteria such as the number taking part, the number involved in violence and the amount and effects of any damage or violence. Such distortion took place primarily in terms of the mode and style of presentation characteristic of most crime reporting: the sensational headlines, the melodramatic vocabulary and the deliberate heightening of those elements in the story considered as news. The regular use of phrases such as 'riot', 'orgy of destruction', 'battle', 'attack', 'siege', 'beat up the town' and 'screaming mob' left an image of a besieged town from which innocent holidaymakers were fleeing to escape a marauding mob.

During Whitsun 1964, even the local papers in Brighton referred to 'deserted beaches' and 'elderly holidaymakers' trying to escape the 'screaming teenagers'. One had to scan the rest of the paper or be present on the spot to know that on the day referred to (Monday, 18 May) the beaches were deserted because the weather was particularly bad. The holidaymakers that *were* present were there to watch the Mods and Rockers. Although at other times (for example, August 1964 at Hastings) there was intimidation, there was very little of this in the Brighton incident referred to. In the 1965 and 1966 incidents, there was even less intimidation, yet the incidents were ritualistically reported in the same way, using the same metaphors, headline and vocabulary.

The full flavour of such reports is captured in the following lines from the *Daily Express* (19 May 1964):

There was Dad asleep in a deckchair and Mum making sandcastles with the children, when the 1964 boys took over the beaches at Margate and Brighton yesterday and smeared the traditional postcard scene with blood and violence.

This type of 'over-reporting' is, of course, not peculiar to the Mods and Rockers. It is characteristic not just of crime reporting as a whole, but mass media inventories of such events as political protests, racial disturbances and so on. What Knopf[2] calls the 'shotgun approach' to such subjects—the front-page build-up, the splashy pictures, the boxscores of the latest riot news—has become accepted in journalism. So accepted, in fact, that the media and their audiences have lost even a tenuous hold on the meaning of the words they use. How is a town 'beaten up' or 'besieged'? How many shop windows have to be broken for an 'orgy of destruction' to have taken place? When can one—even metaphorically—talk of scenes being 'smeared with blood and violence'? Commenting on the way the term 'riot' is used to cover both an incident resulting in 43 deaths, 7000 arrests and $45 million in property damage *and* one in which three people broke a shop window, Knopf remarks: 'The continued media use of the term contributes to an emotionally charged climate in which the public tends to view every event as an "incident", every incident as a "disturbance" and every disturbance as a "riot".'[3]

The sources of over-reporting lay not just in such abuses of language. There was a frequent use of misleading headlines, particularly headlines which were discrepant with the actual story: thus a headline 'violence' might announce a story which, in fact, reports that *no* violence occurred. Then there were more subtle and often unconscious journalistic practices: the use of the generic plural (if a boat was overturned, reports read 'boats were overturned') and the technique, well known to war correspondents, of reporting the same incident twice to look like two different incidents.

Another source of distortion lay in the publication, usually in good faith, of reports which were later to receive quite a different perspective by fresh evidence. The repetition of obviously false stories, despite known confirmation of this, is a familiar finding in studies of the role of the press in spreading mass hysteria.[4] An important example in the Mods and Rockers inventory was the frequently used '£75 cheque story'. It was widely reported that a boy had told the Margate magistrates that he would pay the £75 fine imposed on him with a cheque. This story was true enough; what few papers bothered to publish and what they all knew, was that the boy's offer was a pathetic gesture of bravado. He later admitted that not only did he not have the £75, but he did not even have a bank account and had never signed a cheque in his life. As long as four years after this, though, the story was still being repeated and was quoted to me at a magistrates' conference in 1968 to illustrate the image of the Mods and Rockers as affluent hordes whom 'fines couldn't touch'.

This story had some factual basis, even though its real meaning was lost. At other times, stories of organization, leadership, particular incidents of violence and vandalism were based on little more than unconfirmed rumour. These stories are important because—as I will show in detail—they enter into the consciousness and shape the societal reaction at later stages. It is worth quoting at length a particularly vivid example from the media coverage of an American incident:

In York, Pa., in mid-July, 1968 . . . incidents of rock- and bottle-throwing were reported. Towards the end of the disturbance UPI in Harrisburg asked a stringer to get something on the situation. A photographer took a picture of a motorcyclist with an ammunition belt around his waist and a rifle strapped across his back. A small object dangled from the rifle. On July 18, the picture reached the nation's press. The *Washington Post* said: 'ARMED RIDER—Unidentified motorcyclist drives through heart of York, Pa., Negro district, which was quiet for the first time in six days of sporadic disorders.' The *Baltimore Sun* used the same picture and a similar caption: 'QUIET BUT . . . An unidentified motorcycle rider armed with a rifle and carrying a belt of ammunition, was among those in the heart of York, Pa., Negro district last night. The area was quiet for the first time in six days'.

The implication of this photograph was clear: the 'armed rider' was a sniper. But since when do snipers travel openly in daylight completely armed? Also, isn't there something incongruous about photographing a sniper, presumably 'on his way to work,' when according to the caption, the city 'was quiet'? Actually, the 'armed rider' was a sixteen-year-old boy who happened to be fond of hunting groundhogs—a skill he had learned as a small boy from his father. On July 16, as was his custom, the young man had put on his ammo belt and strapped a rifle across his back, letting a hunting licence dangle so that all would know he was hunting animals, not people. Off he went on his motorcycle headed for the woods, the fields, the groundhogs—and the place reserved for him in the nation's press.[5]

Moving from the form to the content of the inventory, a detailed analysis reveals that much of the image of the deviation presented was, in Lemert's term, putative: '. . . that portion of the societal definition of the deviant which has no foundation in his objective behaviour'.[6] The following is a composite of the mass media inventory:

> Gangs of Mods and Rockers from the suburbs of London invaded, on motor bikes and scooters, a number of seaside resorts. These were affluent young people, from all social classes. They came down deliberately to cause trouble by behaving aggressively towards visitors, local residents and the police. They attacked innocent holidaymakers and destroyed a great deal of public property. This cost the resorts large sums of money in repairing the damage and a further loss of trade through potential visitors being scared to come down.

The evidence for the ten elements in this composite picture is summarized below:

(i) *Gangs*. There was no evidence of any structured gangs. The groups were loose collectivities or crowds within which there was occasionally some more structured grouping based on territorial loyalty, e.g., 'The Walthamstow Boys'.

(ii) *Mods and Rockers*. Initially at least, the groups were not polarized along the Mod-Rocker dimension. At Clacton, for example, the rivalry (already in existence for many years) between on the one hand those from London and on the other locals and youths from the surrounding counties, was a much more significant dimension. The Mod-Rocker polarization was institutionalized later and partly as a consequence of the initial publicity. In addition, throughout the whole life of the phenomenon, many of the young people coming down to the resorts did not identify with either group.

(iii) *Invasion from London*. Although the bulk of day trippers, young and old, were from London, this was simply the traditional bank holiday pattern. Not all offenders were from London; many were either local residents or came from neighbouring towns or villages. This was particularly true of the Rockers who, in Clacton and Great Yarmouth, came mainly from East Anglian villages. The origins of 54 youths, on whom information was obtainable, out of the 64 charged at Hastings (August 1964) was as follows: London or Middlesex suburbs—20; Welwyn Garden City—4; small towns in Kent—9; Sussex—7; Essex—4; and Surrey—10.

(iv) *Motor bikes and scooters*. At every event the majority of young people present came down by train or coach or hitched. The motor bike or scooter owners were always a minority; albeit a noisy minority that easily gave the impression of ubiquity.

(v) *Affluence*. There is no clear-cut information here of the type that could be obtained from a random sample of the crowd. Work on the Brighton Weekend Project and all information from other sources suggest that the young people coming down were not particularly well off. Certainly for those charged in the courts, there is no basis for the affluence image. The average take-home pay in Barker and Little's Margate sample was £11 per week.[7] The original Clacton offenders had on them an average of 75p for the whole Bank Holiday weekend. The best off was a window cleaner earning £15 a week, but more typical were a market assistant earning £7·50 and a 17-year-old office boy earning £5·12.

(vi) *Classless*. Indices such as accent and area of residence, gathered from court reports and observation, suggest that both the crowds and the offenders were predominantly working class. In the Barker-Little sample, the typical Rocker was an unskilled manual worker, the typical Mod a semi-skilled manual worker. All but two had left school at fifteen. At Clacton, out of the 24 charged, 23 had left school at fifteen, and 22 had been to Secondary Moderns. All were unskilled; there were no apprentices or anyone receiving any kind of training.

(vii) *Deliberate intent*. The bulk of young people present at the resorts came down not so much to make trouble as in the hope that there would be some trouble to watch. Their very presence, their readiness to be drawn into a situation of trouble and the sheer accretion of relatively trivial incidents were found inconvenient and offensive; but if there really had been great numbers deliberately intent on causing trouble, there would have been more trouble. The proportion of those whom the police would term 'troublemakers' was always small. This hard core was more evident at Clacton than at any of the subsequent events: 23 out of the 24 charged (97 were originally arrested) had previous convictions.

(viii) *Violence and vandalism*. Acts of violence and vandalism are the most tangible manifestations of what the press and public regard as hooliganism. These acts were therefore played up rather than the less melodramatic effect of the Mods and Rockers which was being a nuisance and inconvenience to many adults. In fact, the total amount of serious violence and vandalism was not great. Only about one-tenth of the Clacton offenders was charged with offences involving violence. At Margate, Whitsun 1964, supposedly one of the most violent events—the one which provoked the *Daily Express* 'blood and violence' report—the only major recorded violence consisted of two stabbings and the dropping of a man on to a flower bed. At Hastings, August 1964, out of 44 found guilty, there were three cases of assaulting the police. At Brighton, Easter 1965, out of 70 arrests there were 7 for assault. Even if the definition of violence were broadened to include obstruction and the use of threatening behaviour, the targets were rarely 'innocent holidaymakers', but members of a rival group, or, more often, the police. The number of recorded cases of malicious damage to property was also small; less than 10 per cent of all cases charged in the courts. The typical offence throughout was obstructing the police or the use of threatening behaviour. In Clacton, although hardly any newspapers mentioned this, a number of the 24 were charged with 'non-hooligan' type offences: stealing half a pint of petrol, attempting to steal drinks from a vending machine and 'obtaining credit to the amount of 7d. by means of fraud other than false pretences' (an ice cream).

(ix) *Cost of damage*. The court figures for malicious damage admittedly underestimate the extent of vandalism because much of this goes undetected. Nevertheless, an examination of the figures given for the cost of the damage suggests that this was not as excessive as reported. Table 1 shows the cost of damage at the first four events.

TABLE 1

COST OF DAMAGE TO FOUR RESORTS: EASTER AND WHITSUN, 1964

Place	Date	No. of arrests	Estimated cost of damage
Clacton	Easter, 1964	97	£513
Bournemouth	Whitsun, 1964	56	£100
Brighton	Whitsun, 1964	76	£400
Margate	Whitsun, 1964	64	£250

SOURCE: Estimates by local authorities quoted in local press.

It must be remembered also that a certain amount of damage to local authority property takes place every Bank Holiday. According to the Deputy Publicity Manager of Margate,[8] for example, the number of deck-chairs broken (50) was not much greater than on an ordinary Bank Holiday weekend; there were also more chairs out on Whit Sunday than ever before.

(x) *Loss of trade*. The press, particularly the local press, laid great emphasis on the financial loss the resorts had suffered and would suffer on account of the Mods and Rockers through cancelled holidays, less use of facilities, loss of trade in shops, restaurants and hotels. The evidence for any such loss is at best dubious. Under the heading, THOSE WILD ONES ARE TO BLAME AGAIN, the Brighton *Evening Argus* quoted figures after Whitsun 1964 to show that, compared with the previous Whitsun, the number of deck-chairs hired had dropped by 8000 and the number using the swimming pool by 1500. But the number using the miniature railway increased by 2000, as did the number of users of the putting green. These figures make sense when one knows that, on the day referred to, the temperature had dropped by 14°F, and it had been raining the night before. This is the main reason why there was less use of deck-chairs and the swimming pool. In Hastings, August 1964, despite a big scare-publicity build up, the number of visitors coming down by train increased by 6000 over the previous year.[9] Newspapers often quoted 'loss of trade' estimates by landlords, hotel keepers and local authority officials, but invariably, final figures of damage fell below the first estimates. These revised figures, however, came too late to have any news value.

Although there were cases of people being scared away by reports of the disturbances, the overall effect was the opposite. The Margate publicity department had a letter from a travel agent in Ireland saying that the events had 'put Margate on the map'. Leaving aside the additional young people themselves attracted by the publicity—they would not be defined as commercial assets—many adults as well came down to watch the fun. I was often asked, on the way down from Brighton station, 'Where are the Mods and Rockers today?', and near the beaches, parents could be seen holding children on their shoulders to get a better view of the proceedings. In an interview with a reporter during which I was present, a man said, 'My wife and I came down with our son (aged 18) to see what all this fun is at the seaside on Bank Holidays.' (*Evening Argus* 30 May 1964). By 1965 the happenings were part of the scene—the pier, the whelks, the Mods and Rockers could all be taken in on a day trip.

Prediction

There is another element in the inventory which needs to be discussed separately because it assumes a special importance in later stages. This is the implicit assumption, present in virtually every report, that what had happened was inevitably going to happen again. Few assumed that the events were transient occurrences; the only questions were where the Mods and Rockers would strike next and what could be done about it. As will be suggested, these predictions played the role of the classical self-

The cumulative effect of such reports was to establish predictions whose truth was guaranteed by the way in which the event, non-event or pseudo-event it referred to was reported.

Symbolization

Communication, and especially the mass communication of stereotypes, depends on the symbolic power of words and images. Neutral words such as place names can be made to symbolize complex ideas and emotions; for example, Pearl Harbour, Hiroshima, Dallas and Aberfan. A similar process occurred in the Mods and Rockers inventory: these words themselves and a word such as 'Clacton' acquired symbolic powers. It became meaningful to say 'We don't want another Clacton here', or 'You can see he's one of those Mod types'.

There appear to be three processes in such symbolization: a word (Mod) becomes symbolic of a certain status (delinquent or deviant); objects (hairstyle, clothing) symbolize the word; the objects themselves become symbolic of the status (and the emotions attached to the status). The cumulative effect of these three processes as they appeared in the inventory was that the terms Mods and Rockers were torn from any previously neutral contexts (for example, the denotation of different consumer styles) and acquired wholly negative meanings. The identical effect is described by Turner and Surace in their classic study of the 1943 Zoot Suit riots[11] and by Rock and myself in tracing how the Edwardian dress style became transformed into the Teddy Boy folk devil.[12]

In their case study, Turner and Surace refer to this process as the creation of 'unambiguously unfavourable symbols'. Newspaper headlines and interpersonal communication following the initial incidents in Los Angeles reiterated the phobia and hatred towards Mexican American youth. References to this group were made in such a way as to strip key symbols (differences in fashion, job style and entertainment) from their favourable or neutral connotations until they came to evoke unambiguously unfavourable feelings. Content analysis showed a switch in the references to Mexicans to the 'Zooter theme', which identified this particular clothing style as the 'badge of delinquency' and coupled such references with mention of zoot suiter attacks and orgies. Invariably the Zooter was identified with the generalized Mexican group. In the same way, the Mods and Rockers status traits were, in later stages of the reaction, to wash off on the generalized adolescent group. Their 'badge of delinquency' emerged as symbols, such as the fur-collared anorak and the scooter, which became sufficient in themselves to stimulate hostile and punitive reactions.[13]

fulfilling prophecy. Unlike the case of natural disasters where the absence of predictions can be disastrous, with social phenomena such as deviance, it is the presence of predictions that can be 'disastrous'.

The predictions in the inventory period took the form of reported statements from local figures such as tradesmen, councillors, and police spokesmen about what should be done 'next time' or of immediate precautions they had taken. More important, youths were asked in TV interviews about their plans for the next Bank Holiday and interviews were printed with either a Mod or a Rocker threatening revenge 'next time'. The following are extracts from two such interviews: 'Southend and places won't let us in any more. It will get difficult here and so next year we'll probably go to Ramsgate or Hastings.' (*Daily Express* 30 March 1964). 'It could have been better—the weather spoiled it a bit. Wait until next Whitsun. Now that will be a real giggle.' (*Daily Mirror* 31 March 1964).

Where predictions were not fulfilled, a story could still be found by reporting non-events. So, for example, when attention was switched to East Anglian resorts in 1966, the *East Anglian Daily Times* (30 May 1966) headed a report on a play attended by a group of long-haired youths, FEARS WHEN TON-UP BOYS WALKED IN GROUNDLESS. Reporters and photographers were often sent on the basis of false tip-offs to events that did not materialize. In Whitsun 1965, a *Daily Mirror* report from Hastings, where nothing at all happened was headed, HASTINGS— WITHOUT THEM. In Whitsun 1966, there was a report (*Daily Mirror* 30 May 1966) on how policemen on a 'Mods and Rockers patrol' in Clacton could only use their specially provided walkie-talkies to help two lost little boys. Again, headlines often created the impression that something had happened: the *Evening Argus* (30 May 1966) used the subheading VIOLENCE to report that 'in Brighton there was no violence in spite of the crowds of teenagers on the beach'.

These non-event stories and other distortions springing from the prediction theme are part of the broader tendency which I will discuss later whereby discrepancies between expectations and reality are resolved by emphasizing those new elements which confirm expectations and playing down those which are contradictory. Commenting on this tendency in their analysis of the media coverage of the October 1968 Vietnam war demonstrations, Halloran et al.[10] draw attention to a technique often employed in the Mods and Rockers inventory '. . . a phrase or sentence describing in highly emotive terms either the expectation of violence or an isolated incident of violence, is followed by a completely contradictory sentence describing the actual situation'.

Symbols and labels eventually acquire their own descriptive and explanatory potential. Thus—to take examples from an earlier folk devil— the label 'Teddy Boy' became a general term of abuse (for example, John Osborne being described as 'an intellectual Teddy Boy'); the devil was seen as a distinct type of personality (drugs were announced to soothe Teddy Boys and make them co-operative for treatment, statements made such as 'some of these soldiers here are just Teddy Boys in army uniform') and the symbols were seen as changing the person ('He was never in trouble before he bought an Edwardian suit'; 'Since my son bought this thing a year ago his personality has changed').

Such symbolization is partly the consequence of the same standard mass communication processes which give rise to exaggeration and distortion. Thus, for example, misleading and inappropriate headlines were used to create unambiguously negative symbols where the actual event did not warrant this at all or at least was ambiguous. Accounts of certain events in Whitsun 1964, for example, were coupled with a report of a 'Mod' falling to his death from a cliff outside Brighton. Similarly in August 1964 there were headlines, MOD DEAD IN SEA. In neither case had these deaths anything to do with the disturbances; they were both pure accidents. A reading of the headlines only, or of early reports not mentioning police statements about the accidents, might have led to a misleading connection. This sort of effect reached its bizarre heights in a headline in the *Dublin Evening Press* (18 May 1964) TERROR COMES TO ENGLISH RESORTS. MUTILATED MOD DEAD IN PARK. The 'mutilated Mod' was, in fact, a man of 21–25 wearing a 'mod jacket'(?) who was found stabbed on the Saturday morning (the day *before* the incidents at the resorts) in a Birmingham park.[14]

Another highly effective technique of symbolization was the use of dramatized and ritualistic interviews with 'representative members' of either group. The *Daily Mirror* (31 March 1964) had Mick 'The Wild One' on WHY I HURLED THAT CHISEL and another boy who said, 'I take pep pills. Everybody does here.' The *Daily Herald* (18 May 1964) quoted one boy clutching his injured head as the police bundled him into a van saying, 'Carry on with the plan.' Another said, 'We're not through yet. We're here for the holiday and we're staying. Margate will wish it was Clacton when we're finished.' The *Evening Standard* (19 May 1964) found 'The Baron' who hated 'Mods and Wogs' and said, 'I like fighting . . . I have been fighting all my life.' The *Daily Mirror* (8 May 1964) found a new angle with THE GIRLS WHO FOLLOW THE WILD ONES INTO BATTLE, and who said about fighting: '. . . it gives you a kick, a thrill, it makes you feel all funny inside. You get butterflies in your stomach and you want the boys to go on and on . . . It's hard luck on the people who get in their way, but you can't do anything about that.'

It is difficult to establish how authentic these interviews are. In some cases they ring so patently absurd a note that they cannot be an accurate transcription of what was actually said. The *Daily Telegraph* (31 May 1964), for example, carried an interview with a Rocker who said, 'We are known as the Rockers and are much more with it.' If any group had a 'with it' self-image and would even contemplate using such a term, it certainly was not the Rockers. It would be fair to describe those interviews and reports as being composite, not necessarily in the sense of being wilfully faked, but as being influenced by the reporter's (or sub-editor's) conception of how anyone labelled as a thug or a hooligan *should* speak, dress and act. This effect may have occasionally been heightened by a certain gullibility about the fantasies of self-styled gang leaders.[15]

Through symbolization, plus the other types of exaggeration and distortion, images are made much sharper than reality. There is no reason to assume that photographs or television reports are any more 'objective'. In a study of the different perceptions experienced by TV viewers and on-the-spot spectators of another crowd situation (MacArthur Day in Chicago), it was shown how the reporting was distorted by the selection of items to fit into already existing expectations.[16] A sharpening up process occurs, producing emotionally toned symbols which eventually acquire their own momentum. Thus the dissemination of overwhelming public support in favour of MacArthur '. . . gathered force as it was incorporated into political strategy, picked up by other media, entered into gossip and thus came to overshadow immediate reality as it might have been recorded by an observer on the scene'.[17]

In this study, observers recorded how their expectations of political enthusiasm and wild mass involvement were completely unfulfilled. Through close ups and a particular style of commentary ('the most enthusiastic crowd ever in our city . . . you can feel the tenseness in the air . . . you can hear the crowd roar') television structured the whole event to convey emotions non-existent to the participants. This effect explains why many spectators at the Mods and Rockers events found them a slight let-down after the mass media publicity. As Boorstin remarks in discussing the effects of television and colour photography: 'Verisimilitude took on a new meaning . . . The Grand Canyon itself became a disappointing reproduction of the Kodachrome original.'[18]

The inventory as manufactured news

The cumulative effects of the inventory can be summarized as follows: (i) the putative deviation had been assigned from which further stereotyping, myth making and labelling could proceed; (ii) the expectation was created that this form of deviation would certainly recur; (iii) a wholly negative symbolization in regard to the Mods and Rockers and objects associated with them had been created; (iv) all the elements in the situation had been made clear enough to allow for full-scale demonology and hagiology to develop: the information had been made available for placing the Mods and Rockers in the gallery of contemporary folk devils.

Why do these sorts of inventories result? Are they in any sense 'inevitable'? What are the reasons for bias, exaggeration and distortion? To make sense of questions such as these, one must understand that the inventory is not, of course, a simple sort of stock-taking in which some errors might accidentally creep in from time to time. Built into the very nature of deviance inventories in modern society are elements of fantasy, selective misperception and the deliberate creation of news. The inventory is not reflective stock-taking but manufactured news.

Before pursuing this notion, let me mention some of the more 'genuine' errors. On one level, much exaggeration and distortion arose simply from the ambiguous and confused nature of the situation. It is notoriously difficult in a crowd setting to estimate the numbers present and some of the overestimates were probably no more than would have occurred after events such as political demonstrations, religious rallies, pop concerts or sporting fixtures. The confusion was heightened by the presence of so many reporters and photographers: their very presence could be interpreted as 'evidence' that something massive and important was happening.

It was a problem for everyone present—police, spectators, participants, newsmen—actually to know what was happening at any one time. In such situations, the gullibility effect is less significant than a general susceptibility to all sorts of rumours. Clark and Barker's classic case study of a participant in a race riot shows this effect very clearly,[19] and in disaster research prospective interviewers are warned, 'People who have discussed their experiences with others in the community can rapidly assimilate inaccurate versions of the disaster. These group versions may quickly come to be accepted by a large segment of the population.'[20]

Important as such errors may be in the short run, they cannot explain the more intrinsic features of deviance inventories: processes such as symbolization and prediction, the direction of the distortions rather than the simple fact of their occurrence, the decision to report the deviance in the first place and to continue to report it in a particular way. Studies of moral panics associated with the Mods and Rockers and other forms of deviance, as well as detailed research on the mass communication process itself (such as that by Halloran and his colleagues) indicate that two interrelated factors determine the presentation of deviance inventories: the first is the institutionalized need to create news and the second is the selective and inferential structure of the news-making process.

The weekend of the Clacton event was particularly dull from a news point of view. Nothing particularly noteworthy happened nationally or internationally. The fact that the event was given such prominence must be due partly at least to the absence of alternative news. The behaviour itself was not particularly new or startling. Disturbances of various sorts—variously called 'hooliganism', 'rowdyism' or 'gang fights'—occurred frequently throughout the late 1950s and early 1960s in coastal resorts favoured by working-class adolescents. In 1958, for example, Southend police had to appeal for outside support after rival groups had fought battles on the pier. In Whitley Bay, Blackpool and other Northern resorts there were disturbances and fighting often more severe than any of the early Mods and Rockers episodes. For years British holidaymakers on day trips or weekend excursions to such European coastal resorts as Calais and Ostend have been involved in considerable violence and vandalism. In Ostend, from the beginning of the 1960s, there was a period of the year referred to as the 'English season' during which holidaymakers and members of amateur football clubs caused considerable damage and trouble, rarely reported in the British press. The Mods and Rockers didn't become news because they were new; they were presented as new to justify their creation as news.

It would be facile to explain the creation of the inventory purely in terms of it being 'good news'; the point is simply that there was room for a story at that initial weekend and that its selection was not entirely due to its intrinsic properties. Labelling theorists have drawn attention to the complex nature of the screening and coding process whereby certain forms of rule-breaking are picked out for attention. Such processes relate to social control as a whole and not just the media. The media reflected the real conflict of interests that existed at various levels: for example, between local residents and police on the one hand and the Mods and Rockers on the other. In such situations the media adjudicate between competing definitions of the situation, and as these definitions are made in a hierarchical context—agents of social control are more likely to be believed than deviants—it is clear which definition will win out in an ambiguous and shifting situation.[21]

Notes and References

1. Peter Laurie, *The teenage revolution* (London, Anthony Blond Ltd, 1965), p. 130.
2. Terry Ann Knopf, 'Media myths on violence', *Columbia Journalism Review* (Spring 1970), pp. 17–18.
3. Ibid., p. 20.
4. See, for example, Norman Jacobs, 'The phantom slasher of Taipei: mass hysteria in a non western society', *Social Problems* 12 (Winter 1965), p. 322.
5. Knopf, op. cit., p. 18.
6. Edwin M. Lemert, *Social pathology* (New York, McGraw-Hill, 1951), p. 55.
7. Paul Barker and Alan Little, 'The Margate offenders: a survey', *New society* (30 July 1964).
8. Interview (23 November 1964).
9. Estimate by Hastings Stationmaster, quoted in *Hastings and St. Leonards Observer* (8 August 1964).
10. James D. Halloran et al., *Demonstrations and communications: A case study* (Harmondsworth, Penguin Books, 1970), p. 112.
11. Ralph H. Turner and Samuel J. Surace, 'Zoot Suiters and Mexicans: symbols in crowd behaviour', *American Journal of Sociology* 62 (1956), pp. 14–20.
12. Paul Rock and Stanley Cohen, 'The Teddy Boy' in V. Bogdanor and P. Skidelsky (eds.), *The age of affluence 1951–1964* (London, Macmillan, 1970).
13. During the inventory period, scooter owners and manufacturers frequently complained about the bad publicity that they were getting. After Clacton, the General Secretaries of the Vespa and Lambretta Scooter Clubs issued a statement dissociating their clubs from the disturbances.
14. Newspapers furthest away from the source invariably carried the greatest distortions and inaccuracies. The *Glasgow Daily Record and Mail* (20 May 1964), for example, described Mods as being dressed in short jacketed suits, with bell bottoms, high boots, bowler or top hats and carrying rolled up umbrellas.
15. Yablonsky has provided numerous examples of how outside observers accept at face value the fantasies of gang leaders and members. See Lewis Yablonsky, *The violent gang* (New York, Free Press, 1962).
16. Kurt and Gladys Lang, 'The unique perspective of television and its effect: A pilot study', *American Sociological Review* 18 (February 1953), pp. 3–12. Halloran and his colleagues (op. cit.) report an identical process in their analysis of the TV coverage of the 1968 anti-Vietnam war demonstrations.
17. Ibid., p. 10.
18. Daniel J. Boorstin, *The image* (Harmondsworth, Penguin Books, 1963), p. 25.
19. Kenneth B. Clark and James Barker, 'The Zoot effect in personality: A race riot participant', *Journal of Abnormal and Social Psychology* 40 (1965), pp. 143–8.

20. I. H. Cissin and W. B. Clark, 'The methodological challenge of disaster research', in G. W. Baker and D. W. Chapman, *Man and society in disaster* (New York, Basic Books, 1962), p. 28.

21. The notion of a 'hierarchy of credibility' in regard to deviance is suggested by Howard S. Becker in his paper 'Whose side are we on?', *Social Problems* 14 (Winter 1967), pp. 239–67.

Sir, Writing by candlelight . . . *

E. P. THOMPSON

Let the power workers dim the street lamps, or even plunge whole districts into utter darkness, the lights of righteousness and duty burn all the brighter from 10,000 darkened drawing-rooms in Chelsea or the Surrey hills.

> Sir,
> May I, writing by candlelight, express my total support for the government in their attempt to halt the unbelievably inflated wage claims now being made?

enquires one correspondent to *The Times* (12 December). Undoubtedly he may and will.

Historians have often paid tribute to this peculiar character of the British. It is in grave adversity, in states of emergency, that they have noted this flaring-up of the British spirit. Only then do those proper guardians of the conscience of the community—the retiring middle classes—shed their usual reticence and openly articulate their values and commitments.

One infallible signal of such a time of bourgeois renaissance is the epistolary *levée en masse* of the readers of *The Times*. Such *levées* are infrequent; when they occur, one senses the presence of History. One such took place in February 1886 after the 'Trafalgar Square Riots', when unorganized unemployed demonstrators—after listening to some exciting rhetoric from John E. Williams, John Burns and H. M. Hyndman of the Social Democratic Federation—broke into a brief rampage through the West End, smashing shop windows, looting and even throwing bricks at select London clubs. Worse riots occurred, in most years, in some parts of the country: but not on such sanctified ground as Pall Mall.

'Sir', wrote one unfortunate gentleman, whose carriage windows were smashed in the rioting: 'I am a subscriber to various charities and hospi-

*From *New Society*, 24 December 1970, pp. 1135–6.

tals, which I shall discontinue. I have always advocated the cause of the people. I shall do so no more.'

But wounded and long-suffering righteousness, on these occasions, takes second place to the firm disciplinary mode. 'Sir', demanded one correspondent in 1886,

> What is the use of having a highly-paid Commissioner of Police, with proportionately highly-paid deputies, if they are afraid of the responsibility attaching to their posts? . . . When there is a kennel riot in any kennel of hounds, the huntsman and whips do not wait to get the special orders of the master, but proceed to restore order at once.

Another correspondent (11 February 1886) produced an example of the genre so rich that it has to be quoted at length:

> Sir,
> On returning from the Prince's Levée I was walking through Pall Mall, in uniform. It was gradually filling with very suspicious-looking 'unemployed' at that time, two of whom, turning towards me, one said, rather significantly, 'Why, who the —— is this chap?'
> As I passed the War Office entrance, formerly the Duke of Buckingham's, a blind fiddler, led by a little girl, came by . . . playing some odd tune or other, when a young guardsman on sentry stepped out and said, in a commanding tone, 'You stop that noise' . . . I thought, 'Now there is a man of common sense and of action.' It was a little thing to stop at the time, but when the snowball which a child or a blind fiddler could set rolling on the top of the hill reaches the bottom it has become in this country an immovable monster, in other countries a destroying avalanche.
> On the 10 April 1848, I was sworn in a special constable between Buckingham Palace and the House of Commons. At the former we had a battery of Horse Artillery hidden in the stable yard. I asked the officer commanding what he was going to do? His answer was, 'We have our scouts, and if we hear of any gatherings we could run out and sweep the Mall or the Birdcage Walk in two minutes, or command St James Street and Pall Mall in three.' He would not wait till mischief was done. Are those days quite gone?
> Your obedient servant,
>
> Wilbraham Taylor

Such high heroics can rarely be repeated, just as the true, physical *levées* of the bourgeoisie against the plebs (the Volunteers against the

Jacobins in 1800, the Yeomanry against the poor of Peterloo, the Specials against the Chartist 10 April, the debs and Oxbridge undergraduates against the General Strike) are too few to satiate the desire dramatically to beat the bounds of class. So the epistolary cry goes out for someone—the government—to discipline *them,* and put them back in kennels.

John E. Williams had been reported, in 1886, as having deplored that the unemployed were not well enough organized—not to riot and destroy property—but to occupy the banks, Stock Exchange and government offices. 'Sir', wrote one *Timesian,* 'if correctly reported Williams must be an atrocious miscreant, compared with whom Gashford in *Barnaby Rudge* is a virtuous person.'

December 1970 has produced little in this genre of comparable quality, perhaps because Electrical Workers' leaders are scarcely typecast as communist or trotskyist fiends. (Perhaps the nearest was the letter—14 December—from Nicolas Bentley, suggesting that Robert Morley, who had dared to declare his solidarity with trade unionism, must be a 'callous reprobate'.) But the old theme of 'there ought to be a law against . . .' has been fully orchestrated. This was very evident in another vintage epistolary year, 1926.

One mine-owner addressed himself (5 June 1926) to the subject of the mineworkers' officials: 'Their one object is to squeeze as much money out of the industry as it will stand, to the detriment of the proprietors who have taken all the risk incidental to coalmining.' (A rigorous statistical examination of the number of coal-owners killed in mining disasters might not bear this out.) The Bishop of Durham came baying up behind (22 June): 'Trade unions now include in their ranks a great number of young men whose boyhood was spent during the war, when every kind of discipline was weakened . . . These lawless youths are well-fitted to become the janissaries of Communist Revolution.'

Trade unions were 'the mocking caricature of anything . . . democratic', and their rank-and-file were 'the hopeless fools of the ruling clique'. They could only be held down by stronger law. The compulsory secret ballot, then as now, was one grand recipe for the extirpation of strikes, from correspondents pathetically anxious to believe that if only the workers expressed their minds *in secret* they would turn out to be chaps just like themselves—or, rather, chaps *convenient to* themselves, compounded of all bourgeois virtues of prudence, self-help, and deference to property, but emasculated of the bourgeois reproductive system—the drive for *money.*

Such themes, announced in 1926, have, if anything, become more pronounced with the epistolary *posse commitatus* of 1970. Should strikes be forbidden by law? asks Sir H. T. Smith, from Wallingford (11 December). On the same day the 'long-suffering public' found a spokesman in H. P. Rae: deeply perturbed about invalids dependent upon 'continuously functioning kidney machines' (which they aren't), he demanded: 'why the hesitation in putting in troops *now*?' 'The vast majority of the public', he assured *Times* readers from his Chelsea address, 'are sick to death of the squalid attempts by the unions to tyrannize' et cetera. Mr. Tennet of Sottermill Ponds, Haslemere, also found (12 December) that the workers were '[mis]using their monopoly position', and Richard Hughes, from the United University Club, suggested 'a national one-day token lockout [by employers] in support of the . . . Industrial Relations Bill'.

Mr Flamank of Solihull (also 12 December) wanted to see the formation of 'an emergency service corps', which could, at the Home Secretary's whistle, 'move in and run the services'. Those encouraging industrial unrest, 'be they communists, shop stewards or militant students, are just as much our enemies as were the Nazis'. (Perhaps one can hear an echo of Wilbraham Taylor and the Horse Artillery over Birdcage Walk?)

Such situations tend to make the bourgeois feel, with a sudden flash of insight, their own value in the world: they bear its weight and (*vide* the coal-owner) its risks upon their shoulders. 'Think what the feeling would be', exclaimed Lord Midleton (28 June 1926), 'if any pit were closed for the day and all wages lost to the men because the managing and controlling staff required a day off!' A similar thought occurred to Mr Reade (14 December 1970): 'Sir, If manual workers can work to rule, why not wages clerks too?' Aha! The argument is final: what if we, who *have* the money, stopped letting you rotters have it!!!

It is not to be thought that in such national emergencies, the bourgeoisie is solely concerned with such paltry matters as money or comfort or class power. Not at all: the full moral idealism blazes out. Thomas Hughes, the Christian Socialist author of *Tom Brown's Schooldays*, came unhesitatingly to his post in the correspondence column in 1886: these modern socialists he found to be 'notorious ruffians', and 'If Mr Chamberlain will consider where he cannot be getting Messrs Hyndman & Co a year or two's oakum picking instead of "receiving their views in writing" he would be doing all honest folk more service, in my judgment.'

At such moments *Timesian* correspondents always know unhesitatingly what are the thoughts and needs of 'all honest folk' or of (see *The Times*, 14 December 1970) 'the welfare of the entire community' (Rose Cottage, Westhumble, Surrey). But it was left to the honest folksman, Sir Alan Lascelles (The Old Stables, Kensington Palace), to come forward as shop steward of 'an immensely larger union—namely, the union of British citizens' (17 December).

In 1926, however, the immediate requirements of the 'entire community' were pointed out to the striking miners in more dulcet tones, since they had made the tragic error of being manoeuvred into a bitter, wasting strike during the summer months, and the readers of *The Times* were suffering, not from empty grates, but from an overfull sense of moral outrage. At such a time the clergy select themselves as the proper admonishers. The Dean of Worcester advised the miners (8 June 1926) that if they capitulated to the coal-owners' terms they 'will have won a great victory—a victory of their nobler over the lower self.' The Archdeacon of Chester addressed the same homily with greater fervour: capitulation by the miners 'would be good Christianity . . . an act of personal self-denial . . . of personal self-renunciation for the sake of others, following the supreme example of the Greatest Figure in history.'

One has yet to notice, in 1970, correspondents congratulating the power workers, who called off their work to rule, on their good Christianity, or likening Frank Chapple to the 'Greatest Figure' in history. (Nor did *The Times* publish such congratulations from rural deans in 1926, when the miners returned to their pits defeated; after all, such letters, if read at the pithead, might have induced moral complacency, and, as events were to show, the nation was to expect a good deal more Christianity from the miners in the coming years.)

But—let us be fair—there has been one change in the genre in recent years: the clergy, generally, do not push themselves forward so obtrusively, nor do they presume so readily to express the conscience of the nation on socially-divisive issues. Their role, as national conscience and admonishers of delinquents, has been passed over, in good part, to David Frost and Malcolm Muggeridge. Some small part, perhaps, has been taken over by that new conscience-bearer, the middle-class housewife, who being out of the hurly-burly and puerility of industrial warfare, can watch all things with a wholly objective eye and instantly detect from her kitchen the national interest. Thus, on 11 December, a correspondent from Prescot, Lancs:

> . . . the radio is dead. The television is dead. The electric heaters are dead. The kettle is dead. The fridge is dead. My washing machine is dead. My iron is dead. All the street lights are dead . . . Goodness knows how many *tragic* deaths may result . . .

It is (she concludes) 'an exhibition of power surely grotesque in its selfishness.'

All dark and comfortless: we stalk the drear world of the psalmist or space-fiction writer: all that inanimate world of consumer goods, animated each quarter by the insertion of money, lies inert, disobedient. All flesh is grass, we know; but what (O ultimate of horrors!) if all gadgets turned out to be grass also? It is the Rebellion of the Robots, recorded by the author of Ecclesiastes.

Grotesque and selfish the power workers' action may have been. How can one know? Facts have been scarcer than homilies. Reading the press one learns that one has been living through little less than cosmic disaster. One had thought that one's neighbours had suffered little more than power cuts for several hours on three or four days, but the mistake is evident. Outside there, in the darkness, the nation had been utterly paralysed for week upon week; invalids dependent upon 'continuously operating' kidney-machines lived two or three to every street; armed robbers prowled the darkness with impunity; not a hospital in the country that was not lit solely by candles, with surgeons operating upon month-old babies by the light of a failing torch.

A comparatively few individuals, wrote a correspondent from Richmond (12 December) were inflicting upon the public 'catastrophic injury'. Why not 'issue an order *withdrawing all legal protection* from the persons and property of the workers concerned', and the officials of their unions? 'Let the community get its own back.' This 'whole community' (another correspondent, 16 December) 'has long been renowned for its patience and forbearance. But surely the time has come,' et cetera. 'We are sick and tired . . . ,' 'the time has come,' 'irresponsible' . . . irresponsible *to us!*

What is, of course, 'grotesque in its selfishness' is the time-worn hypocrisy of the bourgeois response to discomfort. Anyone familiar with the Victorian and Edwardian press cannot fail to detect, in these tones of moral outrage, that old bourgeois theme for moralisms: the 'servant problem'. But the servants now are out of reach; an electric light switch is impervious to the scolding of the mistress; a dust-cart cannot be given a week's wages in lieu of notice.

And anyone who has read his E. M. Forster or his Angus Wilson knows the old British bourgeois propensity to moralize his own convenience and to minister to his own comforts under a cloud of altruism. For 95 per cent of the bluster and outrage was the miasma rising from tens of thousands of petty material inconveniences. The electric alarm failed to go off, mummy fell over the dog in the dark, the grill faded with the fillet steak done on one side only, daddy got stuck for half an hour in the lift on the way to a directors' meeting, the children missed *Top of the Pops*, the fridge de-froze all over the soufflé, the bath was lukewarm, there was nothing to do but go early to a loveless bourgeois bed. But, wait, there was one alternative: 'Sir, Writing by candlelight . . .'

But to mention the *real* occasions might seem petty. It was necessary to generalize these inconveniences into a 'national interest'. The raw unlit fillet steak became an inert kidney-machine, the dripping fridge an operating theatre, the loveless bed became a threat to the 'whole community'. No matter: now the emergency is over these moral fantasies will shrink back to their proper size. The shivering old age pensioners (many of whom will continue to shiver all winter through on their inadequate pensions), the imperilled invalids (many of whom will continue in peril from inadequate medical provision) will cease to obtrude themselves in the correspondence columns of *The Times*.

It has been a notable state of national humbug. It was concluded, as in an obligatory ritual, by David Frost, at peak viewing hours on a Saturday night, bullying a few power workers, with a studio audience, handpicked for their utter insensitive self-righteousness, baying at his back.

Occasions were found, not only to express moral disapprobation, but also approval; the audience applauded to the echo nurses who, underpaid as they are, would never strike because of the needs of their patients. David Frost who, from what one has heard, does not face the same financial dilemmas—and the withdrawal of whose labour would scarcely induce even this government to declare a state of 'national emergency'—was evidently delighted. The bourgeoisie has always been ready to acknowledge virtue in the servant class when it finds it: pliant, loyal, living patiently in the attic, carrying on dutifully a service to the 'whole community'. Aubrey Leatham, physician at St George's Hospital, Hyde Park Corner, saluted the same virtue among the cardiac technicians at his hospital (*The Times*, 16 December) who, earning 'as little as £415 a year, would like to strike, but they do not, because they are humanitarian'.

And how noble they are, indeed, to pace the hearts of emergency patients in the acute care area for only £8 a week! But, surely, if this is so, this also is an outrage, which we should have heard of before, and insistently, and not only as a stick to beat the power workers with? Has Mr Leatham taken up his pen before, to press the astonishing case of his cardiac technicians? Or will he, and the other militant correspondents to *The Times* and so many other papers, relapse into silence now that the inconvenience and discomfort is over?

The grand lesson of the 'emergency' was this: the intricate reciprocity of human needs and services—a reciprocity of which we are, every day, the beneficiaries. In our reified mental world, we think we are dependent upon *things*. What other people do for us is mediated by inanimate objects: the switch, the water tap, the lavatory chain, the telephone receiver, the cheque through the post. That cheque is where the duties of the good bourgeois end. But let the switch or the tap, the chain or the receiver fail, and then the bourgeois discovers—at once—enormous 'oughts' within the reciprocal flow.

But these 'oughts' are always the moral obligations of other people: the sewage workers ought not to kill fish, the dustmen ought not to encourage rats, the power workers ought not to imperil invalids, and—this week it will be—the postmen ought not to deny bronchitic old age pensioners of their Christmas parcels from grandchildren in Australia. Why, all these people owe a duty to the 'community'!

What the duty of the community is to these people is less firmly stated. Certainly, those whose lolly is the theme of the business supplements— those whose salary increases (like those of admirals and university teachers) are awarded quietly and without fuss, and which (it seems) create no national emergency and no dangerous inflationary pressures— have little need to compose letters to *The Times* as to their own moral obligations and duties.

It is the business of the servant class to serve. And it is the logic of this reified bourgeois world that their services are only noticed when they cease. It is only when the dustbins linger in the street, the unsorted post piles up—it is only when the power workers throw across the switches and look out into a darkness of their own making—that the servants know suddenly the great unspoken fact about our society: their own daily power.

The mass media and racial conflict*

PAUL HARTMANN AND CHARLES HUSBAND

Communication between people is possible to the extent that they share common frameworks of interpretation. They need to have similar meanings for the same symbols, and a way of thinking about things in common before they can communicate. Our perceptions are structured by the mental categories available to us for making sense of our world.

Research into attitudes commonly concentrates on differences in attitude between people and groups, and the interpretive frameworks within which such differences occur are either taken for granted or ignored. Where racial prejudice is concerned this emphasis may produce a tendency to seek the origins of prejudice in the personality of the individual or the immediate social situation rather than in the cultural framework itself. This approach was evident in the *Colour and Citizenship*[1] survey and made possible the comforting but misleading conclusion that intense prejudice is a phenomenon rooted in the personality of the individual, an irrational solution to the inadequacies of an undermined personality.[2] But prejudice is not in the first instance the result of immigration, personal pathology or social strain; it is built into the culture. Our whole way of thinking about coloured people, influenced by the colonial past, constitutes a built-in predisposition to accept unfavourable beliefs about them. The very notion of 'tolerance' betrays this cultural bias, for it implies that there is something nasty that requires special virtue to put up with. Even 'authoritarianism', so often cast as the villain of the piece, is not some purely personal aberration; for the beliefs and values that serve to define it are related to our particular social and industrial history and are well embedded in British culture. They have much in common with 'Social Darwinism' and the 'Protestant Ethic'. Only after the underlying cultural predisposition to prejudice had been taken into account does it make sense to ask how variations in prejudice relate to other factors.

*Extracted from Paul Hartmann and Charles Husband, 'The mass media and racial conflict', *Race*, Vol. XII, No. 3 (January 1971), pp. 268–82 Published for the Institute of Race Relations by the Oxford University Press, © Institute of Race Relations, 1971.

The mass media and attitudes

A considerable amount of research effort has been devoted to assessing the influence of the mass media on attitudes and opinions. Results, on the whole, have shown that social attitudes, including prejudice, are relatively resistant to influence through the media. What effects have been demonstrated have typically been of a limited kind. Trenaman and McQuail,[3] for instance, in their study of the effects of the 1959 election campaign on television showed that this produced increases in political knowledge, but were unable to find any effects on attitudes or voting behaviour. Blumler and McQuail's[4] important and complex study of the 1964 election campaign found that various kinds of attitude change did occur as a result of exposure to election television, but the particular kind of attitude change depended on the characteristics of the voter, particularly his motivation, and it was not possible to make across-the-board generalizations that applied to the electorate as a whole. In an early study on prejudice, Cooper and Dinerman[5] found that although many of the *facts* presented in an anti-prejudice film did not get through to the audience, this was not associated with change of attitude, and there was even evidence of 'boomerang' effects.

One of the main explanations for findings of this kind is selection. People select what they read and what they view and tend to avoid communications that they find uncongenial. They are also selective in what they perceive and what they remember. Where the 'message' clashes with existing attitudes or beliefs it is typically the existing outlook that remains intact, while the 'message' is rejected, or distorted to fit the outlook. A study of viewers' reactions to a programme in an ITV series, 'The Nature of Prejudice'[6] carried out in 1967 found that prejudiced viewers evaded the intended anti-prejudice message by a variety of means, ranging from becoming hostile towards the interviewer (who was opposed to prejudice) to finding in the programme confirmation of their own views.

In reviewing research on the effects of mass communications Klapper[7] came to the conclusion that they are much more likely to reinforce existing attitudes (whatever the attitude and whatever the 'message') than to change them. Attitudes may be expected to be particularly resistant to change when they are supported by strong group norms or the prevailing cultural climate.

Work of our own confirms that direct effects on attitude following short-term exposure to media material are unlikely. We studied the effects of the six-part television series, 'Curry and Chips' which caused some controversy in November and December 1969. We gave questionnaires to about 200 secondary schoolchildren, both before the beginning of the series and after it had finished. They had no reason to connect us or the questions with television. The questionnaires included attitude measures as well as open-ended questions designed to elicit beliefs and information about Pakistanis. On the second occasion they were also asked how many of the programmes they had seen. Differences between responses on the two occasions were analysed in relation to the number of programmes viewed. We expected that children who had seen all or most of the series would show changes in information and attitude not found in those who had seen none of the programmes. We found no effects that could be attributed to viewing the programmes. Even when analysed in relation to initial attitude, to whether the children had discussed the series with others, to how true-to-life they had thought it, and other variables, the data yielded no positive results.

This is not to say that the series had no important effects, but only that it appears not to have had the type of effects studied. We do not know the extent to which children's initial opinions were strengthened by viewing the programmes, for instance. It may be that the series helped to make it more acceptable for both children and adults to make fun of immigrants. Letters of complaint appearing in the press and anecdotal evidence suggest that for a time at least this was so. And going on press reports and letters, we have the impression that one of the main effects of the series was to affront the Asian communities. A further possibly important effect was that the programmes provided a focus of discussion in which the questions of immigration and race were aired in informal groups up and down the country. Sixty per cent of the children we surveyed claimed to have discussed the series with others. This must at the very least have resulted in greater awareness of race as a controversial topic and greater familiarity with prevailing norms. All that emerges clearly from our study is that to look for effects in terms of simple changes of attitude may be to look in the wrong place.

More generally we should not conclude from the type of research that we have been discussing that the media have no important influence on public opinion or race relations. Part of the reason for the high incidence of null results in attempts to demonstrate the effects of mass communications lies in the nature of the research questions asked and the limitations of the theoretical orientations of the research tradition. Much of this work was influenced by a view of man as an atomized unit of mass society,

whom stimulus-response psychology saw as responding in a straightforward way to the stimuli or 'messages' of the media. The tradition is
characterized by a search for direct effects, short-term effects, and an
over-reliance on attitude as the index of effect.[8] This kind of model of
mass media influence is still the basis of much thinking on the subject. It
may be that the media have little immediate impact on attitudes as commonly assessed by social scientists, but it seems likely that they have
other important effects. In particular they would seem to play a major
part in defining for people what the important issues are and the terms in
which they should be discussed. Thus the debate surrounding race in
Britain has come to be defined as hinging on immigrant numbers and the
threat to existing social patterns, rather than on integration, housing, or
other issues.

We now present, with some supporting evidence, an outline of one of
the main ways in which we believe the mass media influence the race
relations situation in Britain at the present time. We are concerned with
the news media in particular because these relate directly to the present
social situation, have wide circulation and enjoy the high credibility that
enhances their capacity to influence how people think.[9] They also provide a steady stream of race-related information. Preliminary content
analysis shows that the typical popular national daily contains on average
two items a day in which coloured people in Britain or the U.S.A. figure,
or that deal with explicit race-related topics.

The argument

Briefly, our thesis is that the way race-related material is handled by the
mass media serves both to perpetuate negative perceptions of blacks and
to define the situation as one of intergroup conflict. In communities
where there is a realisitic basis for conflict (e.g., competition for housing)
black-versus-white thinking about the situation will be reinforced by the
media and existing social strains amplified. In multi-racial communities
where there is no 'objective' basis for conflict, conflict may be created
because people come to think in conflict terms. People in all-white communities are particularly liable to accept the interpretation of events
offered by the media because they lack any basis of contact with coloured
people on which to arrive at an alternative way of looking at things—
apart, of course, from the view of blacks provided by traditional culture.

Mass communications regarding race will be interpreted within the
framework of meanings that serve to define the situation within any social

group. At the same time the way race-related material is handled in the media contributes towards this definition of the situation. Attitudes and interpretations prevailing in a community are therefore seen as the result of the interplay between the on-the-ground social situation and the way race is handled by the media. 'Media influence' is seen as operating on interpretive frameworks—the categories people use when thinking about race-related matters—rather than on attitudes directly. The way the media define the situation is seen as resulting from the definitions prevailing in the general culture and from institutional factors that stem from the media themselves.

The media are social institutions located within the overall socio-economic structure, and they have their own characteristics which influence the form and content of their output. In the first place, the nature of the medium itself, the kind of production ideology this generates, together with simple physical limitations of time and space, and the need to attract readers and viewers, imposes constraints both on what events make the news and on the kind of treatment they receive. The well-known preference for action visuals over 'talking heads' in television production, for instance, means that television coverage of a riot, say, is likely to emphasize the violence to the neglect of the causes and background. This was the major criticism made against the television coverage of the 1967 disturbances in America by the Kerner Commission.[10] The Commission concluded that the type of coverage given contributed to the definition of the disturbances as simple black-white confrontations. This is still the generally accepted view, even though the Commission found that the situation was in fact far more complex. 'In fact almost all the deaths, injuries and property damage occurred in all-negro neighbourhoods, and thus the disorders were not "race riots" as that term is generally understood.'[11]

The cultural legacy

There are two main strands to our argument. They are intertwined but it will make for clarity to illustrate each separately. Briefly, the first is this: The British cultural tradition contains elements derogatory to foreigners, particularly blacks. The media operate within the culture and are obliged to use cultural symbols. Hence it is almost inevitable that they will help to perpetuate this tradition in some measure. The prevalence of images and stereotypes deriving mainly from the colonial experience and at least implicitly derogatory to coloured people may be gauged from the existence of a number of traditions of cartoon jokes. These include the missionary in the pot, the fakir on his bed of nails, the snake charmer, and the polygamous Eastern potentate with his harem. Similar themes and images are to be found in nursery rhyme, idiom and literature.

We do not think that these examples are particularly important in themselves, except as an index of the widespread familiarity with, if not acceptance of, the image of coloured people that they carry. It does, however, become disturbing to find this kind of outmoded image obtruding itself into the media handling of current events concerning real people; so that elements of the cultural legacy that are at best ethnocentric and at worst racist come to influence reactions to and interpretations of race-related events in Britain today. The tendency may most clearly be seen in headlines and in cartoon comment, where the use of a phrase or image that will evoke a similar set of associations and meanings in virtually all members of the society to which it is directed enables a complex point to be crystallized unambiguously and memorably in a few words or a single picture. In its front page report of the discovery of the forty illegal Indian immigrants in a Bradford cellar last July the *Daily Express* of 2 July used the heading POLICE FIND FORTY INDIANS IN 'BLACK HOLE'. This is an instantly recognizable allusion to the 'black hole of Calcutta', which, by evoking colonial associations suggests that the appropriate attitude to adopt towards these Indians is that adopted towards the natives in the days of Empire. We are not suggesting that this is what the *Express* intended, only that this is the sort of reaction that the heading is likely to have achieved. The importance of headlines in influencing the way news items are interpreted has been demonstrated by Tannenbaum, and by Warr and Knapper.[12] Headlines have a particularly strong influence when the item itself is not thoroughly read. In the illegal immigrant story, a similar effect was created by the cartoon in the *Sun* on 3 July in which an illegal immigrant asking the way addresses a white man as 'Sahib', and in the cartoon in the *Mirror* on 6 July which showed two lovers on a beach, one of whom was saying 'I thought you said this was a quiet beach' while the beach was being overrun by illegal immigrants in turbans, including a man riding on an elephant, a snake-charmer complete with snake, and a man carrying a bed of nails. The reiteration of this kind of image, not merely at the level of joke or fantasy, but in relation to actual events involving real people, can only perpetuate an outlook which is not only outmoded but antithetical to good race relations and likely to influence perceptions of current events. These examples illustrate the way in which a cultural tradition may be at least party self-sustaining. The image is used because it exists and is known to have wide currency and therefore enables easier communication. By virtue of being used it is kept alive and available for further use.

News value

The second strand of our argument concerns the concept of 'news value' which influences the pattern of coverage of race related topics. We might regard news value as composed of some of the major criteria by which information about events is gathered, selected and published. Johan Galtung's[13] famous analysis of what factors make events newsworthy includes the concepts of unambiguity, meaningfulness, consonance, continuity and negativeness. Though we shall not use these terms our approach is essentially the same. A similar approach was used by Lang and Lang,[14] who showed that the television coverage of a parade in Chicago bore a closer resemblance to the newsmen's anticipations of what the event would be like, than to what actually happened. Similarly, Halloran[15] and his colleagues in their recent study of the anti-Vietnam war demonstration in London in October 1968 showed how the event came to be defined by the media in advance as a violent one, and once this news framework was established, how it structured the coverage of the event itself so that violence was emphasized, and the issues involved and the predominantly peaceful nature of the march neglected.

For present purposes we may distinguish two kinds of characteristics which make events newsworthy. Firstly, conflict, threat, and deviancy all make news, both because information about these has a real importance to society, and because, for various reasons, people enjoy hearing about them. Conflict is the stuff of news just as it is the stuff of drama and literature. Material that can be couched in terms of conflict or threat therefore makes better 'news' than that which cannot. Hence for the story of the forty illegal Indian immigrants referred to above, the front page of the *Daily Mail* of 2 July 1970, carried the headline 40 INDIANS 'INVADE'. The word 'invade' manages to imply that society is somehow threatened by them. This theme was echoed in the *Sun* of 3 July which headed its story THE INVADERS, and in the *Daily Sketch* of the same date which had the headline: 'INVASION OF MIGRANTS' FEAR IN BID TO BEST BAN. Similarly, the police were said to have 'seized' the Indians in the same way as drugs, firearms and other dangerous commodities are seized (*Sun* and *Express*, 2 July). This story was big 'news', being carried on an outside page of seven of the eight major national dailies. That it could be made to carry the inference of threat and conflict would seem to be at least part of the reason that it was thought so newsworthy.

A second feature that makes events more newsworthy is their ability to be interpreted within a familiar framework or in terms of existing images, stereotypes and expectations. The framework and the expectations may originate in the general culture, or they may originate in the news itself and pass from there into the culture. The situation is one of continuous interplay between events, cultural meanings, and news frameworks. The way events are reported helps structure expectations of how coloured people will behave and how race relations situations develop. Subsequent events that conform to the expectation stand a better chance of making the news than those that do not. Thus new events may be interpreted in terms of existing images even if the existing image is not in fact the most appropriate. The use of the image of ethnic conflict derived from the American disorders of the 1960s as the framework for reporting the British situation is a case in point.

In January 1970 the Birmingham *Evening Mail* published a series of feature articles on the race relations situation in the Handsworth area, which explained the background to the social problems there. This was a positive attempt to foster better community relations and was rightly commended as such. The first article of the series, which gave an overview of the situation, provides a good example of what we have been discussing. Its first sentence was 'Must Harlem come to Birmingham?' In the subsequent fifty column inches there were four further explicit parallels drawn between Birmingham and the United States. There were also fourteen separate sentences in which explicit reference was made to violence (this excludes generalized references to crime and robbery). Effectively the situation is defined as one of potential riot. Thus the image of black-white confrontation derived from the media coverage of the American disorders becomes the model for thinking about the British situation, both because it is known to be familiar to the audience, and because it fulfils expectations of how race relations situations develop. The question is, is such an image the most appropriate one for Birmingham today, and does its use not have all the elements of the self-fulfilling prophecy? Might it not be that any benefits resulting from the in-depth explanation and pro-tolerance tone of the *Evening Mail* series were bought at the expense of confirming expectations of civil disorder and amplifying conflict in the area? The author of the article himself seems to be aware of the danger, for he writes:

> The trouble about violence in a multi-racial area like those we have in north Birmingham is that it may be dangerous to the community. People start using emotive words like 'race-riot' and take sides accord-

ing to the colour of their skins. Reports appear in overseas newspapers. Before you know it the community is split into bitter factions.
The problems of the Handsworth area are bad enough as it is.

The fact that he is effectively doing with the best of intentions what he
fears might be done by others and the overseas press illustrates the apparently unconscious nature of many of the assumptions that go to structure
the news.

The numbers game

Public perceptions of the race relations situation depend very heavily on
the type of material made available through the media, the relative prominence given to different types of material and the way it is handled. All
these factors are influenced by considerations of 'news value'. A comparison of the coverage given to two events by the eight major national
dailies provides an illustration of this process in a particularly important
area.

The events were the publication on 10 March 1970 of the Registrar
General's returns which showed that the birth-rate among immigrants
was higher than the national average, and the announcement by the Home
Secretary on 14 May 1970 of the immigration statistics which showed
that the rate of immigration was decreasing and that the number for the
previous quarter was the lowest on record. Our comparisons are of the
coverage of the events on 10 March and 15 May respectively, the days on
which the news was first carried.

Seven of the eight national dailies carried the birth figures, five of them
on the front page. Only four carried the news about the reduction in
immigration, only one of these on the front page. The average headline
for the birth figures occupied four times as much space as the average
headline for the low immigration figures. Altogether there was about five
times as much news-space given to the birth figures and reactions to them
as to the immigration figures (approximately 250 column inches as compared with about 50). Five of the seven papers carried Enoch Powell's
reaction to the birth figures, of which only one, *The Times,* went to the
trouble of trying to balance the story by eliciting reactions from other
sources. This pattern of coverage meant that almost no one who opened a
newspaper on 10 March—or even glanced at his neighbor's on the bus—
could fail to become aware that the coloured population was increasing
and that this was regarded as a matter of great importance; while only the

most diligent newspaper reader on 15 May would have discovered that the rate of immigration was low, and reducing.

Even if we accept that the birth figures were of greater social significance than the reduction in immigration and therefore warranted greater coverage, and allow that Enoch Powell did make a statement, a reportable event, it would still seem necessary to invoke other factors to explain this pattern of coverage.

Specifically, events that carry or can be given connotations of conflict or threat are more newsworthy than others. 'More coloureds' is thus better copy than 'fewer coloureds'. That the threat image was important in making the birth figures newsworthy is clear from the opening paragraph in the *Telegraph's* front page report where it was stated that 'there was no sign of panic over the fact that nearly 12 per cent of the 405,000 babies . . . were conceived by mothers born outside the United Kingdom'. And the front page of the *Sketch* carried the assertion that 'The report adds fuel to Mr Enoch Powell's previous warnings of the rapid breeding rate among coloured families.' Note the use of the word 'warnings' and the acceptance of the Powell definition of the situation. The idea that coloured people constitute some kind of social threat is simply taken for granted— it has become one of the unspoken assumptions of the news framework. The birth figures made a story that fitted this framework, and so the story got big play. The reduction in immigration didn't fit the framework very well, and so it got little play. But even in the reporting of the immigration figures the framework is evident. All four papers that carried the story also reported the Home Secretary's determination to keep the figures low.

Finally the amount of newspace devoted to Powell's statement must be partly explained by the fact that Powell on race has come to be newsworthy in himself. Once a particular kind of news has hit the headlines there appears to be a lowering of the threshold for subsequent news of a similar kind. With Powell one has the impression that since his first immigration speech his every utterance on the question is now thought worth reporting, even if what he says differs in no important respect from what he said the previous week.

Some results

It is one thing to argue from an examination of the media themselves that their handling of race effectively defines the situation in conflict terms, and another to show that this pattern of coverage does in fact influence people's view of the matter. We now present evidence based on a partial analysis of some of the data from our ongoing research that provide support for our general argument. These results cannot be taken as conclusive because our sample is small and confined to white working-class secondary schoolchildren, and the differences we have found do not always reach a high level of statistical significance. A rigorous evaluation of our argument must await the completion of our data collection and analysis. However, the results we have available show a sufficiently coherent pattern to make them worth presenting now.

Unless otherwise stated, the quantitative evidence that follows is based on a combined group of 208 11/12 year old and 14/15 year old children, both boys and girls. Half of them come from areas of high immigration in the West Midlands and West Yorkshire and half from Teesside and Glasgow where immigration has been very low. Schools were chosen in pairs from each area so that one contained an appreciable number of coloured immigrant children (at least 10 per cent, normally 20–40 per cent) and the other few or none. So we have fifty-two children from 'high contact' schools in 'high contact' areas (high-highs), fifty-two low-highs, fifty-two high-lows and fifty-two low-lows. We shall make our comparisons between 'high' and 'low' types of *area,* and our sampling design ensures that the children are roughly equated for amount of personal contact with coloured people, and for social class.

The first thing that has become evident from our interviews is the widespread conviction that the number of coloured people in the country or the rate of immigration is very high and that this poses some kind of threat. This is true even of places where there has been no immigration. In a school in a County Durham village for example (not part of the sample described above) as many as 35 per cent of children expressed something of this kind in response to general open-ended questions. When specifically asked whether they thought anything should be done about coloured immigration to Britain, nearly half (47·4 per cent) advocated restricted entry or more stringent policies. In areas of high immigration the impression of vast numbers is understandably even greater and a clear majority want the numbers limited or reduced. But in an area like our Durham village the only possible major source of this impression is the media. Even apart from that, what is striking is that the idea that 'there are too many here' or 'too many coming in' should be taken as self-evident by such large proportions of children wherever they live. Clearly the message about numbers and their implied threat has got through. It has been equally evident that the message that there is little threat (promoted from time to time, usually in editorials) has not got through. Nor has it got through that whatever threat was posed by unrestricted immigration is now being dealt with. We were confronted with people recommending, as a matter of urgency, the adoption of policies that have been in operation for five years! This is clearly the result of the pattern of reporting about 'numbers' discussed earlier. The inference of threat that any increase in numbers has come to carry is also evident from the fact that when asked how they thought the presence of coloured people in Britain would affect their lives in the future, 23 per cent of all answers referred explicitly to increasing numbers or expressed the fear that the blacks would 'take over'.

Other findings show an interesting pattern. Firstly, children in areas of high immigration are more aware of the major points of 'realistic' competition or conflict between black and white—namely, housing, and employment—than are children in 'low' areas. When asked, 'How do you think the presence of coloured people in Britain might affect your life in the future?', firstly fewer of them foresaw no effect (thirty-eight compared with sixty-one of the 'low' group), and secondly they were more likely to say that their housing or employment opportunities would be threatened (25 per cent of 138 answers given compared with 13 per cent of 117 answers—these include 'no effect' answers. When 'no effect' answers are left out, the percentages change to 35 per cent of 100 answers in 'high' areas, and 27 per cent of fifty-six answers in 'low' areas. Some children gave more than one answer). This fits the commonsense expectation and is also consistent with the pattern of attitude scores which shows that there is more hostility in areas with a realistic basis for conflict.

On this basis we might expect that the ideas of white children in areas of high immigration would be relatively more dominated by the notion of conflict than those living elsewhere. To test this we examined the responses to one of our first questions, 'Can you tell me what you know about coloured people living in Britain today?' Ten per cent of each group gave no answer. Of the remainder we counted the responses having a conflict theme. These fell broadly into three groups: (a) References to direct conflict, e.g., 'They cause trouble.' 'They make riots.' (b) Responses implying incompatibility of interests between black and white, e.g., 'They take all the houses.' 'They take white people's jobs.' 'They'll take over the country soon'; and (c) Responses that showed awareness of hostility of whites to blacks, e.g., 'People dislike them; are prejudiced against them; discriminate against them.' These were counted whether they were said with approval or disapproval. The essential criterion was whether the response explicitly or implicitly contained a definition of the situation in terms of conflict. This is not the same as attitude. Contrary to the hypothesis we found that conflict themes were more common in areas of *low* immigration (29·6 per cent of 159 responses, as compared with 23·0 per cent of 161 responses in areas of high immigration—some gave more than one response).

For each response a child gave we asked him also for the source of his information. 27·4 per cent of the 190 sources mentioned in 'low' areas were media sources, against only 17·5 per cent of 177 sources in 'high' areas. Taking both groups together, 54·2 per cent of the 83 responses attributed to a media source were 'conflict' responses, as against 45·1 per cent of the 62 attributed to other people, and 16·7 per cent of the 222 claimed as personal experience, 'own idea', or 'don't know'. So of all the information children were able to give us, that obtained from the media was more likely to contain the conflict theme than that obtained elsewhere. Looked at in another way, there were 110 responses in all that had the conflict theme of which 45 (41 per cent) were attributed to a media source. There were 41 answers that mentioned cultural differences (religion, clothing, life-style) of which only five (12 per cent) were attributed to media sources. This suggests that while the media seem to play a major role in establishing in people's minds the association of colour with conflict, their role in providing the kind of background information that would help make the race relations situation, including its conflict elements, more understandable, is relatively small.

The picture seems clear, and is what might be expected if our analysis of the handling of race-related matters in the mass media is correct. Children who live in areas of low immigration rely perforce more heavily on the media for their information about coloured people than do others. Media-supplied information carries the inference of conflict more often than that from other sources. As a result these children are more prone to think about race relations in terms of conflict than are those in 'high' contact areas, even though they (the 'lows') live in places where the objective conditions for inter-group competition or conflict are absent. It would seem that while *attitudes* are responsive to the characteristics of the local situation—i.e., the extent of immigration—interpretive frameworks, ways of thinking, are heavily structured by the mass media, particularly in areas where there are few immigrants.

Conclusion

. . . We have argued that a number of factors pertaining to traditional culture, to the media as institutions, the technologies and their related ideologies, and to the interplay between these factors, operate to structure the news coverage of race related matters in a way that causes people to see the situation primarily as one of actual or potential conflict. Blacks come to be seen as conflict-generating *per se* and the chances that people will think about the situation in more productive ways—in terms of the issues involved or of social problems generally—are reduced. The result is that real conflict is amplified, and potential for conflict created. For the media not only operate within the culture, they also make culture and they help shape social reality.

Clearly the factors that we have discussed are not the only ones that structure news coverage. There are obviously others, including the nature of events themselves and editorial policy, but the ones we have discussed do influence what is reported and how it is reported. Although there may be political and other motives at work in the media that influences the coverage of race, it is not necessary to invoke these to explain the kind of pattern we have described. A main point of our argument is that this kind of result may be produced in a quite unintended fashion. The media do not need to *try* to define the situation in terms of conflict. They need merely unreflectingly to follow their normal procedures of news-gathering and selection and to apply their normal criteria of news value.

REFERENCES

1. E. J. B. Rose *et al.*, *Colour and citizenship* (London, Oxford University Press for the Institute of Race Relations, 1969).
2. N. Deakin, *Colour, citizenship and British society* (London, Panther Books, 1970).
3. J. M. Trenaman, D. McQuail, *Television and the political image* (London, Methuen, 1961).
4. Jay G. Blumler and D. McQuail, *Television in politics: its uses and influence* (London, Faber & Faber, 1968).
5. E. Cooper, H. Dinerman, 'Analysis of the film "Don't be a sucker": a study in communication'. *Public Opinion Quarterly*, Vol. 15, No. 2 (1951).
6. The study was carried out by Dr Roger Brown in connection with a production study conducted by Philip Elliott, to be published shortly.
7. J. T. Klapper, *The effects of mass communication* (New York, Free Press, 1960).
8. A good review of work in this tradition is to be found in Klapper (op. cit.). For general reviews and discussion of mass communications research and theory see: D. McQuail, *Towards a sociology of mass communications* (New York, Collier-Macmillan, 1969); M. L. De Fleur, *Theories of mass communication* (New York, McKay, 1966); J. D. Halloran (ed.), *The effects of television* (London, Panther, 1970).

9. See, e.g., Klapper (op. cit.), Chapter V.; C. I. Hovland, I. L. Janis, H. H. Kelley, *Communication and persuasion* (New Haven, Yale University Press, 1953).

10. *Report of the National Advisory Commission on Civil Disorders* (New York, Bantam Books, 1968).

11. Ibid., p. 365.

12. P. H. Tannenbaum, 'The effect of headlines on the interpretation of news stories,' *Journalism Quarterly*, Vol. 30, (1953), p. 189–97; and P. B. Warr and B. Knapper, *The perception of people and events* (New York, John Wiley & Sons, 1968).

13. J. Galtung and M. H. Ruge, 'The structure of foreign news', *Journal of Peace Research*, No. 1 (1965). See extract in this Reader.

14. K. Lang and G. E. Lang, 'The unique perspective of television and its effect: a pilot study', *American Sociological Review*, XVIII (1953), pp. 3–12.

15. J. D. Halloran, P. Elliott and G. Murdock, *Demonstrations and communications: a case study* (Harmondsworth, Penguin Books, 1970). See also article by G. Murdock in this Reader.

16. H. Evans, *The Listener* (16 July 1970).

The British press and the 'placing' of male homosexuality*

FRANK PEARCE

It has often been said that women are the unspoken, denied a voice, a chance to articulate their own needs and desires unmediated by the men in their life or those (tragically) absent. The position of male homosexuals is not dissimilar. Their existence has been denied or they have been displayed or, more recently, display themselves (Larry Grayson, John Inman . . .) only within a rhetoric structured by a paternalistic heterosexual discourse. In the media and, most accessibly in the press, one can find examples of the 'placing' of male homosexuals: thus it is on the press and, particularly the time span from the early 'Fifties to the early 'Seventies, that I focus. And yet, even after the recent 'sexual revolution', one finds that little has changed. The 'revelations' about Anthony Blunt show the resilience of the categories discussed below. It is a commonplace in sociology that in unequal societies, difference is seen as deviance, as a failure, an inability, to accord to an absolute standard. As such the deviant's voice is not to be heard as that of an equal, another in a dialogue, but rather as a symptom, as evidence of pathology.

Thus, in the current political climate, dominated by the 'New Right', other ways of seeing the world, of doing and being, are seen as *de facto* deficient. An absurd yet frightening example of this is in a recent editorial (Mr Robinson and Mr Blunt) in the reborn *Times* (22 November 1979). Not only were Blunt's homosexuality and his communist sympathies seen as indices of the same flaw in Cambridge culture but, the editorial goes on to say, 'Even in the case of Maynard Keynes, perhaps the finest product of this culture, there may be a parallel between his emotional resentment of the monetary rules which prevented inflation, and particularly the gold standard, and his need to reject the conventional sexual morality of his period. He did not like rules.' The theories that guided the economic policy of most capitalist states for the last forty years need no intellectual

*This is an edited and revised version of the paper in the first edition.

The Manufacture of News

contestation—they are self-evidently wrong, the products of a brain overheated by deviant sexuality!

The homosexual as scapegoat

Why is male homosexuality treated with both fear and scorn? Any answer to this question entails an analysis of 'normal' sexuality and particularly the attitude of the Christian church, the major source of public morality. In the Christian tradition, sexual urges are seen as part of base nature, as something to be controlled. Complete control could, of course, not be achieved if for no other reason than that people would only 'increase and multiply' through sexual intercourse. Whilst at different times the churches were more or less optimistic about the degree of control that could be achieved in Victorian Britain, at least publicly, repression was rife.[1] Sexual pleasure was discounted and sexuality tied to reproduction—a functional stress renaming the complex of heterosexual desires as the 'racial instinct'.[2]

Such a view was compatible with both the Malthusian pessimism dominant during most of the nineteenth century and the concern with producing healthy workers and soldiers in the early part of the twentieth century. After further concern in the 1930s about a drop in the birth rate, the 1940s saw the beginning of a change in attitude. Fears about underpopulation and the quality of the population were transformed into a worry about overpopulation. Social concern over this and the custom of smaller families led to a decreasing emphasis on marriage as a baby factory. The relationship between husband and wife gained in importance, and sex was credited with a significant role in this relationship. Only when sex was openly discussed in the newspapers was it possible to focus attention on homosexual practices.

Official morality has long defined such practices as unnatural. As opposed to this view I would argue that people in this society are potentially bisexual (Kinsey's US figures imply that 50% of males have homoerotic feelings[3]) and are brought up in a 'sex-negative' culture, where homosexuality particularly is condemned and is therefore not provided for in any socially accepted way. Exclusive heterosexuality and exclusive homosexuality are not conditions but are rather 'roles' to which people are committed, to a greater or lesser extent. In this society the heterosexual role is publicly valued, highly articulated, socially provided for and also associated with gender identity. At the same time men who wish to engage in homosexual practices after adolescence are virtually forced to utilise the organised homosexual network of meeting places which exist in the interstices of the society. Commitment to a homosexual way of life is likely to result, since some kind of minimal involvement is called for in order to learn the skills and cues necessary for this as any other sexual activity. Thus the average male in this society is constantly pushed towards heterosexual involvement and away from homosexual eroticism, and if he experiments with homosexuality, he is likely with increasing age either to abandon it or virtually to commit himself to it completely by adopting a homosexual role. And so exclusive homosexuality is a logical corollary of enforced exclusive heterosexuality and occurs when a homosexual role has been created.[4]

Homosexuals and the media

I have argued that homoerotic feelings are normal and yet they are still treated in everyday conversation as being exceptional. A potent source of such ideas and of a general image of homosexuality is the newspaper industry. In its treatment of homosexuality it is forced to cope with the disparity between an image of man's naturalness and the continued violation of such a picture. If being sexually attracted to women is the genetic concomitant of possessing a penis, how to explain those who look elsewhere for their pleasures? Men finding other men attractive are anomalies and anomalies, as Mary Douglas points out, endanger the natural moral order of this society. A natural moral order constructed because 'in a chaos of shifting impressions each of us constructs a stable world in which objects have recognisable shapes, are located in depth, and have permanence'.[5]

But our categories are constantly confronted in everyday living with a world which they cannot exhaust, and this becomes serious when there are anomalies which question the validity of the very categories themselves. In such cases she suggests that societies (such as that of the Israelites), have evolved strategies for dealing with the threat to their universality. (1) Negatively we can ignore, just not perceive them or perceiving them, condemn. (2) We can settle for one or other possible interpretation of what they are and thereby reduce ambiguity. (3) We may use the anomaly as a negative reference point, all that something should not be. (4) The anomalous event may be labelled as dangerous and reacted to appropriately, and this may involve violence. I will return to these categories below where I intend to use them in my substantive analysis.

Since reports in papers were infrequent I have concentrated on a limited number of cases that were important news stories, also on feature articles in the Sunday papers. The news stories include those dealing with the trials of Montagu and Wildeblood, the Vassall case and the Wolfenden Report; the feature articles were written in 1952, 1963, 1968 and 1972. Furthermore, although I have read accounts in *The Times* and *Guardian* I have taken most of the examples from the *Daily Mirror*, the *Daily Sketch* and *The Daily Telegraph;* the *Sunday Pictorial/Sunday Mirror* (changed January 1963), the *News of the World*, and *The People*. There is ample justification for such concentration since *The Daily Telegraph* is the most read paper by those in social grade AB, and in 1970 whilst only 45% of this social grade bought a *Sunday Times* or *Observer*, 45% bought the *Sunday Express*, and another 49% bought either the *Sunday Mirror*, the *News of the World* or *The People*. Needless to say the latter three newspapers were the most widely read by the rest of the population.[6]

Suppression of Knowledge

The first method of coping with anomalies is to ignore them. Prior to the 1950s homosexuality was virtually never mentioned and an examination of daily and Sunday newspapers even in the 1950s finds it mentioned relatively infrequently. One survey, on examining press cuttings covering *all* homosexual cases reported in national or provincial papers, from October 1954 to February 1955, found that only 321 individuals were reported as charged. The number of reports fell far short of this since pairs of these individuals were often in the same case.[7] My own examination revealed that only some local papers and the *News of the World* regularly devoted space to brief court reports concerning homosexual activities. This and other information was generally bitty and restricted to a minority of homosexuals, feeding stereotypical pictures of their activities. Occasionally, however, there was a news explosion. During most of 1957 the *Daily Mirror* never mentioned homosexuality, then, after the publication of the Wolfenden Report, in September it devoted to it 963 column inches in two weeks. The following two weeks it had already dropped to 45 column inches, and after that there was virtually no reference to the subject at all.[8] The articles of Swarth in the *Sunday Pictorial* of 1952 were seen by Swarth and the *Daily Mirror's* editor Hugh Cudlipp as an end to this 'conspiracy of silence' about the subject. Cudlipp claimed that these articles

> stripped the subject of the careful euphemistic language in which it has always been concealed. Doctors, social workers and the wretched

homosexuals themselves recognized this as a sincere attempt to get to the root of a spreading fungus.[9]

The blatant dishonesty of such a statement is made evident by Swarth's own proud account of homosexual fears about the effect of his articles. '"This will make life dangerous", one of them said and he named three of his revolting friends, who on the strength of my report, took the boat to Guernsey' ('Evil men', *Sunday Pictorial*, 1 June 1952).

Deviants, social problems and pleasure

In the stereotypical presentation of deviants' identity, the essential self of the deviants is seen to reside in their deviant activity: as murderers, cold-blooded IRA gunmen, junkies, homosexuals. Their 'essential' difference from other men is emphasized by *objectifying* them, using a vocabulary which emphasizes that they are *less than* the normal human citizen. Homosexuals are called 'freaks', 'perverts', 'degenerates' and may be given animal characteristics: Vassall's 'pale eyes flickered like a lizard's towards the domed ceiling and he did not reply . . . He listened unblink-ing, emotionless as a newt.' Meanwhile (!) 'Burgess sits in Moscow like a patient toad awaiting his next willing victim' ('Twilight Traitors', *News of the World*, 28 October 1962). They may also be described as 'sick', 'ill' or 'unfortunate' (even by those who supported the 1967 Sexual Offences Bill). Yet these also objectify, they express the arrogant pity of the 'healthy' for the 'sick'. Sometimes there is an unintended humour in those articles. Vassall was often described as a 'tool of the Russians', and one doctor said that the study of homosexuals was 'still in the groping stage of trial and error' ('Evil men', *Sunday Pictorial*, 8 June 1952).

I have already indicated that all classes read the sensational press. Perhaps they find deviance an interesting phenomenon because 'There are many pleasurable feelings many people are forbidden to experience, imagine, remember, dream about, and they are definitely forbidden to talk about them.'[10] These pleasurable sensations that we have denied but not annihilated may be lived through again by means of the sensational newspaper. By reading a newspaper we are able to stumble across stories about the unthinkable-for-me, pleasurable deviant acts. We can read the details, be disturbed by the salaciousness of what is written, and then condemn what has taken place. We have thereby broken none of our convoluted rules, and yet lived through the forbidden experiences and gained the additional pleasure of moral indignation. Although people complain about the sensationalism, morbidity and triviality of newspapers, 'Sex, crime, violence, scandal and gossip, the very topics deplored, regularly obtain high "thorough readership" scores.'[11]

To analyse adequately the treatment of homosexuals we must take account of its specificity. Guy Burgess in particular and also Oscar Wilde remain ideal-typical models for the affluent homosexuals as in the case of one newspaper account of Vassall's life. Furthermore, there are constant cross-references to various cases, supporting Galtung's contention that news items are reported in images derived from previous stories.[12]

Ambiguity and resolution

The second method of dealing with anomalies is by settling for one or other interpretation. Mary Douglas points out that the Nuer treat monstrous human births as baby hippopotami and lay them down in the river where they belong. Homosexuals violate the natural order—they are men who are attracted to men. Instead of being an animal born to a human they are women born in a man's body. This metaphysical belief that homosexuals are men with women's souls even inspires much medical research as for example experiments trying to find evidence of female chromosomes[13]. This similarly explains the stress by journalists on effeminacy—usually emphasised through juxtaposition with normal masculinity.

'Most people know there are such things—"pansies"—mincing, effeminate, young men who call themselves queers. But simple, decent folk regard them as freaks and rarities.' ('Evil men', *Sunday Pictorial*, 25 May 1952).

Thus they are seen as working in the 'unvirile' professions: Homosexuality is rife in the theatrical profession. Dress designers, hat makers, window-dressers have a high percentage of homosexuals in their ranks. The style and comportment are female. They 'have mincing ways' (Evil Men', *Sunday Pictorial*, 25 May 1952), call 'each other girls' names openly', are 'painted perverts', (*Sunday Pictorial*, 8 June 1952). They wear women's clothes—this was stressed in the Vassall case ('Secrets of the scented flat', *Daily Sketch*, 24 January 1963). Then: 'I watched effeminate-looking men disappear into the "ladies" to titivate their appearance and tidy their waved, dyed hair before going into the back room to dance and cuddle with their "boyfriends".' ('Do we need pubs like this?' *The People*, 24 March 1968.) During the Montagu-Wildeblood case the *Daily Mirror* published a photograph of Wildeblood which made him look extremely effeminate. On close examination the photograph had obviously been touched up so that he looked as though he was wearing lipstick. Finally there is often a stress on a female-like interest in clothes. Vassall had 'nineteen Savile Row suits' (*Daily Sketch,* 23 October 1962).

Having recategorized homosexuals as women in men's bodies resolution can be achieved by uniting the female mind with a female body. The newspapers are sympathetic when operations are performed to effect just such transformations, even when they are writing emotive articles against homosexuals.

Thus the *Daily Sketch* (15 December 1953) had an article entitled 'SEX CHANGE DILEMMA' which dealt sympathetically with the problems faced by somebody wanting a sex-change operation. This was in the middle of the Montagu of Beaulieu case, and just over a month after an article by Donald Soper entitled WHY I WANT A ROYAL COMMISSION TO INVESTIGATE VICE, meaning homosexuality (in which he made the novel prediction 'that a disarmed world would be a world in which homosexuality would die out'.)

The *News of the World* (7 October 1962) had a sympathetic article headlined SEX CHANGE BRIDE; only three weeks later it had a vicious article entitled TWILIGHT TRAITORS. Similarly on the front page of the *News of the World* (9 November 1969) headlined LONDON BOBBY TURNS INTO A GIRL, an article stressing that Miss Linda Grant had always been feminine from the beginning.

The effeminate are generally viewed as harmless, the world laughs at them but it rejoices with them when they resolve their 'identity' problems and match the right mind with the right body.

Moral tales

Needless to say not all homosexuals are so treated. Their existence may also be used, as a negative reference point; as an occasion to reinforce conventional moral values by telling a moral tale. Through these means tensions in the social system can be dealt with and 'conventionalized'.[14] Explicit and implicit contrasts are made between the nature and moral career of 'ordinary men' and that of 'perverts', 'degenerates', 'sick men', 'freaks' and the 'abnormally sexed'. These latter inevitably come to a bad end and the whole incident is used as an occasion to preach 'a little sermon'. Nowhere has this been better demonstrated than in the case of Vassall, the rather insignificant spy of the early 1960s. Vassall was discovered to be a spy after a whole series of scandals during the 1950s — Burgess, Maclean, Philby and the Portdown spy ring. There were allegations that his boss at the Admiralty, Galbraith, was emotionally involved with him, although this seems unlikely. However, it was through

Vassall's homosexual activities that the Russians were able to blackmail him. He was finally sentenced to 18 years' imprisonment and was released in 1972. The whole case was used by the press to demonstrate what happens to the unnatural.

To understand how this was done, it is necessary first to construct the implicit model of the career of the 'normal man'. He is born into a normal, stable family. He is given the appropriate amount of affection by his mother. His father helps him to develop masculine qualities. He then goes to a school befitting his class and intelligence. He works hard there, playing sports well. He then gets a job fitting his abilities, ideally in a useful occupation—not in the intellectual world, not in the world of bars or the retail clothing trade. He marries and has a family. He is proud of his respectable family and his useful job. He respects and is respected by those in other strata. He is patriotic and would go off to war.

Contrast this with the portrayal of Vassall. He had a strong affection for his mother—'I needed mother love and after my mother died they felt they could provide it!' (*Sunday Pictorial*, 11 November 1962). At school he didn't work hard academically and avoided sports. 'He was colourless and rather effeminate,' Captain Noel Elston, the headmaster at his public school said. (*Sketch* 23 October 1962). He had 'no moral fibre'— Defence Counsel (*Daily Telegraph*, 23 October 1962). (That peculiar concept compounded of a Christian belief in free will and some kind of genetic determinism.) At school this was expressed by his homosexual relations with other boys. It expressed itself in failures throughout his life: he failed to gain a commission; he was only an Admiralty clerk; and he also (supposedly) failed with women. (See particularly *Daily Mail*, 23 October 1962). Vassall also claimed to be what he had no right to say he was. He had claimed to be rich (when his father was only a clergyman and he was only a clerk). He matched this presumptuousness with snobbishness. He did not manage his social relationships properly.

Homosexuals are often seen to violate such barriers. Oscar Wilde had been virulently condemned for his relation with the lower classes and Wildeblood was criticized during his trial in 1954 for mixing with 'social inferiors', and much stress was placed on those who were given 'lavish hospitality from men who were their social superiors'.

As Wildeblood points out, the prosecution even relabelled a bottle of cider as a bottle of Champagne. Similarly in the 'Evil men' series Swarth wrote, 'In Swansea police consider the vice most rampant among the "socially elevated classes", although they take their unnatural desires down to the dockland.' (*Sunday Pictorial*, 1 June 1952) The discipline of national life is seen as being endangered and it is precisely in those areas where this is most important that homosexuality is most severely attacked. Sexuality involves some kind of equality, if only through mutual need, hierarchical institutions are threatened by this. Thus the Army, Air Force, Navy and Merchant Navy are excluded from the provisions of the 1967 Act.

It was not surprising then that an unsuccessful Vassall became a spy—a 'Traitorous tool of the RUSSIANS' as *The Daily Telegraph* expressed it (23 October 1962). His vice enabled the Russians to blackmail him—they had photographs of him in compromising positions with other men.

He was seen as true to type; 'After the Burgess and Maclean scandal, civil servants were urged to report any colleagues they suspected of having character defects such as drunkenness or homosexuality' (*Daily Express*, 13 November 1962).

'Who was for years an uncrowned leader in these garish guilty places? A diplomat called Guy Burgess, who disappeared to Moscow eleven years ago' ('Twilight traitors', *News of the World*, 23 October 1962). But now justice was done: 'Men—ordinary men who were patriotic, with normal feelings towards each other—had placed him in the dock, caged him like a rare trapped reptile.'

When characterizing homosexuals as being effeminate and when using them to tell moral tales, a contrast is frequently drawn with 'normal men'. In the Vassall case Colonel John Macafee, Director of Security, was quoted in the *Daily Sketch* (23 October 1962) as saying, 'But if anyone wants to have me sacked, let them try. I walk around with a smile on my face and my shoulders are wide enough to take whatever is coming.' However people who thus could not be homosexuals turn out to be so. Particularly problematic are wartime heroes. For if a man is a brave superpatriot, how can he be a 'degenerate'? Two solutions are available. They are either not homosexuals or they are not really superpatriots. In 1962, on 23 December, less than a month after the article on 'Twilight traitors' in the *News of the World*, there appeared the following news item.

ARMY HERO CLEARS HIS NAME

Wartime hero Michael Abbey Osborn who had been sentenced to be dismissed from the Service won his battle to clear his name in the High Court. Colonel Osborn, holder of the DSC and MC, was accused of indecently assaulting a 15-year old German boy a fortnight after arriving in Germany as Deputy Chief of Staff to the First British Corps of the Rhine Army. The 44-year old Colonel, whose home is in the Old Brompton Road, Kensington, London, was found guilty at a Court Martial at Bielefeld. He appealed to the High Court but the three judges could not agree. Then Lord Parker, the Lord Chief Justice, ordered the appeal to be heard again by five judges. This time the appeal was allowed, and the conviction was quashed (*News of the World*, 23 December 1962).

This news item was also reported by the *Daily Mirror* on 23 January 1963 as THE CLEARED COLONEL WHO IS AFRAID TO BE FRIENDLY. This while they were still reporting the Vassall case.

In the *Sunday Mirror* of 7 April 1973, the front page was devoted to another wartime hero ex-Lieutenant-Commander Christopher Carlisle Swayer. This was headlined WAS JUSTICE DONE? and outlined the dubious evidence on which this man was found guilty in 1956 of indecent assault. Happily he has since cleared his name. One wonders what the verdict would have been of those who followed the *Sunday Mirror's* guide, 'How to spot a possible homo'—only three weeks later on 28 April.

But if the clearly homosexual perform admirable tasks? Their motives are discredited so.

They claim successes not only as writers and in the arts, theatre and poetry, but also as generals, admirals, fighter pilots, engine drivers and boxers. The brilliant war records of many homosexuals are explained by the fact that, as the Spartans, they fought in the company of those whose opinions they valued most highly (*Sunday Pictorial*, June 1952).

So it is for lust, not for patriotism that homosexuals behave bravely.

Dangerous deviants

The above ways of coping with deviants have not particularly viewed them as a threat. When there is a stress on their inadequacies (not really men. . . .) then they can be viewed as sick. They are people who require help and providing that they do not offend public decency, they can be more or less ignored. Further, when homosexuals are used in moral tales, the ending of the tale usually involves some kind of natural justice for them—again suggesting that society working normally will catch them if they are being harmful. The 'commonsense' precautions at embassies will exclude them as liable to blackmail, etc. However, alongside, homosexuality can also be viewed as dangerous, leading to an emphasis on a rather different stereotype from the effeminate male. Homosexuals are seen primarily as corrupters of youth. Society is seen as clearly divided into

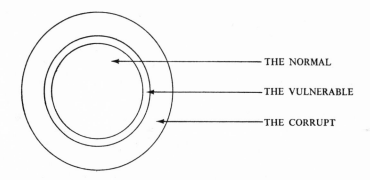

three groups; the normal, the vulnerable and the corrupt. The relative size of each group depends on what is being presented, as does its visibility. Here homosexuals are seen as interested above all in young children. Thus Swarth bemoans that few parents 'recognize the corrupting dangers of the evil men who, in increasing numbers, pervert youngsters to their unnatural ways'. And he exemplified this by referring to the case of a

> 51-year old vicar sent to prison for 15 years for ten offences against boys and a little girl of 13. He asked for 27 other offences to be taken into consideration. The police found a little black book in his posse-ssion, containing the names of 850 boys. Against the names of 382 of them were various symbols (*Sunday Pictorial*, 28 May 1952).

During the *Mirror's* coverage of the Wolfenden Report, it juxtaposed on the same page for several days general articles on the topic with others on a sensational sexual murder case, thus potentially linking this murder in the readers' minds with homosexuality. Information can be received without explicit linking. (One does not have to argue that this was being done to mislead—the fact that these news items were viewed as strongly associated is significant.) This model of homosexuality has the advantage that all homosexuals can be included. Vassall, for example, was seduced by much older boys. So there is an unending tale of childhood corruption. Moreover, one such contact is sometimes seen as enough, as in Swarth's account of the 'Steamers', ageing homosexuals were reputed to look out for youths, job hunting.

> They offer them bed and breakfast, and that, in case after case, is a young man's introduction to perversion. Inevitably he drifts to the clubs that male prostitutes frequent! Furthermore, many men who are not homosexuals go to prison and come out tainted in this way, making

them even more of a social menace than they were before ('Evil men',
Sunday Pictorial, 4 June 1952).

And under extreme circumstances, anybody is vulnerable—in the article
on the Leeds pub, *The Hope and Anchor,* one Rugby player said 'that he
was the only man who had been a regular at the pub for seven years
without going bent' (*The People,* 24 March 1968).

This view of homosexuality is a disease model. It sees homosexuality
as a contagious disease—much as madness was seen in the 18th century
in France. Foucault comments thus:

> Suddenly in the middle of the 18th century a fear arose—a fear formu-
> lated in medical terms but animated basically by a moral truth. People
> were in dread of a mysterious disease that spread, it was said, from the
> houses of confinement, and would soon threaten the cities. They
> spoke of prison fevers; they evoked the wagons of criminals, men in
> chains who passed through the cities, leaving disease in their wake;
> scurvy was thought to cause contagions; it was said that the air, tainted
> by disease, would corrupt the residential quarters. And the great im-
> age of medieval horror reappeared, giving birth, in the metaphors of
> dread, to a second panic. The house of confinement was no longer
> only the Lazar house at the city's edge; it was leprosy itself confronting
> the town.[15]

Similar views but about homosexuals were expressed in the House of
Commons debate on the Sexual Offences Bill in 1966, and in Swarth's
treatment of gays; and it is virtually identical to what James Douglas,
editor of the *Sunday Express,* wrote in 1928 on the occasion of the
publication of Radclyffe Hall's novel of lesbian love, *The well of loneliness.*

> I have seen this plague stalking shamelessly through great social as-
> semblies. I have heard it whispered about by young men and young
> women who do not and cannot grasp its unutterable putrefaction. Both
> aspects of it are thrust upon healthy and innocent minds. The conta-
> gion cannot be escaped, it pervades our social life. Perhaps it is a
> blessing in surprise or a curse in disguise that his novel forces on our
> society, a disagreeable task which it has hitherto shirked, the task of
> cleansing itself from the leprosy of these lepers, and making the air
> clean and wholesome once more (*Sunday Express,* 1928).

Like all these views on homosexuality this helps to solve crucial difficulties caused by the prevalence of the phenomenon. For if it is widespread then it is difficult to describe it as unnatural. It may well be that men can as *rationally* engage in homosexual practices as in heterosexual ones. (Or that men can be socialists as well as stay within the dominant bourgeois political culture, or smoke marijuana as rationally as drink beer. All such deviant activities are on occasion explained by invoking such a model). By treating homosexuality in this way it becomes possible to avoid any confrontation with the real living men who are homosexuals. They can be *legitimately* hounded, locked away and even castrated or destroyed. Of course there is a certain consistency in their view. While these practices are unnatural many may be tempted but only the morally inferior will succumb.

The newspapers' treatment of homosexuality is comprehensible as an attempt to come to terms with the anomalous nature of the activity. Homosexual acts call into question the 'natural' order which has been so necessary for industrial capitalism. I have tried to show how hard the newspapers have to work to suppress the information that destroys both their conception of homosexuality and of the normal moral world. These efforts have been at the expense of homosexual men who have suffered terrible legal and social persecution, stigmatization and psychological stress. One of the worst examples of this very persecution involved the murder of a young man. Michael De Gruchy, on Wimbledon Common on 25 September 1969. Two years later the *Sunday Times* Magazine covered the incident with a story entitled THE QUEER BASH KILLERS (*Sunday Times* 7 February 1971). In this article they discussed the urban anomie in the large estates near the common. They quoted a psychiatrist who thought 'the constraints on violence are missing'. Everybody was shocked at the conduct of the four youths who killed De Gruchy. Nobody however related their behaviour to the attitudes of the wider society to homosexuals. Nobody mentioned that only a year before, *The People*, (1 September 1968) had run an article about THE SICK MEN OF HAMPSTEAD HEATH, which provided a perfect rationale for persecuting homosexuals. Nor did they mention that the boys in their explanations of what they did used *identical* phrases to those used in the original article. 'If they do it in private that's one thing. . . .' The boys recognised the presence of homosexuals by 'the glow of cigarettes': just as *The People's* reporters said that homosexuals could be spotted signalling to each other. Was this anomie? Surely not! After all what were these boys if not agents of a 'public consensus' so artfully created by the papers?

Notes and references

1. M. Ruggoff *Prudery and passion* (London, Hart Davis, 1971); G. Rattray-Taylor, *Sex in history* (London, Thames and Hudson, 1953); M. Foucault, *The history of sexuality* (London, Allen Lane, 1979); F. Pearce and A. Roberts, *The social regulation of sexual behaviour and the development of industrial capitalism in Britain* in R. Bailey & J. Young (eds) *Contemporary social problems in Britain* (Farnborough, D. C. Heath, 1973).
2. See C. W. Saleeby's contribution to A. Emmott, *The nation's morals* (London, Cassell & Co, 1910).
3. M. Schofield, *Sociological aspects of homosexuality* (London, Longmans, 1965).
4. M. Macintosh, 'The homosexual role', *Social Problems,* Volume 16, No 2 (Fall 1968). W. Churchill, *Homosexual behaviour among males* (Englewood Cliffs, Prentice Hall, 1971).
5. M. Douglas, *Purity and danger* (Harmondsworth, Penguin Books, 1966), pp. 49, 51–2.
6. See the readership surveys used by *The Guardian.*
7. During the 12-month period 1955–6 some 5,963 men were charged in England and Wales with homosexual offences. In the five-month period reported this would mean some 2,485 men were prosecuted. See *Criminal Statistics England and Wales 1969* (London, HMSO, 1970). For the newspaper survey see J. Tudor Rees and H. Usill, *They stand apart* (London, Heinemann, 1955), pp. 195–7.
8. I am grateful to Tony Marsden for these figures.
9. H. Cudlipp, *At your peril* (London, Weidenfeld & Nicolson, 1962).
10. R. D. Laing, *The politics of the family* (London, Tavistock Publications, 1971), p. 115.
11. J. Curran, 'The impact of TV on the audience for national newspapers', in J. Tunstall (ed), *Media sociology* (London, Constable, 1970), p. 106.
12. Quoted in J. D. Halloran, P. Elliott and G. Murdock, *Demonstrations and communications, a case study* (Harmondsworth, Penguin Books, 1970), p. 26.
13. C. M. B. Pare, 'Etiology of homosexuality: genetic and chromosomal aspects' in J. Marmour (ed) *Sexual inversion* (New York, Basic Books, 1965), p. 73.
14. In a sense the constant reiteration of similar tales is equivalent to, although much less clearly articulated than, anthropologically interesting myths. They provide a mechanism by which contradictions can be discussed and dealt with. See C. Levi-Strauss, *Structural anthropology* (London, Allen Lane, The Penguin Press, 1968), ch. XI.
15. M. Foucault, *Madness and civilisation* (London, Tavistock Publications, 1965), p. 202.

Images of women in the media*

HELEN BUTCHER ET AL.
(Women's Studies Group,
Centre for Contemporary Cultural Studies)

'I'm going to fly you to Miami like you've never been flown before.
I'm Leslie.
Next time you want to see what you've been missing,
fly my wide-bodied, non stop jet from London to sunny Miami.'

(National Airlines ad in *The Guardian*)

Of course 'Leslie' is also the name of a *National* plane, but how secondary that knowledge is when a smiling woman's face beams down on the
reader. An ad. selling *National* flights? An ad selling woman's sexuality
as if she were a prostitute for sale. An ad which demands from us a more
complex understanding than this. An ad from which we can move in
order to begin to talk about images of women in the media. And
in this paper we do no more than suggest such a beginning. It points to the
way in which images are *produced* images: adverts are so contrived we
can see vividly that they are not representing reality but re-presenting it
(giving us it again) in a transformed way. It points to a hidden history.
Why has woman's sexuality come to be used in this way? Could it not be a
man's? It hints at the contradiction that images of women always betray.
They are rarely there as active, living individuals, but yet it is *one* woman
who is standing for what women *are*, whether it is sexual objects,
mothers or housewives. It suggests the *connotative* value of women's
images: one simple image, a smiling, pretty face and we are already into
the realm of sex or fantasy, happiness or sunshine (she'll fly you to
Miami), excitement or power—for *men*. It persuades us too of *equality*
between men and women: "*I'm* going to fly you . . ." balanced by "you
. . . fly *my* wide-bodied . . ."

Every day on TV and in newspapers, in magazines and at the cinema,
in the street and the underground, we see and hear many similar verbal

---

* These extracts are from a stencilled Occasional Paper of the same title, Women Series SP
no. 31, Centre for Contemporary Cultural Studies, University of Birmingham, November
1974.

317

and visual images of women. Usually we taken them for granted. They are part of our everyday lives. They appear 'natural'. They appear inert not just because we are accustomed to the various media and do not see their processes of production, but because those are the images we are socialised into categorising women in terms of. And although it may be predominantly the media presenting those images to us from our earliest days, it is the social relations predominantly outside the media, in the family and at work which give rise to these categories. In looking at the media we are moving from the specificity in which each medium projects its images to the generalities concerning woman's position in society. So though the media have their own structures and processes, their own codes which translate women into those contexts in specific ways, the level of sexist ideology and its practice arises from a wider base. That sexist ideology, which is lived by us, is the primary determination on the signification of the images of women created in the media.

For instance TV's presentation of the 'Miss World' competition appears because it is a world event and hence newsworthy, because it is entertainment. The Misses of the world are allowed a measure of individuality, if not in terms of their bodily proportions, they do speak about themselves. But are those women that different from the anonymous sexual Leslie of the National ad? The one sells herself as the most perfect object; the other sells National planes as the most perfect planes. Or the housewife. Jeremy Thorpe's election appeal to the 'housewives'—'the women who will decide'—is not produced through the same practices, nor for the same ends as the image we receive from a letter by a 'housewife' who describes when, after a busy and interesting day, an old school friend rings her only to comment: "You poor thing you must be bored as a housewife." (The *Sun* 24 October 74). Jeremy Thorpe's appeal requires that there are such 'housewife' images around.

We have said that images of women are the end-product of media *and* social practices. But the contribution of media practices: to do with the techniques of camera and lighting, the representation of three dimensions in two, as well as the kind of programme or article—news, documentary, fiction, adverts—structures images in such a way that there is a preferred signification. For when all is said and done the purpose of the media is to signify. There is a transparency in the media images which no individual, individuals who are primarily living out a history and only secondarily signifying what their actions are about, can ever have. The media image is complexly structured, but whether verbal or visual is still 'simpler' than 'real life': we have to understand and read it in a particular way. However, although we can interpret 'simplification' in relation to women as a 'reduction' of women, it focuses for us their *fragmentation*. That, real as it is, is usually disguised. Because no woman is just sex object, mother, housewife, whore, she manages to unify these contradictory images of herself. She is on the surface a woman; underneath, those parts. To illustrate the point, the removal of all obnoxious ads like National Airlines' would not necessarily change how men see and treat women. The empty, waiting, sexual vessel *is* how many women are treated by men, but the fact is less obvious when the woman is also a mother and housewife than when she makes a 'simple' appearance in the context of an advert.

This fragmentation is readily evident in the *differential distribution* of images. On TV and radio, if you look and listen long enough, to all programmes, you'll not only see most of the stereotypical images emerging, though in different programmes, and weighted heavily towards some, but also hear individual women doing their best to *negotiate* out of the images they are being persuaded into. In porn there is only the 'lascivious bitch' or 'passive whore'. In women's magazines no elderly, poor or ugly—and so on.

Not only do women appear fragmented, but each of those fragmented images is condensed. The images are familiar and conventional, immediately ripe with connotations, as 'Leslie' is. That simple image which *denotes* just a pretty woman brings together all those associations: she is a symbol for sexuality, excitement, exotic places etc. We will see later that it is adverts which most obviously use woman's image to symbolise. It is however a symbol which is iconic. That is part of the signified remains woman. Theoretically something else could signify those areas, but neither something nor man does: it is woman, and it will be important later to understand why. That it is not woman as such that is important in ads is clear from the use of parts of her body only, her body distorted, a focus on breast or lips, to signify sexuality.

But she is also a symbol or metaphor in a different way. Disguised within her appearance is perhaps the most repressed content of our culture, that which men can only cope with in a *displaced* way. Latently the image of woman often refers not just to women's relation in and to the world, but, not surprisingly since most of these images are constructed and read by men, to men's being in the world. As Anthony Wilden suggests:

> The male myth of 'insatiable' female sexuality is in effect a metaphor of the insatiable demands the socio-economic system makes on men as human beings. It is not the women that men cannot satisfy; what men cannot satisfy are the machines: technique, technology, production and performance.[1]

Or to hint at an area we shall elaborate in detail later, cartoons in the working-class press—the *Sunday Mirror* and *Sun*—ridicule women to an abominable degree: they appear in all their worst attributes, they are stupid, they nag, they are subservient. . . . However does it not make sense that cartoons about man's successful power in the home may also be a displaced way of coping with his lack of power at work? He laughs at women's weakness, not just with scorn, but as a way of distancing himself, defining himself against a state of being he is not allowed to adopt. He cannot be 'just a pretty face', simple and loving; he has to fight in an aggressive competitive world.[2]

Woman as humour

Women, the cartoon and the popular press

'Woman' as a stereotype of media production is nowhere so clearly portrayed as in the cartoon of the popular press. This is for reasons indigenous both to the type of humour and to the nature of the method of communication.

First, the essence of cartooning lies in caricature; in exaggeration of characteristics in order to enable quick and easy recognition (think of the length of Edward Heath's nose in any cartoon!). In the same way, 'woman' becomes very tightly defined by her most easily recognised functions. Secondly, (in the examples that have been chosen) the cartoon is static; it has to make its point in a single statement (short conversation at most) or in a single action, which allows for no subtlety of representation.

The cartoon must also be seen in relation to the audience for which it is intended. Therefore the images which the cartoonist chooses to present will be those which have relevance for the greatest number of his readers. We have all experienced the alienation engendered by lack of understanding of an 'in' joke. The popular press has a distinct, vested, economic interest in avoiding any such alienation of its reading public. Therefore, as Richard Hoggart says, 'the massive popular press must restrict itself to the appeals and attitudes which are most popular. . . . There must be no significant disturbing of assumptions.'

Therefore, 'woman' as seen in the cartoons of the *Sunday Mirror, Daily Mirror, Daily Mail* and the *Sun* is always seen at the level of her highest common factor, at her most stereotyped and paradoxically in her saddest form.

Woman as an object of humour

In order to analyse 'woman' as portrayed in humour, we must look both at the reasons why people laugh, that is the processes involved in producing the physical act and also at the reasons why such a form of humour exists.

In all the examples chosen (from 20th–26th October) the essence of the humour in the cartoon is *ridicule*. That is, laughter *at* somebody, having a joke at somebody else's expense. In all the cases mentioned below, the laughter engendered is at the expense of women. The major emotion that is produced in the reader is one of scorn, and to be scornful it is necessary to convince oneself of one's own superiority. (This superiority can be experienced by both men and women). When an idea of humour is added to that of scorn, then the object of that humour is reduced to a state of debasement.

Max Eastmann, in *The sense of humour,* says, 'And the reason why we hate to be laughed at, is that we experience a feeling of inferiority on such occasions. . . . For no matter how truly the laughers assure us that they are not hostile, but only happy—they feel no scorn but rather a delighted love of our natural blunder—still there remains the fact that we *are* inferior.'

If this kind of woman-objectified humour is produced from reducing woman to a state of inferiority, to a state of debasement, it is important to look behind to the mechanisms which result in this kind of action. Hobbes, in his famous opinion about laughter, said that the passion that aroused laughter was 'sudden glory', which was produced 'either by some sudden act of their own that pleaseth them: or by the apprehension of some deformed thing in another, by comparison thereof, they suddenly applaud themselves. And it is incident most to them, that are conscious of the fewest abilities in themselves: who are forced to keep themselves in their own favour, by observing the imperfections of other men.'

In twentieth-century terms it is therefore possible to see the cartoons of the popular press as a male-contrived, male-produced, male-supporting ego trip, generating laughter which can be seen as the outward expression of an inner contentment which this real or imaginary superiority inspires!

To be more serious, I would like to suggest that the humour of the cartoons is not just an incidental phenomenon which entertains, but that it embodies distinct social mechanisms. These social mechanisms are exactly those which are at work in other forms of the media; those mechanisms by which men maintain their position of social dominance both consciously and unconsciously. I do not think that at this stage it is necessary to debate the reality of our male-orientated society. That is, the ideology which tells us that male action, thoughts and words are *the* reality, the norm, and that women are deviant from that norm. However, that very deviancy has a norm in itself and it is this norm of women which produces the stereotype. As Sheila Rowbotham says, 'The media have considerable power to throw back to us a version of ourselves which is presented as the "norm" '. If we take the male-production oriented norm as given, we begin to see how it is possible that women (as in the examples below) are only defined as related to men.

There are two sides to the humour which binds women to this male norm: two ways in which the mechanism of social dominance controls the image of women in the media.

First, there is the *exclusive* aspect of cartoon humour. This is the aspect which says that masculine and feminine are mutually exclusive and that it is never possible for one sex to do a job which is socially prescribed for the other. This places women completely outside the male norm and then scorns those activities which are traditionally 'feminine', not admitting women to any aspect of the 'real' world. That is, dominance is maintained by not admitting to any comparison of value between the two activities, since there is no common scale of values.

Secondly, there is an *inclusive,* 'social corrective' aspect of humour, by which woman is still seen as deviating from the male norm, but in which she is encouraged to attempt to attain the male world and take on male-based characteristics. The humour is engendered when the woman fails to reach the male norm. That is, maintaining dominance by encouraging woman to a position for which she has not been culturally raised and is therefore likely to remain 'inferior'.

Thus, we return to the old dual concept on which women's theory constantly comes unstuck: the fact that women are both inside and outside the system, that they are both 'fundamental and marginal at the same time'.

This duality of women's position produces another, less obvious idea within the humour of women generally; that there is within the idea of derision a sneaking suspicion of envy by the male responsible for the humour. This means that while the superficial cartoon develops the idea of the small-minded housewife, woman as consumer, emotional, illogical, there is an argument that the male cartoonist might well desire to be able to show those qualities of emotion, of frivolity, of concern for family over 'job', which he is forbidden to show because of his own binding to his own male stereotype.

Specific examples

I would like to look at four cartoons in detail, to see how woman adheres to and deviates from the male norm, adheres to and deviates from the female norm, in what aspect of superiority she is always found wanting, whether the humour is exclusive or inclusive and the results of such controlling mechanisms.

'Eeeny-meeny-miny-mo, is he guilty yes-or-no?'

'I really like you - you're different from the other girls'

'On the other hand, her cooking leaves much to be desired.'

'Why, if it isn't Pan's People!'

No.	Male norm	Female norm	Aspect of superiority	Inclusive Exclusive
1.	Serious, logical thought. (woman deviant)	Illogical, frivolous thought. (woman adherent)	Reason over emotion	Inclusive
2.	Innate mechanical skill (woman adherent)	Innate domestic skill (woman deviant)	Inability of woman to cope with her specified domain	Exclusive
3.	Power, violence, lack of emotion (woman adherent)	Gentle, emotional (woman deviant)	Power over powerlessness	Inclusive
4.	Importance of sexuality (woman deviant)	Importance of domesticity, non-importance of sexuality (woman adherent) modern importance of sexuality (woman deviant)	Broadmindedness (?) over small mindedness	Exclusive

Notes:

1. Derisive humour. Woman in male-dominated occupation unable to cope. Child-like misunderstanding of rule of the game.
2. Mutual exclusiveness of roles. Woman must excel at both, in order to excel as a woman.
3. Woman adhering to male norm half-applauded for recognition of male power sphere, half-derided because incapable of adhering to female.
4. Two female norms—domestic woman and new idea of sexual woman. Even if adhering to former, woman derided for not adhering to latter.

Conclusion

There are no claims to originality in the delineation of the above stereo-types. The importance of the images lies in the cultural context in which they exist and are continually reinforced. The importance is in the *extent* of the stereotyping within certain forms of media presentation. The importance is in the social mechanisms which produce and control these stereotypes on a 'heads I win, tails you lose' formula, by creating both inclusive and exclusive humour, without giving women a position of integrity in either.

So far, from the newspapers and our more extended coverage of 'woman as sex' and 'woman as humour', we find that woman's representation in the media is orientated round the images of 'mother', 'housewife', 'wife', and 'sexual object'. These are the 'norms' within which women are pushed to conform, which individual women have to negotiate. They all represent woman as negativity, woman as oppressed: she only exists through her relationships to men, she can only be consumed by men. But we have begun to see that what is denoted about women is only the first level. Her sexuality, 'a skin glow of sex', however much contained in the commodity form, shifts us to the arena both of 'primitive', more 'natural', more 'animal' and to that idealised simple existence that technological man has lost and relinquished only nostalgically. The image points both backwards to a savage past and forwards to an imagined resolution of man's conflicts in the world. Woman can only be the symbol for all that, while she is not part of the present—while she remains oppressed. That sexual image is a *condensed* one: it holds much inside it. In humour we have seen the fragmentation of woman's different images; the displacement on to her of man's alienation from work and from home.

NOTES AND REFERENCES

1. Anthony Wilden, *System and structure: essays in communication and exchange* (London, Tavistock, 1977), p. 290.
2. At this point, the original paper introduces six separate areas in which the authors present some preliminary material, mainly drawn from the week 20–26 October 1974. These areas are:

   1. Woman as news — mainly newspapers
   2. Woman as sex — papers, films, magazines
   3. Woman as humour — papers
   4. Woman's self-presentation — mainly women's magazines
   5. Woman in ads — mainly women's magazines and colour supplements
   6. Woman in fiction — TV and women's magazines

   Our extract reprints as an example, the discussion about women as humour.

The myth of drug
takers in the mass media*

JOCK YOUNG

The most amazing quality of mass media reporting of the drug problem is their ability to get the wrong end of the stick. Indeed in *The drugtakers* I formulated, with tongue in cheek, Young's Law of Information on Drugs. Namely, that the *greater* the public health risk (measured in number of mortalities) of a psychotropic substance, the *less* the amount of information (including advertising) critical of its effects. Tobacco, alcohol, the barbiturates, amphetamines, heroin, LSD, and marihuana (listed in declining public health risk) would all seem to fit this proposition—apart from those exceptional and short-lived occasions when lung cancer scares occur. It is the explanation of the social basis of this 'Law' with which this article is concerned.

We live in a world which is extremely socially segregated: direct experience of individuals with behaviour different from our own conventions and values is rare. It is in just such a world that we come to rely on the mass media for a sizeable proportion of our information as to the goings on of outsiders to our small discrete social worlds. Criticism of the mass media has centred round the notion that journalists are biased, misinformed or just plain deceitful. The impression is given that if the profession were to revamp its ethics and remove its bias, the body of responsible journalism would be uncovered and the population receive from then on the simple facts of the matter, to interpret as they please. Minor adjustments have to be made to the set after which the picture will focus and the facts be held objectively. I wish to suggest, to the contrary, that 'facts' do not speak for themselves, that they are only given meaning in terms of the frame of reference provided. Further, that the mass media offer an amazingly systematic frame of reference. It is not random bias but a consistent world view which is purveyed. The model of society held by the mass media, and implicit in their reporting of both deviant and

*A revised version of 'Drugs and the mass media', *Drugs and Society,* Vol. 1 (November 1971), pp. 14–18.

normal, I will term consensualist. Its constitution is simplicity itself: namely, that the vast majority of people in society share a common definition of reality—agree as to what activities are praiseworthy and what are condemnable. That this consensus is functional to an organic system which they envisage as society. That behaviour outside this reality is a product of irrationality or sickness, that it is in itself meaningless activity which leads nowhere and is, most importantly, behaviour which has direct and unpleasant consequences for the small minority who are impelled to act this way. The model carries with it a notion of merited rewards and just punishments. It argues for the equitable nature of the *status quo* and draws the parameters of happiness and experience. Specifically, it defines material rewards as the payment for hard work, sexual pleasure as the concomitant of supporting the nuclear family, and religious or mystical experience as not an alternative interpretation of reality but as an activity acceptable only in a disenchanted form which solemnizes (their word) the family and bulwarks the *status quo*. The illicit drug taker is, I want to suggest, the deviant *par excellence*. For his culture disdains work and revels in hedonism, his sexual relations are reputedly licentious and promiscuous, and the psychedelics promise a re-enchantment of the world—a subversive take-on reality.

It is not drugs *per se* which are denigrated—for our culture is historically normal in that drug use is ubiquitous. Rather it is drugs taken for hedonistic reasons. The social drinker who is relaxing between his work bouts, the middle-aged barbiturate addict who needs drugs in order to sleep, the tranquillizer habitué who takes drugs in order to ease his work or marital tensions—or even the physician morphine addict who uses the drug to keep him working under pain or stress: all of these individuals are ignored or treated lightly. It is when drug use is seen as unrelated to productivity, when it leads to 'undeserved' pleasures, when it gives rise to experiences which question the taken-for-granted 'reality', that the forces of condemnation are brought into play.

The mass media carries a mythology of the average man and the deviant—within which Mr Average is seen to prosper and be content in his universe of hard work and industrious consumption and the deviant is portrayed as being beset by forces which lead to ineluctable misfortune. But the real world outside this spectacle differs radically from this. For often the worker doubts the fairness of his rewards, the middle-class housewife surveys her Ideal Home with ambivalence, the husband eyes his secretary and then goes back to his wife, the adolescent Seeker looks at the Established Church and cannot for the life of him see how it refers

to the same reality as that of the Christian mystics. For popular consciousness is a collage of contradictions: it is both sceptical and complacent,
satisfied and discontented, rational and superstitious, conservative and
downright subversive. It is on this base that the mass media act. For
there exists widespread suspicion that the sacrifices made are not worth
the rewards received. This is the basis for what Albert Cohen calls moral
indignation. Thus he writes:

> . . . the dedicated pursuit of culturally approved goals, the adherence
> to normatively sanctioned means—these imply a certain self restraint,
> effort, discipline, inhibition. What is the effect of others who, though
> their activities do not manifestly damage our own interests are morally
> undisciplined, who give themselves up to idleness, self indulgence, or
> forbidden vices? What effect does the propinquity of the wicked have
> upon the peace of mind of the virtuous?[1]

What Cohen is arguing is that deviant activities, even although they
may have no direct effect on the interests of those who observe them, may
be condemned because they represent concrete examples of individuals
who are, so to speak, dodging the rules. For if a person lives by a code of
conduct which forbids certain pleasures, which involves the deferring of
gratification in certain areas, it is hardly surprising that he will react
strongly against those whom he sees to be taking short cuts. This is a
partial explanation of the vigorous repression against what Edwin Schur
calls 'crimes without victims': homosexuality, prostitution, abortion and
drug taking.

The mass media have discovered that people read avidly news which
titillates their sensibilities and confirms their prejudices. The ethos of
'give the public what it wants' involves a constant play on the normative
worries of large segments of the population; it utilizes outgroups as living
Rorschach blots on to which collective fears and doubts are projected.
Moral indignation, if first galvanized by the newspapers and then resolved in a *just* fashion, makes a fine basis for newspaper readership. To
this extent then newspaper men are accurate when they suggest that they
are just giving the public what it wants, only what this represents is
reinforcing the consensual part of the popular consciousness and deni-
grating any subversive notions.

The widespread appeal of the mass media rests, therefore, on its ability
to fascinate and titillate its audience and then reassure by finally condemning. This is a propaganda of a very sophisticated sort, playing on
widespread discontent and insecurities and little resembling the crude

manipulative model of the mass media commonly held in liberal and left circles.

Illicit drug use is custom built for this sort of treatment. A characteristic reaction to drug use is that of ambivalence for, as with so many social relationships between 'normal' and 'deviant', the normal person simultaneously both covets and castigates the deviant action. This after all is the basis of moral indignation, namely that the wicked are undeservedly realizing the covert desires of the virtuous. Richard Blum captured well this fascination-repulsion relationship to drug use when he wrote:

> Pharmaceutical materials do not dispense themselves and the illicit drugs are rarely given away, let alone forced on people. Consequently, the menace lies within the person, for there would be no drug threat without a drug attraction. The amount of public interest in stories about druggies suggests the same drug attraction and repulsion in ordinary citizens. 'Fascination' is the better term since it implies witchcraft and enchantment. People are fascinated with drugs— because they are attracted by the states and conditions drugs are said to produce. That is another side to the fear of being disrupted; it is the desire for release, for escape, for magic, and for ecstatic joys. That is the derivation of the menace in drugs—their representation as keys to forbidden kingdoms inside ourselves. The *dreadful* in the drug is the *dreadful* in ourselves.[2]

This is an explanation of the hostility and attraction which drugs evoke. It makes understandable the findings in opinion polls on both sides of the Atlantic which show the drug pusher to be evaluated a higher community menace that the property criminal. It is rooted in moral indignation. Alasdair MacIntyre captured the attitude well when he wrote:

> Most of the hostility that I have met with comes from people who have never examined the facts at all. I suspect that what makes them dislike cannabis is not the belief that the effects of taking it are harmful but rather a horrifying suspicion that here is a source of pure pleasure which is available to those who have not *earned* it, who do not deserve it.[3]

I want to suggest that the media unwittingly have set themselves up as the guardians of consensus; that as major providers of information about actions, events, groups and ideas they forge this information in a closed consensual image. Further I want to suggest that the myths generated and carried by the media although based on ignorance are not of a random nature. The myths are grounded in a particular view of society which throws up certain contradictions which they attempt to solve. They contain certain simple structures irrespective of whether one considers the myth of the prostitute, the criminal, the striker, the pornographer, the delinquent, or the drug taker.

The mass media are committed, on one hand, to reporting that which is newsworthy and, on the other, to interpreting it within a consensual frame of reference. This leads to the first major contradiction that the media must face: for it is precisely alternative deviant realities such as the world of the illicit drug user which are simultaneously highly newsworthy and, because they are alternative realities, violations of the consensual image of society. For if different realms of meaning exist, and illicit pleasure is in fact pleasurable then the mass media world of the happy worker and joyful consumer is threatened. The contradiction is resolved by a skilful defusing of deviant action. Namely, that much drug taking is a product of personality disorders and is, moreover, unpleasurable. Illicit pleasure, the tinder of moral indignation, is accentuated in reporting in order to maximize its news value. The forbidden is thus potentially all the more tempting. To circumvent this the myth contains the notion of in-built justice mechanisms. Atypical pleasure leads to atypical pain. Thus premarital sexual intercourse gives rise to V.D., LSD to madness and marihuana to pitiful degeneracy. Whatever the outcome the message is the same: *deviancy is unpleasurable*. No one would voluntarily choose to be a drug user of this sort, because of the sticky fate that awaits him. Only the sick person, impelled by forces beyond his control, would find himself involved in such an activity. Thus initially there is a bifurcation of the world and human nature into:

> (a) the normal rational average citizen who lives in well normed communities, shares common values, and displays a well-deserved happiness—he is the vast majority;
> (b) the tiny minority of psychologically sick whose actions are determined by their affliction and are probably a product of social disorganization. Moreover, their deviancy has an in-built punishment. They are unhappy because of their deviancy. Normality is seen to be rewarded and deviance punished. The underlying message is simple: the rational is the pleasurable is the handsomely rewarded is the freely chosen is the meaningful is the non-deviant; the irrational is the painful is the punished is the determined is the meaningless is the deviant. See top diagram opposite.

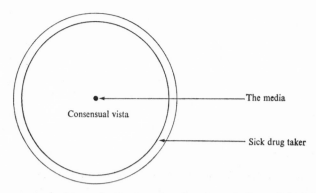

The overtypical 'man in the street' makes free choices to work hard, marry and consume regularly. He relaxes at the right time and place with beer and cigarettes which give him 'luxury' and 'deep pleasure' but do not threaten either the ethos of productivity or the mundane world of taken for granted experience.

Every day attempts are made in the newspapers to lay the ghost of deviation. Every day the same message is repeated, the same morality play enacted, the same parameter drawn, the same doubts and fears dispelled. But the simple bifurcation model comes in certain instances to face further contradictions which must also be met.

Now and then large numbers of individuals engage in activities which are palpably deviant, e.g., strikes, rioting and marihuana smoking. The simple consensual model would not seem to fit this. For the 'normal' young person, the 'normal' working-class individual, the 'normal' woman, etc., must of necessity embrace the consensus. A significant elaboration of the consensual myth is necessary in order to deal with large-scale deviation. Diagrammatically:

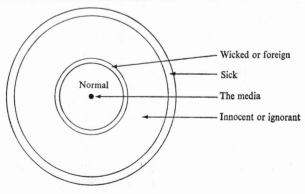

Namely that there exists a body of innocents within society who are corrupted by normal people who are wicked, who seek to gain from their fellows' weakness. Thus we have the following two media descriptions:

> The docks, the car industry, mines, major airports, electricity, the building trade, and the students have all been steadily infiltrated in one guise or another until the militants can disrupt the national life at will.[4]

Drugs: the real criminals

> The drug pusher—the contemptible creature who peddles poison for profit—deserves no mercy from the law. The criminal who sets out to hook young people on drugs deserves far more implacable retribution than the victims of the evil.[5]

N. B. The simple bifurcation of the social universe becomes now a four-fold split:

(a) sick (who can't help it)
(b) innocent (who are corrupted)
(c) wicked (who are corrupt)
and a reduced number of (d) the normal

Thus we have the sick who must be treated and cured, the innocent who must be saved, the wicked who must be punished and the normal who must be congratulated and rewarded.

Deviance then does not ever occur out of volition (for after all it is essentially unpleasurable), it either occurs out of sickness or corruption. Indeed for every example of widespread deviance it is possible to detect the intervention of a corruption. Thus:

strikers	agitators
student sit-ins	foreign agitators
prostitutes	pimps
spiritualists	con-men
illegal immigrants	immigrant runners
marihuana smokers	pushers
junkies	junkie doctors

But the mass media sometimes find themselves in a position where a growing body of opinion insists that certain illicit activites are both pleasurable and harmless. As in the case of marihuana, a crisis of confidence occurs. This is solved by what I shall term the nemesis effect. Namely that those individuals who violate the natural law of happiness and productivity ineluctably suffer in the *long run*. Thus in the long run deviancy must be seen to be unpleasurable. In this mould the stereotype of marihuana has changed. Initially it reflected the exaggerated ambivalence of the mass media towards drugs. Thus, it held promise of uninhibited pleasure, yet plummeted the taker into unmitigated misery. So we had a distorted spectrum ranging from extreme sexuality, through aggressive criminality, to wildly psychotic episodes. The informed journalist, more recently, however, found this model difficult to affix to marihuana usage. He, therefore, switched gear and indicated how the innocuous pleasures of smoking are paid for by the sacrificial few who mysteriously escalate to the nightmares of heroin addiction. Similarly, the American journalist William Braden[6] notes how the press reporting of LSD went through three stages:

1. *Favourable reporting:* in the early 1960s LSD was seen as a therapeutic aid to the mentally ill and the addicted. That is, as a vehicle back to a normality it was in accord with consensual values.

2. *Initial negative reporting:* LSD was simultaneously identified with an ineffable mystical experience and as a cause of suicide, violence and madness. This was concomitant with the movement of LSD out of the hands of the therapists into the psychedelic subculture centring around Timothy Leary.

3. *Secondary negative reporting:* The discovery that LSD *might* result in abnormal chromosome breakage obviated both the sticky problems of mysticism that the psychedelics were giving rise to plus finally providing tangible evidence that LSD was really dangerous after all. As *Chicago's American* put it: LSD: THE 'FLY NOW, DIE LATER' DRUG (the best epithet for the nemesis effect that I've come across). Thus the press found itself armed with a hard 'incontrovertible' fact to use against the growing subculture of pro-LSD advocates.

Every now and then an initially legitimate body of experts will come up with evidence which grossly violates the stereotype. The reception the mass media gave the Wootton Report is fascinating in that we have a government setting up an Advisory Committee to try and elucidate the 'objective' facts about the drug problem which came up with results which violated the political canons that implicitly circumscribed the possible answers that could be accepted as 'objective'! This violation of the consensual myth was dealt with by a flood of invective from the mass media. It:

(a) reaffirmed that corruption was the reason for marihuana smoking—that innocent youngsters had been corrupted by evil pushers;

(b) (most remarkable) suggested that an innocent (ivory-towered) Wootton Committee had been corrupted by a pro-pot lobby.

The corrupter-corrupted imagery was thus used against both the marihuana smoker *and* the Committee that suggested amelioration of their suggestion. As Lady Wootton noted later in the House of Lords:

> The causes of the [hysteria] are familiar to students of social psychology. They occur in other connections as well particularly in relation to sexual crimes, and they are always liable to recur when the public senses that some critical and objective study threatens to block an outlet for indulgence in the pleasures of moral indignation.

To conclude, the mass media portrayal of the drug taker is not a function of random ignorance but a coherent part of a consensual mythology. The mass media are a double-coated pill, for if on the outside they titillate a taste for illicit delights, on the inside, they contain a palliative. They stimulate interest and bromide desire. The myth of the drug user is rooted in moral indignation; it bulwarks the hypothetical world of the normal citizen, it blinkers its audience to deviant realities outside the consensus, it spells out justice for the righteous and punishment for the wicked. Although much of its world view is fantasy, its effects are real enough. For by fanning up moral panics over drug use, it contributes enormously to public hostility to the drug taker and precludes any rational approach to the problem. It also provides a bevy of convenient scapegoats on to which real material and moral discontent can be directed and significant structural changes averted.

REFERENCES

1. A.K. Cohen, 'The sociology of the deviant act', *American Sociological Review* 30 (1965), pp. 5–14.
2. R. Blum, *Society and drugs* (San Francisco, Jossey-Bass Inc., 1969), p. 335.
3. A. MacIntyre, 'The cannabis taboo', *New Society* (5 December 1968), p. 848.
4. *Daily Exress,* 9 December 1970.
5. *Daily Mirror,* 12 March 1970.
6. See W. Braden, 'LSD and the press', reproduced in this Reader.

The social production of
news: Mugging in the media*

STUART HALL, CHAS CHRITCHER, TONY JEFFERSON,
JOHN CLARKE AND BRIAN ROBERTS

The media do not simply and transparently report events which are 'natur-ally' newsworthy *in themselves*. 'News' is the end-product of a complex process which begins with a systematic sorting and selecting of events and topics according to a socially constructed set of categories. As Mac-Dougall puts it:

> At any given moment billions of simultaneous events occur through-out the world . . . All of these occurrences are potentially news. They do not become so until some purveyor of news gives an account of them. The news, in other words, is the account of the event, not something intrinsic in the event itself.[1]

One aspect of the structure of selection can be seen in the routine organi-sation of newspapers with respect to regular types of areas of news. Since newspapers are committed to the regular production of news, these or-ganisational factors will, in turn, affect what is selected. For example, newspapers become predirected to certain types of event and topic in terms of the organisation of their own work-force (e.g. specialist corres-pondents and departments, the fostering of institutional contacts, etc.) and the structure of the papers themselves (e.g. home news, foreign, political, sport, etc.)[2]

Given that the organisation and staffing of a paper regularly direct it to certain categories of items, there is still the problem of selecting, from the many contending items within any one category, those that are felt will be of interest to the reader. This is where the *professional ideology* of what constitutes 'good news'—the newsman's sense of *news values*—begins to structure the process. At the most general level this involves an orienta-tion to items which are 'out of the ordinary', which in some way breach

*These extracts are taken from ch. 3 of Stuart Hall et al., *Policing the crisis* (London, Macmillan, 1978).

our 'normal' expectations about social life, the sudden earthquake or the moon-landing, for example. We might call this the *primary* or *cardinal news value*. Yet, clearly 'extraordinariness' does not exhaust the list, as a glance at any newspaper will reveal: events which concern élite persons or nations; events which are dramatic; events which can be personalised so as to point up the essentially human characteristics of humour, sadness, sentimentality, etc.; events which have negative consequences, and events which are part of, or can be made to appear part of, an existing newsworthy theme, are all possible news stories.[3] Disasters, dramas, the everyday antics—funny and tragic—of ordinary folk, the lives of the rich and the powerful, and such perennial themes as football (in winter) and cricket (in summer), all find a regular place within the pages of a newspaper. Two things follow from this: the first is that journalists will tend to *play up* the extraordinary, dramatic, tragic, etc. elements in a story in order to enhance its newsworthiness; the second is that events which score high on a number of these news values will have greater news potential than ones that do not. And events which score high on *all* dimensions, such as the Kennedy assassinations (i.e. which are *unexpected* and *dramatic,* with *negative* consequences, as well as *human tragedies* involving *élite persons* who were heads of an extremely *powerful nation,* which possesses the status of a *recurrent theme* in the British press), will become so newsworthy that programmes will be interrupted—as in the radio or television news-flash—so that these items can be communicated immediately.

When we come later to consider the case of mugging, we will want to say something about how these news values tend to operate together, as a structure. For our present purposes, however, it is sufficient to say that news values provide the criteria in the routine practices of journalism which enable journalists, editors and newsmen to decide routinely and regularly which stories are 'newsworthy' and which are not, which stories are major 'lead' stories and which are relatively insignificant, which stories to run and which to drop.[4] Although they are nowhere written down, formally transmitted or codified, news values seem to be widely shared as between the different news media (though we shall have more to say later on the way these are differently *inflected* by particular newspapers), and form a core element in the professional socialisation, practice and ideology of newsmen.

These two aspects of the social production of news—the bureaucratic organisation of the media which produces the news in specific types or categories and the structure of news values which orders the selection and ranking of particular stories within these categories—are only part of the process. The third aspect—the moment of the *construction* of the news story itself—is equally important, if less obvious. This involves the presentation of the item to its *assumed* audience, in terms which, as far as the presenters of the item can judge, will make it comprehensible to that audience. If the world is not to be represented as a jumble of random and chaotic events, then they must be identified (i.e., named, defined, related to other events known to the audience), and assigned to a social context (i.e., placed within a frame of meanings familiar to the audience). This process—identification and contextualisation—is one of the most important through which events are 'made to mean' by the media. An event only 'makes sense' if it can be located within a range of known social and cultural identifications. If newsmen did not have available—in however routine a way—such cultural 'maps' of the social world, they could not 'make sense' for their audiences of the unusual, unexpected and unpredicted events which form the basic content of what is 'newsworthy'. Things are newsworthy because they represent the changefulness, the unpredictability and the conflictful nature of the world. But such events cannot be allowed to remain in the limbo of the 'random'—they must be brought within the horizon of the 'meaningful'. This bringing of events within the realm of meanings means, in essence, referring unusual and unexpected events to the 'maps of meaning' which already form the basis of our cultural knowledge, into which the social world is *already* 'mapped'. The social identification, classification and contextualisation of news events in terms of these background frames of reference is the fundamental process by which the media make the world they report on intelligible to readers and viewers. This process of 'making an event intelligible' is a social process—constituted by a number of specific journalistic practices, which embody (often only implicitly) crucial assumptions about what society is and how it works.

One such background assumption is the *consensual* nature of society: the process of *signification*–giving social meanings to events—*both assumes and helps to construct society as a 'consensus'*. We exist as members of one society *because*—it is assumed—we share a common stock of cultural knowledge with our fellow men: we have access to the same 'maps of meanings'. Not only are we all able to manipulate these 'maps of meaning' to understand events, but we have fundamental interests, values and concerns in common, which these maps embody or reflect. We all want to, or do, maintain basically the same perspective *on* events. In this view, what unites us, as a society and a culture—its consensual side—far outweighs what divides and distinguishes us as groups or classes from other groups. Now, at one level, the existence of a cultural consensus is an obvious truth; it is the basis of all social communication.[5] If we were not members of the same language community we literally could not communicate with one another. On a broader level, if we did not inhabit, to some degree, the same classifications of social reality, we could not 'make sense of the world together'. In recent years, however, this basic cultural fact about society has been raised to an extreme ideological level. Because we occupy the same society and belong to roughly the same 'culture', it is assumed that there is, basically, only *one* perspective on events: that provided by what is sometimes called *the* culture, or (by some social scientists) *the* 'central value system'. This view denies any major structural discrepancies between different groups, or between the very different maps of meaning in a society. This 'consensual' viewpoint has important political consequences, when used as the taken-for-granted basis of communication. It carries the assumption that we also all have roughly the same *interests* in the society, and that we all roughly have an equal share of power in the society. This is the essence of the idea of the political consensus. 'Consensual' views of society represent society as if there are no major cultural or economic breaks, no major conflicts of interests between classes and groups. Whatever disagreements exist, it is said, there are legitimate and institutionalised means for expressing and reconciling them. The 'free market' in opinions and in the media is supposed to guarantee the reconciliation of cultural discontinuities between one group and another. The political institutions—parliament, the two-party system, political representation, etc.—are supposed to guarantee equal access for all groups to the decision-making process. The growth of a 'consumer' economy is supposed to have created the economic conditions for everyone to have a stake in the making and distribution of wealth. The rule of law protects us all equally. This consensus view of society is particularly strong in modern, democratic, organised capitalist societies; and the media are among the institutions whose practices are most widely and consistently predicated upon the assumption of a 'national consensus'. So that, when events are 'mapped' by the media into frameworks of meaning and interpretation, it is assumed that we all equally possess and know how to use these frameworks, that they are drawn from fundamentally the same structures of understanding for all social groups and audiences. Of course, in the formation of opinion, as in politics and economic life, it is conceded that there will be differences of outlook, disagreement, argument and opposition; but these are understood as taking place within a broader basic framework of agreement—'the consensus'—to which everyone sub-scribes, and within which every dispute, disagreement or conflict of interest can be reconciled by discussion, without recourse to confronta-tion or violence. The strength of this appeal to consensus was vividly encapsulated in Edward Heath's prime ministerial broadcast, following the settlement of the miners' strike in 1972 (suggesting that open appeals to consensus are particularly prevalent when conflict is most visible):

> In the kind of country we live in there cannot be any 'we' or 'they'. There is only 'us'; all of us. If the Government is 'defeated', then the country is defeated, because the Government is just a group of people elected to do what the majority of 'us' want to see done. That is what our way of life is all about. It really does not matter whether it is a picketline, a demonstration or the House of Commons. We are all used to peaceful argument. But when violence or the threat of violence is used, it challenges what most of us consider to be the right way of doing things. I do not believe you elect any government to allow that to happen and I can promise you that it will not be tolerated wherever it occurs.[6]

Events, as news, then, are regularly interpreted within frameworks which derive, in part, from this notion of the *the consensus* as a basic feature of everyday life. They are elaborated through a variety of 'explanations', images and discourses which articulate what the audience is assumed to think and know about the society. The importance of this process, in *reinforcing* consensual notions, has been recently stressed by Murdock:

> This habitual presentation of news within frameworks which are al-ready familiar has two important consequences. Firstly, it recharges and extends the definitions and images in question and keeps them circulating as part of the common stock of taken-for-granted know-ledge. . . .Secondly, it 'conveys an impression of eternal recurrence, of society as a social order which is made up of movement, but not innovation'.[7] Here again, by stressing the continuity and stability of the social structure, and by asserting the existence of a commonly shared set of assumptions, the definitions of the situation coincide with and reinforce essential consensual notions.[8]

What, then, is the underlying significance of the framing and interpretive function of news presentation? We suggest that it lies in the fact that the media are often presenting information about events which occur outside the direct experience of the majority of the society. The media thus represent the primary, and often the only, source of information about many important events and topics. Further, because news is recurrently concerned with events which are 'new' or 'unexpected', the media are involved in the task of making comprehensible what we would term 'problematic reality'. Problematic events breach our commonly held expectations and are therefore threatening to a society based around the expectation of consensus, order and routine. Thus the media's mapping of problematic events within the conventional understandings of the society is crucial in two ways. The media define for the majority of the population *what* significant events are taking place, but, also, they offer powerful interpretations of *how* to understand these events. Implicit in those interpretations are orientations towards the events and the people or groups involved in them.

Primary and secondary definers

In this section we want to begin to account for the 'fit' between dominant ideas and professional media ideologies and practices. This cannot be simply attributed—as it sometimes is in simple conspiracy theories—to the fact that the media are in large part capitalist-owned (though that structure of ownership is widespread), since this would be to ignore the day-to-day 'relative autonomy' of the journalist and news producers from direct economic control. Instead we want to draw attention to the more routine *structures* of news production to see how the media come in fact, in the 'last instance', to *reproduce the definitions of the powerful*, without being, in a simple sense, in their pay. Here we must insist on a crucial distinction between *primary* and *secondary definers* of social events.

The media do not themselves autonomously create news items; rather they are 'cued in' to specific new topics by regular and reliable institutional sources. As Paul Rock notes:

> In the main journalists position themselves so that they have access to institutions which generate a useful volume of reportable activity at regular intervals. Some of these institutions do, of course, make themselves visible by means of dramatization, or through press releases and press agents. Others are known to regularly produce consequential events. The courts, sports grounds and parliament mechanically manufacture news which is . . . assimilated by the press.[9]

One reason for this has to do with the internal pressures of news production—as Murdock notes:

The incessant pressures of time and the consequent problems of re-source allocation and work scheduling in news organisations can be reduced or alleviated by covering 'pre-scheduled events'; that is, events that have been announced in advance by their convenors. How-ever, one of the consequences of adopting this solution to scheduling problems is to increase the newsmen's dependence on news sources willing and able to preschedule their activities.[10]

The second has to do with the fact that media reporting is underwritten by notions of 'impartiality', 'balance' and 'objectivity'. This is formally en-forced in television (a near-monopoly situation, where the state is directly involved in a regulatory sense) but there are also similar professional ideological 'rules' in journalism.[11] One product of these rules is the carefully structured distinction between 'fact' and 'opinion'. More impor-tantly, here, these professional rules give rise to the practice of ensuring that media statements are, wherever possible, grounded in 'objective' and 'authoritative' statements from 'accredited' sources. This means constantly turning to accredited representatives of major social institutions—M.P.s for political topics, employers and trade-union leaders for industrial matters, and so on. Such institutional representa-tives are 'accredited' because of their institutional power and position, but also because of their 'representative' status: either they represent 'the people' (M.P.s, Ministers, etc.) or organised interest groups (which is how the T.U.C. and the C.B.I. are now regarded). One final 'accredited source' is 'the expert': his calling—the 'disinterested' pursuit of knowledge—not his position or his representativeness, confers on his statements 'objectivity' and 'authority'. Ironically, the very rules which aim to preserve the impartiality of the media, and which grew out of desires for greater professional neutrality, also serve powerfully to orien-tate the media in the 'definitions of social reality' which their 'accredited sources'—the institutional spokesmen—provide.

These two aspects of news production—the practical pressures of constantly working against the clock and the professional demands of impartiality and objectivity—combine to produce a systematically struc-tured *over-accessing* to the media of those in powerful and privileged institutional positions. The media thus tend, faithfully and impartially, to reproduce symbolically the existing structure of power in society's insti-tutional order. This is what Becker has called the 'hierarchy of credibility'—the likelihood that those in powerful or high-status posi-tions in society who offer opinions about controversial topics will have their definitions accepted, because such spokesmen are understood to have access to more accurate or more specialised information on particular topics than the majority of the population.[12] The result of this structured preference given in the media to the opinions of the powerful is that these 'spokesmen' become what we call the *primary definers* of topics.

What is the significance of this? It could rightly be argued that through the requirement of 'balance'—one of the professional rules we have not yet dealt with—alternative definitions do get a hearing: each 'side' *is* allowed to present its case. In point of fact, the setting up of a topic in terms of a debate within which there are oppositions and conflicts is also one way of *dramatising* an event so as to enhance its newsworthiness. The important point about the structured relationship between the media and the primary institutional definers is that it permits the institutional definers to establish the initial definition or *primary interpretation* of the topic in question. This interpretation then 'commands the field' in all subsequent treatment and sets the terms of reference within which all further coverage or debate takes place. Arguments *against* a primary interpretation are forced to insert themselves into *its* definition of 'what is at issue'—they must begin from this framework of interpretation as their starting-point. This initial interpretative framework—what Lang and Lang have called an 'inferential structure'[13]—is extremely difficult to alter fundamentally, once established. For example, once race relations in Britain have been defined as a 'problem of numbers' (i.e. how many blacks there are in the country), then even liberal spokesmen, in proving that the figures for black immigrants have been exaggerated, are nevertheless obliged to subscribe, implicitly, to the view that the debate is 'essentially' *about numbers*. Similarly, Halloran and his co-workers have clearly demonstrated how the 'inferential structure' of violence—once it became established in the lead-up period—dominated the coverage of the second Anti-Vietnam Rally and the events of Grosvenor Square, despite all the first-hand evidence directly contradicting this interpretation.[14] Effectively, then, the primary definition *sets the limit* for all subsequent discussion by *framing what the problem is*. This initial framework then provides the criteria by which all subsequent contributions are labelled as 'relevant' to the debate, or 'irrelevant'—beside the point. Contributions which stray from this framework are exposed to the charge that they are 'not addressing the problem'.[15]

The media, then, do not simply 'create' the news; nor do they simply transmit the ideology of the 'ruling class' in a conspiratorial fashion. Indeed, we have suggested that, in a critical sense, the media are frequently not the 'primary definers' of news events at all; but their structured relationship to power has the effect of making them play a crucial but secondary role in *reproducing* the definitions of those who have privileged access, as of right, to the media as 'accredited sources'. From this point of view, in the moment of news production, the media stand in a position of structured subordination to the primary definers.

It is this structured relationship—between the media and its 'powerful' sources—which begins to open up the neglected question of the *ideological role* of the media. It is this which begins to give substance and specificity to Marx's basic proposition that 'the ruling ideas of any age are the ideas of its ruling class'. Marx's contention is that this dominance of 'ruling ideas' operates primarily because, in addition to its ownership and control of the means of material production, this class also owns and controls the means of 'mental production'. In producing their definition of social reality, and the place of 'ordinary people' within it, they construct a particular image of society which represents particular class interests as the interests of all members of society. Because of their control over material and mental resources, and their domination of the major institutions of society, this class's definitions of the social world provide the basic rationale for those institutions which protect and reproduce their 'way of life'. This control of mental resources ensures that theirs are the most powerful and 'universal' of the available definitions of the social world. Their universality ensures that they are shared to some degree by the subordinate classes of the society. Those who govern, govern also through ideas; thus they govern with the consent of the subordinate classes, and not principally through their overt coercion. Parkin makes a similar point: 'the social and political definitions of those in dominant positions tend to become objectified in the major institutional orders, so providing the moral framework for the entire social system.'[16]

In the major social, political and legal institutions of society, coercion and constraint are never wholly absent. This is as true for the media as elsewhere. For example, reporters and reporting *are* subject to economic and legal constraints, as well as to more overt forms of censorship (e.g. over the coverage of events in Northern Ireland). But the transmission of 'dominant ideas' depends *more* on non-coercive mechanisms for their reproduction. Hierarchical structures of command and review, informal socialisation into institutional roles, the sedimenting of dominant ideas into the 'professional ideology'—all help to ensure, within the media, their continued reproduction in the dominant form. What we have been pointing to in this section is *precisely how one particular professional practice ensures that the media, effectively but 'objectively', play a key role in reproducing the dominant field of the ruling ideologies.*

Media in action: reproduction and transformation

So far we have considered the processes through which the 'reproduction of the dominant ideologies' is secured in the media. As should be clear, this reproduction, in our view, is the product of a set of *structural imperatives,* not of an open conspiracy with those in powerful positions. However, the whole cycle of 'ideological reproduction' is not completed until we have shown the process of *transformation* which the media themselves must perform on the 'raw materials' (facts *and* interpretations) which the powerful provide, in order to process these 'potential' stories into their finished commodity news form. If the former section stressed a relatively passive orientation to powerful 'authoritative' definitions, in this section we are concerned to examine those aspects of news creation in which the media play a more autonomous and active role.

The first point at which the media actively come into their own is with respect to *selectivity.* Not every statement by a relevant primary definer in respect of a particular topic is likely to be reproduced in the media; nor is every part of each statement. By exercising selectivity the media begin to impose their own criteria on the structured 'raw materials'—and thus actively appropriate and transform them. We emphasised earlier how the criteria of selection—a mixture of professional, technical and commercial constraints—served to orientate the media in general to the 'definitions of the powerful'. Here, on the other hand, we wish to stress that such criteria—common to all newspapers—are, nevertheless, *differently* appropriated, evaluated and made operational by each newspaper. To put it simply, each paper's professional sense of the newsworthy, its organisation and technical framework (in terms of numbers of journalists working in particular news areas, amount of column space routinely given over to certain kinds of news items, and so on), and sense of audience or regular readers, is different. Such differences, taken together, are what produce the very different 'social personalities' of papers. The *News of the World's* dominant orientation towards the 'scandalous' and the sexual, and the *Daily Mirror's* concern with the 'human-interest' aspect of stories, are but two obvious examples of such internal differences in 'social personalities'. It is here—as each paper's own 'social personality' comes into play—that the transformatory work proper begins.[17]

An even more significant aspect of 'media work' is the activity of transforming an event into a finished news item. This has to do with the way an item is *coded* by the media into a particular language form. Just as each paper, as we have just argued, has a particular organisational framework, sense of news and readership, so each will also develop a regular and characteristic *mode of address*. This means that the same topic, sources and inferential structures will appear differently even in papers with a similar outlook, since the different rhetorics of address will have an important effect in inflecting the original item. Of special importance in determining the particular mode of address adopted will be the particular part of the readership spectrum the paper sees itself as customarily addressing: its target audience. The language employed will thus be the *newspaper's own version of the language of the public to whom it is principally addressed:* its version of the rhetoric, imagery and underlying common stock of knowledge which it assumes its audience shares and which thus forms the basis of the reciprocity of producer/reader. For this reason we want to call this form of address—different for each news outlet—the *public idiom* of the media.

Although we have stressed here the *different* languages of different papers, this emphasis should not be taken too far. It is not the vast pluralistic range of voices which the media are sometimes held to represent, but a range *within certain distinct ideological limits*. While each paper may see itself as addressing a different section of the newspaper-reading public (or different types of newspapers will be in competition for different sectors of the public), the 'consensus of values' which is so deeply embedded in all the forms of public language is *more limited* than the variety of the forms of public 'language in use' would suggest. Their publics, however distinct, are assumed to fall within that very broad spectrum of 'reasonable men', and readers are addressed broadly in those terms.

The coding of items and topics into variations of the public language provides a significant element of variation in the process of transforming the news into its finished form; but, as with 'objectivity' and 'impartiality' before, this variation is not necessarily structurally at odds with the process we have called 'ideological reproduction'—for translating a news item into a variant of the public language serves, also, to *translate into a public idiom the statements and viewpoints of the primary definers*. This translation of official viewpoints into a public idiom not only makes the former more 'available' to the uninitiated; it invests them with popular force and resonance, naturalising them within the horizon of understandings of the various publics. The following example will serve as an illustration. The *Daily Mirror* of 14 June 1973 reported the presentation by the Chief Inspector of the Constabulary of his *Annual Report*, in which he claimed that 'the increase in violent crimes in England and Wales had aroused justifiable public concern'. What the *Mirror* does in this case is to *translate* the Chief Inspector's concern with rising violent crime amongst the young into a more dramatic, more connotative and more popular form—a news headline which runs, simply, 'AGGRO BRITAIN: "Mindless Violence" of the Bully Boys Worries Top Policeman'. This headline invests the sober *Report* with dramatic news value. It transposes the *Report's* staid officialese into more newsworthy rhetoric. But it also inserts the statement *into* the stock of popular imagery, established over long usage, including that usage created by the paper's own previous coverage of the activities of 'aggro' football hooligans and skinhead 'gangs'. This transformation into a public idiom thus gives the item an *external public reference* and validity in images and connotations already sedimented in the stock of knowledge which the paper and its public share. The importance of this external public reference point is that it serves to *objectify* a public issue. That is, the publicising of an issue in the media can give it more 'objective' status as a *real* (valid) issue of public concern than would have been the case had it remained as merely a report made by experts and specialists. Concentrated media attention confers the status of high public concern on issues which are highlighted; these generally become understood by everyone as the 'pressing issues of the day'. This is part of the media's *agenda-setting* function. Setting agendas also has a reality-confirming effect.

The significance of using a public idiom with which to 'set the agenda' is that it inserts the language of everyday communication *back into the consensus*. While it is true that 'everyday' language is already saturated with dominant inferences and interpretations, the continual process of translating formal official definitions into the terms of ordinary conversation reinforces, at the same time as it disguises, the links between the two discourses. That is, the media 'take' the language of the public and, on each occasion, return it to them *inflected with dominant and consensual connotations*.

This more 'creative' media role is not obviously fully autonomous. Such translations depend on the story's potential-for-translation (its newsworthiness) and on its anchorage in familiar and long-standing topics of concern—hooliganism, crowd violence, 'aggro' gang behaviour. This process is neither totally free and unconstrained, nor is it a simple, direct reproduction. It is a transformation; and such transformations require active 'work' on the part of the media. Their over-all effect is nevertheless to help close the circle by which the definitions of the powerful become part of the taken-for-granted reality of the public by translating the unfamiliar into the familiar world. All this is entailed in the over-simple formula that journalists, after all, know best how to 'get things across to the public'.

The media and public opinion

So far we have been addressing the question of the production of *news reports*. Now we want to draw attention to the relationship between a newspaper's 'public idiom' and its editorial voice. We have so far discussed the transformations involved in transposing a statement made by a primary definer into an everyday language: into the code, or mode of address customarily used by that paper—its 'public idiom'. But the press is also free to editorialise and express an opinion about topics of major concern; it is not limited to 'reproducing', through its own 'code', the statements of the powerful. Now, one common kind of editorialising is for the press to speak *its* own mind, to say what *it* thinks, but *expressed in its public idiom*. In other words the paper's *own* statements and thoughts on an event—the product of editorial judgement—are represented in the paper's public language in the same way as the statements of primary definers: the process is very similar. Whether arguing for or against a line of action, the language employed is that customarily used by the particular paper. However, there is a second type of editorial which adds a further transforming twist; i.e. the editorial which actively claims to *speak for the public*—the editorial which goes beyond expressing *its own views in a public idiom* and actually *claims to be expressing the public's views*. We call this more active process, *taking the public voice* (as opposed to simply *using a public idiom*). Some such editorial voices are so distinctive (e.g. *The Times*) that it might be more accurate to talk of these as the paper's *own* 'voice'. However, it is unlikely that such a voice is ever completely independent in its rhetoric of the editor's sense of the 'public idiom' of his assumed audience. The essence of the difference, which we shall exemplify when we consider briefly some mugging editorials in the final part of this chapter, is that between the editorial which says 'We believe . . . 'and that which says 'The public believes . . .' This 'taking the public voice', this form of articulating what the vast majority of the public are supposed to think, this enlisting of public legitimacy for views which the newspaper *itself* is expressing, represent the media in its most active, *campaigning* role—the point where the media most actively and openly shape and structure public opinion. This kind of editorial usually takes the form either of support for some countervailing action which has been taken, or, even more frequently, of a demand that strong action *should* be taken—because the majority demand it.

In either form of editorialising, the media provide a crucial mediating link between the apparatus of social control and the public. The press can legitimate and reinforce the actions of the controllers by bringing their own independent arguments to bear on the public in support of the actions proposed ('using a public idiom'); or it can bring pressure to bear on the controllers by summoning up 'public opinion' in support of its own views that 'stronger measures are needed' ('taking the public voice'). But, in either case, the editorial seems to provide an objective and external point of reference which can be used either to justify official action or to mobilise public opinion. It should not be overlooked that this playing back of (assumed) public opinion to the powerful, which is the reverse of the earlier process described of translating dominant definitions into an (assumed) public idiom, takes the public as an important point of reference on both occasions (legitimation), while actually bypassing it. By means of a further twist, these representations of public opinion are then often enlisted *by the controllers* as 'impartial evidence' of what the public, in fact, believes and wants. The spirals of amplification are, in this last instance, particularly intricate and tight. (We shall look at some examples from 'mugging' later.)

What we are concerned with here is the general role of the media in the process of actively shaping public opinion. In societies where the bulk of the population has neither direct access to nor power over the central decisions which affect their lives, where official policy and opinion is concentrated and popular opinion is dispersed, the media play a critical mediating and connecting role in the formation of public opinion, and in orchestrating that opinion together with the actions and views of the powerful. The media do not only possess a near-monopoly over 'social knowledge', as the primary source of information about what is happening; they also command the passage between those who are 'in the know' and the structured ignorance of the general public. In performing this connective and mediating role, the media are enhanced, not weakened, by the very fact that they are, formally and structurally, *independent* both of the sources to which they refer and of the 'public' on whose behalf they speak. This picture may now tend to suggest a situation of 'perfect closure', where the free passage of the dominant ideologies is permanently secured. But this tightly conspiratorial image is not an accurate one, and we should beware of its apparent simplicity and elegance. The central factor which prevents such a 'perfect closure', however, is *not* a matter of technical or formal controls, or the randomness of chance, or the good sense and conscience of the professionals.

If the tendency towards ideological closure—the prevailing tendency—is maintained by the way the different apparatuses are structurally linked so as to promote the dominant definitions of events, then the counter-tendency must also depend on the existence of organised and articulate sources which generate *counter*-definitions of the situation. (As Goldman remarked,[18] social groups and collectivities are always the infrastructure of ideologies—and counter-ideologies.) This depends to some degree on whether the collectivity which generates counter-ideologies and explanations is a powerful countervailing force in society; whether it represents an organised majority or substantial minority; and whether or not it has a degree of legitimacy within the system or can win such a position through struggle.[19] Primary definers, acting in or through the media, would find it difficult to establish a complete closure around a definition of a controversial issue in, say, industrial relations without having to deal with an alternative definition generated by spokesmen for the trade unions, since the unions are now a recognised part of the system of institutionalised bargaining in the industrial field, possess an articulate view of their situation and interests, and have *won* 'legitimacy' in the terrain where economic conflict and consensus are debated and negotiated. Many emergent counter-definers, however, have no access to the defining process at all. Even regularly accessed definers, like official trade-union spokesmen, must respond *in terms* pre-established by the primary definers and the privileged definitions, and have a better chance of securing a hearing and influencing the process precisely if they cast their case within the limits of that consensus. The General Secretary of the T.U.C. has an easier passage if he makes a 'reasonable' trade-union case against a reasonable employers' one, if he is arguing and debating and negotiating within the rules, rather than if he is defending unofficial strike action, and so on. If they do not play within the rules of the game, counter-spokesmen run the risk of being defined out of the debate (because they have broken the rules of reasonable opposition)—labelled as 'extremist' or 'irrational' or as acting illegally or unconstitutionally. Groups which have not secured even this limited measure of access are regularly and systematically stigmatised, in their absence, as 'extreme', their actions systematically deauthenticated by being labelled as 'irrational'. The closure of the topic around its initial definition is far easier to achieve against groups which are fragmented, relatively inarticulate, or refuse to order their 'aims' in terms of reasonable demands and a practical programme of reforms, or which adopt extreme oppositional means of struggle to secure their ends, win a hearing or defend their interests. Any of these characteristics make it easier for the privileged definers to label them freely, and to refuse to take their counter-definitions into account.

The media thus help to reproduce and sustain the definitions of the situation which favour the powerful, not only by actively recruiting the powerful in the initial stages where topics are structured,[20] but by favouring certain ways of setting up topics, and maintaining certain strategic areas of silence. Many of these structured forms of communication are so common, so natural, so taken for granted, so deeply embedded in the very communication forms which are employed, that they are hardly visible at all, as ideological constructs, unless we deliberately set out to ask, 'What, other than what has been said about this topic, *could* be said?' 'What questions are omitted?' 'Why do the questions—which always presuppose answers of a particular kind—so often recur in this form? Why do certain other questions never appear?' In the arena of industrial conflict, for example, Westergaard has recently observed:

> The exclusion of wider issues is itself a result of the general 'balance of power' between unions and employers—far more crucial for the analysis of the situation than the upshot of particular disputes within the terms of that restriction. . . . The locus of power has to be sought primarily in the limits which define areas of conflict and restrict the range of alternatives effectively put into dispute. Often indeed, they may be so tightly drawn that there are no alternatives ventilated. There is then no 'decision making' because policies appear as self-evident. They simply flow from assumptions that render all potential alternatives invisible. . . .It follows that the locus of power cannot be seen except from a standpoint outside the parameters of everyday conflict; for those parameters are barely visible from within.[21]

And so, we have tried to indicate the way in which the *routine structures and practices* of the media in relation to news-making serve to 'frame' events within dominant interpretative paradigms, and thus to hold opinions together within what Urry calls 'the same sort of range'.[22]

Since the media are institutionally distinct from the other agencies of the state, they do not automatically take their lead from the state. Indeed, oppositions can and frequently do arise *between* these institutions within the complex of power in society. The media are also impelled by institutional motives and rationales which are different from those of other sectors of the state; for example, the competitive drive to be 'first with the news' may not be immediately in the interest or to the advantage of the state. The media often want to find out things which the primary definers would rather keep quiet. The recurrent conflicts between politicians—especially Labour Party politicians—and the media indicate that the aims of the media and those of the primary definers do not always coincide.[23] Despite these reservations, however, it seems undeniable that the *prevailing tendency* in the media is towards the reproduction, *amidst all their contradictions,* of the definitions of the powerful, of the dominant ideology. We have tried to suggest why this *tendency* is inscribed in the very structures and processes of news making itself, and cannot be ascribed to the wickedness of journalists or their employers.

Crime as news

Now we wish to specify how the general elements and processes of news production operate in the production of crime news as one particular variant of news production. We began by noting that news is shaped by being set in relation to a specific conception of society as a 'consensus'. Against this background newsworthy events are those which seem to interrupt the unchanging consensual calm. Crime marks one of the major boundaries of that consensus. We have already suggested that the consensus is based around legitimate and institutionalised means of action. Crime involves the negative side of that consensus, since the law defines what the society judges to be *illegitimate* types of action. Ultimately, the law, created by Parliament, executed in the courts, embodying the will of the population, provides society with the basic definition of what actions are acceptable and unacceptable; it is the 'frontier' marking 'our way of life' and its connected values. Action to stigmatise and punish those who break the law, taken by the agents formally appointed as the guardians of public morality and order, stands as a *dramatised symbolic reassertion* of the values of the society and of its limits of tolerance. If we conceive of news as mapping problematic reality, then crime is almost by definition 'news', as Erikson has suggested:

> It may be important to note in this connection that confrontations between deviant offenders and the agents of control have always attracted a good deal of public attention . . . A considerable portion of what we call 'news' is devoted to reports about deviant behaviour and its consequences, and it is no simple matter to explain why these items should be considered newsworthy or why they should command the extraordinary attention they do. Perhaps they appeal to a number of psychological perversities among the mass audience, as commentators have suggested, but at the same time they constitute one of our

main sources of information about the normative outlines of our society. In a figurative sense, at least, morality and immorality meet at the public scaffold, and it is during this meeting the line between them is drawn.[24]

Crime, then, is 'news' because its treatment evokes threats to, but also reaffirms, the consensual morality of the society: a modern morality play takes place before us in which the 'devil' is both symbolically and physically cast out from the society by its guardians—the police and the judiciary. Lest this statement be thought over-dramatised, it should be compared with the following *Daily Mail* comment (headed 'The men we take for granted') on the killing of three policemen in 1966:

> The Shepherd's Bush crime reminds Britain of what it really thinks about its police. In Britain the policeman is still the walking sign which says that society has reached and takes for granted a certain stable normality of public order and decency. Bernard Shaw once said that for him the picture of unchanging Britain was symbolized by a policeman standing with the rain glistening on his cape. He is still the man you ask the time, or the way to the Town Hall or whether the last bus has gone. He is still the man, who, when society asks him, goes along into the unlit alley to investigate the noise. That is why the death of a policeman by violence is felt so deeply by us all. The deaths of the three men at Shepherd's Bush, senselessly and deliberately gunned down on the job of maintaining that order and decency, come as a frightful shock that seems to rock the very earth. A dazed incredulity is followed by the realization that order is not to be taken for granted. The jungle is still there. There are still wild beasts in it to be controlled.[25]

Crime news is not of course uniformly of this dramatic nature. Much of it is routine and brief, because the bulk of crime itself is seen as routine. Crime is understood as a permanent and recurrent phenomenon, and hence much of it is surveyed by the media in an equally routinised manner. Shuttleworth, in his study of the reporting of violence in the *Daily Mirror,* has noted the very different kinds of presentation used, depending on the nature of the violence being treated.[26] He commented especially on the relatively small space, and the impersonal and abbreviated manner in which many 'mundane' forms of crime are reported. (The brevity of these reports are further constrained by the *sub judice* rule which prevents the press commenting on a case which is before the courts, and the recent strengthening of the rules against the press presuming guilt before it has been proven.) Many news items about crime therefore do little more than note that another 'serious' crime has been committed. Nevertheless, the media remain highly sensitised to crime as a potential source of news. Much of this 'mundane' reporting of crime still fits our over-all argument—it marks out the transgression of normative boundaries, followed by investigation, arrest, and social retribution in terms of the sentencing of the offender. (The routine work of the police and the courts provide such a permanent category of news that many 'cub reporters' are assigned, as their first task, to the 'crime beat'. If they survive this routine job—most senior editors learn to assume—then they are ready for bigger and more testing news assignments.) The reporting, at greater length, of certain dramatic instances of crime, then, arises from and stands out against the background of this routinised treatment of crime. The alteration in the visibility of certain crime-news items works in conjunction with other organisational and ideological processes within the news media—for example, the relative 'competitiveness' of other news items for space and attention, the item's novelty, or its topicality, and so on. Crime, here, is not significantly different from other kinds of regular news items. What selects particular crime stories for special attention, and determines the relative degree of attention given to them, is the same structure of 'news values' which is applied to other news areas.

One special point about crime as news: this is the special status of *violence* as a news value. Any crime can be lifted into news visibility if violence becomes associated with it, since violence is perhaps the supreme example of the news value 'negative consequences'. Violence represents a basic violation of the person; the greatest personal crime is 'murder', bettered only by the murder of a law-enforcement agent, a policeman. Violence is also the ultimate crime against property, and against the state. It thus represents a fundamental rupture in the social order. The use of violence marks the distinction between those who are fundamentally *of* society and those who are *outside* it. It is coterminous with the boundary of 'society' itself. In the speech quoted earlier, Mr Heath drew the crucial distinction between 'peaceful argument', 'what most of us believe to be the right way of doing things', and 'violence', which 'challenges' that way. The basis of the law is to safeguard that 'right way of doing things'; to protect the individual, property and the state against those who would 'do violence' to them. This is also the basis of law enforcement and of social control. The state, and the state only, has the monopoly of *legitimate* violence, and this 'violence' is used to safeguard society against 'illegitimate' uses. Violence thus constitutes a critical threshold in society; all acts, especially criminal ones, which transgress that boundary, are, by definition, worthy of news attention. It is often complained that in general 'the news' is too full of violence: an item can escalate to the top of the news agenda simply because it contains a 'big bang'. Those who so complain do not understand what 'the news' is about. It is impossible to define 'news values' in ways which would not rank 'violence' at or near the summit of news attention.

We saw previously how the production of news is dependent on the role played by primary definers. In the area of crime news, the media appear to be more heavily dependent on the institutions of crime control for their news stories than in practically any other area. The police, Home Office spokesmen and the courts form a near-monopoly as sources of crime news in the media. Many professional groups have contact with crime, but it is only the police who claim a *professional* expertise in the 'war against crime', based on daily, *personal* experience. This exclusive and particular 'double expertise' seems to give police spokesmen especially authoritative credence. In addition, both the formal and informal social relations of news-making from which the journalist derives his 'crime' material are dependent on a notion of 'trust', e.g. between the police and the crime correspondent; i.e. on reliable and objective reporting by the journalist of the privileged information to which he is allowed access. A 'betrayal' of that trust will lead to the drying up of the flow of information.[27] The Home Office, which is invested with the ultimate political and administrative responsibility for crime control, is accredited because of its responsibility to Parliament and hence, ultimately, to the 'will of the people'. The special status of the courts we have noted earlier. Judges have the responsibility for disposing of the transgressors of society's legal code; this inevitably gives them authority. But the constant media attention to their weighty pronunciations underlines the importance of their *symbolic* role: their status as representatives and 'ventriloquists' for the good and the upright against the forces of evil and darkness. What is most striking about crime news is that it very rarely involves a first-hand account of the crime itself, unlike the 'eye-witness' report from the battlefront of the war correspondent. Crime stories are almost wholly produced from the definitions and perspectives of the institutional primary definers.

This near monopoly situation provides the basis for the *three* typical formats for crime news which together cover most variants of crime stories. First, the report based on police statements about investigations of a particular case—which involve a police reconstruction of the event and details of the action they are taking. Second, the 'state of the war against crime report'—normally based on Chief Constables' or Home Office statistics about current crime, together with an interpretation by the spokesmen of what the bare figures mean—what is the most serious challenge, where there has been most police success, etc. Third, the staple diet of crime reporting—the story based on a court case: some, where the case is held to be especially newsworthy, following the day-to-day events of the trial; others where just the day of sentencing, and especially the judge's remarks, are deemed newsworthy; and still others which consist merely of brief summary reports.

However, the reason why the primary definers of crime figure so prominently in media crime reporting is not exclusively a function of their especially authoritative status. It has also to do with the fact that crime is *less open* than most public issues to competing and alternative definitions. A c. b. i. statement is usually 'balanced' by a t. u. c. statement, but a police statement on crime is rarely 'balanced' by one from a professional criminal, though the latter probably possesses more expertise on crime. But, as an opposition, criminals are neither 'legitimate' nor organised. By virtue of being criminals, they have forfeited the right to take part in the negotiation of the consensus about crime; and in the nature of most criminal activity itself, they are a relatively unorganised, individualised and fragmented stratum. It is only in very recent times that prisoners have become sufficiently organised and articulate on their own behalf to win access to the debate, say, about penal reform, even when this is about prison conditions or methods of prison discipline. By and large, the criminal, by his actions, is assumed to have forfeited, along with other citizenship rights, his 'right of reply' until he has repaid his debt to society. Such organised opposition as does exist—in the form usually of specific reforming groups and experts—often shares the same basic definition of the 'problem' as the primary definers, and is concerned merely to propound alternative means to the same objective: the returning of the criminal to the fold.

What this amounts to, where there seems to be a very wide consensus, and counter-definitions are almost absent, is that dominant definitions command the field of signification relatively unchallenged. What debate there is tends to take place almost exclusively *within the terms of reference* of the controllers. And this tends to repress any play between dominant and alternative definitions; by 'rendering all potential alternatives invisible', it pushes the treatment of the crime in question sharply on to the terrain of the *pragmatic*—given that there *is* a problem about crime, what can we do about it? In the absence of an alternative definition, powerfully and articulately proposed, the scope for any reinterpretation of crime by the public as an issue of public concern is extremely limited. Consequently, one of the areas where the media are most likely to be successful in mobilising public opinion within the dominant framework of ideas is on issues about crime and its threat to society. This makes the avenue of crime a peculiarly one-dimensional and transparent one so far as the mass media and public opinion are concerned: one where issues are simple, uncontroversial and clear cut. For this reason, too, crime and deviance provide two of the main sources for images of pollution and stigma in the public rhetoric.[28] It is not merely coincidental that the language used to justify action against any potential group of troublemakers deploys, as one of its critical boundary markers, the imagery of criminality and illegality, applying it either directly, or indirectly, by association;[29] for example, the signification of student protestors as 'student hooligans', or 'hoodlums', or academic 'thugs'.

Mugging and the media

So far we have been discussing the general characteristics of news production; then more tightly focusing on the forms these take in relation to the production of crime-as-news. In this section we shall connect these analyses of news production with the press treatment of 'mugging' news stories specifically. In examining, chronologically, the changing nature of this press treatment, we shall be able to see not only the application of specific news values, but, more importantly, how these operate as a *structure* in relation to a particular topic—in this case a particular kind of crime—to maintain its newsworthiness.

It might help to start with Table 1, which illustrates the general pattern of press reporting of mugging events during our sample period—August 1972 to August 1973; but first we need to say something about its empirical basis. Our sample was based on a daily reading of both *The Guardian* and the *Daily Mirror* for the thirteen-month sample period. We also had access to substantial files of cuttings referring to mugging events in this same period, which had been collected as a result of an extensive, but not exhaustive, reading of other national dailies, the national Sunday papers and the London evening papers. Because of the slightly different news emphases in both the Sunday papers and the London ones, we have not included stories from these sources in Table 1 or the accompanying text. Our search, based only on the national dailies, yielded thirty-three different events reported as muggings in the *Daily Mirror*, eighteen in the *Guardian*, and sixty over all. In arriving at these figures, we decided to count all the different reports referring to one particular mugging (i.e. 'follow ups' of the same event through to the later stages such as court case, appeal, etc.) as one; and we also decided that the first month in which the event was mentioned should become the month in which it was recorded in the table. Further, we also decided that the 'whole sample' column should include only the total number of different events. Thus in arriving at our figures for each month, the same event reported in, say, four different papers was counted as only one event. In the separate columns for *The Guardian* and the *Daily Mirror,* on the other hand, if the same event appeared in both papers it was recorded in both columns. Foreign mugging reports were excluded from the table. (Those interested in press coverage of mugging generally, as opposed to the coverage of mugging events—reports of crimes or court cases—should consult Table 2 at the end of this chapter.)

It should be clear from Table 1 that the peak of the press coverage of mugging events occurred in October 1972. Thereafter there is a decline in press interest. The maintenance of interest beyond the new year, through March and April, probably owes a lot to the effect of the Handsworth case. After that, only a spate of stories in the *Daily Mirror* in June provide mugging with any appreciable media visibility. Although, as we now know, August 1973 was by no means the end of 'the mugging story', it seems fair to conclude that by August 1973 mugging had concluded 'one cycle' of its newsworthiness. While the figures involved are admittedly small, and not very revealing on their own, when we turn to the *changing* nature of the coverage, a more distinct pattern does emerge— and one which bears out the notion of a 'cycle of newsworthiness'.

'Mugging' breaks as a news story because of its extraordinariness, its novelty. This fits with our notion of the extraordinary as the cardinal news value: most stories seem to require some novel element in order to lift them into news visibility in the first instance; mugging was no exception. The Waterloo Bridge killing, defined by the police as a 'mugging gone wrong', was located and signified to its audience by the *Daily Mirror* as a 'frightening new strain of crime'. Someone stabbed or even killed in the course of a robbery is by no means novel. What *lifts* this particular murder out of the category of the 'run of the mill' is the attribution of a *'new' label;* this *signals* its novelty. Importantly, in line with our earlier argument, this event is *mediated* by the police investigating it; *they* provide the mugging label, and hence the legitimation for its use by the press. The journalist then builds on this skeletal definition. He frames and contextualises the details of the story in line with the operating logic

TABLE 1

MUGGING EVENTS REPORTED IN THE PRESS (AUGUST 1972 TO AUGUST 1973)

Month/Year	Daily Mirror	Guardian	Whole sample
Aug 1972	1	2	2
Sep 1972	4	1	4
Oct 1972	12	9	23
Nov 1972	2	0	4
Dec 1972	0	1	2
Jan 1973	3	2	5
Feb 1973	1	0	4
Mar 1973	2	2	4
Apr 1973	2	0	5
May 1973	0	1	1
Jun 1973	5	0	5
Jul 1973	0	0	0
Aug 1973	1	0	1
Total	33	18	60

of news values; he emphasises its novelty (a 'frightening new strain of crime') and the American connection.

Galtung and Ruge have hypothesised that 'once something has hit the headlines and been defined as "news", then it will continue to be defined as news for some time',[30] and our example certainly validated this. Perhaps more importantly though, for a time, the simple attribution of the mugging label was sufficient to bring many discrete and commonplace crime events into the orbit of the newsworthy. The clearest examples of this process were provided by some of the most publicised early 'mugging' court cases; these were, in fact, trials for pickpocketing (or even 'attempted pickpocketing'). Other examples were the small spate of stories in September/October of attacks committed by girls. Mugging, it would seem, provided something of a focusing element for a latent concern about the growth of female violence—a concern which has since become manifest and independent from the concern about mugging. This process—what Hall has called the 'generative and associative' effect of new labels[31]—was also much in evidence during the period when the 'mod'/'rocker' labels had some novelty.[32]

However, the news value of 'novelty' is eventually expended; through repetition the extraordinary eventually becomes ordinary. Indeed, in relation to any one particular news story, 'novelty' clearly has the most limited life span of all the news values. At this point in the 'cycle' of a news story, other, more enduring news values are needed in order to supplement declining newsworthiness, and so sustain its 'news-life'. Two in particular seemed to play such an augmenting role in relation to mugging: those of the 'bizarre' and 'violence'. In respect of both of these news values, we find a growth in the number of mugging reports, throughout our sample period, which seemed to gain news visibility primarily because of the presence of such supplementary news values. Although the numbers involved are small, they do seem to us to be sufficiently marked to warrant our making inferences about them. On the other hand, the news-value 'élite or famous person' does not appear to play, in our sample anyway, such an augmenting role. In all we found only five stories which seemed to gain news visibility primarily because of the famous name of the victim: two appeared in 1972,[33] and three in 1973.[34]

By the 'bizarre' report we mean one with highly unusual, odd, eccentric, quaint, strange or grotesque characteristics. In our sample such reports could be sub-divided into two—those with a humorous twist and those with more menacing and grotesque overtones—but the term 'bizarre' seems adequate to cover the element of newsworthiness common to both types. During 1972 we found only one such report: *The Guardian* story of 10 November 1972 of a youth marching a man, who had no money, into a bank at knife-point in order to cash a cheque. But between March and July 1973 we found five—some humorous, some grotesque. As an example of each we have chosen two *Daily Mirror* stories.[35] The first, headlined 'Muggers pick on the wrong man', 5 June 1973, was a humorous story full of unusual twists and reversals. The report spoke of an unsuccessful mugging by three 'would-be' muggers. Their intended victim 'waded in with fists flying', left them 'lying dazed and battered', and then called at the nearest police station to inform them of the incident. The police then went to look for the men, not, apparently, to charge them but to see if any of them were 'seriously hurt'. Later in the same month, 27 June 1973, came a report with strange and menacing overtones: the story of the hurling over a cliff, in the small hours, of a hairdresser . . . 'for 30p'.

The bizarre base for this last story is obviously the strange and extreme form that the assault took. But implicit in the story line is a second news angle, which casts an interesting light on the broader social understanding of crime. This second angle is carried in the juxtaposition, in both the headline and the story itself, between the assault and the reward gained by the muggers—'for 30p'. The juxtaposition can only work (creating a dissonance between the two elements) given an implied 'rational calcu-

lus' about crime, and especially about the relation between violence and
the results gained from its use. The implication of the *Mirror's* juxtaposition is that '30p' is not a *rational* motive for the degree of violence
involved in the assault. This implied calculus is often at work in the
public signification of mugging—an implied *disparity* between the violence used in mugging attacks and the 'loot' taken. The contrast implicitly
identifies a subordinate theme which came to be associated with the
social concern about mugging—what was identified by police spokesmen as its 'gratuitous violence'.

Since we found it very difficult to differentiate precisely the purely
'gratuitous' from more 'instrumentally' violent mugging reports—for example, a 'gratuitously violent' headline might belie a more ambiguous,
'instrumental' report[36]—we have no precise, quantitative evidence of an
increase in 'violent' reports of a specifically gratuitous kind. However,
we do have evidence of a relative increase in the number of 'violent'
mugging stories in general which bears out our notion about violence
having an important role to play as a *supplementary* news value in the
case of mugging.

Taking the coverage as a whole, of the sixty different mugging cases
found, thirty-eight were reports of 'violent' muggings (i.e. involving
actual physical assault), whereas only twenty-two were 'non-violent' (i.e.
instances where there was only the threat of violence or no reported
violence): a ratio of slightly under two-to-one. (Our estimates were based
on the reported descriptions of the crimes, not on the formal charges
brought against the defendants.) Yet if we contrast the reports found
during 1972 (twenty violent and fifteen non-violent), with those found
during 1973 (eighteen violent and seven non-violent), we find a change in
the ratio from just over one-to-one to nearly three-to-one; and if we take
only the last five months of the sample period (April–August 1973) we
get a ratio of five-to-one (ten violent reports and two non-violent ones).

Of course, these ratios, and the pattern of intensification around the
violence theme that they reveal, would not be particularly significant if
they corresponded with the official statistics used to justify the reaction to
mugging. Obviously, as our earlier section on statistics should have
demonstrated, the problems of using official crime statistics as a base—
and especially mugging statistics—are many. However, we offer the
following evidence as our basis for saying that of the cases collectively
perceived by the police to be 'part of the mugging problem' in the 1972–3
period, about 50 per cent were 'non-violent', and the ratio of one-to-one
that this revealed remained fairly constant:

So far this year about 450 cases have been reported to the squad [set up to deal with South London 'muggings']. Of these 160 have been substantiated as violent robberies and a further 200 confirmed as thefts from the person, either by snatching or pocketpicking. (*Sunday Times,* 1 October 1972.)

Nor is there such a thing as a typical mugger. But there is a pattern. Go to Brixton Police Station, for example, and it's all there on the wall charts and in the statistics. In the past year, 211 robberies with violence or threats—40 more than the previous year. Snatching without violence—300 cases. (*London Evening News,* 22 March 1973.)

The ratio between the statistics for 'robberies' and 'snatchings' is similar in both sets of statistics, though one set refers to 1972 and the other to early 1973. In fact there are slightly *more* 'non-violent' than 'violent' cases. Since neither article gives any further, separate, figures for 'muggings', it seems fair to assume that both 'robbery' and 'snatching without violence' were being treated, for all practical purposes, as muggings. As a further vindication of this view, we would refer readers to the *Report of the Commissioner of the Metropolitan Police for the Year 1972* which explicitly states that there is little difference between 'snatchings' and 'robbery': 'Although they are not strictly crimes of violence, "snatchings" are included in the table [crimes of violence (selected)] because there is no great distinction between these offences and those of robbery and because a similar increase is evident over the last two years.'[37] The Commissioner is talking—though he claims not to like the term—of 'muggings'. Although the tendency of the media to over report violent crime in general has frequently been noted,[38] what we have been drawing attention to here is the way 'violence' is increasingly used, as a structuring element, in relation to the life cycle of one particular news theme.

In Roshier's look at the selection of crime news in the press, he found four sets of factors to be particularly important: '(1) the seriousness of the offence . . . (2) "Whimsical" circumstances, i.e. humorous, ironic, unusual . . . (3) Sentimental or dramatic circumstances . . . (4) The involvement of a famous or high status person in any capacity (although particularly as offender or victim).'[39] These are very similar factors to the news values we found to be important as supplementary sources of newsworthiness, i.e. the 'famous personality', the 'bizarre' and violence. However, our emphasis has been on how these news values operate as a structure or set: how they operate in relation to the primary value of novelty, principally as different ways of reviving a 'flagging' news story. This emphasis, we believe, justifies our talking of a 'cycle of news-worthiness', and supports our conclusion that by August 1973 this partic-ular cycle was at, or very near, its end.

Reciprocal relations

Finally, we want to look at the *relations of reciprocity* between the primary definers and the media, as exemplified in the mugging case. On 26 September 1972 the *Daily Mirror* carried a story with the headline 'A judge cracks down on muggers in city of fear.' The story perfectly illus-trates the role and status for the media of privileged definitions: the use of the term 'muggers' in the headline is justified by the judge's statement in the main report: 'Mugging is becoming more and more prevalent cer-tainly in London. We are told that in America people are afraid to walk the streets late at night because of mugging.' We must also take note here of the judge's use of American 'mugging' as a reference point against which his sentencing is contextualised; but primarily this example illus-trates the 'anchorage' of news-stories in the authoritative pronouncements of privileged definers *outside* the media.

In October 1972, we find an example of how the media utilises a 'base' in such definitions for its *own* definitional work on such an issue. The *Daily Mirror* on 6 October 1972 accompanied a report of Judge Hines's sentencing three teenage youths to three years' imprisonment for 'mug-ging' with an editorial which picked up his statement that 'The course I feel I am bound to take may not be the best for you young men individu-ally, but it is one I must take in the public interest.' The editorial *adds its own campaigning 'voice'*—its 'public idiom'—to that of the judge: 'Judge Hines is right. There are times when deterrent sentences which normally would seem harsh and unfair, MUST be imposed . . . if mugging is not to get out of hand as it has in America, punishment must be sharp and certain.' Here we can see the press in a more active role—justifying (but simultaneously using as its justification) judicial statements about 'mugging' as a public issue. The circle has become tighter, the topic more closed, the relations between media and primary definers more mutually reinforcing. (Indeed for the *Mirror there is no debate left:* 'Judge Hines is right.')

A week later (13 October 1972), the *Sun,* in an editorial entitled 'Tam-ing the muggers', moved another step towards closure by aligning 'the people' with the dominant definition of the judiciary. In this example, the

Sun does not bring its 'public idiom' to bear—rather, it *takes the public voice;* it becomes the people's 'ventriloquist':

> *WHAT ARE the British people most concerned about today?* Wages? Prices? Immigration? Pornography? People are talking about all these things. But the *Sun* believes there is another issue which has everyone deeply worried and angry: VIOLENCE IN OUR STREETS . . . Nothing could be more utterly against our way of life, based on a common sense regard for law and order. . . . If punitive jail sentences help to stop the violence—and nothing else has done—then they will not only prove to be the only way. They will, regrettably, be the RIGHT way. *And the judges will have the backing of the public.*

If we disregard for a moment differences between individual papers and treat all the newspapers as contributing to a sequence in which critical definitional work on the controversial topic of 'mugging' is carried out, then we can see, in abbreviated form, how the relations between primary definers and the media serve, at one and the same time, to define 'mugging' as a *public issue,* as a matter of *public concern,* and to effect an ideological closure of the topic. Once in play the primary definition commands the field; there is now in existence *an issue of public concern,* whose dimensions have been clearly delineated, which now serves as a continuing point of reference for subsequent news reporting, action and campaigns. For example, it now becomes possible for the police, who are somewhat circumspect about appearing to involve themselves in controversial matters which are not yet settled, to *demand wider powers* to act on an issue of crime control which has now been unambiguously installed as an urgent public matter. Thus:

> *Police may seek more powers on 'mugging'.*
> Police superintendents, alarmed by the increase in violent crime, particularly among young people, may ask the Home Office for stronger powers to combat 'mugging'. (*The Times,* 5 October 1972.)

A few months later it is the judiciary which *recruits the public concern about 'mugging'* (or *takes the public voice*) as a defence for *their* deterrent sentencing policies:

> *Mugger jailed for 3 years. 'And I was lenient', says the judge.* The judge added, 'everybody in this country thinks that offences of this kind—mugging offences—are on the increase and the public have got to be protected. This is a frightful case' (*Daily Mail,* 29 March 1973.)

TABLE 2

THE PRESS COVERAGE OF 'MUGGING' (AUGUST 1972 TO AUGUST 1973)

Month/ Year	Guard- ian (1)	Daily Mirror (2)	(1) and (2) combined	Other dailies	Monthly totals
Aug 1972	5	1	6	3	9
Sep 1972	2	5	7	5	12
Oct 1972	7	18	25	19	44
Nov 1972	5	5	10	13	23
Dec 1972	0	2	2	4	6
Jan 1973	4	5	9	4	13
Feb 1973	0	1	1	7	8
Mar 1973	7	9	16	37	53*
Apr 1973	4	4	8	13	21
May 1973	2	0	2	4	6
Jun 1973	0	5	5	0	5
Jul 1973	0	0	0	0	0
Aug 1973	1	1	2	0	2
Total	37	56	93	109	202

*Includes thirty-four stories on the Handsworth case.

NOTES: (1) As in Table 3.1, the *Guardian* and the *Daily Mirror* were read exhaustively, while the figures for 'other dailies' were reconstructed from press cuttings supplied by N.C.C.L. and the B.B.C.
(2) All items mentioning 'mugging' were counted. Most referred to particular crimes but a substantial number were of a more general kind: reports of Home Office/police activity; features; editorials; etc. Consistently, across papers and months, this latter kind of report provided about a quarter or more of all items.

In this last example 'public opinion' has been *imported back into* the judicial discourse as a way of underpinning and making legitimate a judicial statement about crime. Whereas before the media grounded *its* stories in evidence provided by the courts, now the courts use the public ('everybody thinks') to ground *their* statements. This is an exceedingly limited circle of mutual reciprocities and re-enforcements. But even this twist of the amplification spiral should not blind us to the starting-point of the process: the point where it began and from which it is continually renewed—the role of the primary and privileged definers, who, in classi- fying out the world of crime for media and public, establish the principal categories across which the news media and newsmen run their second- ary themes and variations.

A week previously another judge had added the final twist to the 'spiral', and effectively 'closed the circle'. Sentencing two youths whose counsel had made reference to the heavy sentences handed down in the Handsworth case the previous day, the judge commented that 'The press had now made it known that sentences for street attacks involving robbery "would no longer be light".'[40] Here we see the *reciprocity between the different parts of the control culture* in an extremely clear and explicit form. We have here *exactly the reverse side* of the process we noted earlier in which the media legitimated its coverage in evidence provided by the courts. Now the media themselves have become the 'legitimator' of the control process. We are now at the very heart of the inter-relationships between the control culture and the 'signification culture'. The mutual articulation of these two 'relatively independent' agencies is by this stage so overdetermined that it cannot work in any way other than to create *an effective ideological and control closure* around the issue. In this moment, the media—albeit unwittingly, and through their own 'autonomous' routes—have become effectively an apparatus of the control process itself—an 'ideological state-apparatus'.[41]

NOTES AND REFERENCES

1. C. MacDougall, *Interpretative Reporting* (New York, Macmillan, 1968) p. 12.
2. For a fuller account of the impact of these 'bureaucratic' factors in news production, see P. Rock, 'News as eternal recurrence', p. 64.
3. See J. Galtung and M. Ruge, 'Structuring and selecting news', p. 52.
4. See ibid; K. Nordenstreng, 'Policy for news transmission', in *Sociology of mass communications,* ed. D. McQuail (Harmondsworth, Penguin, 1972); W. Breed, 'Social control in the newsroom? A functional analysis', *Social Forces,* vol 33, May 1955; and S. M. Hall, 'Introduction' in *Paper voices,* ed. Smith *et al.*
5. L. Wirth, 'Consensus and mass communications', *American Sociological Review,* vol. 13, 1948.
6. *The Times,* 28 February 1973; quoted in G. Murdock, 'Political deviance: the press presentation of a militant mass demonstration', p. 206.
7. Rock, 'News as eternal recurrence'.
8. G. Murdock, 'Mass communication and the construction of meaning', in *Rethinking social psychology,* ed. N. Armistead (Harmondsworth, Penguin, 1974) pp. 208–9; but see also S. M. Hall, 'A world at one with itself', *New Society,* 18 June 1970; and J. Young, 'Mass media, deviance and drugs', in *Deviance and social control,* ed. Rock and McIntosh.
9. Rock, 'News as eternal recurrence', p. 64.
10. Murdock, 'Mass communication'.
11. For a historical account of the evolution of those rules, see J. W. Carey, 'The communications revolution and the professional communicator', *Sociological Review Monograph,* vol. 13, 1969.

12. H. Becker, 'Whose side are we on?', in *The relevance of sociology*. ed. J. D. Douglas (New York, Appleton-Century-Crofts, 1972).

13. K. Lang and G. Lang, 'The inferential structure of political communications', *Public Opinion Quarterly*, vol. 19, Summer 1955.

14. J. D. Halloran, P. Elliott and G. Murdock, *Demonstrations and communication: a case study* (Harmondsworth, Penguin, 1970).

15. See S. M. Hall, 'The "structured communication" of events', paper for the Obstacles to Communication Symposium, Unesco/Division of Philosophy (available from Centre for Contemporary Cultural Studies, University of Birmingham); Clarke *et al.*, 'The selection of evidence and the avoidance of racialism'.

16. F. Parkin, *Class inequality and political order* (London, MacGibbon & Kee, 1971) p. 83.

17. On the *Mirror's* transformations, see Smith *et al.*, *Paper voices*.

18. L. Goldmann, *The human sciences and philosophy* (London, Cape, 1969).

19. See I. L. Horowitz and M. Liebowitz, 'Social deviance and political marginality', *Social Problems*, vol. 15(3), 1968; and S. M. Hall, 'Deviancy, politics and the media', in *Deviance and social control*, ed. Rock and McIntosh.

20. See Hall, 'Deviancy, politics and the media'.

21. J. Westergaard, 'Some aspects of the study of modern political society', in *Approaches to sociology*, ed. J. Rex (London, Routledge & Kegan Paul, 1974); see also S. Lukes, *Power: a radical view* (London, Macmillan, 1974); and J. Urry, 'Introduction', in *Power in britain*, ed. J. Urry and J. Wakeford (London, Heinemann, 1973).

22. Urry, 'Introduction', p. 10.

23. For a more detailed analysis of this relationship, see S. M. Hall, I. Connell and L. Curti, 'The unity of current affairs television', *Working Papers in Cultural Studies No. 9*, C.C.C.S., University of Birmingham, 1976.

24. Erikson, *Wayward puritans*, p. 12.

25. *Daily Mail*, 13 August 1966; quoted in S. Chibnall, 'The news media and the police', paper presented to National Deviancy Conference, University of York, September 1973.

26. See A. Shuttleworth *et al.*, *Television violence, crime-drama and the analysis of content*, C.C.C.S., University of Birmingham, 1975.

27. See Chibnall, 'The news media and the police'.

28. See M. Douglas, *Purity and danger* (Harmondsworth, Penguin, 1966).

29. See P. Rock and F. Heidensohn, 'New reflections on violence', in *Anarchy and culture*, ed. D. Martin (London: Routledge & Kegan Paul, 1969); and S. Cohen, 'Protest, unrest and delinquency: convergences in labels or behaviour?', *International Journal of Criminology and Penology*, vol.1, 1973.

30. Galtung and Ruge, 'Structuring and selecting news', p. 52.

31. Hall, 'Deviancy, politics and the media'.

32. See Cohen, *Folk devils and moral panics*, p. 39.

33. See *Daily Mirror*, 7 September 1972; and *Daily Express*, 1 December 1972.

34. See *Sun*, 6 January 1973; *Daily Mail*, 9 February 1973; and *Daily Mirror*, 28 June 1973.

35. See also *Daily Mail*, 29 March 1973; *Sun*, 14 April 1973; and *Daily Mail*, 6 April 1973.

36. See *Daily Mirror,* 12 August 1973.
37. *Report,* p. 44.
38. See B. Roshier, 'The selection of crime news by the press', p. 40.
39. Ibid, pp. 34 – 5.
40. *Daily Telegraph,* 21 March 1973.
41. Althusser, 'Ideology and the State'.

Industrial conflict and the mass media*

DAVID MORLEY

Given that television news broadcasts constitute a prime source of information about events in the world for most people in our society, and that industrial and political militancy is 'problematic' in so far as it 'breaches our expectancies' of how the world should operate,[1] it follows that an analysis of *how* the main news media present to their audience the conflicts that do occur in society will be essential for an understanding of how social and political consensus emerges, is challenged and adapted, and of how the society develops mechanisms for 'containing' and 'explaining' the conflicts that arise within it.

The priority of the message

Geertz has argued that it has been the crucial failure of most analyses of ideology never to give serious consideration to the level of linguistic and symbolic mediation. He remarks:

> Themes are outlined, of course; among the content analysts they are even counted. But they are referred for elucidation not to other themes nor to any sort of sematic theory but either backward to the effect they presumably mirror or forward to the social reality they presumably distort. The problem of how ideologies transform sentiment into significance, and so make it socially available, is shortcircuited . . . .[2]

If we are to take this stricture seriously, then we must see that analysis must give priority to the message in the first instance, as a determinate moment in the communication process. Moreover, we must consider the message, not as a behavioural stimulus, but as a set of symbols organised by a system of rules and categories. We cannot approach the message as if it was simply reducible to its quantifiable 'elements'. In so far as the message is, as Burgelin[3] puts it, 'a structured whole', then the place occupied by the different elements and their relation to each other is more

*This paper originally appeared in *The Sociological Review*, vol. 24, no. 2 (1976).

important than the number of times they recur. Thus I would propose a form of immanent structural analysis as being more appropriate than a quantitative method of content analysis, in the first instance, although at a later stage quantitative methods may provide a useful check on the substantive analysis, and may be useful in developing the analysis of recurring patterns within the totality of the material.

However, a purely formal analysis of the codes which make communication possible is not adequate, for, in so far as ideologies arise in and mediate social practices, they cannot be structured by the formal rules of their production alone, but by their position within a social formation—it is the *interconnections* between social structures and processes, and formal or symbolic structures, that must be the pivot of our analysis. Our focus will be, therefore, not on the linguistic structures of the message, nor on 'ideology' as a set of free-floating 'ideas', but on the ideological structures embedded in the language of the TV message.

Ideology and 'bias'

I shall begin with a critique of the ACTT study, *One week*,[4] as that was the first attempt to provide this kind of analysis. The ACTT enquiry

> sought to discover how far ITV and BBC in their coverage of industrial relations fulfilled the legal obligations which require them to present news and current affairs in an impartial manner.

ACTT used three criteria in the analysis of programmes: neutral language, balance of views and balance of story elements. They concluded, first, that the BBC in particular scandalously failed to maintain impartiality and, second, that industrial affairs are covered in a superficial and haphazard manner.

My criticisms will be concerned with the *'assumptions'* which formed the framework of their analysis. This *'framework'* of *'neutrality/bias'* is inadequate in the sense that it fails to come to grips with the basic problem, that any event must be presented in the media through some particular (inevitably value-loaded) conceptual framework. Neutrality would only be possible if there existed a 'perfect language' in which the pure facts of the world could be recorded without prejudice. Neutrality would then consist of not going beyond these facts, and of not going beyond this sober language which was content to record them. Partiality or bias, on the other hand, would consist of going further, or adding moral evaluations.

But this model suggests that we can add values to facts, or refrain from adding them, as we add milk to tea. The model quite obscures the fact that some values are quite inescapably built into any language we care to employ to characterise and conceptualise things, if only to exclusion of the values built into alternative terminologies. Using this language, as against that, cannot but further some purpose against another. Every language has its opportunity cost: evaluations are already implicit in the concepts, the language in terms of which one observes and records.[5]

Moreover, while it may be significant to show whether a programme is balanced or not, as between different views or story elements, it is much more significant to analyse the basic conceptual and ideological framework through which events are presented and as a result of which they come to be given one dominant/primary meaning rather than another. Thus, during the 1973 gas strike, the media coverage of which forms part of my analysis, programmes were often balanced in the sense that they had a gas board spokesman claiming that the strike, through lowering gas pressures, was causing danger to the public, and a union representative claiming that safety precautions were being observed and that therefore the public were not endangered. But analysis must also deal with the problems of how and why the strike comes to be presented primarily in *these* terms—in this case in terms of the possible dangers it might cause to the public.

The ACTT approach assumes that biased or partial propositions about, or descriptions of an event can be seen as standing in some one-to-one relation with neutral or impartial propositions or descriptions. But the analysis of the manifest text cannot be usefully performed on a word-to-word, proposition-to-proposition basis. This is a limitation which the ACTT study shares with Halloran and colleagues' *Demonstrations and communications*[6]—which took the word as the unit of analysis for press coverage of the demonstration, and simply tried to enumerate the number of times 'favourable' or 'unfavourable' adjectives were used to describe the demonstrators. Rather than this type of 'piecemeal' analysis, which can only uncover specific ideological or biased propositions, what is needed is the identification of the generative set of ideological categories and concepts which can supply the 'code' which relates these propositions to one another.

The most important research in this area to have been published in recent years is, of course, the Glasgow Media Group's *Bad news*[7]—a study of media coverage of industrial affairs during the first half of 1975.

While *Bad news* provides us with a mass of useful and detailed information about specific aspects of the coverage of these issues by television, it is limited as a study by the extent to which it remains locked within the 'bias' problematic—outlined above in relation to ACTT research. To quote the authors out of context, *Bad news* with its extensive statistical tabulations, 'gives us a crude measure . . . but tells us nothing about the "quality" of the actual coverage'.[8] In my own view the study certainly fails to address the crucial question of the structure, as opposed to the detail, of ideology.

Ideology is not a collection of discrete falsehoods, but a matrix of thought firmly grounded in the forms of our social life and organised within a set of interdependent categories, which constitute a network of established, 'given' meanings embedded in the structure of language and common sense; and the signifying role of the media consists principally in the 'assignment' of events to their 'relevant' contexts *within* these pre-established cultural 'maps of meanings'. If what characterises ideology is its rigidity on the level of 'deep structures' combined with the relative flexibility of its surfaced forms, then the primary task of analysis must be the identification of the basic 'set' of categories from which particular messages are constructed.

An analysis of media coverage during February–March 1973

This paper is an attempt at an analysis of the coverage of industrial conflict in the media during February and March 1973. The period was dominated by industrial action against Phase 2 of the Conservative Government's counter-inflation policies. The workers involved were mainly public sector employees—the gasmen, hospital workers, train-drivers, teachers and civil servants—in most cases groups not traditionally noted for their militancy; indeed it was the first ever civil service strike.[9] The material used for my analysis is tape-recordings of the coverage of industrial affairs in sixty-nine television news and current affairs programmes.[10]

The set of categories which I am going to present here, which I would claim constitute the basic elements in the media's signification of industrial conflict, were established by identifying the recurrent patterns found in the totality of the coverage. What I have *not* attempted to do is to establish a clearly defined set of *mutually exclusive* categories, precisely because it is the interrelationships between the different categories, and the way their edges 'blur' into, and depend on, each other which is their crucial characteristic.

Although the characteristic conjunctions do make the relationships between some of the categories clear, my analysis could not claim to be adequate at the level of the TV discourse itself[11]—in so far as I have not systematically established the rules of combination and transformation of the categories, nor have I analysed individual programmes as 'structured wholes'. I could claim that it is adequate only at the level of establishing the basic set of categories *from which that discourse is constructed*.

Moreover, since the analysis is pitched at this level of the 'deep structure' of ideology, a level which only changes slowly, these categories seem to me to be still relevant to the analysis of TV coverage of this area in the later 'Seventies.

In particular, it will be seen that the quotes used to illustrate the categories are taken from politicians, trade union representatives, media reporters, etc., and the significance of their different sources is not explored. They are presented here in a relatively undifferentiated way, while what is necessary is an analysis of individual programmes as 'structured wholes', taking a systematic look at the 'status' of the participants in the debate, for a statement will obviously carry a different weight and meaning coming from a media reporter or presenter, a political or institutional spokesman, an academic expert or media correspondent, an actor in a news event, or a member of the public. Statements reported from persons of accredited high position—for example, the use of a 'summing-up' statement on the industrial situation by Mr Heath at a privileged moment in a news broadcast—can be seen as attempts in the encoding of a message to structure the decoding of that message, by means of 'closures' directing the audience towards a particular meaning.

In a similar way, the status accruing to Michael Barratt as presenter in *Nationwide*—a status deriving from his assumed position as representative of the 'ordinary public'—gives his statements a distinctive 'weight', and the programme can often be seen as structured around perhaps half a dozen 'summing-up' or 'linking' statements made by him at the beginning and end of items in the programme.[12] Taken together, his statements provide a coherent perspective which, if taken over by the audience, 'makes sense' of events in a very particular way.

This is a level of analysis which I have not yet been able to achieve—where one begins to explore the interrelationship between the linguistic structures of the message and the socially defined status of the different speakers—the structure of the message being composed of both these linguistic and social structures.

Fragments of an ideology; the structure of the fragments

1. *The main actors and the stage*
    (a) the image of society

  (b) the image of trade unions
  (c) the image of employers/the state
  (d) the image of the price/wage system
2. *'Explanations' of conflict*
  (a) conspirators model
  (b) 'intransigent attitudes'
3. *Moderation and extremism*
  (a) dedicated workers/irresponsible strikers
  (b) moral obligations and exhortations
4. *The definition of politics*
  (a) the limits of acceptable protest
  (b) subordinate ideology and the opposition
  (c) violence and irrational protest
5. *The 'national interest', the consumer, and 'business as usual'*
  (a) the media, the public and the myth of the two giants
  (b) normal working/the issue of peace
  (c) disruption: strikes cause 'chaos'

1. The main actors and the stage

(a) *the image of society* The prevailing image of society in the media is one of basic social equality, and there are assumed to be no irreconcilable *structural* conflicts of interest. Society is seen to consist of an aggregate of free individuals who form, through association, a number of competing 'interest-groups', whose differing interests are all subordinated to an overall shared 'national interest'. Thus, inflation is a 'national' problem—the concern of the whole community—so we as a nation need to be concerned about 'our' exports, the state of the pound, etc.

Of course, some of these interest groups are weaker than others. These constitute the permanent 'special cases': the old, the poor and the weak—among whom are to be found the remaining 'pockets of poverty' in our society. It is, of course, the role of the state to protect the weak against the strong—for example, the pensioners against the unions—and the parties compete to appear as the most concerned for the welfare of these groups.

In times of crisis the concept of the 'national interest' will be articulated explicitly—for example, see Mr Heath's speech at the end of the miners' strike in February 1972: 'In the kind of country we live in there cannot be any "we" nor "they". There is only "us"; all of us.'[13] Similarly, Mr Heath spoke on 1st March 1973 (BBC, 5·45 p.m.) of the government's obligations 'in the interests of the whole community' to stand by its counter-inflation policies. What we see in the media coverage of the events of 8th March 1973, when bombs exploded in central London on the day of the referendum in Northern Ireland, is a process of redefinition of the boundaries of that community: the striking hospital porters, who had previously been portrayed as a threat to the community, were now praised fulsomely for their response to the authorities' appeals to them to return to work to help with the casualties. Thus *Nationwide* reported that 'In the hospitals *everybody* is buckled down to help', while in Parliament Mr Carr was reported to be 'clearly speaking for *all* MPs' (regardless of inter-party conflicts and disagreements) when he condemned the bombings.

(b) *image of the trade unions* The unions are basically presented as being motivated by a narrowminded concern for their own sectional interest, while the government is presented as being motivated, in a non-sectarian way, by concern for the 'national interest'. Thus Mr Marsh (Chairman of British Rail) portrays ASLEF as a sectional interest group, yet claims his condemnation of their action is 'not partisan': 'it is not partisan . . . to say again and again that the public are being monstrously used.' Likewise Mr Heath described the gasmen's decision to return to work for an offer within the government's pay guidelines as 'a victory for *common sense*.'

Sectionalism is highlighted in the coverage of the inter-union aspects of disputes: the media often came close to taking over wholesale the government's definition of the rail dispute as 'really an inter-union row' between the NUR and ASLEF. Certainly the NUR's criticisms of ASLEF were given prominence. But the high spot of this tendency came on 4 March 1973 (BBC, 10·00 p.m.) in a report on some Welsh miners who were unable to travel on a special train they had chartered to go to a union conference in London on opposition to the Government pay freeze 'because local ASLEF drivers are engaged in a policy of non-co-operation in support of *their own* pay claim'. The moral of the tale? The biter bit, one assumes.

(c) *the image of the employers/the state* (As the state was the employer in most of the disputes occuring during the period of my analysis it was not possible to get discrete images of the employers and the state.)[14] The state is presented as the representative and defender of the 'national interest' and of the rule of law: thus the police are seen to defend against threats to 'law and order'—'police stood by *in case of trouble* when pickets moved into the laundry of Manchester Royal Infirmary . . .' (BBC, 9 March 1973, 5·45 p.m.). The state is presented as the representative of the 'majority of the people'—not of any particular class interest. As Mr Heath said: 'If the government is defeated then the country is defeated, because the government is just a group of people selected to do what the majority of us want to see done.' (Speech after the miners' strike, February 1972).

The authorities are presented as being 'concerned for public welfare' during strikes: Mr Percy Gillett of BR's Eastern Region must have come close to being designated 'the commuters' friend' for his repeatedly concerned accounts of the consumers' sufferings during the rail dispute and his battle-weary efforts to help the commuters through their troubles. On *Nationwide* (BBC, 28 February 1973) we were told that 'police controllers were making emergency arrangements for extra parking for commuters forced to use cars because of ASLEF's action', while in the gas dispute 'to help out, the gas board are providing a telephone answering service for worried consumers'.

The state is further defined as conducting the national fight against inflation/keeping industrial peace/preventing disruption—and these are defined as non-controversial, technocratic tasks. The electors' choice between Labour and Conservative parties is defined as a choice to be made on the basis of a decision as to which party is best at this non-controversial task.

(d) *the image of the price/wage system* The image of the price system is reified, in the sense that price rises are seen to 'happen' in a passive way, while wage claims are seen to be actively *made*. Moreover manufacturers' actions in raising prices in response to an increase in their costs is 'explained' via a built-in assumption of the need to 'maintain profit levels': the Agriculture Minister explained the government's decision to allow meat manufacturers to raise their prices on the grounds that 'these firms had been running at very reduced profits, and might have had to withdraw some of their goods.'

Where the need to maintain profit levels is *argued* rather than assumed, it is argued in terms of the need to encourage profits, which will increase investment, which will increase growth, which is in the national interest. However, at no stage in the coverage was the relationship between profits and investments explored: rather the highly dubious assumption prevailed that an increase in profits would automatically lead to an increase in investment in the home economy.[15]

Trade unions are often presented as the only 'responsible'/free agents in a situation—a union's decision to hold or call off a strike is repeatedly presented as the 'cause' of the event. The authorities are correspondingly presented as 'helpless' in the face of the union's decision. This was nicely put in the BBC 2 *News Review* of 4 March 1973: 'Hospital boards, like the railway board, find the dispute hard to deal with—they can't do a thing, because they haven't got the money, nor permission to give it.'[16]

2. 'Explanations' of conflict

Given the assumption of basic social equality, the very *existence* of industrial conflict is problematic. It is presented as basically *contingent* rather than endemic—it is *these* particular groups who are in conflict over *this* particular issue. There are two main forms of 'explanation' of conflict.

(a) *conspirators model* Here the origin of conflict is 'explained' in terms of the actions of militant leaders or minorities, urging the moderate majority to militant action: 'At Fords . . . workers may reject militant demands for all-out strike action . . . The Dagenham plant has rejected the strike call—a defeat for militants and a victory for common sense', (ITN 28 February, 10 p.m.). Or again, the passage at the TUC conference on 5 March of a resolution calling for a one day strike against the government's pay policy was attributed to the machinations of 'militants'.

Moreover, implications are often made of the 'unrepresentativeness' of these leaders and their militancy. Mr Macmillan, interviewed on *Nationwide*, 15 March, on the rail dispute said: 'I know many drivers, and I don't believe that most of them, in their heart of hearts, would want to have anything like this following from their action.'[17]

(b) *'intransigent attitudes'* A second persistent 'explanation' of conflict is of people 'taking the wrong attitudes': being intransigent, unwilling to compromise. Here there is a displacement in the coverage to the level of attitudes. Correspondingly, the solution to conflict implied is for both sides to adopt more moderate and conciliatory attitudes. Militancy comes to be equated with anger: 'angry gasmen get angrier as the country carries on in the cold . . .' (BBC 2, 4 March, *News Review*). The idea that conflict occurs because of people's 'attitudes' rather than because of structural contradictions was implicit in an important speech by Glen Philips of NALGO reported from the TUC Conference (BBC, 5 March, 9 p.m.), when he spoke of the need to 'combat the increasing *dangers of "us" and "them"* which have become so prevalent in this country.' And in a similar vein, Mr Whitelaw (BBC, 20 March, 5·45 p.m.) urged the people of Northern Ireland, as a solution to the Ulster problem, to 'abandon your prejudices and grievances and look simply to the future'.

3. Moderation and extremism

(a) *dedicated workers/irreponsible strikers* There is a persistent focus on the dedication and responsibility of some workers—for example, nurses, who will stay at their jobs because of their humanitarian concern for their patients. This is persistently presented as a counterpoint to the irresponsible action of strikers. Thus we have the reports of volunteers manning 'emergency services', and of hospitals which are able to stay open 'due to the extra efforts the remaining members of staff are prepared to make.' From this point of view the hospital strike was clearly irresponsible—in the words of a midwife: 'it's not humanity to have a strike in a hospital'.

Also involved here is the idea of the proper, British, response to a crisis: co-operation with the authorities is accredited as the proper, common-sense response. Thus the police appealed to commuters during the rail strike: 'if the public will help us we shall be able to help them' (BBC 1, 27 February, *Nationwide*). Of special concern were the gas consumers who were thought irresponsible not to have turned off their gas appliances when asked to do so by the gas board, and whose irresponsible and selfish action thus created a danger of explosions 'not only to the person who hasn't turned off but to neighbours' (BBC, 4 March, 5·45 p.m.).

As a counterpoint to the long-suffering patience of British commuters during the rail strike we were shown the non-British way of dealing with a crisis: the Tokyo commuter riots, where, in response to a rail go-slow, commuters ran amok beating up railmen, etc.

(b) *moral obligations and exhortations* The moral wrongness of strikes and the moral obligations of strikers are spelt out most clearly at times of crisis, as Thompson points out in 'Sir, Writing by Candlelight':

> 'at times of grave adversity and crisis . . . Oughts are discovered within the reciprocal flow of goods and services on which our society depends—these "oughts" are the moral obligations of the striking workers.'[18]

This theme was particularly applied to the hospital workers, in so far as they were seen as endangering human life. Their strike was described as 'a pretty drastic form of action . . . in an area of life and death' (BBC, 5 March, *Nationwide*), and Sir Keith Joseph pronounced to the workers that 'their *duty* is to get back to their patients'.

For many of the groups on strike in this period, militancy was quite a new thing, and this breakdown of dedication among traditionally non-militant groups made their strikes particularly problematic for the media.

This theme took a new twist when the nurses, who had been held up as a great example of responsibility and dedication throughout the ancillary workers' strike, announced that they were going on strike themselves unless they were awarded a forty per cent. pay increase, although finally they withdrew their threat, and settled for a pay award within the government guidelines.

4. The definition of politics

'Politics' is identified with the procedures of parliamentary debate and trade union negotiation, through which elected representatives debate the 'issues' and arrive at business-like compromises. This is what politics is all about. And this is *all* it is about: any form of opposition which transgresses the limits of these established forms of action is presented as not 'political, but as irrelevant, irrational or criminal'.

(a) *the limits of acceptable protest* A polarity is established between 'talks' and 'disruption'. The basic assumption is that it is reasoned argument, not power, that settles strikes. Those with a grievance are encouraged to 'make their case to the relevant authorities': only once during the period of my analysis did the view emerge that 'the government is not going to take a blind bit of notice of any case, however well argued, unless we punch home the message with a bit of industrial action' (Bill Kendall, CPSA representative at the TUC Conference, BBC, 5 March, 9 p.m.), and this view was immediately labelled as that of a 'militant'. Strikes are defined as being irrelevant to the real business of politics: 'The present wave of strikes is pointless . . . and irrelevant to the real issues facing the nation, industry and the trade unions.' (Mr Heath, BBC, 1 March, 5.54 p.m.)

This definition of industrial action was taken up by the media in interviews with trade union representatives on a number of occasions—for example in an interview with a CPSA representative (ITN, 27 February, 10 p.m.): 'In view of the government's stated determination to stand firm in its pay policy, wasn't today's strikes something of a futile demonstration?'

Interestingly, this affirmation of the values of negotiation rather than force was turned against the government by spokesmen for the Opposition (BBC, 28 February, 9 p.m.) who were able to criticise the government precisely in terms of its having abandoned the proper channels of voluntary negotiation in its statutory pay and prices policy. Moreover, the media, having taken over this definition of politics, will criticise representatives of the state in so far as they fail to appear to be conciliatory and prepared to compromise. Thus Mr Macmillan was subjected to a very hostile interview on *Nationwide* (BBC, 15 March) because he was failing to take a conciliatory role in the rail dispute.

The question of the limits of acceptable protest was raised in many questions put to union representatives—for example, a question put to Ray Buckton of ASLEF: 'Is this a strike against the government's pay policy?' (ITN, 28 February, 10 p.m.)

The question of political strikes reappeared sharply when the special TUC conference (5 March) called for a one day general strike against the government's pay policy, and this event was particularly problematic for the media as the 'very rule of law' had been brought into question at the conference. Jack Jones: 'We cannot say that we will, on the one hand, give support to the gasworkers who are the prisoners of Phase 2 . . . and in the same manner and in the same sentence, say that we will abide by the law . . .' (BBC, 5 March, 9 p.m.). But at a more mundane level, the definition of the limits of acceptable protest was an ongoing aspect of the coverage; in particular these limits were established via *vox pop* interviews. This is an interview with a commuter,

Q. 'Do you have any sympathy for the railmen?'
A. 'No, I don't think this sort of industrial action is the way to go about things.'
(ITN, 7 March, 5:30 p.m.)

'The way to go about things' was conveniently defined by Mr Whitelaw in his speech on the occasion of the publication of the Government White Paper on the future of Northern Ireland (BBC, 20 March, 5:45 p.m.). He said that this was a time for 'politics at the ballot box not on the streets'; he stressed the point that these were 'clear and reasonable proposals that reasonable men can work', and that the proposals 'depended for their success on moderate opinion asserting itself'.

(b) *subordinate ideology and the opposition* The assumption of basic social equality (see 1a) means that any claim for a wage increase has to be 'justified'—a case has to be made out of hardship, etc. *Nationwide* (27 February) dealt with the subject of those workers who were on strike for the first time, asking them why they felt justified in striking 'at this particular time'. Reluctance to strike and dislike of strikers were expressed by those interviewed, but they *justified* their resort to strike action as the only option left open to them to rectify the injustices they felt themselves to be suffering.

The whole question of how much support there is for a group of workers' claim for a pay increase from other workers and from the public is a crucial variable in the media language of 'good cases'. Thus the NUR's criticisms of ASLEF are said to 'weaken their case' while the support for the hospital ancillary workers' claim from some medical staff is said to strengthen theirs.

In so far as the dominant political culture sets the terms of the debate over what *is* 'reasonable', 'realistic' and 'fair' in industrial relations, trade union representatives entering that debate have to enter on these terms, and so have their 'opposition' incorporated within the limits set by the dominant culture.

The language of 'good cases' and 'special cases' adopted by trade union leaders can be seen as what Parkin describes as[19] a 'negotiated version' of the dominant ideology. Union representatives articulating this kind of approach will make a point of affirming their adherence to the central political values of our culture, but will then go on to make a particular case for their claim *within* that framework. The claim is that their case is 'justified' for some *particular* reason—of special hardship, etc. Thus Buckton, throughout the rail dispute, was at pains to point out his adherence to the values of negotiation and compromise, and to stress that ASLEF 'are not in conflict with H.M. Government'.

(c) *violence and irrational protest* Strikes are persistently presented as an irrational form of behaviour. At times this takes the form of a focus on the 'pettiness' of the causes of strikes—as on *Nationwide* on 14 March: 'It's often the simplest of things which lead to the call of "everybody out" . . .', followed by an account of the actions of 'bacon butty protesters' and 'angry onion peelers'. The report was then 'summed up' by Michael Barratt: 'They do seem rather daft reasons for going on strike, don't they?'

Once a dispute is in progress there is often, especially in the coverage of demonstrations, a focus on the irrationality of the form of action—in these cases a focus on the irrationality of the 'chanting mob'. Individuals reason but mobs chant. The point is often made in the coverage, when the camera shows a union representative in the foreground, being interviewed and 'making the case' for the workers' demands in a 'reasonable' manner, while in the background we see and hear a mob of people engaged in ritualistic forms of behaviour, such as chanting in unison and marching around with banners—with the noise from this mob impinging upon, and at times drowning out, the union representative's statements.

A further, related aspect of the coverage is the way in which the political motives of 'protesters' are denigrated, with the implication often being made that they are simply after *'trouble for its own sake'*. Thus teachers on strike in London were said to have 'stayed away'; the situation in the rail dispute was said to depend on whether 'individual drivers turn up for work or not', and *Nationwide's* report on the NUS campaign for increased grants (21 February) was introduced by this comment: 'You can't ignore them, they make the headlines too often for that . . . and today they were at it again . . . demonstrating . . . the main NUS activity is Campaigning . . .'

5. The 'national interest', the consumer and 'business as usual'

(a) *the media, the public and the myth of the two giants* The media interpret their role in the balance requirement as being to speak for the national interest as against the sectional interests of employers and workers. The media project the role of spokesman for the public, supposedly sandwiched between the two mighty and embattled giants (unions and employers) and propose that while the giants stand shoving at each other we, the poor public, suffer.[20]

The implicit image of society here is of a plurality of competing interest groups, rather than a class structure where one class is dominant. The media man's orientation is often one of cynical criticism of the *status quo*, but there is an assumption that one 'interest' is very much like another, and that the only people to be sorry for are the people (like the old) who are not strong interest groups.

The basis of this approach lies in the media presenter usually taking the point of view of the consumer who fails to get his goods and services because of the dispute: as consumers of gas we are all affected by a gas strike. But this elevation of the consumption sphere is very misleading— precisely because it neglects the sphere of production and our different relations to the means of production—which generate the structural conflicts, which cause the disputes by which we *are* all inconvenienced.

This orientation was explicitly spelt out in the introduction to the BBC 2 *News Review* for 4 March:

This hasn't been a happy week for people who one way or another have made the news . . . an awful lot of people who were not interfering with anyone else found themselves the victims of other people's industrial quarrels . . . their only consolation was that however hard they found this week, it wasn't as bad as they can expect next week, according to some union men . . . .

From this standpoint, interviews with hospital workers' representatives repeatedly enquired what their action meant 'in terms of the patients', while a representative of the striking London teachers was asked: 'I'm sure a lot of people will be wondering, where do the children fit into all this . . . aren't they suffering as a result of your battle with the government?' Strikes are particularly regrettable in so far as they cause special hardship to the young, the weak and the old 'who don't have the power of the unions'.

(b) *normal working/the issue of peace* Once a dispute is in progress the 'issue of peace'/restoration of normal working comes to be signified as *the* issue above all else—above all the substantive issues of what a particular dispute is about, where injustice lies, which side is right, etc. In this context the role of the state is defined as the non-controversial, technocratic task of maintaining industrial peace/preventing disruptions and 'improving' industrial relationships. Thus on *Nationwide* (13 March) the Liberal Party 'Stop the Fight' proposals were introduced with: 'What with low gas pressures, disorganised hospitals . . . ANY proposal to IM-PROVE industrial relations must be welcomed . . .'

Implicit here is a consensualist standpoint of judgement from which the industrial situation is said to 'improve' or 'deteriorate'; an assumption that 'improvement' for one is necessarily improvement for all, rather than any idea that what might be a 'solution' to the 'problem' of industrial relations for one class in our society might itself be a 'problem' for another class. Just what constitutes 'good' and 'bad' industrial news from this perspective was very clear in the *Nationwide* round-up (13 March) on the situation in the hospital strike. We were told that 'In Leeds, things are gradually *getting worse* in an atmosphere of increased militancy', while 'In Barnsley, *good news,* the workers have called off their strike'.

(c) *disruption: strikes cause 'chaos'* Strikes are signified as 'problematic' events. They are primarily signified in terms of their *immediate* effects—causing loss of production, inconvenience or danger to the public, damage to the economy and the 'national interest'. Thus, during the period of my analysis, in terms of their primary significations:

    the gas strike *meant* the danger of explosions
    the hospital strike *meant* the danger of patients
    the rail strike *meant* inconvenience to commuters
    the teachers' strike *meant* disruption of children's education
    the customs strike *meant* the creation of a 'drug smuggler's paradise'.

Of particular interest is the fact that this kind of signification of strikes was particularly apparent in the headlines of news broadcasts. Indeed, the sheer existence or threat of 'disruption of normal working', or of the resolution of such disruptive conflict, constituted headline news in its most recurrent form during the period of my analysis. This would seem to be particularly important because it is in the headlines that events are assigned their primary significations. The later reports and comments in a broadcast will take up, expand on, and sometimes in the course of debate call into question, these primary definitions. But it is on the terrain established by these primary definitions that the latter debate will move.

TV news: drama and spectacle

Overlaid on this basic set of categories which I have outlined is a rather different, and quite crucial aspect of the media's operation. This is the basic *'event orientation' of the media*. Brian Groombridge has pointed to the media's tendency towards 'distracting from what matters with a show, and turning what matters into a show' and has remarked of ITN's *News at Ten* that 'the items are orchestrated for mood and variety like a series of revue sketches, complete with tantalising trailers before the commercial break'.[21]

Media practitioners will usually reply that this is mainly a matter of pressure of time—that nothing more *can* be done in a news programme, and that current affairs programmes provide the interested viewer with the necessary 'background'. However, Ros Brunt, in her analysis of *Whicker's World*,[22] has shown that because of the way in which 'facts and figures' are conveyed primarily as unrelated bits of information—as 'accumulations of data' piled up before the spectator—such current affairs programmes may well operate to provide the audience not so much with explanations and understandings of news events as with a sense of 'fascinated distraction'.

Always, the coverage tends to focus on the immediate form of events, on what happened and who was involved, and to ignore the underlying context of the situation, rarely offering any analysis of the relationship between particular events and underlying structural processes. Mystification is inherent in this dehistoricised presentation of the news as a series of 'events'—a series of immediate images of 'actuality without context'.[23] In this respect my findings are exactly in line with those of John Downing when he says that 'compared with the vastly disproportionate weighting given to the effects and implications of strikes, the level of explanation in the coverage as to what the strikes (are) about, how they (have) developed and what their broad antecedents (are), is quite extraordinarily shallow.'[24] Again, substantially the same point is made by Stuart Hall.[25] The overall orientation of the media leads to the presentation of events in a 'collapsed' form; an industrial dispute which is really an instance of the structural conflict between government and organised labour will appear in the news as dramatic pictures of pickets and police locked in struggle. That is, *simply* as a disruptive threat to 'law and order'. This was exactly what happened in the BBC 2 *News Review* (24 March) in their coverage of the Fine Tubes demonstration. It was explicitly characterised as an industrial story which was 'hard to understand'. An extremely truncated account of the background to the strike was given and then we were shown shots of the 'angry demonstration'—mainly close-ups of violent pushing and shoving—an unexplained, violent spectacle.

As we have seen, disputes are primarily signified in terms of the immediate issues—of the effects of the strike, the chances of a quick settlement, etc.—and these issues tend to set the parameters of what is considered relevant to the discussion of a dispute. However, in studio discussions attempts are made by union representatives to introduce wider, background considerations into the debate. For example, on *Nationwide* (13 March), after a consultant had said that the hospital dispute was leading to a 'lowering of standards' in the Health Service, Alan Fisher of NUPE took up the point. Fisher: 'The consultant talked about a "cutting of standards"—well, there have been falling standards in the Health Service for years . . . .' At which point the presenter of the programme cut him short. Presenter: 'Yes, but before you go off on *that* track . . . .'—and brought the discussion back to 'the immediate issues' of the effect of the strike on patients, etc.

In a similar way, on *Nationwide* (8 March), after a report which was the only one I found giving any indication of the historical origins of the rail dispute the presenter immediately 'summed up' in a way that implicitly denied the relevance of such considerations. Presenter: *'Be that as it may,* commuters still have to face the problems of getting to work tomorrow . . .'* The range of considerations deemed relevant in the signification of a dispute is thus at times brought into question, and the limits of that range have to be actively maintained in the studio situation.

Crucially, what is at issue here is the overall tendency of the media towards a fragmentation of the internal connections of 'events' and a concentration on the isolated details of their most 'spectacular' forms of appearance. However, the further and more important point is that it is not *simply* the operation and practices of the media which are involved here: it is the way in which the media's operation articulates with the structure of social reality.

Ideology and reality: an apparent justification

John Mepham suggests that it would be a great mistake to think that:

> the dominance of bourgeois ideology has its basis in the dominance of the bourgeoisie as a class only in the sense that this dominance as a class allows the bourgeoisie to have a monopoly on the production and dissemination of ideas . . . (so that) . . . ideas are transmitted via public communications systems and so on, into the otherwise empty minds of the working class . . .[26]

Of course, Mepham notes, the bourgeoisie's dominance over the 'means for the dissemination of ideas' is a powerful weapon in defence of their class interests. *But,* he goes on,

> to say that the bourgeoisie produces ideas is to ignore the conditions which make this possible, to ignore that which determines which ideas are thus produced, and to conceal the real nature and origins of ideology . . . It is not the bourgeois *class* which produces ideas, but bourgeois *society.* And the effective dissemination of ideas is only possible because, or to the extent that, the ideas thus disseminated are ideas which . . . do have a sufficient degree of effectiveness both in rendering social reality intelligible and in guiding practice within it for them to be apparently acceptable. It is the relation between ideology and reality that is the key to its dominance.

Bearing these remarks in mind, I would make a number of points about the different aspects of 'bourgeois ideology' concerning industrial relations to which I have pointed in my analysis.

(1a) *The image of society.* The concept of 'national interest' is not entirely ideological: we are all involved in the economy. Workers are dependent on it for jobs in a day-to-day sense. What is ideological about this image is precisely that it restricts attention to the level of the phenomenal forms of social life, without considering our differential relations to the means of production and therefore our differential relations to the 'national interest.'

(1b) *The image of the trade unions.* The media do pick up on the inter-union aspects of disputes, as in the case of the emphasis given to the NUR versus ASLEF aspects of the rail dispute, but there is a basis for this in fact—in so far as ASLEF in trying to defend outdated craft union privileges, are engaged in a highly sectional policy.[27]

(1c) *The image of the state*. That the state is the representative of the general will has a certain basis in fact in a democratic welfare state. Thus the state *can* be seen as in some respects 'independent from and superior to all social classes, as being the dominant force in society rather than (*just* as) the instrument of a dominant class'.[28]

(2a) *The conspiritators model*. In so far as conflict is not just generated mechanistically by objective inequalities, 'leaders' and 'interventionists' do play a rôle in the genesis of industrial conflict.

(4c) *Violence and irrational protest*. In noting that the media tend to focus attention on the form of the demonstration, for instance, the violent/chanting mob, one must remember that to some extent the problem is implicit in the form of mass demonstrations. By choosing to work through the medium of public spectacle, demonstrators open themselves to the possibility that they will be 'appropriated' as spectacular entertainment.[29]

(5b and 5c) *Normal working/disruption*. While pointing to the media's overwhelming emphasis on the immediate/negative effects of strikes as being ideological in so far as strikes are seen to have meaning *only* in these terms, it would be pointless to deny the reality of the 'effects' that the media dwelt on—the effects on some patients of the hospital strike, the effects on passers-by of the Old Bailey car bomb, the effect on commuters of the rail strike. The point is that, in all these cases, at a superficial level the media's signification does serve to make these events 'intelligible'. If we return to the theory of ideology, the significance of the 'common sensical' understanding that is provided should become clear.

Mepham proposes that we consider the problem of ideology in this way:

Ideology arises from the opacity of reality, where the opacity of reality is the fact that the forms in which reality "presents itself" to men, or the forms of its appearance, conceal those real relations which themselves produce the appearance, the origin of ideological illusions is in the phenomenal forms of reality itself. The invisibility of real relations derives from the very immediacy and "visibility" of the "natural, self-understood meanings" encountered in social life, the "spontaneous, natural" modes of speech and thought under capitalism. We must reject the view that ideology has its basis in some sort of defective perception of clearly perceptible facts. The basis of ideology is precisely in its *apparent justification* by the perceived forms of empirical social reality.[30]

The media: commonsense and ideology

The tendency of the media to concentrate on the surface forms of events and to present them as discrete and dramatic 'incidents' takes on a particular significance if we consider it in conjunction with Marx's method of analysis in *Capital*. Geras argues that:

> in *Capital* the distinction between essence and appearance is as well as everything else, a distinction also between the totality and its parts. Each single relationship or fact is an appearance whose full meaning or reality is only articulated by integrating it theoretically within its total structure.[31]

To fail to perform this theoretical integration, is then, to fail to penetrate beyond the level of appearances. Earlier in the article cited, Geras has argued that:

> the decisive factor which makes possible the discovery in the production process of the essence of the false appearances of circulation, consists in this: that, in moving from circulation to production, the analysis moves from the consideration of relationships between individuals to that of relationships between classes, of which the former are a function. Only this change of terrain can demystify the appearances.[32]

These comments would seem to throw particular light on the media's tendency to focus on the actions of 'individuals' in case-studies and stories of *personal* hardship or success, but also on their tendency noted earlier (see 5a) to concentrate on the sphere of circulation to the neglect of the sphere of production. However, to argue that this tendency is 'misleading', in so far as the sphere of circulation (the level of the 'phenomenal forms' of social reality in Marx's analysis) is seen to be determined by the sphere of production (the level of 'real relations' in Marx) is *not*, as Geras points out, to argue that:

> the process of analysis which reveals the contents of the forms and the essence of the appearances is 'a journey from illusion to reality'. It is

rather a process of elucidating one reality by disclosing its foundation in and determination by another.[33]

As Lefebvre points out, 'a content is a content only by taking on a form'[34] and the phenomenal forms are the necessary forms of bourgeois productive relationships, given the 'opacity' of reality under capitalism. These phenomenal forms, which arise from the relations of production themselves, provide the basis for the spontaneous forms of everyday consciousness—the set of 'sedimented' typifications which form the dominant pattern of meanings in our society. The point is that this is the field of pre-established meaning on which the media operate at any given moment, and which they participate in constructing, adapting and maintaining over time.

If we look at the news media, and their role in providing for the audience an account of developments in society which is largely restricted to reflecting the surface level of social relations—presenting these as an accumulation of 'spectacular' events—we see that the 'commonsense' understanding of events which they provide, precisely because of its ahistorical, 'foregrounded' nature, is the crucial locus of ideology. It is at this level that the media operate so as to reinforce the ideological structure and content of 'what everybody knows' about our social world.

Towards a dynamic analysis: hegemony and contradiction

I do not mean to imply by the remarks in the previous section that some 'dominant ideology' is simply reproduced and transmitted by TV news programmes in an uncontested fashion. The obligation to reflect viewpoints other than those of the powerful is enshrined in the media's terms of reference, and contradictions do arise between the media systems and the dominant groups.[35]

What we must see is the *process* by which these dominant definitions of the situation are articulated in the programmes, but are also 'negotiated' and challenged by other speakers who may attempt to redefine the terms of the debate. In short, we must see the reproduction of the dominant ideology as performative work since:

> in any instance, the outcome of an encounter in which several contestants are present cannot be fully predicted: in this area, significant battles to win a hearing for alternative points of view *can sometimes* be won: the management of such conflictful situations has to be done *in situ*,[36] and presenters can lose their grip on the situation, though

they rarely do (because they have the ultimate signifying power of defining the events, and are the principal managers of the encounters). . . . Hence situations, while structured in dominance (i.e. showing a systematic tendency to reproduce the hegemony of the dominant definitions of the situation) are not totally pre-determined—each encounter puts the 'structure in dominance' to the test.[37]

The crucial question is 'Who defines whom?' This is the level at which cultural power operates. What we have seen in the foregoing analysis is the greater power of the state to define its own *image,* and the corresponding tendency for the trade unions to have their image *defined for them*—though, of course, the media will not *always* take the state's own projected image for granted, cf. the hostile *Nationwide* interview of Macmillan (15 March).

Similarly the state has greater power to define the overall sphere of politics and to 'set the terms' of specific dates—over what is fair, reasonable, etc.—and the unions' opposition by and large operates *within* these limits. Poulantzas puts this well when he says that:

the dominated classes live their conditions of political existence through the forms of dominant political discourse—(so that) they live even their revolt against the domination of the system within the frame of reference of the dominant legitimacy.[38]

Cultural power can also be seen to operate in terms of 'access on what terms for whom'. The media, via the structure of access, and the systematic 'over-accessing' of representatives of the state, are obliged to transmit and reproduce the state's definitions of the situation. Moreover, the media tend, to quite a large extent, to 'take over' these definitions, which thus often come to 'underlie and permeate the texture of news reporting'.

But despite the 'grip' which this gives the state over the media, it would be incorrect to see the media simply as the ideological servants of the state. The relative autonomy of the media from the state means that they establish a distinctive media culture with its own set of values and orientations which is superimposed upon, and thus comes to modify the definitions articulated by the state.[39] Moreover, that autonomy means that other groups are allowed access, though often on restricted terms, and that negotiations of the dominant definitions and counter-definitions are articulated.

Thus the 'dominant ideology' which is reproduced by the media does not 'simply reflect the (interests) of the dominant class . . . but rather the concrete political relation *between* the dominant and the dominated classes in a social formation[40]—a relation of 'unstable equilibrium' in which 'the interests of the dominant groups prevail, but only up to a certain point . . .'[41]

NOTES AND REFERENCES

1. See Stuart Hall's article: 'Deviancy, politics and the media', in P. Rock and M. McIntosh (eds.), *Deviance and social control*, (Tavistock, London, 1974).
2. C. Geertz, 'Ideology as cultural system', in D. Apter (ed.), *Ideology and discontent*, (New York, Free Press, 1964), quoted in Hall: *op. cit.*, pp. 278–279.
3. Olivier Burgelin, 'Structural analysis and mass communication', in D. McQuail (ed.), *Sociology of mass communications*, (Harmondsworth, Penguin, 1972).
4. ACTT Television Commission: *One week: a survey of television coverage of union and industrial affairs in the week Jan. 8–14, 1971,* (London, ACTT, 1971).
5. Cf. Ernest Gellner, *Thought and change*, (London, Weidenfeld & Nicolson, 1964), pp. 75–77.
6. J. Halloran *et al.: Demonstrations and communications*, (Harmondsworth, Penguin, 1970).
7. *Bad news* (London, Routledge & Kegan Paul, 1976).
8. *Ibid.*, p. 236.
9. See 'Chronicle' in *British Journal of Industrial Relations*, Vol. XI, 1973, pp. 300–312, for details of this period.
10. The breakdown of programmes was as follows: 34 BBC 1 main news broadcasts, 16 ITN main news, 14 editions of *Nationwide* (BBC 1), 4 editions of BBC 2 *News Review* and one BBC 2 late night news broadcast.
11. Most especially because, owing to lack of both theoretical and practical resources, I have not dealt with the visual level of the message. This omission may be partially excused by the extent to which, for much of the time the verbal is 'in dominance' over the visual in news broadcasts. 'For a subsequent attempt to deal with the problem of TV discourse and programme' structure, see C. Brinsdon and D. Morley, 'Everyday television: Nationwide', BFI TV Monograph, no. 10, 1978. See also S. Hall, I. Camel and L. Curti, 'The unity of current affairs TV' in WPCS no. 9. CCCS.
12. See Brinsdon and Morley, *op cit.*, ch. 3 on this.
13. Quoted in Graham Murdock: 'Political deviance: the press presentation of a militant mass demonstration', p. 206.
14. See R. Hyman, 'Industrial conflict and the political economy', in R. Miliband and J. Saville (eds.), *Socialist register 1973*, (London, Merlin, 1973), for an analysis of the changing rôle of the state in industrial relations during this period.
15. See Counter Information Services Anti-Report No. 6: *Three phase trick–A handbook on inflation and phase 3*, (London, C.I.S., 1973), p. 32: 'A

particularly striking example of this is GEC, which despite an outstandingly rapid growth in profits, has been a net disinvestor in productive capacity.'

16. Of course, union spokesmen correspondingly attempt to blame the government for 'forcing' them into strike action.

17. The 'conspirators' model is not given the same prominence in my analysis as in Stuart Hall's, where he describes it as 'the dominant pervasive deep structure' (*op. cit.*, p. 280) underlying reports of industrial conflict. This is because in the period (mid/late 1960s) which he was analysing, unofficial strikes led by militant shop stewards were the norm. In the later period I was analysing, it was a succession of official strikes, by groups such as civil servants, not easily classifiable as deviant/extremist, which was causing the trouble. The model was much harder for the media to apply to this situation.

18. E. P. Thompson, 'Sir, Writing by candlelight . . .' p. 280.

19. Frank Parkin, *Class inequality and political order*, (London, Paladin, 1972), ch. 3.

20. For these points I am particularly indebted to John Downing's excellent work. See his *Some aspects of the coverage of class and race in the British news media*, Ph.D. thesis, London School of Economics, 1975.

21. B. Groombridge, *Television and people*, (Harmondsworth, Penguin, 1972).

22. R. Brunt, *Whicker's World* in 'Working Papers in Cultural Studies No. 3', C.C.C.S., Birmingham, 1973.

23. Cf. G. Gerbner: 'Ideological perspectives and political tendencies in news reporting', *Journalism Quarterly,* Vol. 41, No. 4, Autumn 1964.

24. J. Downing, 'Some aspects of the coverage of class and race in the British news media', Ph.D. Thesis. LSE. 1975.

25. S. Hall, *The structured communication of events,* Centre for Contemporary Cultural Studies, mimeo, Occasional Paper No. 5, C.C.C.S., Birmingham, 1975.

26. J. Mepham, 'The theory of ideology in *Capital'*, *Radical Philosophy,* No. 2.

27. Reports of strikes in the left-wing press often display an opposite distortion—every sectional struggle is presented as *per se* part of the class struggle.

28. R. Miliband, 'Marx and the State', in R. Miliband and J. Saville (eds.), *Socialist register 1965,* (London, Merlin, 1965).

29. See Murdock, *op. cit.*

30. Mepham, *op. cit.*

31. N. Geras, 'Marx and the critique of political economy' in R. Blackburn (ed.), *Ideology in social science* (London, Fontana, 1972), p. 305.

32. Geras, *op. cit.,* p. 300.

33. Geras, *op. cit.,* p. 294.

34. H. Lefebvre, *The sociology of Marx,* (London, Penguin, 1972), p. 111.

35. There remains, of course, the important question of how the media's coverage of these issues is decoded by different sections of the audience: which groups endorse, negotiate or oppose the interpretations of events offered by the media. For the results of research exploring these issues see my (forthcoming—BFI) 'The nationwide audience: structured decoding'.

36. See Krishan Kumar, 'Holding the middle ground: the BBC, the public and the professional broadcaster', *Sociology,* January, 1975.

37. S. Hall, *External influences on broadcasting,* Centre for Contemporary Cultural Studies, mimeo, Occasional Paper No. 8, C.C.C.S., Birmingham, 1975, appendix A.
38. N. Poulantzas, *Political power and social classes* (London, N.L.B. and Sheed and Ward, 1973).
39. Philip Elliott, *The making of a television series,* (London, Constable, 1972) has best developed this notion of a 'media culture'.
40. Poulantzas, *op. cit.,* p. 203.
41. A. Gramsci, *Prison notebooks,* (London, Lawrence & Wishart, 1973), p. 182.

Beyond the Consensual Paradigm: a critique of left functionalism in media theory

JOCK YOUNG

A major convergence in mass media analysis during the 1960s and 70s has been the development of Consensual Paradigm theory. I wish to examine critically the roots and details of such a position in order to suggest directions which will allow us to retain its undoubted gains whilst correcting its theoretical faults.[1]

If Mass Manipulative theory focusses on the power of the controllers in the transmission of news and Market theory on the pivotal nature of the audience, for Paradigm theory it is the message itself which is paramount. Mass media are the major carrier of ideology and the task of the theorist is to decode the literary, auditory and visual images of the media. At heart the theory states that media operatives use a particular paradigm of reality in order to understand events in the real world. This paradigm, or 'inferential structure', is consensual in its basis. That is, it bifurcates the world into a majority of normal people who are possessed of free will and a deviant minority who are determined by forces beyond their control. Deviant realities as threats to this consensus are constantly being defused by being interpreted as sub-human, as not involving the power of free choice which the vast majority of citizens are seen to possess. The phrases 'psychopath', 'mob', 'extremist', 'riot', involve a subtle depiction of the deviant as acting outside of rationality and are constantly contrasted with the same activities of the rational centre of society.

Social reality, according to these theorists, is pluralistic and conflictual. In its radical pluralist version, there is a myriad of groups in society each with a degree of separateness in values and behaviour; in the left-wing version, the class divisions of culture, value and behaviour are hidden by the paradigm just as the conflict between the classes is concealed. The image of consensus is, thus, a mystification foisted upon the public. In *reality,* there are conflicting definitions of what is normal and deviant. Men and women, naturally rational in the pursuit of their own

interests and the development of their own normative systems, are de-
luded by the absolutist mystifications carried by the media.

The key characteristics of Consensual Paradigm theory are a rational,
voluntaristic notion of human action, a notion of society being held
together by a mystification directly functional to the ruling class, and the
coercive nature of reality hidden beneath the surface of consensual appearances.[2]

Whereas theories of Mass Manipulation stress the atomized passivity
of the population, Consensual Paradigm theory stresses the rationality
and voluntarism of the individual. In political terms it celebrates the
intransigence, the spontaneous eruptions of rebellion against the system:
it finds indications from diverse kinds of behaviour within the subordinate population having 'seen through' appearances to the hidden reality of
the system. The central problem of this theory is how, given that in its
own terms the social order is profoundly inequitable and coercive, is it
possible that such a rational and voluntarist population does not openly
and systematically rebel against the system? If reason abounds in the
world and injustice is obvious, why the lack of revolution? The Mass
Manipulative answer to this question—that the disparate yet totalitarian
lies of the media determine consciousness—is inadequate, for in Consensual Paradigm theory we have more recalcitrant, thoughtful actors. The
population is seen to be mystified by a sophisticated, highly developed
mythology; their rationality has been enchanted by a total and systematic
world view which is presented to the individual from cradle to grave.
Moreover, despite the central focus on the mass media by Paradigm
theorists, the media are merely one of a series of institutions which carry
this system of mystification (e.g. education, law, parliamentary democ-
racy) albeit that the media have a central focussing role in the overall
process of delusion.

It is a theory which sees itself as being at core materialist in that it
relates the activities of the ruling class and ruling class institutions to a
simple 1:1 reflex of their material interests and which proclaims that the
behaviour of the working class could be (and often is) a similar voluntaristic recognition of their interests. Their working class actors are either
mystified creatures rendered irrational by false ideas or ones with the
correct ideas who can therefore recognise their material interests. Reality
and ideology are seen as two separate spheres: the world of material
reality and the mystified world of appearances, without any substantive
between theories.

The task of the radical theorist is—in the vernacular—to 'unpack', to
'decode', to 'read' the structures of bourgeois thought and then in some

fashion to convey this analysis to the public. The Marxist fingers will click and the working class dreamers will awake.

We have already in this book examined the fundamental tenets of Consensual Paradigm theory. I wish briefly to place these in order before proceeding to a critique. To do this I will examine how Paradigm theory explains the flow of news formation from selection to the impact on the audience:

1. *Problem of selection (How is news selected from the glut of events?)*

Paradigm theory confronts the problem of why the Western media are obsessed with that which violates the depiction of society as an orderly consensus; for if the social order is seen to be organised in the best interests of all and all rational citizens recognise this, then deviancy and lack of justice and harmony in society are, on the face of it, surprising. Paradigm theory argues that if one starts from a given categorization of the world, then certain events are a perceptual shock. It is these anomalies which are the basis of news because of two interwoven reasons: they violate the public's sense of conceptual order and they violate their sense of justice. They are unreasonable actions—given one's belief in the paradigm—and what is more they are unjust—given that the paradigm insists that, in the long run, merit is rewarded and *vice versa*. The two types of anomaly stemming from this are thus: first, inappropriate role behaviour and secondly inappropriate deserts. Thus (1) good/normal guy acts badly and *vice versa,* e.g. police corruption; (2) good/normal guy gets bad deserts and *vice versa,* e.g. air crash.

In stark contrast to the Mass Manipulative interpretation of the mass media where cognitive confirmation and justice would be the central rules of news formation, here news is that which violates the Consensual Paradigm, in the sense that it is unexpected. The problem here, for the controllers of the media, is the contradiction that whereas, on one hand, they are bound to maintain the Consensual Paradigm, on the other, that which is newsworthy is that which questions it. The solution to this is contained within the consensual depiction of the world, that is violations are regarded as atypical (and the explicit foreground of news) and are contrasted with the overtypical majority of the population (who are the implicit or less conspicuous background of the news). Thus the formula for news is that it is that which is atypical as judged by the concepts and expectations of the Consensual Paradigm.

It is the perception of usual and unusual as seen through such a consensual lens. It is not, therefore, a distortion of the world (as in Manipulative theory) nor a more or less accurate reflection of society (as in Market theory), but an interpretation of reality through the mediating ideology of consensus.

2. *Problem of translation (How are events turned into news?)*

Let us examine the components of the Consensual Paradigm, the posited relationship between the stereotype and reality:

A. It is an anomaly

The morally and cognitively threatening is picked up by the journalist and then interpreted according to the pre-existing inferential stucture of Paradigm theory. That is, first, that the event is atypical and, secondly, that such an atypical event fits the existing stock of stereotypes of deviancy ('the typical atypical').

This process of translation is a two-way process for not only is reality translated into the stereotypes but those parts of deviant reality which are consonant with their stereotypes of atypicality are preferentially selected.

B. It is a morality play where anomaly is resolved

The consensual paradigm does not consist of a series of disparate stereotypes but one where both normal and deviant actors are related together in a series of meaningful structures or patterns.

The paradigm will provide a given aetiology (e.g. strikes are the result of irrational greed, drug use is the result of corruptors, alcoholism is an illness, etc., a given portrait of the actor (e.g. dope fiend, wrecker), a given outcome (e.g. inflation, death) and given victims (e.g. the sick, the children).

That is, it will provide a sophisticated demonology in a morality play which explains away cognitive and material disturbances in the consensual world, reasserting in the long term nemesis and the triumph of justice. Over against the stereotype of the deviant, is the stereotype of the normal: upright citizen, the heroic policeman, the dedicated doctor, the houseproud housewife. We have then a stereotypical categorization of the world which provides an explanatory framework for an ongoing saga of reason and justice. In terms of aetiology, Consensual Paradigm theory points to the existence of deep structures which are repeatedly involved in the explanation of each deviant phenomenon, e.g. the opposition of the 'sick' to the normal, the use of corruption-corrupted imagery.

The theory does not confine itself to news, the stereotypical depictions occur throughout the media: in the advertisements, in short stories, cartoons, women's magazines etc. It is only, however, in news stories that the stress on the atypical is made, but it is in the totality of the media that the fullest outline of the morality play is evident.

The formula: the atypical, contrasted against the overtypical, depicted in a stereotypical way implies that the news process involves a series of resolved anomalies. The journalist lives in a world of institutionalized surprise, his or her job is to translate surprises in reality into the terms provided for in the paradigm. There is little real challenge to the consensual imagery because the very nature of the paradigm is an array of explanations for deviant events and a defence of normality.

3. *Problem of control (How are journalists controlled in their task?)*

The major problem of control which this model confronts is that journalists rarely perceive their role as that of ideological hacks yet, of all people, they daily confront violations of the Consensual Paradigm—for this is the nature of news. The answer given, focusses on the socialization of the journalist into the profession. To become part of a media bureaucracy involves the acquisition of a series of skills. The journalist learns the correct fashion of presentation, the right phrasing, the appropriate visual complement to verbal or printed information etc.

This training into the consensual mode of interpreting reality is in terms of technical competence. For technical criteria of professional acumen hide the political nature of his or her task; and the Consensual Paradigm is represented as the standard for neutrality and objectivity. The journalist is involved in an act of auto-censorship; he or she is unconsciously engaged in the act of translating reality into the terms of the paradigm, a task motivated by the explanatory problems which deviant reality sets up for the paradigm. He or she takes that which on the face of it violates the paradigm, but in the process of translation stereotypically portrays the event and then ideologically explains it in such a way as to reconstitute the boundaries of the paradigm.

But how then is this socialization process maintained? How is it held in a consensual mould? It is at this juncture that the Consensual Paradigm theorists note, like Mass Manipulative theory, that the oligopolization of the media is the key factor. But, unlike Manipulative theorists, they do not view the ruling élite as interfering at every level of media production. Rather, the ruling élite form a ring of steel around the media: ensuring that the parameters of consensus are maintained whilst within the media bureaucracy such limitations are scarcely noticed. Limitations of craftsmanship are noticed: the sub-editor's zeal for housestyle is resented, gross censorship is noticed, the libel laws create problems, etc., but these are problems of exceptional instances or of detail or of technicality—they are not seen as fundamental limitations.

Thus we have the paradox that the Paradigm model despite its overwhelming emphasis on the seductive and mystifying nature of consensual ideas must rely on coercion to explain why the practices do not slip into radicalism, why cynicism does not slip into the discarding of the paradigm itself.

4. *Problem of choice*

The notion of the significant variation of news sources argued for by Market theorists is, in this model, viewed as a myth. It is not—as Manipulative theory would maintain—that variation is non-existent, it is rather a question of what is to be the yardstick of significant variation. Thus it is possible for a particular deviant action to be reported differently by various news sources yet for the notion of absolute consensual standards to be untarnished. Thus, if we have a deviant reality B reported in terms of the consensual framework A, one news source can report this as the result of undersocialization ($A°$), one as evil—an inversion of A (A^-), and the other as an innovative development of absolute standards (A^+). All report it differently—yet in no way is the absolute consensual reality questioned. One must differentiate, therefore, qualitative from merely thematic variation.

Thus, the range of news sources represents no choice outside of the paradigm—the economics of the mass media and the present oligopolization of control ensure this. Indeed Paradigm theory would go beyond this suggesting that the social control apparatus constitutes a coherent totality. That is there is a functional totality of the following sort within the media:

(a) between different sorts of news (e.g. sports reporting and crime reporting)
(b) between different parts of the same media (e.g. advertisements and news)
(c) between different media genres (e.g. news and the mass novel: non-fiction and fiction).

And between the media and the rest of the control apparatus:

(a) in the media representation of parts of the control apparatus (e.g. in the portrayal of the police or judiciary or nuclear family etc.)

(b) in congruence between messages (e.g. between the educational system and the media)
(c) in the division of labour of control (e.g. between predominantly ideological and repressive institutions: the media compared to the police).

Thus we have a totality consisting of an interconnected message which makes up a functional whole, a social control apparatus which is functionally interrelated and the whole configuration which is seen as functional to the posited interests of the ruling class.

From this perspective the public is faced with a constant consensual barrage supportive of capitalism wherein the limited alternatives of available news sources present only variation within a theme: an illusory choice, where the media whether highbrow or lowbrow, visual or literary, parade the same socio-political frame of reference and where the individual is enveloped throughout his or her life with a varied social control apparatus carrying an identical message.

But Paradigm theory not only presents us with a radical critique of the notion of choice, it confronts squarely the major hiatus in Manipulative theory—namely, why, if the media are carrying a message which is alien in terms of the interests and often the posited values of a large section of the population, is such a product devoured so voraciously? For unlike many parts of the control apparatus the mass media have no coercive component to them. Work, education and the family, for example, impose their own direct disciplines, but the media belong to the leisure sphere, to 'free' time. No one is going to test you in the morning about 'News at 10'; the media are chosen voluntarily and are a major—if not the most significant—leisure activity in advanced capitalist societies.

To tackle this central problem Paradigm theory argues that living in the present social order imposes certain demands and sacrifices on the individual. He or she has a need to feel that the sacrifices made are, in fact, worthwhile: that merit is rewarded and evasion of the rules results in appropriate punishment. Indeed, such an equation between merit and reward is the central ideological basis of the modern state. Certain forms of deviancy, especially in the areas of economic and sexual activity, threaten this feeling of the rightness of the moral order and are particularly potent activators of anxiety. The media, it is argued, play on such moral distress: they not only portray the causes of deviancy as irrational, but depict the consequences of such activities as resulting in misfortune. As such, they assure their audience that their decisions are the most rational in a world where, in fact, conformity to consensual norms is

irrational. For in a world where widespread economic explanations exist, it is not deviance that is problematic but conformity. The media are
reassuring to their audience, and it is this that explains both the attractiveness of the media to their audience and the extraordinary fixation on
deviance within the news. Bad news is the order of the day, because such a
morality play of law and order, on one side, and deviation, on the other,
allays the anxieties of the masses. The media select anomalies of social
actors and justice and render them into news stories which in their
dénouement, plump for a suitable aetiology (which does not threaten
social order) and appropriate nemesis (which balances the social accounts). Moreover, the specific deviant groups selected are, in fact, either
innocuous or else comparatively low in any rational list of anti-social
activities. Thus, 'crimes without victims' such as pornography, drug use,
homosexuality and prostitution, which it is maintained are largely freely
chosen transactions between consenting adults, have totally inappropriate and disproportionate attention to them by the media. Furthermore,
crimes with more obvious victims like juvenile delinquency, street violence and burglary are given considerably greater coverage than crimes
such as corporate legal violations, domestic violence or infringement of
factory legislation, despite the fact that the latter crimes are more serious
in their economic and personal impact. Similarly strikes are exaggerated
in their effect on the economy whilst other factors such as lack of investment are ignored.

According to Paradigm theory the attractiveness of mass media is
based on a sophisticated mythology which plays on and exacerbates the
moral indignation and anxieties of its audience displacing them on to
false targets. Here the stress on the voluntarism of the actors—in contrast
to the passivity of Manipulative theory—allows some Paradigm theorists
to move to a position which suggests that the insidious attraction of the
message involves a complicity on the part of the audience. That is, not
only is the illusion immensely persuasive but the audience itself actively
commits an act of bad faith: plumping for the safe target, the reassuring
imagery in order to avoid the haunting doubts as to the irrational nature of
the system.

5. *Problem of effect*

Mass Manipulative theory views attitudes as being engendered directly
by the media—the media are envisaged as a material force which impinges
directly upon the audience's psyche. Market theory sees the media having
either no effect at all on attitudes or—if anything—a simple reinforce-

ment of existing beliefs. For example, if we have two groups of people one with views favourable to a strike (Group A) and one with antagonism to it (Group B), Manipulative theory would predict that media bombardment would reverse those attitudes favourable to the strike: i.e. (A)(B) → (B)(B). Market theory, on the other hand, would predict a reinforcement of attitudes against the strike and a reversal in those for it: i.e. (A)(B) → (A)(B+). The Paradigm model insists that both views are atomistic in their conception of attitudes. For it is not attitudes that are changed but the frame of reference, the contextualization of these attitudes. Thus a strike would be contextualised in terms of a frame of reference which has the notion of the national interest, the limited size of the 'national cake', wage push inflation, etc.

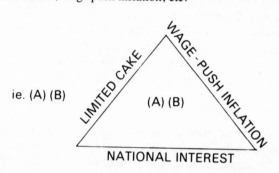

Thus, by talking of the 'national interest', of 'wage-push inflation', of the 'anarchy of free collective bargaining', the person who held positive attitudes to the strike may still remain positive yet the parameters of his or her support will be drastically limited. The effect of the mass media is, therefore, envisaged as providing an overview—a paradigm for understanding the world. Its efficacy is ensured by what is seen as the segregated nature of modern industrial societies. Social knowledge in a complex society is limited both in terms of direct empirical knowledge as to how social groupings different to one's own act, and as to overall understanding of the social order. The media provide such detail and framework: they place the drug user, for example, in a moral scenario wherein there are corruptors ('pushers') and the corrupted ('addicts'). They do not so much change a negative attitude to illicit drug use as pinpoint the lines of causality, those actors who are to be punished and those to be pitied.

The effect of the media is to either (a) supply knowledge and context to an audience for which they have no empirical referents—thus directly shaping this attitude, or (b) where they have definite attitudes, contextualise them within the paradigm. Furthermore, the media are capable of delivering such information suddenly and dramatically. Thus, given the degree of moral anxiety prevalent in society, they can play on these fears with very significant results. Folk devils are created as moral panics develop within the mass of the population. The stereotypical depiction of the atypical serves in a Durkheimian function to unite the population in a sense of their own moral righteousness, fusing their diverse interests into a national unity. But, unlike in Durkheim's writings, such a process is seen to be an illusion: the wild beasts presented as existing at the edge of the social universe are, at least in the beginning, indicative merely of the largely innocuous diversity characteristic of a plural society. They have become social Rorschach blots on to which the media have projected fantasy stereotypes. This effect is two-sided, for it not only unites the audience into a pseudo-consensus, it has a real impact on the deviant. Fantasy is translated into reality: for the population mobilised by means of the moral panic reacts harshly against the deviant, alienating them from the body politic in a deviancy amplification process which, however illusory in its imagery, is real in its consequences.

The paradox of bad news

If one thinks of one word that would sum up the image of the world refracted through the Western media it is crisis. The mysterious natural laws which manipulate the economy are forever depicted as inimical to the patient industry of reasonable men. Wars break out between countries as if some irrational demon had overtaken the aggressor nation. Teenagers who should be contented with their relative abundance commit seemingly meaningless acts of social and personal destruction. Normal workers persist, we are told, in unreasonably holding the country to ransom. The cities created supposedly to serve men constantly manage to cramp and frustrate the lives of their creators. Crisis stalks the streets, each peccadillo chronicled minutely by the media. Now the sharp contrast here is with media within the Soviet bloc where good news and encouraging headlines are the order of the day. Why then do the Western media focus so intensely on bad news? Why is every crack in the structure of capitalism examined with such doleful gusto by a whole profession of doomwatchers? Manipulative theory is clearly out of order here: controlled media invariably purvey good news: I have cited the example of the Soviet media but examples from those parts of the Western media which involve direct controls corroborate this. Thus the closest approximation to the Soviet media is the house magazines of the large corporations. Further examples of good news media are advertisements, which provide a sharp counterpoint to the news parts of the media with which they co-exist alongside like inverted bedfellows, the pull-out supplements of the quality press focussing on particular countries or industries which are lamentably dominated by the advertisers, and the reporting of war under periods of direct censorship.

Market theory is equally incapable of explaining this phenomenon, apart from positing a 'natural' tendency for people to dwell on the negative, an inbuilt Schadenfreude of the Western population. And even if we granted this it is difficult to explain why it is certain types of bad news rather than others that are attractive. For example, street crime rather than corporate crime, armed robbery rather than domestic violence, air crashes rather than industrial accidents.

The problem of bad news is a central concern of Paradigm theory; I have indicated a contradiction lying at the heart of news production. For news is by their definition the atypical as judged against the stereotypical: the deviant as judged against the consensus. Therefore the journalist is in the unenviable position of constantly trying to force intransigent reality into a consensual mould. But it is in dealing with this paradox that the media achieve—as far as Paradigm theory is concerned—an extreme ideological sophistication, which is extremely functional in maintaining the social order. For the mythology *explains away* deviance, it uses that which is, at first sight, most threatening to a consensual depiction of the world to reaffirm this reality. It is not merely that the folk devils are used to present a negative image of ourselves and to lecture the population on the rewards of conformity and the nemesis of deviance. In addition, a process of ideological inversion occurs, where to the question: why are there problems in capitalist society? we have the answer: because of strikes and crime; not that capitalism inevitably produces strikes and crime. The problems endemic to capitalism become the blemishes and the solution to the malaise is to remove the blemishes not to change the system.

The chasm between reality and appearances

Let me emphasize at this stage: Paradigm theory represents a considerable advance on either Mass Manipulative or Market theories. Its stress on the ideological nature of the media, carrying a world-view which both structures and explains the world to an attracted audience, transcends the atomistic views of human nature expressed in earlier theory. For we have neither passive manipulated atoms nor rational calculating ones—the

Consensual Paradigm, however unreal in its basis, creates a common discourse for all men which is real in its consequences. Owners, journalists and audience find their relationship to reality mediated by the all-pervading consensual definitions of media. It is an ideology which makes sense of the world and imposes its own standards of justice. It is an imperative of research that such structures should be analysed and understood. But the model has a profound defect: it does not situate consensual ideology in the material reality which gives rise to it. True, the material interests of the ruling class are seen to ensure that the parameters of consensus are maintained—but it is only at this juncture that material reality intrudes. This defect occurs on two levels: first, that the relationship between the media message and reality is seen to involve a huge gulf (i.e. it is a mere illusion); secondly, that the ideology is seen to be unrelated to the material circumstances of the population (i.e. it is an illusion foisted upon the population).

In Market theory there is no gap between the audience and the media, the latter are merely a reflection of events in the real world as ordered by audience interest. In Manipulative theory there is a yawning gulf between the media and their audience, and between reality and the news message: distorted news is imposed on a passive mass. Paradigm theory maintains this sense of chasm between audience and message, between events and reality. What it ditches in Mass Manipulative theory is its machiavellianism. The whole world exists in an illusion which is ungrounded in material reality. Thus the gulf which is posited between the journalist and his or her experience, between the media message and its audience and between the message and its object in the real world, is forged merely by the tenuous fabrication of illusion. The primacy which Paradigm theory gives to the media as an instrument of social control ignores the material basis of consensual ideology in society; namely that journalists, owners, the audience and the participants themselves all exist in the same social order. It is an idealism because it believes the world is ruled by illusion, it is an idealism because it sees the folk devils which the audience complicitly despise as an act of bad faith. It is an idealism because material reality—or interests—do not impinge directly on consciousness but are a simple reality, out there, to be voluntaristically comprehended by consciousness.

Null Effect theory

I want to turn to a Marxist approach to the mass media which—in sharp contrast to both Manipulative and Paradigm theory—plays down rather than centres around the centrality of the mass media as agencies of social control. It is illuminating to make the following contrasts: in Manipulative theory the media deceive the audience about reality, in the Market model no one is deceived by the responsible journalist, in Paradigm theory the paradigm deceives everyone; the owners, the journalists and the audience: whilst the audience in turn deceive themselves, but in Null Effect theory it is reality itself which is deceptive. As Maurice Godelier put it, in a capitalist society:

> It is not the subject who deceives himself, but *reality* which deceives him, and the appearances in which the structure of the capitalists' production process conceals itself are the starting-point for individuals' conceptions.[3]

This is to suggest that the concepts which the mass media carry are based upon that consciousness spontaneously generated amongst population in their day to day experience of material reality. Thus John Mepham argues:

> I do not of course, intend to deny for one moment that the bourgeoisie do control the means for the dissemination of ideas . . . nor that they do use this contol as a powerful weapon in the defence of their class-interests. But my view is that the bourgeois class is the producer of ideas only in the sense that sleep is the producer of dreams. To say that the bourgeoisie produces ideas is to ignore the conditions that make this possible, to ignore that which determines which ideas are thus produced, and to conceal the real nature and origins of ideology. It is not the bourgeois class that produces ideas but bourgeois society. And the effective dissemination of ideas is only possible because, or to the extent that, the ideas thus disseminated are ideas which, for quite different reasons, do have sufficient degree of effectiveness both in rendering social reality intelligible and in guiding practice within it for them to be apparently acceptable. It is the relation between ideology and reality that is the key to its dominance.[4]

He concludes, later in the article:

> I am not, of course, denying the reality of self-deception. Nor am I denying that there have been and are many who believe what they believe about social relations because they are aware of the connection between such beliefs and the advancement of their own interests.
> . . .Nor am I denying the obvious truth that there are many who

attempt to manipulate others into believing things which they know to be false . . . I have no doubt that such methods or attempted manipulation of people's beliefs are very common, that for example the present President of the United States [Nixon] and many members of his administration are liars, and they and many others not only lie but use their enormous power and wealth to make as sure as possible that their lives fill the media and penetrate into every corner of the language and of people's minds. But I think Marx's theory is an attempt to account for much more puzzling phenomena than this. Namely that at least in certain historical conditions ideological forms of thought are the 'natural self-understood modes of thought'. The bourgeois ideology that has dominated not only the thought of the bourgeoisie but also the theory and practice for example of the English labour movement for over a century has clearly not had its origins in the methods or instruments that are now available to and used by the cynical elite of crisis-torn America. Such methods have not normally been necessary. If we have all been brainwashed then it is by the very forms of social reality itself.[5]

The relation between ideology and reality is not that of an illusion screening a chasm but that of an intimacy. It is an intimacy which is both opaque and contradictory. To find the basis of this we must examine, as Godelier suggests, the structure of capitalist production itself. Here we find two contrasting spheres: the world as it appears from the level of the process of circulation (the market exchange of commodities, in this case labour and wages) and the process of production (in this case, the production of surplus value); on the level of the sphere of circulation of commodities the worker freely sells his labour, he obtains the market equivalent for it, he is an equal before the law, he is not cheated by the individual capitalist. But, if we leave the noisy sphere of human rights and enter the hidden abode of production, we find a different story: instead of freedom we have coercion and necessity; instead of formal equality, substantive inequality; instead of equivalence, exploitation—the extraction of surplus value. Yet, of course, the adult male worker has a qualitatively greater freedom than, for example, under feudalism, or under fascism with state direction of labour, or—most appositely in this context—than those of his contemporaries who are excluded or emarginalized from the labour market (e.g. the unemployed, women, old people, adolescents, racial minorities). For the market economy creates, indeed needs, real freedom, rationality and individualism, at least in *certain sections* of the population.

Thus the phenomenal form (freedom, equality, equivalence) inverts and obfuscates reality (servitude, inequality, exploitation) but it is not a mere illusion. As Jorge Larrain puts it:

> Appearances are not mere illusions nor is the essence more real than the appearance. Both essence and appearance are real. In other words, reality itself is the unity of essence and appearance . . . . phenomenal forms are, therefore, as real as the essence and yet invert the concealed essence[6].

Such a double, opaque and contradictory structure of reality is characteristic of capitalism.

The most immediate superstructural parallel to the wage form is law. Bourgeois law arises in order to safeguard contract and protect property: that is, to maintain equality in the realm of circulation whilst perpetuating and allowing for increasing accumulation at the level of production. The law offering equality of judgement and protection to all once again involves a contrast between formal equality on one level which obscures and perpetuates substantive inequality on the other. Thus, laws are passed which judge people as equal individuals (the legal subject), obscuring the fact that their inequitable class position makes them differentially vulnerable to commit crime in the first place. Whilst the formal equality of protection which laws give in the defence of the property of individuals is, on another hand, simply the right of one class to perpetuate and extend their ownership of the means of production, thus rendering the working class both propertyless and unequal. Thus, to judge people equally is to act inequitably; to protect property equally is to extend inequality. Once again the juridical form is opaque, but once again there is a vital element of reality in the formulation: bourgeois legality is an advance on feudal law (or fascism for that matter), bourgeois society creates crime which threatens the working class and law maintains a degree of protection against the criminal, whilst legal rights allow the individual to organise politically and afford some protection against the intrusions of the ruling class and the state etc.

Let us examine the image of crime and of the law-abiding citizen in this light. Elsewhere, I have argued that the conventional image of the criminal is on one level a mystification (crime is, in fact, ubiquitous, there is no qualitatively separate aetiology of the criminal individual, the cost of street crime is lower than other forms of crime), whilst on another it has a reality (street crime is a product of the emarginalized, the nature of their crime is qualitatively different, the criminal is determined compared to the labourer, the criminal poses a real danger and an injustice to the working class[7]. Thus, the images used by the mass media, tied as they are to the world of appearances, are not mere illusions. It is their cognitive fit with reality that explains their credibility, it is their real sense of justice that generates support for them among the people rather than mere bad faith and mystification.

In a similar vein David Morley notes how the contradictory nature of the concepts of National Interest, the images of the trade unions, the notion of victim and conspiracy are used to depict industrial disputes in the media.

The overall argument then points to the origins of the basic concepts used by the mass media to analyse social phenomena as being generated by popular consciousness—itself a function of the peculiar nature of reality in capitalism. The Consensual Paradigm's image of the normal, the deviant, the threat of the deviant to the normal etc. is not an illusion but something spontaneously generated and grounded in a reality existing prior to the pronouncements of the media. John Mepham puts it: "Bourgeois ideology dominates because within serious limits, *it works* both cognitively and in practice".[8]

Public interest in the news, then, is not based on a mere act of bad faith which embraces a mythological world of illusion. It is a plausible picture of the world, arising out of reality, which presents information about events which really impinge on the audience. Furthermore, bad news about a world which is in reality bad is scarcely surprising: although the *predominance* of bad news and the avid fashion in which Western media are consumed is scarcely explicable in terms of a consciousness that, so to speak, passively and unproblematically reflects reality—albeit a partial distortion of it.

To summarise David Morley, following such an approach suggests that the mass media: 'operate so as to reinforce the ideological structure and content of "what everybody knows" about our social world'[9].

Dreams and nightmares

To ground the 'illusions' carried by the mass media, materially, involves a fundamental critique of Paradigm theory but it at the same time gives rise to certain errors which have as a consequence the relegation of the media to a role of reinforcer, a provider of an overview—an altogether secondary position in the implementation of control.

As against this I want to rephrase Mepham's vivid invocation that:

'the bourgeois class is the producer of ideas only in the sense that sleep is the producer of dreams . . . it is not the bourgeois class that produces ideas but bourgeois society'.

Instead I suggest that on the contrary, bourgeois society produces regularly and inevitably nightmares and it is beholden to the bourgeois class to calm the fears and doubts thus generated.

The mistake which Mepham makes is to assume that capitalist reality produces a popular consciousness which is unequivocal, non-contradictory and in the long run functional to the system. Norman Geras points to two types of mystification occurring in capitalism:

> one type . . . consists of reducing the social objectivity of the forms of capitalist relations to a natural objectivity. This mystification is fetishism. However, Marx also exposes a second type of mystification, one which involves a reduction of these forms, in the opposite direction, from social objectivity to social *subjectivity*[10].

Thus the value of a commodity like gold or silver can be thought of as natural or it can be thought of as a mere fiction of conventional origin. As Larrain comments:

> The phenomenal forms of social relations do not produce by themselves a univocal form of deception or mystification. On the contrary, the practical standpoint of the subject is important. Where the philosopher sees the reign of ideas, the economist may see the reign of things . . . .
> This is important: first of all, it shows that the various forms of ideological distortions in capitalist society are connected in the practical reproduction of social relations and their appearances, and yet remain different in the particular way in which mystification operates; secondly, it shows that ideology is neither a mere subjective creation of the subject's imagination, nor a mere imposition of reality upon the subject's passive consciousness.
> . . . . this very fact, that the mystification stemming from phenomenal forms cannot be reduced to only one form of distortion, excludes the opposite version which sees ideology as the product of external 'given circumstances' which deceive a receptive mind. Phenomenal forms are spontaneously reproduced in consciousness, not as an unavoidable, automatic result, but as a consequence of men's own engagement in the reproductive practice which produces them. If ideology was a

mere attribute of a certain deformed reality contemplated by the human mind from without, how could a non-ideological consciousness be possible?[11].

The two antinomies of bourgeois thought, idealism and vulgar materialism, co-exist and debate on every social issue. But it is not as if this bivocal form of distortion impinges upon consciousness merely to provide a 'talking-shop' of alternatives. The contradiction between the two spheres: circulation and production, which is at the heart of capitalist relations, creates fundamental problems in making sense of the world *both* cognitively and pragmatically. For it is not that the focus on the phenomenal forms of the sphere of circulation merely conceals reality: the sphere of production; it both conceals and exacerbates. That is, the emphasis on freedom, formal rights and equality is consistently undermined by the underlying servitude, exploitation and inequality. The concealed sphere makes a fool of the ideals which are so trenchantly stressed and enacted within the world of appearances. As Holloway and Picciotto put it:

> The contradictions of accumulation derive from the need to extract surplus-value from living labour. The immediate contradictions of this process consist of the continual undermining of the appearance of equality of exchange in the sphere of circulation by the inequality in the sphere of production. These are the contradictions of liberal capitalism and of the liberal moment of the state.
> The forms of the liberal moment of capitalism essentially involve the attempt to overcome the contradictions deriving from capitalist production by resolving all conflicts in the sphere of circulation and in terms of relations of exchange.
> The liberal capitalist state is, therefore, engaged in a continual process of upholding the principles of freedom and equality, while constantly modifying their application in practice, in order to overcome the contradictions continually created by the central contradiction at the heart of the relations of production.
> Hence its ideologies and institutions, based on the equivalence of exchange in the sphere of circulation, are constantly riven by the contradictions engendered by the lack of any such equality in the sphere of production[12].

Equality before the law, freedom of action, egalitarian opportunities, the basic provisions of citizenship: employment, housing and the conventional minima of property, a fair day's work for a fair day's wage and—even *within* the media—the free investigation and propagation of information—all are subverted by reality. Indeed, it is more to the point that such a subversion is a necessity in order to maintain such a reality. The dreams have, therefore, to be worked on actively—the nightmares resolved, for at heart there is a dysfunctionality in the system both materially and within the realm of ideas. The focus on bad news is, therefore, not an artefact of cognitive shock (as in Paradigm theory) nor a natural propensity of human interest (as in Market theory) but a function of the way in which the contradictions of the system generate bad news: ideals that constantly undermine themselves, quiet dreams that turn into nightmares. The frustrations of the material world, the exasperations of consciousness drive the audience to the media, the media in their desire to maximize audiences market bad news.

It is here that a most fundamental conflict in the production of news occurs: namely, between the desire to maximize ratings (the *audience function*) and the desire to maintain political control (the *control function*). For the controllers of the media must try to sell the commodity news but they must also try to keep the commodity within the political and moral limits that they find acceptable. The important point to stress here, is the *active* need of the audience for news, and the *active* dual role of the powerful within the media—in attempting, on one hand, to sell copy, whilst on the other to define and explain the situation in order to maintain hegemony. In order to sell their commodity the controllers open up a Pandora's Box: calamity and mischief fly out and it is their task to keep the lid only partially open and to charm the creatures that they have revealed. *But* the lid has to be kept open if they are to compete for and retain audiences.

In the following table I have illustrated the tension between control and audience functions. A totally controlled media would publish good news, confirm the stereotypes of the heroes and villains, see that they got their appropriate deserts, communicate in the bourgeois language of freewill and consensus, exalt the equation: merit + effort = reward.

But, in fact, this does not occur, instead there is a constant struggle between the two principles. This is evident, for example, in the language of newspapers directed to the working class involving the distinctly non-bourgeois world of fate, luck, inequality and cynicism and undue focus on leisure etc; in the common contradiction between the tone of an article (the *metacommunication* e.g. crime is wicked) and the context of articles (the *communication* e.g. dwelling on the daring or salacious detail of a crime); in the fact that the media can move from exaggerating and dwelling on the success of an act of deviancy to underestimating and condemning it within the same newspaper, or over a short period.

Justice is not always seen to be done: a sense of anomaly, outrage, and injustice sells news, not the soothing principles suggested in Paradigm theory. What I am pointing to is how—because news is a commodity—the control function must constantly accommodate to the audience function. The former will ensure that genuinely radical media never occur, it will select the *sort* of bad news that is discussed, but it cannot completely dominate the content: the audience make the controllers accommodate to them—the controllers ensure that this accommodation stays within limits:

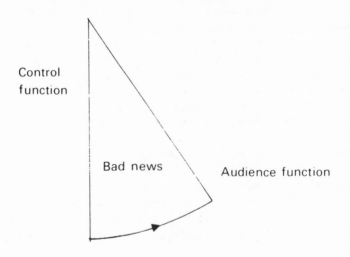

THE CONTRADICTION BETWEEN CONTROL AND AUDIENCE FUNCTION

The Message	Control Function	Audience Function
1. Type of news	Good news	Bad news
2. Stereotypes of actors	Confirmation	Anomaly
3. Justice	Resolved anomaly (Just deserts)	Unresolved anomaly (lack of justice)
4. Conceptualization	Bourgeois concepts	Concepts of audience
5. Communication and metacommunication	Agree	Contradict
6. Internal consistency of message	Coherence	Contradiction

What is important to note here is that the resolution of this contradiction is not a given static outcome but is dependent on the specific importance given by the controllers to a particular new item at a given time and the type of audience that the journalists see themselves as relating to.

With respect to the latter I have pointed to the fashion in which the media orient themselves to a particular audience. The resulting language used is what Hall *et al.* —in the article reproduced in this volume—call the *public idiom*. Such idioms are, of course, markedly different between media directed largely toward professional and those directed towards working class audiences. What is of interest is that in the latter instance it is an attempt to relate to the culture which working class communities evolve in order to deal with precisely those contradictions which we have seen give rise to the sense of anomaly which is the basis of news. That is, the contradiction between the sphere of circulation and the sphere of production, between freedom, equality and equivalence, on one hand, and exploitation, on the other, gives rise to an accommodative working class culture. Paul Willis has ably charted this in his study: *Learning to labour*[13] where he shows how working class culture represents a *penetration* of the world of appearances which in the very process of 'seeing through' the nature of reality erects a further ideology.

> Although inequalities are often seen, exploitation recognised, and injustices and contradictions experienced every day, none of these things seems to point in the same direction. They do not have a common cause. If some exploit and some are exploited, if some are equal and others unequal this does not happen with the systematisation of classes. All have the chance to exploit others as well as be exploited. Nor can any system ever hope to change this. Chance, fate and luck basically deal the cards in any game. A quite marked degree of disenchantment with the prevailing system and a degree of knowledge of exploitation, coupled with culturally mediated (though distorted) and partially lived out penetrations of the capitalist system, can co-exist with a calm acceptance of the system and belief that there is no systematic suppression of personal chances in life. Suppression is recognised, but as no more than a random part of the human condition. Human nature, not capitalism, is the trap. Ideology has helped to produce that—though not simply from its own resources: it is believed, because it is partly self-made.[14]

A break from one form of absolute ideology, that of the bourgeoisie, is replaced by another more realistic but still entrapping absolutism: the law of nature, the law of common sense. Such a 'realism' has both reactionary and progressive components: it is in no way of necessity, functional:

> In the case we have studied cultural penetrations of the special nature of labour in modern capitalism become a strangled muted celebration of masculinity in labour power. Cultural penetrations stop short of any concrete resistance or construction of political alternatives in an unillusioned acceptance of available work roles and a mystified use of them for a certain cultural advantage and resonance—especially concerning sexism and male expressivity. We should not underestimate the surviving degree of rationality and insight here. That working situation is given only the minimum of intrinsic interest and involvement. The self-abnegation of living subordination as equality, and in the terms of the official ideology, in the face of daily evidence and experience to the contrary, is at least denied.[15]

Now what is important here is that Willis is noting, as Larrain suggested, that the world of appearances must be worked upon; that the subject—in this case the working class—penetrates and interprets reality, rather than merely passively reflecting the world of appearances. This accommodative working class culture rises upwards and indeed contradicts official, bourgeois ideology:

> The crucial divisions, distortions and transferences which have been examined arise very often not so much from ideas and values mediated *downward* from the dominant social group, but from internal cultural relationships. Certain aspects of the working class cultural affirmation of manual labour considered here are profoundly important both ideologically and materially, and are, if anything, exported upwards to a largely uncomprehending official ideological apparatus. Division, sexism, racism and expression through manual labour power all occur much more strongly in civil society than in any state institution. In fact liberal democracy seems to set its face against these things. Its agents regard them as evils to be eradicated, not as the conditions of their own existence. This, of course, does not prevent the upwards export of ideological factors being used by the state, nor does it prevent the state from helping to reproduce them in contradictory and unintended ways. Indeed the good faith of state agents in various institutions may be one of the most important conditions for this reproduction under the regime of 'freedom' and 'equality' of the capitalist order.[16]

This is not, as Willis indicates, to reverse the classic flow of ideology; for the downward drift from the state agencies and institutions is crucial.

Rather it is to suggest that the dominant institutions have to deal with and play upon this accommodative culture, 'confirming' only that part of it which is most supportive of the stability and 'dislocating' any critical penetrations that have been achieved. This, I will argue, is precisely the role of the media in their relationship to the working class population—and that because of their need to sell their commodities they are more prone to such influence than any other agency of social control.

Relative autonomy and the media

Both Paradigm and Null Effect theory underplay the possibility of the mass media having a relative autonomy from the ruling class. The commodity nature of news, as I have shown, ensures that there is an autonomous tendency in news production. But there is a further cause of relative autonomy and that is the professional values of journalism. The bourgeois values of balance, lack of bias, objectivity and the creation of a public sphere where the machinations of particular groups are revealed, investigated and assessed, are progressive and set against the control function which is a result of the particular interests of the controllers. Such an information function is also, of course, not identical with audience function which reflects the sway of the accommodative working class culture on the media. We can represent such a triangle of relative autonomy as follows:

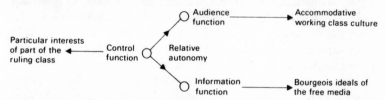

The power of audience and information function against those of control is based on different principles. With the audience, we have, facing those in control of the media, a series of atomised consumers, each of whom have—so to speak—a 'vote' reflecting their accommodative culture, whereas in the case of information function, the outcome is determined by the struggle for better journalism and standards within the media bureaucracy itself.

Left functionalism

Everything fits too neatly. Ideology always pre-exists and pre-empts any authentic criticism. There are no cracks in the billiard ball smoothness of process. All specific contradictions and conflicts are smoothed away in the universal reproductive functions of ideology. This study suggests on the contrary, and in my view more optimistically, that there are deep disjunctions and desperate tensions within social and cultural reproduction. Social agents are not passive bearers of ideology, but active appropriators who reproduce existing structures only through struggle, contestation and a partial penetration of those structures.[17]

The central question is to what extent the dysfunctionality at the heart of capitalism which generates news is resolved by the translation of such events into media messages. I wish to argue that the common assumption of the functionality of the media is tenuous in the extreme. To take the theoretical position most favourable to left functionalism: even if the media were controlled and an elaborate mythology generated in order to conceal or mystify reality, the categorization used to incorporate the plethora of deviant events would be inevitably flawed. For concepts based on the world of appearances, on the sphere of circulation, are incapable of making sense of reality. Corruption imagery for example, which is used to explain everything from strikes, through drug use, to why so many women want to have abortions, is inadequate as a text for the control of such activities and leads inevitably to contradictory results.[18]

But, as I have shown, it is not as if such an assumption of controlled media is correct. Relative autonomy stemming both from audience demand and the struggle for free and principled media leads to media— particularly at specific times and places—which in their focus on anomaly and injustice are far from presenting 'a world at one with itself'.

It is important here to stress the fundamental methodological errors which underlie left functionalism and which are all the more surprising, given the training in criticizing bourgeois functionalism which forms part of the intellectual background of most of its practitioners.

Let me illustrate such a methodology. Say we were concerned with explaining how the media characterize a particular deviant event X. The following explanatory procedure would occur: on one side a unitary ruling class interest is posited, on the other an internally coherent cluster of themes about X are constructed from the available media data. Explanation, then is an elegant solution to the puzzle of linking the two: how are ruling class interests facilitated by the negative way X is reported in the media? The problems with such an approach are manifold:

i. even if the functionalist presumption were correct, this assumes that functional alternatives are unavailable, i.e. other ways of reporting X which would be equally functional.

ii. inevitably given the functionalist premises, the themes are teased out from the data according to functionalist criteria, i.e. what are apposite examples of negative reporting which is functional to the ruling class and/or which help make an internally coherent picture. Thus examples which do not fit such a premise are disregarded.

iii. the assumption of a unitary ruling class interest and the way in which X in a non-contradictory fashion violates it is extremely tenuous.

The method of characterizing the portrayal of X in the media then inevitably plays down: contradictory reporting, variation between media synchronically and over time, and any dysfunctional tendencies which occur in its reporting.

To conclude this article. I want to outline tentatively a way of analysing the various stages in the flow of news from the events to the audience:

1. Problem of selection

I have argued that the element of surprise, the unusual, which is the kernel of news, is not a quality ascribed to certain events from the viewpoint of an external paradigm but arises from the contradictions of reality itself. Constantly bourgeois reality undermines itself: the moment of freedom in the labour market is contradicted by the exploitation of labour freely sold; the universalistic egalitarian ideals of education and law are mocked by the particularism of practice; the commonsense, consensual interdependent world is constantly jolted by crime and strife.

Whereas the American radical phenomenologists such as Molotch and Lester (in this volume) are correct in stressing the prefabrication of news prior to selection by the media—they do not go far enough. The concepts used to describe events are not imposed on an alien reality, they arise out of the phenomenal forms of reality itself. This being said, the concepts do not spring univocally out of reality and one can point to two major processes of interpreting events. First, there are the prepackaged interpretations of the powerful, the *primary definers* as Hall *et al*. call them, and, secondly, there is the accommodative culture of the working class which provides its own interpretation of events.

It is important to stress that such primary definers do not have a unitary definition of events (e.g. compare a corporation and a trade union) and that they must try to sell their definition of events to media which are to some extent autonomous of them. That is, news is a double commodity: it must be sold to the media and the media must sell it to an audience.

2. Problem of translation

The mass media largely work, therefore, on copy which has been already been pre-processed. The 'inferential structure' used by a particular medium is a result of manifold tensions and struggles.[19] The chief of these is the triangle of forces between control, audience and information functions. As a result it is not a monolithic paradigm: it is rather inconsistent, contradictory, changing over time and place and with varying foci and blind spots. To create ideal typical inferential structures, based on functionalist criteria of selection from the media data one has at hand, not surprisingly leads to an analysis which grossly overstresses the internal coherence and external functionality of the message.

3. Problem of control

Unlike Paradigm theory where reality is at odds with the message, there is not such a paramount need to point such a rigid socialization and regimentation of journalists. Reality itself is deceptive although its very contradictory nature still necessitates in this model an element of control. This comes from two forces: the controllers of the media themselves and the market forces arising from selling news to the accommodative culture of a particular audience.

Both of these can contradict the professional standards of the journalist (the information function) which is underlaid by the specific position of journalists in the production process. Namely, that s/he

(i) is in a staff position 'midway' between workers and management in an industry which is notably conflictful and highly unionised.

(ii) in a profession which is relatively speaking meritocratic and individualistic.

(iii) has a peculiar design relationship to the product which conceals the normal relations of production, i.e. the only parallel to a news journalist would be if the designers in Fords made a new model car every day.

I want to suggest that such a particular position in the production process[20] tends to generate a view of the world which is centrist, identifying with universal interest rather than that of workers or management, individualistic, meritocratic, and overemphasises the voluntarism of work. That is, the material position of the journalists corresponds well to a Consensual Paradigm theory of the social universe. Such a position, so responsive to bourgeois ideals, is of necessity often at loggerheads with the sometimes blatant particularism of owners, or the accommodative culture of the audience.

4. Problem of choice

I have pointed to a relative autonomy of the media which at specific times allows for some element of choice. Progressive articles or features do occur within the media (e.g. on abortion, on the police, on homosexuality, on industrial disputes) although, of course, the overwhelming pressure is towards a position which supports the *status quo* (the control function). There is a tendency also in our focus on news—one of the most controlled parts of the media—to ignore far 'freer' areas such as drama. Furthermore, unlike Paradigm theory I have criticised the notion of a monolithic media: the greatest divide being between those media directed to bourgeois audiences and those to predominantly working class audiences.

As far as the attractiveness of the media to its audience: I have pointed to the real basis of public anxiety regarding disruptions in the consensual world rather than relegating this to a mere mistake in thought. The concepts used have a cognitive and pragmatic utility, they do make some sense of a world which materially and ideologically creates constant anxieties. But the media do not merely mirror a deceptive reality nor do they simply reflect the accommodative culture of the audience. The importance of the mass media is that they cater for the desire for news stemming from contradictions at the heart of the system. The massive forces of control within the media attempt to deradicalize these anxieties by playing on only the most conservative elements in the accommodative culture.

5. Problem of effect

For Market theory a constant problematic has been the efficacy of the mass media, for to understand the effect of a message one must first comprehend each specific audience, because surely each audience will read the 'same' message differently. Paradigm theory attempts to solve this problem by arguing that what is provided is a frame of analysis not specific attitudes. For it does not matter that the audience interprets the message in terms of their pre-existing attitudes, if the media provide the frames by which attitudes are contextualised. In Null Effect theory such a problem is minimal for if attitudes are generated in reality, all the media do is to reinforce them. In contrast, the notion of an accommodative culture with a different frame of reference *and* attitudes to that of the dominant culture contradicts these analyses. For the message is not only oriented towards the accommodative culture it is interpreted through it. Thus, for example, messages which say that strikes involve a war of all against all, where the weakest go to the wall, might well be interpreted by certain audiences as underlining the cynical need for muscle in their part of the labour market. Thus there is no necessary functional outcome between the conformist message and its interpretation by an audience.

Furthermore, as I have argued, with regard to the content of the message, whether one takes, on one hand, those instances where the message is completely dominated by the powers that be, or, on the other, where it is most autonomous, there is no necessary conclusion as to its functionality.

To conclude: against the notion of order as being either the product of a beguiling myth or of a beguiling reality, I have pointed to the contradictions in the reality and the inconsistencies of the myth. I have introduced the notion of the active subject struggling to make sense of this world: generating both the desire for news and the accommodative culture. The mass media are a central agency in this process—and it is in this context that we must understand news.

NOTES AND REFERENCES

1. Examples of Paradigm theorists are: in the United States—a radical phenomenological version—Gaye Tuchman, and Harvey Molotch and, in Britain—a left wing version: The Glasgow Media Group, Graham Murdock and some of the earlier work of the editors of this volume.
2. I have developed this critique more fully in my analysis of left idealism in criminology. *Vide* 'Left idealism, reformism and beyond' in *Capitalism and the rule of law* (London, Hutchinson, 1979).
3. M. Godelier in *Ideology and social science* (ed) R. Blackburn (London, Fontana, 1972), p. 296.
4. J. Mepham, 'Theory of ideology in Capital', in *Cultural Studies 6* p. 99–100.
5. *Ibid;* p. 122.

6. J. Larrain, *The concept of ideology* (London, Hutchinson, 1979), p. 57.
7. *Vide* 'Left idealism, reformism and beyond', *op. cit.*
8. *Ibid.*, p. 118.
9. D. Morley, article in this volume.
10. N. Geras, 'Marx and the critique of political economy', in *Ideology in social science,* ed. R. Blackburn (London, Fontana, 1972), p. 297.
11. *Op. cit.*, pp. 59–60.
12. J. Holloway and S. Picciotto, *Capital, crisis and the state,* (2) Summer 1977.
13. P. Willis, *Learning to labour* (London, Saxon House, 1977).
14. *Ibid.*, p. 165.
15. *Ibid.*, p. 174.
16. *Ibid.*, p. 160
17. *Ibid.*, p. 175.
18. We have traced this in V. Greenwood and J. Young, *Abortion in demand* (London, Pluto, 1976).
19. *Vide* A. C. H. Smith's comparison of the *Daily Express* and the *Daily Mirror* in *Paper voices* (London, Chatto and Windus, 1975).
20. Like the classic petit bourgeois described by Nicos Poulantzas.
21. It should be noted, also, that the postulate in Paradigm theory that such a process of framing was often efficacious, because of the limited knowledge of the audience in a segregated society, is not totally accurate. Most people in an interconnected mass society have direct information regarding the work place whether office or factory, and of the impact of strikes or crime. Their attitudes are already formed in the accommodative culture. It is direct knowledge of the *segregated* institutions: the prison, the mental hospital, the university, etc. which is severely limited.

PART THREE

Effects and consequences

The two previous—and largest—parts of this volume dealt with the question of how news about deviance and social problems is selected and then presented in the mass media. To the public and to media experts, though, the question which immediately springs to mind is what *effects* this presentation might have in causing deviant or socially problematic behaviour. From our point of view, the effects question posed in this form is secondary—not in the sense of being unimportant or uninteresting but in being dependent on an adequate theory of how images and news are presented and ideologically signified. It's not that we want to 'play down' media effects—at times, quite the reverse—rather that we want to insist on a more complex theory of how these effects might occur.

Standard research and public debate about this issue—for example, in relationship to censorship—is often over-simplified. The dominant model has tended to use a somewhat crude stimulus-response view of human behaviour; the Stimulus (party political broadcast, soapflake commercial, violent drama, sexually explicit film) is measured against a set of hypothetically direct Responses (voting behaviour, consumer spending, increase of violent crime, sexual offences). We don't propose to reprint extracts from this literature, which is readily available in summary form.[1]

This is not to imply that there are no interesting findings in this body of research—for example about imitative aggression and differential responses to pornography—but in a sense the main feature of this tradition which interests us, is its inconclusiveness. Particularly when using surveys and other sociological methods rather than the experimental or laboratory designs favoured by social psychologists, the current consensus is that direct causal links between media content and actual anti-social behaviour have not been proved. This most clearly applies in the two most frequently researched areas of violence and pornography. And a recent review of the media and violence literature by a prominent British media expert supports our argument that studying the ideological significance of the media—in setting the social and political agenda, in selecting, defining and interpreting news, in legitimating the prevailing system of social control and in managing conflict and dissent—is a more productive line of enquiry than the traditional one: 'This represents a more complex and indirect approach to media influence than is normally postulated, but surely the study of the media in this way is much more valid and rewarding than the relatively simple-minded causal stimulus-response approaches which have been frequently if unproductively utilized in the past'.[2]

Before separating out some of these 'more valid and rewarding' lines of enquiry, it might be useful to identify the contrasting perspectives on mass media effects found in the Manipulative and Commercial models. In the Mass Manipulative Model, the public are passive absorbers of a set of messages which cannot but influence their behaviour and values. Usually the adherents of this model disapprove of the messages and so—from left- or right-wing positions—the point of the enterprise is to identify the effects of the media as being essentially harmful. Sometimes these effects are seen to be short-term and immediate, for example in the charge that TV or cinema violence (assumed or proved to be increasing in content) leads to direct imitation or identification. A typical representative of this position was the psychiatrist Frederic Wertham, who devoted his earlier attention to comic books as the 'seducers of the innocent' and then to TV as the 'school for violence'. His argument was that TV arouses the lust for violence, reinforces it when it is already present, teaches the best method of getting away with it and dulls children's awareness of its wrongness.[3] In the case of pornography, an equivalent set of arguments would be used by Mary Whitehouse and various other moral crusaders in this country.[4] In each debate, 'experts' are used to give scientific legitimacy to the argument, with both sides often citing the same evidence to support what is essentially an ideological position.

In left-wing social criticism about the media, the type of harmful effects usually cited are long-term ones: a gradual debasing of values, a fostering of false consciousness and a seduction of people from their true interests. The media are seen as powerful agents of distortion and mystification, as well as creating an atmosphere of tolerance for individualistic or competitive behaviour. Paradoxically, some of these same charges are made from élitist or right-wing positions—which lay even greater stress on the supposed power of the media in debasing values, standards and morality. Some strands of radical feminist writing about pornography, for example, often look quite similar to standard right wing critiques of such effects as the 'dehumanization of sex'.[5]

The Commercial model, most commonly invoked here by social scientists, as well as journalists themselves, is much more cautious about the question of effects. Influenced by 1940s' media research in the United States in such areas as propaganda and voting behaviour, together with their own rather more critical reading of the laboratory studies of aggression, adherents of this position stress that the public is neither so dumb nor so passive as all that. It will only seek out particular messages if they fulfil an existing need or fit into an existing set of opinions. How else to explain why not *everyone* exposed to the same violent images on TV becomes violent? Or—to take an extremely influential example—how could Democratic governments get elected in the United States when the media were overwhelmingly Republican?

Market models, then, play down the effects of the media. Thus in regard to the TV violence debate, psychological versions work with such concepts as the 'predisposed personality' in whom the media can, at the most, trigger off violent behaviour. Sociological versions talk of behavioural and attitudinal changes stemming from or being mediated through such intermediate influences as primary groups and reference groups.

None of these positions is particularly consistent. Some left manipulative critics, for example, might take an extreme Laissez-faire market position in the violence debate, while some commercial interests take it wholly for granted that the media have powerful effects on such matters as consumer choice. Indeed we have to some extent caricatured these two positions here—and they can only be properly understood in terms of the broader debate about the media in mass society.[6]

Our own position—as we indicated in the Selection and Model sections—is not simply a 'compromise' between these two extremes. It denies neither that overt manipulation sometimes occurs nor that market forces operate. A theory is needed to incorporate both these observations—and to be sensitive to other areas which both the Manipulative and Market models ignore.

For example: Market models, in a reaction to the exaggerated rhetoric of the Manipulative model and also because of a liberal democratic distrust of censorship, miss some of the more important effects of the media. Such effects are not monolithic, because there is some degree of choice, but more important *they are not directly dependent on the content of the media message*. As we stressed earlier, the media provide a setting or a frame, which allows different audiences to interpret the 'same' message in quite different ways. The question, for example, of whether the reporting of industrial conflict will lead to pro or anti union attitudes cannot be 'read off' from the reports in any straightforward way.

In public debates, political programmes, or legal principles, these more subtle effects obviously cannot be easily accommodated and protagonists invariably get drawn into either of the extreme Manipulative or Commercial positions. We might illustrate this with reference to the 1972 obscenity trial against the underground magazine *Oz*.[7]

Here the one side was arguing that the contents of the particular edition of the magazine would corrupt its younger readers. Advertisements for homosexual contacts, features presenting a tolerant attitude towards certain forms of drug use, cartoons depicting school authority in an obscene and derogatory way, articles and advertisements drawing attention to sexual deviation—all would have a harmful effect on values and behaviour. The opposed position drew attention to the selective nature of the audience (not everyone would buy the magazine) and the unlikelihood that the objectionable messages would actually have any effect on individuals not already committed towards that particular line of action or thought.

Both of us found ourselves involved in this case as potential witnesses for the defence. We had no doubt of the weaknesses of the prosecution's case on both legal and sociological grounds and would have drawn attention to the relevant evidence on such matters as for example, the effects of exposure to explicit sexual material.[8] In addition, our own values made us totally opposed to prosecutions of this sort. We should, therefore, have been ideal defence witnesses. But at some point in our initial briefing by the defence lawyers we realized that we were being put in a somewhat false position. We were being asked to support an extreme Laissez-Faire Market model which we knew in this case to be patently absurd. Clearly the publishers and editors of *Oz had* intended to change people's values and opinions, otherwise why produce the magazine at all? And if some members of the audience saw the voice of *Oz* as providing an authoritative source of alternative definitions of reality, why shouldn't these definitions affect attitudes to sex, drugs, authority? And weren't the adverts for various sexual couplings precisely designed to attract people or their money? When the defence lawyers saw that we were unable to completely suspend our theoretical doubts about the way they had to argue their case, we were quietly dropped from their line-up.

These doubts—and their reflections in such settings as courtrooms, academic theorizing and, increasingly, the media themselves as they get more introspective about their own roles—exemplify most of the problems inherent in the effects debate. Our readings in this Part cannot represent this whole debate—and indeed only Hartman's article comes close to providing the sort of information needed to understand how the media might actually produce the sort of effects which interest us.

We have separated out five main effects of this sort:

1. On the information stock

The master effect of the mass media's portrayal of deviance and social problems is in terms of the quantity and quality of the information which the public receives and uses as a basis for action. In modern urban societies there is an extreme social segregation between different groups.

The media are the major and at times the sole source of information about a whole range of phenomena. What McLuhan terms the 'implosive factor' in the media points to continual bombardment by images of phenomena that otherwise could conveniently be forgotten. For reasons we discussed in Part One, many such phenomena are not selected for attention at all, others are given continual exposure (for example, the 'violence problem') while yet others are suddenly thrust into the public consciousness. The quantity of the information, as we have suggested (see Wilkins, Roshier, Fishman), has a curious relationship to the real world. In Ben Hecht's often quoted words, 'Trying to determine what is going on in the world by reading the newspaper is like trying to tell the time by watching the second hand of a clock'.

The quality of the information is curious also. In our type of society information about deviance and social problems is invariably received at second hand. This means that it arrives after going through complex selective filters (see Molotch and Lester) and then being processed by the media. It tends to be of a flat, one-dimensional quality unlike the multi-dimensional picture which is seen as characteristic of the archetypal pre-industrial society whose information stock relied more on personal experience. The information is presented—as our examples in Part Two show—in a stereotypical manner, with elements of fantasy and selective misperception.

This is not to suggest that misperception and fantasy are exclusive attributes of those industrial societies where the mass media are so pervasive. On the contrary, the stereotypical accounts transmitted through such informal processes as rumour and gossip involve parallel distortions and are similar to the moral panics precipitated by contemporary mass media. Note, for example, how the medieval persecution of witches, devils, mystics and other 'deviants' depended entirely on pre-media and pre-literate forms of communication.

There still remain important differences, though. The manufacture of news is essentially an élitist endeavour whereas the process of rumour formation without the help of the mass media is marked by a series of 'democratic' innovations by each person in the chain. It is true, of course, that in order to communicate and persuade, the newsman uses a consensual paradigm which is—at least in part—embraced by large numbers. But the conservative direction of this framework is more structured and the chances of any innovation or alternative interpretations are more severely limited than in face-to-face communication. Rumour can be 'radical' and it possesses a fluidity of structure whereas the media present their audience with a fixed interpretation. When the media themselves trigger off rumour, the message is again more structured and related to the consensual paradigm. Social segregation in advanced industrial societies ensures that the experiential knowledge against which one might measure stereotypes is comparatively poor and restricted. This is not to make the romantic suggestion that pre-industrial man had wider social horizons: obviously people growing up in industrial society have an extraordinary range of social knowledge and much of this derives from the media. But the quality of this knowledge is different. *Within* small-scale societies social knowledge is more multidimensional and directly experienced, and also the restricted overall *quantity* of such information is less subject to the sudden implosions of concern which allow the mass media to introduce a social problem one day and forget about it on the next.

Students of the mass media, then, before trying to find stimulus/response links or any other such patterns, must look for the master effect which changes the nature of the 'stimulus'—i.e., the information that is actually used to build up society's stock of images. Research and theory about this master effect, though, must be extremely careful not to assume a direct relationship between media content and audience perception. This would be to perpetuate the worst errors of the Mass Manipulative model: to depict the public as passive 'cultural dummies' and to ignore alternative sources of information. Much more research is needed of the sort represented by Hartmann's article reprinted here: a systematic empirical comparison of the way industrial relations are presented in the news media and the way they are received and perceived (at least as revealed in a survey) by members of different social classes.

2. On the consensus

The media do not just transmit neutral information; they present a particular set of images about what the social world *should* be like. They reinforce the same image of society which they themselves draw upon. This is a complicated relationship to conceptualize, for the media both reflect dominant values and at the same time act as active *socializing agents* for these values. Take, for example, the effect of the media in sex role stereotyping and the trivialization of women: of course these tendencies already exist, but the evidence is compelling (see Tuchman) that the media augment or distort these tendencies in quite distinctive ways, for example, in leading girls to believe that their social horizons and life alternatives are even *more* limited than is the actual case.

As we have suggested in other contexts, the media are not monolithically and consistently conservative in this way. They present contradictory modes of consciousness, sometimes (usually inadvertently) highly radical in the sense of undermining or casting doubts on such cherished values as the work ethic, deferred gratification, or the good faith of authority. Women—to repeat our above example—can certainly obtain from some contemporary media products all sorts of images which contradict or confuse the traditional, consensually allocated roles of wife, mother or sex object. But we have to grasp dominant tendencies—and these certainly appear to reinforce a consensual image of society. This is so even when no open advocacy, partisanship, or 'taking of sides' is involved and the pretence is just towards 'recording the facts'. As Hunter Thompson remarks: ' . . . When you're in the business of recording history, you don't declare war on the people who're making it.' In the dominant imagery, the majority in any society is seen to share a consensus about reality. This involves agreement about what is normal, praiseworthy and acceptable. Those who are abnormal, who deviate or who present problems to the dominant value system are seen to inhabit a territory beyond the boundaries of society. They are allowed no history, no real alternative conception of reality and no status other than objects of social control. They are recurrent objects of attention not just because they entertain and interest us, or fulfil some psychological need for identification but because they inform us about the boundaries of reality. As Erikson notes: 'a considerable portion of what we call "news" is devoted to reports about deviant behaviour and its consequences'.[9] Such news is a main source of information about the normative contours of a society. It informs us about right and wrong, about the parameters beyond which one should not venture and about the shapes that the devil can assume. A gallery of folk types—heroes and saints, as well as fools, villains and devils—is publicized not just in oral-tradition and face-to-face contact, but to much larger audiences and with much greater dramatic resources.

This provides—as all our readings in Part Two variously show—certain structured sets, frames or discourses by which social problems are understood. Conceptions of race held by children for example (see Hartmann and Husband) are mainly structured by media imagery—particularly in areas where there is little contact with immigrants. Similarly, the 'crime problem', the 'drug problem', 'strikes' become virtually impossible to discuss apart from the way they are typically framed by the media.

The mass media provide a major source of knowledge in a segregated society of what the consensus actually is and what is the nature of deviation from it. They conjure up for each group with its limited stock of social knowledge, what 'everyone else' believes. They counterpose the reification of 'the average man' against the reality of individual group experience. The deviant's own knowledge of how 'most' others perceive him derives from this mass media portrayal; indeed in the case of the isolated deviant, even his knowledge of others involved in the same form of action might derive from this source.[10] This makes each social problem group feel more marginal when facing what they often presume to be a monolith of agreement. Such a perception is a vital link in the process of deviancy amplification which we discuss later.

In this fashion the mass media present frame-works, grounded in conservative thought, by which social problems are to be interpreted. Market theorists would comment that, if this is so, it is because: (a) such consensual models are the correct interpretations of reality; and (b) they are only taken up by the population because they are, in fact, widely accepted definitions already. We have already commented on such objections. It is obviously the case that in order to communicate at all, the mass media must talk in the same language as the audience—'language'—not just in the sense of vocabulary and syntax, but in the sense of some shared assumptions about reality. And some of these assumptions *are* essentially conservative in nature. But to talk about a conservative culture cannot be to characterize the totality of consciousness. The conservative part of the population's thinking may well be constantly reinforced by the impact of media material, while the radical portion is constantly denied. For consciousness, at least in our society, commonly displays a contradictory mode: our public rhetoric celebrates a world which our private discourse and personal feelings often denigrate. The journalist, as part of such a society, is placed in a role where competence is measured in terms of an ability to write in such an official language, he finds his promotion linked to the notion of 'responsible journalism' which in turn reflects such a way of thinking. It is not necessary, therefore, for him to be machiavellian in his adoption of conservative imagery even though his peace of mind may, at times, be disturbed by the obdurate nature of events. Manipulation, then, can occur, but it is of a more subtle kind than that suggested in the Mass Manipulative model, allowing as it does for a willing journalist and a partially responsive audience.

3. On moral panics

The mass media are the main agents and carriers of moral panics. Sociologists have recently devoted increasing attention to the elements involved in the creation of social problems.[11] The presence of a condition about which people feel anxious or threatened, the element of moral indignation,[12] a belief system to legitimate social control and the activities of enterprising individuals who facilitate public awareness of the condition are among the many elements studied. Thus Becker[13] and Gusfield[14] have taken the cases of the Marihuana Tax Act and the Prohibition laws respectively to show how public concern about a particular condition is generated and a 'symbolic crusade' mounted. This, with publicity and the actions of certain interest groups, results in what Becker calls *moral enterprise:* ' . . . the creation of a new fragment of the moral constitution of society'.[15]

The student of moral enterprise cannot but pay particular attention to the role of the mass media in defining and shaping social problems. The media have long operated as agents of moral indignation in their own right: even if they are not self-consciously engaged in crusading or muck raking, their very reporting of certain 'facts' can be sufficient to generate concern, anxiety, indignation or panic. When such feelings coincide with a perception that particular values need to be protected, the preconditions for new rule creation or social problem definition are present. The outcome might not always be as definite as the actual creation of new rules or the more rigid enforcement of existing ones. What may result is the sort of symbolic process which Gusfield describes in his conception of 'moral passage', namely a change in the public designation of deviance.[16] In his example, the problem drinker changes over time from 'repentant' to 'enemy' to 'sick'. Even less concretely, the media might leave a diffuse feeling of anxiety about the situation: 'Something should be done about it.' 'This sort of thing can't go on for ever.'

Such vague feelings are crucial in laying the ground for further moral enterprise. The media play on the normative concerns of the public and by thrusting certain moral directives into the universe of discourse, can create social problems suddenly and dramatically.[17] This potential is consciously exploited by those whom Becker calls 'moral entrepreneurs' to aid them in their attempt to win public support. A good recent example of the combined entrepreneurial power of politicians and the media, is the emergence in Britain over the 'Seventies of the welfare 'scrounger' as a folk devil—a moral categorization made possible by exploiting the deep-seated public ambiguity about welfare and social security.[18]

Moral enterprise is not, of course, always successful and the media's attempts to whip up a moral panic might not 'take'. Here, for example, is an editorial from the *Sun* (6 October 1972):

MURDER IN THE WARD: A Jordanian doctor ran amok and killed three children in a Blackpool hospital last February. Now Sir Keith Joseph

refuses a formal enquiry. 'The killings were completely unpredictable'
he says.

NOT SO, SIR KEITH.

PARENTS with children in hospital want to be reassured that there are
not any more mad medicos with daggers about.

Whatever the merits of an enquiry in this particular case, it seems hardly
likely that the majority of the *Sun*'s readers were consciously worried
every time they sent their children to hospital that 'mad medicos with
daggers' were lurking about the wards. This particular enterprise looked
unlikely to take off and one significant area for sociological research is to
uncover the conditions under which the media are or are not successful in
creating moral panics.

4. On social control

Both in their role as purveyors of information and transmitters of moral
panics, the media have a crucial effect on society's agents of social
control. What Lemert calls the societal control culture, the laws, procedures, programmes and organizations which in the name of a collectivity
help, rehabilitate, punish or otherwise manipulate deviants,[19] contains
not just a set of institutions (courts, prisons, hospitals) and personnel
(policemen, magistrates, social workers) but also typical modes and
models of understanding and explaining deviance. To a large extent,
these modes and models are provided for the control culture by the mass
media. There is little reason to suppose that control agents are somehow
immune to the messages transmitted by the media. Indeed the segregated
position of some control agents—such as policemen in regard to the
reality of, say, subcultural drug taking—makes them peculiarly suscept-
ible to certain media images. It becomes difficult for the police and courts
not to see themselves as front line defenders of the social order. And as
studies of moral panics show, the media transmit the belief systems
which legitimate or justify particular forms of social control.

Once the action against the deviant or social problem is taken, it is the
media which provide a commentary on the nature of the 'solution'. Philip
Slater has nicely captured the essence of this commentary in his discussion of what he calls the 'compulsive American tendency to avoid confrontation of chronic social problems':[20]

> We are, as a people, perturbed by our inability to anticipate the conse-
> quences of our acts, but we still wait optimistically for some magic

telegram, informing us that the tangled skein of misery and self-deception into which we have woven ourselves has vanished in the night. Each month popular magazines regale their readers with such telegrams: announcing that our transportation crisis will be solved by a bigger plane or a wider road, mental illness with a pill, poverty with a law, slums with a bulldozer, urban conflict with a gas, racism with a goodwill gesture. Perhaps the most grotesque of all these telegrams was an article in *Life* showing a group of suburbanites participating in a 'Clean-Up Day' in an urban slum. Foreigners are surprised when Americans exhibit this kind of naïveté and/or cynicism about social problems, but their surprise is inappropriate. Whatever realism we may display in technical areas, our approach to social issues inevitably falls back on cinematic tradition, in which social problems are resolved by gesture. Deeply embedded in the somnolent social consciousness of the broom-wielding suburbanites is a series of climactic movie scenes in which a long column of once surly natives, marching in solemn silence and as one man, framed by the setting sun, turn in their weapons to the white chief who has done them a good turn, or menace the white adventurer's enemy (who turns pale at the sight), or rebuild the missionary's church, destroyed by fire.

When a social problem persists (as they tend to do) longer than a few days, those who call attention to its continued presence are viewed as 'going too far' and 'causing the pendulum to swing the other way'. We can make war on poverty but shrink from the extensive readjustments required to stop breeding it. Once a law is passed, a commission set up, a study made, a report written, the problem is expected to have been 'wiped out' or 'mopped up'. Bombs abroad are matched by 'crash programmes' at home—the terminological similarity reveals a psychological one.

Or—to put Slater's critique in terms of our own model—the peculiar effect on social control of the way in which the media select and present information is simultaneously to direct attention to some conditions (through moral panics etc.) and to selectively avoid others. The tendency to avoid certain conditions is reflected in our way of segregating, particularly through institutionalization, the awkward, threatening or embarrassing elements in our society. This thought pattern is called by Slater the 'Toilet Assumption':

the notion that unwanted matter, unwanted difficulties, unwanted complexities and obstacles will disappear if they are removed from our immediate field of vision. We do not connect the trash we throw from the car window with the trash in our streets, and we assume that replacing old buildings with new expensive ones will alleviate poverty in the slums. We throw the aged and psychotic into institutional holes where they cannot be seen. Our approach to social problems is to decrease their visibility: out of sight, out of mind. This is the real foundation of racial segregation, especially in its most extreme case, the Indian 'reservation'. The result of our social efforts has been to remove the underlying problems of our society farther and farther from daily experience and daily consciousness, and hence to decrease, in the mass of the population, the knowledge, skill, resources, and motivation necessary to deal with them.

When these discarded problems rise to the surface again—a riot, a protest, an exposé in the mass media—we react as if a sewer had backed up. We are shocked, disgusted and angered, and immediately call for the emergency plumber (the special commission, the crash programme) to ensure that the problem is once again removed from consciousness.

The Toilet Assumption is not merely a facetious metaphor. Prior to the widespread use of the flush toilet all of humanity was daily confronted with the immediate reality of human waste and its disposal. They knew where it was and how it got there. Nothing miraculously vanished. Excrement was conspicuously present in the outhouse or chamber pot, and the slops that went out the window went visibly and noticeably into the street. The most aristocratic Victorian ladies strolling in fashionable city parks thought nothing of retiring to the bushes to relieve themselves. Similarly, garbage did not disappear down a disposal unit—it remained nearby.

As with physical waste, so with social problems. The biblical adage, 'the poor are always with us,' had a more literal meaning before World War I. The poor were visible and all around. Psychosis was not a strange phenomenon in a textbook but a familiar neighbour or village character. The aged were in every house. Everyone had seen animals slaughtered and knew what they were eating when they ate them; illness and death were a part of everyone's immediate experience.

In contemporary life the book of experience is filled with blank and mysterious pages. Occupational specialization and plumbing have exerted a kind of censorship over our understanding of the world we live in and how it operates. And when we come into immediate contact with anything that does not seem to fit into the ordinary pattern of our somewhat bowdlerized existence our spontaneous reaction is to try somehow to flush it away, bomb it away, throw it down the jail.

But in some small degree we also feel bored and uneasy with the orderly chrome and porcelain vacuum of our lives, from which so much of life has been removed. Evasion creates self-distaste as well as comfort, and radical confrontations are exciting as well as disruptive. The answering chord that they produce within us terrifies us, and although we cannot entirely contain our fascination, it is relatively easy to project our self-disgust on to the perpetrators of the confrontations.

This ambivalence is reflected in the mass media. The hunger for confrontation and experience attracts a lot of attention to social problems, but these are usually dealt with in such a way as to reinforce the avoidance process. The TV documentary presents a tidy package with opposing views and an implication of progress. Reports in popular magazines attempt to provide a substitute for actual experience. Important book and film reviews, for example, give just the blend of titillation and condescension to make the reader imagine that he is already 'in' and need not undergo the experience itself—that he has not only participated in the novel adventure but already outgrown it. Thus the ultimate effect of the media is to reinforce the avoiding response by providing an effigy of confrontation and experience.[21]

5. On deviance and social problems

It is only against the background of such broader effects of the mass media—the master effect in shaping information about deviance, the effects on the consensus, moral panics, control agents—that we can begin to think about the effects on the actual people or behaviour labelled as socially deviant or problematic. And again, the obvious effects questions—Is the programme or story likely to cause the viewer or reader anxiety? Will it be used as a model for anti-social behaviour?—must be approached in terms of how the audience 'at risk' perceives or defines the message; 'we can no longer be content to speak vaguely of television "reinforcing" trends in viewers that were already present; the reinforcement only becomes relevant when it is seen by the viewers as relevant.'[22]

This type of theory of the audience as active interpreters is not, of course, to be taken as endorsing a totally free market model of the media. Reality is not entirely up for grabs and the interpretations are made *within* what we have variously conceptualized as the sets, agendas, frames or discourses which the media provide. Often, the sheer power and exclusiveness of these frames will not allow for much element of interpretation, perceived relevance or choice. But even among groups supposedly the most powerless to resist the media—for example, pre-school children in their exposure to television—internal variation is possible.[23]

And in most cases that matter, an active process of selection, interpretation and decoding is being carried out by consumers as well as producers of the media. The results of this process might simply confirm the media message, might take sceptical distance from it[24] or might wholly undermine it. A vivid example of how people are not just *used by* the media but actively *use them* for their own ends, is provided by the internal development of delinquent or deviant youth subcultures.[25] We include in this Part, a small extract from David Robins and Philip Cohen's study of a North London housing estate which shows how the kids absorb and adopt media culture (in this case, Kung Fu movies) into their own lives.

The readings in this section start, though, with two examples from our own work suggesting more straightforward media effects on the development of deviance: *amplification* and *sensitization*.

REFERENCES

1. In the case of violence—the most common research topic—see for example: D. Howitt and G. Cumberbatch, *Mass media violence and society* (London, Elek, 1975), and G. Comstock, *The evidence of television violence* (Santa Monica, Cal., Rand, 1976).
2. James D. Halloran, 'Studying violence and the media: a sociological approach', in C. Winick (ed.), *Deviance and mass media* (Beverly Hills, Sage Publications, 1978).
3. See Frederic Wertham, *The seduction of the innocent* (New York, Holt, Rinehart & Winston, 1954), and 'School for violence', *New York Times* (5 July 1964), reprinted in Otto N. Larsen (ed.), *Violence and the mass media* (New York, Harper & Row, 1968).
4. For interesting sociological material on moral crusades against 'obscenity' in the media, see: L. Zurcher and R. Kirkpatrick, *Citizens for decency* (Austin, University of Texas Press, 1976), and M. Tracy and D. Morrison, *Whitehouse* (London, Macmillan, 1979).
5. For example, D. Holbrook, *Sex and dehumanization* (London, Pitman, 1972).
6. Key texts in the mass society debate include (A. Dexter and D. M. White, eds.), *People, society and mass communications* (New York, Free Press, 1964); W. Kornhauser, *The politics of mass society* (London, Routledge & Kegan Paul, 1964); H. Gans, *Popular culture and high culture* (New York, Basic Books, 1974). For relevant general text on the media, see D. McQuail

(ed.), *Sociology of mass communication* (Harmondsworth, Penguin, 1972); P. Golding, *The mass media* (London, Longmans, 1975); R. Williams, *Communications* (Harmondsworth, Penguin, 1966); C. Seymour-Ure, *The political impact of mass media* (London, Constable, 1974); J. Curran *et al., Mass communication and society* (London, Edward Arnold, 1977); A. Swingewood, *The myth of mass culture* (London, Macmillan, 1977).

7. For details, see Tony Palmer, *The trials of Oz* (London, Hutchinson, 1972).

8. A standard summary of this literature is the *Report of the Commission on Obscenity and Pornography* (New York, Bantam Books, 1970).

9. Kai T. Erikson, *Wayward puritans: a study in the sociology of deviance* (New York, John Wiley, 1966).

10. For an elaboration of this notion of perceived consensus and the effects on deviants, see J. Young, 'The consensual myth' in P. Rock and M. McIntosh (eds.), *Deviance and social control* (London, Tavistock Publications, 1973).

11. See Introduction, Howard Becker (ed.), *Social problems* (New York, John Wiley, 1964), and Malcolm Spector and John Kitsuse, *Constructing social problems* (California, Cummings, 1977).

12. See S. Ranulf, *Moral indignation and middle class psychology* (New York, Schocken Books, 1964), and Albert K. Cohen, 'The sociology of the deviant act', *American Sociological Review* 30 (1965) pp. 5–14.

13. Howard S. Becker, *Outsiders: studies in the sociology of deviance* (New York, Free Press, 1963), chs. 7 and 8.

14. Joseph Gusfield, *Symbolic crusade: status politics and the American temperance movement* (Urbana, University of Illinois, 1963).

15. Becker (1963) *op. cit.*, p. 145. Note though, some criticisms suggesting that such formulations underplay the *material* interests behind such instances of enterprise. See, e.g. J. Galliher and A. Walker, "The puzzle of social origins of the Marijuana Tax Act of 1937," *Social Problems* Vol. 24 No. 3 pp. 367–77.

16. Joseph Gusfield, 'Moral passage: the symbolic process in public designations of deviance', *Social Problems* 15 (Fall, 1967), pp. 175–88.

17. For further details on the role of the mass media in creating moral panics, see Paul Rock and Stanley Cohen, 'The Teddy Boy', in V. Bogdanor and R. Skidelsky (eds.), *The age of affluence 1951–1964* (London, Macmillan, 1970); Jock Young, *The drug takers* (London, Paladin, 1971); Stanley Cohen, *Folk devils and moral panics: the creation of the Mods and Rockers* (London, MacGibbon & Kee, 1972); and Stuart Hall *et al., Policing the crisis* (London, Macmillan, 1978).

18. See Peter Golding and Susan Middleton, *Images of welfare: the mass media, public attitudes and the welfare state* (London, Macmillan, forthcoming).

19. Edwin M. Lement, *Social pathology* (New York, McGraw Hill, 1952), p. 557.

20. Philip Slater, *The pursuit of loneliness: American culture at the breaking point* (Boston, Beacon Press, 1970), ch. 1.

21. *Ibid.*, pp. 15–17.

22. David Chaney, 'Involvement realism and the perception of aggression in television programmes', *Human Relations*, Vol. 23 No. 5 (1970), pp. 373–81.

23. On the ways in which the pattern of television learning by pre-school children is influenced by such factors as the particular parent-child relationship, see Gwen Dunn, *The box in the corner: television and the under fives* (London, Macmillan, 1977), and Grant Noble, *Children in front of the small screen* (London, Constable, 1975).

24. The notion of a sceptical distancing from the artefacts of mass culture is explained in S. Cohen and L. Taylor, *Escape attempts: the Sociology of resistance to everyday life* (Harmondsworth, Penguin, 1978).

25. For a selection of recent work in this area, see S. Hall and T. Jefferson (eds.), *Resistance through ritual* (London, Hutchinson, 1976), and G. Mungham and G. Pearson (eds.), *Working class youth culture* (London, Routledge, 1976).

The amplification of drug use*

JOCK YOUNG

This section is based on a participant observation study on the relationship between the police and the marihuana smoker in Notting Hill over the period 1967–1969. First it is necessary to introduce the concept of deviance amplification. This process, originally elaborated by Leslie Wilkins[1] must be understood in the context of what we have said about the nature of information about deviance in contemporary society. The argument is that under certain conditions, society will define as deviant a group of people who depart from valued norms in some ways. This negative societal reaction—with its concomitant exclusion and restriction on the possibilities of normal action—might merely serve to increase the possibility that the group will act even more deviantly. If it does so, societal reaction will increase at the same pace, more deviancy will be induced and, in turn, the reaction further escalated. As a result, a deviancy amplification spiral is entered into where each increase in social control is matched by a corresponding increase in deviancy.

Diagrammatically:

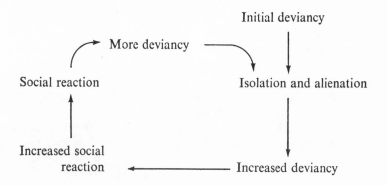

*This is a revised version of part of Jock Young's paper 'The role of the police as amplifiers of deviancy, negotiators of reality and translators of fantasy: some consequences of our present system of drug control as seen in Notting Hill', in S. Cohen (ed.), *Images of deviance* (Harmondsworth, Penguin, 1971).

441

It should not be thought that the deviant group is, so to speak, a pinball inevitably propelled in a deviant direction, or that the agencies of social control are the cushions of the machine that will inevitably reflex into a reaction triggered by the changing course of the deviant. Although the notion of deviancy amplification is often used mechanically there is no need for us to limit ourselves to such an interpretation. Thus, the drug-taking group creates its own circumstances to the extent that it interprets and makes meaningful the reactions of the police against it; both the police and the group evolve theories which attempt to explain each other and test them out in terms of the actual course of events: the arrest situation, encounters on the street, portrayals in the mass media and conversations with friends. These hypotheses of the police about the nature of drug use, and of the drug taker about the mentality of the police, determine the direction and intensity of the deviancy amplification process.

It is obvious that a prime factor in this exchange between police and deviant group will be the nature of the information that each has of the other. We must examine how the extent to which the mass media provide this information and by this means threaten to precipitate a deviancy amplification spiral.

The position of the policeman in a segregated society

The police occupy a particularly segregated part of the social structure. This is because:

1. A policy of limited isolation is followed, based on the premiss that if you become too friendly with the community you are liable to corruption.

2. Public attitudes range from a ubiquitous suspicion to (in such areas as Notting Hill) downright hostility.

3. In terms of actual contacts, the Royal Commission Survey on the police found that just under half of city police and three-quarters of country police thought they would have had more friends if they had a different job. Two-thirds of all police thought their job adversely affected their outside friendships.

4. A fair proportion of policemen are residentially segregated. Thus a quarter of city police live in groups of six or more police houses.

5. In the particular instance of middle-class drug takers in Notting Hill, the police have very little direct knowledge, outside the arrest situation, of the normal behaviour of middle-class youth.

Because of this segregation the police are particularly exposed to the stereotypical accounts of deviants prevalent in the mass media. They have, of course, by the very nature of their role, a certain degree of face-to-face contact with deviants; but these contacts are of a type which, because of the policeman's position of power, make for a reinforcement rather than an elimination of mass media stereotypes.

A person in a position of power whose direct empirical knowledge of a group is restricted to situations where he is exerting that authority will tend to elicit stereotypical responses from that group. That is, they will negotiate the situation by telling the police what they want to hear in order to minimize their likely punishment.[2]

The vested interests of police and media

The police have a bureaucratic interest in apprehending the marihuana smoker to the extent that this avoids public recrimination of failing in their duty. They have also a certain moral indignation about drug use. For the hedonism and expressivity of bohemian drug takers challenges the moral validity of their sense of the work ethic and just reward. They will tend in such circumstances to have an image of marihuana smoking as a pursuit which although pleasurable is dangerous and an appraisal of the bohemian way of life as being a miserable one compared to their own. Drug use is not freely chosen but a result of corruption and innocence. In this fashion they evolve a myth of the marihuana smoker which protects the validity of their own way of life. Their own role is immediately derived from such an ethos: they must save the innocent (i.e. the drug user) in a humanitarian fashion and punish the wicked (i.e., the drug 'pusher'). As suggested in Young's earlier article (Part Two) on the mass media portrayal of drug users, the media have learnt that the fanning up of moral indignation is a remarkable commercial success. They, therefore, play on and continue such distorted imagery. But the relationship between police and mass media is closer and more intricate than this. For a symbiotic relationship exists between the police and the crime reporter: the police providing information and the journalists holding back news in such a fashion as to aid police investigations. Precisely such a cooperative relationship exists over the control of drug use. Robert Traini, the Chairman of the Crime Reporters Association, has indicated how the moral panic over drug use was initiated in this country by the police approaching journalists and informing them that 'the situation had got out of hand'.[3] The mass media responded enthusiastically and police of all ranks become exposed to a playback and subsequent elaboration of their prejudices.

The mass media representing a reified public opinion was a major pressure on the police. The moral panic which evolved in the middle 1960s soon got firmly on its way.

The fantasy and reality of drug taking

One might contrast the social world of the marihuana smoker in Notting Hill, as it was in 1967, with the fantasy stereotype of the drug taker available in the mass media:

1. It is a typical bohemian scene, that is, it is a highly organized community involving tightly interrelated friendship nets and especially intense patterns of visiting.

The stereotype held in the mass media is that of the isolated drug taker living in a socially disorganized area, or at the best, a drifter existing in a loose conglomeration of misfits.

2. The values of the hippie marihuana smoker are relatively clear-cut and in opposition to the values of the wider society. The focal concerns of the culture are short-term hedonism, spontaneity, expressivity, disdain for work.

The stereotype held is of a group of individuals who are essentially *asocial,* who lack values, rather than propound alternative values. They are prey to wicked pushers who play on their naïveté and inexperience.

3. Drug taking is—at least to start with—irregular. It is not an essential prerequisite of membership. Rather it is used instrumentally for hedonistic and expressive purposes and symbolically as a sign of the exotic 'differentness' of the bohemian. Drugs are thus an important, although not central focus of such groups.

Drugs hold a great fascination for the non-drug taker, and in the stereotype drugs are held to be the primary—if not exclusive—concern of such groups. Thus a peripheral activity is misperceived as a central group activity.

4. The marihuana user and the marihuana seller are not, on the street level, fixed roles in the culture. At one time a person may sell marihuana, at another he may be buying it. This is because at street level supply is irregular, and good 'connections' appear and disappear rapidly. The supply of marihuana at that time derived from two major sources: tourists returning from abroad, and 'hippie' or immigrant entrepreneurs. The latter are unsystematic, deal in relatively small quantities and make a restricted and irregular profit. The tourists' total contribution to the mar-

ket is significant. Both tourists and entrepreneurs restrict their criminal activities to marihuana importation. The dealer in the street buys from these sources and sells in order to maintain himself in drugs and sustain subsistence living. He is well thought of by the group, is part of the hippie culture, and is not known as a 'pusher'. The criminal underworld has little interest in the entrepreneur, the tourist, or the dealer in the street.

The stereotype, in contrast, is on the lines of the corruptor and the corrupted, that is the 'pusher' and the 'victim'. The pusher is perceived as having close contacts with the criminal underworld and being part of a 'drug pyramid'.

5. The culture consists of largely psychologically stable individuals. The stereotype sees the drug taker essentially as an immature, psychologically unstable young person corrupted by unscrupulous pushers.

6. The marihuana user has in fact a large measure of disdain for the heroin addict. There is an interesting parallel between the marihuana user's perception of the businessman and of the heroin addict. Both are considered to be 'hung up', obsessed and dominated by money or heroin respectively. Hedonistic and expressive values are hardly likely to be realized by either, and their way of life has no strong attraction for the marihuana user. Escalation, then, from marihuana to heroin is a rare phenomenon which would involve a radical shift in values and life style.

In the stereotype the heroin addict and the marihuana user are often indistinguishable, the values of both are similar, and escalation is seen as part of a progressive search for more effective 'kicks'.

7. The marihuana user is widely prevalent in Notting Hill. A high proportion of young people in the area have smoked pot at some time or another.

The stereotype based on numbers known to the police is small compared with the actual number of smokers, yet is perceived as far too large at that and increasing rapidly.

8. The effects of marihuana are mildly euphoric; psychotic effects are rare and only temporary.

The stereotypical effects of marihuana reflect the exaggerated ambivalence of the mass media towards drugs. Thus they hold promise of uninhibited pleasure, yet plummet the taker inevitably into unmitigated misery.

Results of the moral panic

Over time, police action on the marihuana smoker in Notting Hill results in (a) the intensification of the deviancy of the marihuana user, that is the

consolidation and accentuation of his deviant values as deviancy amplifies: and (b) a change in the life style and reality of marihuana use, so that
certain facets of the stereotype become actuality. That is a translation of
fantasy into reality.

I wish to consider the various aspects of the social world of the marihuana user which I outlined earlier and note the cumulative effects of
intensive police action:

1. Intensive police action serves to increase the organization and cohesion of the drug-taking community, uniting its members in a sense of
injustice felt at harsh sentences and mass media distortions. The severity
of the conflict compels bohemian groups to evolve theories to explain the
nature of their position in society, thereby heightening their consciousness of themselves as a group with definite interests over and against
those of the wider society. Conflict welds an introspective community
into a political faction with a critical ideology, and deviancy amplification results.

2. A rise in police action increases the necessity for the drug taker to
segregate himself from the wider society of non-drug takers. The greater
his isolation the less chance there is that the informal face-to-face forces
of social control will come into operation, and the higher his potentiality
for further deviant behaviour. At the same time the creation by the bohemian of social worlds centring around hedonism, expressivity, and drug
use makes it necessary for the non-drug taker, the 'straight', to be excluded not only for reasons of security but also to maintain definitions of
reality unchallenged by the outside world. Thus after a point in the
process of exclusion of the deviant by society, the deviant himself will
cooperate in the policy of separation.

3. The further the drug taker evolves deviant norms, the less chance
there is of his re-entering the wider society. Regular drug use, bizarre
dress, long hair, and lack of a workaday sense of time, money, rationality
and rewards, all militate against his re-entry into regular employment. To
do so after a point would demand a complete change of identity; besides
modern record systems would make apparent any gaps which have occurred in his employment or scholastic records, and these might be seen
to indicate a personality which is essentially shiftless and incorrigible.
Once he is out of the system and labelled by the system in this manner, it
is very difficult for the penitent deviant to re-enter it, especially at the
level of jobs previously open to him. There is a point therefore beyond
which an ossification of deviancy can be said to occur.[4]

4. As police concern with drug taking increases, drug taking becomes
more and more a secret activity. Because of this, drug taking in itself

becomes of greater value to the group as a symbol of their difference, and of their defiance of perceived social injustices. That is, marihuana comes to be consumed not only for its euphoric effects but as a symbol of bohemianism and rebellion against the unjust system.

Drug taking and trafficking thus move from being peripheral activities of the groups, a mere vehicle for the better realization of hedonistic, expressive goals, to become a central activity of great importance. The stereotype begins to be realized, and fantasy is translated into reality.

5. The price of marihuana rises, the gains to be made from selling marihuana become larger and the professional pusher begins to emerge as police activity increases. Importation becomes more systemized, long term and concerned with large regular profits. Because of increased vigilance at the customs, the contribution of returning tourists to the market declines markedly. International connections are forged by importers linking supply countries and profitable markets and involving large sums of capital. Other criminal activities overlap with marihuana importation, especially those dealing in other saleable drugs. On the street level the dealer becomes more of a 'pusher', less part of the culture, and motivated more by economic than social and subsistence living considerations. The criminal underworld becomes more interested in the drug market, overtures are made to importers: a few pushers come under pressure to buy from them and to sell a wider range of drugs, including heroin and methedrine. A drug pyramid, as yet embryonic, begins to emerge. Once again fantasy is being translated into reality.

6. The marihuana user becomes increasingly secretive and suspicious of those around him. How does he know that his activities are not being observed by the police? How does he know that seeming friends are not police informers? Ugly rumours fly around about treatment of suspects by the police, long terms of imprisonment, planting and general social stigmatization. The effects of drugs are undoubtedly related to the cultural milieu in which drugs are taken. A Welsh rugby club drinks to the point of aggression, an all-night party to the point of libidinousness; an academic sherry party unveils the pointed gossip of competitiveness lurking under the mask of a community of scholars. Similarly, the effects of marihuana being smoked in the context of police persecution invite feelings of paranoia and semi-psychotic episodes. Thus stereotypical effects become in part reality.

7. As police activity increases, the marihuana user and the heroin addict begin to feel some identity as joint victims of police persecution. Interaction between heroin addicts and marihuana users increases. The general social feeling against all drugs creates a stricter control of the

supply of heroin to the addict. He is legally bound to obtain his supplies from one of the properly authorized clinics. Lack of personnel who are properly trained, or who even have an adequate theoretical knowledge of dealing with the withdrawal problems of the heroin addict, results in the alienation of many from the clinics. The addict who does attend either is kept on maintenance doses or else has his supply gradually cut. Either way euphoria becomes more difficult to obtain from the restricted supply, and the 'grey market' of surplus National Health heroin, which previously catered for addicts who required extra or illicit supplies, disappears. In its place a black market springs up, often consisting of Chinese heroin diluted with adulterants. This provides a tentative basis for criminal underworld involvement in drug selling and has the consequence of increasing the risks of overdosage (because the strength is unknown) and infection (because of the adulterants).

But the supply of black-market heroin alone is inadequate. Other drugs are turned to in order to make up the scarcity, the precise drugs varying with their availability, and the ability of legislation to catch up with this phenomenon of drugs displacement. Chief of these are methadone, a drug addictive in its own right and which is used to wean addicts off heroin, and freely prescribed barbiturates. As a result of displacement a body of methadone and barbiturate addicts emerges, the barbiturates being probably more dangerous than heroin and causing even greater withdrawal problems. For a while the over-prescription by doctors creates, as once occurred with heroin, an ample grey market of methadone and barbiturates. But the pressure on the doctors restricts at least the availability of methadone, and the ranks of saleable black-market drugs are increased in the process. Because many junkies share some common bohemian traditions with hippies (they often live in the same areas, smoke pot, and affect the same style of dress), the black market of heroin, methadone, barbiturates and marihuana will overlap. The heroin addict seeking money in order to maintain his habit at a desirable level and the enterprising drug seller may find it profitable to make these drugs available to marihuana smokers.

Some marihuana users will pass on to these hard drugs, but let me emphasize *some,* as, in general, heavy use of such drugs is incompatible with hippie values. For full-blown physical addiction involves being at a certain place at a certain time every day; it involves an obsession with one substance to the exclusion of all other interests; it is anathema to the values of hedonic expressivity and autonomy. But the number of known heroin addicts in Britain is comparatively small (only 1555 in 1971), while the estimates of the marihuana smoking population range up to one million and beyond. Thus it would need only a minute proportion of marihuana smokers to escalate for the heroin addiction figures to rise rapidly. Besides, the availability of methadone and barbiturates gives rise to alternative avenues of escalation. Methadone, once a palliative for heroin addicts, becomes a drug of addiction for individuals who have never used heroin. To this extent increased social reaction against the drug taker would make real the stereotype held by the public about escalation. But the transmission of addiction, unlike the transmission of disease, is not a matter of contact, it is a process that is dictated by the social situation and values of the person who is in contact with the addict. The values of marihuana smokers and the achievement of subterranean goals are not met by intensive heroin use. Escalation to heroin (or methadone and the barbiturates) will occur only in atypical cases where the structural position of the marihuana user changes sufficiently to necessitate the evolution of values compatible with heroin use as solutions to his newly emergent problems.[5] Availability of a drug alone is insufficient to precipitate addiction, there has to be a meaningful reason for its use. At the moment, the widespread structural unemployment in Britain may provide—along American lines—precisely such a cause. Increased availability *plus* the desperation associated with exclusion from the means of earning a living is the sort of combination which might spell a serious heroin problem in the future. The irony is that if it comes it will strike hardest amongst the lower-class youth on the edge of the drug culture. The middle-class marihuana smoker will have a degree of immunity to the solution heroin offers.

8. As the mass media fan public indignation over marihuana use, pressure on the police increases; the public demands that they solve the drug problem. The number of marihuana users known to the police is a mere tip of the iceberg of actual smokers. Given their desire to behave in accordance with public opinion and to legitimize their position, the police will act with great vigilance and arrest more offenders. All that happens is that they dig deeper into the undetected part of the iceberg; the statistics for marihuana offenders soar; the public, the press and the magistrates view the new figures with even greater alarm. Increased pressure is put on the police, the latter dig even deeper into the iceberg, the figures increase once again, and public concern becomes even greater. We have entered a fantasy crime wave, where the supposed statistical increase in marihuana use bears little relationship to the actual rate of increase. Because of the publicity, however, the notion of marihuana smoking occurs for the first time to a larger number of people, and through their desire to experiment there will be some real increase in the rate of smoking. We must not

overlook here the fact that moral panic over drug taking results in the setting up of drug squads which by their very bureaucratic creation will ensure a regular contribution to the offence figures which had never been evidenced before.

Police action not only has a deviance amplification effect because of the unforeseen consequences of the exclusion of the marihuana smoker from 'normal' society. It has also an effect on the content of the bohemian culture within which marihuana smoking takes place. The important feature to note is that there has been change, and that this has been in part the product of social reaction. For many social commentators and policy makers, however, this change has merely reinforced their initial presumptions about the nature of drug takers; individuals with near psychopathic personalities, a weak super-ego, an unrealistic ego and inadequate masculine identification. Inevitably these people, it is suggested, will pass on to heroin, and the figures show that this has actually occurred. Similarly journalists and the police, convinced that drug use is a function of a few pushers, will view the deviancy amplification of the bohemian and the emergence of a drug pyramid as substantiation of their theory that we have been too permissive all along. False theories are taken by many to be a proof of their initial presumptions. Similarly, the drug taker, evolving theories as to the repressive nature of the police, finds them progressively proven as the gravity of the situation escalates.

References

1. L. Wilkins, 'Some sociological factors in drug addiction control', in D. Wilner and G. Kassebaum (eds.), *Narcotics* (New York, MacGraw Hill, 1965).
2. See the discussion in T. Scheff, 'Negotiating reality', *Social Problems,* 16 (Summer 1968).
3. R. Traini, *The work of the Crime Reporters Association* (Paper read at the 8th National Deviancy Symposium, University of York, 10–11 July 1971).
4. For a discussion of the deviancy amplification of bohemians, see J. Young, 'The hippie solution' in I. Taylor and L. Taylor (eds.), *The politics of deviancy* (Harmondsworth, Penguin, 1973).
5. See J. Young, *The drugtakers* (London, Paladin, 1971).

Sensitization: the case of the Mods and Rockers*

STANLEY COHEN

At each Bank Holiday scene during the peak of the Mods and Rockers phenomenon in the middle 1960s, the mass media operated to reinforce and give shape to the crowd's sense of expectancy and provide the content of rumours and shared definitions with which ambiguous situations were restructured. Although popular commentators on the Mods and Rockers often blamed 'publicity' for what happened (and the press responded with indignant editorials about its 'duty' to publish the 'facts'), the term 'publicity' was used in a somewhat restricted sense. It either referred to the publicity immediately before the event which advertised the disturbances and pinpointed the resorts where they would take place, or to the gratification young people supposedly derived from exposure to publicity during the event.

The first of these factors operated in the gross sense of publicizing the event in such a way that it might look attractive, but it is unlikely to have directly influenced the choice of target: asked where they got the idea from (of going to Margate), 82·3 per cent of a sample of offenders mentioned friends as their source, only 2·9 per cent mentioned newspapers and 2·9 per cent television. Only a handful I spoke to at any stage said that anything in the press or television *initially* decided them on a particular resort. The media more likely reinforced rather than initiated rumours already current. There were certain exceptions, though, when during the weekend a sensational report or TV interview might have directly attracted new crowds. One notorious BBC interview in which two Rockers said that reinforcements would be arriving, was followed by a sudden influx of both Mods and Rockers, large numbers of whom might have been attracted by the excitement the interview promised.

There were also signs of direct publicity-seeking behaviour in the sense that on-the-spot attention from journalists, reporters and photogra-

*This is an adapted version of Stanley Cohen, *Folk devils and moral panics: the creation of the Mods and Rockers* (London, MacGibbon & Kee, 1972), Chapter 5.

phers was a stimulus to action. The following account is by one of the boys arrested at Margate:

> By the railway station a cameraman asked 'Give us a wave'. So me and a group ran about and waved some flags we bought. My picture was in the paper. We were pleased; anybody would be.

If one is in a group of twenty, being stared at by hundreds of adults and being pointed at by two or three cameras, the temptation to do something—even if only to shout an obscenity, make a rude gesture or throw a stone—is very great and made greater by the knowledge that one's actions will be recorded for others to see. The participant in such situations might exaggerate the extent of his involvement and look for some recognition of it. Thus at every weekend, young people could be observed at newspaper kiosks buying each edition of the evening paper as it appeared and scanning it for news of disturbances. The exploitative element in this feedback is reflected in the rumours—which, at least in one case, I am certain were firmly based—that press photographers were asking suitably attired young males to pose kicking in a window or telephone kiosk.

The cumulative effects of the mass media, though, were at the same time more subtle and more potent than simply giving the events pre-publicity or gratifying the participants' need for attention. Through a complex process that is not yet fully understood the mere reporting of one event has, under certain circumstances, the effect of triggering off events of a similar order. This effect is well documented in regard to the spread of crazes, fashions, fads and other forms of collective behaviour, such as mass delusion or hysteria. The main reason why this process has been misunderstood in regard to deviance—particularly collective and novel forms—is that too much attention has been placed on the supposed direct effects (imitation, attention, gratification, identification) on the deviants, rather than the effects on the control system and culture and hence (via such processes as amplification) on the deviance.

The simple suggestibility type effect can be seen even in apparently individual forms of deviance such as suicide. A particularly vivid example is the spread in the self-immolation as a form of suicide following the report in 1963 of a Vietnamese monk burning himself to death as an act of political protest. This is a form of suicide almost completely unknown in the West; in the period 1960–1963, there was only one such case in England, yet in 1963, there were three and in 1964, nine. A similar progression in numbers occurred in the United States. In this case, the effect was in the technique rather than the motivation behind the act and must be explained in terms of what the 'new' stimulus meant and how it was interpreted. Cases where the motive as well as the technique is suggested by mass communication might be the spread of prison riots, prison escapes and racial and political riots. A particularly well-documented example is the Swastika Epidemic of 1959–1960. The contagion effect could be clearly shown in plotting the curve of the 'epidemic.'[1]

An example closer to the Mods and Rockers is the spread during the 1950s of the Teddy Boy riots and similar phenomena elsewhere in Europe. Most commentators on these events acknowledged the role of publicity in stimulating imitative or competitive forms of behaviour[2] and some studies have been made on the mass media coverage of such events.[3] At the time, though, blame was put on 'publicity' in the restricted sense and there was little awareness of the complex ways in which mass communication operates before during and after each event. The causative nature of mass communication—in the whole context of the societal reaction to such phenomena—is still usually misunderstood.

The common element in all these diverse examples of the amplification of violence is that an adequate medium of communication must be present for spreading the hostile belief and mobilizing potential participants. The mass communication of the news of one outbreak is a condition of structural conduciveness for the development of a hostile belief. This, in turn, has to sensitize the 'new' crowd (or individual deviant) to incipient or actual action and lower the threshold of readiness by providing readily identifiable symbols. The symbolization process (see Part Two, page 272) becomes crucial during the event, shaping the content of the rumours[4] spread through the crowd that something was going to happen and locating the targets for action.

The inventory reporting (see Part Two, page 276) can be seen as having a reinforcing effect on already existing tendencies to expect and look forward to trouble. Constant repetition of the violence and vandalism images and reports about preparations for the next 'invasion' generated an atmosphere in which something *had* to happen. Once a dominant perception is established the tendency is to assimilate all subsequent happenings to it. This is how to view the relatively trivial incidents which attracted attention and sometimes triggered off trouble. Through the process of sensitization, incidents which would not have been defined as unusual or worthy of attention during a normal Bank Holiday weekend acquired a new meaning. Thus:

Two boys stopped to watch a very drunk old tramp dancing about on the beach. They started throwing pennies at his feet. Within 45 seconds there were at least 100 people gathered round and in 60 seconds the police were there. I turned my back on the crowd to watch the spectators gathering on the promenade above and by the time I turned back, two policemen were leading a boy away from the crowd.

(Notes, Brighton, Easter 1965)

The mass media provided the images and stereotypes with which ambiguous situations could be restructured; a stone-throwing incident might not have progressed beyond the 'milling stage' if there were no readily available collective images to give meaning to the activity. These images provide the basis for rumours about 'random' events: so, an incident in which a girl was carried on a stretcher to an ambulance was variously explained by the crowd gathering round as 'this bloke with her must have knifed her', 'too many pills if you ask me', 'these Rockers' birds just drink all the time'.

Different versions of such events are circulated and eventually assimilated into one theme that receives collective sanction. Each link in the chain of assimilation involves preconceptions derived from sources such as the mass media. Without publicity about 'stabbings on the beach' or 'drug orgies' the rumours about the girl being carried to the ambulance would have assumed an entirely different form. Rumours further serve to validate a particular course of action: the deviant, as well as the control agent, uses collective imagery (which may be objectively false) to justify action. Symbolization provides a short-circuited definition of the situation whereby culturally sanctioned signs and symbols are used as a basis for action. The inventory symbols prepared the crowd for action because shared images and objects contribute to uniformity: if a dance hall becomes defined as 'The Top Mod Spot of the South', then the defence of it against invading Rockers takes on a symbolic significance. So not only was the likelihood of deviance increased—one almost *had* to try to see or take part in trouble—but the content of the behaviour influenced. The societal reaction increases the deviant's chance of acting and—given his interpretation of the new situation—provides him with some lines and stage directions.

The crucial effect here is the way in which deviant behaviour is shaped by the normative expectations of how people in that particular deviant role should act. Much of the Mods and Rockers behaviour can be conceptualized in terms of a role-playing model. Posing for photos, chanting slogans, making warlike gestures, fantasying about super-gangs, wearing distinctive insignia, making a mock raid on an ice-cream van, whistling at girls, jeering at the 'other side': all these acts of 'hooliganism' may be seen as analogous to the impersonation of mental illness resorted to by those defined as mentally ill. The actor incorporates aspects of the typecast role into his self-concept and when the deviant role is public—as hooliganism is by definition—and the situation increases the chances of mutual suggestibility, then this incorporation is often more conscious and deliberate than in those types of 'private' deviance such as mental illness, homosexuality and drug taking, to which a role-playing perspective has been applied.

New recruits might search for and positively try to exemplify the values and imagery portrayed in the stereotypes. The media created some sort of diversionary sideshow in which all could seek their appropriate parts. The young people on the beaches knew very well that they had been typecast as folk devils and they saw themselves as targets for abuse. When the audiences, TV cameras and police started lining themselves up, the metaphor of role playing becomes no longer a metaphor, but the real thing. One acute observer at the live TV coverage of the Mod Ball at Wembley (a week after the initial Clacton event) described a girl in front of the cameras worshipping a hair salvaged off Mick Jagger's trousers as being like a man acting drunk when he is hardly tipsy, 'acting out this adoration. She sees she is being watched, grins sheepishly and then laughs outright.'[5]

The content of the typecast role was present in the inventory and crystallized more explicitly in the process of spurious attribution or labelling. This is not to say that a new one-to-one link between the labelling and the behaviour was formed. For one thing, the typecast hooligan role was known to the potential actors before the deviance even began; like the labellers themselves, they could draw upon an existent folklore and mythology. The point, however, was that the normative element in the role was reinforced by the societal reaction; although the actors might already have been familiar with the lines and the stage directions, they were now confirmed in their roles. In the same way as the 'chronic' schizophrenic begins to approximate closer to the schizophrenic role, so did the Mods and Rockers phenomenon take on every time an increasing ritualistic and stereotypical character.

Although the hooligan role was ready made and had only to be confirmed by the labelling process, there were other elements in the behaviour which could be directly traced to the societal reaction.

One was the way in which the gap between the Mods and Rockers became increasingly wider and obvious. Although the Mods and Rockers reprsented two different consumer styles—the Mods the more glossy fashion-conscious teenager, the Rockers the tougher, reactionary tradition—the antagonism betwen the two groups was not initially very marked. Despite their real differences in life styles—visible in symbols such as the Mods' scooters and the Rockers' motor bikes—the groups had a great deal in common, particularly their working-class membership. There was, initially at least, nothing like the gang rivalry that is supposed to characterize the type of violent gang conflict enshrined in folklore by the 'Sharks' and 'Jets' of *West Side Story*. Indeed, one could not justifiably talk of 'gangs' at all in any meaningful sociological sense. The only structured grouping one could find in the early crowds was based on slight territorial loyalty and it was tenuous enough to be broken up in the crowd situation.

Constant repetition of the warring gangs' image, however, had the effect of giving these loose collectivities a structure they never possessed and a mythology with which to justify the structure. This image was disseminated in the inventory, reinforced through the symbolization process, repeated in opinions which exaggerated the stylistic differences and the degree of pre-planning, used to advantage in the form of commercial exploitation and repeated during the warning phase. Even if these images were not directly absorbed by the actors, they were used to justify control tactics, which still further structured the groups and hardened the barriers between them. Police action, for example, increased the deviance by unwittingly solidifying the amorphous crowd forces into more viable groups for engaging in violence and by further polarizing the deviants against the community. Such solidification and polarization takes place not simply in the face of attack, but attack that is perceived as harsh, indiscriminate and unfair. Even if these elements had not been present the ambiguous crowd situation offered the maximum possible opportunity for rumours of such police action to spread. In the same way that the Mods and Rockers were perceived symbolically and stereotypically by the police, the police too were perceived by the crowd as the 'enemy'. By seeing the crowd as a homogeneous mass, to be controlled on the basis of the visible stigmata of dress, a greater sense of cohesion develops. If subject to indiscriminate harassment or even if only witnessing the use of violence by the police, the crowd could quite easily develop a sense of resentment and grievance. This could be the first step towards a sense of identity and common purpose with the real or imagined 'hard core', with 'police brutality' as a rallying point.

The presence of the media—actually, in the form of cameras and reporters, symbolically in the form of the next day's stories—gave police and courtroom confrontations with the deviants a ritualistic dramatic quality. These were arenas for acting out society's morality plays. And they had to be reported as 'news', so the amplification effects of the control culture were fed back into the mass media, which further exaggerated them, thus producing another link in the sequence. If the policemen did not see themselves as the 'brave men in blue' fighting with the evil mob, nor the magistrates themselves as society's chosen mouthpiece for denouncing evil, the polarizations were made on their behalf by others.

The mass media—and the ideological exploitation of deviance—reinforced the polarization: between the Mods and Rockers on one hand, and the whole adult community on the other. If one is seen as the 'enemy' in the 'war against crime', it is not difficult to respond in similar spirit: one 'rejects the rejectors' and 'condemns the condemners'. The specialized effect of the Lunatic Fringe theme (a derivation of the consensus model which sees most youth as decent and conformist) is to segregate and label those involved by emphasizing their difference from the majority. A striking parallel from a similar form of deviance was the labelling by the motor cycling 'Establishment' of riders identified with the Hell's Angels image as the one per cent who cause all the trouble: the term 'one percenter' was then used by the groups as an honorific epithet, reinforcing their commitment.

In summary then, the societal reaction in general and the mass media in particular could plausibly be thought to have had the following sort of effects on the nature, extent and development of the deviance:

1. Reinforcing and magnifying a predisposition to expect trouble: 'something's going to happen'.
2. Providing the content for rumours and the milling process, thereby structuring the 'something' into potential or actual deviance; such rumours and images facilitated deviance by solidifying the crowd and validating its moods and actions.
3. Creating a set of culturally identifiable symbols which further structured the situation and legitimized action.
4. Spreading hostile beliefs and mobilizing the participants for action.
5. Providing the content for deviant role playing by transmitting the stereotypical expectations of how persons in particular deviant roles should act.

6. Magnifying the Mods-Rockers dichotomy and giving the groups a tighter structure and common ethos than they originally possessed.
7. Polarizing the deviants further against the community and—through the actions of the police and courts—setting up a spiral of deviancy amplification.

REFERENCES

1. See David Caplowitz and Candace Rogers, *Swastika 1960: the epidemic of anti-Semitic vandalism in America* (New York, Anti-Defamation League of Benai Brith, 1961). A noteworthy feature of this epidemic was that initial reporting indicated other avenues for expressing grievances: at the peak, targets for hostility other than anti-Semitic ones were chosen and, in fact, these general incidents out-numbered the specifically anti-Semitic. This is similar to the ways the Mods and Rockers changed their targets of action. All such processes are heavily dependent on the mass media.
2. See, for example, T. R. Fyvel, *The insecure offenders* (London, Chatto & Windus, 1961) and C. Bondy et al., *Jugendliche Stören die Ordnung* (München, Juventa Verlag, 1957).
3. See Britt-Marie Blegvad, 'Newspapers and Rock and Roll riots in Copenhagen', *Acta Sociologica* 7 (1963), pp. 151–78, and Paul Rock and Stanley Cohen, 'The Teddy Boy', in V. Bogdanor and R. Skidelsky, (eds.), *The age of affluence: 1951–1964* (London, Macmillan, 1970).
4. For a relevant formulation on the sociology of rumour, see Tamotsu Shibutani, *Improvised news* (Indianapolis, Bobbs-Merrill, 1966).
5. Peter Laurie, *The teenage revolution* (London, Anthony Blond Ltd, 1965), p. 105.
6. See Hunter Thompson, *Hell's Angels* (Harmondsworth, Penguin, 1967) and Robert Shellow and Derek Roemer, 'The riot that didn't happen,' *Social Problems* 14 (Fall 1966), pp. 221–33.

News and public perceptions of industrial relations*

PAUL HARTMANN

The idea of 'news as ideology' has been central to much recent mass communication research. This focus represents an attempt to tackle one aspect of the broader sociological question of how it comes about that one rather than another among conflicting definitions of reality can be 'made to stick' within a society.[1] Concern with the ideological character of news has been particularly evident in writings about industrial relations news, of which the *Bad News* study of the Glasgow University Media Group[2] has attracted most attention. The authors conclude from their analysis of television news that industrial relations coverage is such as to discredit union activity in industrial disputes and to uphold assumptions about the economic and social order favourable to dominant class interests. Similar arguments appear in various articles in Beharrell and Philo,[3] and the general thesis has been foreshadowed in earlier more impressionistic discussions of the topic such as those to be found in Milliband,[4] Toynbee[5] and Morley.[6]

All of this work has depended heavily on assessment of the content of industrial relations news and has involved the assumption that the way audience perceptions and values are shaped by attention to news can be inferred from news content. Such an assumption is now without foundation if only on the basis of availability. If, as seems obvious, most people are dependent on news for their information about events, and if news presentation reflects a dominant ideological perspective, then it seems likely that popular understandings of industrial conflict will at least bear traces of this dominant perspective. There is, on the other hand, little reason to assume a one-to-one relationship between audience perceptions and news content. It is now a truism that different groups—particularly members of different social classes—bring different subcultural perspec-

*This paper originally appeared in *Media, Culture and Society* (1979), vol. 1, Copyright© 1979 by Academic Press Inc (London) Ltd.

tives to bear upon mass communications and that the same news may be differently interpreted in different sections of society. It has also been persuasively argued[7] that though news tends to reflect a version of events consistent with the interests of a ruling class, the news organizations do not automatically reproduce a dominant ideology, but enjoy a degree of autonomy from both state and dominant power groupings so that their output is mediated through a 'professional code' that may overlay news significations with meanings not necessarily wholly consistent with those of the 'dominant code'. In other words whatever cultivation of public consciousness takes place through news presentation, the process is clearly not a simple one.

What has generally been lacking in this area of research is any thorough-going attempt to relate audience reception of news empirically to its content. The only substantial study has been that of Blumler and Ewbank[8] who examined relationships between news exposure and views on a number of union-related issues among union members and union officials. They found only very limited evidence that different views were related to amount and type of media exposure. The focus of this study was, however, narrow and it was conceptually limited in that beliefs and attitudes were seen primarily as characteristics of individuals rather than as aspects of structurally based cultural or subcultural meaning systems.

The present article is a report of some results from a study that sought to explore empirically the relationships between the way industrial relations are presented in the news media and the way they are perceived by members of different social classes.[9]

The study was carried out in two parts—an examination of news content, and a social survey.

News content

The results of the quantitative content analysis have been reported elsewhere.[10] It covered all industrial relations news appearing in the *Daily Telegraph, Daily Express, Daily Mirror, Morning Star, Coventry Evening Telegraph*, the BBC Nine O'Clock News, ITN's News at Ten, and the One O'Clock News on Radio 4 during an eight week period in the spring of 1973. Briefly the data showed that there was a steady flow of material on the topic, the greatest emphasis being given to industrial action and the activities of trade unions. The government was also shown as an important protagonist. The activities of employers and managements, on the other hand, seldom made news in an industrial relations context. The treatment of strikes tended to emphasize their effects, and generally explanations of both causes and effects were superficial. The coverage of the period was dominated by reference to wage control, the Counter-Inflation and Industrial Relations Acts, inflation, and the cost of living. This pattern of attention was broadly similar to that later found by McQuail,[11] and consistent with the findings of the Glasgow University Media Group[12] though these workers organized their data differently.

In the present study the papers and programmes examined showed remarkably similar patterns of coverage and emphasis. The biggest differences found between them could be attributed to the difference between local and national media or to the amount of space available, rather than to differing political orientations. Only in the case of the *Morning Star* were clear politically-linked differences apparent from the quantitative data.

The quantitative findings were supplemented by a detailed analysis of newspaper editorials during the sample period and during the crisis, miners' strike, and General Election periods of December 1973 and February 1974. During these latter periods the other national papers were also included in the analysis. Differences in interpretation and approach between the papers became evident from this qualitative analysis but important similarities remained. In the popular press in particular there was a persistent tendency to explain industrial conflict in terms of personalities and personal motivations and emotions rather than in structural terms. There was also frequent insistence that in industry and society there is no 'them and us'.

The overall conclusions from the content work as a whole were that, except in the case of the *Morning Star,* industrial relations are handled in the British media in such a way as to cast doubt on the legitimacy of trade union activity and aspirations, and that the essential justice of the British social order is never seriously called into question. Though there are differences in interpretation of news events to be found in different newspapers, related to the papers' particular political stances and to their estimates of the concerns of their readerships, the variety of viewpoint offered is within the prevailing political consensus.

Audience perceptions

The main aim of the survey was to seek indications of differences in perspectives on industrial relations between working class and middle class groups, and to relate these to the findings on content. A second aim was to assess the part played by the media in structuring audience perceptions. The overall theoretical framework derives from those who, like Parkin,[13] have argued that to capture the cultural complexity of Western democracies it is necessary to view the normative order as a number of competing meaning systems having their base in the collective experience of different class groups. The research was therefore not conceived primarily as an 'effects' study or an examination of individual opinion formation (though it bears upon these questions), but as a means of elucidating class-based interpretive frameworks available in our society and their relationship to media interpretations, as a contribution to the 'news as ideology' debate.

Sampling

Three hundred and twenty-three people were interviewed in Coventry (210 men and 113 women). The sample was selected so as to make it possible to compare working class and middle class perceptions. A common way of doing this is to take a random sample of the population and then to divide it into blue-collar and white-collar subgroups. While this normally yields a blue-collar sample that can reasonably be called working class, there are a number of problems about identifying a random white-collar sample as middle class. The main difficulty is that random samples tend to produce a very high proportion of people in routine clerical occupations whose background, education and life styles may differ little from many in blue-collar occupations. They may well earn less and their opportunities may be no better than those of skilled manual workers. There are reasons why those in routine clerical grades might be regarded as more working class than middle class. As well as producing a large number of ambiguously placed white-collar workers, random sampling also yields comparatively few people from the managerial and professional strata, about whose middle class status there is little doubt.

The sampling was therefore carried out in such a way as to identify a blue-collar sample that could unambiguously be regarded as working class, and a white-collar sample that was a better approximation to a middle class group than would be obtained by ordinary random sampling. To achieve this the latest available detailed census records (1966) for the City and County Borough of Coventry were examined. Enumeration districts with a high proportion of residents in the Registrar General's social class IV and a low proportion in classes I and II were identified as working class areas. Similarly enumeration districts high on classes I and

II but low on class IV were taken as middle class areas. The streets to be sampled in the middle class areas were further delimited by visiting them and choosing only those with a better type of housing. In this way a list of streets was produced from which a random sample of addresses was drawn, based on the addresses listed in the electoral register. Of the 512 persons contacted for interviews (heads of household or their spouses), 63% were willing to be interviewed (60% in middle class areas and 66% in working class areas).

Of course some white-collar respondents were located in the working class areas and a proportion of those contacted in middle class areas had blue-collar occupations. The colour-of-collar distribution between the two types of sampling area, the overall composition of the sample by socio-economic status, and the relation of this to a random sampling expectation are all shown in Table 1, which shows that the sample was fairly well polarized by class. (Occupation of head of household was used as the criterion.)

TABLE 1.

CLASS DISTRIBUTION BY AREA

		Middle class areas	Working class areas	Total	Approx. random expectation[1]
A.	Upper middle class	21 17.1%	2 1.0%	23 7.1%	14%
B.	Middle class	34 27.6%	3 1.5%	37 11.5%	
C1	Lower middle class	33 26.8%	17 8.5%	50 15.5%	22%
C2	Skilled working class	24 19.5%	58 29.0%	82 25.4%	31%
D.	Other working class	8 6.5%	108 54.0%	116 35.9%	33%
E.	Lowest levels of subsistence	0 —	11 5.5%	11 3.4%	
	No information	3 2.4%	1 0.5%	4 1.2%	
Total		123 100%	200 100%	323 100%	

[1]Source: IPC *Marketing Manual of the United Kingdom,* 1971.

In the results reported below the blue/white-collar (manual/non-manual) distinction is used as an approximation to a working middle class split in the sample. (Classes A, B and C1 were combined as white-collar, and C2, D and E as blue-collar.) On type of school attended, age of leaving school, and house ownership there were clear differences between the two sections of the sample of the kind to be expected between working class and middle class groups. In addition, while 71% of the blue-collar group had no educational qualifications, only 28% of the white-collar were unqualified. Of those in employment 71% of the manual group and 39% of the non-manual group belonged to trade unions. Fifty-nine per cent of the white-collar sample were men, and 62% of the blue-collar; 93% of men were employed, as against 54% of women. The blue-collar group were on average two and a half years older than the white-collar, and men about seven years older than women, in both groups. (Overall mean age 44.9.)

The interviews were carried out between 23 January and 28 February 1974. This was a 'crisis' period and the interviewing overlapped with part of the general election campaign. There is never an 'ideal' time for a survey and this period had some disadvantages. For one thing the crisis appears to have increased the refusal rate; interviewers reported that some refusers said they did not want to be interviewed 'at this time' or 'in the circumstances'. It is also possible that the ongoing public discussion of topics covered in the survey led people to answer questions in terms of the party political rhetoric current at the time. In quieter times they might have answered differently, but there is no way of knowing. The introduction to the interview and a number of questions were phrased in such a way as to take this kind of problem into account. The period had the advantage that the crisis and the election must have heightened public awareness of the questions being studied and so produced more considered and meaningful answers; the 'no answer' rate on most of the questions was fairly low.

The interviewing was carried out by the field force of Social and Community Planning Research. Initial design and piloting of the questionnaire was done by the author who also personally conducted the briefing of the interviewers.

Media exposure

A number of questions were included in the interview to discover the media habits of the respondents. These proved to be very much what might be expected on the basis of existing audience and readership surveys.[14] The vast majority of respondents claimed to see at least one television news broadcast per day; over 40% claimed to see more than one, with a tendency for the blue-collar group to be more heavily exposed to television news than the others. A majority of each group also said they saw a television documentary about once a week; the white-collar group watched slightly more documentaries than the manual sample.

Almost all claimed to look at at least one national daily paper each day. *The Daily Telegraph,* the *Daily Express,* and the *Daily Mail* were the most read papers among the white-collar respondents, each being seen by 17–18% of this sample. The *Mirror* was read by 12% and the *Sun, Times, Guardian* and *Financial Times* by between 9% and 6%. The *Mirror* and the *Sun* were read by 36% and 35% of the blue-collar respondents respectively, followed by the *Daily Express* (10%), the *Daily Mail (8%),* and *The Daily Telegraph* (6%). Hardly any of the blue-collar group saw the *Times, Guardian* or *Financial Times.* Over two thirds of the blue-collar group saw the *Coventry Evening Telegraph* every evening; the figure was a little under two thirds for white-collar respondents. Nobody read the *Morning Star.*

Despite overlap between the two sections of the sample in types of paper read, the more middle class readership was clearly skewed towards the more middle class oriented and quality papers and the working class readership towards the more working class oriented papers.

Explanations of strikes

Early in the interview respondents were asked what they thought were the 'main causes or reasons behind strikes in Britain'. This people found easy to answer: only five persons, all working class, said they did not know. Results are shown in Table 2. The most common reason given was the need for money, the rising cost of living, or some equivalent explanation. This was mentioned by 41% of all respondents. Seventeen per cent attributed strikes, somewhat tautologically, to lack of co-operation or bad relations between management and workers. References to distrust, bitterness and discontent were included under this heading. There were no significant class differences in the frequency of these two answers though the working class were more likely to mention need for money than the middle class to an extent that approached statistical significance. (These comparisons were carried out by means of the chi-squared test which has been used throughout.) This response was significantly more often given by women than men in either class (significant at the 0.1% level), presumably reflecting the experience of housewives. The third most common explanation, given by 15% of the sample, was that strikes resulted from poor communication. This was a distinctively white-collar response being given by 19% of non-manual respondents and only 7% of manual respondents and the difference was significant (at the 1% level). Another fairly common answer was that strikes could be attributed to greed on the part of workers. This was carefully distinguished in the coding from simple statements of the need for money because of its moral overtones. Explanations in terms of greed were significantly more often given by women (1% level) but upon examination this difference turned out to be due to the number of middle class women rather than working class women giving the response. When women alone were considered this difference appeared also as a class difference (5% level of significance). Other reasons, each given by 7% or 8% of the sample, included poor working conditions, militancy, political motivation, general references to 'misunderstanding' (as opposed to specific mention of lack of communication) and bad management. None of these differed significantly by class though there was some tendency for political motivation to be favoured as an explanation by middle class respondents.

In the explanations for strikes offered we can already see that in spite of the overall similarity of response patterns between classes there are also differences clearly indicative of class-based differences in economic position, experience and characteristic outlook. The 'breakdown of communication' explanation offered mainly by middle class respondents is a popular theory of industrial relations that was at one time much in vogue in management education. It has as its underlying premise the notion that there is no real conflict of interest between employers and workers; what is good for the firm is good for the work-force. Any realistic basis for industrial conflict is therefore denied and strikes are explained as lamentable lapses from the norm of mutually beneficial co-operation brought about by a failure to communicate effectively. The suggestion is that if only the work-force understood properly what the management was up to they would co-operate willingly. To this end a small industry has sprung up offering courses in 'effective communication in industry' for junior management and even shop stewards, in technical colleges and other institutions up and down the country.

The condemnation of strikes as resulting from greed, volunteered by nearly a third of middle class women, clearly reflects the concern with abstract individual morality that has traditionally been one of the more tender-minded and 'religious' aspects of middle class consciousness. This was a theme in a much publicized speech by the Archbishop of Canterbury towards the end of our interview period (19 February) which may account for some of the references to greed in our data. If so, it is interesting that it should be picked up by middle class women more than others. A similar interpretation of the nation's ills was put forward by the Archbishop's successor in October 1975. He said 'Grabbing and getting is a poor creed. Envy is a cancer' (*The Times,* 16 October 1975). This is a particular kind of middle class notion that carries the implication that people should be happy with what they have got. It may be seen as an element in the dominant ideology—in Parkin's[15] terms as part of 'the moral framework that promotes the endorsement of existing inequality'. By contrast the (near significant) tendency in our data for working class

TABLE 2.

CAUSES OF STRIKES

	White collar	Blue collar	Total
Need for money, rising living costs, etc.	37 34%	94 45%	133 41%
Greed for money—unfavourable moral judgment	18 16%	24 12%	44 14%
Misunderstandings	8 7%	17 8%	25 8%
Lack of co-operation, bloody-mindedness, etc.	22 20%	31 15%	55 17%
Bad communication (explicit reference)	21 19%	15 7%	36 11%
Conditions—all kinds including payment systems	8 7%	18 9%	26 8%
Militancy, union power	9 8%	16 8%	25 8%
Political motivation, leftists, etc.	12 11%	11 5%	23 7%
Bad management/supervision, other than communications	8 7%	14 7%	22 7%
Apathy of ordinary workers	2 2%	4 2%	6 2%
Other	14 13%	18 9%	32 10%
Don't know/no answer	0 —	5 2%	5 1%
$N =$	110	209	323[1]

[1]Information on class location of four respondents was not available. These therefore appear in the Total column only, not in the class breakdown, in this and subsequent tables.

respondents to attribute strikes to the rising cost of living more than the middle class would seem to reflect a degree of difficulty in making ends meet that outweighs generalized moral precepts, and a different way of looking at life.

A somewhat similar difference in experience was reflected in answers to a later question about the results of strikes. The most frequently given response in both class groups referred to the loss of wages by the strikers. But whereas 20% of the white-collar group gave this reply, 31% of the manual group did so and the class difference was significant ($P < 0.05$). (While only 20% of the white-collar group said they had been on strike themselves, 53% of the manual group had.) The second most common answer to the question was that strikes tend to be successful and the workers get what they want. Twenty-two per cent of all respondents said this. Nearly as many, however, (21% of all) said that strikes changed nothing—'they get nowhere', 'the men lose', 'everyone loses'. Fourteen per cent referred to a legacy of bitterness and distrust resulting from strikes, 14% mentioned damage to the economy (lost production and exports and so on) and 10% said strikes added to inflation. There were no significant differences in these answers, though there was a slight tendency for damage to the economy to be mentioned more often by white-collar respondents and the success of strikes by manual respondents.

To explore further people's conceptions of strikes they were asked firstly in general terms whether there were any kinds of reason for going on strike that they were inclined to feel sympathetic towards, and also whether there were any they were unsympathetic to. There were only slight class differences in answers to these questions, the details of which need not concern us here.

Respondents were then asked to give an example of a recent strike that they had been sympathetic to and what had made them sympathetic. Similarly, they were asked to recall a recent strike they had been against and why they had been against it. Though the previous more general questions about the legitimacy of strikes had thrown up only minor differences between the class groups, posed in this more specific form some interesting differences did emerge.

In the first place, whereas 71% of the white-collar group could give reasons justifying strikes in the abstract, only 55% of them could think of any actual strike they had favoured. With the manual group, on the other hand, this kind of disparity was barely apparent. Seventy-five per cent of them could give abstract justifications for striking and 73% could give actual examples of strikes they had sympathized with. (They were asked to exclude any strike they had taken part in themselves.) The strike that commanded greatest sympathy was the miners'. Forty-five per cent of the manual group expressed sympathy with the miners, but only 23 % of the white-collar group, a difference significant at the 0.1 % level of probability. Low pay for the poor conditions was the main reason they gave for their support of the miners. Other strikes supported were very miscellaneous, and no single one received any substantial number of mentions.

When the sample was asked for examples of unjustified strikes the picture was similar. While 77 % of the white-collar group could give generalized reasons for being against strikes, even more of them (86 %) could think of particular strikes that they opposed. Again, the manual group did not show this disparity. Sixty-nine per cent of them could give reasons for being unsympathetic to strikes and 70 % could give instances of strikes they were unsympathetic to.

One of the points to emerge from this analysis is that there is some disparity in the answers obtained when a question is posed in general terms and when it refers to specifics, and that this disparity appears to be most marked among middle class respondents. To some extent this is one of the hazards of survey research, but it also suggests a difference in consciousness between the two groups. Specifically it might be suggested that middle class expressions of sympathy with strikes owe more to an abstract belief in the right to strike than to support for particular groups of strikers, while working class perceptions are conditioned by more direct experience of industrial conflict. The working class responses suggest less disjunction between abstract and concrete levels of perception. While it would be foolish to make too much of a minor finding, we may take this difference as another indication of different frames of reference between the class groups.

Counter-inflation policy

The interviewing took place against the background of the Conservative government's counter-inflation policy. Respondents were asked how far they thought the policy for controlling prices had been effective. The question was repeated for wages and profits.

There was a definite tendency to see the price control policies as lacking in effectiveness and the wage control as effective. There was general scepticism about how well profits were being controlled, and in answer to this question many people said they did not know; some apparently were unaware that the policy had profit control provisions. Over all three questions the white-collar group expressed greater belief in the efficacy of government policies than the manual group. This difference was significant in the case of prices and wages and approached significance in the case of profits.

Respondents were then asked who they thought would benefit most from these policies in the long run. Here quite distinct class differences were evident. The most common white-collar response was that everyone would benefit and this was given by 41% of this group but by only 15% of the manual group (0.1% level). The most common working class response was owners, bosses, investors, management, etc., given by 27% of the manual group but only 16% of the white-collar group (5% level). Fifteen per cent of the working class said the Government would benefit as against only 2% of the white-collar group (0.1% level). (Upon examination this answer turned out to be given almost entirely by women.) Other answers, for which there were no significant class differences, were workers, the working man, the low paid, etc., given by 10% of all, and 'nobody', given by 5%.

The answers to this question are particularly interesting for the great suspicion of government motives that they reveal among the working class respondents along with a suggestion that many of this group perceived a definite conflict of interests between 'bosses', for instance, and others. The white-collar respondents on the other hand were much more inclined to accept the consensual line that the policy was for the good of all and were apparently less likely to think of the situation in terms of opposed interests.

Finally, people were asked how strongly they supported the government's attempts to hold down pay increases. Here again there was a significant class difference ($P < 0.001$) with 81% of the non-manual group clearly behind the policy and the manual group far less convinced (41%).

Class differences

The answers given to the questions we have considered so far reflect the common-sense understanding of industrial relations that is to be found in our society. They contain few sentiments or explanations that cannot readily be heard at dinner-table or public house discussions of these matters. Furthermore, when the class groupings are considered separately there are broad similarities in what people had to say. Even where statistically significant differences appear there is still considerable overlap in the response patterns of different classes. So we are not dealing with a situation where views are completely polarized along class lines. The differences do, however, indicate a tendency for people in different class situations to view industrial relations in different ways. It will be worthwhile to summarize the main distinguishing features of these different perspectives that have surfaced in fragmentary form in the present data.

In the first place the views of our manual respondents were characterized by a greater emphasis on money than was found in the white-collar group. Not only was the need for money seen as a major cause of strikes but respondents expressed sympathy for the miners because they felt they were underpaid for the unpleasant work they had to do. In addition in questions not detailed here the manual respondents showed a generally higher level of support for trade unions and greater approval of their activities, were very much aware of the loss of earnings that results from going on strike, and saw the achievement of better pay as an important benefit of unionism. This was to be seen in their support for the miners, in the relatively smaller numbers mentioning strikes of which they disapproved or advancing criticisms of unions. A third feature of working class answers was the suspicion of the government's incomes policy and the comparative lack of support for it coupled with a tendency to view questions of prices and incomes in terms of opposed interests.

White-collar respondents, on the other hand, showed a greater tendency to use non-economic explanations of industrial conflict, particularly in the 'failure of communication' thesis with its underlying assumption of a harmony of interests, and the explanation in terms of moral shortcomings or 'greed'. This group also expressed a lower level of approval of unions and their activities, especially in their views on concrete instances as opposed to abstract principles. This was clear from their relatively greater opposition to strikes in general, and the miners' action in particular. A further feature of the white-collar answers to other questions was the comparative frequency of reference to left-wing militancy and political motivation in criticizing union activity, with its counterpart in the view offered in response to another question that the apathy of members allowed activists to manipulate the situation. Finally, non-manual respondents showed more faith in the efficacy of the counter-inflation policy and much greater support for it, expressing the view that the policy was to everyone's advantage and showing a disinclination to see the situation in terms of conflicting interests.

It should be emphasized again that the two class groups were broadly similar in what they had to say and that the common ground in their answers was more noticeable than the differences between them. The differences do however indicate elements of distinctively different views of the world that might reasonably be called working class and middle class perspectives.

These findings are what might be expected; indeed it would have been surprising had no class differences appeared. The characteristic differences between middle class and working class outlooks are well documented and those that we have found can readily be explained in terms both of the social histories and immediate situations of the two groups. The traditional loyalty of manual workers to trade unions as defensive organizations of the working class and the traditional hostility to them by business interests and those in or close to managerial roles makes the different levels of approval of unions we have observed unremarkable. Similarly, along with unionism, a them-and-us perspective has always been more typical of those in blue-collar occupations than of white-collar sections of the community—with the possible exception of persons whose wealth and power derive most directly from the ownership of capital, a group notably absent from our white-collar sample. It is also fairly obvious why manual workers should have greater reservations about wage restraint than those in white-collar occupations. Though an incomes policy may operate equally on the pay of manual and non-manual employees, the latter tend on the whole to enjoy higher pay and better job security and prospects and ought therefore to find wage restraint less difficult to bear. Moreover, white-collar personnel are more often paid on an incremental scale rather than on the basis of a simple agreed rate so that even with a total wage freeze many of them would still receive increments though the scale itself might remain static. Such differences of position would also help to account for the greater concern with cash income among the manual group.

Explanations of this kind could readily be extended and elaborated to account for the data, the general pattern of which would seem to conform to expectations. It might even reasonably be asked why the observed class differences were not more pronounced than they were. A partial explanation of this is probably to be found in the fact that, in spite of the method of sampling, the white-collar sample contained many whose background, economic and social position approximated closely to that of the manual group. In other words, it might well be argued that many of those in lower clerical grades should be regarded as working class and could more appropriately have been included in the analysis together with the manual workers and their wives. The incidence of union membership among them would support this interpretation. For present purposes, it is not necessary to dwell at length on this type of problem. It is sufficient to focus on indicative differences between the groups and to ask how the differences in outlook they suggest relate to the perspectives offered by the news media.

News perspectives and social perspectives

The news media handling of industrial relations has already been summarized. In broad terms it was characterized by a heavy emphasis on
industrial action and an overall handling that tended to suggest that
unions are organizations that need watching and that the legitimacy and
consequences of their activity are often suspect. It is clear that the perspective on industrial relations that is dominant in the media has far more
in common with the characteristically 'middle class' way of looking at the
world indicated by the survey data than with the alternative perspective
most noticeable among the working class.

More specifically, the white-collar tendency to refer to militancy and
political motivation in their comments on unions echoes the emphasis
given by the media to these themes (each occurring in about one news
item in 15 in the main media). Their tendency to employ non-economic
explanations—as in 'greed' and 'bad communications'—parallels the tendency of the media to analyse industrial relations in terms of personal
motivations and shortcomings and to present conflicts as unfortunate
aberrations from a normal state of harmony. The proportion of white-
collar respondents apparently accepting the counter-inflation legislation
as being 'to everyone's benefit' is reflected in editorial insistence that
there is no 'them and us'. Probably of most significance, however, is the
parallel between the comparative lack of sympathy for strikes that distinguished white-collar respondents from the others and the media's opposition to strikes, even though the right to strike and the worth of unions
might be defended in principle. Finally there is close correspondence
between white-collar belief in and support for the counter-inflation policy and the main newspapers' unanimous approval of the aim of wage
restraint, if not always of the detailed provisions of the policy. On the
other hand, many of the features of the interview answers that distinguished the manual respondents from the rest—especially the degree of
support expressed for unions and strikes, the reservations about wage
restraint, and the tendency to see industrial relations in terms of opposed
economic interests—were views that the news media, particularly in the
editorial columns, were at pains to discredit.

The significance of these observations is not simply that middle class
views on industrial relations are similar to those embodied in media
output and might therefore be derived from the media—a possibility to be
examined shortly—but that media perspectives are more representative
of a middle class than working class outlook. While attitudes and explanations that can be regarded as essentially middle class are widely

endorsed, both explicitly and implicitly in the news media, those that distinguish working class groups from the rest seldom are. While this is what might be expected *a priori*, given that the ownership, control and production of news media are in the hands of people whose position, backgrounds and affiliations are clearly more middle class than working class, the observation does run counter to the rhetoric of media apologists who take pride in the variety of viewpoints said to be available in the British media.

It should further be noted that the tendency for the construction placed upon industrial relations matters by the manual group to differ from that characteristic of both more middle class groups and the mass media, is not a simple parallel with the differences found among the main newspapers themselves. For the differences among papers were mainly differences within the consensus. The elements of the working class outlook that distinguish this group most clearly from the white-collar sample (albeit to only a small extent) are ones that hint strongly at a point of view that goes beyond differences of opinion presented as acceptable by the main media. The significance of these points should not be missed in the consideration of media influence to which we now turn.

Sources of information

On the question about the reasons or causes behind strikes, for each cause given (up to two were recorded), respondents were asked, 'You say that . . . (reason given) is the reason for strikes. Can you tell me where you got that idea *from?*' In probing for sources particular care was taken not to hint at the media as a possible answer. Many people gave several sources, and duplication of media sources in statements like 'The papers, and television' was quite common. The frequency of mention of different sources by the 318 people giving an answer was as follows:

		% of all mentions
Other people—talking to friends, etc.	84	15
Spouse	14	2
Own experience—observation, 'I know because of the prices in the shops' etc.	198	35
Newspapers (any)	140	25
Television	73	13
Other media—radio, magazines, etc.	24	4
Own opinion—own idea, 'I just know' etc.	29	5
Don't know/no answer	2	—

It can be seen that newspapers were very important, television intermediate, and radio and other media comparatively unimportant. For convenience of subsequent analysis the media categories were collapsed to show simply whether the respondent had referred to the media or not. The 237 references to media were made in 170 answers and it is upon this latter figure that the results that follow are based. Note that these 170 answers were given by fewer than 170 people because some gave two answers. (This is true when data are viewed as a whole. When particular responses and their sources are examined, the frequencies are the actual number of people, since no person could give the same answer twice.) In a similar way the categories 'spouse' and 'other people' were collapsed to 'people'.

Before examining the results in more detail a comment is required on the interpretation of this sort of data. In the first place people may often be unclear where they got a particular idea or piece of information from, particularly when this is of a ubiquitous kind. In this situation, asked how they know something to be the case, they may mention the media simply because this is a plausible answer. For similar reasons, or out of a desire to present themselves as able to arrive at their own conclusions, they may say simply that the view expressed is their own opinion, even though they may originally have heard it from someone else or from the media. Again, to say they know something from their own experience at work might mean that someone at work told them about it. Furthermore, as we noted earlier, we are concerned not just with facts but with the construction people put on them. Thus people might interpret information and experience within a frame of reference derived from the media, or within the subcultural perspectives of groups to which they belong, or more likely an outlook derived from interactions among different available perspectives. The data are therefore problematic as an indication of the origins of information or ideas as such. On the other hand, it can be accepted as having comparative validity in the sense that if more people say they learned A through the media than B, then it is reasonable to conclude that the media are a more important source of information or ideas of type A than of type B; or if one group mentions media more than another group then media may be taken as a more important source for them.

Table 3 shows the number and percentage of people referring to media as the source of their information in respect of different causes given for strikes. Looked at overall, the first thing to note from the figures is that the white-collar group made comparatively more frequent reference to the media. This is because the manual group gave other types of source in preference to the media more often. This tends to confirm the earlier suggestion that the manual group were more likely to have a wider range of more direct sources of information about industrial relations than the white-collar group. Where no media source was given, the manual group gave a 'people' source to 20% of answers and 'personal experience' to 56%. The latter figure exceeds that for media sources. Comparative figures are 11% and 51% for the white-collar group, who appear to make less use of interpersonal sources in particular.

Looked at by response category, it is clear that the kinds of information and view most frequently linked with media sources were that strikes occur because of the need for money, the rising cost of living and so on; because of politically motivated leftwing activity; because of greed; militancy or union power; or conditions of employment or work. The strong association between the idea that strikes result from the desire for more money and the media as a source, is in line with the content analysis finding that wage claims are the most frequently given cause of strikes. It should be noted that the link between media and the notion of greed as a cause of strikes is strong only among the white-collar respondents. This would seem to be a clear case of groups with differing perspectives putting different constructions on similar information. Media-derived explanations in terms of militancy or union power, and political motivation, are also what might be expected in view of the frequency of these themes in the media. The idea of political motivation, which we earlier saw to be a characteristic of the white-collar group, appears to be another example of differential interpretation in that it is strongly linked with media only among the non-manual respondents. When manual respondents did hold this view they tended to attribute it to other kinds of source. The 'bad communications' thesis is an example of a different kind. We noted earlier that this is a stock explanation of industrial conflict in certain white-collar circles and we find that white-collar respondents who advanced this explanation seldom gave the media as its source. When manual respondents gave it, on the other hand, the media appear as a fairly prominent source, as though the idea were not so readily available from local subcultures as for the non-manual group.

While this analysis on its own does not constitute conclusive proof of anything it serves to clarify the picture in three ways. First, it gives added plausibility to our previous observation that the world of industrial relations as presented in the media has more in common with a middle class view of the world than a working class view. Second, it suggests that the media may help to sustain the prevalence of this particular framework as a way of making sense of industrial relations. And third, the analysis

TABLE 3.

CAUSES OR REASONS BEHIND STRIKES—PERCENTAGES
GIVING MEDIA AS SOURCE OF INFORMATION.
(THE PERCENTAGE IS FOLLOWED BY THE N UPON WHICH IT IS BASED.
WHERE N $<$ 12 FIGURES ARE GIVEN IN BRACKETS.
PERCENTAGES OVER 30% ARE STARRED WHERE N $>$ 11)

	White collar	Blue collar	All
Need for money, rising living costs, etc.	70%* $(N = 37)$	43%* $(N = 94)$	51%* $(N = 133)$
Greed for money—unfavourable moral judgment	61%* $(N = 18)$	29%* $(N = 24)$	45%* $(N = 43)$
Misunderstandings	(38%) $(N = 8)$	18% $(N = 17)$	24% $(N = 25)$
Lack of co-operation, bloody-mindedness, etc.	50%* $(N = 22)$	19% $(N = 31)$	27% $(N = 55)$
Bad communication (explicit reference)	14% $(N = 21)$	33%* $(N = 15)$	22% $(N = 36)$
Conditions—all kinds including payment systems	(63%) $(N = 8)$	33%* $(N = 18)$	42%* $(N = 26)$
Militancy, union power	(56%) $(N = 9)$	38%* $(N = 16)$	44%* $(N = 25)$
Political motivation, leftists, etc.	67%* $(N = 12)$	(27%) $(N = 11)$	48%* $(N = 23)$
Bad management/supervision, other than communications	(38%) $(N = 8)$	(21% $(N = 14)$	27% $(N = 22)$
Total media references as percentage of sample size	73% $N = 110$	41% N = 209	53% N = 323

makes it clear that the media do not influence public conceptions on any simple one to one basis. For one thing, generally speaking, people from white-collar backgrounds seem to accept the media version of industrial relations most readily, partly it would seem because they tend to have fewer alternative sources of information, but probably also because what the media present is similar to what might be called the 'natural' middle class perspective. Of perhaps more significance, however, is the suggestion from the data that working class people also derive ideas on industrial relations from the media and that to some extent this involves accepting interpretations running counter to those most characteristic of this group as a whole with its traditional sympathy for unions and tendency to construe industrial conflict in oppositional terms. However, the situation is far from clear-cut, and there are definite indications from the data that other sources of interpretation may be preferred to the media, and that media output may be interpreted or reinterpreted within subculturally derived perspectives. Clearly what are at work are not simple cause and effect relationships but a number of sometimes conflicting tendencies that produce a great deal of complexity and unpredictability.

Summary

We have focused on the views elicited in the survey as manifestation of different kinds of class subcultures, rather than as differences between individuals. The rather complex pattern of relationships indicated by the data may be summarized as follows.

(1) The same news may be interpreted differently by persons differently located in the class structure; different social perspectives may lend different meanings to the same information. Psychologically speaking, people may find support in the news for the views they already hold; sociologically speaking, the views they hold will tend to be those most characteristic of their class.

(2) In spite of this tendency towards selective interpretation, it is mostly views characteristic of a middle class rather than working class outlook that are derived from the news media. On the one hand, middle class people derive their interpretations from the media more than do manual workers partly because the latter have access to alternative sources of interpretation and partly because the perspective on industrial relations that predominates in news is similar to typical middle class outlooks. On the other hand, where working class people hold views of a characteristically 'middle class' kind—for example, the explanation of strikes as due to 'bad communication'—there are indications that the media may be an important source of this kind of interpretation. (This does not mean that they are the only source, of course.)

(3) The data is, furthermore, entirely consistent with the suggestion that the comparatively low prevalence of oppositional points of view among the sample results, in part at least, from lack of endorsement of such views in the news media. Whereas the middle class person is likely to find in the news a perspective on life that is generally taken for granted among his own social group, the working class person will find little endorsement or authentication of oppositional types of view that may nonetheless enjoy some currency among friends, family and work-mates. This point cannot be proved by these results but the data are certainly in line with the idea that the news media may among other things serve as a means by which—to paraphrase Goldthorpe[16]—it is made more difficult for members of the working class to become 'aware of their common interests and conscious of the importance of class relations within their society'.

NOTES AND REFERENCES

1. J. H. Goldthorpe, 'Class, status and party in modern Britain: some recent interpretations, Marxist and Marxisant,' in *European Journal of Sociology,* Vol. XIII, No. 2, 1972.

2. Glasgow University Media Group, *Bad news* (London, Routledge & Kegan Paul, 1976).

3. P. Beharrell and G. Philo, *Trade unions and the media* (London, Macmillan, 1977).

4. R. Milliband, *The state in capitalist society* (London, Weidenfeld & Nicolson, 1969).

5. P. Toynbee, 'The language of inequality,' in R. Blackburn and A. Cockburn (eds), *The incompatibles: trade union militancy and the consensus* (Harmondsworth, Penguin, 1967).

6. D. Morley, 'Industrial conflict and the mass media,' *Sociological Review,* Vol. XXIV, No. 2, 1976. Reprinted in this volume.

7. S. Hall, 'The structured communication of events,' in *Getting the message across* (Paris, Unesco, 1975).

8. J. G. Blumler and A. J. Ewbank, 'Trade unionists, the mass media, and unofficial strikes,' *British Journal of Industrial Relations,* Vol. VIII, 1970, pp. 32–54.

9. The research was supported by a grant from the Leverhulme Trust Fund.

10. P. Hartmann, 'Industrial relations in the news media,' *Industrial Relations Journal,* Vol. VI, No. 4, Winter 1975/6.

11. D. McQuail, *Analysis of newspaper content,* Royal Commission on the Press (London, HMSO, 1977).

12. Glasgow Mass Media Group, *op. cit.*

13. F. Parkin, *Class inequality and political order* (St Albans, Paladin, 1972).

14. Grateful acknowledgement is made to the Joint Industry Committee for National Readership Surveys for permission to use information on newspaper readership, and to the Joint Industry Committee for Television Advertising Research for television audience information.

15. Parkin, *op. cit.,* p. 81.

16. Goldthorpe, *op. cit.,* p. 328.

Enter the dragon*

DAVID ROBINS AND PHILIP COHEN

Micky Spyer was a member of [a skinhead] crew in an area of South Islington which had been [one of their] strongholds.

> Well, some of us go to work, and then we go to clubs, or pubs sometimes, to have fights, but the weekends are best, that's when we have the big fights, with about ten of us outside the fish and chip shop. You've got to fight to protect yourself and you can get a bit of a name and you've got to fight to protect it, you can't just bottle it and walk away, and then you get really slagged off . . . There's about ten of us like, we're all together, all mates from round the flats . . . and when we get into fights then the birds we're with fight with the other birds [i.e. of the other crew]. They're worse than us, they use bottles as well, they're fucking mad sometimes . . . They're all good fighters in our crew, well, that's the idea, isn't it, there's a few no good, well they just hang about with us like, they're not really in it. If a kid's not a good fighter than he don't go about with us and that's that. If we think a geezer's all mouth and not really a good fighter, then we just have a fight with him to show him up . . . they're the real idiots, the right mouthy geezers.'

Elements of the old fighting code can still be seen in this account, but they no longer have any work to do. The code no longer has any purchase on social reality outside itself. And not surprisingly this results in a kind of regression of age roles in the fighting crew.

The kind of routine fighting which characterizes young children's groups in the playground or street is both random and highly competitive, but still playful, essentially 'friendly'. Its function is both to learn and display fighting prowess, as well as to establish hierarchies of prestige

---

*This is part of a chapter, 'configurations of youth' from David Robins and Philip Cohen, *Knuckle sandwich: growing up in the working class city* (Harmondsworth, Penguin, 1978). The study as a whole deals with youth in a large London housing estate and this extract shows how they find their needs reflected in the media.

within the peer group. The fighting crew of older youth remains fixated at this stage; the same mechanisms are carried over, but with one big difference—now they operate for 'real', and are projected on to randomly selected 'enemies' outside the group. In terms of sex roles though, this development must be seen as also containing a progressive aspect. For, as Micky's account makes clear and as our own observations corroborated, what had been a male preserve, and an index of male sexual dominance, opened up to the opposite sex. But the credit for this belongs not so much to the crew itself, as to the advent of Bruce Lee on to the silver screen. For Bruce could not only be idolized by girls in traditional terms as Super-male, his films demonstrated that the so-called weaker sex could master a technique which meant that they could fight on equal terms with boys—and win. Even if his girl fans didn't in practice follow the way of the dragon, Bruce Lee ratified their entry into the precincts of the fighting crew.

The traditions of the Martial arts imported from the Far East thus provided a new source of orientation, but not just for these crews. They appealed to larger sections of youth precisely because they spoke to a widespread sense of cultural displacement experienced during this period, 1972–4. In kung fu, kendo and karate, fighting technique is culti-vated as an end in itself, a pure metaphysic of bodily control, split off from external reality, rather than what it had always been in the working class, a means of social control. In addition, the mass media intervened to blend all three elements, the native brawling tradition, youthful styles of aggro, and the martial arts, into a single *mise en scène* of contemporary violence.

There were no fighting crews on the Monmouth or Denby estates at this time (summer 1973). If there had been, then they would certainly have provided a 'solution' for lads like Bobby Munro. But the older fighting code still exerted an influence on most local youth, albeit at an increasing distance. The way Neil or Phil talked about fights or fighting was still a long way away from Micky Spyer's account. And those lads whose personal styles of aggro went over the limits were quickly isolated as 'nutters' and steered clear of as far as possible.

This did not mean that interest in karate and kung fu wasn't high. Many of the members of the Wall gang boasted of their prowess in such matters. But none showed any signs of expertise, or the inclination to submit themselves to the rigorous physical and mental discipline needed to ac-quire it. One night over the summer months, a group from the Wall went up the West End to see Bruce Lee in *Fist of fury*. Afterwards, one of them attempted to emulate his new-found hero by chopping down a window. Result: a cracked arm and seven stitches! The irony of the story is that the imagery of kung fu appeals most strongly to those kids who are often least equipped, in real terms, to master its techniques. The majority of the Wall, for example, had long since rejected the whole ethos of physical self-discipline and sustained effort which goes with success in organized sport.

The girls too had their stake in the martial arts. Since there was no fighting crew, they formed one of their own. This they modelled after the sixties bike gangs—a number of the lads were roaring around the estate on Suzukis at the time, and so provided the initial 'image' to emulate. The Denby Lady Hells Angels Club was formed. The girls didn't have bikes, of course, but they did have Bruce Lee, and they set off to practise their skills on the boys. There was nothing pretend about this. One lad was set on by a group of girls and so badly beaten up that he had to be sent to hospital. Needless to say, this aggro did nothing to alter the girls' fundamental one-down position in the local youth culture—as in other areas of their lives.

In other words, the fascination of kung fu movies for these kids was not simply due to the fact that they presented a new and exotic fighting style. Their interest was much more sociological.

Bruce Lee in his movies finds himself, just as much as his fans in real life, caught up in a social system which he neither understands nor controls, because it is 'remote controlled' by superior, often institutional, forces, whose power is as hidden as it is all-pervasive. But unlike the heroes of the Western, ganster or fantasy stories (which in movie or comic form constitute these kids' staple cultural diet), Bruce Lee shuns the advanced weaponry of 'the Man' to fight back, just as he scorns ideological ruses. He takes on the technology of 'the system' armed with nothing but his fists, and his superior techniques of body control. And unlike these kids, he manages to salvage victory out of defeat.

The *mise en scène* of martial arts movies is, however, already familiar to the audience—from their comics and film-going, as much as from the narrative context of their everyday lives: rival mobs fighting over territory, plenty of ritual insults, even more physical injuries. For example, if we compare the narrative structure of *Fist of Fury* with the kids' own story-telling about the exploits and encounters they live through, we can see an almost point by point correspondence between the two. The story of *Fist of Fury* goes like this: The leader of the kung fu school has died. He has left behind a scroll of instructions on how his disciples are to carry on the tradition. It contains a key *interdict*[1]—kung fu is to be used only in self-defence, and in the last resort when attacked. While the members of the school are pondering this, and their *lack of a leader* and how to replace him, in other words the *tasks* the founding father has *assigned* to them, they are interrupted by a visit of a 'mob' from a rival, Japanese school of martial arts. They have come not to praise the name of the dead master, but to *insult* him—and issue a challenge to his disciples to take them on in unarmed combat to see which of the two schools is superior. The elders hold to their master's instructions, and refuse to be provoked, so the Japanese leave, jeering at their cowardice, and taking with them the 'sacred text'. The kung fu school are in a dilemma. A *new task* has been *assigned*—to retrieve the scroll, but its *accomplishment* will inevitably mean *violating* the founder's *interdict*. They are caught in a *trap*. Young Bruce Lee rises to the challenge, even though he knows that it means banishment from the school. Alone and outcast, or rather since this is a movie with Hollywood pretensions, aided by an attractive young female accomplice who runs away from the school to join him, he succeeds in *avenging the insult* and retrieving the scroll. But this only brings further trouble from the Japanese mob, and the familar pattern of *attack* and *counter-attack* follows. In the process, Bruce Lee of course takes the place of the dead master, the school has found a *new leader*. But the authorities present them with an ultimatum: either Bruce Lee surrenders or the school is closed down. Bruce knows that he has successfully *accomplished the task* set by his dead teacher—the reputation and tradition of the kung fu school have been secured by his victories in battle—and will survive his own death. But if the school closes down everything he has fought for will be lost. So he gives himself up. And the school is left back where it was at the beginning of the story, *lacking a leader*.

The fascination of the content of such movies for working-class kids thus goes side by side with their unconscious recognition of its narrative style or 'grammar' as one which is identical with their own. They can read it effortlessly. Sometimes, at the level of motif, the links are more explicitly recognized, as in this poem written by a thirteen-year-old girl from Denby estate:

> *Tribute to Bruce Lee*
> When you were young, you used to roam
> the streets and alleys of Hong Kong
> You learn't your martial arts and then
> you tried it out on everywun.

You led a gang or so they say
and terrorized the town
a rebel you will always be
nowun can keep you down

Your dead i know I've seen the proof
your image still lives on
you're worshipped now throughout the world
even tho youre gone

The waterfronts you used to go
to fight and show your skill
you always wun cos youre the guy
nowun could ever kill

You never thought of death i know
cos death woud mean defeat
and thats the thing you never knew
how to win or beat.[2]

In recent years there has been a lot of talk to the effect that violence in the mass media has produced the teenage rampage—working-class kids acting out the images and situations they see portrayed on the screen in real life. It should be clear from the analysis so far that what is in play is the linkage of two forms of 'collective representation' which have radically different historical origins and institutional supports. If the linkage is possible at all, it is because there is an objective correspondence between some oral traditions in working-class culture and *some* genres produced by the mass media. It is a correspondence of form, rather than content, and where it doesn't exist, the impact of the mass media on working-class consciousness is entirely negligible. Finally, both in the history of the class, and in the life history of those growing up into it, the narrative forms of oral culture predate those of the mass media and constitute a kind of permanent infra-structure, which condition and limit the effectivity of the latter.

The following discussion between two fourteen-year-old best mates living on the Monmouth may help to illustrate this. They are trying to reconstruct a subcultural past which they've experienced only at second hand, through the stories told by elder brothers or from what they've read in newspapers or books, or seen on TV or film. Images drawn from the mass media are inextricably interwoven with those drawn from real lives around the estate. But although they may be 'overdramatizing' this past, it is done with a self-critical awareness and no sentimentalism:

FRANK: Well, when I was young I used to really like the mods, but I couldn't st... the rockers. I thought they were a load of hooligans, you know. But as you grow older you kind of find out they was as bad as each other. I used to think of the rockers going round with chains and hatchets and things like that, but the mods used to go round just as much with bare fists. They'll just mob a couple of rockers, splatter them against the wall, rearrange their faces a little, and then the kid will go and get a couple of rockers to get the kids that got him and do exactly the same back . . .

TERRY: And when you was little, remember people used to come up and say 'who do you want, mods or rockers?' and there was two lots of gangs of us round here, one supported the rockers, and the other mods, and it just went on like that and there was fights over that.

FRANK: You know people used to reckon the teddy boys were the biggest, but the skins were thousands, tens of thousands all over Britain, and they were in the papers every day like the teds . . . Skins, bovver, all over the papers. Skins hit Brixton, Skins hit this, Skins hit that . . . there was a book out not long ago, you know it was really good, but it was a load of bollocks as well, if you know what I mean. It was called *Skinhead*. It was all about this geezer called Joe Hawkins and his mob and all the fights they used to have down Southend and all that. And after that he was sent to jail. And after he came out and became a suedehead and by the time you finished the book he was back in prison again for stabbing some Paki in the throat, with an umbrella, blood running all over him and that was that.

TERRY: It's like that film we see the other night, didn't we. *Heavy Traffic*. There was three greasers and they was trying to get this other kid to have it off with this bird, 'cos to become one you got to do it, you know, overnight, and anyway this kid doesn't know what to do, so they start mucking him about, hitting him over the head, and you see all the blood coming out, and they're pulling out chains and all sorts, and in the end they was all flaked out on the floor with half a leg missing here and there, and that. It was really tasty, but I don't think it's like that, 'cos me brother had a mate who was a greaser and he had a bike, you know, a big BMW, and he went on runs, the lot, but he never said anything about anything like that . . .

The Mary Whitehouse brigade would by now be getting quite excited picturing two young psychopathic thugs who set out each night to brutally translate these media fantasies into reality on whoever they can get their hands on. Concerned liberals may be worrying that these two lads are internalizing a 'stereotyped image of deviance', and acting up to *that*. The truth, however, is quite otherwise, and far more mundane.

Both Terry and Frank were popular members of the Wall fraternity, and well liked on the estate generally. Both their families were decidedly 'respectable' Irish, though not well off. Terry in particular had been an articulate supporter of the disco lobby described earlier. They both had a reputation locally as 'comedians' and in fact had quite a nice little double act going. They both knew how to 'handle themselves' and, for that reason, rarely got into fights. Equally, they'd both been in the odd bit of bother with the law, but only for trivial 'offences' to do with hanging about the Wall, and not involving violence of any kind. They didn't see themselves, and weren't seen by anyone else, as deviant, or as in any way different from the majority of the young people on the estate.

It becomes evident from this that such lads readily draw on the resources of the mass media where it supports their imaginative capacities as story-tellers of their own lives.

Sometimes there is an objective correspondence between situations portrayed in a given movie and the more subterranean realities of living in a 'hard' working-class area. In the following account, Terry draws on a media analogy to make the distinction—correctly from our own observations—between different roles in a well-known Islington fighting crew. But towards the end, media imagery spills out of its context and 'takes over the account'.

TERRY: . . . you usually find it's a dim bitch that's got all the bottle. If you look at *Clockwork Orange,* the one in there, he was dim, he had all the bottle there. You usually get that in crews . . . like we've got this kid, he's called Willy, he's as dim as they come, and every time there's a fight he don't care what the odds are, he just steams in, but then this other kid, they more or less take him for leader, Steve Taylor, when the fight starts off, he's usually at the back, he may be the best fighter there, but he's clever like. So it's the poor mugs blind at the front that gets the first chunk of lead and all their face just going splut all over the place and all you hear is chop chop and little groans and grunts, and little kids crawling out with half their jaws missing . . .

But this doesn't mean that Terry, Frank or any of the other lads have any difficulty in 'telling' fantasy from reality *when it matters*. The major subterranean tradition of violence in this part of London was carried on by the fraternity of professional villains whose base was in the Cross Keys pub opposite the Black Horse. The local lads' attitude to these men was nothing if not ambivalent. They admired their trappings of affluence, the expensive suits, cars and the rest, and the fact that they had got this without having to work. But the other trappings of their trade, the scars, the broken noses, their justified reputation for calculated violence, the spells in prison, this inspired only fear. They might watch at a safe distance, but they didn't aspire to be any part of it.

FRANK: But then you get these really hard nuts, about twenty and up. You know, there's really big fights. Like we were up the hospital the other day, and this geezer come in, he works up the Riverside, and he's been slashed across the face and he's been stabbed twice in the back by some other geezer from another mob, reckoned he should have the job or something, so he puts him out of commission like. I think that's pretty stupid, you know, but if any of that lot are around, the kids stand around like little goody boys . . .

In fact these kids have a very solid, and material sense of their own reality—and it is from that base-line that they criticize its distortion and misrepresentations by press and TV. For example, another lad, in his early twenties, a keen Arsenal supporter but now grown out of the North Bank, comments on a TV discussion programme in which a panel of experts have given their views on the nature and causes of contemporary teenage violence:

Well there was this geezer sitting there who thought he knew all about it, but he didn't know nothing if you ask me . . . He was going on about soccer hooligans and how they carry on down the ends, and he says, well, it's all because they don't like the middle classes taking over the game, getting in the act like. Well, anyone who ever been down the North Bank'll tell you they don't give a sod for the students and all the other wankers and pooftas that turn up. They never go down the end anyway, they're too scared. All the North Bank care about is their team and the other end and that's all there is to it.

NOTES

1. The italics indicate the narrative function.
2. This poem is not a bad bit of writing. But the standard of literacy or rather non-literacy revealed by a survey we carried out on 330 letters sent to a Bruce Lee fan mag *(Kung Fu Monthly)* was quite staggering. We estimated that the average 'literacy' age of the majority of these letter-writers was 10–11 years. A readership survey of this magazine revealed the following profile:

Age: 7–14 17%, 15–21 69%, 21 and over 14%

Sex: Male 62%, Female 38%

Ethnic origins (parents): West Indian 31%, Asian 28%, Greek or other immigrant 18%, UK 27%

Social class (parents): Professional and Managerial 4%, Skilled manual/White collar 35%, Unskilled manual/White collar 61%

Total estimated readership of *Kung Fu Monthly:* 285,000.

This survey shows that a large majority of this audience were kids who for various reasons would be likely to experience the maximum difficulty in mastering techniques of literacy as taught in school; but because of their background they were likely to be highly sensitized to techniques of story-telling carried through the oral traditions of their own culture.

PART FOUR

Do-it-yourself media sociology

The first edition of this book drew attention to the paucity of empirical material about deviance and social problems in the mass media. Now, nearly a decade later, this deficiency has only been partly remedied and many research gaps still remain. As we originally said, this is odd in the light of the fact that the mass media, by definition are so widely available and accessible.

There are, broadly speaking, four types of research which can be done on the mass media: the first deals with questions of ownership and control; the second with the actual processes of selection and manufacturing of news; the third, with the images and content eventually presented and the fourth, with the effects of this presentation. The second and last of these categories obviously present formidable research problems—of access, technique and methodology. The other two, though, are much more amenable to small scale research, without massive funding, hardware or personnel. There is no struggle to get permission to have access to the data and there are no arcane research skills to be learnt. Even television research is becoming feasible given the greater availability of video recorders.

On the assumption that small scale research (in at least the two areas of ownership/control and content/images) is possible and that it provides an active mode of learning, we have concluded this Reader with some suggestions for do-it-yourself research. Charting the patterns of ownership and control of the mass media is relatively straightforward. Local librarians will usually be able to provide directories which will allow you to trace the interlocking directorships between various companies and the percentages of the market held in specified areas. More detailed information can be obtained from stock, shareholder and company reports. (Beware of invisible links through third parties—for example accountants and lawyers who represent corporate interests on certain boards.) For some background information and references, see:

G. Murdock and P. Golding, 'Capitalism, communication and class relations', in J. Curran *et al*. (eds.), *Mass communication and society* (London, Arnold, 1977).

G. Murdock, 'Course Unit 10: Patterns of ownership and questions of control', Open University Course DE 353 *Mass Communication and Society*.

J. Tunstall, *The media are American* (London, Constable, 1979).

It is, however, the third of the research areas we distinguished—the analysis of the images and content of media messages—which provides the most interesting and feasible research and it is here that we concentrate our suggestions. The projects we suggest are often just a systematic way of using everyday experience. Every now and then you read a report about an event that you personally participated in, scratch your head and say, 'That's not how it was when I was there', and find that most people who were with you agree. Or you watch a television documentary which has a faint air of unreality. Or get annoyed at the intrusion into someone's private grief in interviews with victims or their relatives. Sometimes, people are indignant enough to make these feelings public.

But on the whole, people keep such indignation and doubts to themselves and their day-to-day reactions to the media never get documented in a systematic way.

We hope that the projects suggested here are not only of intrinsic interest and educational value, but also of some practical use—for example, in providing political and reform groups some way of monitoring their concerns in the media. Few of these projects—some of which are more suitable for groups or teams rather than individuals working on their own—make great technical or financial demands. We have confined ourselves to suggestions which should be well within the resources available to most groups of students in schools, colleges and universities. Besides some familiarity with the sort of issues we have raised in this volume and with the readings already suggested, the main qualities needed are imagination, resourcefulness and patience.

And unlike ten years ago—when we first made these suggestions for do-it-yourself research—there exists now a large critical literature on the media and the business of journalism. This comes either from outside observers or—more interestingly—from working journalists themselves in the form of what is usually called the 'new journalism'. Anyone starting media research should certainly look at some of these sources. Recent useful studies of the media include:

Hans Magnus Enzenberger, *The consciousness industry* (New York, Seabury Press, 1974).

Gaye Tuchman, *Making news: a study in the construction of reality* (New York; Free Press, 1978).

Herbert J. Gans, *Deciding what's news: a study of CBS Evening News, NBC Nightly News, Newsweek and Time.* (London, Constable, 1980).

Note also the journal *Media, culture and society* (published quarterly by the Academic Press).

Various types of 'new' or 'alternative' journalism in America are discussed or represented in: E. Dennis and C. Rivers (eds.), *Other voices: the new journalism in America* (1974); C. Flippen, *Liberating the media* (1974) and M. Fishwick (ed.), *New journalism* (1975). The 'new' elements in this journalism are either its more open advocacy or participatory stance, its stylistic and literary departures or its deliberate tone of personal involvement. The exemplar who combines (outrageously) all these innovations is Hunter S. Thompson and no one can look at the media in quite the same way after reading him.[1] New journalism doesn't guarantee an automatic transcendance of all the conventions of newsmaking we have discussed in this Reader—but it at least allows a vision of other possibilities. And most sociological research would benefit from this sort of vision and from the suspension of that numbing cynicism which does not allow for alternatives.

What sort of projects and strategies are suitable for do-it-yourself research? The answer obviously depends on how ambitious your aims are. You might want to (or have to) limit yourself to one form of mass media—for example, the press—and to one form of deviance or social problem—for example, vandalism. You might use media sources only, or you might compare the media to other sources of information. The projects and strategies we suggest below should cover most choices and they can be used in various permutations.

Making comparisons

Every piece of research included and discussed in this Reader involves a series of implicit or explicit comparisons: either *within* the media or *between* the media and some other source of information. This is a list of some of the main *internal* comparisons which can be made, i.e. comparisons which only use mass media sources:

1. Between different products of the same medium. Compare, for example, daily newspapers (The *Sun* with *The Guardian*) or weekly newspapers *(The Observer* with the *News of the World)* or different news channels: the BBC *Nine O'Clock News* with ITV's *News at Ten*. Which items are selected by one and not by the other? Or given prominence (size of headlines; page position; order of appearance). Then compare the models of presentation (see Checklist of Questions below).

2. Between two or more forms of communication: for example, television and the press. (Besides the standard Checklist of Questions, note how each medium feeds off the other).

3. Between the media in different socially defined boundaries—for example, local papers from the North and South of England. Or the media in different countries.

4. Between different parts of the same news medium: television documentaries, for example might seem to be more 'radical' than the news coverage. And how does the image of women on the 'women's page' of the daily newspaper compare to the same image elsewhere in the paper? Or industrial news as reported by industrial correspondents rather than non-specialist reporters?

5. Across time: one- or five-year comparisons may be made or a longer time span—say, before and after the war might be used. If there has been a major social change in the area you are studying you should consider a before-and-after design. For example, if you are looking at abortion or gambling, you should compare media images before, during and after the recent legal changes in these areas. Or compare sex-role imagery in such sources as women's magazines for the decades before, during and after the women's movement gained influence at the beginning of the 1970s.

6. Compare the media image of various groups as 'objects' with the way these groups prefer to present themselves as 'subjects' in their own alternative media. Political militants, prisoners, students and gays all have their own magazines or newsletters of restricted circulation and these can be compared with the 'straight' media.

7. Between the information channels of the media—the news, features, documentaries etc.,—and various fictional, dramatic or fantasy representations. (Though this Reader has concentrated on *news* in the media, each subject we've covered—race, industrial conflict, sex roles, violence, law and order, political marginality, sexual deviance, alcoholism—might be approached through a study of their fictional representations. Indeed, the feedback between dramatic and real images is an important element in the construction of contemporary modes of understanding deviance. The dramatic form might embody the archetypal consensus about what things are really like or—the opposite—the news might be constructed in terms of traditional dramatic themes: tragedies, heroes, villains, fools, comedies, martyrs.[2] A suitable topic for this sort of comparison might be images of the police: compare the treatment of the police in news and current affairs programmes, with that in police dramas such as *Z Cars, The Sweeney, Starsky and Hutch* or *Kojak*.[3]

These are seven examples of the type of *internal* media comparisons which can be made relatively easily. Each of them probably implies some degree of *external* comparison: this is how the police are presented on the news, this is how they seem on *The Sweeney* but what are they really like?

But to make these external comparisons systematically, careful thought and planning is required—and, invariably, extra time and money. Some of the more obvious sources of knowledge with which the media can be compared include:

1. Your own personal experience—either as a member of the category to which the media refer or as a participant in some event—strike, sit-in, football match—which the media have reported. (We expand below on how to exploit the 'event as news'.)

2. Established bodies of knowledge—standard research findings in criminology for example, about the extent of crime or class background of convicted criminals. Or comparisons with expert opinion. (See Nunnally's paper on mental illness.)

3. Public attitude and opinion—especially as influenced by the media (see Hartmann's paper).

The decision on which sort of comparisons to make is partly determined by practical factors—just how much time and resources you have; partly by how ambitious the level of generality or abstractness you are aiming for, and partly by how readily the particular subject you have chosen lends itself to a certain type of analysis. You might have chosen to look at, say, the media presentation of environmental pollution as a social problem, but because this is a relatively new problem, you might not be able to establish a 'baseline' of public or expert opinion.

To help make these choices, we first give some examples of media research in a few selected areas. This is followed by an explanation of the 'event as news' strategy. We then give a checklist of questions that would be asked in most research which follows the line of this book, and then conclude with some more adventurous and active research strategies.

1. Pick a problem

The most straightforward approach in media research is simply to pick a form of deviance or social problem which interests you. Then make one or more of the series of comparisons we have suggested above. Any of the topics included in this volume would be suitable and you might in fact prefer to use one of these to follow up any lines of argument which the article raised. Other suitable topics include: gambling; prostitution; organized crime; political corruption; environmental pollution; traffic problems; poverty (both in your own country and Third World societies); population problems; abortion and birth control; pornography; prisons; mental hospitals; police; courts; public spending cuts; unemployment.

Any standard textbook or book of readings in such fields as criminology, sociology of deviance, social problems and social policy will suggest other suitable examples as well as references to the recent specialist literature.

Here is a selection of references to some recent media studies (excluding those already reprinted in this Reader) in the four areas of (i) *crime and delinquency;* (ii) *industrial conflict* and (iii) *sexual divisions and images of women* and (iv) *race*.

(i) Crime and delinquency

Steve Chibnall, *Law and order news* (London, Tavistock, 1977)

Steve Chibnall, 'The Metropolitan Police and the news media', in S. Holdaway (ed.), *The British police* (London, Edward Arnold, 1979).

Joseph R. Dominick, 'Crime and law enforcement in the mass media', in C. Winick (ed.), *Deviance and the mass media* (Beverly Hills, Sage, 1978).

Stuart Hall *et al., Policing the crisis: mugging, the state and law and order* (London, Macmillan, 1978).

Stuart Hall, *Mugging: a case study in the media* (Open University, D.101 Making Sense of Society).

D. Payne, 'Newspapers and crime: what happens during strike periods', *Journalism Quarterly* 51 (4), 1974, pp. 233–238.

Sanford Sherizen, 'Social creation of crime news: all the news fitted to print,' in C. Winick (ed.) *Deviance and the mass media* (Beverly Hills, Sage, 1978).

(ii) Industrial conflict and trade unions

Peter Beharrell and Greg Philo (eds.), *Trade unions and the media* (London, Macmillan 1977).

Glasgow University Media Group, *Bad news* (London, Routledge & Kegan Paul, 1976).

Glasgow University Media Group, *More bad news* (London, Routledge & Kegan Paul, 1980).

Paul Hartmann, 'Industrial relations in the news media', *Industrial Relations Journal,* Vol. 6 No. 4 (Winter 1975/6).

(iii) Images of women and sex roles

Centre for Contemporary Cultural Studies Woman's Study Group, *Women take issue* (London, Hutchinson, 1978).

Leslie Friedman, *Sex role stereotyping in the mass media: an annotated bibliography* (New York; Garland Press, 1974).

Erving Goffman, *Gender advertisements* (London, Macmillan, 1979).

Josephine King and Mary Stott (eds.), *Is this your life? Images of women in the media* (London, Virago, 1977). Various papers on radio, TV, newspapers, films, advertisements etc.

Gaye Tuchman *et al.* (eds.), *Hearth and home: images of women in the mass media* (New York, OUP, 1978). Includes 15 separate papers on TV, women's magazines, newspapers and detailed annotated bibliography (pp. 273–299) on women in television.

Gaye Tuchman "Women's depiction by the mass media" *Signs: Journal of Women in Culture and Society* Vol. 4, No. 3 (1979)

(iv) Race

Campaign Against Racism in the Media (CARM) *In black and white* (London, 1977).

J. Downing, *Some aspects of the coverage of class and race in the British media* (Ph.D. thesis, London School of Economics, 1975).

P. Evans, *Publish and be damned?* (London, Runnymede Trust, 1976).

P. Hartmann *et al.*, 'Race as news: a study of the handling of race in the British national press from 1963–1970', in *Ethnicity and the media* (Paris, Unesco, 1974).

P. Hartmann and C. Husband, *Racism and the mass media* (London, Davis Poynter, 1974).

C. Husband (ed.), *White media and black Britain* (London, Arrow Books, 1975).

D. MacShane, *Black and front: journalists and race reporting* (London, NUJ, 1978).

B. Troyna, 'Images of race and racist images in the British news media', in J. D. Halloran (ed.), *Mass media and mass communications* (Leicester University Press, forthcoming).

B. Troyna, *Race, the media and the National Front* (London, Constable, forthcoming).

2. *The event as news*

Projects which work with media images only, can be interesting enough. But they have the inbuilt limitation of not being able *directly* to relate these images to the world outside the media. A satisfying way of dealing with this limitation, is to build a project around the organizing principle of 'the event as news'. Not only does this allow some insight into the processes of selection—how certain events are selected as newsworthy in the first place—but it confronts some of the relativistic strands in media theory. Do news and events 'really' exist or are they artefacts of some process in the social construction of reality?[4]

Simple 'one-shot' research of this type can be done around the following sort of events, which you might observe either as a full participant or an outsider: a pop festival; a football match; a strike; a march, meeting, demonstration or other political event; a court hearing; a public speech.

Record your own observations and, if possible, check them with someone else present. If your observations take place over a long period—for example, a sit-in at a college—you need to be more aware of some of the standard problems of participant observation research in sociology.

Your next step is to make your comparisons with the media. Say you have been to a protest march: try to have the TV and radio news tape-recorded and look at every newspaper the next day, asking the following sorts of questions:

1. Which paper ignored the event altogether? Is there any sort of pattern to this inattention? For example, have only the left-wing papers picked up the march?

2. Are there any major discrepancies with your own observations? For example, are the numbers of marchers or strength of the police consistently underestimated? Do such discrepancies occur in all the papers?

3. Which paper/type of paper gives the event most coverage? Look at the size of headline, column inches (not absolute, but relative to paper's whole size); location in the paper (front page or inside), etc.

4. What are the main models and conventions used in reporting the event? (See 'Checklist of Questions' below.)

5. What is suggested by internal comparisons of the way in which the media report the event? (See Comparisons above.)

An event need not be so dramatic as a march, a pop festival or a demonstration. By definition, 'events' do not happen very often and the media sometimes have to create them out of nothing or transform routine everyday matters into events. Thus on the TV news, simple technical aids such as graphs, charts, summarized expert opinions, interviews or reports from special correspondents can add drama to such mundane matters as a completely uninteresting set of monthly trade figures. Such regular monthly or annual 'events' make excellent case studies for do-it-yourself research. Start by finding a media report of one of the following, for example:

sets of annual statistics (crime, housing, divorce, venereal disease, illegitimate births, immigration, strikes)
annual meetings (political parties, professional associations, trade union conferences).

Make all the relevant event-comparisons we suggested earlier; in addition look up papers for at least five previous years to check which particular aspect of the 'event' is picked out as newsworthy and, indeed, whether it is mentioned at all. Taking the criminal statistics, for example, you might find them given the full banner treatment one year (DRAMATIC IN-CREASES, DISTURBING FIGURES, SHOCK STATISTICS) with very little coverage the year before. You might further find that the statistics for the supposed 'quiet year' were in fact quite the same for the current 'shock, horror' year. Is there any evident reason for the reporting to have been so different?

And what about comparisons within the media? On pp. 504 is an example of a comparison which reveals clearly the different pictures of the 'same' news received by readers of two newspapers.

Here—and in whatever type of media research you do—you will benefit by learning something about content analysis and other techniques for collecting, classifying, coding and quantifying your material. These techniques range from strict content analysis—very precise and repeatable operations for counting say, numbers of references per column inch—through much looser thematic analysis to the highly inferential forms of 'reading', decoding and textualizing influenced by semiotic and structuralist theory. Here are some useful standard sources:

(a) Conventional media research

G. Gerbner, *The analysis of communication content* (New York, John Wiley & Sons, 1969).

O. R. Holsti, *Content analysis for the social sciences and humanities* (Reading, Mass., Addison Wesley, 1968).

W. P. Davison and F. T. C. Yu (eds.), *Mass communications research: major issues and future directions* (New York, Praeger, 1974).

P. Clarke (ed.), *New models for mass communication research* (Beverly Hills, Sage, 1973).

I. Pool *et al.* (eds.), *Handbook of communications* (Stanford Universities/Rand McNally, 1973).

(b) Semiotic and structural analysis

Roland Barthes, *Elements of semiology* (London, Cape, 1967).

Anthony Wilden, *System and structure: Essays in communication and exchange* (London, Tavistock, 1977).

Umberto Eco, 'Towards a semiotic enquiry into the television message', Working Papers in Cultural Studies, University of Birmingham No. 3 (1972).

Umberto Eco, *A theory of semiotics* (London, Macmillan, 1977).

A checklist of questions

Whatever set of internal or external comparisons you make there is a similar series of questions to look out for. Items on the following checklist obviously have to be modified according to the particular problem you have chosen.

1. What patterns of selection are immediately apparent? Is this a subject which has just been picked up by the media and if so, why? What significant aspects of the phenomena might have been left out? What ideological or bureaucratic factors might have been operative? See Part One, (particularly the readings by Edwards, Fishman, Roshier and Rock) for ideas on what sort of questions to ask about selection.

2. What model is being transmitted of the particular form of deviance or social problem you are examining? In particular:

    (a) Is the phenomenon explained in terms of a free will or a deterministic model of causation?

    (b) Are notions such as sickness, pathology, disease being used? (See Pearce, Linsky, and Young for the variations applied to homosexuality, alcoholism and drug taking.)

    (c) Are conspiracy theories or their variants invoked?

    (d) Are the actors involved seen to accept passively society's definitions of them or actively fight such definitions?

3. Is a particular model of social control 'framed' in a taken-for-granted way? Is it simply assumed, for example, that this is something which the police (or doctors? or politicians?) should be doing something about?

4. Are there obvious contradictions apparent in these dominant models? For example, are free will and deterministic theories used simultaneously? Or 'lunatic fringe' and 'everybody's-doing-it' images? Or radical

and conservative implications? Are these contradictions worked through or left unresolved?

5. Is the tendency to personalize the phenomenon or to allow it to be seen in structural terms? Are such political conflicts as Northern Ireland, for example, reported predominantly in terms of the best known individuals involved?

6. Are any obvious recurrent myths being unfolded—(for example, 'Crime doesn't pay', 'All decent people would condemn this . . .')? And are there identifiable heroes and villains—such as the 'handful of brave men in blue' versus 'the screaming mob'? (See Chibnall.)

7. What hidden biases can be detected in the actual techniques of reporting? Try detecting hidden bias in a presentation deliberately set up to present 'both sides', for example, a TV confrontation or debates on programmes such as *Midweek, Panorama* or *Man Alive*. If you can find a clear spectrum on issues such as abortion and euthanasia, where on the spectrum do the sides come from? Thus, in the following diagram, is the debate A versus Z or really G versus T or A versus T?

8. What elements of spurious or putative deviation are present? That is, what properties are assigned to a phenomenon, with little or no evidence of their actual existence? And why should these particular properties be chosen?

9. Is there evidence of a parasitic or symbiotic relationship between the media? That is, does the story or model in question originate primarily from other mass media outlets? For example, see the documentation of how the media's handling of the 1968 Grosvenor Square demonstration was heavily influenced by an initial story in *The Times*.[5]

10. Can a particular moral panic be charted? That is, can one trace in the media the creation and definition of a problem through the fanning up of public indignation?

11. An allied question is whether there are recognizable stages and sequences which can be traced in the evolution of reporting on the topic. Or else fixed conventions (see Chibnall on crime reporting). Note, for example, the 'signification spiral' identified in the mugging study:

1. Identification of specific issue
2. Identification of culprits: 'Subversive minority', 'Lunatic fringe'

3. Convergence: Linking of issue to other problems ('It's not only this' . . .)
4. Notion of thresholds—once they are crossed, further escalation must result; 'slippery slope to anarchy'
5. Explaining and prophesying—analogies to what happened elsewhere
6. Call for firm steps—clamp down hard

12. In regard to each of these eleven questions, look, where appropriate, for some or other of the internal or external comparisons listed above.

Guerrilla Research

If the media contain elements of the mythical, why not observe the process of myth making from the beginning? Here are ideas for some more active research projects:
1. Try to get a story into the media about some event you have participated in or know something about. This could be as dramatic as witnessing a bank robbery or as mundane as attending a school prize-giving. Phone newspapers directly (asking for the news desk or a special correspondent), local stringers if you know them, news agencies, TV stations etc. Keep a careful record of their response—for example, do they immediately say they're not interested? How much care is taken to check your story?—and then analyse what eventually appears.

You can vary:
(a) the number and type of media outlets you contact;
(b) the angle or content of the story;
(c) your own involvement:
and then see how each of these variations affects the final story. Say, for example, that you hear about a pupil from a school in your area being expelled or not allowed to write his exams because his hair is too long. Find out some background details, then phone a number of newspapers emphasizing one set of details to half of them and another to the other half. Now see what happens!
2. Find a story about an event, group or organization and then check on what sort of selection and what distortions, if any, have taken place in the report. Then—with the permission of the group or organization if this is relevant—contact the news' source and try to get them to correct their original report. See how far you get—if anywhere. A good example would have been the publicity given to the foundation of PROP, the prisoners' union, and the demonstrations they organized in the middle of

1972. A large proportion of the 'news'—including especially numerous cartoons—emphasized PROP's demands for conjugal visits: one might have gathered from some stories that 'More sex for prisoners' was the union's *only* demand. If one had contacted PROP or even looked over one of its official publicity handouts (from which most of the news stories were derived) quite a different picture would have emerged.

3. Try the "Cohen-Young Letter Scale Test". Find an issue on which opinions are easily polarized—for example, the total legalization of cannabis or the removal of all age-of-consent restrictions on sex. Then at an appropriate time, draw up say 20 letters, carefully scaled from an extreme pro through to an extreme anti position. Now using fictitious names and addresses, send all the letters to each national newspaper. Which ones will they print? There are endless variations on the Letter-Scale Test: for example, varying the name and status of the 'writer' as well as the opinion expressed.

4. A much more hazardous type of guerrilla research involves using *on* the media, the same techniques of disguise, deception and concealment which have often been adapted in investigative journalism itself. Many "new journalists" have included in their reports an account not just of the matters being reported but of the whole business of newsmaking.[7] And— more controversially—some intrepid investigators have deliberately infiltrated media organizations in order to study their operations. Perhaps the most intrepid and best known of these has been the West German investigative journalist, Günter Wallraff who, armed with faked identity papers, an invented life history and a disguise, spent four months on the staff of *Bild,* the mass circulation paper owned by the Springer group.[8] He then proceeded systematically to detail how *Bild's* stories misinterpreted reality. For obvious reasons, this is not a strategy we can recommend to everyone . . . but its advantages are clear.[9]

Feedback

Once your research project is completed, you should consider whether it can be *used* in some way, in particular by feeding it back to groups concerned with the area you have investigated. Research on the media coverage of an industrial dispute, for example, could be presented to local trade union groups or other individuals involved in the strike. Copies of the report could also be submitted to local community papers or trade union journals.

Such feedback can often be extremely effective. Wallraff, for example, cites a large company where the chairman of the works council

Daily Mail

WEDNESDAY, JUNE 7, 1973

Gangs of young thugs link with 'Fagins'

JUNIOR CRIME WAVE SHOCK

By PETER BURDEN, Crime Reporter

INCREASING numbers of youngsters are taking to serious crime. Many operate in gangs. Some link up with Fagin-type adult crooks.

Of all people arrested for serious offences last year, nearly half were under 21.

The figures are revealed in the annual Scotland Yard crime report for the London area, published yesterday.

National figures are still being completed, but reports indicate that they will confirm the London trend : that youth is on a growing crime rampage.

The Yard's figures show :

Age ten to 13 : Arrests for serious crime up 12 per cent. to 10,006 ;

Age 14 to 16 : Up 17·2 per cent. to 15,936 ;

Age 17 to 20 : Up 3·6 per cent. to 17,031.

Violence

Arrests for robbery (theft where violence is used or threatened) in the under "1 group rose by 35·8 per cent. Nearly two-thirds of all robbery arrests were of youngsters between ten and 20.

Another gloomy sign : police have found that many arrested young people have previous records.

A Yard man commented : 'Experience shows that once convicted the chances increase that the boy or girl will go on pursuing crime as a "career."

The total arrests in the Metropolitan area in 1971 for serious crimes were 86,287, a 6·6 per cent. increase ; 42,973 were of people under 21.

Gangs

The report, by Sir John Waldron, the just-retired Commissioner, says: 'The tendency for young criminals to operate in gangs : both with others of their own age group and with adults, has continued to grow.'

● At Witham, Essex, children are banned from the Iaddnost Jones's toy shop unless accompanied by an adult or they come to buy a specific toy. The owner: £3,000 worth of toys have vanished from his shelves in 12 months.

504

Two newspapers' versions
of the 'same' news

On left
Daily Mail, 7 June 1972
Top of front page

Below
The Guardian, 7 June 1972
Bottom of inside page

More London police in trouble
but fewer complaints

The number of police officers in London facing serious criminal or disciplinary charges rose last year, though fewer public complaints were made against the police, Sir John Waldron says today in his last annual report as Metropolitan Police Commissioner.

Sir John says he feels bound to comment on this "unwelcome trend," but he also emphasises the small number of officers involved, in view of the false impression which might be projected by the disproportionate publicity each case attracts.

"It is perhaps indicative of the small size of the problem in relation to the large number of police officers in the force that each individual case remains newsworthy," he says. And during 1971, only 3,165 complaints were made against the police by the public—344 (9.8 per cent) fewer than in 1970 and the lowest figure since 1968.

Sir John explains that in recent years, officers have been promoted at a younger age, and,

By PETER HARVEY

though capable of supervising the technical work of the men under them, they often had insufficient experience to identify weaknesses of character in subordinate officers. That phase is passing, he says, and there is now a much greater awareness of their responsibilities among supervising officers which should continue to ensure that any indiscipline is exposed.

Crimes of violence in London rose by more than 15 per cent during 1971, and Sir John says that violence caused him the greatest concern during his last year in office. Robbery and assault with intent to rob were up by 15.1 per cent, to a total of 2,727 cases. Firearms were used on almost 400 occasions and other offensive weapons—including pickaxe handles and noxious fluids, were used 804 times.

But in line with other parts of the country sexual offences showed a marked decrease. During 1970, cases of rape

increased by 29 per cent, to 141. Last year they fell by 24.1 per cent to 107. Other sexual offences decreased by 12.5 per cent, to a total of 1,833.

Crime in general increased in London by 6 per cent during the year, but the clear-up rate also showed an increase; from 22.3 per cent in 1966 to 29.4 per cent last year.

Sir John's report also refers to a subject causing growing discontent in the police; the number of people given bail in spite of police objections—thus "defeating" the value of arrest. During 1971, 2,094 people were arrested for indictable offences committed while on bail. In 780 of these cases, the police had objected to bail, and "by and large we detect only a third of the crime committed, so it would be perhaps fair to assume that at least twice as many again as the number set out above commit crime on bail and get away with it."

505

publishes a regular 'Truth behind *Bild* stories' in the workers' information sheets. A poll revealed that only 35 out of the 1,500 workers still continued to read *Bild,* otherwise the best selling newspaper in West Germany.[10]

Research might also have valuable lessons for how various organizations might deal with the media. The increasing realization that news is not an objectively given category has led to groups other than the powerful and their publicity officers (who have always known this) to become more sensitive to strategies for selecting and creating news.[11]

REFERENCES

1. For a representative collection of his work, see Hunter S. Thompson, *The great shark hunt: strange tales from a strange time* (New York; Summit Books, 1979).
2. See Orrin E. Klapp, *Symbolic leaders* (Chicago, Aldine, 1965), and *Heroes, villains and fools* (Englewood Cliffs, N.J., Prentice Hall, 1963).
3. See for example, Geoff Hurd, 'The television presentation of the police', in S. Holdaway (ed.), *The British police* (London, Edward Arnold, 1979).
4. Note here particularly, Molotch and Lester's paper reprinted in Part One and their other publications on the subject: 'Accidents scandals and routines: resources for insurgent methodology', *Insurgent Sociologist,* Vol. 3 (1973) pp. 1–11, and 'Accidental news: the great oil spill', *American Journal of Sociology* Vol. 81 (1975), pp. 235–260.
5. James D. Halloran *et al., Demonstrations and communications: a case study* (Harmondsworth, Penguin, 1970), and article by Graham Murdock in this Reader.
6. Stuart Hall *et al., Policing the crisis: mugging, the state and law and order* (London, Macmillan, 1978).
7. See references on the 'New journalism' and, in the case of political reporting, Tim Crouse *The boys on the bus* (New York, 1978), and war reporting, Michael Herr, *Dispatches* (London, Pan Books, 1978).
8. See G. Wallraff, *Wallraff: the undesirable journalist* (London, Pluto Press, 1978).
9. The editors of the English edition of a collection of Wallraff's reports note: 'The only objection to Wallraff's method made in 1970 by Heinrich Böll was this: its effectiveness is limited because Wallraff has become too well known. In 1978 other and more immediate dangers threaten the one German journalist who sometimes risks his life to awaken public opinion. Böll says, 'I can only see one way out—to create five, six, a dozen Wallraffs.' *Ibid.,* p. 6.
10. *Ibid.,* p. 135.
11. For some useful practical suggestions for dealing with the media, see Dennis MacShane, *Using the media* (London, Pluto, 1979).